k_{ps}	Cost of preferred stock
k_{RF}	Rate of return on a risk-free security
k_s	(1) Cost of retained earnings
	(2) Required return on a stock
M	Maturity value of a bond
M/B	Market-to-book ratio
MCC	Marginal cost of capital
MIRR	Modified internal rate of return
N	Calculator key denoting number of periods
n	(1) Life of a project
	(2) Number of shares outstanding
NPV	Net present value
NWC	Net working capital
P	(1) Price of a share of stock; P_0 = price of the stock today
	(2) Sales price per unit of product sold
P/E	Price/earnings ratio
PMT	Periodic level payment of an annuity
PV	Present value
PVA_n	Present value of an annuity for n years
PVIF	Present value interest factor for a lump sum
PVIFA	Present value interest factor for an annuity
Q	Quantity produced or sold
r	Correlation coefficient
ROA	Return on assets
ROE	Return on equity
RP	Risk premium
RP_M	Market risk premium
S	Sales
SML	Security Market Line
Σ	Summation sign (capital sigma)
σ	Standard deviation (lowercase sigma)
σ^2	Variance
t	Time period
T	Marginal income tax rate
TIE	Times interest earned
V	Variable cost per unit
V_B	Bond value
VC	Total variable costs
WACC	Weighted average cost of capital
YTC	Yield to call
YTM	Yield to maturity

FUNDAMENTALS

OF

FINANCIAL

MANAGEMENT

THE CONCISE EDITION

FUNDAMENTALS

OF

FINANCIAL

MANAGEMENT

THE CONCISE EDITION

EUGENE F. BRIGHAM
JOEL F. HOUSTON
UNIVERSITY OF FLORIDA

THE DRYDEN PRESS
HARCOURT BRACE COLLEGE PUBLISHERS

FORT WORTH   PHILADELPHIA   SAN DIEGO   NEW YORK   ORLANDO   AUSTIN   SAN ANTONIO
TORONTO   MONTREAL   LONDON   SYDNEY   TOKYO

Associate Editor: Shana Lum
Project Editor: Sandy Walton
Production Manager: Ann Coburn
Permissions Editor: Adele Krause

Text and Cover Designer: Linda Miller
Project Management: Elm Street Publishing Services, Inc.
Compositor: The Clarinda Company
Text Type: 10/12 Minion

Address orders:
The Dryden Press
6277 Sea Harbor Drive
Orlando, FL 32887
1-800-782-4479, or 1-800-433-0001 (in Florida)

Address editorial correspondence:
The Dryden Press
301 Commerce Street, Suite 3700
Fort Worth, TX 76102

ISBN: 0-03-015958-X

Library of Congress Catalog Number: 95-68008

Printed in the United States of America

5 6 7 8 9 0 1 2 3 4   048   9 8 7 6 5 4 3 2 1

The Dryden Press
Harcourt Brace College Publishers

The Dryden Press Series in Finance

Amling and Droms
Investment Fundamentals

Berry and Young
**Managing Investments:
A Case Approach**

Bertisch
Personal Finance

Brigham
**Fundamentals of Financial
Management**
Seventh Edition

Brigham, Aberwald, and Gapenski
Finance with Lotus 1-2-3
Second Edition

Brigham and Gapenski
**Cases in Financial Management:
Dryden Request**

Brigham and Gapenski
**Cases in Financial Management:
Module A**

Brigham and Gapenski
**Cases in Financial Management:
Module C**

Brigham and Gapenski
**Financial Management:
Theory and Practice**
Seventh Edition

Brigham and Gapenski
Intermediate Financial Management
Fifth Edition

Brigham and Houston
**Fundamentals of Financial
Management: The Concise Edition**

Chance
An Introduction to Derivatives
Third Edition

Clark, Gerlach, and Olson
Restructuring Corporate America

Cooley
**Advances in Business Financial
Management: A Collection
of Readings**
Second Edition

Cooley
Business Financial Management
Third Edition

Dickerson, Campsey, and Brigham
**Introduction to Financial
Management**
Fourth Edition

Eaker, Fabozzi, and Grant
International Corporate Finance

Evans
**International Finance: A Markets
Approach**

Fama and Miller
The Theory of Finance

Gardner and Mills
**Managing Financial Institutions:
An Asset/Liability Approach**
Third Edition

Gitman and Joehnk
Personal Financial Planning
Seventh Edition

Greenbaum and Thakor
**Contemporary Financial
Intermediation**

Harrington and Eades
**Case Studies in Financial Decision
Making**
Third Edition

Hayes and Meerschwam
**Financial Institutions: Contemporary
Cases in the Financial Services
Industry**

Hearth and Zaima
**Contemporary Investments: Security
and Portfolio Analysis**

Johnson
**Issues and Readings in Managerial
Finance**
Fourth Edition

Koch
Bank Management
Third Edition

Leahigh
A Pocket Guide to Finance

Maisel
Real Estate Finance
Second Edition

Martin, Cox, and MacMinn
**The Theory of Finance: Evidence
and Applications**

Mayes and Shank
**Financial Analysis with Lotus
for Windows**

Mayes and Shank
**Financial Analysis with Microsoft
Excel**

Mayo
**Financial Institutions, Investments,
and Management: An Introduction**
Fifth Edition

Mayo
Investments: An Introduction
Fourth Edition

Pettijohn
PROFIT+

Reilly
**Investment Analysis and Portfolio
Management**
Fourth Edition

Reilly and Norton
Investments
Fourth Edition

Sears and Trennepohl
Investment Management

Seitz and Ellison
Capital Budgeting and Long-Term Financing Decisions
Second Edition

Siegel and Siegel
Futures Markets

Smith and Spudeck
Interest Rates: Principles and Applications

Stickney
Financial Reporting and Statement Analysis: A Strategic Perspective
Third Edition

Weston, Besley, and Brigham
Essentials of Managerial Finance
Eleventh Edition

THE HB COLLEGE OUTLINE SERIES

Baker
Financial Management

PREFACE

Finance is an exciting, challenging, and ever-changing discipline. *Fundamentals of Financial Management* was first published 18 years ago, and since then we have tried to reflect changes in the world of finance in each new edition, along with the latest innovations in education and publishing. These changes have resulted in a better, more complete textbook, but one that is much longer than it was originally. This may present a problem: today, covering the textbook in a single term is increasingly difficult. Not only is size an issue, but cost is, as well.

When we became aware of the problem, we turned to students and other professors for advice. Some students and professors advised us not to worry about the size issue. They argued that a larger, more complete textbook is better because it provides professors more flexibility in designing their courses, is better as a reference for students after they complete the course, and is better because it allows interested students to read chapters not covered in the course on their own. Others took a different position, arguing that as a textbook gets larger, it becomes increasingly difficult to develop a manageable syllabus, and that many students buy a larger, more expensive textbook than they want or need. In the end, we concluded that both arguments have merit, so we decided to create *Fundamentals of Financial Management: The Concise Edition (FFM-C)* for those who like *Fundamentals* but think a smaller, more concise textbook would better serve their needs.

THE PRICE FACTOR

Another motivating factor behind the development of *FFM-C* was to reduce the price of the textbook. When asking professors about our ideas for streamlining the textbook, we heard the importance of price. It makes sense that a "smaller" textbook should be less expensive. Dryden priced this textbook at a suggested retail price of $39.99, which we believe is an educational value whose low cost and high quality will benefit students.

INTENDED MARKET AND USE

Like *Fundamentals, FFM-C* is intended for use in the introductory finance course. Unlike the larger textbook, it is possible to cover *FFM-C* in a single term, and perhaps even to supplement it with a few outside readings or cases. *FFM-C* may also be used in courses in which the material is covered in two terms, allowing professors the flexibility to assign even more additional cases, readings, and exercises.

Although the chapters in *FFM-C* are sequenced logically, they are written in a flexible, modular format, allowing instructors to cover the material in a different sequence.

STEPS TAKEN TO STREAMLINE THE TEXTBOOK

We debated streamlining the textbook either by covering the same topics in less depth or by covering fewer topics, but with the same depth and rigor as in *Fundamentals.* We chose to retain the depth and level of rigor in *Fundamentals,* while eliminating some dispensable topics. While these topics are interesting and important, they are typically covered in subsequent courses. Consequently, many instructors do not attempt to cover them in the introductory course. Such core topics as the time value of money, the relationship between risk and return, the financial environment, and financial statements are still discussed in great detail.

Accordingly, we reduced *FFM-C* from 22 to 16 chapters, or by 6 chapters, in two steps. First, we eliminated the three chapters on hybrid securities, mergers, and international finance. We address these issues in other parts of the textbook, but in less depth than was contained in the deleted chapters. Second, we consolidated (a) the three chapters on stocks, bonds, and security valuation into two chapters; (b) the three chapters on capital budgeting into two chapters; and (c) the three chapters on working capital into two chapters. Thus, these consolidations eliminated three more chapters.

These consolidations produced some unexpected benefits. First, moving the institutional material on bonds and stocks from late in the textbook to the beginning of the new valuation chapters enables students to understand better the nature of bonds, stocks, and the markets in which they trade, which helps students understand the valuation process. Second, consolidating the capital budgeting and working capital chapters enabled us to delete details that do little to help students understand the basic issues. To some extent, students had difficulty seeing the forest for the trees, and it helped to remove a few trees.

FFM-C is significantly different from *Fundamentals,* but most of the chapters will be familiar to users of *Fundamentals.* While we pruned some material and clarified, updated, and otherwise improved all the chapters, *FFM-C* should still be regarded as an alternative version of *Fundamentals* rather than as a *de novo* textbook.

FEATURES OF THE BOOK

Although *FFM-C* is a streamlined version of *Fundamentals,* we did retain all the pedagogical elements and supporting materials which helped make the larger textbook so successful. Included are the following items:

■ Each chapter opens with a vignette describing how an actual corporation has contended with the issues discussed in the chapter. These vignettes heighten students' interest by pointing out the real-world relevance and applicability of what might otherwise seem to be dry, technical material.

■ Throughout the book, there are boxes which provide additional real-world illustrations of how the finance concepts covered in the chapter are applied in practice.

■ An "Integrated Case," generally relating to the vignette, appears at the end of each chapter, illustrating the topics covered in the chapter. These cases are ideal for use as the basis for lectures—going through them systematically covers the key material in the chapter. Instructors can also assign the cases as comprehensive study problems.

■ A large number of end-of-chapter questions, problems, and exam-type problems varying in level of difficulty thoroughly cover the various topics.

■ Most chapters contain a "Computer-Related Problem," enabling students to use a computer spreadsheet program such as *Lotus 1-2-3* or *Microsoft Excel* to answer a set of questions. These problems reinforce the concepts covered in the chapter and provide students with an opportunity to become more proficient with computers. Our models for these problems are available to instructors, who can, if they choose, make them available to students.

■ Throughout the textbook, key terms are highlighted in the text and defined in the margins. This enables students to quickly find and review key topics within the chapter. International references are also defined in the margins.

■ Self-Test questions are provided after each major section within each chapter. These questions provide useful check points for students to test their understanding.

THE INSTRUCTIONAL PACKAGE: AN INTEGRATED SYSTEM

FFM-C includes a broad range of ancillary materials designed to enhance the student's learning experience, while making it easier for the instructor to prepare for and conduct classes. The ancillaries are described below:

1. **Instructor's Manual.** This comprehensive manual contains answers to all text questions and problems, as well as detailed solutions to the integrated cases. At the suggestion of numerous instructors, the format of the *Instructor's Manual* was changed from the format of *Fundamentals' Instructor's Manual* so that all elements for a given chapter (lecture tips, answers to questions, solutions to problems, solutions to integrated cases, and solutions to computer-related problems) are given together. If a computerized version of the IM would help in class preparation, instructors can contact The Dryden Press for a copy.

2. **Lecture Presentation Software or Computerized Lecture Slide Show.** This ancillary, formatted in Microsoft PowerPoint, is a computer graphics slide show covering all the essential issues presented in the chapter. Graphs, tables, lists of points, and calculations are developed sequentially, much as one might develop them on a blackboard. However, the slides are more crisp and clear with use of color coding to tie elements of a given slide together, and they are generally more polished than anything previously available. The slides for *FFM-C* are similar to those provided with *Fundamentals,* which were initially developed with the assistance of Dr. Larry Wolken of Texas A&M University. On their end-of-course evaluations, our students over-

whelmingly liked the slides and recommended that we continue using them as an integral part of our lectures.

When we first began using the slide show, we were concerned about the lack of flexibility in the classroom, thinking that although one can navigate easily from slide to slide, one cannot change the slides themselves in the classroom. Our fears were unfounded. We had spent a great deal of time designing the slides, using examples and materials that would be appropriate in almost any lecture situation. When we used the slide show in class, we discovered that we can easily depart from it by going to the blackboard, which also provides variety and spontaneity. Now, the slides provide the backbone of our lectures, and we spice them up by going to the blackboard to address current events, present alternative examples, and answer questions.

The fact that the *FFM-C* set of slides is available in *PowerPoint* should also allow more flexibility for instructors. It is our understanding that *Microsoft Office* is one of, if not *the*, most popular packages in the country. We reasoned that if the vast majority of professors already had access to *Power Point,* the slide show would be of even greater benefit because of the ease of making any type of changes to it—colors, text, organization, and style, to name a few.

3. **Blueprints.** This supplement was first developed several years ago for the purpose of guiding students through the chapter material. Since the integrated cases systematically cover the key points in the chapters, and the examples in these cases are designed to explain both logical relationships and calculations, we use them as the basis for both *Blueprints* and the lectures.

As lectures move away from the blackboard, it becomes increasingly important to provide students with a hard copy of the lecture materials, thus enabling students to focus on the lecture and still develop a complete set of notes. With this in mind, we have continually modified *Blueprints* to maximize its benefit to students.

Originally, *Blueprints* contained the lecture case and partially completed solutions which the students completed during the course of the lecture. It worked well, receiving favorable feedback from our students and from other instructors who used it in their classes. However, once we chose the slide show format, we concluded that students would best be served with a completely revamped version of *Blueprints.* Each chapter of the new *Blueprints* begins with the case itself, followed by copies of the slides—with space for notes and comments. At the end of each chapter, we include several exam-type problems which are either covered in class or left up to the students to solve on their own. Now students can watch and listen to the lecture, yet still end up with a good set of notes.

The new *Blueprints* has several other advantages. First, it offers more flexibility for presenting alternative examples and discussing current events because, as mentioned previously, students have a complete set of notes, regardless of whether all of the materials in the case (chapter) are discussed in the lecture. Second, because the professor's notes are also the lecture notes, and because the professor's comments about the slides can be placed next to the slides in the space provided, the slides and alternative examples reinforce one another. This helps students to better relate the professor's comments to the slides and to develop a better set of notes.

Each term, we use a course pack consisting of the syllabus, some old exams, and *Blueprints,* made available to students through an off-campus copy center. We also make available 10- to 12-page write-ups on several popular calculators (see "Technology Supplement" below) which can be selectively added to the course pack by students.

4. **Test Bank.** Although some instructors do not prefer multiple-choice questions, they do provide a good means of testing students in many situations. It is critically important, however, that the questions be unambiguous and be consistent with the lectures and assigned readings. To meet this need, a revised and enlarged *Test Bank* with more than 1,200 class-tested questions and problems is available both in book form and on diskettes. A number of new and thoroughly class-tested conceptual questions and problems, which range in level of difficulty, have been added to the *Test Bank* for *FFM-C*. Information regarding the topics covered, the degree of difficulty, and the correct answer, along with complete solutions for all numerical problems, is provided with each question. Questions which require the use of a financial calculator are grouped together in a separate section at the end of each chapter.

A complete *Test Bank* is offered in the *WordPerfect* format for instructors who are more comfortable with that program. Answer keys are automatically generated for each version of an exam—the solutions always following the problems. One can, of course, utilize all the features of *WordPerfect* to customize tests.

The *Test Bank* is also available in Dryden's **computerized test bank form (EXAMaster+).** This software has many features that make test preparation, scoring, and grade recording easy. For example, **EXAMaster+** allows automatic conversion of multiple-choice questions and problems into free-response questions. The order of test questions can be altered to make different versions of a given test. In addition, the software permits the user to add to and edit the existing test items, and, through key-word searches and qualifier screening, the user can easily compile a test covering specific topics.

5. **Supplemental Test Bank.** A *Supplemental Test Bank* will be provided in the future each year. Instructors obviously use the *Test Bank* for exams, but some also like to provide students with samples of *Test Bank* questions for study purposes. Instructors also use *Test Bank* questions for pre-exam reviews. This multiple usage can exhaust even the largest of *Test Banks*. Since we develop new problems in our own classes each term, we decided to provide these new problems on a more timely basis through the use of this annual *Supplemental Test Bank*.

6. **Supplemental Problems.** A set of additional problems similar to the end-of-chapter problems, organized according to topic and level of difficulty, is available with this textbook. The Dryden Press will provide this problem set to instructors upon request.

7. **Problem Diskette.** A diskette containing spreadsheet models for the computer-related end-of-chapter problems is also available. To obtain the diskette, contact The Dryden Press.

8. **Data Disk.** In the textbook itself we incorporate many real-company examples to better illustrate how the concepts apply to actual companies. However, several professors involved in a focus group suggested that we should take this emphasis one step further and provide instructors with real-company data in a computerized form. Although in most introductory

courses students do not have the opportunity to do much computer work, this may change in the not-so-distant future. Thus, with the help of Stan Eakins of East Carolina University, we have put together a set of financial data from several companies along with a set of key economic statistics, including interest rates and stock market indices.

9. **Technology Supplement.** The *Technology Supplement* contains tutorials for five commonly used financial calculators and for *Lotus 1-2-3*. The *1-2-3* tutorial can be used, with slight modifications, with *Microsoft Excel* or other spreadsheets. The calculator tutorials cover everything a student needs to know about the calculator to work the problems in the text, and we provide them as a part of our course pack. These tutorials are generally about 12 typewritten pages. Some students are intimidated by the rather large manuals that accompany the calculators, and they find our brief, course-specific versions easier to use to get started.

10. **Video Package: Integrating Print and Video Technologies.** We live in a visually oriented world, so it is important that we take advantage of the educational tools available through video. It was a long process, but with the tremendous help of Sarah Bryant and Scott Weiss of George Washington University and Brett Spalding of Archipelago Productions, a complete video package consisting of 10-minute tapes to accompany each chapter was developed for the seventh edition of *Fundamentals*. The videos were developed on the assumption that students will view them in class before the relevant chapter is covered. In addition to introducing the main ideas of the chapter, each video includes either news footage regarding the company and/or situation presented in the chapter's opening vignette, or a very similar situation. The video closes with a lead-in to the chapter and, in general terms, to the integrated case at the end of the chapter.

Instructors do not have to assign or utilize either the opening vignette or the integrated case to show the videos, or vice versa. There are many different classroom settings and course objectives, and our video format will not meet all needs. However, we believe that many of you will find these videos extremely useful. To hold costs down, the videos were not edited or updated to coincide with the changes made in the concise version of *Fundamentals*. Nevertheless, the *Fundamentals* videos will go well with *FFM-C*, and The Dryden Press will provide them to instructors who adopt this textbook.

11. **Finance by FAX.** One of the difficulties inherent in textbooks is trying to keep them current in a constantly changing world. When Orange County goes bankrupt or Barings Bank collapses or Procter & Gamble loses $200 million, it would be useful to relate these events to the textbook. Fortunately, a new communications technology—the fax machine—can help us keep up to date. By contacting your Dryden sales representative and providing your departmental fax number, you, the instructor, can receive a one-page fax every two weeks. This faxed information will cite one or two recent articles in *The Wall Street Journal, Business Week,* and other major business publications and provide summaries, discussion questions, and references to the text to facilitate the incorporation of late-breaking news in class discussions. One can also use the accompanying questions for quizzes and exams.

In addition to updates via the fax machine, this information will also be available on The Dryden Press Bulletin Board, "Dryden On-Line." With a modem and communication software, professors can connect with Dryden

On-Line by dialing 1-800-950-1299. The Dryden Bulletin Board is developing quickly with teaching information posted regularly.

A number of additional items are offered for students, as described here:

1. **Study Guide.** This supplement outlines the key sections of each chapter, provides students with self-test questions, and provides a set of problems and solutions similar to those in the text and in the *Test Bank.*

2. **Cases and Casebooks.** A set of 64 cases written by Eugene F. Brigham, Louis C. Gapenski, and others is now in a custom case bank which allows instructors to select cases for their own customized casebook. These cases can be used to illustrate the various topics covered in the textbook. The cases come in directed and nondirected versions (with and without guidance questions), with most of the cases having accompanying spreadsheet models. The models are not essential for working the cases, but they do reduce number crunching and thus leave more time for students to consider conceptual issues.

3. **Finance with Lotus 1-2-3: Text and Models.** In its second edition, this textbook by Eugene F. Brigham, Dana A. Aberwald, and Louis C. Gapenski (Dryden Press, 1992) enables students to learn, on their own, how to use *Lotus 1-2-3* and apply it to financial decisions. This textbook takes students from formatting and copying diskettes to the development of macros and other complex procedures, and it also provides students with substantially more information about spreadsheet modeling than does the *Technology Supplement.*

The Dryden Press will provide complimentary supplements or supplement packages to those adopters qualified under their adoption policy. Please contact your sales representative to learn how you may qualify. If as an adopter or potential user you receive supplements you do not need, please return them to your sales representative or send them to the following address: Attn: Returns Department, Troy Warehouse, 465 South Lincoln Drive, Troy, MO 63379.

ACKNOWLEDGMENTS

This textbook reflects the efforts of a great many people who have worked on *Fundamentals* over a number of years, as well as those who have worked specifically on this concise version. First, we would like to thank Dana Aberwald Clark, who worked closely with us at every stage of the revision—her assistance was absolutely invaluable. Also, our colleagues Lou Gapenski and Carolyn Takeda gave us many useful suggestions regarding the ancillaries and many parts of the book, including the integrated cases. Next, we would like to thank the following professors, who reviewed this edition in detail and provided may useful comments and suggestions: Thomas Berry, DePaul University; Laurence E. Blose, University of North Carolina–Charlotte; Bob Boldin, Indiana University of Pennsylvania; Michael Bond, Cleveland State University; Waldo Born, Eastern Illinois University; Paul Bursik, St. Norbert College; K. C. Chen, California State University–Fresno; Steven M. Dawson, University of Hawaii; John W. Ellis, Colorado State University; Suzanne Erickson, Seattle University; Linda Hittle, San Diego State University; Steve Johnson, University of Texas–El Paso; Ravi Kamath, Cleveland State University; James Keys, Florida International University; Reinhold Lamb, University of North

Carolina–Charlotte; David E. LeTourneau, Winthrop University; Judy Maese, New Mexico State University; Abbas Mamoozadeh, Slippery Rock University; James McNulty, Florida Atlantic University; Scott Moore, John Carroll University; William O'Connell, College of William and Mary; Stuart Rosenstein, Clemson University; Marjorie Rubash, Bradley University; David Suk, Rider College; Bruce Swenson, Adelphi University; Philip Swenson, Utah State University; Holland J. Toles, West Texas A&M University; Paul Vanderheiden, University of Wisconsin–Eau Claire; and Al Webster, Bradley University.

We would also like to thank the following professors, whose reviews and comments on companion books have contributed to this edition: Robert Adams, Mike Adler, Syed Ahmad, Ed Altman, Bruce Anderson, Ron Anderson, Bob Angell, Vince Apilado, Harvey Arbalaez, Henry Arnold, Bob Aubey, Gil Babcock, Peter Bacon, Kent Baker, Robert Balik, Tom Bankston, Babu Baradwai, Les Barenbaum, Charles Barngrover, Bill Beedles, Moshe Ben-Horim, Bill Beranek, Tom Berry, Will Bertin, Scott Besley, Dan Best, Roger Bey, Dalton Bigbee, John Bildersee, Russ Boisjoly, Keith Boles, Geof Booth, Kenneth Boudreaux, Helen Bowers, Oswald Bowlin, Don Boyd, G. Michael Boyd, Pat Boyer, Joe Brandt, Elizabeth Brannigan, Greg Bauer, Mary Broske, Dave Brown, Kate Brown, Bill Brueggeman, Bill Campsey, Bob Carlson, Severin Carlson, David Cary, Steve Celec, Mary Chaffin, Don Chance, Antony Chang, Susan Chaplinsky, Jay Choi, S. K. Choudhary, Lal Chugh, Maclyn Clouse, Bruce Collins, Margaret Considine, Phil Cooley, Joe Copeland, David Cordell, Marsha Cornett, M. P. Corrigan, John Cotner, Charles Cox, David Crary, John Crockett, Jr., Roy Crum, Brent Dalrymple, Bill Damon, Joel Dauten, Steve Dawson, Sankar De, Fred Dellva, Chad Denson, James Desreumaux, Bodie Dickerson, Bernard Dill, Gregg Dimkoff, Les Dlabay, Mark Dorfman, Gene Drzycimski, Dean Dudley, David Durst, Ed Dyl, Richard Edelman, Charles Edwards, John Ellis, Dave Ewert, John Ezzell, Michael Ferri, Jim Filkins, John Finnerty, Susan Fischer, Steven Flint, Russ Fogler, Jennifer Fraizer, Dan French, Michael Garlington, David Garraty, Sharon Garrison, Jim Garven, Adam Gehr, Jr., Jim Gentry, Philip Glasgo, Rudyard Goode, Walt Goulet, Bernie Grablowsky, Theoharry Grammatikos, Owen Gregory, Ed Grossnickle, John Groth, Alan Grunewald, Manak Gupta, Darryl Gurley, Sam Hadaway, Don Hakala, Gerald Hamsmith, William Hardin, John Harris, Paul Hastings, Bob Haugen, Steve Hawke, Del Hawley, Robert Hehre, David Heskel, George Hettenhouse, Hans Heymann, Kendall Hill, Roger Hill, Tom Hindelang, Linda Hittle, Ralph Hocking, J. Ronald Hoffmeister, Robert Hollinger, Jim Horrigan, John Houston, John Howe, Keith Howe, Steve Isberg, Jim Jackson, Vahan Janjigian, Kose John, Craig Johnson, Keith Johnson, Ramon Johnson, Ray Jones, Frank Jordan, Manuel Jose, Alfred Kahl, Gus Kalogeras, Rajiv Kalra, Michael Keenan, Bill Kennedy, Carol Kiefer, Joe Kiernan, Richard Kish, Don Knight, Ladd Kochman, Dorothy Koehl, Jaroslaw Komarynsky, Duncan Kretovich, Harold Krogh, Charles Kroncke, Don Kummer, Joan Lamm, Larry Lang, P. Lange, Howard Lanser, Edward Lawrence, Martin Lawrence, Wayne Lee, Jim LePage, Jules Levine, John Lewis, Jason Lin, Chuck Linke, Bill Lloyd, Susan Long, Judy Maese, Bob Magee, Ileen Malitz, Phil Malone, Terry Maness, Chris Manning, S. K. Mansinghka, Terry Martell, David Martin, D. J. Masson, John Mathys, Ralph May, John McAlhany, Andy McCollough, Ambrose McCoy, Thomas McCue, Bill McDaniel, John McDowell, Charles McKinney, Robyn McLaughlin, Jeanette Medewitz-Diamond, Jamshid Mehran, Larry Merville, Rick Meyer, Jim Millar, Ed Miller, John Miller, John Mitchell, Carol Moerdyk, Bob Moore, Barry Morris, Gene Morris, Fred Morrissey, Chris Muscarella, David Nachman, Tim Nantell, Don Nast, Bill Nelson, Bob Nelson, Bob Niendorf, Tom O'Brien, Dennis O'Connor, John O'Donnell, Jim Olsen, Robert Olsen, Jim Pappas, Stephen Parrish, Helen Pawlowski, Michael Pescow, Glenn Petry, Jim Pettijohn, Rich Pettit, Dick

Pettway, Aaron Phillips, Hugo Phillips, H. R. Pickett, John Pinkerton, Gerald Pogue, Eugene Poindexter, R. Potter, Franklin Potts, R. Powell, Chris Prestopino, Jerry Prock, Howard Puckett, Herbert Quigley, George Racette, Bob Radcliffe, Bill Rentz, Ken Riener, Charles Rini, John Ritchie, Pietra Rivoli, Antonio Rodriguez, James Rosenfeld, E. N. Roussakis, Dexter Rowell, Bob Ryan, Jim Sachlis, Abdul Sadik, Thomas Scampini, Kevin Scanlon, Frederick Schadeler, Mary Jane Scheuer, Carl Schweser, John Settle, Alan Severn, James Sfiridis, Sol Shalit, Frederic Shipley, Dilip Shome, Ron Shrieves, Neil Sicherman, J. B. Silvers, Clay Singleton, Joe Sinkey, Stacy Sirmans, Jaye Smith, Patricia Smith, Steve Smith, Don Sorensen, David Speairs, Ken Stanley, Ed Stendardi, Alan Stephens, Don Stevens, Jerry Stevens, Glen Strasburg, Katherine Sullivan, Philip Swensen, Ernest Swift, Paul Swink, Gary Tallman, Dular Talukdar, Dennis Tanner, Craig Tapley, Russ Taussig, Richard Teweles, Ted Teweles, Francis C. Thomas, Andrew Thompson, John Thompson, Dogan Tirtirogu, George Tsetsekos, William Tozer, Emery Trahan, George Trivoli, David Upton, Howard Van Auken, Pretorious Van den Dool, Pieter Vandenberg, Paul Vanderheiden, JoAnn Vaughan, Jim Verbrugge, Patrick Vincent, Steve Vinson, Susan Visscher, John Wachowicz, Mike Walker, Sam Weaver, Kuo-Chiang Wei, Bill Welch, Fred Weston, Norm Williams, Tony Wingler, Ed Wolfe, Criss Woodruff, Don Woods, Michael Yonan, Dennis Zocco, and Kent Zumwalt.

Special thanks are due to Chris Barry, Texas Christian University, and Shirley Love, Idaho State University, who wrote many of the boxes relating to small business issues; to Dilip Shome, Virginia Polytechnic Institute, who helped greatly with the capital structure chapter; to Art Herrmann, University of Hartford, who helped us with the bankruptcy material; and to Larry Wolken, Texas A&M University, who offered his hard work and advice for the development of the *Lecture Presentation Software*. Carol Stanton and Susan Sternberg typed and helped proof the various manuscripts. Finally, The Dryden Press and Elm Street Publishing Services staffs, especially Karen Hill, Craig Johnson, Shana Lum, Sue Nodine, and Mike Reynolds, helped greatly with all phases of the textbook's development and production.

ERRORS IN THE TEXTBOOK

At this point, most authors make a statement like this: "We appreciate all the help we received from the people listed here but any remaining errors are, of course, our own responsibility." And generally there are more than enough remaining errors. Having experienced difficulties with errors ourselves, both as students and as instructors, we resolved to avoid this problem in *Fundamentals of Financial Management: The Concise Edition.* As a result of our detection procedures, we are convinced that the book is relatively free of significant errors, meaning those that either confuse or distract readers.

Partly because of our confidence that few such errors remain, but primarily because we want very much to detect those errors that may have slipped by to correct them in subsequent printings, we decided to offer a reward of $10.00 per error to the first person who reports it to us. For purposes of this reward, errors are defined as misspelled words, nonrounding numerical errors, incorrect statements, and any other error that inhibits comprehension. Typesetting problems such as irregular spacing and differences in opinion regarding grammatical or punctuation conventions do not qualify for the reward. Finally, any qualifying error that has follow-through effects is counted as two errors only. Please report any errors to us at the address given below.

CONCLUSION

Finance is, in a real sense, the cornerstone of the enterprise system—good financial management is vitally important to the economic health of business firms, and hence to the nation and the world. Because of its importance, finance should be widely and thoroughly understood, but this is easier said than done. The field is relatively complex, and it is undergoing constant change in response to shifts in economic conditions. All of this makes finance stimulating and exciting but also challenging and sometimes perplexing. We sincerely hope that this concise edition of *Fundamentals* will meet its own challenge by contributing to a better understanding of our financial system.

EUGENE F. BRIGHAM
JOEL F. HOUSTON
College of Business
University of Florida
Gainesville, Florida 32611-7160

August 1995

BRIEF CONTENTS

CONTENTS

I

INTRODUCTION TO FINANCIAL MANAGEMENT

1 AN OVERVIEW OF FINANCIAL MANAGEMENT

It was called "Marlboro Friday." On April 2, 1993, Philip Morris, in a move to improve its declining market share, sharply cut cigarette prices on its flagship brand. Following the announcement, Philip Morris' stock price tumbled $14, reducing the company's market value by a staggering $13.4 billion. Analysts estimate that this action also slashed $2.3 billion in profits from the company's tobacco operations, and, for the first time in 25 years, the company failed to increase its dividend.

Shares of other large companies with major brands such as Coca-Cola, Procter & Gamble, H.J. Heinz, Quaker Oats, and Pepsico also tumbled, as investors feared that Philip Morris' announcement reflected a broad consumer shift away from major brands. Roger Enrico, head of Pepsi's Frito-Lay subsidiary, commented, "In the annals of business history, Philip Morris's action is bigger than New Coke. MBAs will study this decision for the next century."

Philip Morris has made many changes in the two years following Marlboro Friday. A new management team is running the company. Market share has improved. The stock price has rebounded somewhat, triggered in part by an increase in the dividend and a buy-back of the company's shares. Nevertheless, many of Philip Morris' largest shareholders, representing major institutions such as pension funds and the company's labor union, remain unconvinced, and many of these same disgruntled shareholders stormed out of a private meeting with senior management in late 1994. Their discontent stems from what they perceive to be management's unwillingness to listen to their concerns and the lack of vigilance among the company's board of directors. In particular, shareholders were upset at management's refusal to spin off the company's food divisions from its tobacco operations.

While tobacco is currently quite profitable, it is under siege on a variety of fronts. Health concerns have triggered numerous lawsuits, adverse publicity, regulation on public smoking, and increased taxes. The new management team has taken a decidedly more aggressive approach in these issues. Unlike Michael Miles, the previous CEO and a nonsmoker who rose through the ranks in the food services business, the current CEO, Geoff Bible, is an avowed smoker who has already begun fighting back. The company has sued the Environmental Protection Agency to contest its findings that second-hand smoke causes cancer and ABC News for suggesting that tobacco companies "spiked" cigarettes with nicotine to promote addiction. When New York City considered a strong antismoking law, Philip Morris threatened to move its headquarters out of the city, and it reminded city leaders that such a pullout would jeopardize the company's long-standing contributions to promote the arts in the city. As a result, many in the arts community came out against the ban.

The recent travails of Philip Morris raise a number of important issues concerning operating strategy, the stock market's response to new information, the role of directors and large shareholders in overseeing management, and the ethics of producing a product that is legal but widely acknowledged to have significant health concerns.

The purpose of this chapter is to give you an overview of financial management. After you finish the chapter, you should have a reasonably good idea of what finance majors might do after graduation, and you should also have a better understanding of (1) some of the forces that will affect financial management in the future; (2) the way businesses are organized; (3) the place finance has in a firm's organization; (4) the relationships between financial managers and their counterparts in accounting, marketing, production, and personnel departments; (5) the goals of a firm; and (6) the way financial managers can contribute to the attainment of these goals.

CAREER OPPORTUNITIES IN FINANCE

Finance consists of three interrelated areas: (1) *money and capital markets*, which deals with securities markets and financial institutions; (2) *investments*, which focuses on the decisions of investors, both individuals and institutions, as they choose securities for their investment portfolios; and (3) *financial management*, or "business finance," which involves the actual management of a firm. The career opportunities within each field are many and varied, but financial managers must have a knowledge of all three areas if they are to do their jobs well.

MONEY AND CAPITAL MARKETS

Many finance majors go to work for financial institutions, including banks, insurance companies, investment companies, savings and loans, and credit unions. For success here, you need a knowledge of the factors that cause interest rates to rise and fall, the regulations to which financial institutions are subject, and the various types of financial instruments (mortgages, auto loans, certificates of deposit, and so on). You also need a general knowledge of all aspects of business administration, because the management of a financial institution involves accounting, marketing, personnel, and computer systems. An ability to communicate, both orally and in writing, is important, and "people skills," or the ability to get others to do their jobs, is critical.

The most common entry-level job in this area is a bank officer trainee, where you go into bank operations and learn about the business, from tellers' work to cash management to making loans. You could expect to spend a year or so being rotated among these different areas, after which you would settle into a department, often as an assistant manager in a branch. Alternatively, you might become a specialist in some area such as real estate and be authorized to make loans going into the millions of dollars, or in the management of trusts, estates, and pension funds. Similar career paths are available in insurance companies, investment companies, credit unions, and consumer loan companies.

INVESTMENTS

Finance graduates who go into investments generally work for a brokerage house such as Merrill Lynch, either in sales or as a security analyst. Others work for banks, mutual funds, or insurance companies in the management of investment portfolios, or for financial consulting firms which advise individual investors or pension funds on how to invest their funds. The three main functions in the investments area are (1) sales, (2) the analysis of individual securities, and (3) determining the optimal mix of securities for a given investor.

FINANCIAL MANAGEMENT

Financial management is the broadest of the three areas, and the one with the greatest number of job opportunities. Financial management is important in all types of businesses, including banks and other financial institutions, as well as industrial and retail firms. Financial management is also important in governmental operations, from schools to hospitals to highway departments. The types of jobs encountered in financial management range from decisions regarding plant expansions to choosing what types of securities to issue to finance expansion. Financial managers also decide the credit terms under which customers may buy, how much inventory the firm should carry, how much cash to keep on hand, whether to acquire other firms (merger analysis), and how much of the firm's earnings to plow back into the business versus pay out as dividends.

Regardless of which area a finance major goes into, he or she will need a knowledge of all three areas. For example, a banker lending to businesses cannot do his or her job well without a good understanding of financial management, because he or she must be able to judge how well a business is operated. The same is true for Merrill Lynch's security analysts and stockbrokers, who must have an understanding of general financial principles if they are to give intelligent advice to their customers. At the same time, corporate financial managers need to know what their bankers consider important, and how investors are likely to judge their corporations' performances and thus determine their stock prices. So, if you decide to make finance your career, you will need to know something about all three areas.

Suppose you do not plan to major in finance. Is the subject still important to you? Absolutely: (1) You need a knowledge of finance to make many personal decisions, ranging from investing your savings to determining the best alternative for a car loan. (2) In practically any job, you will see that most important decisions are "business decisions" that require inputs from marketing, production, personnel, finance, and accounting people. In particular, marketing programs always have financial implications, so marketing people must work with the finance staff to reach good decisions. For example, if Ford were considering a new rebate offer, or Nike the hiring of Michael Jordan, these decisions would be made by teams consisting of marketing and finance people. The issues would be (1) what will it cost, (2) how much will it boost sales, and (3) will revenues increase more than enough to offset the costs? So, if you want to get ahead in business, you will have to be a good "team player," and that requires an understanding of what the other team members are doing.

SELF-TEST QUESTIONS

What are the three main areas of finance?

If you have definite plans to go into one area of finance, why is it necessary that you know something about the other two areas?

Why is it necessary for business students who do not plan to major in finance to know something about finance?

FINANCIAL MANAGEMENT IN THE 1990s

When financial management emerged as a separate field of study in the early 1900s, the emphasis was on the legal aspects of mergers, the formation of new firms, and the various types of securities firms could issue to raise capital. During the Depression era of the 1930s, the emphasis shifted to bankruptcy and reorganization, corporate liquidity, and regulation of security markets. During the 1940s and early 1950s, finance continued to be taught as a descriptive, institutional subject, viewed more from the standpoint of an outsider rather than from that of management. However, a movement toward theoretical analysis began during the late 1950s, and the focus of financial management shifted to managerial decisions regarding the choice of assets and liabilities with the goal of maximizing the value of the firm. The focus on valuation has continued on into the 1990s, but the analysis has been expanded to include (1) *inflation* and its effects on business decisions; (2) *deregulation* of financial institutions and the resulting trend toward large, broadly diversified financial services companies; (3) the dramatic increase in the use of *computers* for analysis and the electronic transfer of information; and (4) the increased importance of *global* markets and operations. The two most important trends during the 1990s are likely to be the continued globalization of business and a further increase in the use of computer technology.

THE GLOBALIZATION OF BUSINESS

Four factors have led to the increased globalization of business: (1) Improvements in transportation and communications, which have lowered shipping costs and made international trade more feasible. (2) The increasing political clout of consumers who desire low-cost, high-quality products, which has helped lower trade barriers that protected inefficient, high-cost domestic manufacturers. (3) As technology has become more advanced, the cost of developing new products has increased, so higher unit sales are necessary if the firm is to spread its fixed costs and be competitive. (4) In a world populated by multinational firms able to shift production to wherever costs are lowest, a firm whose manufacturing operations are restricted to one country cannot compete effectively unless costs in its home country happen to be low, a condition that does not necessarily exist for many U.S. corporations. As a result of these four factors, survival requires that most manufacturers produce and sell globally.

Service companies, including banks, advertising agencies, and accounting firms, are also being forced to "go global," because such firms can better serve their multinational clients if they have worldwide operations. There will, of course, always be some purely domestic companies, but you should keep in mind that the most dynamic growth, and the best job and investment opportunities, are often with companies that operate worldwide.

Even businesses which operate exclusively in local U.S. markets cannot escape the effects of the globalization of business. For example, a homebuilder in central Illinois will be affected by interest rates — which are determined by worldwide conditions — and by employment in the local area — which will be affected by U.S. exports. So, some knowledge of the global situation is important to almost everyone, not just to those employed by multinational companies or companies that buy or sell in international markets.

COMPUTER TECHNOLOGY

The remainder of the 1990s will see continued advances in computer and communications technology, and this technology will revolutionize the way financial decisions are made. Companies have and will continue to develop networks of personal computers linked to one another, to other computer systems, and to their customers' and suppliers' computers. Thus, financial managers will be able to share data and programs and to have "face-to-face" meetings with distant colleagues through video teleconferencing. The ability to access and analyze data on a real-time basis will also mean that quantitative analyses will be used routinely to "test out" alternative courses of action. As a result, the next generation of financial managers will need stronger computer and quantitative skills than were required in the past.

SELF-TEST QUESTIONS

How has financial management changed from the early 1900s to the 1990s?

How might a person become better prepared for a career in financial management?

What are two key trends to look for in the 1990s and beyond?

INCREASING IMPORTANCE OF FINANCIAL MANAGEMENT

The historical trends discussed above have greatly increased the importance of financial management. In earlier times the marketing manager would project sales, the engineering and production staffs would determine the assets necessary to meet those demands, and the financial manager's job was simply to raise the money needed to purchase the required plant, equipment, and inventories. That situation no longer exists — decisions are now made in a much more coordinated manner, and the financial manager generally has direct responsibility for the control process.

Eastern Airlines and Delta can be used to illustrate both the importance of financial management and the effects of financial decisions. In the 1960s, Eastern's stock sold for more than $60 per share, while Delta's sold for $10. By the 1990s, Delta had become one of the world's strongest airlines, and its stock was selling for more than $50 per share. Eastern, on the other hand, had gone bankrupt and was no longer in existence. Although many factors combined to produce these divergent results, financial decisions exerted a major influence. Because Eastern had traditionally used a great deal of debt while Delta had not, Delta had more flexibility to respond to changes in the economic environment. For example, when fuel price increases made it imperative for the airlines to buy new, fuel-efficient planes, Delta was able to do so, but Eastern was not. Also, when the airlines were deregulated, Delta was strong enough to expand into developing markets and to cut prices as necessary to attract business, but Eastern was not.

The Delta-Eastern story, and others like it, is now well known. As a result, all companies today are greatly concerned with financial planning, and this has increased the importance of corporate financial staffs. Indeed, the importance of financial management is reflected in the fact that more chief executive officers (CEOs) in the top 1,000 U.S. companies started their careers in finance than in any other functional area.

It is also becoming increasingly important for people in marketing, accounting, production, personnel, and other areas to understand finance in order to do a good job in their own fields. Marketing people, for instance, must understand how marketing decisions affect and are affected by funds availability, by inventory levels, by excess plant capacity, and so on. Similarly, accountants must understand how accounting data are used in corporate planning and are viewed by investors.

Thus, there are financial implications in virtually all business decisions, and nonfinancial executives simply must know enough finance to work these implications into their own specialized analyses.[1] Because of this, every student of business, regardless of major, should have a basic knowledge of finance.

SELF-TEST QUESTIONS

Why is financial management important to today's chief executives?

Why do marketing people need to know something about financial management?

THE FINANCIAL STAFF'S RESPONSIBILITIES

The financial staff's task is to acquire and use funds so as to maximize the value of the firm. Here are some specific activities which are involved:

1. **Forecasting and planning.** The financial staff must interact with people from other departments as they look ahead and lay the plans which will shape the firm's future position.

2. **Major investment and financing decisions.** A successful firm usually has rapid growth in sales, which requires investments in plant, equipment, and inventory. The financial staff must help determine the optimal sales growth rate, and finance people must help decide on the specific assets to acquire and the best way to finance those assets. For example, should the firm finance with debt or equity, and if debt is used, should it be long term or short term?

3. **Coordination and control.** The financial staff must interact with other personnel to ensure that the firm is operated as efficiently as possible. All business decisions have financial implications, and all managers — financial and otherwise — need to take this into account. For example, marketing decisions affect sales growth, which in turn affects investment requirements. Thus, marketing decision makers must take account of how their actions affect (and are affected by) such factors as the availability of funds, inventory policies, and plant capacity utilization.

4. **Dealing with the financial markets.** The financial staff must deal with the money and capital markets. As we shall see in Chapter 4, each firm affects and is affected by the general financial markets where funds are raised, where the firm's securities are traded, and where its investors are either rewarded or penalized.

---

[1] It is an interesting fact that the course "Financial Management for Nonfinancial Executives" has the highest enrollment in most executive development programs.

In summary, people working in financial management make decisions regarding which assets their firms should acquire, how those assets should be financed, and how the firm should manage its existing resources. If these responsibilities are performed optimally, financial people will help maximize the values of their firms, and this will also maximize the long-run welfare of those who buy from or work for the company.

SELF-TEST QUESTION

What are four specific activities with which finance people are involved?

ALTERNATIVE FORMS OF BUSINESS ORGANIZATION

There are three main forms of business organization: (1) sole proprietorships, (2) partnerships, and (3) corporations. In terms of numbers, about 80 percent of businesses are operated as sole proprietorships, while the remainder are divided equally between partnerships and corporations. Based on dollar value of sales, however, about 80 percent of all business is conducted by corporations, about 13 percent by sole proprietorships, and about 7 percent by partnerships. Because most business is conducted by corporations, we will concentrate on them in this book. However, it is important to understand how the three forms differ.

SOLE PROPRIETORSHIP

Sole Proprietorship
An unincorporated business owned by one individual.

A **sole proprietorship** is an unincorporated business owned by one individual. Going into business as a sole proprietor is easy — one merely begins business operations. However, even the smallest establishments must often be licensed by a governmental unit.

The proprietorship has three important advantages: (1) It is easily and inexpensively formed, (2) it is subject to few government regulations, and (3) the business pays no corporate income taxes.

The proprietorship also has three important limitations: (1) It is difficult for a proprietorship to obtain large sums of capital; (2) the proprietor has unlimited personal liability for business debts, so business losses can result in personal bankruptcy; and (3) the life of a business organized as a proprietorship is limited to the life of the individual who created it. For these three reasons, sole proprietorships are restricted primarily to small business operations. However, businesses are frequently started as proprietorships and then converted to corporations when their growth causes the disadvantages of being a proprietorship to outweigh the advantages.

PARTNERSHIP

Partnership
An unincorporated business owned by two or more persons.

A **partnership** exists whenever two or more persons associate to conduct a noncorporate business. Partnerships may operate under different degrees of formality, ranging from informal, oral understandings to formal agreements filed with the secretary of the state in which the partnership does business. The major advantage of a partnership is its low cost and ease of formation. The disadvantages are similar to those associated with proprietorships: (1) unlimited liability, (2) limited life of the organization, (3) difficulty of transferring ownership, and (4) difficulty of raising large amounts of capital. The tax treatment of a partnership is similar to that for a proprietorship and thus is often more favorable than that for corporations, as we demonstrate in Chapter 2.

Regarding liability, the partners can potentially lose all of their personal assets, even those assets not invested in the business, because under partnership law each partner is liable for the business's debts. Therefore, if any partner is unable to meet his or her pro rata claim in the event the partnership goes bankrupt, the remaining partners must make good on the unsatisfied claims, drawing on their personal assets if necessary. The partners of the national accounting firm Laventhol and Horwath, a huge partnership which went bankrupt recently as a result of suits filed by investors who relied on faulty audit statements, learned about the perils of doing business as a partnership. Thus, a Texas partner who audits a savings and loan which goes under can bring ruin to a millionaire New York partner who never went near the S&L.[2]

The first three disadvantages — unlimited liability, impermanence of the organization, and difficulty of transferring ownership — lead to the fourth, the difficulty partnerships have in attracting substantial amounts of capital. This is no particular problem for a slow-growing business, but if a business's products really catch on, and if it needs to raise large amounts of capital in order to capitalize on its opportunities, the difficulty in attracting capital becomes a real drawback. Thus, growth companies such as Hewlett-Packard and Apple Computer generally begin life as a proprietorship or partnership, but at some point they find it necessary to convert to a corporation.

CORPORATION

Corporation
A legal entity created by a state, separate and distinct from its owners and managers, having unlimited life, easy transferability of ownership, and limited liability.

A **corporation** is a legal entity created by a state. It is separate and distinct from its owners and managers. This separateness gives the corporation three major advantages: (1) *Unlimited life* — A corporation can continue after its original owners and managers are deceased. (2) *Easy transferability of ownership interest* — Ownership interests can be divided into shares of stock, which in turn can be transferred far more easily than can proprietorship or partnership interests. (3) *Limited liability* — To illustrate the concept of limited liability, suppose you invested $10,000 in a partnership which then went bankrupt owing $1 million. Because the owners are liable for the debts of a partnership, you could be assessed for a share of the company's debt, and you could be held liable for the entire $1 million if your partners could not pay their shares. Thus, an investor in a partnership is exposed to unlimited liability. On the other hand, if you invested $10,000 in the stock of a corporation which then went bankrupt, your potential loss on the investment would be limited to your $10,000 investment.[3] These three factors — unlimited life, easy transferability of ownership interest, and limited liability — make it much easier

---

[2]However, it is possible to limit the liabilities of some of the partners by establishing a *limited partnership*, wherein one partner is designated the *general partner* and others *limited partners*. Limited partnerships are quite common in the area of real estate investment, but they do not work well with most types of businesses, including accounting firms, because one partner is rarely willing to assume all of the business's risk.

[3]In the case of small corporations, the limited liability feature is often a fiction because bankers and credit managers generally require personal guarantees from the stockholders of small, weak businesses.

for corporations than for proprietorships or partnerships to raise money in the general capital markets.

Although the corporate form offers significant advantages over proprietorships and partnerships, it does have two important disadvantages: (1) Corporate earnings are subject to double taxation — the earnings of the corporation are taxed, and then any earnings paid out as dividends are taxed again as income to the stockholders. (2) Setting up a corporation, and filing required state and federal reports, is more complex and time-consuming than for a proprietorship or a partnership.

Although a proprietorship or a partnership can commence operations without much paperwork, setting up a corporation requires that the founders hire a lawyer to prepare a charter and a set of bylaws. The *charter* includes the following information: (1) name of the proposed corporation, (2) types of activities it will pursue, (3) amount of capital stock, (4) number of directors, and (5) names and addresses of directors. The charter is filed with the secretary of the state in which the firm will be incorporated, and, when it is approved, the corporation is officially in existence.[4] Then, after the corporation is in operation, quarterly and annual financial and tax reports must be filed with state and federal authorities.

The *bylaws* are a set of rules drawn up by the founders of the corporation to aid in governing its internal management. Included are such points as (1) how directors are to be elected (all elected each year, or perhaps one-third each year for three-year terms); (2) whether the existing stockholders will have the first right to buy any new shares the firm issues; and (3) procedures for changing the bylaws themselves, should conditions require it.

The value of any business other than a very small one will probably be maximized if it is organized as a corporation for these three reasons:

1. Limited liability reduces the risks borne by investors, and, other things held constant, *the lower the firm's risk, the higher its value.*

2. A firm's value is dependent on its *growth opportunities*, which in turn are dependent on the firm's ability to attract capital. Since corporations can attract capital more easily than unincorporated businesses, they have superior growth opportunities.

3. The value of an asset also depends on its *liquidity*, which means the ease of selling the asset and converting it to cash at a "fair market value." Since an investment in the stock of a corporation is much more liquid than a similar investment in a proprietorship or partnership, this enhances the value of a business.

As we will see later in the chapter, most firms are managed with value maximization in mind, and this, in turn, has caused most large businesses to be organized as corporations.

 ## SELF-TEST QUESTIONS

What are the key differences between sole proprietorships, partnerships, and corporations?

Explain why the value of any business other than a very small one will probably be maximized if it is organized as a corporation.

---

[4]Note that more than 60 percent of major U.S. corporations are chartered in Delaware, which has, over the years, provided a favorable legal environment for corporations. It is not necessary for a firm to be headquartered, or even to conduct operations, in its state of incorporation.

FINANCE IN THE ORGANIZATIONAL STRUCTURE OF THE FIRM

Organizational structures vary from firm to firm, but Figure 1-1 presents a fairly typical picture of the role of finance within a corporation. The chief financial officer — who has the title of vice-president: finance — reports to the president. The financial vice-president's key subordinates are the treasurer and the controller. In most firms the treasurer has direct responsibility for managing the firm's cash and marketable securities, for planning its capital structure, for selling stocks and bonds to raise capital, and for overseeing the corporate pension fund. The treasurer also supervises the credit manager, the inventory manager, and the director of capital budgeting (who analyzes decisions related to investments in fixed assets). The controller is responsible for the activities of the accounting and tax departments.

SELF-TEST QUESTION

Identify two key subordinates who report to the firm's chief financial officer, and indicate the primary responsibilities of each.

THE GOALS OF THE CORPORATION

Stockholder Wealth Maximization The primary goal for management decisions; considers the risk and timing associated with expected earnings per share in order to maximize the price of the firm's common stock.

Business decisions are not made in a vacuum — decision makers have specific objectives in mind. *Throughout this book we operate on the assumption that management's primary goal is* **stockholder wealth maximization,** which, as we shall see, translates into *maximizing the price of the firm's common stock.* Firms do, of course, have other objectives — in particular, the managers who make the actual decisions are interested in their own personal satisfaction, in their employees' welfare, and in the good of the community and of society at large. Still, for the reasons set forth in the following sections, *stock price maximization is the most important goal of most corporations.*

MANAGERIAL INCENTIVES TO MAXIMIZE SHAREHOLDER WEALTH

Stockholders own the firm and elect the board of directors, who then appoint the management team. Management, in turn, is supposed to operate in the best interests of the stockholders. We know, however, that because the stock of most large firms is widely held, managers of large corporations have a great deal of autonomy. This being the case, might not managers pursue goals other than stock price maximization? For example, it has been argued that managers of a large, well-entrenched corporation could work just hard enough to keep stockholder returns at a "reasonable" level and then devote the remainder of their efforts and resources to public service activities, to employee benefits, to higher executive salaries, or to golf.

It is almost impossible to determine whether a particular management team is trying to maximize shareholder wealth or is merely attempting to keep stockholders satisfied while pursuing their own personal goals. For example, how can we tell whether employee or community benefit programs are in the long-run best inter-

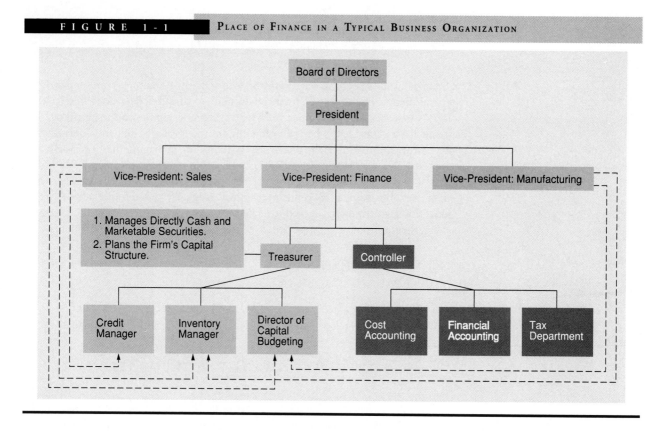

ests of the stockholders? Similarly, was it really necessary for Coca-Cola to pay its chairman more than $50 million to obtain his services, or was this just another example of a manager taking advantage of stockholders?

It is impossible to give definitive answers to these questions. However, we do know that managers of firms operating in competitive markets will be forced to undertake actions that are reasonably consistent with shareholder wealth maximization. If they depart from this goal, they run the risk of being removed from their jobs through a hostile takeover or a proxy fight.

Hostile Takeover
The acquisition of a company over the opposition of its management.

Proxy Fight
An attempt to gain control of a firm by soliciting stockholders to vote for a new management team.

A **hostile takeover** is the purchase by one company of the stock of another over the opposition of its management, whereas a **proxy fight** involves an attempt to gain control by getting stockholders to vote a new management group into place. Both actions are facilitated by low stock prices, so for the sake of self-preservation, managers try to keep stock prices as high as possible. Therefore, while some managers may be more interested in their own personal positions than in maximizing shareholder wealth, the threat of losing their jobs still motivates them to try to maximize stock prices. We will have more to say about the conflict between managers and shareholders later in the chapter.

SOCIAL RESPONSIBILITY

Social Responsibility
The concept that businesses should be actively concerned with the welfare of society at large.

Another issue that deserves consideration is **social responsibility:** Should businesses operate strictly in their stockholders' best interests, or are firms also responsible for the welfare of their employees, customers, and the communities in which they operate? Certainly, firms have an ethical responsibility to provide a safe working

ARE CEOS OVERPAID?

At first glance the number is hard to believe: $203 million. That's what Disney's chief, Michael Eisner, received as compensation in 1993. This happened in a year when Disney's net income fell 63 percent, partly in response to losses at EuroDisney. In fact, Eisner's compensation was not that much less than Disney's 1993 net income, which totaled $229.8 million. A cynic might think, "If someone reduced net income by 63 percent and still earned $203 million, how much would the company pay if earnings actually rose?"

What is interesting is that Eisner's compensation received little or no resistance from the company's shareholders. Why? During his tenure as Disney's CEO, Eisner has made shareholders rich. Disney's market value has skyrocketed from $2.2 billion in 1984, when he took over as CEO, to $22.7 billion at the end of 1993. If you had invested $1,000 in Disney stock in 1984, it would be worth nearly $15,000 today.

Eisner's record haul came largely in the form of stock options. His salary and bonus totaled only $750,000, but he exercised long-term stock options worth more than $202 million. Clearly, those stock options provided Eisner with a significant incentive to raise the company's stock price, and he delivered.

Concerns about "excessive compensation" are most likely to arise when CEOs receive exorbitant levels of pay at the same time the firm's stock price is underperforming the market. Even in these instances, the issues may not be all that straightforward. The stock price may fall for reasons having nothing to do with the CEO — indeed, you could argue that CEOs probably work especially hard when the company's fortunes are declining. Also, you need to look at the long-run track record of the CEO and the firm. In Disney's case, the company's performance over time has been outstanding, even though during the year in which Eisner exercised his options and had a reported income of $203 million, the company's performance was lackluster.

Some critics argue that although performance incentives are entirely appropriate as a method of compensation, the overall level of CEO compensation is still too high. Would Eisner have been unwilling to take the job if he had been offered only half as many stock options? Would he have put forth less effort, and would the stock price not have gone up as much? It is hard to say.

Eisner's compensation was extraordinary, but it was largely a one-time payment. The typical CEO of a large corporation generally receives annual compensation of less than $1 million. Although this certainly is respectable, it pales compared with the salaries sports stars and other entertainers receive. For example, it has been estimated that director Steven Spielberg earned more than $165 million in 1994, while the preschool icon Barney the Dinosaur earned $59 million for his creators in 1993 and another $25 million in 1994.

Normal Profits/Rates of Return
Those profits and rates of return that are close to the average for all firms and are just sufficient to attract capital.

environment, to avoid polluting the air or water, and to produce safe products. However, socially responsible actions have costs, and it is questionable whether businesses would incur these costs voluntarily. If some firms do act in a socially responsible manner while others do not, then the socially responsible firms will be at a disadvantage in attracting capital. To illustrate, suppose the firms in a given industry have **profits** and **rates of return on investment** that are close to **normal,** that is, close to the average for all firms and just sufficient to attract capital. If one company attempts to exercise social responsibility, it will have to raise prices to cover the added costs. If the other businesses in its industry do not follow suit, their costs and prices will be lower. The socially responsible firm will not be able to compete, and it will be forced to abandon its efforts. Thus, any voluntary socially responsible acts that raise costs will be difficult, if not impossible, in industries that are subject to keen competition.

What about oligopolistic firms with profits above normal levels — cannot such firms devote resources to social projects? Undoubtedly they can, and many large, successful firms do engage in community projects, employee benefit programs, and the like to a greater degree than would appear to be called for by pure profit or wealth maximization goals.[5] Still, publicly owned firms are constrained in such ac-

---

[5]Even firms like these often find it necessary to justify such projects at stockholder meetings by stating that these programs will contribute to long-run profit maximization.

tions by capital market factors. To illustrate, suppose a saver who has funds to invest is considering two alternative firms. One firm devotes a substantial part of its resources to social actions, while the other concentrates on profits and stock prices. Most investors are likely to shun the socially oriented firm, thus putting it at a disadvantage in the capital market. After all, why should the stockholders of one corporation subsidize society to a greater extent than those of other businesses? For this reason, even highly profitable firms (unless they are closely held rather than publicly owned) are generally constrained against taking unilateral cost-increasing social actions.

Does all this mean that firms should not exercise social responsibility? Not at all, but it does mean that most significant cost-increasing actions will have to be put on a *mandatory* rather than a voluntary basis, at least initially, to ensure that the burden falls uniformly on all businesses. Thus, such social benefit programs as fair hiring practices, minority training, product safety, pollution abatement, and antitrust actions are most likely to be effective if realistic rules are established initially and then enforced by government agencies. Of course, it is critical that industry and government cooperate in establishing the rules of corporate behavior, that the costs as well as the benefits of such actions be accurately estimated and taken into account, and that firms follow the spirit as well as the letter of the law in their actions.

In spite of the fact that many socially responsible actions must be mandated by government, in recent years numerous firms have been voluntarily taking actions, especially in the area of environmental protection, because these actions help sales. For example, many detergent manufacturers now use recycled paper for their containers, and food companies are packaging more and more products in materials that consumers can recycle or that are biodegradable. To illustrate, McDonald's has replaced its styrofoam boxes, which take years to break down in landfills, with paper wrappers that are less bulky and decompose more rapidly. Some companies, such as the Body Shop and Ben & Jerry's Ice Cream, go to great lengths to be socially responsible. According to the president of the Body Shop, the role of business is to promote the public good, not just the good of the firm's shareholders. Furthermore, she believes that it is impossible to separate business from social responsibility. For some firms, socially responsible actions may not even be very costly because the companies can advertise such actions, and many consumers prefer to buy from "green" companies rather than from companies that shun social responsibility.

STOCK PRICE MAXIMIZATION AND SOCIAL WELFARE

If a firm attempts to maximize its stock price, is this good or bad for society? In general, it is good. Aside from such illegal actions as attempting to form monopolies, violating safety codes, and failing to meet pollution control requirements, *the same actions that maximize stock prices also benefit society*. First, note that stock price maximization requires efficient, low-cost plants that produce high-quality goods and services at the lowest possible cost. Second, stock price maximization requires the development of products that consumers want and need, so the profit motive leads to new technology, to new products, and to new jobs. Finally, stock price maximization necessitates efficient and courteous service, adequate stocks of merchandise, and well-located business establishments — these factors are all necessary to make sales, and sales are necessary for profits. Therefore, actions which help a firm increase the price of its stock are also beneficial to society at large. This is why profit-motivated, free-enterprise economies have been so much more successful than socialist and communist economic systems. Since financial management plays a crucial role in the operation of successful firms, and since successful firms are absolutely necessary for a healthy, productive economy, it is easy to see why finance is important from a social standpoint.[6]

SELF-TEST QUESTIONS

What is management's primary goal?

What actions could be taken to remove management if it departed from the goal of maximizing shareholder wealth?

Explain the difference between a hostile takeover and a proxy fight. How does a firm's stock price influence the likelihood of those actions?

What would happen if one firm attempted to exercise costly social responsibility, while its competitors did *not* exercise social responsibility?

How does the goal of stock price maximization benefit society at large?

BUSINESS ETHICS

The word *ethics* is defined in Webster's dictionary as "standards of conduct or moral behavior." Business ethics can be thought of as a company's attitude and conduct toward its employees, customers, community, and investors. High standards of ethical behavior demand that a firm treat each party that it deals with in a fair and honest manner. A firm's commitment to business ethics can be measured by the tendency of the firm and its employees to adhere to laws and regulations relating to such factors as product safety and quality, fair employment practices, fair marketing and selling practices, the use of confidential information for personal gain, community involvement, and bribery.

There are many instances of firms engaging in unethical behavior. For example, in recent years the employees of several prominent Wall Street investment banking houses have been sentenced to prison for illegally using insider information on proposed mergers for their own personal gain, and E. F. Hutton, a large brokerage firm, lost its independence through a forced merger after it was convicted of cheating its banks out of millions of dollars in a check kiting scheme. Drexel Burnham Lambert, one of the largest investment banking firms, went bankrupt, and its "junk bond king," Michael Milken, who had earned $550 million in just one year, was sentenced to 10 years in prison plus charged a huge fine for securities-law violations. Recently, Salomon Brothers Inc. was implicated in a Treasury-auction bidding scandal which resulted in the removal of its top officers and a significant reorganization of the firm.

In spite of all this, the results of a recent study indicate that the executives of most major firms in the United States believe that their firms should, and do, try

---

[6]People sometimes argue that firms, in their efforts to raise profits and stock prices, increase product prices and gouge the public. In a reasonably competitive economy, which we have, prices are constrained by competition and consumer resistance. If a firm raises its prices beyond reasonable levels, it will simply lose its market share. Even giant firms like General Motors lose business to the Japanese and Germans, as well as to Ford and Chrysler, if they set prices above levels necessary to cover production costs plus a "normal" profit. Of course, firms *want* to earn more, and they constantly try to cut costs, to develop new products, and so on, and thereby to earn above-normal profits. Note, though, that if they are indeed successful and do earn above-normal profits, those very profits will attract competition, which will eventually drive prices down, so the main long-term beneficiary is the consumer.

to maintain high ethical standards. Further, most executives believe that there is a positive correlation between ethics and long-run profitability. For example, Chemical Bank suggested that ethical behavior has increased its profitability because such behavior (1) avoids fines and legal expenses, (2) builds public trust, (3) attracts business from customers who appreciate and support its policies, (4) attracts and keeps employees of the highest caliber, and (5) supports the economic viability of the communities in which it operates.

Most firms today have in place strong codes of ethical behavior, and about half of all large firms conduct training programs designed to ensure that employees understand the correct behavior in different business situations. However, it is imperative that top management — the chairman, president, and vice-presidents — be openly committed to ethical behavior and that they communicate this commitment through their own personal actions as well as through company policies, directives, and punishment/reward systems.

Situations often arise in which profits and ethics conflict. Sometimes ethical considerations are so strong that they offset profit considerations, but often the ethical issue is not overwhelmingly important, and reasonable people might dispute if or how it should affect the decision. For example, if Norfolk and Southern knows that its coal trains are polluting the air along their routes, but the pollution is within legal limits and cleaning it up would be costly, should the company clean up its act anyway? And if the decision is "yes," just how clean should it make its trains, given that the cleaner the train, the higher the cost? There is no obvious answer to questions such as these, but companies must deal with them and reach decisions.

SELF-TEST QUESTIONS

How would you define "business ethics"?

Is "being ethical" good for profits in the long run? In the short run?

AGENCY RELATIONSHIPS

An *agency relationship* exists any time one or more people (the principals) hire another person (the agent) to perform a service and also delegate decision-making authority to that agent. For our purposes, the two most important agency relationships are those (1) between managers and stockholders and (2) between stockholders (acting through the firm's managers) and creditors (debtholders).

STOCKHOLDERS VERSUS MANAGERS

Agency Problem
A potential conflict of interest between the agent (manager) and (1) the outside stockholders or (2) the creditors (debtholders).

A potential **agency problem** arises whenever the manager of a firm owns less than 100 percent of the firm's common stock. If a firm is a proprietorship managed by the owner, the owner-manager will presumably operate so as to improve his or her own welfare, with welfare measured in the form of increased personal wealth, more leisure, or perquisites.[7] However, if the owner-manager incorporates and sells some of the firm's stock to outsiders, a potential conflict of interests immediately arises. For example, the owner-manager may now decide not to work as hard to maxi-

---

[7]*Perquisites* are executive fringe benefits such as luxurious offices, use of corporate planes and yachts, personal assistants, and general use of business assets for personal purposes.

mize shareholder wealth because less of this wealth will go to him or her, or to take a higher salary and enjoy more perquisites because part of those costs will fall on the outside stockholders. This potential conflict between the principals (outside shareholders) and the agent (manager) is an agency problem.

Leveraged Buyout (LBO)
A situation in which a group which generally includes the firm's management uses credit to purchase the outstanding shares of the company's stock.

Tender Offer
An offer to buy the stock of a firm directly from its shareholders.

Another potential conflict between management and stockholders arises in a **leveraged buyout (LBO)**, a term used to describe the situation in which management itself (1) arranges a line of credit, (2) makes a **tender offer** to buy the stock not already owned by the management group, and then (3) "takes the company private." Dozens of such buyouts of major corporations have occurred recently, and a potential conflict clearly exists whenever one is contemplated. For example, RJR Nabisco's President, Ross Johnson, attempted in 1988 to take RJR private in an LBO. If he had been successful, Johnson and several other RJR executives would have ended up owning about 20 percent of the company, worth more than a billion dollars. Management tried to pave the way for the LBO in various ways that were questionable from the stockholders' point of view. Management argued that its bid was in all stockholders' interests, but many disagreed: If management itself was buying the stock, it clearly would be in management's own best interest to keep the price down until the deal was completed, and thus a clear conflict of interest existed.

If a potential conflict of interest exists, what can be done to ensure that management treats the outside stockholders fairly? For one thing, the U.S. Securities and Exchange Commission (SEC), which regulates our securities markets, now requires that management disclose all material information relating to a proposed deal, and also that a committee of outside (i.e., nonofficer) directors be established (1) to seek other bids for the company, (2) to evaluate and compare any other bids with that of management, and (3) to recommend the best bid to stockholders. Further, the outside directors' committee members cannot have any interest in the reorganized company; this requirement is designed to ensure their independence, and lawsuits would quickly be filed if a conflicting situation developed.

In RJR's case, the outside directors' committee received bids from several groups, including one from Kohlberg Kravis Roberts (KKR), an investment company that specializes in LBOs using pension funds as its primary source of equity capital. (KKR generally finances with about 10 percent equity and 90 percent debt, with the debt divided between short-term bank loans and longer-term junk bonds.) A bidding war ensued, and in the end KKR beat out the management group by making a bid of $109 per share, up from management's original $75 offer. The final management and KKR bids were similar, but the outside directors recommended KKR in part because of the widespread feeling that management had tried to "steal" the company. This whole episode is a good example of the fact that leveraged buyouts constitute an important type of agency problem between stockholders and managers.

Several mechanisms are used to motivate managers to act in the shareholders' best interests. These include (1) the threat of firing, (2) the threat of takeover, and (3) managerial compensation.

1. **The threat of firing.** Until recently, the probability of a large firm's management being ousted by its stockholders was so remote that it posed little threat. The ownership of most firms was widely distributed, and management's control over the proxy (voting) mechanism was so strong that it was almost impossible for dissident stockholders to gain enough votes to overthrow the managers. However, today 55 percent of the stock of an average large corporation is owned by a relatively few large institutions rather than by thou-

sands of individual investors, and the institutional money managers have the clout to influence a firm's operations. Examples of major corporations where individual managers or entire management teams have been ousted include General Motors, IBM, Borden, United Airlines, and Eastman Kodak.

2. **The threat of takeover.** Hostile takeovers (where management does not want the firm to be taken over) are most likely to occur when a firm's stock is undervalued relative to its potential. In a hostile takeover, the managers of the acquired firm are generally fired, and any who are able to stay on lose the autonomy they had prior to the acquisition. Thus, managers have a strong incentive to take actions which maximize stock prices. In the words of one company president, "If you want to keep control, don't let your company's stock sell at a bargain price."

   Actions to increase the firm's stock price and to keep it from being a bargain are obviously good from the standpoint of the stockholders, but other tactics that managers can use to ward off a hostile takeover may not be. Two examples of questionable tactics are *poison pills* and *greenmail*. A **poison pill** is an action that a firm can take which practically kills it and thus makes it unattractive to potential suitors. Examples include Disney's plan to sell large blocks of its stock at low prices to "friendly" parties, Scott Industries' decision to make all of its debt immediately payable if its management changed, and Carleton Corporation's decision to give huge retirement bonuses, which represented a large part of the company's wealth, to its managers if the firm was taken over (such payments are called *golden parachutes*).

   Greenmail, which is like blackmail, occurs when (a) a potential acquirer (firm or individual) buys a block of stock in a company, (b) the target company's management becomes frightened that the acquirer will make a tender offer and gain control of the company, and (c) to head off a possible takeover, management offers to pay greenmail, buying the stock owned by the potential raider at a price above the existing market price without offering the same deal to other stockholders. A good example of greenmail was Disney's buy-back of 11.1 percent of its stock from Saul Steinberg's Reliance Group, giving Steinberg a quick $60 million profit. A group of stockholders sued, and Steinberg and the Disney directors were forced to pay $45 million to Disney stockholders.

3. **Managerial compensation.** Managers obviously must be compensated, and the structure of the compensation package can and should be designed to meet two primary objectives: (a) to attract and then retain able managers and (b) to align the manager's actions as closely as possible with the interests of the firm's stockholders, which is primarily stock price maximization. Different companies follow different compensation practices, but a typical senior executive's compensation is structured in three parts: (a) a specified annual salary necessary to meet living expenses; (b) a bonus paid at the end of the year which depends on the company's profitability during the year; and (c) options to buy stock, or actual shares of stock, which reward the executive for the firm's long-term performance.

   Managers are more likely to focus on maximizing stock price if they are themselves large shareholders. Often, companies grant senior management **performance shares,** where the executive receives a number of shares dependent upon the company's actual performance. For example, in 1991 Coca-Cola granted one million shares of stock valued at $81 million to its CEO, Roberto Goizueta. The award was based on Coke's performance under Goi-

Poison Pill
An action taken by management to make a firm unattractive to potential buyers and thus to avoid a hostile takeover.

Greenmail
A situation in which a firm, in trying to avoid a takeover, buys back stock from a raider at a price above the existing market price.

Performance Shares
Stock which is awarded to executives on the basis of the company's performance.

Executive Stock Option
An option to buy stock at a stated price within a specified time period that is granted to an executive as part of his or her compensation package.

zueta's leadership, but it also stipulated that Goizueta would receive the shares only if he stayed with the company for the remainder of his career.

Most large corporations also provide **executive stock options,** which allow managers to purchase stock at some future time at a given price. Obviously, a manager who has an option to buy, say, 10,000 shares of stock at a price of, say, $10 during the next 5 years will have an incentive to help raise the stock's value to an amount greater than $10.

The number of performance shares or options awarded is generally based on objective criteria. Years ago, the primary criteria were accounting measures such as earnings per share (EPS) and return on equity (ROE). Today, though, the focus is more on the market value of the firm's shares or, better yet, on the performance of its shares relative to other stocks' performance. Various procedures are used to structure compensation programs, and good programs are relatively complicated. Still, it has been thoroughly established that a well-designed compensation program can do wonders to improve a company's financial performance.

STOCKHOLDERS VERSUS CREDITORS

A second agency problem involves conflicts between stockholders (acting through the firm's managers) and creditors (debtholders). Creditors lend funds to the firm at rates that are based on (1) the riskiness of the firm's existing assets, (2) expectations concerning the riskiness of future asset additions, (3) the firm's existing capital structure (that is, the amount of debt financing it uses), and (4) expectations concerning future capital structure changes. These are the controllable factors that determine the riskiness of the firm's debt, and creditors base the interest rate they charge on expectations regarding these factors.

Now suppose the stockholders, acting through management, cause the firm to take on new ventures that have much more risk than was anticipated by the creditors. This increased risk will cause the value of the outstanding debt to fall. If the risky ventures turn out to be successful, all the benefits will go to the stockholders, because the creditors get only a fixed return. However, if things go sour, the bondholders will have to share the losses. What this amounts to, from the stockholders, point of view, is a game of "heads I win, tails you lose," which is obviously not a good game for the bondholders.

Similarly, if the firm increases its use of debt in an effort to boost the return to stockholders, the value of the old debt will decrease, so we have another "heads I win, tails you lose" situation. To illustrate, consider what happened to RJR Nabisco's bondholders when RJR's CEO announced his plan to take the company private in an LBO. Stockholders saw their shares jump in value from $56 to more than $90 in just a few days, but RJR's bondholders suffered a loss of 20 percent. Investors realized that the LBO would cause the amount of RJR's debt to rise dramatically, and thus its riskiness would soar. This, in turn, led to a huge decline in the price of RJR's outstanding bonds.

The entire industrial bond market was shaken by the RJR announcement because bond investors realized that virtually any company could become an LBO target. Indeed, the state of Ohio's pension fund administrator announced that he was liquidating the fund's entire industrial bond portfolio and switching to Treasury bonds because of the danger of other corporate LBOs.

The bond market's disarray caught many experts by surprise. Even though bond investors had been stung many times in recent years by LBOs and restructurings, the gargantuan size of the RJR Nabisco deal made investors realize that no firm is too large to be a target. "Now, bond investors are going to have to pay much closer attention to the fine print in the credit agreements," said one analyst. He went on to say that "anybody who holds an industrial bond that is not protected against something like this is sitting on a credit toxic waste site."

The RJR situation is an illustration of what has become known as *event risk,* the probability that some event (such as an LBO) will occur, increase the firm's chance of default and, therefore, reduce the value of outstanding bonds.

Also, the RJR situation increased the use of "poison puts." A *put* is an option which gives the holder the right to sell something at a stipulated price, and a *poison put* is a provision in a bond agreement which permits the holder of the bond to sell it back to the issuer at par in the event of an LBO or some similar corporate action.

Can and should stockholders, through their managers/agents, try to expropriate wealth from the firm's creditors? In general, the answer is no. First, because such attempts have been made in the past, creditors today protect themselves reasonably well against stockholder actions through poison puts and other restrictions in credit agreements. Second, if potential creditors perceive that a firm will try to take advantage of them in unethical ways, they will either refuse to deal with the firm or else will require a much higher than normal rate of interest to compensate for the risks of such "sneaky" actions. Thus, firms which try to deal unfairly with creditors either lose access to the debt markets or are saddled with higher interest rates, both of which decrease the long-run value of the stock.

In view of these constraints, it follows that the goal of maximizing shareholder wealth requires fair play with creditors: Stockholder wealth depends on continued access to capital markets, and access depends on fair play and abiding by both the letter and the spirit of credit agreements. Managers, as agents of both the creditors and the shareholders, must act in a manner which is fairly balanced between the interests of these two classes of security holders. Similarly, because of other constraints and sanctions, management actions which would expropriate wealth from any of the firm's *stakeholders* (employees, customers, suppliers, and so on) will ultimately be to the detriment of shareholders. Therefore, maximizing shareholder wealth requires the fair treatment of all stakeholders.

 SELF-TEST QUESTIONS

What is an agency relationship, and what two major agency relationships affect financial management?

Give some examples of potential agency problems between stockholders and managers.

List several factors which motivate managers to act in shareholders' interests.

Give an example of how an agency problem might arise between stockholders and creditors.

MANAGERIAL ACTIONS TO MAXIMIZE SHAREHOLDER WEALTH

Profit Maximization
The maximization of the firm's net income.

To maximize the price of a firm's stock, what types of actions should management take? First, consider the question of stock prices versus profits: Will **profit maxi-**

Earnings Per Share (EPS)
Net income divided by the number of shares of common stock outstanding.

mization result in stock price maximization? In answering this question, we must consider the matter of total corporate profits versus **earnings per share (EPS)**.

For example, suppose Xerox had 100 million shares outstanding and earned $400 million, or $4 per share. If you owned 100 shares of the stock, your share of the total profits would be $400. Now suppose Xerox sold another 100 million shares and invested the funds received in assets which produced $100 million of income. Total income would rise to $500 million, but earnings per share would decline from $4 to $500/200 = $2.50. Now your share of the firm's earnings would be only $250, down from $400. You (and other current stockholders) would have suffered an *earnings dilution*, even though total corporate profits had risen. Therefore, other things held constant, *if management is interested in the well-being of its current stockholders, it should concentrate on earnings per share rather than on total corporate profits.*

Will maximization of expected earnings per share always maximize stockholder welfare, or should other factors be considered? Think about the *timing of the earnings*. Suppose Xerox had one project that would cause earnings per share to rise by $0.20 per year for 5 years, or $1 in total, while another project would have no effect on earnings for 4 years but would increase earnings by $1.25 in the fifth year. Which project is better — in other words, is $0.20 per year for 5 years better or worse than $1.25 in Year 5? The answer depends on which project adds the most to the value of the stock, which in turn depends on the time value of money to investors. Thus, timing is an important reason to concentrate on wealth as measured by the price of the stock rather than on earnings alone.

Another issue relates to *risk*. Suppose one project is expected to increase earnings per share by $1, while another is expected to raise earnings by $1.20 per share. The first project is not very risky — if it is undertaken, earnings will almost certainly rise by about $1 per share. However, the other project is quite risky, so while our best guess is that earnings will rise by $1.20 per share, we must recognize the possibility that there may be no increase whatsoever, or even a loss. Depending on how averse stockholders are to risk, the first project might be preferable to the second.

The riskiness inherent in projected earnings per share (EPS) also depends on *how the firm is financed*. As we shall see, many firms go bankrupt every year, and the greater the use of debt, the greater the threat of bankruptcy. *Consequently, while the use of debt financing may increase projected EPS, debt also increases the riskiness of projected future earnings.*

Dividend Policy Decision
The decision as to how much of current earnings to pay out as dividends rather than to retain for reinvestment in the firm.

Another issue is the matter of paying dividends to stockholders versus retaining earnings and reinvesting them in the firm, thereby causing the earnings stream to grow over time. Stockholders like cash dividends, but they also like the growth in EPS that results from plowing earnings back into the business. The financial manager must decide exactly how much of the current earnings to pay out as dividends rather than to retain and reinvest — this is called the **dividend policy decision**. The optimal dividend policy is the one that maximizes the firm's stock price.

We see, then, that the firm's stock price is dependent on the following factors:

1. Projected earnings per share
2. Timing of the earnings stream
3. Riskiness of the projected earnings
4. Use of debt
5. Dividend policy

Every significant corporate decision should be analyzed in terms of its effect on these factors and hence on the price of the firm's stock. For example, suppose Occidental Petroleum's coal division is considering opening a new mine. If this is done, can it be expected to increase EPS? Is there a chance that costs will exceed estimates, that prices and output will fall below projections, and that EPS will be reduced because the new mine was opened? How long will it take for the new mine to show a profit? How should the capital required to open the mine be raised? If debt is used, by how much will this increase Occidental's riskiness? Should Occidental reduce its current dividends and use the cash thus saved to finance the project, or should it maintain its dividends and finance the mine with external capital? Financial management is designed to help answer questions like these, plus many more.

SELF-TEST QUESTIONS

Will profit maximization always result in stock price maximization?

Identify five factors which affect the firm's stock price, and explain the effects of each of them.

THE EXTERNAL ENVIRONMENT

Although managerial actions affect the value of a firm's stock, external factors also influence stock prices. Included among these factors are legal constraints, the general level of economic activity, tax laws, and conditions in the stock market. Figure 1-2 diagrams these general relationships. Working within the set of external constraints shown in the box at the extreme left, management makes a set of long-run strategic policy decisions which chart a future course for the firm. These policy decisions, along with the general level of economic activity and the level of corporate income taxes, influence the firm's expected profitability, the timing of its cash

FIGURE 1-2   SUMMARY OF MAJOR FACTORS AFFECTING STOCK PRICES

flows, their eventual transfer to stockholders in the form of dividends, and the degree of risk inherent in projected earnings and dividends. Profitability, timing, and risk all affect the price of the firm's stock, but so does another factor — conditions in the stock market as a whole — because all stock prices tend to move up and down together to some extent.

SELF-TEST QUESTION

Identify some factors beyond a firm's control which influence its stock price.

ORGANIZATION OF THE BOOK

The primary goal of management is to help maximize the value of the firm. To achieve this goal, managers must have a general understanding of how businesses are organized, how financial markets operate, how interest rates are determined, how the tax system operates, and how accounting data are used to evaluate a business's performance. In addition, managers must have a good understanding of some fundamental concepts, including time value of money, risk measurement, asset valuation, and evaluation of specific investment opportunities. This background information is essential for anyone involved with the kinds of decisions that affect the value of a firm's securities.

The organization of this book reflects these considerations, so in Part I we present four background chapters. Chapter 1 discusses the goals of the firm and the "philosophy" of financial management. Chapter 2 describes the key financial statements, discusses what they are designed to do, and then discusses how our tax system affects both stock prices and managerial decisions. Chapter 3 shows how financial statements are analyzed, and Chapter 4 explains how financial markets operate and how interest rates are determined.

Part II considers two of the most fundamental concepts in financial management. First, in Chapter 5, we see how risk is measured and how it affects security prices and rates of return. Next, Chapter 6 discusses the time value of money and its effects on asset values and rates of return.

The issues involved when investing in financial assets — stocks, bonds, and other securities — are covered in Part III. Chapter 7 focuses on bonds, and Chapter 8 considers stocks. Both chapters describe the relevant institutional details, and they also explain how risk and time value jointly determine stock and bond values.

Part IV, "Investing in Long-Term Assets: Capital Budgeting," applies the concepts covered in earlier chapters to long-term, fixed asset decisions. First, Chapter 9 explains how to measure the cost of funds used to acquire fixed assets, or the cost of capital. Next, Chapter 10 shows how this information is used to evaluate potential capital investments. The key issue is this: Can we expect a project to provide a higher rate of return than the cost of the funds used to finance it? Only if the expected return exceeds the cost of capital will accepting the project increase the wealth of the firm's stockholders. Chapter 11 goes into more detail on capital budgeting decisions, looking at replacement projects versus expansion projects, the effects of inflation, and risk analysis in capital budgeting.

Part V discusses how firms should finance their long-term assets. First, Chapter 12 examines capital structure theory, or the issue of how much debt versus equity the firm should use. Then, Chapter 13 considers dividend policy, or the decision to retain earnings versus paying them out as dividends.

In Part VI, our focus shifts from long-term, strategic decisions to short-term, day-to-day operating decisions. Operating decisions are made within the context of a financial plan, or forecast, so we begin, in Chapter 14, with a discussion of financial planning and forecasting. Then, in Chapters 15 and 16, we see how the proper amounts of cash, inventories, and accounts receivable are determined, and the best way of financing these current assets.

It is worth noting that some instructors may choose to cover the chapters in a different sequence from their order in the book. The chapters are written in a modular, self-contained manner, so such reordering should present no major difficulties.

SUMMARY

This chapter has provided an overview of financial management. The key concepts covered are listed below.

- Finance consists of three interrelated areas: (1) **money and capital markets,** (2) **investments,** and (3) **financial management.**
- **Financial managers** are responsible for **obtaining and using funds** in a way that will **maximize the value of their firms.**
- The three main forms of business organization are the **sole proprietorship,** the **partnership,** and the **corporation.**
- Although each form of organization offers some advantages and disadvantages, **most business is conducted by corporations because this organizational form maximizes most firms' values.**
- The primary goal of management should be to **maximize stockholders' wealth,** and this means **maximizing the price of the firm's stock.** However, actions which maximize stock prices also increase social welfare.
- An **agency problem** is a potential conflict of interests that can arise between a principal and an agent. Two important agency relationships are those between (1) the owners of the firm and its management or (2) the managers, acting for stockholders, and the creditors (debtholders).
- There are a number of ways to **motivate managers to act in the best interests of stockholders,** including (1) the **threat of firing,** (2) the **threat of takeovers,** and (3) properly structured **managerial incentives.**
- The **price of the firm's stock** depends on the firm's **projected earnings per share,** the **timing of its earnings,** the **riskiness of the projected earnings,** its **use of debt,** and its **dividend policy.**

QUESTIONS

1-1 What are the three principal forms of business organization? What are the advantages and disadvantages of each?

1-2 Would the "normal" rate of return on investment be the same in all industries? Would "normal" rates of return change over time? Explain.

1-3 Would the role of a financial manager be likely to increase or decrease in importance relative to other executives if the rate of inflation increased? Explain.

1-4 Should stockholder wealth maximization be thought of as a long-term or a short-term goal — for example, if one action would probably increase the firm's stock price from a current level of $20 to $25 in 6 months and then to $30 in 5 years but another action would probably keep the stock at $20 for several years but then increase it to $40 in 5 years, which action would be better? Can you think of some specific corporate actions which might have these general tendencies?

1-5 Drawing on your background in accounting, can you think of any accounting differences that might make it difficult to compare the relative performance of different firms?

1-6 Would the management of a firm in an oligopolistic or in a competitive industry be more likely to engage in what might be called "socially conscious" practices? Explain your reasoning.

1-7 What's the difference between stock price maximization and profit maximization? Under what conditions might profit maximization *not* lead to stock price maximization?

1-8 If you were the president of a large, publicly owned corporation, would you make decisions to maximize stockholders' welfare or your own personal interests? What are some actions stockholders could take to ensure that your interests and theirs coincided? What are some other factors that might influence management's actions?

1-9 The president of Southern Semiconductor Corporation (SSC) made this statement in the company's annual report: "SSC's primary goal is to increase the value of the common stockholders' equity over time." Later on in the report, the following announcements were made:
   a. The company contributed $1.5 million to the symphony orchestra in Birmingham, Alabama, its headquarters city.
   b. The company is spending $500 million to open a new plant in Mexico. No revenues will be produced by the plant for 4 years, so earnings will be depressed during this period versus what they would have been had the decision not been made to open the new plant.
   c. The company is increasing its relative use of debt. Whereas assets were formerly financed with 35 percent debt and 65 percent equity, henceforth the financing mix will be 50-50.
   d. The company uses a great deal of electricity in its manufacturing operations, and it generates most of this power itself. Plans are to utilize nuclear fuel rather than coal to produce electricity in the future.
   e. The company has been paying out half of its earnings as dividends and retaining the other half. Henceforth, it will pay out only 30 percent as dividends.
   Discuss how each of these actions would be reacted to by SSC's stockholders and customers, and then how each action might affect SSC's stock price.

1-10 Assume that you are serving on the board of directors of a medium-sized corporation and that you are responsible for establishing the compensation policies of senior management. You believe that the company's CEO is very talented, but your concern is that she is always looking for a better job and may want to boost the company's short-run performance (perhaps at the expense of long-run profitability) to make herself more marketable to other corporations. What effect would these concerns have on the compensation policy you put in place?

1-11 If the overall stock market is extremely volatile, and if many analysts foresee the possibility of a stock market crash, how might these factors influence the way, corporations choose to compensate their senior executives?

1-12 Teacher's Insurance and Annuity Association–College Retirement Equity Fund (TIAA–CREF) is the largest institutional shareholder in the United States, controlling $125 billion in pension funds. Traditionally, TIAA–CREF has acted as a passive investor. However, TIAA–CREF announced a tough new corporate governance policy beginning October 5, 1993.

In a statement mailed to all 1,500 companies in which it invests, TIAA–CREF outlined a policy designed to improve corporate performance, including a goal of higher stock prices for the $52 billion in stock assets it holds, and to encourage corporate boards to have a majority of independent (outside) directors. TIAA–CREF wants to see management more accountable to shareholder interests, as evidenced by its statement that the fund will vote against any director "where companies don't have an effective, independent board which can challenge the CEO."

Historically, TIAA–CREF did not quickly sell poor-performing stocks. In addition, the fund invested a large part of its assets to match performance of the major market indexes, locking TIAA–CREF into ownership of certain companies. Further complicating the problem, TIAA–CREF owns stakes of from 1 percent to 10 percent in several companies, and selling such large blocks of stock would depress their prices.

Common stock ownership confers a right to sponsor initiatives to shareholders regarding the corporation. A corresponding voting right exists for shareholders.
   a. Is TIAA–CREF an ordinary shareholder?
   b. Due to its asset size, TIAA–CREF assumes large positions with which it plans to actively vote. However, who owns TIAA–CREF?
   c. Should the investment managers of a fund like TIAA–CREF determine the voting practices of the fund's shares, or should the voting rights be passed on to TIAA–CREF's stakeholders?

SELF-TEST PROBLEM *(Solution Appears in Appendix B)*

ST-1 Key terms Define each of the following terms:
— a. Sole proprietorship; partnership; corporation
— b. Stockholder wealth maximization
   c. Hostile takeover; proxy fight; tender offer
   d. Social responsibility; business ethics
   e. Normal profits; normal rate of return
— f. Agency problem; agency costs
   g. Leveraged buyout (LBO)
   h. Poison pill; greenmail
   i. Performance shares; executive stock option
   j. Profit maximization
   k. Earnings per share
   l. Dividend policy decision

FINANCIAL STATEMENTS, CASH FLOW, AND TAXES

2

DOING YOUR HOMEWORK WITH FINANCIAL STATEMENTS

Y ou are a small investor who knows a little bit about finance and accounting. Can you ever expect to compete against large institutional investors armed with fleets of analysts, high-powered computers, and state-of-the-art trading strategies?

The answer, according to one Wall Street legend, is a resounding yes! Peter Lynch, who had an outstanding track record as manager of the $10 billion Fidelity Magellan fund and who has gone on to become the best selling author of *One Up on the Street* and *Beating the Street,* has long argued that small investors can beat the market by using common sense and information available to all of us as we go about our day-to-day lives.

For example, a college student may be more adept at scouting out new and inter-esting products which are likely to become tomorrow's success stories than is an investment banker who works 75 hours a week in a New York office. Parents of young children are likely to know which baby foods will succeed or which diapers are best. Couch potatoes may know which tortilla chips have a future, or whether a new remote control device is worth its price.

The trick is to find a product which will boom, yet whose manufacturer's stock is undervalued. If this sounds too easy, it is. Lynch argues that once you have discovered a good product, there is still homework to be done. Doing your homework involves combing through the vast amount of financial information that is regularly provided by the company to investors. It also requires taking a closer and more critical look at how the company conducts its business — Lynch refers to this as "kicking the tires."

To illustrate his point, Lynch relates his experience with Dunkin' Donuts. As a consumer, Lynch was impressed with the quality of the product — particularly the coffee. This impression led him to take a closer look at the company's financial statements and operations. He liked what he saw, and Dunkin' Donuts became one of the strongest performers in his portfolio.

The next two chapters discuss financial statements and financial statement analysis. Once you have come up with a good product as a possible investment, the principles discussed in the next two chapters will help you "do your homework."

The quantitative and verbal information are equally important. The financial statements report *what has actually happened* to earnings and dividends over the past few years, whereas the verbal statements attempt to explain why things turned out the way they did.

For illustrative purposes, we shall use data taken from Allied Food Products, a processor and distributor of a wide variety of staple foods, to discuss the basic financial statements. Formed in 1977 when several regional firms merged, Allied has grown steadily and has earned a reputation for being one of the best firms in its industry. Allied's earnings dropped a bit in 1995, to $113.5 million versus $118 million in 1994. Management reported that the drop resulted from losses associated with a drought and from increased costs due to a 3-month strike. However, management then went on to paint a more optimistic picture for the future, stating that full operations had been resumed, that several unprofitable businesses had been eliminated, and that 1996 profits were expected to rise sharply. Of course, an increase in profitability may not occur, and analysts should compare management's past statements with actual results. In any event, *the information contained in an annual report is used by investors to form expectations about future earnings and dividends.* Therefore, the annual report is obviously of great interest to investors.

SELF-TEST QUESTIONS

What is the annual report, and what two types of information are given in it?

Why is the annual report of great interest to investors?

THE BALANCE SHEET

Balance Sheet
A statement of the firm's financial position at a specific point in time.

The left-hand side of Allied's year-end 1994 and 1995 **balance sheets,** which are given in Table 2-1, shows the firm's assets, while the right-hand side shows the liabilities and equity, or the claims against these assets. The assets are listed in order of their "liquidity," or the length of time it typically takes to convert them to cash. The claims are listed in the order in which they must be paid: Accounts payable must generally be paid within 30 days, notes are payable within 90 days, and so on, down to the stockholders' equity accounts, which represent ownership and need never be "paid off."

Some additional points about the balance sheet are worth noting:

1. **Cash versus other assets.** Although the assets are all stated in terms of dollars, only cash represents actual money. Receivables are bills others owe Allied; inventories show the dollars the company has invested in raw materials, work-in-process, and finished goods available for sale; and fixed assets reflect the amount of money Allied paid for its plant and equipment when it acquired those assets at some time in the past. Allied can write checks at present for a total of $10 million (versus current liabilities of $310 million due within a year). The noncash assets should produce cash over time, but they do not represent cash in hand, and the amount of cash they would bring if they were sold today could be higher or lower than the values at which they are carried on the books.

2. **Liabilities versus stockholders' equity.** The claims against assets are of two types — liabilities (or money the company owes) and the stockholders' own-

| TABLE 2-1 | ALLIED FOOD PRODUCTS: DECEMBER 31 BALANCE SHEETS (MILLIONS OF DOLLARS) | | | | | |

ASSETS	1995	1994	LIABILITIES AND EQUITY	1995	1994
Cash and marketable securities	$ 10	$ 80	Accounts payable	$ 60	$ 30
Accounts receivable	375	315	Notes payable	110	60
Inventories	615	415	Accruals	140	130
Total current assets	$1,000	$ 810	Total current liabilities	$ 310	$ 220
Net plant and equipment	1,000	870	Long-term bonds	754	580
			Total debt	$1,064	$ 800
			Preferred stock (400,000 shares)	40	40
			Common stock (50,000,000 shares)	130	130
			Retained earnings	766	710
			Total common equity	$ 896	$ 840
Total assets	$2,000	$1,680	Total liabilities and equity	$2,000	$1,680

Note: The bonds have a sinking fund requirement of $20 million a year. Sinking funds are discussed in Chapter 7, but in brief, a sinking fund simply involves the repayment of long-term debt. Thus, Allied was required to pay off $20 million of its mortgage bonds during 1995. The current portion of the long-term debt is included in notes payable here, although in a more detailed balance sheet it would be shown as a separate item under current liabilities.

Common Stockholders' Equity (Net Worth)
The capital supplied by common stockholders — capital stock, paid-in capital, retained earnings, and, occasionally, certain reserves. *Total equity* is common equity plus preferred stock.

ership position.[2] The **common stockholders' equity**, or **net worth**, is a residual:

$$\text{Assets} - \text{Liabilities} - \text{Preferred stock} = \frac{\text{Common}}{\text{stockholders' equity.}}$$

$$\$2,000,000,000 - \$1,064,000,000 - \$40,000,000 = \$896,000,000.$$

Suppose assets decline in value — for example, suppose some of the accounts receivable are written off as bad debts. Liabilities and preferred stock remain constant, so the value of the common stockholders' equity must decline. Therefore, the risk of asset value fluctuations is borne by the common stockholders. Note, however, that if asset values rise (perhaps because of inflation), these benefits will accrue exclusively to the common stockholders.

3. **Preferred versus common stock.** Preferred stock is a hybrid, or a cross between common stock and debt. In the event of bankruptcy, preferred stock ranks below debt but above common stock. Also, the preferred dividend is fixed, so preferred stockholders do not benefit if the company's earnings grow. Finally, many firms do not use any preferred stock, and those that do generally do not use very much of it. Therefore, when the term "equity" is used in finance, we generally mean "common equity" unless otherwise noted.

4. **Breakdown of the common equity accounts.** The common equity section is divided into two accounts — "common stock" and "retained earnings." The

---

[2]One could divide liabilities into (1) debts owed to someone and (2) other items, such as deferred taxes, reserves, and so on. Because we do not make this distinction, the terms *debt* and *liabilities* are used synonymously. It should be noted that firms occasionally set up reserves for certain contingencies, such as the potential costs involved in a lawsuit currently in the courts. These reserves represent an accounting transfer from retained earnings to the reserve account. If the company wins the suit, retained earnings will be credited, and the reserve will be eliminated. If it loses, a loss will be recorded, cash will be reduced, and the reserve will be eliminated.

$2.27 per share in 1995, down from $2.36 in 1994, but it still raised the dividend from $1.06 to $1.15.

While the balance sheet can be thought of as a snapshot in time, the income statement reports on operations *over a period of time,* for example, during the calendar year 1995. During 1995 Allied had sales of $3 billion, and its net income available to common stockholders was $113.5 million. Income statements can cover any period of time, but they are usually prepared monthly, quarterly, or annually. Of course, sales, costs, and profits will be higher the longer the reporting period, and the sum of the last 12 monthly (or 4 quarterly) income statements should equal the values shown on the annual income statement.

For planning and control purposes, management generally forecasts monthly (or perhaps quarterly) income statements, and it then compares actual results to the budgeted statements. If revenues are below and costs above the forecasted levels, then management should take corrective steps before the problem becomes too serious.

SELF-TEST QUESTIONS

What is an income statement, and what information does it provide?

Why is earnings per share called "the bottom line"?

Regarding the time period reported, how does the income statement differ from the balance sheet?

STATEMENT OF RETAINED EARNINGS

Statement of Retained Earnings
A statement reporting how much of the firm's earnings were retained in the business rather than paid out in dividends. The figure for retained earnings that appears here is the sum of the annual retained earnings for each year of the firm's history.

Changes in retained earnings between balance sheet dates are reported in the **statement of retained earnings.** Table 2-3 shows that Allied earned $113.5 million during 1995, paid out $57.5 million in common dividends and plowed $56 million back into the business. Thus, the balance sheet item "Retained earnings" increased from $710 million at the end of 1994 to $766 million at the end of 1995.

Note that "Retained earnings" represents a *claim against assets,* not assets per se. Note also that firms retain earnings primarily to expand the business, and this means investing in plant and equipment, in inventories, and so on, *not* piling up cash in a bank account. Changes in retained earnings occur because common stockholders allow the firm to reinvest in the business funds that otherwise could be

TABLE 2-3	ALLIED FOOD PRODUCTS: STATEMENT OF RETAINED EARNINGS FOR YEAR ENDING DECEMBER 31, 1995 (MILLIONS OF DOLLARS)

Balance of retained earnings, December 31, 1994	$710.0
Add: Net income, 1995	113.5
Less: Dividends to common stockholders	(57.5)[a]
Balance of retained earnings, December 31, 1995	$766.0

[a]Here, and throughout the book, parentheses are used to denote negative numbers.

distributed as dividends. *Thus, retained earnings as reported on the balance sheet do not represent cash and are not "available" for the payment of dividends or anything else.*[3]

SELF-TEST QUESTIONS

What is the statement of retained earnings, and what information does it provide?

Why do changes in retained earnings occur?

Explain why the following statement is true: "Retained earnings as reported on the balance sheet do not represent cash and are not 'available' for the payment of dividends or anything else."

ACCOUNTING INCOME VERSUS CASH FLOW

When you studied income statements in accounting, the emphasis was probably on determining the net income of the firm. In finance, however, we focus on **cash flow.** The value of an asset (or a whole firm) is determined by the cash flow it generates. The firm's net income is important, but cash flow is even more important because dividends must be paid in cash and because cash is necessary to purchase the assets required to continue operations.

As we discussed in Chapter 1, the goal of the firm should be to maximize the price of its stock. Since the value of any asset, including a share of stock, depends on the cash flow produced by the asset, managers should strive to maximize the cash flow available to investors over the long run. A business's cash flow is generally equal to cash from sales, minus cash operating costs, minus interest charges, and minus taxes. Before we go any further though, we need to discuss *depreciation,* which is an operating cost.

Recall from accounting that **depreciation** is an annual charge against income which reflects the estimated dollar cost of the capital equipment used up in the production process. For example, suppose a machine with a life of 5 years and a zero expected salvage value was purchased in 1994 for $100,000. This $100,000 cost is not expensed in the purchase year; rather, it is charged against production over the machine's 5-year depreciable life. If the depreciation expense were not taken, profits would be overstated, and taxes would be too high. So, the annual depreciation charge is deducted from sales revenues, along with such other costs as labor and raw materials, to determine income. However, because the $100,000 was actually expended back in 1994, the depreciation charged against income in 1995 through 1999 is not a cash outlay, as are labor or raw materials charges. *Depreciation is a noncash charge, so it must be added back to net income to obtain the cash flow from operations.*

Cash Flow
The actual net cash, as opposed to accounting net income, that a firm generates during some specified period.

Depreciation
The charge for assets used in production. Depreciation is not a cash outlay.

---

[3]The amount reported in the retained earnings account is *not* an indication of the amount of cash the firm has. Cash (as of the balance sheet date) is found in the cash account — an asset account. A positive number in the retained earnings account indicates only that in the past, according to generally accepted accounting principles, the firm has earned an income, but its dividends have been less than its reported income. Even though a company reports record earnings and shows an increase in the retained earnings account, it still may be short of cash.

The same situation holds for individuals. You might own a new BMW (no loan), lots of clothes, and an expensive stereo, and hence have a high net worth, but if you had only 23 cents in your pocket plus $5 in your checking account, you would still be short of cash.

SHERLOCK HOLMES OR CORPORATE ENEMY NUMBER 1?

Is there more than meets the eye when it comes to looking at financial statements? One American University accounting professor certainly thinks so. His name is Howard Schilit, and he is recognized as a leading forensic accountant. As an independent consultant, Schilit works as a detective to search for the truth among the financial statements that companies make available to the public. *Business Week* has labeled Schilit the "Sherlock Holmes of Accounting." It is safe to say that many of the companies that have been targeted by Schilit would characterize his work less charitably.

Schilit pores over financial statements and looks for cases where companies adopt accounting practices which overstate their true health. These practices, which are generally legal and often consistent with generally accepted accounting principles (GAAP), are fre-

quently referred to as "window dressing." In many instances, companies have considerable latitude in deciding how to account for various activities in their financial statements. Schilit objects, however, when he believes these statements result in an inaccurate picture of a company's financial health.

Business Week also reported that in a recent one-year period, Schilit investigated 39 companies and wrote negative reports on 24 of these companies. During this time, the average price of these 24 companies' stocks fell by 31 percent. Schilit has particularly targeted firms which have recently gone public (issued shares of stock to the public for the first time). These firms are often under particular pressure to quickly demonstrate strong performance, and they may use accounting gimmicks to boost profits.

Take the case of Kendall Square Research Corporation, which went public in 1992 at a price of $10 per share. Within the first year, its stock price more than doubled to $22 a share, and its revenues increased from less than $1 million to nearly $21 million. Fidelity Investments, a large institutional investor, hired Schilit to see if this was too good to be true. Schilit concluded that it was. His report, along with a later report by the company's independent auditor, led to a dramatic restatement of the company's financial statements. The company reported a large loss of 1993, and in early 1994, its stock price fell to just over $2 per share. In an additional blow to investors, the company was delisted by the National Association of Securities Dealers (NASDAQ).

SOURCE: "The Sherlock Holmes of Accounting," *Business Week*, September 5, 1994, 48–52.

To see how depreciation affects cash flow, consider the following simplified income statement (Column 1) and cash flow statement (Column 2). Here we assume that all sales revenues were received in cash during the year and that all costs except depreciation were paid in cash during the year. By examining the data, you can see that cash flow is equal to net income plus depreciation:

	INCOME STATEMENT (1)	CASH FLOW STATEMENT (2)
Sales revenues	$1,500	$1,500
Costs except depreciation	1,050	1,050
Depreciation (DEP)	150	—
Total costs	$1,200	$1,050 (Cash costs)
Earnings before taxes	$ 300	$ 450 (Pretax cash flow)
Taxes (40%)	120	120 (From Column 1)
Net income (NI)	$ 180	
Add back depreciation	150	
Net cash flow = NI + DEP	$ 330	$ 330

As we shall see in Chapter 8, a stock's value is based on the *present value of the cash flows* which investors expect it to provide in the future. Although any individual investor could sell the stock and receive cash for it, the *cash flow* provided by the stock itself is the expected future dividend stream, and that expected dividend stream provides the fundamental basis for the stock's value.

Accounting Profit
A firm's net income as reported on its income statement.

Because dividends are paid in cash, a company's ability to pay dividends depends on its cash flow. Cash flow is generally related to **accounting profit,** which is simply net income as reported on the income statement. Although companies with relatively high accounting profits generally have relatively high cash flows, the relationship is not precise. Therefore, investors are concerned about cash flow projections as well as profit projections.

Firms can be thought of as having two separate but related bases of value: *existing assets,* which provide profits and cash flows, and *growth opportunities,* which represent opportunities to make new investments that will increase future profits and cash flows. The ability to take advantage of growth opportunities often depends on the availability of the cash needed to buy new assets, and the cash flow from existing assets is often the primary source of the funds used to make profitable new investments. This is another reason why both investors and managers are concerned with cash flows as well as profits.

Operating Cash Flow
That cash flow which arises from normal operations; the difference between sales revenues and cash expenses.

For our purposes, it is useful to divide cash flows into two classes: (1) *operating cash flows* and (2) *other cash flows.* **Operating cash flows** arise from normal operations, and they are, in essence, the difference between sales revenues and cash expenses, including taxes paid. Other cash flows arise from the issuance of stock, from borrowing, or from the sale of fixed assets. Our focus here is on operating cash flow.

Operating cash flow can differ from accounting profits (or net income) for three primary reasons:

1. All the taxes reported on the income statement may not have to be paid during the current year, or, under certain circumstances, the actual cash payments for taxes may exceed the tax figure deducted from sales to calculate net income. The reasons for these tax cash flow differentials are discussed in detail in accounting courses.

2. Sales may be on credit, hence not represent cash.

3. Some of the expenses (or costs) deducted from sales to determine profits may not be cash costs. Most important, depreciation is not a cash cost.

Thus, operating cash flow could be larger or smaller than accounting profits during any given year.

THE CASH FLOW CYCLE

As a company like Allied Food goes about its business, it makes sales, which lead (1) to a reduction of inventories, (2) to an increase in cash, and, (3) if the sales price exceeds the cost of the item sold, to a profit. These transactions cause the balance sheet to change, and they are also reflected in the income statement. It is critical that you understand (1) that businesses deal with *physical* units like autos, computers, or aluminum; (2) that physical transactions are translated into dollar terms through the accounting system; and (3) that the purpose of financial analysis is to examine the accounting numbers in order to determine how efficiently the firm is producing and selling physical goods and services.

Several factors make financial analysis difficult. One is the variations that exist in accounting methods among firms. As we discussed earlier, different methods of inventory valuation and depreciation can lead to differences in reported profits for otherwise identical firms. Therefore, a good financial analyst must be able to adjust for these differences if he or she is to make valid comparisons among companies. Another factor involves timing — actions are taken at one point in time, but their full effects cannot be accurately measured until a later date.

Cash Flow Cycle
The way actual cash, as opposed to accounting income, flows into or out of the firm during some specified period.

To understand how timing influences the financial statements, one must understand the **cash flow cycle** as set forth in Figure 2-1. Rectangles represent balance sheet accounts — assets and claims against assets — whereas circles represent actions which affect the income statement. Each rectangle may be thought of as a reservoir, and there is a certain dollar amount of the asset or liability in the reservoir on each balance sheet date. Only the cash account represents real cash; the other accounts show the dollar value of the assets in the account.

Various transactions cause changes in the accounts, just as adding or subtracting water changes the level in a reservoir. For example, collecting an account receivable reduces the receivables reservoir, but this transaction also increases the cash reservoir.

The cash (and marketable securities) account is the focal point of the figure. Certain events, such as collecting accounts receivable or borrowing money from the bank, will cause the cash account to increase, while the payment of taxes, interest, dividends, and accounts payable will cause it to decline. Similar comments could be made about all the balance sheet accounts — their balances rise, fall, or remain constant depending on events that occur during the period under study, which for Allied is January 1, 1995, through December 31, 1995.

Projected increases in sales may require the firm to raise cash by borrowing from its bank, by selling additional bonds, or by selling new stock. For example, if Allied anticipates an increase in sales, it will (1) expend cash to buy or build fixed assets through the capital budgeting process; (2) step up purchases of raw materials, thereby increasing both raw materials inventories and accounts payable; (3) increase production, which will lead to an increase in both accrued wages and work-in-process; and (4) eventually build up its finished goods inventory. Cash will have been expended and hence removed from the cash account, and the firm will have obligated itself to expend still more cash within a few weeks to pay off its accounts payable and accrued wages. These cash-using events will have occurred *before* any new cash has been generated from sales. Even when the expected sales do occur, there will still be a lag in the generation of cash — because Allied grants credit for 30 days, it will have to wait 30 days after a sale is made before cash comes in. Depending on how much cash the firm had at the beginning of the buildup, on the length of its production-sales-collection cycle, and on how long it can delay payment of its own payables and accrued wages, Allied may have to obtain substantial amounts of additional cash by selling stock or bonds or by borrowing from the bank.

If the firm is profitable, its sales revenues will exceed its costs, and its cash inflows will eventually exceed its cash outlays. However, even a profitable business can experience a cash shortage if it is growing rapidly. It may have to pay for plant, materials, and labor before cash from the expanded sales starts flowing in. For this reason, rapidly growing firms generally require large bank loans plus capital from other sources.

An unprofitable firm such as Eastern Airlines before its bankruptcy will have larger cash outlays than inflows. This, in turn, will drain the cash account and also cause a buildup of accrued wages and accounts payable, and lead to heavy borrowings. As a result, liabilities rise to excessive levels in unprofitable firms. Similarly, an overly ambitious expansion plan may result in excessive inventories and fixed assets, while too lenient a credit/collection policy will result in high accounts receivable, which may eventually result in bad debts and reduced profits.

FIGURE 2-1   CASH AND MATERIALS FLOWS WITHIN THE FIRM

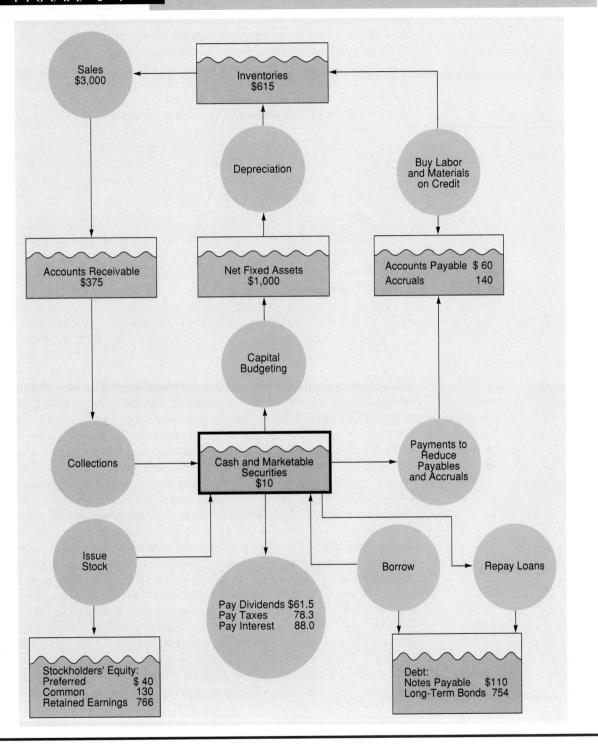

Financial Distress
A situation that occurs when a firm runs out of cash and has trouble meeting its obligations.

If a firm runs out of cash and cannot obtain enough to meet its obligations, then it cannot operate. Firms in this predicament are characterized as being in **financial distress.** Firms in financial distress often try to restructure their obligations so that they can continue operating. However, this may not be successful, in which case the firm may be forced out of business.

In fact, thousands of companies declare bankruptcy every year. Therefore, an accurate cash flow forecast is a critical element in financial management. Financial analysts are well aware of all this, and they use the analytical techniques discussed in the remainder of this chapter to help identify cash flow problems before they become serious.

SELF-TEST QUESTIONS

Differentiate between operating cash flow and net income.

List three reasons why operating cash flows can differ from net income.

In accounting, the emphasis is on the determination of net income. What is emphasized in finance, and why is that emphasis important?

Assuming that depreciation is the only noncash cost, how can someone calculate a business's cash flow?

STATEMENT OF CASH FLOWS

Statement of Cash Flows
A statement reporting the impact of a firm's operating, investing, and financing activities on cash flows over an accounting period.

The graphic cash flow analysis set forth in Figure 2-1, when converted into numerical form, is reported in annual reports as the **statement of cash flows.** This statement is designed to show how the firm's operations have affected its cash position and to help answer questions such as these: Is the firm generating the cash needed to purchase the additional assets required to grow? Is the firm generating extra cash that can be used to repay debt or to invest in new products? This information is useful both for financial managers and investors, so the statement of cash flows is an important part of the annual report. A detailed discussion of how to create the statement of cash flows is presented in financial accounting texts, but we are more concerned with the use of the statement of cash flows rather than its construction. Table 2-4 is Allied's statement of cash flows as it would appear in the company's annual report.

The top part of Table 2-4 shows cash flows generated by and used in operations —for Allied, operations provided net cash flows of *minus* $2.5 million. The operating cash flows are generated in the normal course of business, and this amount is determined by adjusting the net income figure to account for depreciation plus other cash flows related to operations. Allied's day-to-day operations in 1995 provided $257.5 million of funds; however, the increase in receivables and inventories more than offset this amount, resulting in a *negative* cash flow from operations.

The second section shows long-term investing activities. Allied purchased fixed assets totaling $230 million; this was the only long-term investment it made during 1995.

Allied's financing activities, shown in the third section of Table 2-4, included borrowing from banks (notes payable), selling new bonds, and paying dividends on its common and preferred stock. Allied raised $224 million by borrowing, but it paid $61.5 million in preferred and common dividends, so its net inflow of funds from financing activities during 1995 was $162.5 million.

TABLE 2-4	ALLIED FOOD PRODUCTS: STATEMENT OF CASH FLOWS FOR 1995 (MILLIONS OF DOLLARS)

OPERATING ACTIVITIES

Net income	$117.5
Additions (Sources of Cash)	
Depreciation[a]	100.0
Increase in accounts payable	30.0
Increase in accruals	10.0
Subtractions (Uses of Cash)	
Increase in accounts receivable	(60.0)
Increase in inventories	(200.0)
Net cash provided by operating activities	($ 2.5)

LONG-TERM INVESTING ACTIVITIES

Cash used to acquire fixed assets[b]	($230.0)

FINANCING ACTIVITIES

Increase in notes payable	$ 50.0
Increase in bonds	174.0
Payment of common and preferred dividends	(61.5)
Net cash provided by financing activities	$162.5
Net decrease in cash and marketable securities	($ 70.0)
Cash and securities at beginning of year	80.0
Cash and securities at end of year	$ 10.0

[a]Depreciation is a noncash expense that was deducted when calculating net income. It must be added back to show the correct cash flow from operations.

[b]The net increase in fixed assets is $130 million; however, this net amount is after a deduction for the year's depreciation expense. Depreciation expense should be added back to show the increase in gross fixed assets. From the company's income statement, we see that 1995 depreciation expense is $100 million; thus, the acquisition of fixed assets equals $230 million.

When all of these sources and uses of cash are totaled, we see that Allied's cash outflows exceeded its cash inflows by $70 million during 1995. It met that shortfall by drawing down its cash and marketable securities holdings by $70 million, as shown in Table 2-1, the firm's balance sheet.

Allied's statement of cash flows should be worrisome to its managers and to outside analysts. The company had a $2.5 million cash shortfall from operations, it spent an additional $230 million on new fixed assets, and it paid out another $61.5 million in dividends. It covered these cash outlays by borrowing heavily and by selling off most of its marketable securities. Obviously, this situation cannot continue year after year, so something will have to be done. In Chapter 3, we will consider some of the actions Allied's financial staff might recommend to ease the cash flow problem.[4]

---

[4]We should also mention the term "free cash flow," which is defined as the difference between operating cash inflows and the required expenditures necessary to maintain operating cash flows in the future. Management has discretion in the use of free cash flow, so the larger the free cash flow, the greater the firm's potential for expanding, increasing dividends, paying off debt, and so forth. Consequently, financial analysts give much attention to free cash flow. Allied had negative free cash flow during 1995.

SELF-TEST QUESTION

What is the statement of cash flows, and what types of questions does it answer?

THE FEDERAL INCOME TAX SYSTEM

The value of any financial asset, including stocks, bonds, and mortgages, as well as most real assets such as plants or even entire firms, depends on the stream of cash flows produced by the asset. Cash flows from an asset consist of *usable* income plus depreciation, and usable income means income *after taxes*.

Our tax laws can be changed by Congress, and in recent years changes have occurred almost every year. Indeed, a major change has occurred, on average, every three to four years since 1913, when our federal income tax system began. Further, certain parts of our tax system are tied to the rate of inflation, so changes occur automatically each year, depending on the rate of inflation during the previous year. Therefore, although this section will give you a good background on the basic nature of our tax system, you should consult current rate schedules and other data published by the Internal Revenue Service (available in U.S. post offices) before you file your personal or business tax return.

Currently (1995), federal income tax rates for individuals go up to 39.6 percent, and, when social security, Medicare, and state and city income taxes are included, the marginal tax rate on an individual's income can easily exceed 50 percent. Business income is also taxed heavily. The income from partnerships and proprietorships is reported by the individual owners as personal income and, consequently, is taxed at federal-plus-state rates going up to 50 percent or more. Corporate profits are subject to federal income tax rates of up to 39 percent, in addition to state income taxes. Because of the magnitude of the tax bite, taxes play a critical role in many financial decisions.

As this text is being written, a new Republican Congress and a Democratic administration are debating the merits of different changes in the tax laws. To stimulate investment, depreciation schedules may be liberalized, and capital gains may be taxed at a lower rate. Even in the unlikely event that no explicit changes are made in the tax laws, changes will still occur because certain aspects of the tax calculation are tied to the inflation rate. Thus, by the time you read this chapter, tax rates and other factors will almost certainly be different from those we provide. Still, if you understand the chapter, you will also understand the basics of our tax system, and you will know how to operate under the revised tax code.

Taxes are so complicated that university law schools offer master's degrees in taxation to practicing lawyers, many of whom are also CPAs. In a field complicated enough to warrant such detailed study, only the highlights can be covered in a book such as this. This is really enough, though, because business managers and investors should and do rely on tax specialists rather than trusting their own limited knowledge. Still, it is important to know the basic elements of the tax system as a starting point for discussions with tax experts.

INDIVIDUAL INCOME TAXES

Individuals pay taxes on wages and salaries, on investment income (dividends, interest, and profits from the sale of securities), and on the profits of proprietorships

Progressive Tax

A tax system where the tax rate is higher on higher incomes. The personal income tax in the United States, which goes from 0 percent on the lowest increments of income to 39.6 percent, is progressive.

Taxable Income

Gross income minus exemptions and allowable deductions as set forth in the Tax Code.

and partnerships. Our tax rates are **progressive** — that is, the higher one's income, the larger the percentage paid in taxes. Table 2-5 gives the tax rates for single individuals and married couples filing joint returns under the rate schedules that were in effect in 1994.

1. **Taxable income** is defined as gross income less a set of exemptions and deductions which are spelled out in the instructions to the tax forms individuals must file. When filing a tax return in 1995 for the tax year 1994, each taxpayer received an exemption of $2,450 for each dependent, including the taxpayer, which reduces taxable income. However, this exemption is indexed to rise with inflation, and the exemption is phased out for high-income taxpayers. Also, certain expenses including mortgage interest paid, state and local income taxes paid, and charitable contributions, can be deducted and thus be used to reduce taxable income, but again, high-income taxpayers lose some of this benefit.

TABLE 2-5	INDIVIDUAL TAX RATES FOR **1994**

Single Individuals

IF YOUR TAXABLE INCOME IS	YOU PAY THIS AMOUNT ON THE BASE OF THE BRACKET	PLUS THIS PERCENTAGE ON THE EXCESS OVER THE BASE	AVERAGE TAX RATE AT TOP OF BRACKET
Up to $22,750	$ 0	15.0%	15.0%
$22,750–$55,100	3,413	28.0	22.6
$55,100–$115,000	12,471	31.0	27.0
$115,000–$250,000	31,040	36.0	31.9
Over $250,000	79,640	39.6	39.6

Married Couples Filing Joint Returns

IF YOUR TAXABLE INCOME IS	YOU PAY THIS AMOUNT ON THE BASE OF THE BRACKET	PLUS THIS PERCENTAGE ON THE EXCESS OVER THE BASE	AVERAGE TAX RATE AT TOP OF BRACKET
Up to $38,000	$ 0	15.0%	15.0%
$38,000–$91,850	5,700	28.0	22.6
$91,850–$140,000	20,778	31.0	25.5
$140,000–$250,000	35,705	36.0	30.1
Over $250,000	75,305	39.6	39.6

Notes:

a. These are estimated tax rates for 1994 and beyond. The income ranges at which each tax rate takes effect, as well as the ranges for the additional taxes discussed below, are indexed with inflation each year, so they will change from those shown in the table.

b. The average tax rate approaches 39.6 percent as taxable income rises without limit. At $1 million of taxable income, the average tax rates for single individuals and married couples filing joint returns are 37.7 percent and 37.2 percent, respectively, while at $10 million it is 39.4 percent.

c. In 1994, a *personal exemption* of $2,450 per person or dependent could be deducted from gross income to determine taxable income. Thus, a husband and wife with two children would have a 1994 exemption of 4 × $2,450 = $9,800. The amount of the exemption is scheduled to increase with inflation. However, if the gross income exceeds certain limits ($167,700 for joint returns and $111,800 for single individuals in 1994), the exemption is phased out, and this has the effect of raising the effective tax rate on incomes over the specified limit by about 0.5 percent per family member, or 2.0 percent for a family of four. In addition, taxpayers can claim *itemized deductions* for charitable contributions and certain other items, but these deductions are reduced if the gross income exceeds $111,800 (for both single individuals and joint returns), and this raises the effective tax rate for high-income taxpayers by another 1 percent or so. The combined effect of the loss of exemptions and the reduction of itemized deductions is about 3 percent, so the marginal federal tax rate for high-income individuals goes up to about 42.6 percent.

In addition, there is the social security tax, which amounts to 6.2 percent (12.4 percent for a self-employed person) on up to $60,600 of earned income, plus a 1.45 percent Medicare payroll tax (2.9 percent for self-employed individuals) on *all* earned income. Finally, older high-income taxpayers who receive social security payments must pay taxes on 85 percent of their social security receipts, up from 50 percent in 1994. All of this pushes the effective tax rate up even further.

Marginal Tax Rate
The tax rate applicable to the last unit of a person's income.

2. The **marginal tax rate** is defined as the tax rate on the last unit of income. Marginal rates begin at 15 percent and rise to 39.6 percent. Note, though, that when consideration is given to the phase-out of exemptions and deductions, to social security and Medicare taxes, and to state taxes, the marginal tax rate can actually exceed 50 percent.

Average Tax Rate
Taxes paid divided by taxable income.

3. One can calculate **average tax rates** from the data in Table 2-5. For example, if Jill Smith, a single individual, had taxable income of $35,000, her tax bill would be $3,413 + ($35,000 − $22,750)(0.28) = $3,413 + $3,430 = $6,843. Her *average tax rate* would be $6,843/$35,000 = 19.6% versus a *marginal rate* of 28 percent. If Jill received a raise of $1,000, bringing her income to $36,000, she would have to pay $280 of it as taxes, so her after-tax raise would be $720. In addition, her social security and Medicare taxes would increase by $76.50, which would cut her net raise to $643.50.

Bracket Creep
A situation that occurs when progressive tax rates combine with inflation to cause a greater portion of each taxpayer's real income to be paid as taxes.

4. As indicated in the notes to the table, current legislation provides for tax brackets to be indexed to inflation to avoid the **bracket creep** that occurred during the 1970s and that in reality raised tax rates substantially.[5]

TAXES ON DIVIDEND AND INTEREST INCOME.   Dividend and interest income received by individuals from corporate securities is added to other income and thus is taxed at rates going up to about 50 percent.[6] Since corporations pay dividends out of earnings that have already been taxed, there is *double taxation* of corporate income — income is first taxed at the corporate rate, and when what is left is paid out as dividends, it is taxed again at the personal rate.

It should be noted that under U.S. tax laws, interest on most state and local government bonds, called *municipals* or *"munis,"* is not subject to federal income taxes. Thus, investors get to keep all of the interest received from most municipal bonds but only a fraction of the interest received from bonds issued by corporations or by the U.S. government. This means that a lower-yielding muni can provide the same after-tax return as a higher-yielding corporate bond. For example, a taxpayer in the 39.6 percent marginal tax bracket who could buy a muni that yielded 5.5 percent would have to receive a before-tax yield of 9.11 percent on a corporate or U.S. Treasury bond to have the same after-tax income:

$$\frac{\text{Equivalent pretax yield}}{\text{on taxable bond}} = \frac{\text{Yield on muni}}{1 - \text{Marginal tax rate}}$$

$$= \frac{5.5\%}{1 - 0.396} = 9.11\%.$$

[5]For example, if you were single and had a taxable income of $22,750, your tax bill would be $3,413. Now suppose inflation caused prices to double and your income, being tied to a cost-of-living index, rose to $45,500. Because our tax rates are progressive, if tax brackets were not indexed, your taxes would jump to $9,783. Your after-tax income would thus increase from $19,337 to $35,717, but, because prices have doubled, your real income would *decline* from $19,337 to $17,859 (calculated as one-half of $35,717). You would be in a higher tax bracket, so you would be paying a higher percentage of your real income in taxes. If this happened to everyone, and if Congress failed to change tax rates sufficiently, real disposable incomes would decline because the federal government would be taking a larger share of the national product. This is called the federal government's "inflation dividend." However, since tax brackets are now indexed, if your income doubled due to inflation, your tax bill would double, but your after-tax real income would remain constant at $19,337. Bracket creep was a real problem during the 1970s and early 1980s, but indexing — if it stays in the law — puts an end to it.

[6]You do not pay social security and Medicare taxes on interest, dividends, and capital gains, only on earned income. But state taxes are imposed on dividends, interest, and capital gains.

If we know the yield on the taxable bond, we can use the following equation to find the equivalent yield on a muni:

$$\text{Equivalent yield on muni} = \left(\begin{array}{c} \text{Pretax yield} \\ \text{on taxable} \\ \text{bond} \end{array} \right) (1 - \text{Marginal tax rate})$$

$$= 9.11\% \, (1 - 0.396) = 9.11\%(0.604) = 5.5\%.$$

The exemption from federal taxes stems from the separation of federal and state powers, and its primary effect is to help state and local governments borrow at lower rates than would otherwise be available to them.

Munis generally yield from 2 to 4 percentage points less than corporate bonds with the same risk. It would make no sense for someone in a very low tax bracket to buy munis, but it would make sense for high tax bracket investors to buy them. Therefore, most munis are owned by high-bracket investors.

Capital Gain or Loss
The profit (loss) from the sale of a capital asset for more (less) than its purchase price.

CAPITAL GAINS VERSUS ORDINARY INCOME.   Assets such as stocks, bonds, and real estate are defined as *capital assets.* If you buy a capital asset and later sell it for more than your purchase price, the profit is called a **capital gain;** if you suffer a loss, it is called a **capital loss.** An asset sold within one year of the time it was purchased produces a *short-term gain or loss,* whereas one held for more than one year produces a *long-term gain or loss.* Thus, if you buy 100 shares of Disney stock for $42 per share and sell it for $52 per share, you make a capital gain of $100 \times \$10$, or $1,000. However, if you sell the stock for $32 per share, you will have a $1,000 capital loss. If you hold the stock for more than one year, the gain or loss is long-term; otherwise, it is short-term. If you sell the stock for exactly $42 per share, you make neither a gain nor a loss; you simply get your $4,200 back, and no tax is due.

Short-term capital gains are added to such ordinary income as wages, dividends, and interest and then are taxed at the same rate as ordinary income. However, long-term capital gains are taxed differently in that the rate on long-term capital gains is capped at 28 percent. Thus, if in 1994 you were in a tax bracket of 28 percent or less, any capital gains you earned would be taxed just like ordinary income, but if you were in the 31, 36, or 39.6 percent bracket, your long-term capital gains would only be taxed at a 28 percent rate. Thus, long-term capital gains are better than ordinary income for many people because more of it is left after taxes.

Capital gains tax rates have varied over time, but they have generally been lower than rates on ordinary income. The reason is simple — Congress wants the economy to grow. For that to happen we need investment in productive assets, and low capital gains tax rates encourage investment. To see why, suppose you owned a company that earned $1 million after corporate taxes. Because it is your company, you could have it pay out the entire profit as dividends, or you could have it retain and reinvest all or part of the income to expand the business. If it pays dividends, they will be taxable to you at a rate of 39.6 percent. However, if the company reinvests its income, that reinvestment should cause the company's earnings and stock price to increase. Now, if you wait for a year, then sell some of your stock at a now-higher price, you will have earned capital gains, which will be taxed at only 28 percent. Further, you can postpone the capital gains tax by simply not selling the stock.

It should be clear that a lower tax rate on capital gains will encourage investment. The owners of small businesses will want to reinvest income to get capital gains, as will stockholders in large corporations. Individuals with money to invest will understand the tax advantages associated with investing in newly formed companies versus buying bonds, so new ventures will have an easier time attracting equity capital. All in all, lower capital gains tax rates stimulate capital formation and investment.[7]

CORPORATE INCOME TAXES

The corporate tax structure, shown in Table 2-6, is relatively simple. To illustrate, if a firm had $75,000 of taxable income, its tax bill would be

$$\text{Taxes} = \$7,500 + 0.25(\$25,000)$$
$$= \$7,500 + \$6,250 = \$13,750,$$

and its average tax rate would be $13,750/$75,000 = 18.3%. Note that corporate income above $18,333,333 has an average and marginal tax rate of 35 percent.[8]

TABLE 2-6	CORPORATE TAX RATES		
IF A CORPORATION'S TAXABLE INCOME IS	IT PAYS THIS AMOUNT ON THE BASE OF THE BRACKET	PLUS THIS PERCENTAGE ON THE EXCESS OVER THE BASE	AVERAGE TAX RATE AT TOP OF BRACKET
Up to $50,000	$ 0	15%	15.0%
$50,000–$75,000	7,500	25	18.3
$75,000–$100,000	13,750	34	22.3
$100,000–$335,000	22,250	39	34.0
$335,000–$10,000,000	113,900	34	34.0
$10,000,000–$15,000,000	3,400,000	35	34.3
$15,000,000–$18,333,333	5,150,000	38	35.0
Over $18,333,333	6,416,667	35	35.0

[7]The 1993 tax act called for capital gains on the newly issued stock of certain small companies to be taxed at one-half the regular capital gains tax rate if the stock is held for five years or longer. Thus, if one bought newly issued stock from a qualifying small company and held it for at least five years, any capital gains would be taxed at a maximum rate of 14 percent. This provision was designed to help small businesses obtain equity capital.

[8]Prior to 1987, many large, profitable corporations such as General Electric and Boeing paid no income taxes. The reasons for this were as follows: (1) expenses, especially depreciation, were defined differently for calculating taxable income than for reporting earnings to stockholders, so some companies reported positive profits to stockholders but losses — hence no taxes — to the Internal Revenue Service; and (2) some companies which did have tax liabilities used various tax credits to offset taxes that would otherwise have been payable. This situation was effectively eliminated in 1987.

    The principal method used to eliminate this situation is the Alternative Minimum Tax (AMT). Under the AMT, both corporate and individual taxpayers must figure their taxes in two ways, the "regular" way and the AMT way, and then pay the higher of the two. The AMT is calculated as follows: (1) Figure your regular taxes. (2) Take your taxable income under the regular method and then add back certain items, especially income on certain municipal bonds, depreciation in excess of straight line depreciation, certain research and drilling costs, itemized or standard deductions (for individuals), and a number of other items. (3) The income determined in (2) is defined as AMT income, and it must then be multiplied by the AMT tax rate to determine the tax due under the AMT system. An individual or corporation must then pay the higher of the regular tax or the AMT tax. In 1994, there were two AMT tax rates for individuals (26 percent and 28 percent, depending on the level of AMT income and filing status); the corporate AMT remained unchanged at 20 percent.

INTEREST AND DIVIDEND INCOME RECEIVED BY A CORPORATION. Interest income received by a corporation is taxed as ordinary income at regular corporate tax rates. *However, 70 percent of the dividends received by one corporation from another is excluded from taxable income, while the remaining 30 percent is taxed at the ordinary tax rate.*[9] Thus, a corporation earning more than $18,333,333 and paying a 35 percent marginal tax rate would pay only $(0.30)(0.35) = 0.105 = 10.5\%$ of its dividend income as taxes, so its effective tax rate on intercorporate dividends would be 10.5 percent. If this firm had $10,000 in pretax dividend income, its after-tax dividend income would be $8,950:

$$
\begin{aligned}
\frac{\text{After-tax}}{\text{income}} &= \text{Before-tax income} - \text{Taxes} \\
&= \text{Before-tax income} - (\text{Before-tax income})(\text{Effective tax rate}) \\
&= \text{Before-tax income}(1 - \text{Effective tax rate}) \\
&= \$10,000 \, [1 - (0.30)(0.35)] \\
&= \$10,000(1 - 0.105) = \$10,000(0.895) = \$8,950.
\end{aligned}
$$

If the corporation pays its own after-tax income out to its stockholders as dividends, the income is ultimately subjected to *triple taxation:* (1) the original corporation is first taxed, (2) the second corporation is then taxed on the dividends it received, and (3) the individuals who receive the final dividends are taxed again. This is the reason for the 70 percent exclusion on intercorporate dividends.

If a corporation has surplus funds that can be invested in marketable securities, the tax factor favors investment in stocks, which pay dividends, rather than in bonds, which pay interest. For example, suppose GE had $100,000 to invest, and it could buy either bonds that paid interest of $8,000 per year or preferred stock that paid dividends of $7,000. GE is in the 35 percent tax bracket; therefore, its tax on the interest, if it bought bonds, would be $0.35(\$8,000) = \$2,800$, and its after-tax income would be $5,200. If it bought preferred (or common) stock, its tax would be $0.35[(0.30)(\$7,000)] = \$735$, and its after-tax income would be $6,265. Other factors might lead GE to invest in bonds, but the tax factor certainly favors stock investments when the investor is a corporation.[10]

INTEREST AND DIVIDENDS PAID BY A CORPORATION. A firm's operations can be financed with either debt or equity capital. If it uses debt, it must pay interest on this debt, whereas if it uses equity, it will pay dividends to the equity investors (stockholders). The interest paid by a corporation is deducted from its operating income to obtain its taxable income, but dividends paid are not deductible. Therefore, a firm

---

[9]The size of the dividend exclusion actually depends on the degree of ownership. Corporations that own less than 20 percent of the stock of the dividend-paying company can exclude 70 percent of the dividends received; firms that own more than 20 percent but less than 80 percent can exclude 80 percent of the dividends; and firms that own more than 80 percent can exclude the entire dividend payment. Since most companies own less than 20 percent of other companies, we will, in general, assume a 70 percent dividend exclusion.

[10] This illustration demonstrates why corporations favor investing in lower-yielding preferred stocks over higher-yielding bonds. When tax consequences are considered, the yield on the preferred stock, $[1 - 0.35(0.30)](7.0\%) = 6.265\%$, is higher than the yield on the bond, $(1 - 0.35)(8.0\%) = 5.200\%$. Also, note that corporations are restricted in their use of borrowed funds to purchase other firms' preferred or common stocks. Without such restrictions, firms could engage in *tax arbitrage,* whereby the interest on borrowed funds reduces taxable income on a dollar-for-dollar basis, but taxable income is increased by only $0.30 per dollar of dividend income. Thus, current tax laws reduce the 70 percent dividend exclusion in proportion to the amount of borrowed funds used to purchase the stock.

TABLE 2-7	CASH FLOWS TO INVESTORS UNDER BOND AND STOCK FINANCING	

	USE BONDS (1)	USE STOCK (2)
Sales	$5,000,000	$5,000,000
Operating costs	3,500,000	3,500,000
Earnings before interest and taxes (EBIT)	$1,500,000	$1,500,000
Interest	1,500,000	0
Taxable income	$ 0	$1,500,000
Federal-plus-state taxes (40%)	0	600,000
After-tax income	$ 0	$ 900,000
Income to investors	$1,500,000	$ 900,000
Rate of return on $10 million of assets	15.0%	9.0%

needs $1 of pretax income to pay $1 of interest, but if it is in the 40 percent federal-plus-state tax bracket, it needs $1.67 of pretax income to pay $1 of dividends:

$$\text{Pretax income needed to pay \$1 of dividends} = \frac{\$1}{1 - \text{Tax rate}} = \frac{\$1}{0.60} = \$1.67.$$

Proof: After-tax income = $1.67 − Tax = $1.67 − $1.67(0.4) = $1.67(1 − 0.4) = $1.00.

Table 2-7 shows the situation for a firm with $10 million of assets, sales of $5 million, and $1.5 million of earnings before interest and taxes (EBIT). As shown in Column 1, if the firm were financed entirely by bonds, and if it made interest payments of $1.5 million, its taxable income would be zero, taxes would be zero, and its investors would receive the entire $1.5 million. (The term *investors* includes both stockholders and bondholders.) As shown in Column 2, if the firm had no debt and was therefore financed only by stock, all of the $1.5 million of EBIT would be taxable income to the corporation, the tax would be $1,500,000(0.40) = $600,000, and investors would receive only $0.9 million versus $1.5 million under debt financing. The rate of return to investors on their $10 million investment is also much higher if debt is used.

Of course, it is generally not possible to finance exclusively with debt capital, and the risk of doing so would offset the benefits of the higher expected income. *Still, the fact that interest is a deductible expense has a profound effect on the way businesses are financed — our corporate tax system favors debt financing over equity financing.* This point is discussed in more detail in Chapters 9 and 12.

CORPORATE CAPITAL GAINS.   Before 1987, corporate long-term capital gains were taxed at lower rates than ordinary income, as is true for individuals. Under current law, however, corporations' capital gains are taxed at the same rates as their operating income.

Tax Loss Carry-Back and Carry-Forward

Ordinary corporate operating losses can be carried backward for 3 years or forward for 15 years to offset taxable income in a given year.

CORPORATE LOSS CARRY-BACK AND CARRY-FORWARD.   Ordinary corporate operating losses can be carried back (**carry-back**) to each of the preceding 3 years and forward (**carry-forward**) for the next 15 years to offset taxable income in those years. For example, an operating loss in 1996 could be carried back and used to reduce taxable income in 1993, 1994, and 1995, and forward, if necessary, and used in 1997, 1998, and so on, to the year 2011. The loss is typically applied first to the earliest year, then to the next earliest year, and so on, until losses have been used up or the 15-year carry-forward limit has been reached.

To illustrate, suppose Apex Corporation had $2 million of *pretax* profits (taxable income) in 1993, 1994, and 1995, and then, in 1996, Apex lost $12 million. Also, assume that Apex's federal-plus-state tax rate is 40 percent. As shown in Table 2-8, the company would use the carry-back feature to recompute its taxes for 1993, using $2 million of the 1996 operating losses to reduce the 1993 pretax profit to zero. This would permit it to recover the amount of taxes paid in 1993. Therefore, in 1997 Apex would receive a refund of its 1993 taxes because of the loss experienced in 1996. Because $10 million of the unrecovered losses would still be available, Apex would repeat this procedure for 1994 and 1995. Thus, in 1997 the company would pay zero taxes for 1996 and also would receive a refund for taxes paid from 1993 through 1995. Apex would still have $6 million of unrecovered losses to carry forward, subject to the 15-year limit, until the entire $12 million loss had been used to offset taxable income. The purpose of permitting this loss treatment is, of course, to avoid penalizing corporations whose incomes fluctuate substantially from year to year.

Improper Accumulation
Retention of earnings by a business for the purpose of enabling stockholders to avoid personal income taxes.

IMPROPER ACCUMULATION TO AVOID PAYMENT OF DIVIDENDS. Corporations could refrain from paying dividends to permit their stockholders to avoid personal income taxes on dividends. To prevent this, the Tax Code contains an **improper accumulation** provision which states that earnings accumulated by a corporation are subject to penalty rates *if the purpose of the accumulation is to enable stockholders to avoid personal income taxes.* A cumulative total of $250,000 (the balance sheet item "retained earnings") is by law exempted from the improper accumulation tax for most corporations. This is a benefit primarily to small corporations.

The improper accumulation penalty applies only if the retained earnings in excess of $250,000 are *shown to be unnecessary to meet the reasonable needs of the business.* A great many companies do indeed have legitimate reasons for retaining more than $250,000 of earnings. For example, earnings may be retained and used

TABLE 2-8	APEX CORPORATION: CALCULATION OF LOSS CARRY-BACK AND CARRY-FORWARD FOR 1993–1995 USING A $12 MILLION 1996 LOSS		
	1993	**1994**	**1995**
Original taxable income	$ 2,000,000	$2,000,000	$2,000,000
Carry-back credit	− 2,000,000	− 2,000,000	− 2,000,000
Adjusted profit	$ 0	$ 0	$ 0
Taxes previously paid (40%)	800,000	800,000	800,000
Difference = Tax refund	$ 800,000	$ 800,000	$ 800,000

Total refund check received in 1997: $800,000 + $800,000 + $800,000 = $2,400,000.

Amount of loss carry-forward available for use in 1997–2011:

1996 loss	$12,000,000
Carry-back losses used	$ 6,000,000
Carry-forward losses still available	$ 6,000,000

to pay off debt, to finance growth, or to provide the corporation with a cushion against possible cash drains caused by losses. How much a firm should properly accumulate for uncertain contingencies is a matter of judgment. We shall consider this matter again in Chapter 13, which deals with corporate dividend policy.

CONSOLIDATED CORPORATE TAX RETURNS.   If a corporation owns 80 percent or more of another corporation's stock, it can aggregate income and file one consolidated tax return; thus, the losses of one company can be used to offset the profits of another. (Similarly, one division's losses can be used to offset another division's profits.) No business ever wants to incur losses (you can go broke losing $1 to save 35¢ in taxes), but tax offsets do make it more feasible for large, multidivisional corporations to undertake risky new ventures or ventures that will suffer losses during a developmental period.

TAXATION OF SMALL BUSINESSES: S CORPORATIONS

S Corporation
A small corporation which, under Subchapter S of the Internal Revenue Code, elects to be taxed as a proprietorship or a partnership yet retains limited liability and other benefits of the corporate form of organization.

The Internal Revenue Code provides that small businesses which meet certain restrictions as spelled out in the code may be set up as corporations and thus receive the benefits of the corporate form of organization — especially limited liability — yet still be taxed as proprietorships or partnerships rather than as corporations. These corporations are called **S corporations.** ("Regular" corporations are called C corporations.) If a corporation elects S corporation status for tax purposes, all of the business's income is reported as personal income by the owners, and it is taxed at the rates that apply to individuals. This would be preferred by owners of small corporations in which all or most of the income earned each year is distributed as dividends, because then the income would be taxed only once, at the individual level.

? SELF-TEST QUESTIONS

Explain what is meant by the statement: "Our tax rates are progressive."

Are tax rates continuously progressive, or does progressivity eventually level out?

Explain the difference between marginal tax rates and average tax rates.

What are capital gains and losses, and how do they differ from ordinary income?

How are dividends received by a corporation taxed versus dividends received by an individual? Why is this distinction made?

Briefly explain how tax loss carry-back and carry-forward procedures work.

What is a "municipal bond," and how are these bonds taxed?

DEPRECIATION

Congress specifies in the tax code the life over which assets can be depreciated for tax purposes, and the methods that can be used to calculate depreciation. Since these factors have a major influence on the amount of depreciation a firm can take in a given year, and thus on the firm's taxable income, depreciation has an important effect on taxes paid and on cash flows from operations. We will discuss in detail how depreciation is calculated, and how it affects income and cash flows, when we take up capital budgeting, in Chapters 10 and 11.

SUMMARY

The primary purposes of this chapter were (1) to describe the basic financial statements, (2) to present some background information on cash flows, and (3) to give an overview of the federal income tax system. The key concepts covered are listed below.

- The four basic statements contained in the **annual report** are the balance sheet, the income statement, the statement of retained earnings, and the statement of cash flows. Investors use the information provided in these statements to form expectations about the future levels of earnings and dividends, and about the firm's riskiness.

- A firm's **balance sheet** shows its assets on the left-hand side and its liabilities and equity, or claims against assets, on the right-hand side. The balance sheet may be thought of as a snapshot of the firm's financial position at a particular point in time.

- A firm's **income statement** reports the results of operations over a period of time, and it shows earnings per share as its "bottom line."

- A firm's **statement of retained earnings** shows the change in retained earnings between the balance sheet dates. Retained earnings represent a claim against assets, not assets per se.

- **Operating cash flows** differ from reported **accounting profits.** Investors are more interested in a firm's projected cash flows than in reported earnings because it is cash, not paper profits, that is paid out as dividends and plowed back into the business to produce growth.

- The **cash flow cycle** is the way in which actual net cash, as opposed to accounting net income, flows into or out of a firm during some specified period.

- A firm's **statement of cash flows** reports the impact of operating, investing, and financing activities on cash flows over an accounting period.

- The value of any asset depends on the stream of **after-tax cash flows** it produces. Tax rates and other aspects of our tax system are changed by Congress every year or so.

- In the United States, tax rates are **progressive** — the higher one's income, the larger the percentage paid in taxes, up to a point.

- Assets such as stocks, bonds, and real estate are defined as **capital assets.** If a capital asset is sold for more than its cost, the profit is called a **capital gain.** If the asset is sold for a loss, it is called a **capital loss.** Assets held for over a year provide **long-term** gains or losses.

- Operating income paid out as dividends is subject to **double taxation:** the income is first taxed at the corporate level, and then shareholders must pay personal taxes on their dividends.

- **Interest income** received by a corporation is taxed as **ordinary income;** however, 70 percent of the dividends received by one corporation from another are excluded from **taxable income.** The reason for this exclusion is to reduce **triple taxation** of corporate income.

- Interest paid by a corporation is a **deductible** expense, but dividends are not. As a result, our corporate tax system favors debt over equity financing.

- Ordinary corporate operating losses can be **carried back** to each of the preceding 3 years and **carried forward** for the next 15 years to offset taxable income in those years.

- **S corporations** are small businesses which have the limited-liability benefits of the corporate form of organization yet obtain the benefits of being taxed only once at the individual level like a partnership or a proprietorship.

QUESTIONS

2-1 What four statements are contained in most annual reports?

2-2 If a "typical" firm reports $20 million of retained earnings on its balance sheet, could its directors declare a $20 million cash dividend without any qualms whatsoever?

2-3 Explain the following statement: "While the balance sheet can be thought of as a snapshot of the firm's financial position *at a point in time,* the income statement reports on operations *over a period of time.*"

2-4 Differentiate between accounting income and cash flow. Why might these two numbers differ?

2-5 What do the numbers on financial statements actually represent?

2-6 Who are some of the basic users of financial statements, and how do they use them?

2-7 Suppose you owned 100 shares of General Motors stock, and the company earned $6 per share during the last reporting period. Suppose further that GM could either pay all its earnings out as dividends (in which case you would receive $600) or retain the earnings in the business, buy more assets, and cause the price of the stock to go up by $6 per share (in which case the value of your stock would rise by $600).
   a. How would the tax laws influence what you, as a typical stockholder, would want the company to do?
   b. Would your choice be influenced by how much other income you had? Why might the desires of a 45-year-old doctor differ with respect to corporate dividend policy from those of a pension fund manager or a retiree living on a small income?
   c. How might the corporation's decision with regard to dividend policy influence the price of its stock?

2-8 What does *double taxation of corporate income* mean?

2-9 If you were starting a business, what tax considerations might cause you to prefer to set it up as a proprietorship or a partnership rather than as a corporation?

2-10 Explain how the federal income tax structure affects the choice of financing (use of debt versus equity) of U.S. business firms.

2-11 For someone planning to start a new business, is the average or the marginal tax rate more relevant?

SELF-TEST PROBLEMS *(Solutions Appear in Appendix B)*

ST-1 Key terms Define each of the following terms:
   a. Annual report; balance sheet; income statement
   b. Common stockholders' equity, or net worth; paid-in capital; retained earnings
   c. Cash flow; accounting profit; cash flow cycle
   d. Statement of retained earnings; statement of cash flows
   e. Depreciation; inventory valuation methods
   f. Operating cash flow; financial distress
   g. Progressive tax
   h. Marginal and average tax rates
   i. Bracket creep
   j. Capital gain or loss
   k. Tax loss carry-back and carry-forward
   l. Improper accumulation
   m. S corporation

ST-2 Effect of form of organization on taxes Mary Henderson is planning to start a new business, MH Enterprises, and she must decide whether to incorporate or to do business as a sole proprietorship. Under either form, Henderson will initially own

100 percent of the firm, and tax considerations are important to her. She plans to finance the firm's expected growth by drawing a salary just sufficient for her family living expenses, which she estimates will be about $40,000, and by retaining all other income in the business. Assume that as a married woman with one child, Henderson has income tax exemptions of 3 × $2,450 = $7,350, and she estimates that her itemized deductions for each of the 3 years will be $9,700. She expects MH Enterprises to grow and to earn income of $52,700 in 1996, $90,000 in 1997, and $150,000 in 1998. Which form of business organization will allow Henderson to pay the lowest taxes (and retain the most income) during the period from 1996 to 1998? Assume that the tax rates given in the chapter are applicable for all future years. (Social security taxes would also have to be paid, but ignore them.)

PROBLEMS

Note: By the time this book is published, Congress might have changed rates and/or other provisions of current tax law — as noted in the chapter, such changes occur fairly often. Work all problems on the assumption that the information in the chapter is applicable.

2-1 Financial statements   The Smythe-Davidson Corporation just issued its annual report. The current year's balance sheet and income statement as they appeared in the annual report are given below. Answer the questions that follow based on information given in the financial statements.

SMYTHE-DAVIDSON CORPORATION: BALANCE SHEET AS OF DECEMBER 31, 1995 (MILLIONS OF DOLLARS)

Assets		Liabilities and Equity	
Cash and marketable securities	$ 15	Accounts payable	$ 120
Accounts receivable	515	Notes payable	220
Inventories	880	Accruals	280
Total current assets	$1,410	Total current liabilities	$ 620
Net plant and equipment	2,590	Long-term bonds	1,520
		Total debt	$2,140
		Preferred stock (800,000 shares)	80
		Common stock (100 million shares)	260
		Retained earnings	1,520
		Common equity	$1,780
Total assets	$4,000	Total liabilities and equity	$4,000

SMYTHE-DAVIDSON CORPORATION: INCOME STATEMENT FOR YEAR ENDING DECEMBER 31, 1995 (MILLIONS OF DOLLARS)

Sales	$6,250
Operating costs excluding depreciation	5,230
Depreciation	220
EBIT	$ 800
Less: Interest	180
EBT	$ 620
Taxes (40%)	248
Net income before preferred dividends	372
Preferred dividends	8
Net income available to common stockholders	$ 364
Common dividends paid	$ 146
Earnings per share	$3.64

a. Assume that all of the firm's revenues were received in cash during the year and that all costs except depreciation were paid in cash during the year. What is the firm's net cash flow available to common stockholders for the year? How is this number different from the accounting profit reported by the firm?

b. Construct the firm's Statement of Retained Earnings for December 31, 1995.

c. How much money has the firm reinvested in itself over the years instead of paying out dividends?

d. At the present time, how large a check could the firm write without it bouncing?

e. How much money must the firm pay its current creditors within the next year?

2-2 Income and cash flow analysis The Menendez Corporation expects to have sales of $12 million in 1996. Costs other than depreciation are expected to be 75 percent of sales, and depreciation is expected to amount to $1.5 million. All sales revenues will be collected in cash, and costs other than depreciation must be paid for during the year. Menendez's federal-plus-state tax rate is 40 percent.

a. Set up an income and cash flow statement (two columns on one statement). What is Menendez's expected cash flow from operations?

b. Suppose Congress changed the tax laws so that Menendez's depreciation expenses doubled. No changes in operations occurred. What would happen to reported profits and to cash flows?

c. Now suppose that Congress, instead of doubling Menendez's depreciation, reduced it by 50 percent. How would profits and cash flows be affected?

d. If this were your company, would you prefer Congress to cause your depreciation expense to be doubled or halved? Why?

e. In the situation in which depreciation doubled, would this possibly have an adverse effect on the company's stock price and on its ability to borrow money?

2-3 Loss carry-back, carry-forward The Herrmann Company has made $150,000 before taxes during each of the last 15 years, and it expects to make $150,000 a year before taxes in the future. However, in 1995 the firm incurred a loss of $650,000. The firm will claim a tax credit at the time it files its 1995 income tax return, and it will receive a check from the U.S. Treasury. Show how it calculates this credit, and then indicate the firm's tax liability for each of the next 5 years. Assume a 40 percent tax rate on *all* income to ease the calculations.

2-4 Loss carry-back, carry-forward The projected taxable income of the McAlhany Corporation, formed in 1996, is indicated in the table below. (Losses are shown in parentheses.) What is the corporate tax liability for each year? Use tax rates as shown in the text.

YEAR	TAXABLE INCOME
1996	($ 95,000)
1997	70,000
1998	55,000
1999	80,000
2000	(150,000)

2-5 Form of organization Susan Visscher has operated her small restaurant as a sole proprietorship for several years, but projected changes in her business's income have led her to consider incorporating.

Visscher is married and has two children. Her family's only income, an annual salary of $52,000, is from operating the business. (The business actually earns more than $52,000, but Susan reinvests the additional earnings in the business.) She itemizes deductions, and she is able to deduct $8,600. These deductions, combined with her four personal exemptions for 4 × $2,450 = $9,800, give her a taxable income of $52,000 − $8,600 − $9,800. (Assume the personal exemption remains at $2,450.) Of course, her actual taxable income, if she does not incorporate, would be higher by the amount of reinvested income. Visscher estimates that her business earnings before salary and taxes for the period 1996 to 1998 will be:

YEAR	EARNINGS BEFORE SALARY AND TAXES
1996	$ 70,000
1997	$ 95,000
1998	$110,000

a. What would her total taxes (corporate plus personal) be in each year under
  (1) A non-S corporate form of organization? (1996 tax = $7,740.)
  (2) A proprietorship? (1996 tax = $9,508.)

b. Should Visscher incorporate? Discuss.

2-6 Personal taxes Mary Jarvis has this situation for the year 1995: salary of $82,000; dividend income of $12,000; interest on Disney bonds of $5,000; interest on state of Florida municipal bonds of $10,000; proceeds of $22,000 from the sale of Disney stock purchased in 1984 at a cost of $9,000; and proceeds of $22,000 from the November 1995 sale of Disney stock purchased in October 1995 at a cost of $21,000. Jarvis gets one exemption ($2,450), and she has allowable itemized deductions of $4,900; these amounts will be deducted from her gross income to determine her taxable income.

   a. What is Jarvis's federal tax liability for 1995?

   b. What are her marginal and average tax rates?

   c. If she had $5,000 to invest and was offered a choice of either state of Florida bonds with a yield of 6 percent or more Disney bonds with a yield of 8 percent, which should she choose, and why?

   d. At what marginal tax rate would Jarvis be indifferent in her choice between the Florida and Disney bonds?

EXAM-TYPE PROBLEMS

The problems included in this section are set up in such a way that they could be used as multiple-choice exam problems.

2-7 Corporate tax liability The Talley Corporation had a 1995 taxable income of $365,000 from operations after all operating costs but before (1) interest charges of $50,000, (2) dividends received of $15,000, (3) dividends paid of $25,000, and (4) income taxes. What is the firm's income tax liability and its after-tax income? What are the company's marginal and average tax rates on taxable income?

2-8 Corporate tax liability The Wendt Corporation had $10.5 million of taxable income from operations in 1995.

   a. What is the company's federal income tax bill for the year?

   b. Assume the firm receives an additional $1 million of interest income from some bonds it owns. What is the tax on this interest income?

   c. Now assume that Wendt does not receive the interest income but does receive an additional $1 million as dividends on some stock it owns. What is the tax on this dividend income?

2-9 After-tax yield The Shrieves Corporation has $10,000 which it plans to invest in marketable securities. It is choosing between AT&T bonds, which yield 7.5 percent, state of Florida muni bonds, which yield 5 percent, and AT&T preferred stock, with a dividend yield of 6 percent. Shrieves's corporate tax rate is 35 percent, and 70 percent of the dividends received are tax exempt. Assuming that the investments are equally risky and that Shrieves chooses strictly on the basis of after-tax returns, which security should be selected? What is the after-tax rate of return on the highest-yielding security?

2-10 After-tax yield Your personal tax rate is 36 percent. You can invest in either corporate bonds which yield 9 percent or municipal bonds (of equal risk) which yield 7 percent. Which investment should you choose? (Ignore state income taxes.)

INTEGRATED CASE

D'LEON INC., PART I

2-11 SECTION I: Financial statements Donna Jamison, a 1993 graduate of the University of Florida with two years of banking experience, was recently brought in as assistant to the chairman of the board of D'Leon Inc., a small food producer which operates in north Florida and whose specialty is high-quality pecan and other nut products sold in the snack-foods market. D'Leon's president, Al Watkins, decided in 1994 to undertake a major expansion and to "go national" in competition with Frito-Lay, Eagle, and other major snack food companies. Watkins felt that D'Leon's products were of a higher quality than the competition's, that this quality differential would enable it to charge a premium price, and that the end result would be greatly increased sales, profits, and stock price.

The company doubled its plant capacity, opened new sales offices outside its home territory, and launched an expensive advertising campaign. D'Leon's results were not satisfactory, to put it mildly. Its board of directors, which consisted of its president and vice-president plus its major stockholders (who were all local business people) was most upset when directors learned how the expansion was going. Suppliers were being paid late and were unhappy, and the bank was complaining about the deteriorating situation and threatening to cut off credit. As a result, President Watkins was informed that changes would have to be made, and quickly, or he would be fired. Also, at the board's insistence Donna Jamison was brought in and given the job of assistant to Fred Campo, a retired banker who was D'Leon's chairman and largest stockholder. Campo agreed to give up a few of his golfing days and to help nurse the company back to health, with Jamison's help.

Jamison began by gathering the financial statements and other data given in Tables IC2-1, IC2-2, and IC2-3. Assume that you are Jamison's assistant, and you must help her answer the following questions for Campo. (Note: We will continue with this case in Chapter 3, and you will feel more comfortable with the analysis there, but answering these ques-

TABLE IC2-1   BALANCE SHEETS

	1995	1994
Assets		
Cash	$ 7,282	$ 57,600
Accounts receivable	632,160	351,200
Inventories	1,287,360	715,200
Total current assets	$1,926,802	$1,124,000
Gross fixed assets	$1,202,950	$ 491,000
Less accumulated depreciation	263,160	146,200
Net fixed assets	$ 939,790	$ 344,800
Total assets	$2,866,592	$1,468,800
Liabilities and Equity		
Accounts payable	$ 524,160	$ 145,600
Notes payable	720,000	200,000
Accruals	489,600	136,000
Total current liabilities	$1,733,760	$ 481,600
Long-term debt	$1,000,000	$ 323,432
Common stock (100,000 shares)	$ 460,000	$ 460,000
Retained earnings	(327,168)	203,768
Total equity	$ 132,832	$ 663,768
Total liabilities and equity	$2,866,592	$1,468,800

tions will help prepare you for Chapter 3. Provide clear explanations, not just yes or no answers!)

a. Refer to Figure 2-1 in Chapter 2. What happened to D'Leon's "cash reservoir" rectangle during 1995? What happened to the other asset and liability reservoirs?

b. D'Leon purchases materials on 30-day terms, meaning that it is supposed to pay for purchases within 30 days of receipt. Judging from its 1995 balance sheet, do you think D'Leon pays suppliers on time? Explain. If not, what problems might this lead to?

c. D'Leon spends money for labor, materials, and fixed assets (depreciation) to make products, and still more money to sell those products. Then, it makes sales which result in receivables, which eventually result in cash inflows. Does it appear that D'Leon's sales price exceeds its costs per unit sold? How does this affect the "cash reservoir," or cash balance?

d. Suppose D'Leon's sales manager told the sales staff to start offering 60-day credit terms rather than the 30-day terms now being offered. D'Leon's competitors react by offering similar terms, so sales remain constant. What effect would this have on the cash account? How would the cash account be affected if sales doubled as a result of the credit policy change?

e. Can you imagine a situation in which the sales price exceeds the cost of producing and selling a unit of output, yet a dramatic increase in sales volume causes the cash balance to decline?

f. In general, could a company like D'Leon increase sales without a corresponding increase in inventory and other assets? Would the asset increase occur before the increase in sales, and, if so, how would that affect the cash account and the statement of cash flows?

g. Did D'Leon finance its expansion program with internally generated funds (additions to retained earnings plus depreciation) or with external capital? How does the choice of financing affect the company's financial strength?

h. Refer to Tables IC2-2 and IC2-3. Suppose D'Leon broke even in 1995 in the sense that sales revenues equaled total operating costs plus interest charges. Would the asset expansion have caused the company to experience a cash shortage which required it to raise external capital?

i. If D'Leon started depreciating fixed assets over 7 years rather than 10 years, would that affect (1) the physical stock of assets, (2) the balance sheet account for fixed assets, (3) the company's reported net income, and (4) its cash position? Assume the same depreciation method is used for

TABLE IC2-2	INCOME STATEMENTS	

	1995	1994
Sales	$5,834,400	$3,432,000
Cost of goods sold	5,728,000	2,864,000
Other expenses	680,000	340,000
Depreciation	116,960	18,900
Total operating costs	$6,524,960	$3,222,900
EBIT	($ 690,560)	$ 209,100
Interest expense	176,000	62,500
EBT	($ 866,560)	$ 146,600
Taxes (40%)	(346,624)	58,640
Net income	($ 519,936)	$ 87,960
EPS	($ 5.199)	$ 0.880
DPS	$ 0.110	$ 0.220
Book value per share	$ 1.328	$ 6.638
Stock price	$ 2.25	$ 8.50
Shares outstanding	100,000	100,000
Tax rate	40.00%	40.00%
Lease payments	40,000	40,000
Sinking fund payments	0	0

stockholder reporting and for tax calculations, and the accounting change has no effect on assets' physical lives.

j. Explain how (1) inventory valuation methods, (2) the accounting policy regarding expensing versus capitalizing research and development, and (3) the policy with regard to funding future retirement plan costs (retirement pay and retirees' health benefits) could affect the financial statements.

k. D'Leon's stock sells for $2.25 per share even though the company had large losses. Does the positive stock price indicate that some investors are irrational?

l. D'Leon followed the standard practice of paying dividends on a quarterly basis. It paid a dividend during the first two quarters of 1995, then eliminated the dividend when management realized that a loss would be incurred for the year. The dividend was cut before the losses were announced, and at that point the stock price fell from $8.50 to $3.50. Why would an $0.11, or even a $0.22, dividend reduction lead to a $5.00 stock price reduction?

m. Explain how earnings per share, dividends per share, and book value per share are calculated, and what they mean. Why does the market price per share *not* equal the book value per share?

n. How much new money did D'Leon borrow from its bank during 1995? How much additional credit did its suppliers extend? Its employees and the taxing authorities?

o. If you were D'Leon's banker, or the credit manager of one of its suppliers, would you be worried about your job? If you were a current D'Leon employee, a retiree, or a stockholder, should you be concerned?

p. The 1995 income statement shows negative taxes, that is, a tax credit. How much taxes would the company have had to pay in the past to actually get this credit? If taxes paid within the last 3 years had been less than $346,624, what would have happened? Would this have affected the statement of cash flows and the ending cash balance?

SECTION II: Taxes

q. Working with Jamison has required you to put in a lot of overtime, so you have had very little time to spend on your private finances. It's now April 1, and you have only two weeks left to file your income tax return. You have managed to get all the information together that you will need to complete your return. D'Leon paid you a salary of $45,000, and you received $3,000 in dividends from common stock that you own. You are single, so your personal exemption is $2,450, and your itemized deductions are $4,550.

(1) On the basis of the information above and the 1994 individual tax rate schedule, what is your tax liability?

(2) What are your marginal and average tax rates?

TABLE IC2-3	STATEMENT OF CASH FLOWS, 1995

OPERATING ACTIVITIES	
Net income	($ 519,936)
Additions (Sources of Cash)	
Depreciation	116,960
Increase in accounts payable	378,560
Increase in accruals	353,600
Subtractions (Uses of Cash)	
Increase in accounts receivable	(280,960)
Increase in inventories	(572,160)
Net cash provided by operating activities	($ 523,936)
LONG-TERM INVESTING ACTIVITIES	
Cash used to acquire fixed assets	($ 711,950)
FINANCING ACTIVITIES	
Increase in notes payable	$ 520,000
Increase in long-term debt	676,568
Payment of cash dividends	(11,000)
Net cash provided by financing activities	$1,185,568
Sum: net decrease in cash	($ 50,318)
Plus: cash at beginning of year	57,600
Cash at end of year	$ 7,282

r. Assume that a corporation has $100,000 of taxable income from operations plus $5,000 of interest income and $10,000 of dividend income. What is the company's tax liability?

s. Assume that after paying your personal income tax as calculated in Part q, you have $5,000 to invest. You have narrowed your investment choices down to California bonds with a yield of 7 percent or equally risky Exxon bonds with a yield of 10 percent. Which one should you choose and why? At what marginal tax rate would you be indifferent to the choice between California and Exxon bonds?

COMPUTER-RELATED PROBLEM

Work the problem in this section only if you are using the computer problem diskette.

2-12 Effect of form of organization on taxes The problem requires you to rework Problem 2-5, using the data given below. Use File C2 on the computer problem diskette.

a. Suppose Visscher decides to pay out (1) 50 percent or (2) 100 percent of the after-salary corporate income in each year as dividends. Would such dividend policy changes affect her decision about whether or not to incorporate?

b. Suppose business improves, and actual earnings before salary and taxes in each year are twice the original estimate. Assume that if Visscher chooses to incorporate she will continue to receive a salary of $52,000, and to reinvest additional earnings in the business. (No dividends would be paid.) What would be the effect of this increase in business income on Visscher's decision to incorporate or not incorporate?

BORDEN: STRATEGIC ERRORS COST THE COMPANY AND ITS INVESTORS

In the span of one very bad year at Borden Inc., CEO Anthony S. D'Amato has undergone a startling transformation. Once robust and energetic, he now looks ashen. Barely graying at the temples last fall, his hair has now gone almost completely gray. To look at him is to understand the strain of running a company that is its industry's poorest performer.

As this 1993 quote from *Business Week* makes clear, Borden Inc., the $7 billion packaged-foods company best known for its Elsie the cow logo, has been under siege. *Value Line,* a leading investment advisory service, reported that Borden's stock price dropped 50 percent in just a few months, even as the Dow Jones average was hitting record highs. The dividend had been cut in half, which increased stockholders' pain. In addition, Standard & Poor's, the major bond rating agency, downgraded Borden's debt, making it more difficult and expensive for the company to borrow money.

Problems such as Borden experienced can be caused by general economic conditions or by industry-specific events which take all firms in the industry down together. However, neither of these conditions af-

fected Borden — the general market was strong, and Borden's competitors were setting records even as it crashed. Rather, Borden's problems were of its own making — management's strategic errors harmed the company and its investors.

Borden's fall cost stockholders about $3.5 billion. These losses were shared equally by institutional investors such as pension funds and mutual funds, which hold about half of Borden's outstanding stock, and by individual investors. One fund manager bet heavily on Borden, bought shares as they began their fall, and ended up with huge losses. He lost his job. Anthony D'Amato also lost his job — at the end of 1993, he was forced to resign. Even worse, a number of Borden retirees had most of their life savings invested in the company, and they now face their "golden years" having to move in with their children. D'Amato is more fortunate. He was given a severance package valued at $3.6 million, to be received over four years, in return for his 32 years of service at Borden.

The Borden saga continued in 1994, when the investment firm of Kohlberg Kravis Roberts (KKR), best known for its

1988 leveraged buyout of RJR Nabisco, announced plans to acquire Borden. KKR will have to take bold steps to sell off the company's nonperforming segments, which most observers think is the only way to boost Borden's sagging profits and stock price.

While KKR paid a premium over Borden's pre-offer stock price, many of Borden's institutional investors were irate that the company's current managers were unable to get a higher bid. At the same time, though, some KKR investors felt strongly that the offer price was too high. Only time will tell who is right.

As you study this chapter, think about Borden's situation. An analysis of financial statements can highlight a company's shortcomings, and that information can then be used to avoid problems such as Borden's. This type of analysis can also be used to estimate how strategic decisions such as the sale of divisions, major marketing programs, or expansion plans are likely to affect future financial statements. KKR undoubtedly used such analysis before it made its offer to determine how much it could afford to pay for the company.

QUICK, OR ACID TEST, RATIO

Quick (Acid Test) Ratio
This ratio is calculated by deducting inventories from current assets and dividing the remainder by current liabilities.

The **quick,** or **acid test, ratio** is calculated by deducting inventories from current assets and then dividing the remainder by current liabilities:

$$\text{Quick, or acid test, ratio} = \frac{\text{Current assets} - \text{Inventories}}{\text{Current liabilities}}$$

$$= \frac{\$385}{\$310} = 1.2 \text{ times.}$$

Industry average = 2.1 times.

Inventories are typically the least liquid of a firm's current assets, hence they are the assets on which losses are most likely to occur in the event of liquidation. Therefore, a measure of the firm's ability to pay off short-term obligations without relying on the sale of inventories is important.

The industry average quick ratio is 2.1, so Allied's 1.2 ratio is low in comparison with the ratios of other firms in its industry. Still, if the accounts receivable can be collected, the company can pay off its current liabilities without having to liquidate its inventory.

 ## SELF-TEST QUESTIONS

Identify two ratios that are used to analyze a firm's liquidity position, and write out their equations.

What are the characteristics of a liquid asset? Give some examples.

Which type of current asset is typically the least liquid?

ASSET MANAGEMENT RATIOS

Asset Management Ratios
A set of ratios which measure how effectively a firm is managing its assets.

The second group of ratios, the **asset management ratios,** measures how effectively the firm is managing its assets. These ratios are designed to answer this question: Does the total amount of each type of asset as reported on the balance sheet seem reasonable, too high, or too low in view of current and projected sales levels? When they acquire assets, Allied and other companies must borrow or obtain capital from other sources. If a firm has too many assets, its cost of capital will be too high, hence its profits will be depressed. On the other hand, if assets are too low, profitable sales will be lost. Ratios which analyze the different types of assets are described in this section.

INVENTORY TURNOVER

Inventory Turnover Ratio
The ratio calculated by dividing sales by inventories.

The **inventory turnover ratio** is defined as sales divided by inventories:

$$\text{Inventory turnover ratio} = \frac{\text{Sales}}{\text{Inventories}}$$

$$= \frac{\$3,000}{\$615} = 4.9 \text{ times.}$$

Industry average = 9.0 times.

As a rough approximation, each item of Allied's inventory is sold out and restocked, or "turned over," 4.9 times per year. "Turnover" is a term that originated many years ago with the old Yankee peddler, who would load up his wagon with goods, then go off on his route to peddle his wares. The merchandise was his "working capital" because it was what he actually sold, or "turned over," to produce his profits, whereas his "turnover" was the number of trips he took each year. Annual sales divided by inventory equaled turnover, or trips per year. If he made 10 trips per year, stocked 100 pans, and made a gross profit of $5 per pan, his annual gross profit would be (100)($5)(10) = $5,000. If he went faster and made 20 trips per year, his gross profit would double, other things held constant. So, his turnover directly affected his profits.

Allied's turnover of 4.9 times is much lower than the industry average of 9 times. This suggests that Allied is holding excessive stocks of inventory; excess stocks are, of course, unproductive, and they represent an investment with a low or zero rate of return. Allied's low inventory turnover ratio also makes us question the current ratio. With such a low turnover, we must wonder whether the firm is actually holding damaged or obsolete goods not worth their stated value.[3]

Note that sales occur over the entire year, whereas the inventory figure is for one point in time. For this reason, it is better to use an average inventory measure.[4] If the firm's business is highly seasonal, or if there has been a strong upward or downward sales trend during the year, it is essential to make some such adjustment. To maintain comparability with industry averages, however, we did not use the average inventory figure.

DAYS SALES OUTSTANDING

Days Sales Outstanding (DSO)
The ratio calculated by dividing accounts receivable by average sales per day; indicates the average length of time the firm must wait after making a sale before receiving cash.

Days sales outstanding (DSO), also called the "average collection period" (ACP), is used to appraise accounts receivable, and it is calculated by dividing average daily sales into accounts receivable to find the number of days' sales that are tied up in receivables. Thus, the DSO represents the average length of time that the firm must wait after making a sale before receiving cash, which is the average collection period. Allied has 45 days sales outstanding, well above the 36-day industry average.[5]

---

[3]A problem arises calculating and analyzing the inventory turnover ratio. Sales are stated at market prices, so if inventories are carried at cost, as they generally are, the calculated turnover overstates the true turnover ratio. Therefore, it would be more appropriate to use cost of goods sold in place of sales in the numerator of the formula. However, established compilers of financial ratio statistics such as Dun & Bradstreet use the ratio of sales to inventories carried at cost. To develop a figure that can be compared with those published by Dun & Bradstreet and similar organizations, it is necessary to measure inventory turnover with sales in the numerator, as we do here.

[4]Preferably, the average inventory value should be calculated by summing the monthly figures during the year and dividing by 12. If monthly data are not available, one can add the beginning and ending figures and divide by 2; this will adjust for growth but not for seasonal effects.

[5]Note that by convention the financial community generally uses 360 rather than 365 as the number of days in the year for purposes such as this. Finally, it would be better to use *average* receivables, either an average of the monthly figures or (beginning receivables + ending receivables)/2 = ($315 + $375)/2 = $345 in the formula. Had the annual average receivables been used, Allied's DSO would have been $345.00/$8.333 = 41 days. The 41-day figure is the more accurate one, but because the industry average was based on year-end receivables, we used 45 days for our comparison. The DSO is discussed further in Chapter 15.

$$DSO = \begin{array}{c} \text{Days} \\ \text{sales} \\ \text{outstanding} \end{array} = \frac{\text{Receivables}}{\text{Average sales per day}} = \frac{\text{Receivables}}{\text{Annual sales}/360}$$

$$= \frac{\$375}{\$3,000/360} = \frac{\$375}{\$8.333} = 45 \text{ days.}$$

Industry average = 36 days.

The DSO can also be evaluated by comparison with the terms on which the firm sells its goods. For example, Allied's sales terms call for payment within 30 days, so the fact that 45 days' sales, not 30 days', are outstanding indicates that customers, on the average, are not paying their bills on time. This deprives Allied of funds which it could use to invest in productive assets. Moreover, in some instances the fact that a customer is late paying its bills may signal that the customer is in financial trouble, in which case Allied may have a hard time ever collecting what is owed. Therefore, if the trend in DSO over the past few years has been rising, but the credit policy has not been changed, this would be strong evidence that steps should be taken to expedite the collection of accounts receivable.

FIXED ASSETS TURNOVER

Fixed Assets Turnover Ratio
The ratio of sales to net fixed assets.

The **fixed assets turnover ratio** measures how effectively the firm uses its plant and equipment. It is the ratio of sales to net fixed assets:

$$\text{Fixed assets turnover ratio} = \frac{\text{Sales}}{\text{Net fixed assets}}$$

$$= \frac{\$3,000}{\$1,000} = 3.0 \text{ times.}$$

Industry average = 3.0 times.

Allied's ratio of 3.0 times is equal to the industry average, indicating that the firm is using its fixed assets about as intensively as are the other firms in the industry. Allied seems to have about the right amount of fixed assets in relation to other firms.

A major potential problem can exist when the fixed assets turnover ratio is used to compare different firms. Recall from accounting that fixed assets reflect the historical costs of the assets. Inflation has caused the value of many assets that were purchased in the past to be seriously understated. Therefore, if we were comparing an old firm which had acquired many of its fixed assets years ago at low prices with a new company which had acquired its fixed assets only recently, we probably would find that the old firm had a higher fixed assets turnover ratio. However, this would be more reflective of the inability of accountants to deal with inflation than of any inefficiency on the part of the new firm. The accounting profession is trying to devise ways of making financial statements reflect current values rather than historical values. If balance sheets were actually stated on a current value basis, this would help us make better comparisons, but at the moment the problem still exists. Since financial analysts typically do not have the data necessary to make adjustments, they simply recognize that a problem exists and deal with it judgmentally. In Allied's case, the issue is not a serious one because all firms in the industry have been expanding at about the same rate; thus, the balance sheets of the comparison firms are reasonably comparable.[6]

---

[6]See FASB #33, *Financial Reporting and Changing Prices* (September 1979), for a discussion of the effects of inflation on financial statements.

TOTAL ASSETS TURNOVER

Total Assets Turnover Ratio
The ratio calculated by dividing sales by total assets.

The final asset management ratio, the **total assets turnover ratio**, measures the turnover of all the firm's assets; it is calculated by dividing sales by total assets:

$$\text{Total assets turnover ratio} = \frac{\text{Sales}}{\text{Total assets}}$$

$$= \frac{\$3,000}{\$2,000} = 1.5 \text{ times.}$$

$$\text{Industry average} = 1.8 \text{ times.}$$

Allied's ratio is somewhat below the industry average, indicating that the company is not generating a sufficient volume of business given its total asset investment. Sales should be increased, some assets should be disposed of, or a combination of these steps should be taken.

 SELF-TEST QUESTIONS

Identify four ratios that are used to measure how effectively a firm is managing its assets, and write out their equations.

What problem might arise with the inventory turnover ratio?

What potential problem arises when comparing different firms' fixed assets turnover ratios?

DEBT MANAGEMENT RATIOS

Financial Leverage
The use of debt financing.

The extent to which a firm uses debt financing, or **financial leverage**, has three important implications: (1) By raising funds through debt, stockholders can maintain control of a firm while limiting their investment. (2) Creditors look to the equity, or owner-supplied funds, to provide a margin of safety, so if the stockholders have provided only a small proportion of the total financing, the risks of the enterprise are borne mainly by its creditors. (3) If the firm earns more on investments financed with borrowed funds than it pays in interest, the return on the owners' capital is magnified, or "leveraged."

To understand better how financial leverage affects risk and return, consider Table 3-1. Here we analyze two companies that are identical except for the way they are financed. Firm U (for "unleveraged") has no debt, whereas Firm L (for "leveraged") is financed half with equity and half with debt that costs 15 percent. Both companies have $100 of assets and $100 of sales, and their expected operating income (also called earnings before interest and taxes, or EBIT) is $30. Thus, both firms *expect* to earn $30, before taxes, on their assets. Of course, things could turn out badly, in which case EBIT would be lower; in the second column of the table, we show EBIT declining from $30 to $2.50 under bad conditions.

Even though both companies' assets have the same expected EBIT, under normal conditions Firm L should provide its stockholders with a return on equity of 27 percent versus only 18 percent for Firm U. This difference is caused by Firm L's use of debt. Financial leverage raises the expected rate of return to stockholders for two reasons: (1) Since interest is deductible, the use of debt lowers the tax bill and leaves more of the firm's operating income available to its investors. (2) If the ex-

TABLE 3-1	EFFECTS OF FINANCIAL LEVERAGE ON STOCKHOLDERS' RETURNS

FIRM U (UNLEVERAGED)

Current assets	$ 50	Debt	$ 0
Fixed assets	50	Common equity	100
Total assets	$100	Total liabilities and equity	$100

	EXPECTED CONDITIONS (1)	BAD CONDITIONS (2)
Sales	$100.00	$82.50
Operating costs	70.00	80.00
Operating income (EBIT)	$ 30.00	$ 2.50
Interest	0.00	0.00
Earnings before taxes (EBT)	$ 30.00	$ 2.50
Taxes (40%)	12.00	1.00
Net income (NI)	$ 18.00	$ 1.50
ROE_U = NI/Common equity = NI/$100 =	18.00%	1.50%

FIRM L (LEVERAGED)

Current assets	$ 50	Debt (interest = 15%)	$ 50
Fixed assets	50	Common equity	50
Total assets	$100	Total liabilities and equity	$100

	EXPECTED CONDITIONS (1)	BAD CONDITIONS (2)
Sales	$100.00	$82.50
Operating costs	70.00	80.00
Operating income (EBIT)	$ 30.00	$ 2.50
Interest	7.50	7.50
Earnings before taxes (EBT)	$ 22.50	($ 5.00)
Taxes (40%)	9.00	(2.00)
Net income (NI)	$ 13.50	($ 3.00)
ROE_L = NI/Common equity = NI/$50 =	27.00%	(6.00%)

pected rate of return on assets (EBIT/Total assets) exceeds the interest rate on debt, as it generally does, then a company can use debt to acquire assets, pay the interest on the debt, and have something left over as a "bonus" for its stockholders. For our hypothetical firms, these two effects have combined to push Firm L's expected rate of return on equity up far above that of Firm U. Thus, debt can be used to "leverage up" the rate of return on equity.

However, financial leverage can cut both ways. As we show in Column 2 of the income statements, if sales are lower and costs are higher than were expected, the return on assets will also be lower than was expected. Under these conditions, the leveraged firm's return on equity falls especially sharply, and losses occur. For example, under the "bad conditions" in Table 3-1, the debt-free firm still shows a profit, but the firm which uses debt shows a loss, and a negative return on equity. This occurs because Firm L needs cash to service its debt, while Firm U does not. Firm U, because of its strong balance sheet, could ride out the recession and be ready for the next boom. Firm L, on the other hand, must pay interest of $7.50 regardless of its level of sales. Since in the recession its operations do not generate enough income to meet the interest payments, cash would be depleted and the firm probably would need to raise additional funds. Because it would be running a loss, Firm L would have a hard time selling stock to raise capital, and its losses would cause lenders to raise the interest rate, increasing L's problems still further. As a final result, Firm L just might not survive to enjoy the next boom.

We see, then, that firms with relatively high debt ratios have higher expected returns when the economy is normal, but they are exposed to risk of loss when the economy goes into a recession. Thus, firms with low debt ratios are less risky, but they also forgo the opportunity to leverage up their return on equity. The prospects of high returns are desirable, but investors are averse to risk. Therefore, decisions about the use of debt require firms to balance higher expected returns against increased risk. Determining the optimal amount of debt for a given firm is a complicated process, and we defer a discussion of this topic until Chapter 12. For now, we will simply look at two procedures analysts use to examine the firm's debt: (1) They check the balance sheet to determine the extent to which borrowed funds have been used to finance assets, and (2) they review the income statement to see the extent to which fixed charges are covered by operating profits.

TOTAL DEBT TO TOTAL ASSETS

Debt Ratio
The ratio of total debt to total assets.

The ratio of total debt to total assets, generally called the **debt ratio**, measures the percentage of funds provided by creditors:

$$\text{Debt ratio} = \frac{\text{Total debt}}{\text{Total assets}}$$

$$= \frac{\$310 + \$754}{\$2,000} = \frac{\$1,064}{\$2,000} = 53.2\%.$$

$$\text{Industry average} = 40.0\%.$$

Total debt includes both current liabilities and long-term debt. Creditors prefer low debt ratios because the lower the ratio, the greater the cushion against creditors' losses in the event of liquidation. The stockholders, on the other hand, may want more leverage because it magnifies expected earnings.

Allied's debt ratio is 53.2 percent; this means that its creditors have supplied more than half the firm's total financing. As we will discuss in Chapter 12, there are a variety of factors which determine a company's optimal debt ratio. Even within the same industry, optimal debt ratios may differ considerably. Nevertheless, the fact that Allied's debt ratio exceeds the industry average of 40 percent raises some concern and may make it costly for Allied to borrow additional funds without first raising more equity capital. Creditors may be reluctant to lend the firm more money, and management would probably be subjecting the firm to the risk of bankruptcy if it sought to increase the debt ratio any further by borrowing additional funds.[7]

TIMES INTEREST EARNED

Times-Interest-Earned (TIE) Ratio
The ratio of earnings before interest and taxes (EBIT) to interest charges; measures the ability of the firm to meet its annual interest payments.

The **times-interest-earned (TIE) ratio** is determined by dividing earnings before interest and taxes (EBIT in Table 2-2) by the interest charges:

$$\text{Times-interest-earned (TIE) ratio} = \frac{\text{EBIT}}{\text{Interest charges}}$$

$$= \frac{\$283.8}{\$88} = 3.2 \text{ times.}$$

$$\text{Industry average} = 6.0 \text{ times.}$$

The TIE ratio measures the extent to which operating income can decline before the firm is unable to meet its annual interest costs. Failure to meet this obligation can bring legal action by the firm's creditors, possibly resulting in bankruptcy. Note that earnings before interest and taxes, rather than net income, is used in the numerator. Because interest is paid with pre-tax dollars, the firm's ability to pay current interest is not affected by taxes.

Allied's interest is covered 3.2 times. Since the industry average is 6 times, Allied is covering its interest charges by a relatively low margin of safety. Thus, the TIE ratio reinforces our conclusion based on the debt ratio that Allied would face difficulties if it attempted to borrow additional funds.

FIXED CHARGE COVERAGE

Fixed Charge Coverage Ratio
This ratio expands upon the TIE ratio to include the firm's annual long-term lease and sinking fund obligations.

The **fixed charge coverage ratio** is similar to the times-interest-earned ratio, but it is more inclusive because it recognizes that many firms lease assets and also must make sinking fund payments.[8] Leasing has become widespread in certain industries in recent years, making this ratio preferable to the times-interest-earned ratio for many purposes. Allied's annual lease payments are $28 million, and it must make an annual $20 million sinking fund payment to help retire its debt. Because sinking fund payments must be paid with after-tax dollars, whereas interest and lease payments are paid with pre-tax dollars, the sinking fund payment must be "grossed up" by dividing by (1 − Tax rate) to find the before-tax income required to pay taxes and still have enough left to make the sinking fund payment.[9]

---

[7]The ratio of debt to equity is also used in financial analysis. The debt to assets (D/A) and debt to equity (D/E) ratios are simply transformations of each other:

$$D/E = \frac{D/A}{1 - D/A}, \text{ and } D/A = \frac{D/E}{1 + D/E}.$$

[8]Generally, only rental payments on 1-year or longer leases are defined as fixed charges and are included in the fixed charge coverage ratio. A sinking fund is a required annual payment designed to reduce the balance of a bond or preferred stock issue. Sinking funds are discussed in Chapter 7.

[9]Note that $20/0.6 = $33.33. Therefore, if the company had pre-tax income of $33.33, it could pay taxes at a 40 percent rate and have exactly $20 left with which to make the sinking fund payment. Thus, a $20 sinking fund requirement requires $20/0.6 = $33.33 of pre-tax income. Dividing by (1 − T) is called "grossing up" an after-tax value to find the corresponding pre-tax value.

Fixed charges include interest, annual long-term lease obligations, and sinking fund payments, and the fixed charge coverage ratio is defined as follows:

$$\text{Fixed charge coverage ratio} = \frac{\text{EBIT} + \text{Lease payments}}{\underset{\text{charges}}{\text{Interest}} + \underset{\text{payments}}{\text{Lease}} + \frac{\text{Sinking fund payments}}{(1 - \text{Tax rate})}}$$

$$= \frac{\$283.8 + \$28}{\$88 + \$28 + \dfrac{\$20}{0.6}} = 2.1 \text{ times.}$$

Industry average = 5.5 times.

Allied's fixed charges are covered only 2.1 times, versus an industry average of 5.5 times. Again, this indicates that the firm is weaker than average, and this reinforces the argument that Allied would probably encounter difficulties if it attempted to increase its debt.

SELF-TEST QUESTIONS

How does the use of financial leverage affect stockholders' control position?

In what way do taxes influence a firm's willingness to finance with debt?

In what way does the decision to use debt involve a risk-versus-return tradeoff?

Explain the following statement: "Analysts look at both balance sheet and income statement ratios when appraising a firm's financial condition."

Name three ratios that are used to measure the extent to which a firm uses financial leverage, and write out their equations.

PROFITABILITY RATIOS

Profitability is the net result of a number of policies and decisions. The ratios examined thus far provide useful clues as to the effectiveness of a firm's operations, but the **profitability ratios** show the combined effects of liquidity, asset management, and debt on operating results.

PROFIT MARGIN ON SALES

Profitability Ratios

A group of ratios which show the combined effects of liquidity, asset management, and debt on operating results.

Profit Margin on Sales

This ratio measures income per dollar of sales; it is calculated by dividing net income by sales.

The **profit margin on sales,** calculated by dividing net income by sales, gives the profit per dollar of sales:

$$\text{Profit margin on sales} = \frac{\text{Net income available to common stockholders}}{\text{Sales}}$$

$$= \frac{\$113.5}{\$3,000} = 3.8\%.$$

Industry average = 5.0%.

Allied's profit margin is below the industry average of 5 percent. This sub-par result occurs because costs are too high. High costs, in turn, generally occur because of inefficient operations. However, Allied's low profit margin is also a result of its heavy use of debt. Recall that net income is income *after interest.* Therefore, if two firms have identical operations in the sense that their sales, operating costs, and EBIT are the same, but if one firm uses more debt than the other, it will have higher interest charges. Those interest charges will pull net income down, and since sales are constant, the result will be a relatively low profit margin. In such a case, the low profit margin would not indicate an operating problem, just a difference in financing strategies, and the firm with the low margin might well end up with a higher rate of return on its stockholders' investment due to its use of financial leverage. We will see exactly how profit margins and the use of debt interact to affect stockholder returns shortly.

BASIC EARNING POWER (BEP)

Basic Earning Power (BEP) Ratio
This ratio indicates the ability of the firm's assets to generate operating income; calculated by dividing EBIT by total assets.

The **basic earning power (BEP) ratio** is calculated by dividing earnings before interest and taxes (EBIT) by total assets:

$$\text{Basic earning power ratio (BEP)} = \frac{\text{EBIT}}{\text{Total assets}}$$

$$= \frac{\$283.8}{\$2,000} = 14.2\%.$$

$$\text{Industry average} = 17.2\%.$$

This ratio shows the raw earning power of the firm's assets, before the influence of taxes and leverage, and it is useful for comparing firms with different tax situations and different degrees of financial leverage. Because of its low turnover ratios and low profit margin on sales, Allied is not getting as high a return on its assets as is the average food-processing company.[10]

RETURN ON TOTAL ASSETS

Return on Total Assets (ROA)
The ratio of net income to total assets.

The ratio of net income to total assets measures the **return on total assets (ROA)** after interest and taxes:

$$\frac{\text{Return on}}{\text{total assets}} = \text{ROA} = \frac{\text{Net income available to common stockholders}}{\text{Total assets}}$$

$$= \frac{\$113.5}{\$2,000} = 5.7\%.$$

$$\text{Industry average} = 9.0\%.$$

Allied's 5.7 percent return is well below the 9 percent average for the industry. This low return results from (1) the company's low basic earning power plus (2) its above-average use of debt, both of which cause its net income to be relatively low.

---

[10]Notice that EBIT is earned throughout the year, whereas the total assets figure is an end-of-the-year number. Therefore, it would be conceptually better to calculate this ratio as EBIT/Average assets = EBIT/ [(Beginning assets + Ending assets)/2]. We have not made this adjustment because the published ratios used for comparative purposes do not include it, but when we construct our own comparative ratios, we do make the adjustment. Incidentally, the same adjustment would also be appropriate for the next two ratios, ROA and ROE.

ECONOMIC VALUE ADDED (EVA) — TODAY'S HOTTEST FINANCIAL IDEA

According to *Fortune* magazine, "Economic Value Added (EVA)" is today's hottest financial idea. Developed and popularized by the consulting firm Stern Stewart & Co., EVA helps managers ensure that a given business unit is adding to stockholder value, while investors can use it to spot stocks that are likely to increase in value. Right now, relatively few managers and investors are using it, so those who do use it have a competitive advantage. However, *Fortune* thinks this situation won't last long, as more managers and investors are catching the EVA fever every day.

What exactly is EVA? EVA is a way to measure an operation's true profitability. The cost of debt capital (interest expense) is deducted when calculating net income, but no cost is deducted to account for the cost of common equity. Therefore, in an economic sense, net income overstates "true" income. EVA overcomes this flaw in conventional accounting.

EVA is found by taking the after-tax operating profit and subtracting the annual cost of *all* the capital a firm uses. Such highly successful giants as Coca-Cola, AT&T, Quaker Oats, Briggs & Stratton, and CSX have jumped on the EVA bandwagon and attribute much of their success to its use. According to AT&T financial executive William H. Kurtz, EVA played a major role in AT&T's decision to acquire McCaw Cellular. In addition, AT&T made EVA the primary measure of its business unit managers' performance. Quaker Oats's CEO William Smithburg said, "EVA makes managers act like shareholders. It's the true corporate faith for the 1990s."

Surprisingly, many corporate executives have no idea how much capital they are using, or what that capital costs. The cost of debt capital is easy to determine because it shows up in financial statements as interest expense; however, the cost of equity capital, which is actually much larger than the cost of debt capital, does not appear in financial statements. As a result, managers often regard equity as free capital, even though it actually has a high cost. So, until a management team determines its cost of capital, it cannot know whether it is covering all costs and thereby adding value to the firm.

Although EVA is perhaps the most widely discussed concept in finance today, it is not new; the need to earn more than the cost of capital is actually one of the oldest ideas in business. However, the idea is often lost because of a misguided focus on conventional accounting.

John Snow, the chief executive officer who introduced the EVA concept to CSX Corporation in 1988, notes that CSX has lots of capital tied up in its fleets of locomotives, containers, trailers, and railcars, and in its tracks and rights-of-way, and that CSX's effectiveness in using that capital determines its market value. Snow's stiffest challenge has been in the fast-growing, but low-margin, intermodal business, where trains rush freight to waiting trucks or ships. In 1988, CSX Intermodal lost $70 million after all capital costs were considered — thus, its EVA was a negative $70 million. The division was told that it must break even by 1993 or be sold. Intermodal's employees realized what would happen to their jobs if the division were sold, so they worked hard and were able to increase freight volume by 25 percent even as they reduced capital by selling off containers, trailers, and locomotives. Wall Street has noticed the improvement, too. CSX's stock price was $28 when Snow introduced the EVA concept in 1988, but it had climbed to $82.50 by 1993.

Briggs & Stratton, a maker of gasoline engines, tells a similar success story. When EVA was introduced there in 1990, management was earning a return of only 7.7 percent on capital versus a cost of 12 percent. Drastic changes were made, the return on capital was pushed up over its cost, and, as a result, the stock price quadrupled in four years.

Coca-Cola formally introduced the EVA concept to its managers after Roberto Goizueta took over as CEO in 1981. Since then, Coke has restructured its business, sharply lowered its average cost of capital, and increased its EVA even more sharply. As a result, its stock price increased from $3 to $57.

One of EVA's greatest virtues is its direct link to stock prices. AT&T found an almost perfect correlation between its EVA and its stock price. Moreover, security analysts have found that stock prices track EVA far more closely than other factors such as earnings per share, operating margin, or return on equity. This correlation occurs because EVA is what investors really care about, namely, the net cash return on their capital. Therefore, more and more security analysts are calculating companies' EVAs and using them to help identify good buys in the stock market.

EVA can be determined at divisional levels within the company as well as for the company as a whole. Therefore, EVA provides a useful basis for determining the compensation of managers at all levels.

We will have more to say about EVA, and explain how it is calculated, after we discuss the cost of capital in Chapter 9.

SOURCES: "The Real Key to Creating Wealth," *Fortune,* September 20, 1993, 38–44; and "America's Best Wealth Creators," *Fortune,* November 28, 1994, 143–162.

RETURN ON COMMON EQUITY

Return on Common Equity (ROE)
The ratio of net income to common equity; measures the rate of return on common stockholders' investment.

The ratio of net income to common equity measures the **return on common equity (ROE),** or the *rate of return on stockholders' investment*:

$$\text{Return on common equity} = \text{ROE} = \frac{\text{Net income available to common stockholders}}{\text{Common equity}}$$

$$= \frac{\$113.5}{\$896} = 12.7\%.$$

Industry average = 15.0%.

Allied's 12.7 percent return is below the 15 percent industry average, but not as far below as the return on total assets. This somewhat better result is due to the company's greater use of debt, a point that is analyzed in detail later in the chapter.

SELF-TEST QUESTIONS

Identify four ratios that show the combined effects of liquidity, asset management, and debt management on profitability, and write out their equations.

Why is the basic earning power ratio useful?

What does ROE measure?

MARKET VALUE RATIOS

Market Value Ratios
A set of ratios that relate the firm's stock price to its earnings and book value per share.

A final group of ratios, the **market value ratios,** relates the firm's stock price to its earnings and book value per share. These ratios give management an indication of what investors think of the company's past performance and future prospects. If the firm's liquidity, asset management, debt management, and profitability ratios are all good, then its market value ratios will be high, and its stock price will probably be as high as can be expected.

PRICE/EARNINGS RATIO

Price/Earnings (P/E) Ratio
The ratio of the price per share to earnings per share; shows the dollar amount investors will pay for $1 of current earnings.

The **price/earnings (P/E) ratio** shows how much investors are willing to pay per dollar of reported profits. Allied's stock sells for $23, so with an EPS of $2.27 its P/E ratio is 10.1:

$$\text{Price/earnings (P/E) ratio} = \frac{\text{Price per share}}{\text{Earnings per share}}$$

$$= \frac{\$23.00}{\$2.27} = 10.1 \text{ times.}$$

Industry average = 12.5 times.

As we will see in Chapter 8, P/E ratios are higher for firms with high growth prospects, other things held constant, but they are lower for riskier firms. Since Allied's P/E ratio is below the average for other food processors, this suggests that the company is regarded as being somewhat riskier than most, as having poorer growth prospects, or both.

MARKET/BOOK RATIO

The ratio of a stock's market price to its book value gives another indication of how investors regard the company. Companies with relatively high rates of return on equity generally sell at higher multiples of book value than those with low returns. First, we find Allied's book value per share:

$$\text{Book value per share} = \frac{\text{Common equity}}{\text{Shares outstanding}}$$

$$= \frac{\$896}{50} = \$17.92.$$

Market/Book (M/B) Ratio
The ratio of a stock's market price to its book value.

Now we divide the market price per share by the book value to get a **market/book (M/B) ratio** of 1.3 times:

$$\text{Market/book ratio} = \text{M/B} = \frac{\text{Market price per share}}{\text{Book value per share}}$$

$$= \frac{\$23.00}{\$17.92} = 1.3 \text{ times.}$$

$$\text{Industry average} = 1.7 \text{ times.}$$

Investors are willing to pay less for a dollar of Allied's book value than for one of an average food-processing company.

The average company followed by the *Value Line Investment Survey* had a market/book ratio of about 2.34 during 1994. Since M/B ratios typically exceed 1.0, this means that investors are willing to pay more for stocks than their accounting book values. This situation occurs primarily because asset values, as reported by accountants on corporate balance sheets, do not reflect either inflation or "goodwill." Thus, assets purchased years ago at preinflation prices are carried at their original costs, even though inflation might have caused their actual values to rise substantially, and going concerns have a value greater than their historical costs.

If a company earns a low rate of return on its assets, then its M/B ratio will be relatively low versus an average company. Thus, many airlines, which have not fared well in recent years, sell at M/B ratios below 1.0, while very successful firms such as Microsoft (which makes the operating systems for virtually all PCs) achieve high rates of return on their assets, and their market values are well in excess of their book values. In 1995, Microsoft's book value per share was $7.63 versus a market price of $63, so its market/book ratio was $63/$7.63 = 8.3 times.

SELF-TEST QUESTIONS

Describe two ratios that relate a firm's stock price to its earnings and book value per share, and write out their equations.

How do market value ratios reflect what investors think about a stock's risk and expected rate of return?

What does the price/earnings (P/E) ratio show? If one firm's P/E ratio is lower than that of another firm, what factors might explain the difference?

How is book value per share calculated? Explain how inflation and goodwill cause book values to deviate from market values.

TREND ANALYSIS

Trend Analysis
An analysis of a firm's financial ratios over time; used to determine the improvement or deterioration in its financial situation.

It is important to analyze trends in ratios as well as their absolute levels, for trends give clues as to whether the financial situation is likely to improve or to deteriorate. To do a **trend analysis**, one simply plots a ratio over time, as shown in Figure 3-1. This graph shows that Allied's rate of return on common equity has been declining since 1992, even though the industry average has been relatively stable. All the other ratios could be analyzed similarly.

SELF-TEST QUESTIONS

How does one do a trend analysis?

Why is it important to include a trend analysis in a study of ratios?

TYING THE RATIOS TOGETHER: THE DU PONT CHART

Du Pont Chart
A chart designed to show the relationships among return on investment, asset turnover, the profit margin, and leverage.

Table 3-2 summarizes Allied's ratios, and Figure 3-2, which is called a modified **Du Pont chart** because that company's managers developed the general approach, shows how the return on equity is affected by asset turnover, the profit margin, and leverage. The left-hand side of the chart develops the *profit margin on sales*. The various expense items are listed and then summed to obtain Allied's total cost, which is subtracted from sales to obtain the company's net income. When we divide net income by sales, we find that 3.8 percent of each sales dollar is left over for stockholders. If the profit margin is low or trending down, one can examine the individual expense items to identify and then correct problems.

The right-hand side of Figure 3-2 lists the various categories of assets, totals them, and then divides sales by total assets to find the number of times Allied "turns its assets over" each year. The company's total assets turnover ratio is 1.5 times.

FIGURE 3-1   RATE OF RETURN ON COMMON EQUITY, 1991–1995

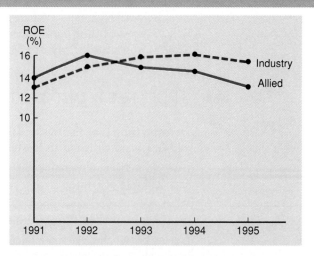

| TABLE 3-2 | ALLIED FOOD PRODUCTS: SUMMARY OF FINANCIAL RATIOS (MILLIONS OF DOLLARS) | | | | |

RATIO	FORMULA FOR CALCULATION	CALCULATION	RATIO	INDUSTRY AVERAGE	COMMENT
Liquidity					
Current	$\dfrac{\text{Current assets}}{\text{Current liabilities}}$	$\dfrac{\$1,000}{\$310}$	= 3.2×	4.2×	Poor
Quick, or acid, test	$\dfrac{\text{Current assets} - \text{Inventories}}{\text{Current liabilities}}$	$\dfrac{\$385}{\$310}$	= 1.2×	2.1×	Poor
Asset Management					
Inventory turnover	$\dfrac{\text{Sales}}{\text{Inventories}}$	$\dfrac{\$3,000}{\$615}$	= 4.9×	9.0×	Poor
Days sales outstanding (DSO)	$\dfrac{\text{Receivables}}{\text{Annual sales}/360}$	$\dfrac{\$375}{\$8.333}$	= 45 days	36 days	Poor
Fixed assets turnover	$\dfrac{\text{Sales}}{\text{Net fixed assets}}$	$\dfrac{\$3,000}{\$1,000}$	= 3.0×	3.0×	OK
Total assets turnover	$\dfrac{\text{Sales}}{\text{Total assets}}$	$\dfrac{\$3,000}{\$2,000}$	= 1.5×	1.8×	Somewhat low
Debt Management					
Total debt to total assets	$\dfrac{\text{Total debt}}{\text{Total assets}}$	$\dfrac{\$1,064}{\$2,000}$	= 53.2%	40.0%	High (risky)
Times-interest-earned (TIE)	$\dfrac{\text{Earnings before interest and taxes (EBIT)}}{\text{Interest charges}}$	$\dfrac{\$283.8}{\$88}$	= 3.2×	6.0×	Low (risky)
Fixed charge coverage	$\dfrac{\text{Earnings before interest and taxes} + \text{Lease payments}}{\text{Interest charges} + \text{Lease payments} + \dfrac{\text{SF payments}}{(1-T)}}$	$\dfrac{\$311.8}{\$149.3}$	= 2.1×	5.5×	Low (risky)
Profitability					
Profit margin on sales	$\dfrac{\text{Net income available to common stockholders}}{\text{Sales}}$	$\dfrac{\$113.5}{\$3,000}$	= 3.8%	5.0%	Poor
Basic earning power (BEP)	$\dfrac{\text{Earnings before interest and taxes (EBIT)}}{\text{Total assets}}$	$\dfrac{\$283.8}{\$2,000}$	= 14.2%	17.2%	Poor
Return on total assets (ROA)	$\dfrac{\text{Net income available to common stockholders}}{\text{Total assets}}$	$\dfrac{\$113.5}{\$2,000}$	= 5.7%	9.0%	Poor
Return on common equity (ROE)	$\dfrac{\text{Net income available to common stockholders}}{\text{Common equity}}$	$\dfrac{\$113.5}{\$896}$	= 12.7%	15.0%	Poor
Market Value					
Price/earnings (P/E)	$\dfrac{\text{Price per share}}{\text{Earnings per share}}$	$\dfrac{\$23.00}{\$2.27}$	= 10.1×	12.5×	Low
Market/book (M/B)	$\dfrac{\text{Market price per share}}{\text{Book value per share}}$	$\dfrac{\$23.00}{\$17.92}$	= 1.3×	1.7×	Low

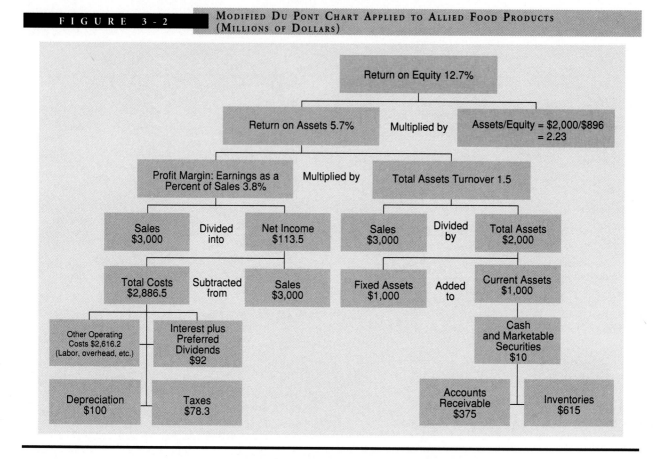

Du Pont Equation
A formula that gives the rate of return on assets by multiplying the profit margin by the total assets turnover.

The profit margin times the total assets turnover is called the **Du Pont equation,** and it gives the rate of return on assets (ROA):

$$\text{ROA} = \text{Profit margin} \times \text{Total assets turnover}$$

$$= \frac{\text{Net income}}{\text{Sales}} \times \frac{\text{Sales}}{\text{Total assets}} \quad (3\text{-}1)$$

$$= 3.8\% \times 1.5 = 5.7\%.$$

Allied made 3.8 percent, or 3.8 cents, on each dollar of sales, and assets were "turned over" 1.5 times during the year, so the company earned a return of 5.7 percent on its assets.

If the company were financed only with common equity, the rate of return on assets (ROA) and the return on equity (ROE) would be the same because the total assets would equal the common equity:

$$\text{ROA} = \frac{\text{Net income}}{\text{Total assets}} = \frac{\text{Net income}}{\text{Common equity}} = \text{ROE}.$$

This equality holds if and only if Total assets = Common equity, i.e., if the company uses no debt. Allied does use debt, so its common equity is less than total assets. Therefore, the return to the common stockholders (ROE) must be greater than the ROA of 5.7 percent. Specifically, the rate of return on assets (ROA) can be multiplied by the *equity multiplier,* which is the ratio of assets to common equity, to see how the rate of return on equity (ROE) is related to the firm's ROA and its use of leverage:[11]

$$
\begin{aligned}
\text{ROE} &= \text{ROA} \quad \times \text{Equity multiplier} \\
&= \frac{\text{Net income}}{\text{Total assets}} \times \frac{\text{Total assets}}{\text{Common equity}} \\
&= \quad 5.7\% \quad \times \quad \$2{,}000/\$896 \\
&= \quad 5.7\% \quad \times \quad 2.23 \\
&= \quad 12.7\%.
\end{aligned}
\tag{3-2}
$$

We can combine Equations 3-1 and 3-2 to form the extended Du Pont equation, which shows how the profit margin, the assets turnover ratio, and the equity multiplier combine to determine the ROE:

$$
\begin{aligned}
\text{ROE} &= (\text{Profit margin}) \, (\text{Total assets turnover}) \, (\text{Equity multiplier}) \\
&= \frac{\text{Net income}}{\text{Sales}} \times \frac{\text{Sales}}{\text{Total assets}} \times \frac{\text{Total assets}}{\text{Common equity}}.
\end{aligned}
\tag{3-3}
$$

For Allied, we have

$$
\begin{aligned}
\text{ROE} &= (3.8\%)\,(1.5)\,(2.23) \\
&= 12.7\%.
\end{aligned}
$$

The 12.7 percent rate of return could, of course, be calculated directly: Net income/Common equity = $113.5/$896 = 12.7%. However, the Du Pont equation shows how the profit margin, the total assets turnover ratio, and the use of debt interact to determine the return on equity.[12]

Allied's management can use the Du Pont system to analyze ways of improving the firm's performance. Focusing on the left, or "profit margin," side of its modified Du Pont chart, Allied's marketing people can study the effects of raising sales prices (or lowering them to increase volume), of moving into new products or markets with higher margins, and so on. The company's cost accountants can study various expense items and, working with engineers, purchasing agents, and other operating personnel, seek ways to hold down costs. On the "turnover" side, Allied's financial analysts, working with both production and marketing people, can investigate ways to reduce the investment in various types of assets. At the same time, the treasury staff can analyze the effects of alternative financing strategies, seeking to hold down interest expense and the risk of debt while still using leverage to increase the rate of return on equity.

As a result of such an analysis, Al Jackson, Allied's president, recently announced a series of moves designed to cut operating costs by more than 20 percent per year.

---

[11]Note that we could also find the ROE by "grossing up" the ROA, by dividing the ROA by the common equity fraction: ROE = ROA/Equity fraction = 5.7%/0.448 = 12.7%. The two procedures are algebraically equivalent.

[12]Another ratio that is frequently used is the following:

$$
\text{Rate of return on investors' capital} = \frac{\text{Net income} + \text{Interest}}{\text{Debt} + \text{Equity}}.
$$

The numerator shows the dollar returns to investors, the denominator shows the total amount of money investors have put up, and the ratio itself shows the rate of return on all investors' capital. This ratio is especially important in the public utility industries, where regulators are concerned about the companies' using their monopoly positions to earn excessive returns on investors' capital. In fact, regulators try to set utility prices (service rates) at levels that will force the return on investors' capital to equal a company's cost of capital as defined in Chapter 9.

Jackson also announced that the company intended to concentrate its capital in markets where profit margins are reasonably high, and that if competition increases in certain of its product markets (such as the low-price end of the canned fruit market), Allied will withdraw from those markets. Allied is seeking a high return on equity, and Jackson recognizes that if competition drives profit margins too low in a particular market, it will be impossible to earn high returns on the capital invested to serve that market. Therefore, if it is to achieve a high ROE, Allied may have to develop new products and shift capital into new areas. The company's future depends on this type of analysis, and the Du Pont system can help it achieve success.

Jackson himself, and other Allied executives, have a strong incentive for improving the company's financial performance because their compensation is based to a large extent on how well the company does. Allied's executives receive a salary which is sufficient to cover their living costs, but their compensation package also includes "performance shares" which will be awarded if and only if the company meets or exceeds target levels for earnings and the stock price. These target levels are based on Allied's performance relative to other food companies. So, if Allied does well, then Jackson and the other executives — and the stockholders — will also do well. But if things deteriorate, Jackson could suffer the same fate as Borden's Anthony D'Amato.

 ## SELF-TEST QUESTIONS

Explain how the modified Du Pont equation and chart can be used to reveal the basic determinants of ROE.

What is the equity multiplier?

How can management use the Du Pont system to analyze ways of improving the firm's performance?

COMPARATIVE RATIOS AND "BENCHMARKING"

Comparative Ratio Analysis
An analysis based on a comparison of a firm's ratios with those of other firms in the same industry.

Benchmarking
The process of comparing a particular company with a group of "benchmark" companies.

The preceding analysis is called a **comparative ratio analysis** because the company's ratios were compared with those of other firms in the same industry, that is, to industry average figures. However, like most firms, Allied managers go one step further — they also compare their ratios with those of a smaller set of leading food companies. This technique is called **benchmarking,** and the companies used for the comparison are called *benchmark companies.* Allied's management benchmarks against the following companies: Campbell Soup, a leading manufacturer of canned soups and fruit and vegetable juices; Dean Foods, a processor of canned and frozen vegetables; Dole Food Company, a processor of fruits and vegetables; H.J. Heinz, which makes ketchup and other products; Pet Inc., a packaged-foods company; and Borden Inc., which makes pasta, dairy products, and snack foods. The ratios are calculated for each company, and then the ratios are listed in descending order as shown below for the profit margin on sales as reported by *Value Line* for 1995:

	PROFIT MARGIN
Campbell Soup	8.9%
Heinz	7.7
Pet Inc.	7.3

	PROFIT MARGIN
Allied Food Products	3.8
Dean Foods	2.9
Dole Food Company	2.7
Borden	2.0

The benchmarking setup makes it easy for Allied's management to see exactly where they stand relative to their competition. As the data show, Allied is ranked in the middle with respect to its profit margin, so the company has room for improvement.

Comparative ratios are available from a number of sources. One useful set is compiled by Dun & Bradstreet (D&B), which provides various ratios calculated for a large number of industries; nine of these ratios are shown for a small sample of industries in Table 3-3. Useful ratios can also be found in the *Annual Statement Studies* published by Robert Morris Associates, which is the national association of bank loan officers. The U.S. Commerce Department's *Quarterly Financial Report*, which is found in most libraries, gives a set of ratios for manufacturing firms by industry group and size of firm. Trade associations and individual firms' credit departments also compile industry average financial ratios. Finally, financial statement data for thousands of publicly owned corporations are available on magnetic tapes

TABLE 3-3	**DUN & BRADSTREET RATIOS FOR SELECTED INDUSTRIES: UPPER QUARTILE, MEDIAN, AND LOWER QUARTILE[a]**

SIC CODES, LINE OF BUSINESS, AND NUMBER OF CONCERNS REPORTING	QUICK RATIO	CURRENT RATIO	TOTAL LIABILITIES TO NET WORTH	DAYS SALES OUTSTANDING	NET SALES TO INVENTORY	TOTAL ASSETS TO NET SALES	RETURN ON NET SALES	RETURN ON TOTAL ASSETS	RETURN ON NET WORTH
	×	×	%	DAYS	×	%	%	%	%
2879	1.8	4.4	27.5	23.0	16.2	36.8	23.1	24.2	35.3
Agricultural chemicals	1.2	2.4	59.3	37.2	9.5	48.4	6.4	6.5	19.8
(52)	0.5	1.3	165.2	62.8	6.4	85.1	2.3	0.5	2.6
3724	2.1	4.2	25.6	41.8	13.2	53.1	5.7	6.3	11.4
Aircraft parts, including	1.0	2.3	65.6	52.1	5.4	72.5	3.1	2.0	6.0
engines (80)	0.7	1.4	203.1	65.2	3.7	89.3	(0.6)	(1.2)	(2.0)
2051	1.8	2.4	41.5	17.4	61.9	22.8	8.4	14.7	45.2
Bakery products	0.9	1.3	95.1	23.7	39.2	30.6	2.8	6.6	17.9
(172)	0.6	0.9	227.5	34.9	20.5	42.6	0.3	0.6	1.9
2086	2.4	3.7	23.2	17.7	25.6	31.6	6.3	10.0	24.9
Beverages	1.0	1.7	72.8	29.4	18.0	44.0	1.8	3.3	11.1
(115)	0.5	1.0	178.6	44.1	10.4	100.3	(0.3)	0.2	2.7
3312	2.3	3.1	42.7	32.1	27.5	31.4	7.9	16.6	47.5
Blast furnaces and steel	1.1	1.8	120.1	43.1	11.4	46.9	2.9	4.0	11.8
mills (271)	0.7	1.2	263.5	55.9	6.7	77.4	0.2	0.3	1.8
2731	2.5	4.8	23.5	32.7	8.7	41.0	13.9	17.2	37.0
Book publishing	1.1	2.4	64.8	49.6	4.9	63.1	5.5	6.1	13.0
(394)	0.6	1.4	180.2	81.8	3.0	94.5	1.3	1.3	2.7

SOURCE: Industry Norms and Key Business Ratios, 1993–94 Edition, Dun & Bradstreet Credit Services.

[a]The median and quartile ratios can be illustrated by an example. The median quick ratio for agricultural chemical manufacturers, as shown in this table, is 1.2. To obtain this figure, the ratios of current assets less inventories to current debt for each of the 52 concerns were arranged in a graduated series, with the largest ratio at the top and the smallest at the bottom. The median ratio of 1.2 is the ratio halfway between the top and the bottom. The ratio of 1.8, representing the upper quartile, is one-quarter of the way down from the top (or halfway between the top and the median). The ratio 0.5, representing the lower quartile, is one-quarter of the way up from the bottom (or halfway between the median and the bottom). SIC codes are "Standard Industrial Classification" codes used by the U.S. government to classify companies.

and diskettes, and since brokerage houses, banks, and other financial institutions have access to these data, security analysts can and do generate comparative ratios tailored to their specific needs.

Each of the data-supplying organizations uses a somewhat different set of ratios designed for its own purposes. For example, D&B deals mainly with small firms, many of which are proprietorships, and it sells its services primarily to banks and other lenders. Therefore, D&B is concerned largely with the creditor's viewpoint, and its ratios emphasize current assets and liabilities, not market value ratios. So, when you select a comparative data source, you should be sure that your emphasis is similar to that of the agency whose ratios you plan to use. Additionally, there are often definitional differences in the ratios presented by different sources, so before using a source, be sure to verify the exact definitions of the ratios to ensure consistency with your own work.

SELF-TEST QUESTIONS

Differentiate between trend analysis and comparative ratio analysis.

Why is it useful to conduct comparative ratio analysis?

What is benchmarking, and how is it different from comparative ratio analysis?

USES AND LIMITATIONS OF RATIO ANALYSIS

As noted earlier, ratio analysis is used by three main groups: (1) *managers,* who employ ratios to help analyze, control, and thus improve their firms' operations; (2) *credit analysts,* such as bank loan officers or bond rating analysts, who analyze ratios to help ascertain a company's ability to pay its debts; and (3) *stock analysts,* who are interested in a company's efficiency and growth prospects. In later chapters we will look more closely at the basic factors which underlie each ratio, and at that point you will get a better idea about how to interpret and use ratios.

While ratio analysis can provide useful information concerning a company's operations and financial condition, it does have limitations that necessitate care and judgment. Some potential problems are listed below:

1. Many large firms operate different divisions in different industries, and this makes it difficult to develop a meaningful set of industry averages for comparative purposes. Therefore, ratio analysis is more useful for small, narrowly focused firms than for large, multidivisional ones.

2. Most firms want to be better than average, so merely attaining average performance is not necessarily good. As a target for high-level performance, it is best to focus on the industry leaders' ratios. Benchmarking helps in this regard.

3. Inflation may have badly distorted firms' balance sheets — recorded values are often substantially different from "true" values. Further, since inflation affects both depreciation charges and inventory costs, profits are also affected. Thus, a ratio analysis for one firm over time, or a comparative analysis of firms of different ages, must be interpreted with judgment.

4. Seasonal factors can also distort a ratio analysis. For example, the inventory turnover ratio for a food processor will be radically different if the balance

sheet figure used for inventory is the one just before versus just after the close of the canning season. This problem can be minimized by using monthly averages for inventory (and receivables) when calculating ratios such as turnover.

"Window Dressing" Techniques
Techniques employed by firms to make their financial statements look better than they really are.

5. Firms can employ **"window dressing" techniques** to make their financial statements look stronger. To illustrate, a Chicago builder borrowed on a two-year basis on December 28, 1995, held the proceeds of the loan as cash for a few days, and then paid off the loan ahead of time on January 2, 1996. This improved his current and quick ratios, and made his year-end 1995 balance sheet look good. However, the improvement was strictly window dressing; a week later the balance sheet was back at the old level.

6. Different accounting practices can distort comparisons. As noted earlier, inventory valuation and depreciation methods can affect financial statements and thus distort comparisons among firms. Also, if one firm leases a substantial amount of its productive equipment, then its assets may appear low relative to sales because leased assets often do not appear on the balance sheet. At the same time, the lease liability may not be shown as a debt. Therefore, leasing can artificially improve both the turnover and the debt ratios. However, the accounting profession has taken steps to reduce this problem.

7. It is difficult to generalize about whether a particular ratio is "good" or "bad." For example, a high current ratio may indicate a strong liquidity position, which is good, or excessive cash, which is bad (because excess cash in the bank is a nonearning asset). Similarly, a high fixed assets turnover ratio may denote either a firm that uses its assets efficiently or one that is undercapitalized and cannot afford to buy enough assets.

8. A firm may have some ratios that look "good" and others that look "bad," making it difficult to tell whether the company is, on balance, strong or weak. However, statistical procedures can be used to analyze the *net effects* of a set of ratios. Many banks and other lending organizations use statistical procedures to analyze firms' financial ratios, and, on the basis of their analyses, classify companies according to their probability of getting into financial trouble.[13]

Ratio analysis is useful, but analysts should be aware of these problems and make adjustments as necessary. Ratio analysis conducted in a mechanical, unthinking manner is dangerous, but used intelligently and with good judgment, it can provide useful insights into a firm's operations. Your judgment in interpreting a set of ratios is necessarily weak at this point, but it will improve as you go through the remainder of the book.

 SELF-TEST QUESTIONS

List three types of users of ratio analysis. Would these different types of users emphasize different types of ratios?

List several potential problems with ratio analysis.

---

[13]The technique used is discriminant analysis. For a discussion, see Edward I. Altman, "Financial Ratios, Discriminant Analysis, and the Prediction of Corporate Bankruptcy," *Journal of Finance,* September 1968, 589–609, or Eugene F. Brigham and Louis C. Gapenski, *Intermediate Financial Management,* 5th ed., 1996, Chapter 26.

FINANCIAL ANALYSIS IN THE SMALL FIRM

Financial ratio analysis is especially useful for small businesses, and readily available sources provide comparative data by size of firm. For example, Robert Morris Associates provides comparative ratios for a number of small-firm classes, including the size range of zero to $250,000 in annual sales. Nevertheless, analyzing a small firm's statements presents some unique problems. We examine here some of those problems from the standpoint of a bank loan officer, one of the most frequent users of ratio analysis.

When evaluating a small business credit prospect, a banker is essentially making a prediction about the ability of the company to repay its debt. In making this prediction, the banker will be especially concerned about indicators of liquidity and about continuing prospects for profitability. Bankers like to do business with a new customer if it appears that loans can be paid off on a timely basis and that the company will remain in business and therefore be a customer of the bank for some years to come. Thus, both short-run and long-run viability are of interest to the banker. At the same time, the banker's perceptions about the business are important to the owner-manager, because the bank will probably be the firm's primary source of funds.

The first problem the banker is likely to encounter is that, unlike the bank's bigger customers, the small firm may not have audited financial statements. Further, the statements that are available may have been produced on an irregular basis (for example, in some months or quarters but not in others). If the firm is young, it may have historical financial statements for only one year, or perhaps none at all. Also, the financial statements may not have been produced by a reputable accounting firm but by the owner's brother-in-law.

The poor quality of its financial data may therefore be a hinderance for a small business that is attempting to establish a banking relationship. This could keep the firm from getting credit even though it is really on solid financial ground. Therefore, it is in the owner's interest to make sure that the firm's financial data are credible, even if it is more expensive to do so. Furthermore, if the banker is uncomfortable with the data, the firm's management should also be uncomfortable: Because many managerial decisions depend on the numbers in the firm's accounting statements, those numbers should be as accurate as possible.

For a given set of financial ratios, a small firm may be riskier than a larger one. Small firms often produce a single product, rely heavily on a single customer, or both. For example, several years ago a company called Yard Man Inc. manufactured and sold lawn equipment. Most of Yard Man's sales were to Sears, so most of its revenues and profits were due to its Sears account. When Sears decided to drop Yard Man as a supplier, the company was left without its most important customer. Yard Man is no longer in business. Because large firms typically have a broad customer base, they are not as exposed to the sudden loss of a large portion of their business.

A similar danger applies to a single-product company. Just as the loss of a key customer can be disastrous for a small business, so can a shift in the tides of consumer interest in a particular fad. For example, Coleco manufactured and sold the extremely popular Cabbage Patch dolls. The phenomenal popularity of the dolls was a great boon for Coleco, but the public is fickle. One can never predict when such a fad will die out, leaving the company with a great deal of capacity to make a product that no one will buy, and with a large amount of overvalued inventory. Exactly that situation hit Coleco, and it was forced into bankruptcy.

The extension of credit to a small company, especially to a small owner-managed company, often involves yet another risk that is less of a problem for larger firms — dependence on the leadership of a single key individual whose unexpected death could cause the company to fail. Similarly, if the company is family owned and managed, there is typically one key decision maker, even though several other family members may be involved in helping to manage the company. In the case of the family business, the loss of the top person may not wipe out the company, but it often creates the equally serious problem of who will assume the leadership role. The loss of a key family member is often a highly emotional event, and it is not at all unusual for it to be followed by an ugly and prolonged struggle for control of the business. It is in the family's interest, and certainly in the creditors' interests, to see that a plan of management succession is clearly specified before trouble arises. If no good plan can be worked out, perhaps the firm should be forced to carry "key person insurance," payable to the bank and used to retire the loan in the event of the key person's death.

In summary, to determine the creditworthiness of a small firm, the financial analyst must "look beyond the ratios" and analyze the viability of the firm's products, customers, management, and market. Still, ratio analysis is the first step in a sound credit analysis.

SUMMARY

The primary purpose of this chapter was to discuss techniques used by investors and managers to analyze financial statements. The key concepts covered are listed below.

- **Financial statement analysis** generally begins with the calculation of a set of **financial ratios** designed to reveal the relative strengths and weaknesses of a company as compared with other companies in the same industry, and to show whether its position has been improving or deteriorating over time.

- **Liquidity ratios** show the relationship of a firm's current assets to its current liabilities, and thus its ability to meet maturing debts.

- Two commonly used liquidity ratios are the **current ratio** and the **quick, or acid test, ratio.**

- **Asset management ratios** measure how effectively a firm is managing its assets.

- Asset management ratios include **inventory turnover, days sales outstanding, fixed assets turnover,** and **total assets turnover.**

- **Debt management ratios** reveal (1) the extent to which the firm is financed with debt and (2) its likelihood of defaulting on its debt obligations.

- Debt management ratios include the **debt ratio, times-interest-earned,** and the **fixed charge coverage ratio.**

- **Profitability ratios** show the combined effects of liquidity, asset management, and debt management policies on operating results.

- Profitability ratios include the **profit margin on sales,** the **basic earning power ratio,** the **return on total assets,** and the **return on common equity.**

- **Market value ratios** relate the firm's stock price to its earnings and book value per share, and they give management an indication of what investors think of the company's past performance and future prospects.

- Market value ratios include the **price/earnings ratio** and the **market/book ratio.**

- **Trend analysis,** where one plots a ratio over time, is important, because it reveals whether the firm's ratios are improving or deteriorating over time.

- The **Du Pont chart** is designed to show how the profit margin on sales, the assets turnover ratio, and the use of debt interact to determine the rate of return on equity. The firm's management can use the Du Pont system to analyze ways of improving the firm's performance.

- **Benchmarking** is the process of comparing a particular company with a group of "benchmark" companies.

- In analyzing a small firm's financial position, ratio analysis is a useful starting point. However, the analyst must also (1) examine the quality of the financial data, (2) ensure that the firm is sufficiently diversified to withstand shifts in customers' buying habits, and (3) determine whether the firm has a plan for the succession of its management.

Ratio analysis has limitations, but used with care and judgment, it can be very helpful.

QUESTIONS

3-1 Financial ratio analysis is conducted by four groups of analysts: managers, equity investors, long-term creditors, and short-term creditors. What is the primary emphasis of each of these groups in evaluating ratios?

3-2 Why would the inventory turnover ratio be more important when analyzing a grocery chain than an insurance company?

3-3 Over the past year, M. D. Ryngaert & Co. has realized an increase in both its current ratio and its total assets turnover ratio. However, the company's sales, quick ratio, and fixed assets turnover ratio have remained constant. What explains these changes?

3-4 Profit margins and turnover ratios vary from one industry to another. What differences would you expect to find between a grocery chain like Safeway and a steel company? Think particularly about the turnover ratios, the profit margin, and the Du Pont equation.

3-5 How does inflation distort ratio analysis comparisons, both for one company over time (trend analysis) and when different companies are compared? Are only balance sheet items or both balance sheet and income statement items affected?

3-6 If a firm's ROE is low and management wants to improve it, explain how using more debt might help.

3-7 How might (a) seasonal factors and (b) different growth rates distort a comparative ratio analysis? Give some examples. How might these problems be alleviated?

3-8 Why is it sometimes misleading to compare a company's financial ratios with other firms which operate in the same industry?

3-9 Indicate the effects of the transactions listed in the following table on total current assets, current ratio, and net income. Use (+) to indicate an increase, (−) to indicate a decrease, and (0) to indicate either no effect or an indeterminate effect. Be prepared to state any necessary assumptions, and assume an initial current ratio of more than 1.0. (Note: A good accounting background is necessary to answer some of these questions; if yours is not strong, just answer the questions you can handle.)

	TOTAL CURRENT ASSETS	CURRENT RATIO	EFFECT ON NET INCOME
a. Cash is acquired through issuance of additional common stock.			
b. Merchandise is sold for cash.			
c. Federal income tax due for the previous year is paid.			
d. A fixed asset is sold for less than book value.			
e. A fixed asset is sold for more than book value.			
f. Merchandise is sold on credit.			
g. Payment is made to trade creditors for previous purchases.			
h. A cash dividend is declared and paid.			
i. Cash is obtained through short-term bank loans.			
j. Short-term notes receivable are sold at a discount.			
k. Marketable securities are sold below cost.			
l. Advances are made to employees.			
m. Current operating expenses are paid.			
n. Short-term promissory notes are issued to trade creditors in exchange for past due accounts payable.			
o. Ten-year notes are issued to pay off accounts payable.			
p. A fully depreciated asset is retired.			
q. Accounts receivable are collected.			
r. Equipment is purchased with short-term notes.			
s. Merchandise is purchased on credit.			
t. The estimated taxes payable are increased.			

SELF-TEST PROBLEMS *(Solutions Appear in Appendix B)*

ST-1 Key terms   Define each of the following terms:
  a. Liquidity ratios: current ratio; quick, or acid test, ratio
  b. Asset management ratios: inventory turnover ratio; days sales outstanding (DSO); fixed assets turnover ratio; total assets turnover ratio
  c. Financial leverage: debt ratio; times-interest-earned (TIE) ratio; fixed charge coverage ratio
  d. Profitability ratios: profit margin on sales; basic earning power (BEP) ratio; return on total assets (ROA); return on common equity (ROE)
  e. Market value ratios: price/earnings (P/E) ratio; market/book (M/B) ratio; book value per share
  f. Trend analysis; comparative ratio analysis; benchmarking
  g. Du Pont chart; Du Pont equation
  h. "Window dressing"; seasonal effects on ratios

ST-2 Debt ratio   K. Billingsworth & Co. had earnings per share of $4 last year, and it paid a $2 dividend. Total retained earnings increased by $12 million during the year, while book value per share at year-end was $40. Billingsworth has no preferred stock, and no new common stock was issued during the year. If Billingsworth's year-end debt (which equals its total liabilities) was $120 million, what was the company's year-end debt/assets ratio?

ST-3 Ratio analysis   The following data apply to A.L. Kaiser & Company (millions of dollars):

Cash and marketable securities	$100.00
Fixed assets	$283.50
Sales	$1,000.00
Net income	$50.00
Quick ratio	2.0×
Current ratio	3.0×
DSO	40 days
ROE	12%

Kaiser has no preferred stock — only common equity, current liabilities, and long-term debt.
  a. Find Kaiser's (1) accounts receivable (A/R), (2) current liabilities, (3) current assets, (4) total assets, (5) ROA, (6) common equity, and (7) long-term debt.
  b. In Part a, you should have found Kaiser's accounts receivable (A/R) = $111.1 million. If Kaiser could reduce its DSO from 40 days to 30 days while holding other things constant, how much cash would it generate? If this cash were used to buy back common stock (at book value), thus reducing the amount of common equity, how would this affect (1) the ROE, (2) the ROA, and (3) the total debt/total assets ratio?

PROBLEMS

3-1 Ratio analysis   Data for Barry Computer Company and its industry averages follow.
  a. Calculate the indicated ratios for Barry.
  b. Construct the extended Du Pont equation for both Barry and the industry.
  c. Outline Barry's strengths and weaknesses as revealed by your analysis.
  d. Suppose Barry had doubled its sales as well as its inventories, accounts receivable, and common equity during 1995. How would that information affect the validity of your ratio analysis? (Hint: Think about averages and the effects of rapid growth on ratios if averages are not used. No calculations are needed.)

BARRY COMPUTER COMPANY: BALANCE SHEET AS OF DECEMBER 31, 1995 (IN THOUSANDS)

Cash	$ 77,500	Accounts payable	$ 129,000
Receivables	336,000	Notes payable	84,000
Inventories	241,500	Other current liabilities	117,000
Total current assets	$ 655,000	Total current liabilities	$ 330,000
Net fixed assets	292,500	Long-term debt	256,500
		Common equity	361,000
Total assets	$ 947,500	Total liabilities and equity	$ 947,500

BARRY COMPUTER COMPANY: INCOME STATEMENT FOR YEAR ENDED DECEMBER 31, 1995 (IN THOUSANDS)

Sales		$1,607,500
Cost of goods sold		
Materials	$717,000	
Labor	453,000	
Heat, light, and power	68,000	
Indirect labor	113,000	
Depreciation	41,500	1,392,500
Gross profit		$ 215,000
Selling expenses		115,000
General and administrative expenses		30,000
Earnings before interest and taxes (EBIT)		$ 70,000
Interest expense		24,500
Earnings before taxes (EBT)		$ 45,500
Federal and state income taxes (40%)		18,200
Net income		$ 27,300

RATIO	BARRY	INDUSTRY AVERAGE
Current assets/current liabilities	_____	2.0×
Days sales outstanding	_____	35 days
Sales/inventories	_____	6.7×
Sales/total assets	_____	3.0×
Net income/sales	_____	1.2%
Net income/total assets	_____	3.6%
Net income/common equity	_____	9.0%
Total debt/total assets	_____	60.0%

3-2 Balance sheet analysis Complete the balance sheet and sales information in the table that follows for Hoffmeister Industries using the following financial data:

Debt ratio: 50%
Quick ratio: 0.80×
Total assets turnover: 1.5×
Days sales outstanding: 36 days
Gross profit margin on sales: (Sales − Cost of goods sold)/Sales = 25%
Inventory turnover ratio: 5×

BALANCE SHEET

Cash	_____	Accounts payable	_____
Accounts receivable	_____	Long-term debt	60,000
Inventories	_____	Common stock	_____
Fixed assets	_____	Retained earnings	97,500
Total assets	$300,000	Total liabilities and equity	_____
Sales	_____	Cost of goods sold	_____

3-3 Du Pont analysis The Ferri Furniture Company, a manufacturer and wholesaler of high-quality home furnishings, has been experiencing low profitability in recent years. As a result, the board of directors has replaced the president of the firm with a new president, Helen Adams, who has asked you to make an analysis of the firm's financial position using the Du Pont chart. The most recent industry average ratios, and Ferri's financial statements, are as follows:

INDUSTRY AVERAGE RATIOS

Current ratio	2×	Sales/fixed assets	6×
Debt/total assets	30%	Sales/total assets	3×
Times-interest-earned	7×	Profit margin on sales	3%
Sales/inventory	10×	Return on total assets	9%
Days sales outstanding	24 days	Return on common equity	12.9%

FERRI FURNITURE COMPANY: BALANCE SHEET AS OF DECEMBER 31, 1995 (MILLIONS OF DOLLARS)

Cash	$ 45	Accounts payable	$ 45
Marketable securities	33	Notes payable	45
Net receivables	66	Other current liabilities	21
Inventories	159	Total current liabilities	$111
Total current assets	$303	Long-term debt	24
		Total liabilities	$135
Gross fixed assets	225		
Less depreciation	78	Common stock	114
Net fixed assets	$147	Retained earnings	201
		Total stockholders' equity	$315
Total assets	$450	Total liabilities and equity	$450

FERRI FURNITURE COMPANY: INCOME STATEMENT FOR YEAR ENDED DECEMBER 31, 1995 (MILLIONS OF DOLLARS)

Net sales	$795.0
Cost of goods sold	660.0
Gross profit	$135.0
Selling expenses	73.5
Depreciation expense	12.0
Earnings before interest and taxes	$ 49.5
Interest expense	4.5
Earnings before taxes (EBT)	45.0
Taxes (40%)	18.0
Net income	$ 27.0

Primary Markets
Markets in which corporations raise capital by issuing new securities.

Secondary Markets
Markets in which securities and other financial assets are traded among investors after they have been issued by corporations.

5. *World, national, regional,* and *local markets* also exist. Thus, depending on an organization's size and scope of operations, it may be able to borrow all around the world, or it may be confined to a strictly local, even neighborhood, market.

6. **Primary markets** are the markets in which corporations raise new capital. If J.C. Penney were to sell a new issue of common stock to raise capital, this would be a primary market transaction. The corporation selling the newly created stock receives the proceeds from the sale in a primary market transaction. **Secondary markets** are markets in which existing, already outstanding, securities are traded among investors. Thus, if Edgar Rice decided to buy 1,000 shares of AT&T stock, the purchase would occur in the secondary market. The New York Stock Exchange is a secondary market, since it deals in outstanding, as opposed to newly issued, stocks and bonds. Secondary markets also exist for mortgages, various other types of loans, and other financial assets. The corporation whose securities are being traded is not involved in a secondary market transaction and, thus, does not receive any funds from such a sale.

Other classifications could be made, but this breakdown is sufficient to show that there are many types of financial markets. Also, note that the distinctions among markets are often blurred and unimportant, except as a general point of reference. For example, it makes little difference if a firm borrows for 11, 12, or 13 months, hence, whether we have a "money" or "capital" market transaction. You should recognize the big differences among types of markets but not get hung up trying to distinguish them at the boundaries.

A healthy economy is dependent on efficient transfers of funds from people who are net savers to firms and individuals who need capital. Without efficient transfers, the economy simply could not function: Carolina Power & Light could not raise capital, so Raleigh's citizens would have no electricity; the Johnson family would not have adequate housing; Carol Hawk would have no place to invest her savings; and so on. Obviously, the level of employment and productivity, hence our standard of living, would be much lower. Therefore, it is absolutely essential that our financial markets function efficiently — not only quickly, but also at a low cost.[1]

Table 4-1 on page 98 gives a listing of the most important instruments traded in the various financial markets. The instruments are arranged from top to bottom in ascending order of typical length of maturity. As we go through the book, we will look in much more detail at many of these instruments. For example, we will see that there are many varieties of corporate bonds, ranging from "plain vanilla" bonds to bonds that are convertible into common stocks and to bonds whose interest payments vary depending on the rate of inflation. Still, the table gives an idea of the characteristics and costs of the instruments traded in the major financial markets.

RECENT TRENDS AND INNOVATIONS[2]

OVERVIEW OF RECENT TRENDS.   The financial services industry between 1980 and 2000 will witness three different time periods. The decade of the 1980s was marked by

---

[1]As the countries of the former Soviet Union and other Eastern European nations move toward capitalism, just as much attention must be paid to the establishment of cost-efficient financial markets as to electrical power, transportation, communications, and other infrastructure systems. Economic efficiency is simply impossible without a good system for allocating capital within the economy.

[2]Parts of this discussion are taken from " '90s Shape Up as Era of Global Opportunity," *The American Banker,* June 22, 1992, 4–5; "Wall Street Moves in on Futures Products," *The Wall Street Journal,* February 4, 1992, C1; and "Greenspan Says New Ways to Limit Risk from Financial Markets Are Needed," *The Wall Street Journal,* August 23, 1993, A2, A4.

growth, innovation, and speculative excess. It witnessed a stock market boom, the megamerger and leveraged buyout wave, the development of the junk bond market, and a sharp increase in corporate leverage. Growth in financial services was high, and innovation flourished, but speculative excesses led to an unsustainable situation.

From 1987 to 1994, we witnessed a period of adjustment. Because of losses and market retrenchments which resulted from the excesses of the 1980s, banks and other financial firms scaled back their capital market activities. During this period, the banking industry's focus turned toward consumer financial services rather than corporate services because consumer services seemed to offer greater stability.

The years from 1995 to 2000 are shaping up to be a time of resurgence. Capital market activities, corporate lending, and investing are rebounding. However, domestic growth will be moderate — the real growth opportunities in the latter half of the 1990s will probably be in international markets.

Technology, globalization, competition, and deregulation all have combined to revolutionize worldwide financial markets, and the result is an efficient, internationally linked market. But these developments have created potential problems. At a recent conference, Federal Reserve Board Chairman Alan Greenspan stated that modern financial markets "expose national economies to shocks from new and unexpected sources, and with little if any lag." He went on to say that central banks must develop new ways to evaluate and limit risks to the financial system. Large volumes of capital move quickly around the world in response to changes in interest and exchange rates, and these movements can be disruptive to local institutions and economies.

With globalization has come the need for greater cooperation among regulators at the international level. Various committees are currently in place and working to improve coordination, but the task is not easy. Factors that complicate coordination include (1) the differing structures of the various nations' banking and securities industries, (2) the trend in Europe toward financial service conglomerates, and (3) a reluctance on the part of individual countries to give up complete control over their national monetary policies. Still regulators are unanimous about the need to close the gaps in the supervision of worldwide markets, and many believe that these committees can help accomplish that goal.

Derivative
Any financial asset whose value is derived from the value of some other "underlying" asset.

RECENT TRENDS. Securities firms have been busy developing fancy new financial products called **derivatives.** A derivative is any security whose value is *derived* from the price of some other "underlying" asset. An option to buy IBM stock is a derivative, as is a contract to buy Japanese yen six months from now. The value of the IBM option will depend on the price performance of IBM's stock, and the value of the Japanese yen "future" will depend on the exchange rate between yen and dollars. The market for derivatives has grown faster than any other market in recent years, providing corporations with additional opportunities but also exposing them to additional risks.

Derivatives can be used either to reduce risks or as speculative investments, which increase risk. As an example of a risk-reducing usage, suppose a company's net income tends to fall whenever the dollar falls relative to the yen. That company could reduce its risk by purchasing derivatives which increase in value whenever the dollar declines. This would be called a "hedging operation," and its purpose is to reduce risk exposure. Speculation, on the other hand, is done in the hope of high returns, but it does raise risk exposure. For example, Procter & Gamble recently disclosed that it lost $150 million on derivative investments, and Orange County (California) went bankrupt as a result of derivatives speculation.

| **TABLE 4-1** | | **SUMMARY OF MAJOR MARKET INSTRUMENTS, MARKET PARTICIPANTS, AND SECURITY CHARACTERISTICS** | | | |

| | | | SECURITY CHARACTERISTICS | | |
INSTRUMENT (1)	MARKET (2)	MAJOR PARTICIPANTS (3)	RISKINESS (4)	MATURITY (5)	INTEREST RATE ON 12/19/94[a] (6)
U.S. Treasury bills	Money	Sold by U.S. Treasury to finance federal expenditures	Default-free	91 days to 1 year	7.1%
Banker's acceptances	Money	Firm's promise to pay, guaranteed by a bank	Low degree of risk if guaranteed by a strong bank	Up to 180 days	6.6
Commercial paper	Money	Issued by financially secure firms to large investors	Low default risk	Up to 270 days	6.3
Negotiable certificates of deposit (CDs)	Money	Issued by major money-center commercial banks to large investors	Default risk depends on the strength of the issuing bank	Up to 1 year	6.6
Money market mutual funds	Money	Invest in Treasury bills, CDs, and commercial paper; held by individuals and businesses	Low degree of risk	No specific maturity (instant liquidity)	5.1
Eurodollar market time deposits	Money	Issued by banks outside U.S.	Default risk depends on the strength of the issuing bank	Up to 1 year	6.8
Consumer credit loans	Money	Issued by banks/credit unions/finance companies to individuals	Risk is variable	Variable	Variable
U.S. Treasury notes and bonds	Capital	Issued by U.S. government	No default risk, but price will decline if interest rates rise	2 to 30 years	7.8

[a]Interest rates are for longest maturity securities of the type and for the strongest securities of a given type. Thus, the 8.6% interest rate shown for corporate bonds reflects the rate on 30-year, Aaa bonds. Lower-rated bonds had higher interest rates.

How does the introduction of these new derivative products influence the financial markets? The size and complexity of derivatives transactions have concerned regulators, academics, and members of Congress. Fed Chairman Greenspan noted that, in theory, derivatives should allow banks to manage risk better, but he stated that it is not clear whether these recent innovations have "increased or decreased the inherent stability of the financial system."

 SELF-TEST QUESTIONS

Distinguish between physical asset markets and financial asset markets.

What is the difference between spot and futures markets?

Distinguish between money and capital markets.

			SECURITY CHARACTERISTICS		
INSTRUMENT (1)	MARKET (2)	MAJOR PARTICIPANTS (3)	RISKINESS (4)	MATURITY (5)	INTEREST RATE ON 12/19/94[a] (6)
Mortgages	Capital	Borrowings from commercial banks and S&Ls by individuals and businesses	Risk is variable	Up to 30 years	9.5
State and local government bonds	Capital	Issued by state and local governments to individuals and institutional investors	Riskier than U.S. government securities, but exempt from most taxes	Up to 30 years	6.4
Corporate bonds	Capital	Issued by corporations to individuals and institutional investors	Riskier than U.S. government securities, but less risky than preferred and common stocks; varying degree of risk within bonds depending on strength of issuer	Up to 40 years[b]	8.6
Leases	Capital	Similar to debt in that firms can lease assets rather than borrow and then buy the assets	Risk similar to corporate bonds	Generally 3 to 20 years	Similar to bond yields
Preferred stocks	Capital	Issued by corporations to individuals and institutional investors	Riskier than corporate bonds, but less risky than common stock	Unlimited	6 to 8%
Common stocks[c]	Capital	Issued by corporations to individuals and institutional investors	Risky	Unlimited	10 to 15%

[b]Just recently (1993), a few corporations have issued 100-year bonds; however, the majority have issued bonds with maturities of up to 40 years.
[c]Common stocks are expected to provide a "return" in the form of dividends and capital gains rather than interest. Of course, if you buy a stock, while you may *expect* to earn 10 percent on your money, the stock's price may decline and cause you to experience a 100 percent loss.

What is the difference between primary and secondary markets?

Why are financial markets essential for a healthy economy?

What are derivatives, and how is their value determined?

FINANCIAL INSTITUTIONS

Transfers of capital between savers and those who need capital take place in the three different ways diagrammed in Figure 4-1:

1. *Direct transfers* of money and securities, as shown in the top section, occur when a business sells its stocks or bonds directly to savers, without going

ORANGE COUNTY BLUES

It was too good true to be true. For more than 20 years, the investment fund managed by California's Orange County produced impressive returns. However, this all came to an end in December 1994, when the county announced that the fund had generated more than $2 billion in losses. The county's treasurer, Robert Citron, was forced to resign, and both the county and its fund were declared bankrupt.

What happened? During the 1980s, fund manager Citron had followed a strategy of investing in long-term securities. The trend in interest rates was downward; when rates decline, long-term bond prices rise, so Citron's fund had earned both interest and capital gains. Furthermore, Citron started borrowing at low short-term rates and investing in higher-yielding long-term bonds, which further increased the fund's net interest income and capital gains.

Such a strategy works wonderfully during a period of declining rates: The fund's record was outstanding, and Citron was a hero in Orange County. However, Citron's confidence in his ability to beat the market turned to overconfidence, and he failed to display a reasonable degree of prudence. In November 1993, he became convinced that interest rates were poised for another dramatic decline, so he began borrowing heavily and using the money to purchase "high octane" — exceptionally risky — derivative products whose values were extremely sensitive to changes in interest rates. One of Citron's favorites was a derivative called an "inverse floater," whose interest payments rise when interest rates fall, and vice versa. Another favorite was a complicated derivative product that was designed to go up in value if the yield curve steepened, that is, if long-term rates increased relative to short-term rates.

Citron was betting (1) that interest rates in general were going to decline and (2) that short-term rates were going to decline more than long-term rates. However, his predictions were completely wrong. The economy strengthened in 1994, causing the Fed to raise interest rates on six separate occasions. Further, short-term rates went up almost 4 percentage points versus less than 2 percentage points for long-term rates, so the yield curve flattened instead of growing steeper.

These changes reduced the value of inverse floaters and yield curve derivatives, and the general increase in rates also reduced the value of the "plain vanilla" securities the fund held. Further, the problem was exacerbated because the fund had borrowed on a short-term basis to finance its investments, and its own interest expenses rose steadily as interest rates increased.

The fund used its investments as collateral for its loans. It took in some $7.5 billion in tax receipts, fees, and the like from school districts, cities in the county such as Anaheim (home of Disneyland), and water districts. This money was "invested" in derivatives and other securities until such time as it was needed for payrolls and the like, and its "investments" were then used as collateral for loans to buy still more derivatives.

Interestingly, most of the securities in which Orange County invested were issued by or backed by the federal government, but they declined in value even though there will be no default on their promised cash payments. Of

through any type of financial institution. The business delivers its securities to savers, who in turn give the firm the money it needs.

2. As shown in the middle section, transfers may also go through an *investment banking house* such as Merrill Lynch, which serves as a middleman and facilitates the issuance of securities. The company sells its stocks or bonds to the investment bank, which in turn sells these same securities to savers. The businesses' securities and the savers' money merely "pass through" the investment banking house. However, the investment bank does buy and hold the securities for a period of time, so it is taking a risk — it may not be able to resell them to savers for as much as it paid. Because new securities are involved, hence the corporation receives the proceeds of the sale, this is a primary market transaction.

3. Transfers can also be made through a *financial intermediary* such as a bank or mutual fund. Here the intermediary obtains funds from savers in exchange for its own securities, and it then uses this money to purchase and then hold a business's securities. For example, a saver might give dollars to a bank, re-

course, if the amount of cash received declines, as it would on an inverse floater if interest rates rise, the value of the security will decline, and such a security is certainly not riskless.

Orange County is the fifth largest county in the country — and one of the wealthiest — and it will undoubtedly recover from Mr. Citron's folly. But recovery will be painful. The county's debt has been downgraded from AA to junk, causing its interest costs to soar. Highway and other projects have been canceled, and school teachers and other employees have been laid off. Moreover, companies that had planned to move into or expand in Orange County are holding off, exacerbating an already serious unemployment problem. To illustrate, Disney had been planning to expand its Disneyland park, but that project has been put on hold.

In the aftermath of the Orange County fiasco, *The Wall Street Journal* published several fascinating articles on derivatives. In one, it described a $500 million bond issue that Merrill Lynch underwrote for Orange County during the summer of 1994. Mr. Citron borrowed the $500 million to get money to buy more derivatives for use as collateral for past loans. That was a questionable operation, but what really raised

eyebrows — and may be the basis of lawsuits against Merrill Lynch — is that neither Orange County's financial condition nor the fact that the $500 million was to be used to buy derivatives which would be turned over to creditors was revealed to the buyers of the new bonds. When Orange County declared bankruptcy a few months later and defaulted on the bonds, their value was cut in half, and their holders raised the question of whether the county, Merrill Lynch, and others associated with the issue had complied with the securities laws, which require full disclosure of all material facts when bonds are issued. Lawsuits may well arise from this situation.

A second story described the way major Wall Street investment banks market their structured notes. Wall Street firms create different types of notes, all backed by federally guaranteed mortgages. They then sell the relatively safe notes to large, sophisticated investors, but dispose of those in which the risks have been concentrated (called "toxic waste") to "boiler shop operators" who, in turn, sell the securities to naive investors. The boiler shops are concentrated in Houston, and their salesmen use deceptive, high-pressure tactics to dispose of the risky

paper. In their sales pitches, the sales reps point out that the notes are "backed by an agency of the federal government," which is true, and then imply that the notes are, therefore, essentially riskless, which is utterly false. Some losers include the Vermilion, Ohio, school system, which saw a $200,000 investment decline to $16,000; the Shoshone Tribe of Wyoming, which lost almost $4 million; and the City Colleges of Chicago, which lost $47 million.

Based on stories like these, some authorities have suggested that financial derivatives should be banned. Others, including the authors of this book, absolutely disagree. Derivatives serve many useful purposes, and the fact that they can be abused is no reason to abolish them. However, sellers of these instruments should be required to inform buyers of what they are getting, and investors should exercise prudence when they make investment decisions. In addition, it would probably make sense for voters to impose rules which would prevent officials from doing what Orange County's Mr. Citron did. However, it would not be good policy for Congress or any other body to ban all uses of derivatives.

ceiving from it a certificate of deposit, and then the bank might lend the money to a small business in the form of a mortgage loan. Thus, intermediaries literally create new forms of capital — in this case, certificates of deposit, which are both safer and more liquid than mortgages and thus are better securities for most savers to hold. The existence of intermediaries greatly increases the efficiency of money and capital markets.

For simplicity, we assumed that the entity needing capital is a business, and specifically a corporation, but it is easy to visualize the demander of capital as a home purchaser, a government unit, and so on.

Direct transfers of funds from savers to businesses are possible and do occur on occasion, but it is generally more efficient for a business to enlist the services of an **investment banking house.** Merrill Lynch, Salomon Brothers, Dean Witter, and Goldman Sachs are examples of financial service corporations which offer investment banking services. Such organizations (1) help corporations design securities with features that are currently attractive to investors, (2) buy these securities from the corporation, and (3) resell them to savers. Although the securities are sold twice,

Investment Banking House
An organization that underwrites and distributes new investment securities and helps businesses obtain financing.

FIGURE 4-1   DIAGRAM OF THE CAPITAL FORMATION PROCESS

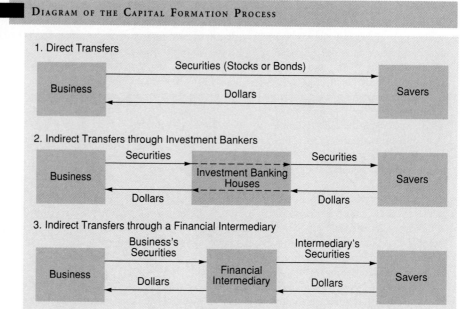

Financial Intermediaries
Specialized financial firms that facilitate the transfer of funds from savers to demanders of capital.

this process is really one primary market transaction, with the investment banker acting as a broker to help transfer capital from savers to businesses.

The **financial intermediaries** shown in the third section of Figure 4-1 do more than simply transfer money and securities between firms and savers — they literally create new financial products. Since the intermediaries are generally large, they gain economies of scale in analyzing the creditworthiness of potential borrowers, in processing and collecting loans, and in pooling risks and thus helping individual savers diversify, that is, "not put all their financial eggs in one basket." Further, a system of specialized intermediaries can enable savings to do more than just draw interest. For example, individuals can put money into banks and get both interest income and a convenient way of making payments (checking), or put money into life insurance companies and get both interest income and protection for their beneficiaries.

In the United States and other developed nations, a set of specialized, highly efficient financial intermediaries has evolved. The situation is changing rapidly, however, and different types of institutions are performing services that were formerly reserved for others, causing institutional distinctions to become blurred. Still, there is a degree of institutional identity, and here are the major classes of intermediaries:

1. *Commercial banks,* the traditional "department stores of finance," serve a wide variety of savers and borrowers. Historically, commercial banks were the major institutions which handled checking accounts and through which the Federal Reserve System expanded or contracted the money supply. Today, however, several other institutions also provide checking services and significantly influence the money supply. Conversely, commercial banks are providing an ever-widening range of services, including stock brokerage services and insurance.

Note that commercial banks are quite different from investment banks. Commercial banks lend money, whereas investment banks help companies raise capital from other parties. Prior to 1933, commercial banks offered investment banking services, but the Glass-Steagall Act, which was passed in that year, prohibited commercial banks from engaging in investment banking. Thus, the Morgan Bank was broken up into two separate organizations, one of which is now the Morgan Guaranty Trust Company, a commercial bank, while the other is Morgan Stanley, a major investment banking house. Note also that Japanese and European banks can offer both commercial and investment banking services. This hinders U.S. banks in global competition, so efforts are being made to get Glass-Steagall repealed or modified.

2. *Savings and loan associations (S&Ls),* which have traditionally served individual savers and residential and commercial mortgage borrowers, take the funds of many small savers and then lend this money to home buyers and other types of borrowers. Because the savers obtain a degree of liquidity that would be absent if they bought the mortgages or other securities directly, perhaps the most significant economic function of the S&Ls is to "create liquidity" which would otherwise be lacking. Also, the S&Ls have more expertise in analyzing credit, setting up loans, and making collections than individual savers, so they reduce the cost and increase the availability of real estate loans. Finally, the S&Ls hold large, diversified portfolios of loans and other assets and thus spread risks in a manner that would be impossible if small savers were making mortgage loans directly. Because of these factors, savers benefit by being able to invest in more liquid, better managed, and less risky accounts, whereas borrowers benefit by being able to obtain more capital, and at lower costs, than would otherwise be possible.

In the 1980s, the S&L industry experienced severe problems when (1) short-term interest rates paid on savings accounts rose well above the returns being earned on the existing mortgages held by S&Ls and (2) commercial real estate suffered a severe slump, resulting in high mortgage default rates. Together, these events forced many S&Ls to either merge with stronger institutions or close their doors. Today, the S&L industry is smaller and more focused, with companies either playing the traditional S&L role discussed above or acting as mortgage originators and collection agents, wherein the mortgages originated are immediately sold to a governmental agency such as the Government National Mortgage Association (GNMA). GNMA uses the mortgages it buys as collateral for bonds, which it then sells to the public to raise money to buy still more mortgages. This process helps increase the availability of funds, and lowers their cost, to home buyers.

3. *Mutual savings banks,* which are similar to S&Ls, operate primarily in the northeastern states, accept savings primarily from individuals, and lend mainly on a long-term basis to home buyers and consumers.

4. *Credit unions* are cooperative associations whose members have a common bond, such as being employees of the same firm. Members' savings are loaned only to other members, generally for auto purchases, home improvement loans, and even home mortgages. Credit unions often are the cheapest source of funds available to individual borrowers.

5. *Pension funds* are retirement plans funded by corporations or government agencies for their workers and administered primarily by the trust depart-

ments of commercial banks or by life insurance companies. Pension funds invest primarily in bonds, stocks, mortgages, and real estate.

6. *Life insurance companies* take savings in the form of annual premiums; invest these funds in stocks, bonds, real estate, and mortgages; and finally make payments to the beneficiaries of the insured parties. In recent years, life insurance companies have also offered a variety of tax-deferred savings plans designed to provide benefits to the participants when they retire.

7. *Mutual funds* are corporations which accept money from savers and then use these funds to buy stocks, long-term bonds, or short-term debt instruments issued by businesses or government units. These organizations pool funds and thus reduce risks by diversification. They also achieve economies of scale, which lower the costs of analyzing securities, managing portfolios, and buying and selling securities. Different funds are designed to meet the objectives of different types of savers. Hence, there are bond funds for those who desire safety, stock funds for savers who are willing to accept significant risks in the hope of higher returns, and still other funds that are used as interest-bearing checking accounts (the **money market funds**). There are literally thousands of different mutual funds with dozens of different goals and purposes.

Money Market Fund
A mutual fund that invests in short-term, low-risk securities and allows investors to write checks against their accounts.

Mutual funds have grown more rapidly than any other institution in recent years, in large part because of a change in the way corporations provide for employees' retirement. Before the 1980s, most corporations said, in effect, "Come work for us, and when you retire, we will give you a retirement income based on the salary you were earning during the last five years before you retired." The company was then responsible for setting aside funds each year to make sure that it had the money available to pay the agreed-upon retirement benefits. That situation is rapidly changing. Today, new employees are likely to be told, "Come work for us, and we will give you some money each payday which you can invest for your future retirement. You can't get the money until you retire (without paying a huge tax penalty), but if you invest wisely, you can retire in comfort." Most employees know they don't know how to invest wisely, so they turn their retirement funds over to a mutual fund. Hence, mutual funds are growing rapidly. Excellent information on the objectives and results of the various funds are provided in publications such as *Value Line Investment Survey* and *Morningstar Mutual Funds*, and are available in most libraries.

Financial institutions have historically been heavily regulated, with the primary purpose of this regulation being to ensure the safety of the institutions and thus to protect investors. However, these regulations — which have taken the form of prohibitions on nationwide branch banking, restrictions on the types of assets the institutions can buy, ceilings on the interest rates they can pay, and limitations on the types of services they can provide — have tended to impede the free flow of capital and thus have hurt the efficiency of our capital markets. Recognizing this fact, Congress has authorized some major changes, and more will be forthcoming.

Financial Service Corporation
A firm which offers a wide range of financial services, including investment banking, brokerage operations, insurance, and commercial banking.

The result of the ongoing regulatory changes has been a blurring of the distinctions between the different types of institutions. Indeed, the trend in the United States today is toward huge **financial service corporations,** which own banks, S&Ls, investment banking houses, insurance companies, pension plan operations, and mutual funds, and which have branches across the country and even around the world. Examples of financial service corporations, most of which started in one area and have now diversified to cover most of the financial spectrum, include Transamerica, Merrill Lynch, American Express, Citicorp, Fidelity, and Prudential.

 ## SELF-TEST QUESTIONS

Identify three different ways capital is transferred between savers and borrowers.

What is the difference between a commercial bank and an investment bank?

Distinguish between investment banking houses and financial intermediaries.

List the major types of intermediaries and briefly describe each one's function.

THE STOCK MARKET

As noted earlier, secondary markets are those in which outstanding, previously issued securities are traded. By far the most active secondary market, and the most important one to financial managers, is the *stock market*. Here the prices of firms' stocks are established, and, since the primary goal of financial management is to maximize the firm's stock price, a knowledge of this market is important to anyone involved in managing a business.

THE STOCK EXCHANGES

There are two basic types of stock markets: (1) *organized exchanges,* which include the New York Stock Exchange (NYSE), the American Stock Exchange (AMEX), and several regional exchanges and (2) the less formal *over-the-counter market.* Since the organized exchanges have actual physical market locations and are easier to describe and understand, we shall consider them first.

Organized Security Exchanges
Formal organizations having tangible physical locations that conduct auction markets in designated ("listed") securities. The two major U.S. stock exchanges are the New York Stock Exchange (NYSE) and the American Stock Exchange (AMEX).

The **organized security exchanges** are tangible physical entities. Each of the larger ones occupies its own building, has a limited number of members, and has an elected governing body — its board of governors. Members are said to have "seats" on the exchange, although everybody stands up. These seats, which are bought and sold, give the holder the right to trade on the exchange. There are more then 1,300 seats on the New York Stock Exchange, and recently NYSE seats were selling for about $900,000.

Most of the larger investment banking houses operate *brokerage departments,* which own seats on the exchanges and designate one or more of their officers as members. The exchanges are open on all normal working days, with the members meeting in a large room equipped with telephones and other electronic equipment that enable each member to communicate with his or her firm's offices throughout the country.

Like other markets, security exchanges facilitate communication between buyers and sellers. For example, Merrill Lynch (the largest brokerage firm) might receive an order in its Atlanta office from a customer who wants to buy 100 shares of AT&T stock. Simultaneously, Dean Witter's Denver office might receive an order from a customer wishing to sell 100 shares of AT&T. Each broker communicates by wire with the firm's representative on the NYSE. Other brokers throughout the country are also communicating with their own exchange members. The exchange members with *sell orders* offer the shares for sale, and they are bid for by the members with *buy orders*. Thus, the exchanges operate as *auction markets*.[3]

THE OVER-THE-COUNTER MARKET

Over-the-Counter Market
A large collection of brokers and dealers, connected electronically by telephones and computers, that provides for trading in unlisted securities.

In contrast to the organized security exchanges, the **over-the-counter market** is a nebulous, intangible organization. An explanation of the term "over-the-counter" will help clarify exactly what this market is. The exchanges operate as auction markets — buy and sell orders come in more or less simultaneously, and exchange members match these orders. If a stock is traded less frequently, perhaps because it is the stock of a new or a small firm, few buy and sell orders come in, and matching them within a reasonable length of time would be difficult. To avoid this problem, some brokerage firms maintain an inventory of such stocks — they buy when individual investors want to sell and sell when investors want to buy. At one time, the inventory of securities was kept in a safe, and the stocks, when bought and sold, were literally passed over the counter.

Today, the over-the-counter market is defined to include all facilities that are needed to conduct security transactions not conducted on the organized exchanges. These facilities consist of (1) the relatively few *dealers* who hold inventories of over-the-counter securities and who are said to "make a market" in these securities; (2) the thousands of brokers who act as *agents* in bringing the dealers together with investors; and (3) the computers, terminals, and electronic networks that provide a communications link between dealers and brokers. The dealers who make a market in a particular stock continuously quote a price at which they are willing to buy the stock (the *bid price*) and a price at which they will sell shares (the *asked price*). Each dealer's prices, which are adjusted as supply and demand conditions change, can be read off computer screens all across the country. The spread between bid and asked prices represents the dealer's markup, or profit.

Brokers and dealers who make up the over-the-counter market are members of a self-regulating body known as the *National Association of Securities Dealers (NASD),* which licenses brokers and oversees trading practices. The computerized trading network used by NASD is known as the NASD Automated Quotation System (NASDAQ), and *The Wall Street Journal* and other newspapers provide information on NASDAQ transactions.

---

[3]The NYSE is actually a modified auction market, wherein people (through their brokers) bid for stocks. Originally — about 200 years ago — brokers would literally shout, "I have 100 shares of Erie for sale; how much am I offered?" and then sell to the highest bidder. If a broker had a buy order, he or she would shout, "I want to buy 100 shares of Erie; who'll sell at the best price?" The same general situation still exists, although the exchanges now have members known as *specialists* who facilitate the trading process by keeping an inventory of shares of the stocks in which they specialize. If a buy order comes in at a time when no sell order arrives, the specialist will sell off some inventory. Similarly, if a sell order comes in, the specialist will buy and add to inventory. The specialist sets a *bid price* (the price the specialist will pay for the stock) and an *asked price* (the price at which shares will be sold out of inventory). The bid and asked prices are set at levels designed to keep the inventory in balance. If many buy orders start coming in because of favorable developments or sell orders come in because of unfavorable events, the specialist will raise or lower prices to keep supply and demand in balance. Bid prices are somewhat lower than asked prices, with the difference, or *spread,* representing the specialist's profit margin.

Special facilities are available to help institutional investors such as mutual funds or pension funds sell large blocks of stock without depressing their prices. In essence, brokerage houses which cater to institutional clients will purchase blocks (defined as 10,000 or more shares) and then resell the stock to other institutions or individuals. Also, when a firm has a major announcement which is likely to cause its stock price to change sharply, it will ask the exchanges to halt trading in its stock until the announcement has been made and digested by investors. Thus, when Texaco announced that it planned to acquire Getty Oil, trading was halted for one day in both Texaco and Getty stocks.

In terms of numbers of issues, the majority of stocks are traded over the counter. However, because the stocks of most large companies are listed on the exchanges, about two-thirds of the dollar volume of stock trading takes place on the exchanges. In recent years, many large companies — including Microsoft, Intel, MCI, and Apple — have elected to remain NASDAQ stocks, so the over-the-counter market is growing faster than the exchanges.

SOME TRENDS IN SECURITY TRADING PROCEDURES

From the NYSE's inception in 1792 until the 1970s, the majority of all stock trading occurred on the Exchange and was conducted by member firms. The NYSE established a set of minimum brokerage commission rates, and no member firm could charge a commission lower than the set rate. This was a monopoly, pure and simple. However, on May 1, 1975, the Securities and Exchange Commission (SEC), with strong prodding from the Antitrust Division of the Justice Department, forced the NYSE to abandon its fixed commissions. Commission rates declined dramatically, falling in some cases as much as 90 percent from former levels.

These changes were a boon to the investing public, but not to the brokerage industry. A number of "full-service" brokerage houses went bankrupt, and others were forced to merge with stronger firms. The number of brokerage houses has declined from literally thousands in the 1960s to a much smaller number of large, strong, nationwide companies, many of which are units of diversified financial service corporations. Deregulation has also spawned a number of "discount brokers," some of which are affiliated with commercial banks or mutual fund investment companies.[4]

There has also been a rise in "third market" activities, where large financial institutions trade both listed and unlisted stocks among themselves on a 24-hour basis. Buyers and sellers in this market are located all around the globe — New York, San Francisco, Tokyo, Singapore, Zurich, and London — and this makes the 24-hour trading day a necessity. The exchanges have resisted going to longer days because it inconveniences members, but competition is too strong for them to resist. Right now, institutional investors, and even some individuals, can turn on their computers any time, day or night, and execute trades. That situation will be easy and universal in a very few years.

SELF-TEST QUESTIONS

What are the two basic types of stock markets, and how do they differ?

How has deregulation changed security trading procedures?

THE COST OF MONEY

Capital in a free economy is allocated through the price system. *The interest rate is the price paid to borrow debt capital, whereas in the case of equity capital, investors*

---

[4]Full-service brokers give investors information on different stocks and make recommendations as to which stocks to buy. Discount brokers do not give advice — they merely execute orders. Some brokerage houses (institutional houses) cater primarily to institutional investors such as pension funds and insurance companies, while others cater to individual investors and are called "retail houses." Large firms such as Merrill Lynch generally have both retail and institutional brokerage operations.

| FIGURE 4-4 | RELATIONSHIP BETWEEN ANNUAL INFLATION RATES AND LONG-TERM INTEREST RATES, 1955–1994 |

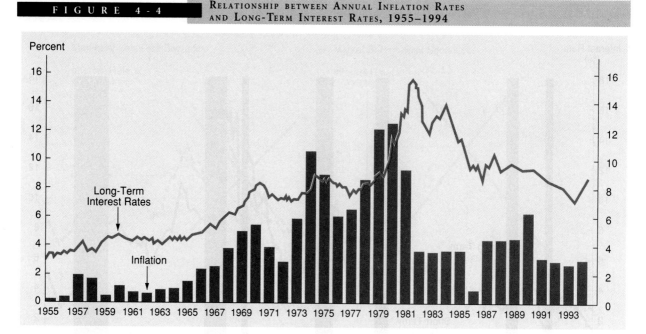

Notes:

a. Interest rates are those on AAA long-term corporate bonds.

b. Inflation is measured as the annual rate of change in the Consumer Price Index (CPI).

SOURCE: *Federal Reserve Bulletin.*

Gradually, though, people began to realize that the Federal Reserve was serious about keeping inflation down, that global competition was keeping U.S. auto producers and other corporations from raising prices as they had in the past, and that constraints on corporate prices were diminishing labor unions' ability to push through cost-increasing wage hikes. As these realizations set in, interest rates declined, and the "current real rate of interest," which is the difference between the current interest rate and the current inflation rate, declined as shown in Figure 4-4.

In recent years, inflation has been running at about 3 percent a year. However, in early 1995 the economy strengthened, unemployment declined, and capacity utilization rose to high levels. As a result, investors began to fear a resurgence of inflation, which caused long-term interest rates to rise. At present (January 1995), the cost of long-term debt to strong corporations is about 8.6 percent. In the years ahead, the level of interest rates will move up or down depending primarily on what happens to the rate of inflation.

 SELF-TEST QUESTIONS

How are interest rates used to allocate capital among firms?

What happens to market-clearing, or equilibrium, interest rates in a capital market when the demand for funds declines? What happens when inflation increases or decreases?

Why does the price of capital change during booms and recessions?

How does risk affect interest rates?

THE DETERMINANTS OF MARKET INTEREST RATES

In general, the quoted (or nominal) interest rate on a debt security, k, is composed of a real risk-free rate of interest, k*, plus several premiums that reflect inflation, the riskiness of the security, and the security's marketability (or liquidity). This relationship can be expressed as follows:

$$\text{Quoted interest rate} = k = k^* + IP + DRP + LP + MRP. \tag{4-1}$$

Here

k = the quoted, or nominal, rate of interest on a given security.[8] There are many different securities, hence many different quoted interest rates.

k^* = the real risk-free rate of interest. k^* is pronounced "k-star," and it is the rate that would exist on a riskless security if zero inflation were expected.

k_{RF} = the quoted risk-free rate of interest. This is the quoted interest rate on a security such as a U.S. Treasury bill which is very liquid and also free of most risks. Note that k_{RF} includes a premium for expected inflation because $k_{RF} = k^* + IP$.

IP = inflation premium. IP is equal to the average expected inflation rate over the life of the security. The expected future rate of inflation is not necessarily equal to the current rate of inflation, so IP is not necessarily equal to current inflation as reported in Figure 4-4.

DRP = default risk premium. This premium reflects the possibility that the issuer will not pay interest or principal at the stated time and in the stated amount. DRP is zero for U.S. Treasury securities, but it rises as the riskiness of issuers increases.

LP = liquidity, or marketability, premium. This is a premium charged by lenders to reflect the fact that some securities cannot be converted to cash on short notice at a "reasonable" price. LP is very low for Treasury securities, but it is relatively high on securities issued by very small firms.

MRP = maturity risk premium. As we will explain later, longer-term bonds are exposed to a significant risk of price declines, and a maturity risk premium is charged by lenders to reflect this risk.

Since $k_{RF} = k^* + IP$, we can rewrite Equation 4-1 as follows:

$$k = k_{RF} + DRP + LP + MRP. \tag{4-2}$$

We discuss the components whose sum makes up the quoted, or nominal, rate on a given security in the following sections.

---

[8]The term *nominal* as it is used here means the *stated* rate as opposed to the *real* rate, which is adjusted to remove the effects of inflation. If you bought a 10-year Treasury bond in April 1995, the quoted, or nominal, rate would be about 7.2 percent, but if inflation averages 4 percent over the next 10 years, the real rate would be about 7.2% − 4% = 3.2%. In Chapter 6, the term *nominal* is used in yet another way: to distinguish between quoted rates and equivalent annual rates when compounding occurs more frequently than once a year.

THE REAL RISK-FREE RATE OF INTEREST, k*

Real Risk-Free Rate of Interest, k*
The rate of interest that would exist on default-free U.S. Treasury securities if no inflation were expected.

The **real risk-free rate of interest, k*,** is defined as the interest rate that would exist on a riskless security if no inflation were expected, and it may be thought of as the rate of interest on short-term U.S. Treasury securities in an inflation-free world. The real risk-free rate is not static — it changes over time depending on economic conditions, especially (1) on the rate of return corporations and other borrowers expect to earn on productive assets and (2) on people's time preferences for current versus future consumption. Borrowers' expected returns on real asset investments set an upper limit on how much they can afford to pay for borrowed funds, while savers' time preferences for consumption establish how much consumption they are willing to defer, hence the amount of funds they will lend at different rates of interest. It is difficult to measure the real risk-free rate precisely, but most experts think that in the United States k* has fluctuated in the range of 1 to 4 percent in recent years.[9]

THE NOMINAL, OR QUOTED, RISK-FREE RATE OF INTEREST, k_{RF}

Nominal (Quoted) Risk-Free Rate, k_{RF}
The rate of interest on a security that is free of all risk; k_{RF} is proxied by the T-bill rate or the T-bond rate. k_{RF} includes an inflation premium.

The **nominal,** or **quoted, risk-free rate, k_{RF},** is the real risk-free rate plus a premium for expected inflation: $k_{RF} = k* + IP$. To be strictly correct, the risk-free rate should mean the interest rate on a totally risk-free security — one that has no risk of default, no maturity risk, no liquidity risk, and no risk of loss if inflation increases. There is no such security, hence there is no observable truly risk-free rate. However, there is one security that is free of most risks — a U.S. Treasury bill (T-bill), which is a short-term security issued by the U.S. government. Treasury bonds (T-bonds), which are longer-term government securities, are free of default and liquidity risks, but T-bonds are exposed to some risk due to changes in the general level of interest rates.

If the term "risk-free rate" is used without either the modifier "real" or the modifier "nominal," people generally mean the quoted (nominal) rate, and we will follow that convention in this book. Therefore, when we use the term risk-free rate, k_{RF}, we mean the nominal risk-free rate, which includes an inflation premium equal to the average expected inflation rate over the life of the security. In general, we use the T-bill rate to approximate the short-term risk-free rate, and the T-bond rate to approximate the long-term risk-free rate. So, whenever you see the term "risk-free rate," assume that we are referring either to the quoted U.S. T-bill rate or to the quoted T-bond rate.

INFLATION PREMIUM (IP)

Inflation has a major impact on interest rates because it erodes the purchasing power of the dollar and lowers the real rate of return on investments. To illustrate, suppose you saved $1,000 and invested it in a Treasury bill that matures in 1 year

---

[9]The real rate of interest as discussed here is different from the *current* real rate as discussed in connection with Figure 4-4. The current real rate is the current interest rate minus the current (or latest past) inflation rate, while the real rate, without the word "current," is the current interest rate minus the *expected future* inflation rate. In the press, the term "real rate" generally means the current real rate, but in economics and finance, hence in this book unless otherwise noted, the real rate means the one based on expected inflation rates.

and will pay 5 percent interest. At the end of the year, you will receive $1,050 — your original $1,000 plus $50 of interest. Now suppose the inflation rate during the year is 10 percent, and it affects all items equally. If gas had cost $1 per gallon at the beginning of the year, it would cost $1.10 at the end of the year. Therefore, your $1,000 would have bought $1,000/$1 = 1,000 gallons at the beginning of the year, but only $1,050/$1.10 = 955 gallons at the end. In *real terms*, you would be worse off — you would receive $50 of interest, but it would not be sufficient to offset inflation. You would thus be better off buying 1,000 gallons of gas (or some other storable asset such as land, timber, apartment buildings, wheat, or gold) than buying the Treasury bill.

Investors are well aware of all this, so when they lend money, they build in an **inflation premium (IP)** equal to the average expected inflation rate over the life of the security. As discussed previously, for a short-term, default-free U.S. Treasury bill, the actual interest rate charged, $k_{\text{T-bill}}$, would be the real risk-free rate, k^*, plus the inflation premium (IP):

$$k_{\text{T-bill}} = k_{\text{RF}} = k^* + IP.$$

Inflation Premium (IP)

A premium for expected inflation that investors add to the real risk-free rate of return.

Therefore, if the real risk-free rate of interest were $k^* = 3\%$, and if inflation were expected to be 4 percent (and hence IP = 4%) during the next year, then the quoted rate of interest on 1-year T-bills would be 7 percent. In early January of 1995, the expected 1-year inflation rate was about 4 percent, and the yield on 1-year T-bills was about 7 percent. This implies that the real risk-free rate on short-term securities at that time was about 3 percent.

It is important to note that the rate of inflation built into interest rates is the *rate of inflation expected in the future,* not the rate experienced in the past. Thus, the latest reported figures might show an annual inflation rate of 3 percent, but that is for a past period. If people on the average expect a 6 percent inflation rate in the future, then 6 percent would be built into the current rate of interest. Note also that the inflation rate reflected in the quoted interest rate on any security is the *average rate of inflation expected over the security's life.* Thus, the inflation rate built into a 1-year bond is the expected inflation rate for the next year, but the inflation rate built into a 30-year bond is the average rate of inflation expected over the next 30 years.[10]

Expectations for future inflation are closely, but not perfectly, correlated with rates experienced in the recent past. Therefore, if the inflation rate reported for last month increased, people would tend to raise their expectations for future inflation, and this change in expectations would cause an increase in interest rates.

 Note that Germany, Japan, and Switzerland have had lower inflation rates than the United States, hence their interest rates have been relatively low. Italy and most South American countries have experienced high inflation, and that is reflected in their interest rates.

---

[10]To be theoretically precise, we should use a *geometric average.* Also, since millions of investors are active in the market, it is impossible to determine exactly the consensus expected inflation rate. Survey data are available, however, which give us a reasonably good idea of what investors expect over the next few years. For example, in 1980 the University of Michigan's Survey Research Center reported that people expected inflation during the next year to be 11.9 percent and that the average rate of inflation expected over the next five to 10 years was 10.5 percent. Those expectations led to record-high interest rates. However, the economy cooled in 1981 and 1982, and, as Figure 4-4 showed, actual inflation dropped sharply after 1980. This led to gradual reductions in the *expected future* inflation rate. In early 1995, as we write this, the expected future inflation rate is about 4 percent. As inflationary expectations dropped, so did quoted market rates of interest.

TREASURIES WITH A TWIST

Investors who purchase bonds must constantly worry about inflation. If inflation turns out to be greater than expected, bonds will provide a lower-than-expected real return. To protect themselves against rising (as opposed to expected) inflation, investors build an inflation risk premium into their required rate of return. This raises the overall interest rate and makes it more expensive for governments, households, and corporations to borrow money.

In early 1995, inflation was running at about 3 percent a year, yet long-term Treasury rates were nearly 8 percent. A considerable portion of the 8 percent rate can be attributed to the market's fear that inflation will rise in the years ahead. Therefore, long-term rates should decline if investors can be convinced that inflation is under control. Indeed, the actions taken by the Federal Reserve in 1995 were designed primarily to convince the bond market that the Fed was not going to tolerate rising inflation.

The Clinton administration, in conjunction with the Fed, is considering another way to help convince the bond market that it should not fear rising inflation — issue Treasury securities that are indexed to inflation. With indexed bonds, if inflation rises, the yield on the bonds also rises, leaving investors with a constant real return.

For example, if indexed bonds were issued with a real risk-free rate of 3 percent, the nominal rate received each year would equal 3 percent plus the level of inflation. If inflation remained at 3 percent, investors would receive an interest rate of 6 percent for the year (which is considerably lower than the current 8 percent long-term rate). If inflation rose to 6 percent the following year, these indexed bonds would yield 9 percent.

It is by no means certain that the U.S. Treasury will ever issue indexed bonds. First, it would have to iron out a number of technical issues such as

how the bonds would be taxed, what measure of inflation would be used to adjust the bonds, and how frequently the interest rate would be reset. Because of these issues, indexed bonds probably cannot be issued before 1996.

Ultimately, though, whether or not indexed bonds are issued will depend largely on whether the U.S. Treasury thinks that these bonds would have a higher or lower cost, over their life, than regular fixed-rate bonds. Since indexing would remove some risk for investors, a lower required rate of return and thus a lower average cost over the bonds' life should be reflected in these bonds. Note also that indexed bonds have been used successfully in Britain, and within the United States, many investors would jump at the chance to eliminate most, if not all, risk of inflation.

Source: "Treasuries with a Twist," *Business Week*, November 21, 1994, 116.

Default Risk Premium (DRP)

The risk that a borrower will *default* on a loan, which means not pay the interest or the principal, also affects the market interest rate on a security: the greater the default risk, the higher the interest rate lenders charge. Treasury securities have no default risk; thus, they carry the lowest interest rates on taxable securities in the United States. For corporate bonds, the higher the bond's rating, the lower its default risk, and, consequently, the lower its interest rate.[11] Here are some representative interest rates on long-term bonds during December 1994:

	Rate	DRP
U.S. Treasury	7.9%	—
AAA	8.5	0.6%
AA	8.6	0.7
A	8.7	0.8

[11]Bond ratings, and bonds' riskiness in general, will be discussed in detail in Chapter 7. For now, merely note that bonds rated AAA are judged to have less default risk than bonds rated AA, while AA bonds are less risky than A bonds, and so on. Ratings are designated AAA or Aaa, AA or Aa, and so forth, depending on the rating agency. In this book, the designations are used interchangeably.

Default Risk Premium (DRP)
The difference between the interest rate on a U.S. Treasury bond and a corporate bond of equal maturity and marketability.

The difference between the quoted interest rate on a T-bond and that on a corporate bond with similar maturity, liquidity, and other features is the **default risk premium (DRP).** Therefore, if the bonds listed above were otherwise similar, the default risk premium would be DRP = 8.5% − 7.9% = 0.6 percentage point for AAA corporate bonds, 8.6% − 7.9% = 0.7 percentage point for AA, and 8.7% − 7.9% = 0.8 percentage point for A corporate bonds. Default risk premiums vary somewhat over time, but the December 1994 figures are representative of levels in recent years.

Also, countries such as the United States, Japan, Germany, and Switzerland, which have enjoyed political and economic stability, have lower DRP's than less stable nations, and this is reflected in international capital markets.

LIQUIDITY PREMIUM (LP)

Liquidity is generally defined as the ability to convert an asset to cash quickly and at a "fair market value." Assets have varying degrees of liquidity, depending on the characteristics of the market in which they are traded. For instance, there exist very active and efficient secondary markets for financial assets such as government notes and bonds, and for the stocks and bonds of large corporations, but the markets for real estate are much more limited. Therefore, most financial assets are considered more liquid than real assets. Of course, the most liquid asset of all is cash, and the more easily an asset can be converted to cash at a "fair market value," the more liquid it is considered. Because liquidity is important, investors evaluate liquidity and include **liquidity premiums (LP)** when market rates of securities are established. Although it is very difficult to accurately measure liquidity premiums, a differential of at least two and probably four or five percentage points exists between the least liquid and the most liquid financial assets of similar default risk and maturity.

Liquidity Premium (LP)
A premium added to the equilibrium interest rate on a security if that security cannot be converted to cash on short notice and at close to the original cost.

Again, capital market liquidity varies across countries, which affects firms' ability to attract capital at reasonable rates and thus to compete in international markets. This presents a challenge to developing nations and to Russia, China, and Eastern Bloc countries as they try to convert to market economies.

MATURITY RISK PREMIUM (MRP)

Interest Rate Risk
The risk of capital losses to which investors are exposed because of changing interest rates.

U.S. Treasury securities are free of default risk in the sense that one can be virtually certain that the federal government will pay interest on its bonds and will also pay them off when they mature. Therefore, the default risk premium on Treasury securities is essentially zero. Further, active markets exist for Treasury securities, so their liquidity premiums are also close to zero. Thus, as a first approximation, the rate of interest on a Treasury bond should be the risk-free rate, k_{RF}, which is equal to the real risk-free rate, k^*, plus an inflation premium, IP. However, an adjustment is needed for long-term Treasury bonds. The prices of long-term bonds decline sharply whenever interest rates rise, and since interest rates can and do occasionally rise, all long-term bonds, even Treasury bonds, have an element of risk called **interest rate risk.** As a general rule, the bonds of any organization, from the U.S. government to Continental Airlines, have more interest rate risk the longer

Maturity Risk Premium (MRP)
A premium which reflects interest rate risk.

the maturity of the bond.[12] Therefore, a **maturity risk premium (MRP),** which is higher the longer the years to maturity, must be included in the required interest rate.

The effect of maturity risk premiums is to raise interest rates on long-term bonds relative to those on short-term bonds. This premium, like the others, is extremely difficult to measure, but (1) it seems to vary over time, rising when interest rates are more volatile and uncertain, then falling when interest rates are more stable, and (2) in recent years, the maturity risk premium on 30-year T-bonds appears to have generally been in the range of one or two percentage points.[13]

Reinvestment Rate Risk
The risk that a decline in interest rates will lead to lower income when bonds mature and funds are reinvested.

We should mention that although long-term bonds are heavily exposed to interest rate risk, short-term bills are heavily exposed to **reinvestment rate risk.** When short-term bills mature and the funds are reinvested, or "rolled over," a decline in interest rates would necessitate reinvestment at a lower rate, and hence would lead to a decline in interest income. To illustrate, suppose you had $100,000 invested in 1-year T-bills, and you lived on the income. In 1981, short-term rates were about 15 percent, so your income would have been about $15,000. However, your income would have declined to about $9,000 by 1983, and to just $3,500 by 1993. Had you invested your money in long-term T-bonds, your income (but not the value of the principal) would have been stable.[14] Thus, although "investing short" preserves one's principal, the interest income provided by short-term T-bills varies from year to year, depending on reinvestment rates.

 SELF-TEST QUESTIONS

Write out an equation for the nominal interest rate on any debt security.

Distinguish between the *real* risk-free rate of interest, k*, and the *nominal,* or *quoted,* risk-free rate of interest, k_{RF}.

How is inflation dealt with when interest rates are determined by investors in the financial markets?

Does the interest rate on a T-bond include a default risk premium? Explain.

Distinguish between liquid and illiquid assets, and identify some assets that are liquid and some that are illiquid.

Briefly explain the following statement: "Although long-term bonds are heavily exposed to interest rate risk, short-term bills are heavily exposed to reinvestment rate risk. The maturity risk premium reflects the net effects of these two opposing forces."

---

[12]For example, if someone had bought a 30-year Treasury bond for $1,000 in 1972, when the long-term interest rate was 7 percent, and held it until 1981, when long-term T-bond rates were about 14.5 percent, the value of the bond would have declined to about $514. That would represent a loss of almost half the money, and it demonstrates that long-term bonds, even U.S. Treasury bonds, are not riskless. However, had the investor purchased short-term T-bills in 1972, and subsequently reinvested the principal each time the bills matured, he or she would still have had $1,000. This point will be discussed in detail in Chapter 7.

[13]The MRP has averaged 1.4 percentage points over the last 67 years. See *Stocks, Bonds, Bills, and Inflation: 1995 Yearbook* (Chicago: Ibbotson Associates, 1995).

[14]Long-term bonds also have some reinvestment rate risk. If one is saving and investing for some future purpose, say, to buy a house or for retirement, then to actually earn the quoted rate on a long-term bond, the interest payments must be reinvested at the quoted rate. However, if interest rates fall, the interest payments must be reinvested at a lower rate; thus, the realized return would be less than the quoted rate. Note, though, that reinvestment rate risk is lower on a long-term bond than on a short-term bond because only the interest payments (rather than interest plus principal) on the long-term bond are exposed to reinvestment rate risk. Zero coupon bonds, which are discussed in Chapter 7, are completely free of reinvestment rate risk during their life.

THE TERM STRUCTURE
OF INTEREST RATES

Term Structure of Interest Rates
The relationship between bond
yields and maturities.

A study of Figure 4-3 reveals that at certain times such as in 1994, short-term interest rates were lower than long-term rates, whereas at other times such as in 1980 and
1981, short-term rates were higher than long-term rates. The relationship between
long- and short-term rates, which is known as the **term structure of interest rates,**
is important to corporate treasurers, who must decide whether to borrow by issuing
long- or short-term debt, and to investors, who must decide whether to buy long- or
short-term bonds. Thus, it is important to understand (1) how long- and short-term
rates are related to each other and (2) what causes shifts in their relative positions.

To begin, we can look up in a source such as *The Wall Street Journal* or the
Federal Reserve Bulletin the interest rates on Treasury bonds of various maturities
at a given point in time. For example, the tabular section of Figure 4-5 presents

| FIGURE 4 - 5 | U.S. TREASURY BOND INTEREST RATES ON DIFFERENT DATES |

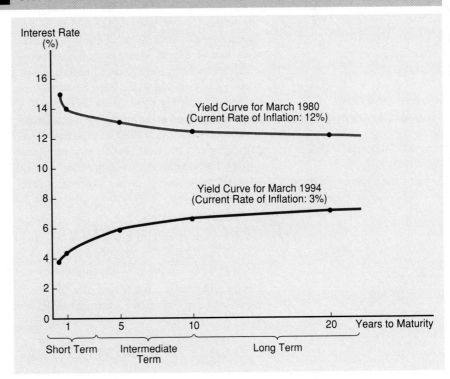

TERM TO MATURITY	INTEREST RATE	
	MARCH 1980	MARCH 1994
6 months	15.0%	3.9%
1 year	14.0	4.4
5 years	13.5	5.9
10 years	12.8	6.6
20 years	12.5	7.1

Yield Curve
A graph showing the relationship between bond yields and maturities.

interest rates for different maturities on two dates. The set of data for a given date, when plotted on a graph such as that in Figure 4-5, is called the **yield curve** for that date. The yield curve changes both in position and in slope over time. In March 1980, all rates were relatively high, and short-term rates were higher than long-term rates, so the yield curve on that date was *downward sloping*. However, in March 1994, all rates had fallen, and short-term rates were lower than long-term rates, so the yield curve at that time was *upward sloping*. Had we drawn the yield curve during January 1982, it would have been essentially horizontal, for long-term and short-term bonds on that date had about the same rate of interest. (See Figure 4-3.) In recent months interest rates have increased sharply, particularly for short-term bonds. Consequently, the present yield curve (January 1995) remains upward sloping, but it is considerably flatter than it was in March 1994.

Figure 4-5 shows yield curves for U.S. Treasury securities, but we could have constructed them for corporate bonds; for example, we could have developed yield curves for AT&T, Exxon, Chrysler, or any other company that borrows money over a range of maturities. Had we constructed such curves and plotted them on Figure 4-5, the corporate yield curves would have been above those for Treasury securities on the same date because the corporate yields would include default risk premiums, but they would have had the same general shape as the Treasury curves. Also, the riskier the corporation, the higher its yield curve; thus Chrysler, which is in a relatively weak financial position, would have had a yield curve substantially higher than that of Exxon, which has a higher bond rating.

"Normal" Yield Curve
An upward-sloping yield curve.

Inverted ("Abnormal") Yield Curve
A downward-sloping yield curve.

Historically, in most years long-term rates have been above short-term rates, so usually the yield curve has been upward sloping. For this reason, people often call an upward-sloping yield curve a **"normal" yield curve** and a yield curve which slopes downward an **inverted,** or **"abnormal," yield curve.** Thus, in Figure 4-5 the yield curve for March 1980 was inverted, but the one for March 1994 was normal. We explain in the next section why an upward slope is the normal situation, but briefly, the reason is that short-term securities have less interest rate risk than longer-term securities, hence short-term rates are normally lower than long-term rates.

SELF-TEST QUESTIONS

What is a yield curve, and what information would you need to draw this curve?

Distinguish between the shapes of a "normal" yield curve and an "abnormal" yield curve, and explain when each might exist.

TERM STRUCTURE THEORIES

Several theories have been proposed to explain the shape of the yield curve. The three major ones are (1) the expectations theory, (2) the liquidity preference theory, and (3) the market segmentation theory.

Expectations Theory
A theory which states that the shape of the yield curve depends on investors' expectations about future inflation rates.

EXPECTATIONS THEORY

The **expectations theory** states that the yield curve depends on expectations about future inflation rates. To begin, the expectations theory indicates that long-term interest rates are a weighted average of current and expected short-term interest rates. For example, if 1-year Treasury bills currently yield 7 percent and 1-year bills are expected to yield 7.5 percent a year from now, investors will expect to earn an average of 7.25 percent over the next 2 years. According to the expectations theory, this implies that a 2-year Treasury note purchased today should also yield 7.25 percent[15]:

$$[(1)(7\%) + (1)(7.5\%)]/2 = 7.25\%.$$

Similarly, if 10-year bonds yield 9 percent today, and if 5-year bonds are expected to yield 7.5 percent 10 years from now, then investors will expect to earn an average return of 8.5 percent over the next 15 years:

$$[(10)(9\%) + (5)(7.5\%)]/15 = 8.5\%.$$

Consequently, a 15-year bond should also yield 8.5 percent.

To understand the logic behind this averaging process, ask yourself what would happen if long-term yields were not an average of expected short-term yields. For example, suppose 2-year bonds yielded only 7 percent, not the 7.25 percent calculated above. Bond traders would be able to earn a profit by adopting the following trading strategy:

1. Borrow money for 2 years at a cost of 7 percent.
2. Invest the money in a series of 1-year bonds. The expected return over the 2-year period would be (7.0 + 7.5)/2 = 7.25%.

In this case, bond traders would rush to borrow money (demand funds) in the 2-year market and invest (or supply funds) in the 1-year market. Recall from Figure 4-2 that an increase in the demand for funds raises interest rates, whereas an increase in the supply of funds reduces interest rates. Therefore, bond traders' actions would push up the 2-year yield but reduce the yield on 1-year bonds. The net effect would be to bring about a market equilibrium in which 1-year rates were a weighted average of expected 1-year rates.

The pure expectations theory assumes that investors establish bond prices and interest rates strictly on the basis of expectations for inflation. This means that they are indifferent with respect to maturity in the sense that they do not view long-term bonds as being riskier than short-term bonds. Therefore, according to the pure expectations theory, the maturity risk premium (MRP) is equal to zero.

Expressed as an equation, according to the pure expectations theory, k_t, the nominal interest rate on a U.S. Treasury bond that matures in t years, would be found as follows:

$$k_t = k^* + IP_t.$$

Here k^* is the real risk-free rate and IP_t is an inflation premium found as the average inflation rate over t years until the bond matures. The real risk-free rate tends to be fairly constant over time; therefore, changes in interest rates are driven largely by changes in expected inflation. Note also that under the pure expectations theory, the MRP is assumed to be zero, and for Treasury securities, the default risk premium (DRP) and liquidity premium (LP) are also zero.

---

[15]Technically, we should be using geometric averages rather than arithmetic averages, but the differences are not material in this example. For a discussion of this point, see Robert C. Radcliffe, *Investment: Concepts, Analysis, and Strategy,* 4th ed. (Glenview, Ill.: Scott, Foresman, 1993), Chapter 6.

To illustrate the pure expectations theory, suppose that in early March 1995 the real risk-free rate of interest was $k^* = 3\%$ and expected inflation rates for the next 3 years were as follows:

	EXPECTED ANNUAL (1-YEAR) INFLATION RATE	EXPECTED AVERAGE INFLATION RATE FROM 1995 TO INDICATED YEAR
1996	3%	3%/1 = 3.0%
1997	5%	(3% + 5%)/2 = 4.0%
1998	7%	(3% + 5% + 7%)/3 = 5.0%

Given these expectations, the following pattern of interest rates should exist:

	REAL RISK-FREE RATE (k^*)		INFLATION PREMIUM, WHICH IS EQUAL TO THE AVERAGE EXPECTED INFLATION RATE (IP_t)		NOMINAL TREASURY BOND RATE FOR EACH MATURITY $(k_{T\text{-BOND}})$
1-year bond	3%	+	3.0%	=	6.0%
2-year bond	3%	+	4.0%	=	7.0%
3-year bond	3%	+	5.0%	=	8.0%

Had the pattern of expected inflation rates been reversed, with inflation expected to fall from 7 percent to 5 percent and then to 3 percent, the following situation would have existed:

	REAL RISK-FREE RATE		AVERAGE EXPECTED INFLATION RATE		TREASURY BOND RATE FOR EACH MATURITY
1-year bond	3%	+	7.0%	=	10.0%
2-year bond	3%	+	6.0%	=	9.0%
3-year bond	3%	+	5.0%	=	8.0%

These hypothetical data are plotted in Figure 4-6. According to the pure expectations theory, an upward-sloping yield curve implies that interest rates are expected to increase in the future. This increase could be due to an increase in expected inflation (as is the case in the example above) or to an increase in the expected real risk-free rate. By contrast, a downward-sloping yield curve would suggest that interest rates are expected to decline.

In practice, we can never actually observe the marginal investor's expected inflation rate or real risk-free rate. However, if the pure expectations theory were correct, we could "back out" of the yield curve the bond market's best guess about future interest rates. If, for example, you observe that Treasury securities with 1- and 2-year maturities yield 7 percent and 8 percent, respectively, this information can be used to back out the market's forecast of what 1-year rates will yield one year from now. If the pure expectations theory is correct, the rate on 2-year bonds is the average of the current 1-year rate and the 1-year rate expected one year from now. Since the current 1-year rate is 7 percent, this implies that the 1-year rate is expected to be 9 percent:

$$2\text{-year yield} = 8\% = \frac{7\% + X\%}{2}$$

$X = 9\% = $ 1-year yield expected next year.

FIGURE   4-6   HYPOTHETICAL EXAMPLE OF THE TERM STRUCTURE OF INTEREST RATES

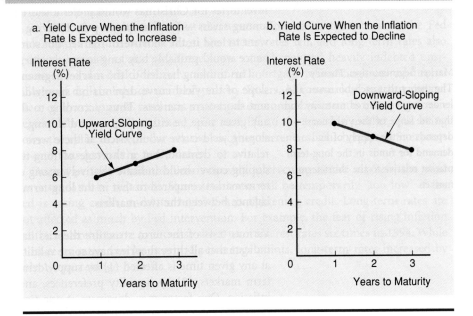

LIQUIDITY PREFERENCE THEORY

The pure expectations theory assumes that the maturity risk premium (MRP) is zero. However, convincing evidence suggests that there is a positive maturity risk premium; that is, investors require higher rates of return on longer-term bonds, other things held constant.

Liquidity Preference Theory
The theory that lenders, other things held constant, would prefer to make short-term loans rather than long-term loans; hence, they will lend short-term funds at lower rates than long-term funds.

This has given rise to the **liquidity preference theory,** which states that long-term bonds normally yield more than short-term bonds for two reasons: (1) Investors generally prefer to hold short-term securities because such securities are more liquid in the sense that they can be converted to cash with little danger of loss of principal. Investors will, therefore, generally accept lower yields on short-term securities, and this leads to relatively low short-term rates. (2) Borrowers, on the other hand, generally prefer long-term debt because short-term debt exposes them to the risk of having to repay the debt under adverse conditions. Accordingly, borrowers are willing to pay a higher rate, other things held constant, for long-term funds than for short-term funds, and this also leads to relatively low short-term rates. Thus, lender and borrower preferences both operate to cause short-term rates to be lower than long-term rates. Taken together, these two sets of preferences — hence the liquidity preference theory — imply that under normal conditions, a positive maturity risk premium (MRP) exists, and the MRP increases with years to maturity, causing the yield curve to be upward sloping.

MARKET SEGMENTATION THEORY

The expectation theory is based on the assumption that investors have no maturity preferences. However, empirical studies suggest that different lenders and borrowers have different preferred maturities. For example, a person borrowing to buy a loan will reflect the then-current short-term rate. Interest rates could return to their March 1980 levels, in which case you would be paying 14 percent, or $140,000, per year. These high interest payments would cut into, and perhaps eliminate, your profits. Your reduced profitability could easily increase your firm's risk to the point where its bond rating would be lowered, causing lenders to increase the risk premium built into the interest rates they charge. That would force you to pay even higher rates, which would further reduce your profitability, worrying lenders even more, and making them reluctant to renew your loan. If your lenders refused to renew the loan and demanded payment, as they have every right to do, you might have to sell assets at a loss, which could lead to bankruptcy.

On the other hand, if you used long-term financing in 1994, your interest costs would remain constant at $71,000 per year, so an increase in interest rates in the economy would not hurt you. You might even be able to buy up some of your bankrupt competitors at bargain prices — bankruptcies increase dramatically when interest rates rise, primarily because many firms do use short-term debt.

Does all this suggest that firms should always avoid short-term debt? Not necessarily. If inflation falls in the next few years, so will interest rates. If you had borrowed on a long-term basis for 7.1 percent in March 1994, your company would be at a major disadvantage if it was locked into 7.1 percent debt while its competitors (who used short-term debt in 1994 and thus rode interest rates down in subsequent years) had a borrowing cost of only 3 or 4 percent.

Financing decisions would be easy if we could develop accurate forecasts of future interest rates. Unfortunately, predicting future interest rates with consistent accuracy is somewhere between difficult and impossible — people who make a living by selling interest rate forecasts say it is difficult, but many others say it is impossible.

Even if it is difficult to predict future interest rate *levels,* it is easy to predict that interest rates will *fluctuate* — they always have, and they always will. This being the case, sound financial policy calls for using a mix of long- and short-term debt, as well as equity, to position the firm so that it can survive in any interest rate environment. Further, the optimal financial policy depends in an important way on the nature of the firm's assets — the easier it is to sell off assets and thus to pay off debts, the more feasible it is to use large amounts of short-term debt. This makes it more feasible to finance current assets than fixed assets with short-term debt. We will return to this issue later in the book, when we discuss working capital policy.

SELF-TEST QUESTIONS

If short-term interest rates are lower than long-term rates, why might a firm still choose to finance with long-term debt?

Explain the following statement: "The optimal financial policy depends in an important way on the nature of the firm's assets."

SUMMARY

In this chapter, we discussed the nature of financial markets, the types of institutions that operate in these markets, how interest rates are determined, and some of the ways in which interest rates affect business decisions. The key concepts covered are listed below.

- There are many different types of **financial markets.** Each market serves a different region or deals with a different type of security.

- **Physical asset markets,** also called tangible or real asset markets, are those for such products as wheat, autos, and real estate.

- **Financial asset markets** deal with stocks, bonds, notes, mortgages, and other claims on real assets.

- **Spot markets** and **futures markets** are terms that refer to whether the assets are being bought or sold for "on-the-spot" delivery or for delivery at some future date.

- **Money markets** are the markets for debt securities with maturities of less than one year.

- **Capital markets** are the markets for long-term debt and corporate stocks.

- **Primary markets** are the markets in which corporations raise new capital.

- **Secondary markets** are markets in which existing, already outstanding, securities are traded among investors.

- Transfers of capital between borrowers and savers take place (1) by **direct transfers** of money and securities; (2) by transfers through **investment banking houses,** which act as middlemen; and (3) by transfers through **financial intermediaries,** which create new securities.

- Among the major classes of intermediaries are **commercial banks, savings and loan associations, mutual savings banks, credit unions, pension funds, life insurance companies,** and **mutual funds.**

- One result of ongoing regulatory changes has been a blurring of the distinctions between the different financial institutions. The trend in the United States has been toward **financial service corporations** which offer a wide range of financial services, including investment banking, brokerage operations, insurance, and commercial banking.

- The **stock market** is an especially important market because this is where stock prices (which are used to "grade" managers' performances) are established.

- There are two basic types of stock markets — the **organized exchanges** and the **over-the-counter market.**

- Capital is allocated through the price system — a price must be paid to "rent" money. Lenders charge **interest** on funds they lend, while equity investors receive dividends and capital gains in return for letting firms use their money.

- Four fundamental factors affect the cost of money: (1) **production opportunities,** (2) **time preferences for consumption,** (3) **risk,** and (4) **inflation.**

- The **risk-free rate of interest, k_{RF},** is defined as the real risk-free rate, k^*, plus an inflation premium (IP): $k_{RF} = k^* + IP$.

- The **nominal** (or **quoted**) **interest rate** on a debt security, **k,** is composed of the real risk-free rate, k^*, plus premiums that reflect inflation (IP), default risk (DRP), liquidity (LP), and maturity risk (MRP):

$$k = k^* + IP + DRP + LP + MRP.$$

- If the **real risk-free rate of interest and the various premiums were constant over time,** interest rates would be stable. However, both the real rate and the premiums — especially the premium for expected inflation — **do change over time, causing market interest rates to change.** Also, Federal

Reserve intervention to increase or decrease the money supply, as well as international currency flows, lead to fluctuations in interest rates.

■ The relationship between the yields on securities and the securities' maturities is known as the **term structure of interest rates,** and the **yield curve** is a graph of this relationship.

■ The yield curve is normally **upward sloping** — this is called a **normal yield curve**. However, the curve can slope downward (an **inverted yield curve**) if the demand for short-term funds is relatively strong or if the rate of inflation is expected to decline.

■ A number of theories have been proposed to explain the shape of the yield curve at any point in time. These theories include the **expectations theory,** the **liquidity preference theory**, and the **market segmentation theory.**

■ **Interest rate levels have a profound effect on stock prices.** Higher interest rates (1) slow down the economy, (2) increase interest expenses and thus lower corporate profits, and (3) cause investors to sell stocks and transfer funds to the bond market. Thus, higher interest rates depress stock prices.

■ Because interest rate levels are difficult if not impossible to predict, **sound financial policy** calls for using a mix of short- and long-term debt, and also for positioning the firm to survive in any future interest rate environment.

QUESTIONS

4-1 What are financial intermediaries, and what economic functions do they perform?

4-2 Suppose interest rates on residential mortgages of equal risk were 7 percent in California and 9 percent in New York. Could this differential persist? What forces might tend to equalize rates? Would differentials in borrowing costs for businesses of equal risk located in California and New York be more or less likely to exist than differentials in residential mortgage rates? Would differentials in the cost of money for New York and California firms be more likely to exist if the firms being compared were very large or if they were very small? What are the implications of all this for the pressure now being put on Congress to permit banks to engage in nationwide branching?

4-3 What would happen to the standard of living in the United States if people lost faith in the safety of our financial institutions? Why?

4-4 How does a cost-efficient capital market help to reduce the prices of goods and services?

4-5 Which fluctuate more, long-term or short-term interest rates? Why?

4-6 Suppose you believe that the economy is just entering a recession. Your firm must raise capital immediately, and debt will be used. Should you borrow on a long-term or a short-term basis? Why?

4-7 Suppose the population of Area Y is relatively young while that of Area O is relatively old, but everything else about the two areas is equal.
   a. Would interest rates likely be the same or different in the two areas? Explain.
   b. Would a trend toward nationwide branching by banks and savings and loans, and the development of nationwide diversified financial corporations, affect your answer to Part a?

4-8 Suppose a new process was developed which could be used to make oil out of seawater. The equipment required is quite expensive, but it would, in time, lead to very low prices for gasoline, electricity, and other types of energy. What effect would this have on interest rates?

4-9 Suppose a new and much more liberal Congress and administration were elected, and their first order of business was to take away the independence of the Federal Reserve System, and to force the Fed to greatly expand the money supply. What effect would this have
   a. On the level and slope of the yield curve immediately after the announcement?
   b. On the level and slope of the yield curve that would exist two or three years in the future?

4-10 It is a fact that the federal government (1) encouraged the development of the savings and loan industry; (2) virtually forced the industry to make long-term, fixed-interest-rate mortgages; and (3) forced the savings and loans to obtain most of their capital as deposits that were withdrawable on demand.
    a. Would the savings and loans have higher profits in a world with a "normal" or an inverted yield curve?
    b. Would the savings and loan industry be better off if the individual institutions sold their mortgages to federal agencies and then collected servicing fees or if the institutions held the mortgages that they originated?

4-11 Suppose interest rates on Treasury bonds rose from 7 to 14 percent as a result of higher interest rates in Europe. What effect would this have on the price of an average company's common stock?

SELF-TEST PROBLEMS *(Solutions Appear in Appendix B)*

ST-1 Key terms Define each of the following terms:
    a. Money market; capital market
    b. Primary market; secondary market
    c. Investment banker; financial service corporation
    d. Financial intermediary
    e. Mutual fund; money market fund
    f. Organized security exchanges; over-the-counter market
    g. Production opportunities; time preferences for consumption
    h. Real risk-free rate of interest, k^*; nominal risk-free rate of interest, k_{RF}
    i. Inflation premium (IP)
    j. Default risk premium (DRP)
    k. Liquidity; liquidity premium (LP)
    l. Interest rate risk; maturity risk premium (MRP)
    m. Reinvestment rate risk
    n. Term structure of interest rates; yield curve
    o. "Normal" yield curve; inverted ("abnormal") yield curve
    p. Expectations theory
    q. Market segmentation theory; liquidity preference theory
    r. Derivatives

ST-2 Inflation rates Assume that it is now January 1, 1996. The rate of inflation is expected to be 4 percent throughout 1996. However, increased government deficits and renewed vigor in the economy are then expected to push inflation rates higher. Investors expect the inflation rate to be 5 percent in 1997, 6 percent in 1998, and 7 percent in 1999. The real risk-free rate, k^*, is expected to remain at 2 percent over the next 5 years. Assume that no maturity risk premiums are required on bonds with 5 years or less to maturity. The current interest rate on 5-year T-bonds is 8 percent.
    a. What is the average expected inflation rate over the next 4 years?
    b. What should be the prevailing interest rate on 4-year T-bonds?
    c. What is the implied expected inflation rate in 2000, or Year 5, given that bonds which mature in that year yield 8 percent?

PROBLEMS

4-1 Yield curves Suppose you and most other investors expect the rate of inflation to be 7 percent next year, to fall to 5 percent during the following year, and then to remain at a rate of 3 percent thereafter. Assume that the real risk-free rate, k^*, will remain at 2 percent and that maturity risk premiums on Treasury securities rise from zero on very short-term bonds (those that mature in a few days) to a level of 0.2 percentage point for 1-year securities. Furthermore, maturity risk premiums increase 0.2 percentage point for each year to maturity, up to a limit of 1.0 percentage point on 5-year or longer-term T-bonds.
    a. Calculate the interest rate on 1-, 2-, 3-, 4-, 5-, 10-, and 20-year Treasury securities, and plot the yield curve.
    b. Now suppose Exxon, an AAA-rated company, had bonds with the same maturities as the Treasury bonds. As an approximation, plot an Exxon yield curve on the same graph with the Treasury bond yield curve. (Hint: Think about the default risk premium on Exxon's long-term versus its short-term bonds.)
    c. Now plot the approximate yield curve of Long Island Lighting Company, a risky nuclear utility.

FIGURE 5-5   RATE OF RETURN DISTRIBUTIONS FOR TWO PERFECTLY NEGATIVELY CORRELATED STOCKS ($r = -1.0$) AND FOR PORTFOLIO WM

a. Rates of Return

b. Probability Distributions of Returns

Year	Stock W ($\bar{k}_W$)	Stock M ($\bar{k}_M$)	Portfolio WM ($\bar{k}_p$)
1991	40%	(10%)	15%
1992	(10)	40	15
1993	35	(5)	15
1994	(5)	35	15
1995	15	15	15
Average return	15%	15%	15%
Standard deviation	22.6%	22.6%	0.0%

statistical terms, we say that the returns on Stocks W and M are *perfectly negatively correlated*, with r = −1.0.

The opposite of perfect negative correlation, with r = −1.0, is *perfect positive correlation*, with r = +1.0. Returns on two perfectly positively correlated stocks would move up and down together, and a portfolio consisting of two such stocks would be exactly as risky as the individual stocks. This point is illustrated in Figure 5-6, where we see that the portfolio's standard deviation is equal to that of the individual stocks. *Thus, diversification does nothing to reduce risk if the portfolio consists of perfectly positively correlated stocks.*

Figures 5-5 and 5-6 demonstrate that when stocks are perfectly negatively correlated (r = −1.0), all risk can be diversified away, but when stocks are perfectly positively correlated (r = +1.0), diversification does no good whatsoever. In reality, most stocks are positively correlated, but not perfectly so. On average, the correlation coefficient for the returns on two randomly selected stocks would be about +0.6, and for most pairs of stocks, r would lie in the range of +0.5 to +0.7. *Under such conditions, combining stocks into portfolios reduces risk but does not eliminate it completely.* Figure 5-7 illustrates this point with two stocks whose correlation coefficient is r = +0.67. The portfolio's average return is 15.0 percent, which is exactly the same as the average return for each of the two stocks, but its standard deviation is 20.6 percent, which is less than the standard deviation of either stock. Thus, the portfolio's risk is *not* an average of the risks of its individual stocks — diversification has reduced, but not eliminated, risk.

From these two-stock portfolio examples, we have seen that in one extreme case (r = −1.0), risk can be completely eliminated, while in the other extreme case (r = +1.0), diversification does nothing to limit risk. In between these extremes, combining two stocks into a portfolio reduces, but does not eliminate, the riskiness inherent in the individual stocks.

What would happen if we included more than two stocks in the portfolio? *As a rule, the riskiness of a portfolio will decline as the number of stocks in the portfolio increases.* If we added enough partially correlated stocks, could we completely eliminate risk? In general, the answer is no, but the extent to which adding stocks to a portfolio reduces its risk depends on the *degree of correlation* among the stocks: The smaller the positive correlation coefficient, the lower the risk in a large portfolio. If we could find a set of stocks whose correlations were zero or negative, all risk could be eliminated. *In the real world, where the correlations among the individual stocks are generally positive but less than +1.0, some, but not all, risk can be eliminated.*

To test your understanding, would you expect to find higher correlations between the returns on two companies in the same or in different industries? For example, would the correlation of returns on Ford's and General Motors's stocks be higher, or would the correlation coefficient be higher between either Ford or GM and AT&T, and how would those correlations affect the risk of portfolios containing them?

Answer: Ford's and GM's returns have a correlation coefficient of about 0.9 with one another because both are affected by auto sales, but only about 0.6 with those of AT&T.

Implications: A two-stock portfolio consisting of Ford and GM would be less well diversified than a two-stock portfolio consisting of Ford or GM, plus AT&T. Thus, to minimize risk, portfolios should be diversified across industries.

Before leaving this section we should issue a warning — in the real world, it is *impossible* to find stocks like W and M, whose returns are expected to be perfectly negatively correlated. *Therefore, it is impossible to form completely riskless stock portfolios.* Diversification can reduce risk, but it cannot eliminate it. The real world is closer to the situation depicted in Figure 5-7.

DIVERSIFIABLE RISK VERSUS MARKET RISK

As noted earlier, it is difficult if not impossible to find stocks whose expected returns are not positively correlated — most stocks tend to do well when the national economy is strong and badly when it is weak.[7] Thus, even very large portfolios endup with a substantial amount of risk, but not as much risk as if all the money were invested in only one stock.

To see more precisely how portfolio size affects portfolio risk, consider Figure 5-8, which shows how portfolio risk is affected by forming larger and larger portfolios of randomly selected NYSE stocks. Standard deviations are plotted for an average one-stock portfolio, a two-stock portfolio, and so on, up to a portfolio consisting of all 1,500-plus common stocks that were listed on the NYSE at the time the data were graphed. The graph illustrates that, in general, the riskiness of a portfolio consisting of average NYSE stocks tends to decline and to approach some limit as the size of the portfolio increases. According to data accumulated in recent years, σ_1, the standard deviation of a one-stock portfolio (or an average stock), is approximately 35 percent. A portfolio consisting of all stocks, which is called the *market portfolio,* would have a standard deviation, σ_M, of about 20.6 percent, which is shown as the horizontal dashed line in Figure 5-8.

Thus, almost half of the riskiness inherent in an average individual stock can be eliminated if the stock is held in a reasonably well-diversified portfolio, which is one containing 40 or more stocks. Some risk always remains, however, so it is virtually impossible to diversify away the effects of broad stock market movements that affect almost all stocks.

That part of the risk of a stock which *can* be eliminated is called *diversifiable risk,* while that part which *cannot* be eliminated is called *market risk.*[8] The fact that a large part of the riskiness of any individual stock can be eliminated is vitally important.

Diversifiable risk is caused by such random events as lawsuits, strikes, successful and unsuccessful marketing programs, winning or losing of major contracts, and other events that are unique to a particular firm. Since these events are random, their effects on a portfolio can be eliminated by diversification — bad events in one firm will be offset by good events in another. **Market risk,** on the other hand, stems from factors which systematically affect most firms: war, inflation, recessions, and high interest rates. Since most stocks will tend to be negatively affected by these factors, market risk cannot be eliminated by diversification.

We know that investors demand a premium for bearing risk; that is, the higher the riskiness of a security, the higher its expected return must be to induce investors to buy (or to hold) it. However, if investors are primarily concerned with *portfolio risk* rather than the risk of the individual securities in the portfolio, how should the riskiness of an individual stock be measured? One answer is provided by the **Capital Asset Pricing Model (CAPM),** an important tool used to analyze the relationship between risk and rates of return.[9] The primary conclusion of the CAPM

Diversifiable Risk
That part of a security's risk associated with random events; it *can* be eliminated by proper diversification.

Market Risk
That part of a security's risk that *cannot* be eliminated by diversification.

Capital Asset Pricing Model (CAPM)
A model based on the proposition that any stock's required rate of return is equal to the risk-free rate of return plus a risk premium which reflects only the risk remaining after diversification.

[7]It is not too hard to find a few stocks that happened to have risen because of a particular set of circumstances in the past while most other stocks were declining, but it is much harder to find stocks that could logically be *expected* to go up in the future when other stocks are falling. Payco American, the collection agency discussed earlier, seems to be one of those rare exceptions.

[8]Diversifiable risk is also known as *company-specific,* or *unsystematic,* risk. Market risk is also known as *nondiversifiable,* or *systematic,* or *beta,* risk; it is the risk that remains after diversification.

[9]Indeed, the 1990 Nobel Prize was awarded to the developers of the CAPM, Professors Harry Markowitz and William F. Sharpe. The CAPM is a relatively complex subject, and only its basic elements are presented in this text. For a more detailed discussion, see any standard investments textbook.

The basic concepts of the CAPM were developed specifically for common stocks, and therefore, the

FIGURE 5-8	EFFECTS OF PORTFOLIO SIZE ON PORTFOLIO RISK FOR AVERAGE STOCKS

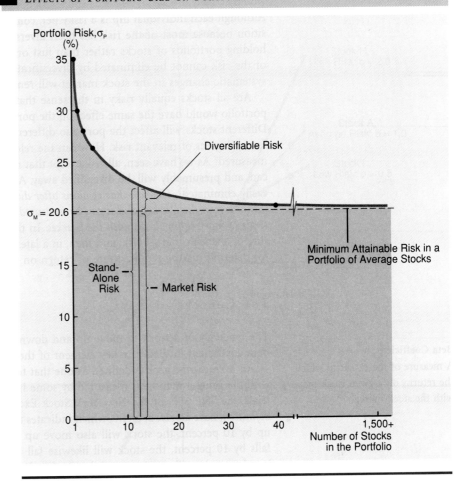

is this: *The relevant riskiness of an individual stock is its contribution to the riskiness of a well-diversified portfolio.* In other words, the riskiness of General Electric's stock to a doctor who has a portfolio of 40 stocks or to a trust officer managing a 150-stock portfolio is the contribution that the GE stock makes to the portfolio's riskiness. The stock might be quite risky if held by itself, but if half its risk can be eliminated by diversification, then its **relevant risk,** which is its *contribution to the portfolio's risk,* is much smaller than its stand-alone risk.

A simple example will help make this point clear. Suppose you are offered the chance to flip a coin once; if a head comes up, you win $20,000, but if it comes up tails, you lose $16,000. This is a good bet — the expected return is $0.5(\$20,000) + 0.5(-\$16,000) = \$2,000$. However, it is a highly risky proposition, because you have a 50 percent chance of losing $16,000. Thus, you might well refuse to make the bet. Alternatively, suppose you were offered the chance to flip a coin 100 times, and you would win $200 for each head but lose $160 for each tail. It is possible that you would flip all heads and win $20,000, and it is also possible that

Relevant Risk

The risk of a security that cannot be diversified away, or its *market risk*. This reflects a security's contribution to the riskiness of a portfolio.

---

theory is examined first in this context. However, it has become common practice to extend the concepts to capital budgeting and to speak of firms having "portfolios of tangible assets and projects." In Chapter 11, we discuss the implications of the CAPM for capital budgeting and corporate diversification.

FIGURE 5-11   **SHIFT IN THE SML CAUSED BY AN INCREASE IN INFLATION**

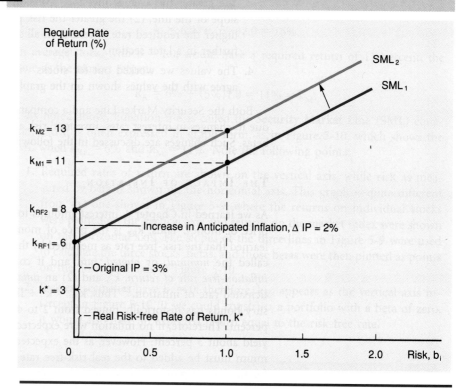

CHANGES IN RISK AVERSION

The slope of the Security Market Line reflects the extent to which investors are averse to risk — the steeper the slope of the line, the greater the average investor's risk aversion. Suppose investors were indifferent to risk; that is, they are not risk averse. If k_{RF} were 6 percent, then risky assets would also provide an expected return of 6 percent: If there were no risk aversion, there would be no risk premium, so the SML would be horizontal. As risk aversion increases, so does the risk premium, and this causes the slope of the SML to become steeper.

Figure 5-12 illustrates an increase in risk aversion. The market risk premium rises from 5 to 7.5 percent, causing k_M to rise from $k_{M1} = 11\%$ to $k_{M2} = 13.5\%$. The returns on other risky assets also rise, and the effect of this shift in risk aversion is more pronounced on riskier securities. For example, the required return on a stock with $b_i = 0.5$ increases by only 1.25 percentage points, from 8.5 to 9.75 percent, whereas that on a stock with $b_i = 1.5$ increases by 3.75 percentage points, from 13.5 to 17.25 percent.

CHANGES IN A STOCK'S BETA COEFFICIENT

As we shall see later in the book, a firm can affect its market risk through changes in the composition of its assets and also through its use of debt financing. A company's beta can also change as a result of external factors such as increased competition in its industry, the expiration of basic patents, and the like. When such

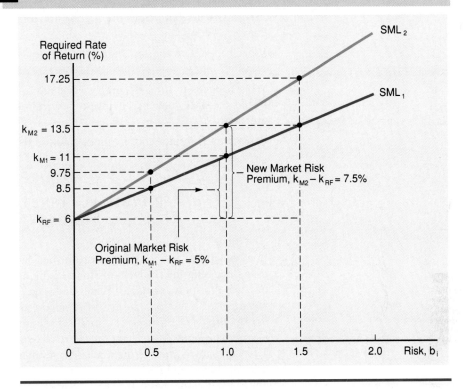

FIGURE 5-12   **SHIFT IN THE SML CAUSED BY INCREASED RISK AVERSION**

changes occur, the required rate of return also changes, and, as we shall see in Chapter 8, this will affect the price of the firm's stock. For example, consider Allied Food Products, with a beta of 1.40. Now suppose some action occurred which caused Allied's beta to increase from 1.40 to 2.00. If the conditions depicted in Figure 5-10 held, Allied's required rate of return would increase from 13 to 16 percent:

$$k_1 = k_{RF} + (k_M - k_{RF})b_i$$
$$= 6\% + (11\% - 6\%)1.40$$
$$= 13\%$$

to

$$k_2 = 6\% + (11\% - 6\%)2.0$$
$$= 16\%.$$

Any change which affects the required rate of return on a security, such as a change in its beta coefficient or in expected inflation, will have an impact on the price of the security. We will discuss the relationship between a stock's required rate of return and its price in Chapter 8.

 ## SELF-TEST QUESTIONS

Differentiate between the expected rate of return ($\hat{k}$) and the required rate of return (k) on a stock. Which would have to be larger to get you to buy the stock?

What are the differences between the relative volatility graph (Figure 5-9), where "betas are made," and the SML graph (Figure 5-10), where "betas are used"? Discuss both how the graphs are constructed and the information they convey.

What happens to the SML graph in Figure 5-10 when inflation increases or decreases?

What happens to the SML graph when risk aversion increases or decreases? What would the SML look like if investors were indifferent to risk, i.e., had zero risk aversion?

How can a firm influence its market risk as reflected in its beta?

PHYSICAL ASSETS VERSUS SECURITIES

In a book on financial management for business firms, why do we spend so much time discussing the riskiness of stocks? Why not begin by looking at the riskiness of such business assets as plant and equipment? *The reason is that, for a management whose goal is stock price maximization, the overriding consideration is the riskiness of the firm's stock, and the relevant risk of any physical asset must be measured in terms of its effect on the stock's risk.* For example, suppose Goodyear Tire Company is considering a major investment in a new product, recapped tires. Sales of recaps, and hence earnings on the new operation, are highly uncertain, so on a stand-alone basis the new venture appears to be quite risky. However, suppose returns in the recap business are negatively correlated with Goodyear's regular operations — when times are good and people have plenty of money, they buy new tires, but when times are bad, they tend to buy more recaps. Therefore, returns would be high on regular operations and low on the recap division during good times, but the opposite situation would occur during recessions. The result might be a pattern like that shown earlier in Figure 5-5 for Stocks W and M. Thus, what appears to be a risky investment when viewed on a stand-alone basis might not be very risky when viewed within the context of the company as a whole.

This analysis can be extended to the corporation's stockholders. Because Goodyear's stock is owned by diversified stockholders, the real issue each time the company makes a major asset investment is this: How does this investment affect the risk of our stockholders? Again, the stand-alone risk of an individual project may look quite high, but viewed in the context of the project's effect on stockholders' risk, it may not be very large. We will address this issue again in Chapter 11, where we examine the effects of capital budgeting on companies' beta coefficients and thus on stockholders' risks.

SELF-TEST QUESTIONS

Explain the following statement: "The stand-alone risk of an individual project may look quite high, but viewed in the context of a project's effect on stockholders, the project's risk may not be very large."

How would the correlation between returns on a project and returns on the firm's other assets' returns affect the project's risk?

IS BETA DEAD?

The Capital Asset Pricing Model (CAPM) is more than just an abstract theory described in textbooks — it is also widely used by analysts, investors, and corporations. Therefore, it is reasonable to ask, "Is the CAPM correct in the sense that stocks with higher betas have higher returns?"

A recent study by two University of Chicago professors, Eugene Fama and Kenneth French, concluded that the answer is no. They found no historical relationship between stocks' returns and their betas, confirming a position long held by a number of professors and stock market analysts. Nevertheless, the strength of the Fama-French findings surprised many people, and it led some to conclude that "beta is dead."

If beta does not determine returns, what does? Fama and French found two variables which are consistently related to stock returns: (1) the firm's size and (2) its market/book ratio. They found that after adjusting for other factors, smaller firms have provided relatively high returns and also that returns are higher on stocks whose equity book values are high relative to their market values. By contrast, after controlling for the size of firm and market-to-book ratios, they found that there is no relationship between a stock's beta and its return.

Given Fama and French's findings, should you just ignore everything said about beta in this chapter? In other words, is beta really dead? Probably not. Proponents of the CAPM argue that the theory is right, but the evidence is flawed. In particular, the CAPM states that there is a relationship between a firm's *expected future* volatility and its *expected future* return. In practice, however, we have only historical data, so Fama and French were forced to test the CAPM using historical instead of expected future data. This also forced them to assume that investors expect the future to be like the past. However, there is no guarantee that investors expect historical relationships to be maintained. Therefore, studies such as Fama-French cannot prove or disprove the CAPM.

Practitioners and academicians have long recognized the limitations of the CAPM, and they are constantly working on ways to improve it. For example, procedures have been developed to calculate "adjusted" betas, which provide a better indication of a stock's future relative volatility than purely historical betas. Also, people recognize that factors other than market risk (beta) — including the size of the company, oil prices, unemployment, and the like — probably affect returns. Therefore, "multifactor" CAPM procedures are being developed and used.

Overall, the CAPM is the most logical and intuitively appealing method ever devised to measure risk and relate it to required returns. Therefore, while beta may not be in the best of health, it is certainly not dead.

A WORD OF CAUTION

As we discuss in the box entitled "Is Beta Dead?" a word of caution about betas and the Capital Asset Pricing Model (CAPM) is in order. Although these concepts are logical, the entire theory is based on *ex ante,* or expected, conditions, yet we have available only *ex post,* or past, data. Thus, the betas we calculate show how volatile a stock has been in the *past.* However, conditions do change, and the stock's *future volatility,* which is the item of real concern to investors, might be quite different from its past volatility. Therefore, while the CAPM represents a significant step forward in security pricing theory, it does have some potentially serious deficiencies when applied in practice, and estimates of k_i found through use of the SML may be subject to considerable error.

RISK IN A GLOBAL CONTEXT

 It seems reasonable to think that investments outside the United States are, for a U.S. citizen or company, riskier than investments in U.S. assets. However, this is not necessarily true — because returns on foreign investments are not perfectly positively correlated with returns on U.S. assets, it has been argued that multinational corporations may be less risky than companies which operate strictly within the boundaries of any one country. Similarly, portfolio managers have argued that to minimize risk, investors should diversify not only across stocks but also across countries.[14] A study of global diversification would go beyond the scope of this text, but you should at this point be able to see how global diversification might be able to improve investment performance.

SUMMARY

The primary goals of this chapter were (1) to show how risk is measured in financial analysis and (2) to explain how risk affects rates of return. The key concepts covered are listed below.

■ **Risk** can be defined as the chance that some unfavorable event will occur.

■ The riskiness of an asset's cash flows can be considered on a **stand-alone basis** (each asset by itself) or in a **portfolio context,** where the investment is combined with other assets and its risk is reduced through diversification.

■ Most rational investors hold **portfolios of assets,** and they are more concerned with the risks of their portfolios than with the risks of individual assets.

■ The **expected return** on an investment is the mean value of its probability distribution of returns.

■ The **higher the probability** that the actual return will be far below the expected return, the **greater the risk** associated with the asset.

■ The average investor is **risk averse,** which means that he or she must be compensated for holding risky assets. Therefore, riskier assets have higher required returns than less risky assets.

■ An asset's risk consists of (1) **diversifiable risk,** which can be eliminated by diversification, plus (2) **market risk,** which cannot be eliminated by diversification.

■ The **relevant risk** of an individual asset is its contribution to the riskiness of a well-diversified **portfolio,** which is the asset's **market risk.** Since market risk cannot be eliminated by diversification, investors must be compensated for bearing it.

■ A stock's **beta coefficient, b,** is a measure of the stock's market risk. Beta measures the extent to which the stock's returns move relative to the market.

■ A **high-beta stock** is more volatile than an average stock, while a **low-beta stock** is less volatile than an average stock. An **average stock** has $b = 1.0$.

■ The **beta of a portfolio** is a **weighted average** of the betas of the individual securities in the portfolio.

■ The **Security Market Line (SML)** equation shows the relationship between a security's risk and its required rate of return. The return required for any

---

[14]Over the past 10 years, adding even a small percentage of foreign stocks to a U.S. portfolio actually decreased the portfolio's overall risk while increasing its overall return. In fact, a portfolio with 50 percent foreign stocks and 50 percent domestic stocks had approximately the same risk as a 100 percent U.S. portfolio, yet its average annual return over the past 10 years was almost 2 percentage points higher.

security i is equal to the **risk-free rate** plus the **market risk premium** times the **security's beta:** $k_i = k_{RF} + (k_M - k_{RF})b_i$.

■ Even though the expected rate of return on a stock is generally equal to its required return, a number of things can happen to cause the required rate of return to change: (1) **the risk-free rate can change** because of changes in anticipated inflation, (2) **a stock's beta can change,** and (3) **investors' aversion to risk can change.**

■ Because returns on assets in different countries are not perfectly correlated, **global diversification** may result in lower risk for multinational companies and globally diversified portfolios.

In the next three chapters, we will see how a security's rate of return affects its value. Then, in the remainder of the book, we will examine the ways in which a firm's management can influence a stock's riskiness and hence its price.

QUESTIONS

5-1 The probability distribution of a less risky expected return is more peaked than that of a riskier return. What shape would the probability distribution have for (a) completely certain returns and (b) completely uncertain returns?

5-2 Security A has an expected return of 7 percent, a standard deviation of expected returns of 35 percent, a correlation coefficient with the market of −0.3, and a beta coefficient of −0.5. Security B has an expected return of 12 percent, a standard deviation of returns of 10 percent, a correlation with the market of 0.7, and a beta coefficient of 1.0. Which security is riskier? Why?

5-3 Suppose you owned a portfolio consisting of $250,000 worth of long-term U.S. government bonds.
  a. Would your portfolio be riskless?
  b. Now suppose you hold a portfolio consisting of $250,000 worth of 30-day Treasury bills. Every 30 days your bills mature and you reinvest the principal ($250,000) in a new batch of bills. Assume that you live on the investment income from your portfolio and that you want to maintain a constant standard of living. Is your portfolio truly riskless?
  c. Can you think of any asset that would be completely riskless? Could someone develop such an asset? Explain.

5-4 A life insurance policy is a financial asset. The premiums paid represent the investment's cost.
  a. How would you calculate the expected return on a life insurance policy?
  b. Suppose the owner of a life insurance policy has no other financial assets — the person's only other asset is "human capital," or lifetime earnings capacity. What is the correlation coefficient between returns on the insurance policy and returns on the policyholder's human capital?
  c. Life insurance companies have to pay administrative costs and sales representatives' commissions; hence, the expected rate of return on insurance premiums is generally low, or even negative. Use the portfolio concept to explain why people buy life insurance in spite of negative expected returns.

5-5 If investors' aversion to risk increased, would the risk premium on a high-beta stock increase more or less than that on a low-beta stock? Explain.

5-6 If a company's beta were to double, would its expected return double?

5-7 Is it possible to construct a portfolio of stocks which has an expected return equal to the risk-free rate?

SELF-TEST PROBLEMS *(Solutions Appear in Appendix B)*

ST-1 Key terms Define the following terms, using graphs or equations to illustrate your answers wherever feasible:
  a. Stand-alone risk; risk; probability distribution
  b. Expected rate of return, k̂
  c. Continuous probability distribution
  d. Standard deviation, σ; variance, σ^2; coefficient of variation, CV

e. Risk aversion; realized rate of return, $\bar{k}$
f. Risk premium for Stock i, RP_i; market risk premium, RP_M
g. Capital Asset Pricing Model (CAPM)
h. Expected return on a portfolio, $\hat{k}_p$
i. Correlation coefficient, r
j. Market risk; diversifiable risk; relevant risk
k. Beta coefficient, b; average stock's beta, b_A
l. Security Market Line (SML); SML equation
m. Slope of SML as a measure of risk aversion

ST-2 Realized rates of return Stocks A and B have the following historical returns:

YEAR	STOCK A's RETURNS, k_A	STOCK B's RETURNS, k_B
1991	(10.00%)	(3.00%)
1992	18.50	21.29
1993	38.67	44.25
1994	14.33	3.67
1995	33.00	28.30

a. Calculate the average rate of return for each stock during the period 1991 through 1995. Assume that someone held a portfolio consisting of 50 percent of Stock A and 50 percent of Stock B. What would have been the realized rate of return on the portfolio in each year from 1991 through 1995? What would have been the average return on the portfolio during this period?
b. Now calculate the standard deviation of returns for each stock and for the portfolio. Use Equation 5-3a in Footnote 5.
c. Looking at the annual returns data on the two stocks, would you guess that the correlation coefficient between returns on the two stocks is closer to 0.9 or to −0.9?
d. If you added more stocks at random to the portfolio, which of the following is the most accurate statement of what would happen to σ_p?
  (1) σ_p would remain constant.
  (2) σ_p would decline to somewhere in the vicinity of 21 percent.
  (3) σ_p would decline to zero if enough stocks were included.

PROBLEMS

5-1 Expected returns Suppose you won the Florida lottery and were offered (1) $0.5 million or (2) a gamble in which you would get $1 million if a head were flipped but zero if a tail came up.
a. What is the expected value of the gamble?
b. Would you take the sure $0.5 million or the gamble?
c. If you choose the sure $0.5 million, are you a risk averter or a risk seeker?
d. Suppose you actually take the sure $0.5 million. You can invest it in either a U.S. Treasury bond that will return $537,500 at the end of a year or a common stock that has a 50-50 chance of being either worthless or worth $1,150,000 at the end of the year.
  (1) What is the expected dollar profit on the stock investment? (The expected profit on the T-bond investment is $37,500.)
  (2) What is the expected rate of return on the stock investment? (The expected rate of return on the T-bond investment is 7.5 percent.)
  (3) Would you invest in the bond or the stock?
  (4) Exactly how large would the expected profit (or the expected rate of return) have to be on the stock investment to make *you* invest in the stock, given the 7.5 percent return on the bond?
  (5) How might your decision be affected if, rather than buying one stock for $0.5 million, you could construct a portfolio consisting of 100 stocks with $5,000 invested in each? Each of these stocks has the same return characteristics as the one stock — that is, a 50-50 chance of being worth either zero or $11,500 at year-end. Would the correlation between returns on these stocks matter?

5-2 Security Market Line The Kish Investment Fund, in which you plan to invest some money, has total capital of $500 million invested in five stocks:

STOCK	INVESTMENT	STOCK'S BETA COEFFICIENT
A	$160 million	0.5
B	120 million	2.0
C	80 million	4.0
D	80 million	1.0
E	60 million	3.0

The beta coefficient for a fund like Kish Investment can be found as a weighted average of the fund's investments. The current risk-free rate is 6 percent, whereas market returns have the following estimated probability distribution for the next period:

PROBABILITY	MARKET RETURN
0.1	7%
0.2	9
0.4	11
0.2	13
0.1	15

a. What is the estimated equation for the Security Market Line (SML)? (Hint: First determine the expected market return.)
b. Compute the fund's required rate of return for the next period.
c. Suppose Bridget Nelson, the president, receives a proposal for a new stock. The investment needed to take a position in the stock is $50 million, it will have an expected return of 15 percent, and its estimated beta coefficient is 2.0. Should the new stock be purchased? At what expected rate of return should the fund be indifferent to purchasing the stock?

5-3 Realized rates of return Stocks A and B have the following historical returns:

YEAR	STOCK A's RETURNS, k_A	STOCK B's RETURNS, k_B
1991	(18.00%)	(14.50%)
1992	33.00	21.80
1993	15.00	30.50
1994	(0.50)	(7.60)
1995	27.00	26.30

a. Calculate the average rate of return for each stock during the period 1991 through 1995.
b. Assume that someone held a portfolio consisting of 50 percent of Stock A and 50 percent of Stock B. What would have been the realized rate of return on the portfolio in each year from 1991 through 1995? What would have been the average return on the portfolio during this period?
c. Calculate the standard deviation of returns for each stock and for the portfolio.
d. Calculate the coefficient of variation for each stock and for the portfolio.
e. If you are a risk-averse investor, would you prefer to hold Stock A, Stock B, or the portfolio? Why?

5-4 Financial calculator needed; Expected and required rates of return You have observed the following returns over time:

YEAR	STOCK X	STOCK Y	MARKET
1991	14%	13%	12%
1992	19	7	10
1993	−16	−5	−12
1994	3	1	1
1995	20	11	15

Assume that the risk-free rate is 6 percent and the market risk premium is 5 percent. (Hint: See Appendix 5A.)
a. What are the betas of Stocks X and Y?
b. What are the required rates of return for Stocks X and Y?
c. What is the required rate of return for a portfolio consisting of 80 percent of Stock X and 20 percent of Stock Y?
d. If Stock X's expected return is 22 percent, is Stock X under- or overvalued?

EXAM-TYPE PROBLEMS

The problems included in this section are set up in such a way that they could be used as multiple-choice exam problems.

5-5 Expected returns The market and Stock J have the following probability distributions:

PROBABILITY	k_M	k_J
0.3	15%	20%
0.4	9	5
0.3	18	12

a. Calculate the expected rates of return for the market and Stock J.
b. Calculate the standard deviations for the market and Stock J.
c. Calculate the coefficients of variation for the market and Stock J.

5-6 Expected returns Stocks X and Y have the following probability distributions of expected future returns:

PROBABILITY	X	Y
0.1	(10%)	(35%)
0.2	2	0
0.4	12	20
0.2	20	25
0.1	38	45

a. Calculate the expected rate of return, $\hat{k}$, for Stock Y. ($\hat{k}_X = 12\%$.)
b. Calculate the standard deviation of expected returns for Stock X. (That for Stock Y is 20.35 percent.) Now calculate the coefficient of variation for Stock Y. Is it possible that most investors might regard Stock Y as being *less* risky than Stock X? Explain.

5-7 Required rate of return Suppose $k_{RF} = 5\%$, $k_M = 10\%$, and $k_A = 12\%$.
a. Calculate Stock A's beta.
b. If Stock A's beta were 2.0, what would be A's new required rate of return?

5-8 Required rate of return Suppose $k_{RF} = 9\%$, $k_M = 14\%$, and $b_i = 1.3$.
a. What is k_i, the required rate of return on Stock i?
b. Now suppose k_{RF} (1) increases to 10 percent or (2) decreases to 8 percent. The slope of the SML remains constant. How would this affect k_M and k_i?
c. Now assume k_{RF} remains at 9 percent but k_M (1) increases to 16 percent or (2) falls to 13 percent. The slope of the SML does not remain constant. How would these changes affect k_i?

5-9 Portfolio beta Suppose you hold a diversified portfolio consisting of a $7,500 investment in each of 20 different common stocks. The portfolio beta is equal to 1.12. Now, suppose you have decided to sell one of the stocks in your portfolio with a beta equal to 1.0 for $7,500 and to use these proceeds to buy another stock for your portfolio. Assume the new stock's beta is equal to 1.75. Calculate your portfolio's new beta.

5-10 Portfolio required return Suppose you are the money manager of a $4 million investment fund. The fund consists of 4 stocks with the following investments and betas:

STOCK	INVESTMENT	BETA
A	$ 400,000	1.50
B	600,000	(0.50)
C	1,000,000	1.25
D	2,000,000	0.75

If the market required rate of return is 14 percent and the risk-free rate is 6 percent, what is the fund's required rate of return?

5-11 Portfolio beta You have a $2 million portfolio consisting of a $100,000 investment in each of 20 different stocks. The portfolio has a beta equal to 1.1. You are considering selling $100,000 worth of one stock which has a beta equal to 0.9 and using the proceeds to purchase another stock which has a beta equal to 1.4. What will be the new beta of your portfolio following this transaction?

5-12 Required rate of return Stock R has a beta of 1.5, Stock S has a beta of 0.75, the expected rate of return on an average stock is 13 percent, and the risk-free rate of return is 7 percent. By how much does the required return on the riskier stock exceed the required return on the less risky stock?

INTEGRATED CASE

MERRILL FINCH INC.

5-13 Risk and return Assume that you recently graduated with a major in finance, and you just landed a job as a financial planner with Merrill Finch Inc., a large financial ser-vices corporation. Your first assignment is to invest $100,000 for a client. Because the funds are to be invested in a business at the end of one year, you have been instructed to plan for a one-year holding period. Further, your boss has restricted you to the following investment alternatives, shown with their probabilities and associated outcomes. (Disregard for now the items at the bottom of the data; you will fill in the blanks later.)

RETURNS ON ALTERNATIVE INVESTMENTS

STATE OF THE ECONOMY	PROBABILITY	T-BILLS	HIGH TECH	COLLECTIONS	U.S. RUBBER	MARKET PORTFOLIO	2-STOCK PORTFOLIO
				ESTIMATED RATE OF RETURN			
Recession	0.1	8.0%	(22.0%)	28.0%	10.0%*	(13.0%)	3.0%
Below average	0.2	8.0	(2.0)	14.7	(10.0)	1.0	
Average	0.4	8.0	20.0	0.0	7.0	15.0	10.0
Above average	0.2	8.0	35.0	(10.0)	45.0	29.0	
Boom	0.1	8.0	50.0	(20.0)	30.0*	43.0	15.0
k̂				1.7%	13.8%	15.0%	
σ		0.0		13.4	18.8	15.3	3.3
CV				7.9	1.4	1.0	0.3
b				−0.86	0.68		

*Note that the estimated returns of U.S. Rubber do not always move in the same direction as the overall economy. For example, when the economy is below average, consumers purchase fewer tires than they would if the economy was stronger. However, if the economy is in a flat-out recession, a large number of consumers who were planning to purchase a new car may choose to wait and instead purchase new tires for the car they currently own. Under these circumstances, we would expect U.S. Rubber's stock price to be higher if there is a recession than if the economy was just below average.

Merrill Finch's economic forecasting staff has developed probability estimates for the state of the economy, and its se-curity analysts have developed a sophisticated computer pro-gram which was used to estimate the rate of return on each alternative under each state of the economy. High Tech Inc. is an electronics firm; Collections Inc. collects past-due debts; and U.S. Rubber manufactures tires and various other rubber and plastics products. Merrill Finch also maintains an "index fund" which owns a market-weighted fraction of all publicly traded stocks; you can invest in that fund, and thus obtain average stock market results. Given the situation as described, answer the following questions.

a. (1) Why is the T-bill's return independent of the state of the economy? Do T-bills promise a completely risk-free re-turn? (2) Why are High Tech's returns expected to move with the economy whereas Collections' are expected to move counter to the economy?

b. Calculate the expected rate of return on each alternative and fill in the blanks on the row for k̂ in the table above.

c. You should recognize that basing a decision solely on ex-pected returns is only appropriate for risk-neutral individu-als. Since your client, like virtually everyone, is risk averse, the riskiness of each alternative is an important aspect of the decision. One possible measure of risk is the standard deviation of returns. (1) Calculate this value for each alternative, and fill in the blank on the row for σ in the table above. (2) What type of risk is measured by the standard deviation? (3) Draw a graph which shows *roughly* the shape of the probability distributions for High Tech, U.S. Rubber, and T-bills.

d. Suppose you suddenly remembered that the coefficient of variation (CV) is generally regarded as being a better measure of stand-alone risk than the standard deviation when the alternatives being considered have widely differing expected returns. Calculate the missing CVs and fill in the blanks on the row for CV in the table above. Does the CV produce the same risk rankings as the standard deviation?

e. Suppose you created a 2-stock portfolio by investing $50,000 in High Tech and $50,000 in Collections. (1) Calculate the expected return ($\hat{k}_p$), the standard deviation (σ_p), and the coefficient of variation (CV_p) for this portfolio and fill in the appropriate blanks in the table above. (2) How does the riskiness of this 2-stock portfolio compare to the riskiness of the individual stocks if they were held in isolation?

f. Suppose an investor starts with a portfolio consisting of one randomly selected stock. What would happen (1) to the riskiness and (2) to the expected return of the portfolio as more and more randomly selected stocks were added to the portfolio? What is the implication for investors? Draw two graphs to illustrate your answer.

g. (1) Should portfolio effects impact the way investors think about the riskiness of individual stocks? (2) If you decided to hold a 1-stock portfolio, and consequently were exposed to more risk than diversified investors, could you expect to be compensated for all of your risk; that is, could you earn a risk premium on that part of your risk that you could have eliminated by diversifying?

h. The expected rates of return and the beta coefficients of the alternatives as supplied by Merrill Finch's computer program are as follows:

Security	Return ($\hat{k}$)	Risk (Beta)
High Tech	17.4%	1.29
Market	15.0	1.00
U.S. Rubber	13.8	0.68
T-bills	8.0	0.00
Collections	1.7	(0.86)

(1) What is a beta coefficient, and how are betas used in risk analysis? (2) Do the expected returns appear to be related to each alternative's market risk? (3) Is it possible to choose among the alternatives on the basis of the information developed thus far? Use the data given at the start of the problem to construct a graph which shows how the T-bill's, High Tech's, and Collections's beta coefficients are calculated. Then discuss what betas measure and how they are used in risk analysis.

i. (1) Write out the Security Market Line (SML) equation, use it to calculate the required rate of return on each alternative, and then graph the relationship between the expected and required rates of return. (2) How do the expected rates of return compare with the required rates of return? (3) Does the fact that Collections has an expected return which is less than the T-bill rate make any sense? (4) What would be the market risk and the required return of a 50-50 portfolio of High Tech and Collections? Of High Tech and U.S. Rubber?

j. (1) Suppose investors raised their inflation expectations by 3 percentage points over current estimates as reflected in the 8 percent T-bill rate. What effect would higher inflation have on the SML and on the returns required on high- and low-risk securities? (2) Suppose instead that investors' risk aversion increased enough to cause the market risk premium to increase by 3 percentage points. (Inflation remains constant.) What effect would this have on the SML and on returns of high- and low-risk securities?

COMPUTER-RELATED PROBLEM

Work the problem in this section only if you are using the computer problem diskette.

5-14 Realized rates of return Using the computerized model in the File C5, rework Problem 5-3, assuming that a third stock, Stock C, is available for inclusion in the portfolio. Stock C has the following historical returns:

Year	Stock C's Returns, k_C
1991	32.00%
1992	(11.75)
1993	10.75
1994	32.25
1995	(6.75)

a. Calculate (or read from the computer screen) the average return, standard deviation, and coefficient of variation for Stock C.

b. Assume that the portfolio now consists of 33.33 percent of Stock A, 33.33 percent of Stock B, and 33.33 percent of Stock C. How does this affect the portfolio return, standard deviation, and coefficient of variation versus when 50 percent was invested in A and in B?

c. Make some other changes in the portfolio, making sure that the percentages sum to 100 percent. For example, enter 25 percent for Stock A, 25 percent for Stock B, and 50 percent for Stock C. (Note that the program will not allow you to enter a zero for the percentage in Stock C.) Notice that $\hat{k}_p$ remains constant and that σ_p changes. Why do these results occur?

d. In Problem 5-3, the standard deviation of the portfolio decreased only slightly, because Stocks A and B were highly positively correlated with one another. In this problem, the addition of Stock C causes the standard deviation of the portfolio to decline dramatically, even though $\sigma_C = \sigma_A = \sigma_B$. What does this indicate about the correlation between Stock C and Stocks A and B?

e. Would you prefer to hold the portfolio described in Problem 5-3 consisting only of Stocks A and B or a portfolio that also included Stock C? If others react similarly, how might this affect the stocks' prices and rates of return?

Here the interest rate is 5 percent during the first period, but it rises to 10 percent during the second period. If the interest rate is constant in all periods, we show it only in the first period, but if it changes, we show all the relevant rates on the time line.

Time lines are essential when you are first learning time value concepts, but even experts use them to analyze complex problems. We will be using time lines throughout the book, and you should get into the habit of using them when you work problems.

SELF-TEST QUESTION

Draw a 3-year time line to illustrate the following situation: (1) An outflow of $10,000 occurs at Time 0. (2) Inflows of $5,000 then occur at the end of Years 1, 2, and 3. (3) The interest rate during the three years is 10 percent.

FUTURE VALUE

Compounding
The arithmetic process of determining the final value of a cash flow or series of cash flows when compound interest is applied.

A dollar in hand today is worth more than a dollar to be received in the future because, if you had it now, you could invest it, earn interest, and end up with more than one dollar in the future. The process of going from today's values, or present values (PV), to future values (FV) is called **compounding.** To illustrate, suppose you deposit $100 in a bank that pays 5 percent interest each year. How much would you have at the end of one year? To begin, we define the following terms:

PV = present value, or beginning amount, in your account. Here PV = $100.

i = interest rate the bank pays per year. The interest earned is based on the balance at the beginning of each year, and we assume that it is paid at the end of the year. Here i = 5%, or, expressed as a decimal, i = 0.05. Throughout this chapter, we designate the interest rate as i (or I) because that symbol is used on most financial calculators. Note, though, that in later chapters we use the symbol k to denote interest rates because k is used more often in the financial literature.

INT = dollars of interest you earn during the year = Beginning amount $\times$ i. Here INT = $100(0.05) = $5.

FV_n = future value, or ending amount, in your account at the end of n years. Whereas PV is the value now, or the *present value*, FV_n is the value n years into the *future*, after the interest earned has been added to the account.

n = number of periods involved in the analysis. Here n = 1.

In our example, n = 1, so FV_n can be calculated as follows:

$$FV_n = FV_1 = PV + INT$$
$$= PV + PV(i)$$
$$= PV(1 + i).$$
$$= \$100(1 + 0.05) = \$100(1.05) = \$105.$$

Future Value (FV)

The amount to which a cash flow or series of cash flows will grow over a given period of time when compounded at a given interest rate.

Thus, the **future value (FV)** at the end of one year, FV_1, equals the present value multiplied by 1.0 plus the interest rate, so you will have $105 after one year.

What would you end up with if you left your $100 in the account for five years? Here is a time line set up to show the amount at the end of each year:

	0	1	2	3	4	5
		5%				
Initial deposit:	−100	$FV_1 = ?$	$FV_2 = ?$	$FV_3 = ?$	$FV_4 = ?$	$FV_5 = ?$
Interest earned:		5	5.25	5.51	5.79	6.08
Amount at the end of each period:		105	110.25	115.76	121.55	**127.63**

Note the following points: (1) You start by depositing $100 in the account — this is shown as an outflow at t = 0. (2) You earn $100(0.05) = $5 of interest during the first year, so the amount at the end of Year 1 (or t = 1) is $100 + $5 = $105. (3) You start the second year with $105, earn $5.25 on the now larger amount, and end the second year with $110.25. Your interest during Year 2, $5.25, is higher than the first year's interest because you earned $5(0.05) = $0.25 interest on the first year's interest. (4) This process continues, and because the beginning balance is higher in each succeeding year, the annual interest earned increases. (5) The total interest earned, $27.63, is reflected in the final balance at t = 5, $127.63.

Note that the value at the end of Year 2, $110.25, is equal to

$$FV_2 = FV_1(1 + i)$$
$$= PV(1 + i)(1 + i)$$
$$= PV(1 + i)^2$$
$$= \$100(1.05)^2 = \$110.25.$$

Continuing, the balance at the end of Year 3 is

$$FV_3 = FV_2(1 + i)$$
$$= PV(1 + i)^3$$
$$= \$100(1.05)^3 = \$115.76,$$

and

$$FV_5 = \$100(1.05)^5 = \$127.63.$$

In general, the future value of an initial sum at the end of n years can be found by applying Equation 6-1:

$$FV_n = PV(1 + i)^n. \tag{6-1}$$

Equation 6-1 and most other time value of money equations can be solved in three ways: numerically with a regular calculator, with interest tables, or with a financial calculator.

 NUMERICAL SOLUTION

One can use a regular calculator and either multiply $(1 + i)$ by itself $n - 1$ times or else use the exponential function to raise $(1 + i)$ to the nth power. With most calculators, you would enter $1 + i = 1.05$ and multiply it by itself four times, or

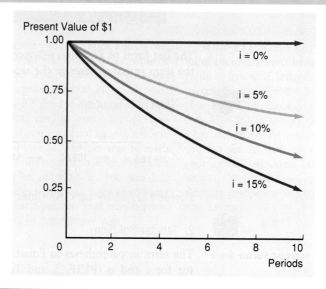

How does the present value of an amount to be received in the future change as the time is extended and as the interest rate increases?

SOLVING FOR TIME AND INTEREST RATES

At this point, you should realize that the compounding and discounting processes are reciprocals of one another, and that we have been dealing with one equation in two different forms:

FV Form:

$$FV_n = PV(1 + i)^n. \tag{6-1}$$

PV Form:

$$PV = \frac{FV_n}{(1 + i)^n}. \tag{6-2}$$

There are four variables in these equations — PV, FV, i, and n — and if you know the values of any three, you (or your financial calculator) can find the value of the fourth. Thus far, we have always given you the interest rate (i) and the number of years (n) plus either the PV or the FV. In many situations, though, you will need to solve for i or n, as we discuss below.

SOLVING FOR i

Suppose you can buy a security for $78.35 which will pay you $100 after 5 years. Here we know PV, FV, and n, but we do not know i, the interest rate you will earn on your investment. Problems such as this are solved as follows:

Time Line:

Equation:

$$FV_n = PV(1 + i)^n \qquad (6\text{-}1)$$

$$\$100 = \$78.35(1 + i)^5. \text{ Solve for i.}$$

1. Numerical Solution:

Go through a trial-and-error process in which you insert different values of i into Equation 6-1 until you find a value which "works" in the sense that the right-hand side of the equation equals $100. The solution value is i = 0.05, or 5 percent. The trial-and-error procedure is extremely tedious and inefficient for most problems, so no one in the "real world" uses it.

2. Tabular Solution:

$$FV_n = PV(1 + i)^n = PV(FVIF_{i,n})$$

$$\$100 = \$78.35(FVIF_{i,5})$$

$$FVIF_{i,5} = \$100/\$78.35 = 1.2763.$$

Now, look across the Period 5 row in Table A-3 until you find FVIF = 1.2763. This value is in the 5% column, so the interest rate at which $78.35 grows to $100 over 5 years is 5 percent. This procedure can be used only if the interest rate is in the table; therefore, it will not work for fractional interest rates or where n is not a whole number. Approximation procedures can be used, but they are laborious and inexact.

3. Financial Calculator Solution:

Enter N = 5, PV = −78.35, PMT = 0, and FV = 100, and then press I to get I = 5%. This procedure can be used for any interest rate or for any value of n, including fractional values.

SOLVING FOR **n**

Suppose you know that a security will provide a return of 5 percent per year, that it will cost $78.35, and that you will receive $100 at maturity, but you do not know when the security matures. Thus, you know PV, FV, and i, but you do not know n, the number of periods. Here is the situation:

Time Line:

0   5%   1   2   ···   n − 1   n = ?
├────────┼────────┼──── ··· ───┼─────────┤
−78.35   100

THE $40 MILLION MAN

If you are a football fan, you've probably heard of Steve Young, the MVP quarterback of the San Francisco 49ers. Young first became famous in 1984, when he graduated from college and signed a contract with the L.A. Express, a team in the now-defunct United States Football League (USFL).

Under the terms of his contract, the Express agreed to pay Young a mind-boggling $40 million. Even in the sports industry, where million dollar contracts are commonplace, the size of Young's contract caught everyone's attention. Why would the Express be willing to pay $40 million to a rookie quarterback who had not yet thrown a pass as a professional?

The time value of money provides most of the answer. Although Young's contract was for four years, the actual payments were spread out over a period of 43 years. Over the first four years, Young was to receive $5.9 million in cash as salary and bonus. Then, starting in 1990, Young's contract called for the commencement of $34.5 million in deferred compensation in the form of a series of rising annuities, beginning with $200,000 per year through 1999 and rising to a final annuity payment of $3.173 million in the year 2027.

Given that the deferred payments were not to be received for several years, the Express was able to provide for the annuities at a cost considerably less than $34.5 million. Overall, the present value of Young's contract was estimated to be worth about $5.5 million — not too shabby, but a far cry from $40 million.

Later on in 1984, Herschel Walker, one of the big stars of the USFL, signed a four-year contract with the New Jersey Generals. While Walker's contract was for "only" $6 million, most of it was paid in up-front money. This led Donald Trump, owner of the Generals, to comment:

> You have to bring the contract down to present value . . . . I know numbers, and if I had my choice between Herschel's contract and Steve Young's contract, I'd take Herschel's.

Less than two years later, the Express and the USFL were struggling, and Young was able to buy out the remaining years of his contract. He signed with the Tampa Bay Buccaneers in the National Football League, and he was later traded to the 49ers. He continues to be well paid, but his current contract is considerably less interesting than his first one.

PERPETUITIES

Perpetuity
A stream of equal payments expected to continue forever.

Most annuities call for payments to be made over some finite period — for example, $100 per year for three years. However, some annuities go on indefinitely, or perpetually, and these annuities are called **perpetuities.** The present value of a perpetuity is found by applying Equation 6-5.[7]

$$\text{PV(Perpetuity)} = \frac{\text{Payment}}{\text{Interest rate}} = \frac{\text{PMT}}{i}. \tag{6-5}$$

Consol
A perpetual bond issued by the British government to consolidate past debts; in general, any perpetual bond.

Perpetuities can be illustrated by some British securities issued after the Napoleonic Wars. In 1815, the British government sold a huge bond issue and used the proceeds to pay off many smaller issues that had been floated in prior years to pay for the wars. Since the purpose of the bonds was to consolidate past debts, the bonds were called **consols.** Suppose each consol promised to pay $100 per year in perpetuity. (Actually, interest was stated in pounds.) What would each bond be worth if the opportunity cost rate, or discount rate, was 5 percent? The answer is $2,000:

$$\text{PV (Perpetuity)} = \frac{\$100}{0.05} = \$2,000 \text{ if } i = 5\%.$$

---

[7]The derivation of Equation 6-5 is given in Appendix 4A of Eugene F. Brigham and Louis C. Gapenski, *Intermediate Financial Management,* 5th ed. (Forth Worth, Tex.: Dryden Press, 1996).

Suppose the interest rate rose to 10 percent; what would happen to the consol's value? The value would drop to $1,000:

$$\text{PV (Perpetuity)} = \frac{\$100}{0.10} = \$1,000 \text{ at i} = 10\%.$$

We see that the value of a perpetuity changes dramatically when interest rates change. Perpetuities are discussed further in Chapter 8.

SELF-TEST QUESTIONS

What happens to the value of a perpetuity when interest rates increase?
What happens when interest rates decrease? Why do these changes occur?

UNEVEN CASH FLOW STREAMS

The definition of an annuity includes the words *constant amount*—in other words, annuities involve payments that are equal in every period. Although many financial decisions do involve constant payments, some important decisions involve uneven, or nonconstant, cash flows; for example, common stocks typically pay an increasing stream of dividends over time, and fixed asset investments such as new equipment normally do not generate constant cash flows. Consequently, it is necessary to extend our time value discussion to include **uneven cash flow streams.**

Uneven Cash Flow Stream
A series of cash flows in which the amount varies from one period to the next.

Throughout the book, we will follow convention and reserve the term **payment (PMT)** for annuity situations where the cash flows are equal amounts, and we will use the term **cash flow (CF)** to denote uneven cash flows. Financial calculators are set up to follow this convention, so if you are using one and dealing with uneven cash flows, you will need to use the cash flow register.

Payment (PMT)
This term designates equal cash flows coming at regular intervals.

Cash Flow (CF)
This term designates uneven cash flows.

PRESENT VALUE OF AN UNEVEN CASH FLOW STREAM

The PV of an uneven cash flow stream is found as the sum of the PVs of the individual cash flows in the stream. For example, suppose we must find the PV of the following cash flow stream, discounted at 6 percent:

0	6%	1	2	3	4	5	6	7
PV = ?		100	200	200	200	200	0	1,000

The PV will be found by applying this general present value equation:

$$PV = CF_1\left(\frac{1}{1+i}\right)^1 + CF_2\left(\frac{1}{1+i}\right)^2 + \cdots + CF_n\left(\frac{1}{1+i}\right)^n$$

$$= \sum_{t=1}^{n} CF_t\left(\frac{1}{1+i}\right)^t = \sum_{t=1}^{n} CF_t(PVIF_{i,t}). \tag{6-6}$$

Simply input the CF values into the cash flow register and then press the IRR key. IRR stands for "internal rate of return," which is the return on an investment. We will defer further discussion of this calculation for now, but we will take it up later, in our discussion of capital budgeting methods in Chapter 10.[8]

SELF-TEST QUESTIONS

Give two examples of financial decisions that would typically involve uneven cash flows.

What is meant by the term "terminal value"?

SEMIANNUAL AND OTHER COMPOUNDING PERIODS

Annual Compounding
The arithmetic process of determining the final value of a cash flow or series of cash flows when interest is added once a year.

Semiannual Compounding
The arithmetic process of determining the final value of a cash flow or series of cash flows when interest is added twice a year.

In all of our examples thus far, we have assumed that interest is compounded once a year, or annually. This is called **annual compounding.** Suppose, however, that you put $100 into a bank which states that it pays a 6 percent annual interest rate but that interest is credited each six months. This is called **semiannual compounding.** How much would you have accumulated at the end of one year, two years, or some other period under semiannual compounding?

To illustrate semiannual compounding, assume that $100 is placed into an account at an interest rate of 6 percent and left there for 3 years. First, consider again what happens under *annual* compounding:

1. Time Line, Equation, and Numerical Solution:

$$
\begin{array}{ccccc}
0 & & 1 & 2 & 3 \\
\vdash & 6\% & \dashv & \dashv & \dashv \\
-100 & & & & FV = ?
\end{array}
$$

$$FV_n = PV(1 + i)^n = \$100(1.06)^3$$

$$= \$119.10.$$

2. Tabular Solution:

$$FV_3 = \$100(FVIF_{6\%,3}) = \$100(1.1910) = \$119.10.$$

3. Financial Calculator Solution:

Inputs:	3	6	−100	0	
	N	**I**	**PV**	**PMT**	**FV**
Output:					= 119.10

However, our bank account pays semiannually, which is more frequent than once a year. Note that virtually all bonds pay interest semiannually, most stocks pay dividends quarterly, and most mortgages, student loans, and auto loans require monthly payments. Therefore, it is essential that you understand how to deal with non-annual compounding.

---

[8]To obtain an IRR solution, at least one of the cash flows must have a negative sign, indicating that it is an investment. Since none of the CFs in our example were negative, the cash flow stream has no IRR. However, had we input a cost for CF_0, say −$1,000, we could have obtained an IRR, which would be the rate of return earned on the $1,000 investment. Here IRR = 13.96%.

Whenever payments occur more frequently than once a year, or if interest is stated to be compounded more than once a year, then you must convert the stated interest rate to a "periodic rate" and the number of years to "number of periods," as follows:

Periodic rate = Stated rate/Number of payments per year.

Number of periods = Number of years × Periods per year.

In our example, where we must find the value of $100 after 3 years when the stated interest rate is 6 percent, compounded semiannually (or twice a year), you would begin by making the following conversion:

Periodic rate = 6%/2 = 3%.

Periods = N = 3 × 2 = 6.

In this situation, the investment will earn 3 percent every 6 months over 6 periods, not 6 percent per year for 3 years. As we shall see, there is a significant difference between these two procedures.

You should make the conversions as your first step when working on such a problem *because calculations must be done using number of periods and the periodic rate, not the number of years and the stated rate.* Periodic rates and number of periods, not yearly rates and number of years, should normally be shown on time lines and entered into your calculator whenever you are dealing with anything other than one payment per year (or annual compounding).[9]

With that background, we can now find the value of $100 after 3 years if it is held in an account that pays a stated rate of 6 percent, semiannual compounding. Here is the time line:

Time Line:

 1. Equation and Numerical Solution:

$$FV_n = PV(1 + i)^n = \$100(1.03)^6$$
$$= \$100(1.1941) = \$119.41.$$

Here i = rate per period = annual rate/compounding periods per year = 6%/2 = 3%, and n = the total number of periods = years × periods per year = 3 × 2 = 6.

 2. Tabular Solution:

$$FV_6 = \$100(FVIF_{3\%,6}) = \$100(1.1941) = \$119.41.$$

Look up FVIF for 3%, 6 periods in Table A-3 and complete the arithmetic.

---

[9]With some financial calculators, you can enter the annual (nominal) rate and the number of compounding periods rather than make the conversion we recommend. We prefer making the conversion because it is easier to see the setup of the problem in a time line, and also because it is easy to forget to readjust your calculator after working a problem and to then make an error on the next problem because of an incorrect calculator setting.

3. Financial Calculator Solution:

Inputs:	6	3	−100	0	
	N	**I**	**PV**	**PMT**	**FV**
Output:					= 119.41

Enter N = Years × Periods per year = 3 × 2 = 6, I = Annual rate/Periods per year = 6/2 = 3, PV = −100, and PMT = 0. Then press FV to find the answer, $119.41 versus $119.10 under annual compounding. The FV is larger under semi-annual compounding because interest on interest is being earned more frequently.

Throughout the world economy, different compounding periods are used for different types of investments. For example, bank accounts generally pay interest daily; most bonds pay interest semiannually; and stocks generally pay dividends quarterly.[10] If we are to properly compare securities with different compounding periods, we need to put them on a common basis. This requires us to distinguish between **nominal, or quoted, interest rates** and **effective, or equivalent, annual rates.**[11]

The nominal, or quoted, or stated, interest rate in our example is 6 percent. *The effective (or equivalent) annual rate (EAR, also called EFF%) is defined as that rate which would produce the same ending (future) value if annual compounding had been used.* In our example, the effective annual rate is the once-a-year rate which would produce an FV of $119.41 at the end of Year 3.

We can determine the effective annual rate, given the nominal rate and the number of compounding periods per year, by solving this equation:

$$\text{Effective annual rate} = \text{EAR (or EFF\%)} = \left(1 + \frac{i_{Nom}}{m}\right)^m - 1.0. \quad \textbf{(6-8)}$$

Here i_{Nom} is the nominal, or quoted, interest rate, and m is the number of compounding periods per year. For example, to find the effective annual rate if the nominal rate is 6 percent and semiannual compounding is used, we have[12]

$$\text{Effective annual rate} = \text{EAR (or EFF\%)} = \left(1 + \frac{0.06}{2}\right)^2 - 1.0$$

$$= (1.03)^2 - 1.0$$

$$= 1.0609 - 1.0 = 0.0609 = 6.09\%.$$

The points made about semiannual compounding can be generalized as follows. When compounding occurs more frequently than once a year, we can use a modified version of Equation 6-1 to find the future value of any lump sum:

$$\text{Annual compounding: } FV_n = PV(1 + i)^n. \quad \textbf{(6-1)}$$

$$\text{More frequent compounding: } FV_n = PV\left(1 + \frac{i_{Nom}}{m}\right)^{mn}. \quad \textbf{(6-9)}$$

---

[10]Some banks and savings and loans even pay interest compounded *continuously.* Continuous compounding is discussed in Appendix 6A.

[11]The term *nominal rate* as it is used here has a different meaning than the way it was used in Chapter 4. There, nominal interest rates referred to stated market rates as opposed to real (zero inflation) rates. In this chapter, the term *nominal rate* means the stated, or quoted, annual rate as opposed to the effective annual rate. In both cases, though, *nominal* means *stated,* or *quoted,* as opposed to some adjusted rate.

[12]Most financial calculators are programmed to find the EAR or, given the EAR, to find the nominal rate. This is called "interest rate conversion," and you simply enter the nominal rate and the number of compounding periods per year and then press the EFF% key to find the effective annual rate.

Nominal (Quoted, or Stated) Interest Rate
The contracted, or quoted, or stated, interest rate.

Effective (or Equivalent) Annual Rate (EAR or EFF%)
The annual rate of interest actually being earned, as opposed to the quoted rate. Also called the "equivalent annual rate."

Here i_{Nom} is the nominal, or quoted, rate, m is the number of times compounding occurs per year, and n is the number of years. For example, when banks pay daily interest, the value of m is set at 365 and Equation 6-9 is applied.[13]

To illustrate further the effects of compounding more frequently than annually, consider the interest rate charged on credit cards. Many banks charge 1.5 percent per month, and, in their advertising, they state that the **Annual Percentage Rate (APR)** is $1.5 \times 12 = 18.0$ percent. However, the "true" rate is the effective annual rate of 19.6 percent:[14]

Annual Percentage Rate (APR)
The periodic rate × the number of periods per year.

$$\text{Effective annual rate} = \text{EAR (or EFF\%)} = \left(1 + \frac{0.18}{12}\right)^{12} - 1$$

$$= (1.015)^{12} - 1.0$$

$$= 0.196 = 19.6\%.$$

Semiannual and other compounding periods can also be used for discounting, and for both lump sums and annuities. First, consider the case where we want to find the PV of an ordinary annuity of $100 per year for 3 years when the interest rate is 8 percent, compounded annually:

Time Line:

```
        0   8%   1        2        3
        +---------+--------+--------+
PV = ?       100      100      100
```

1. Numerical Solution:

Find the PV of each cash flow and sum them. The PV of the annuity is $257.71.

2. Tabular Solution:

$$\text{PVA}_n = \text{PMT}(\text{PVIFA}_{i,n})$$
$$= \$100(\text{PVIFA}_{8\%,3}) = \$100(2.5771) = \$257.71.$$

3. Financial Calculator Solution:

Inputs:	3	8		100	0
	N	**I**	**PV**	**PMT**	**FV**
Output:			= −257.71		

---

[13]To illustrate, the future value of $1 invested at 10 percent for 1 year under daily compounding is $1.1052:

$$\text{FV}_n = \$1\left(1 + \frac{0.10}{365}\right)^{365(1)} = \$1(1.105156) = \$1.1052.$$

Note also that banks sometimes use 360 as the number of days per year for this and other calculations.

[14]The *annual percentage rate (APR)* is the rate used in bank loan advertisements since it meets the requirements contained in "truth in lending" laws. Typically, the APR is defined as (Periodic rate)(Number of periods in one year), which also equals the nominal rate. For example, the APR on a credit card with interest charges of 1.5 percent per month is 1.5%(12) = 18.0%. The APR understates the effective annual rate, so banks tend to use the APR when advertising what they charge on loans. However, they often use the EAR when advertising rates on savings accounts and certificates of deposit because they want to make their deposit rates look high. This switch is somewhat sneaky, but legal.

Now, let's change the situation to one where the annuity calls for payments of $50 each 6 months rather than $100 per year, and the rate is 8 percent, compounded semiannually. Here is the time line:

Time Line:

```
0           1       2       3       4       5       6 6-month periods
|----4%-----|-------|-------|-------|-------|-------|
PV = ?     50      50      50      50      50      50
```

1. Numerical Solution:

Find the PV of each cash flow by discounting at 4 percent. Treat each tick mark on the time line as a period, so there would be 6 periods. The PV of the annuity is $262.11 versus $257.71 under annual compounding.

2. Tabular Solution:

$$PVA_n = PMT(PVIFA_{i,n})$$
$$= \$50(PVIFA_{4\%,6}) = \$50(5.2421) = \$262.11.$$

3. Financial Calculator Solution:

Inputs:	6	4		50	0
	N	**I**	**PV**	**PMT**	**FV**

Output: = −262.11

The semiannual payments come in sooner, so the $50 semiannual annuity is more valuable than the $100 annual annuity.

SELF-TEST QUESTIONS

What changes must you make in your calculations to determine the future value of an amount that is being compounded at 8 percent semiannually versus one being compounded annually at 8 percent?

Why is semiannual compounding better than annual compounding from a saver's standpoint?

Define the terms "annual percentage rate," "effective (or equivalent) annual rate," and "nominal interest rate."

How does the term "nominal rate" as used in this chapter differ from the term as it was used in Chapter 4?

COMPARISON OF DIFFERENT TYPES OF INTEREST RATES

People in finance often work with three types of interest rates: nominal rates, i_{Nom}; periodic rates, i_{PER}; and effective annual rates, EAR or EFF%. Therefore, it is essential that you understand what each one is and when it should be used.

1. **Nominal, or quoted, rate.** This is the rate that is quoted by borrowers and lenders. Practitioners in the stock, bond, mortgage, commercial loan, consumer loan, banking, and other markets express all financial contracts in terms of nominal rates. So, if you talk with a banker, broker, mortgage

lender, auto finance company, or student loan officer about rates, the nominal rate is the one he or she will normally quote you. However, to be meaningful, the quoted nominal rate must also include the number of compounding periods per year. For example, a bank might offer 8.5 percent, compounded quarterly, on CDs, or a mutual fund might offer 8 percent, compounded monthly, on its money market account.

Nominal rates can be compared with one another, *but only if the instruments being compared use the same number of compounding periods per year.* Thus, you could compare the quoted yields on two bonds if they both pay interest semiannually. However, to compare an 8.5 percent, annual payment CD with an 8 percent, daily payment money market fund, we would need to put both instruments on an *effective (or equivalent) annual rate (EAR)* basis as discussed later in this section.

Note again that the nominal rate is never shown on a time line, and it is never used as an input in a financial calculator (unless compounding occurs only once a year, in which case i_{Nom} = periodic rate = EAR). If more frequent compounding occurs, you should generally use the periodic rate as discussed below.

2. **Periodic rate, i_{PER}.** This is the rate charged by a lender or paid by a borrower each period. It can be a rate per year, per 6-month period, per quarter, per month, per day, or per any other time interval (usually one year or less). For example, a bank might charge 1.5 percent per month on its credit card loans, or a finance company might charge 3 percent per quarter on consumer loans. We find the periodic rate as follows:

$$\text{Periodic rate, } i_{PER} = i_{Nom}/m, \tag{6-10}$$

which implies that

$$\text{Nominal annual rate} = i_{Nom} = (\text{Periodic rate})(m). \tag{6-11}$$

Here i_{Nom} is the nominal annual rate and m is the number of compounding periods per year. To illustrate, consider a finance company loan at 3 percent per quarter:

$$\text{Nominal annual rate} = i_{Nom} = (\text{Periodic rate})(m) = (3\%)(4) = 12\%,$$

or

$$\text{Periodic rate} = i_{Nom}/m = 12\%/4 = 3\% \text{ per quarter.}$$

If there is one payment per year, or if interest is added only once a year, then m = 1, and the periodic rate is equal to the nominal rate.

The periodic rate is the rate which is generally shown on time lines and used in calculations. The only exception is in situations where (1) annuities are involved and (2) the payment periods do not correspond to the compounding periods.[15] To illustrate use of the periodic rate, suppose you make

---

[15]If an annuity is involved, and if its payment periods do not correspond to the compounding periods — for example, if you are making quarterly payments into a bank account to build up a specified future sum, but the bank pays interest on a daily basis — then the calculations are more complicated. For such problems, one can proceed in two alternative ways. (1) Determine the periodic (daily) interest rate by dividing the nominal rate by 360 (or 365 if the bank uses a 365-day year), then compound each payment over the exact number of days from the payment date to the terminal point, and then sum the compounded payments to find the future value of the annuity. This is what would generally be done in the real world. Using a computer, it would be a simple process. (2) Calculate the EAR based on daily compounding, then find the corresponding nominal rate based on quarterly compounding (because the annuity payments are made quarterly), then find the quarterly periodic rate, and then use that rate with standard annuity procedures. The second procedure is faster with a calculator, but hard to explain and generally not used in practice given the ready availability of computers.

the following 8 quarterly payments of $100 each into an account which pays 12 percent, compounded quarterly. How much would you have after two years?

Time Line and Equation:

$$FVA_n = \sum_{t=1}^{n} PMT(1 + i)^{n-t} = \sum_{t=1}^{8} \$100(1.03)^{8-t}.$$

1. Numerical Solution:

Compound each $100 payment at 12/4 = 3 percent for the appropriate number of periods, and then sum these individual FVs to find the FV of the payment stream, $889.23.

2. Tabular Solution:

Look up FVIFA for 3%, 8 periods, in Table A-4, and complete the arithmetic:

$$FVA_n = PMT(FVIFA_{i,n})$$
$$= \$100(FVIFA_{3\%,8}) = \$100(8.8923) = \$889.23.$$

3. Financial Calculator Solution:

Inputs:	8	3	0	−100	
	N	**I**	**PV**	**PMT**	**FV**
Output:					= 889.23

Input N = 2 × 4 = 8, I = 12/4 = 3, PV = 0, and PMT = −100, and then press the FV key to get FV = $889.23.

3. **Effective (or equivalent) annual rate (EAR).** This is the annual rate which produces the same result as if we had compounded at a given periodic rate m times per year. The EAR is found as follows:

$$EAR \text{ (or EFF\%)} = \left(1 + \frac{i_{Nom}}{m}\right)^m - 1.0. \qquad \textbf{(6-8)}$$

You could also use the interest conversion feature of a financial calculator.

In the EAR equation, i_{Nom}/m is the periodic rate, and m is the number of periods per year. For example, suppose you could borrow using either a credit card which charges 1 percent per month or a bank loan with a 12 percent quoted nominal interest rate that is compounded quarterly. Which should you choose? To answer this question, the cost rate of each alternative must be expressed as an EAR:

$$\text{Credit card loan: EAR} = (1 + 0.01)^{12} - 1.0 = (1.01)^{12} - 1.0$$

$$= 1.126825 - 1.0 = 0.126825 = 12.6825\%.$$

$$\text{Bank loan: EAR} = (1 + 0.03)^{4} - 1.0 = (1.03)^{4} - 1.0$$

$$= 1.125509 - 1.0 = 0.125509 = 12.5509\%.$$

Thus, the credit card loan is slightly more costly than the bank loan. This result should have been intuitive to you — both loans have the same 12 percent nominal rate, yet you would have to make monthly payments on the credit card versus quarterly payments under the bank loan.

The EAR rate generally is not used in calculations. Rather, it is used to compare the effective cost or rate of return on loans or investments when payment periods differ, as in the credit card versus bank loan example.

SELF-TEST QUESTIONS

Define the nominal (or quoted) rate, the periodic rate, and the effective annual rate.

How are the nominal rate, the periodic rate, and the effective annual rate related? Name the one situation where all three of these rates will be the same.

Which rate should generally be shown on time lines and used in calculations?

FRACTIONAL TIME PERIODS[16]

In all the examples used thus far in the chapter, we have assumed that payments occur at either the beginning or the end of periods, but not at some date *within* a period. However, sometimes fractional periods are involved. For example, suppose you deposited $100 in a bank that pays 10 percent interest, compounded annually. How much would be in your account after 9 months, or 0.75 percent of the way through the year? The answer is $100; since interest is added only at the end of the year, no interest would have been added after only 9 months. Years ago, before computers made daily compounding easy, banks really did compound interest annually, but today they generally credit interest daily.

Now let's ask a different question: If a bank adds interest to your account daily, that is, uses daily compounding, and the nominal rate is 10 percent with a 360-day year, how much will be in your account after 9 months? The answer is $107.79:[17]

$$\text{Periodic rate} = i_{PER} = 0.10/360 = 0.00027778 \text{ per day.}$$

$$\text{Number of days} = 0.75(360) = 270.$$

$$\text{Ending amount} = \$100(1.00027778)^{270} = \$107.79.$$

---

[16]This section is relatively technical, and it can be omitted without loss of continuity.

[17]Here we assumed a 360-day year, and we also assumed that the 9 months all have 30 days. In real-world calculations, the bank's computer (and many financial calculators) would have a built-in calendar, and if you input the beginning and ending dates, the computer or calculator would tell you the exact number of days, taking account of 30-day months, 31-day months, and 28- or 29-day months. See Footnote 15.

6-7 Effective rate of interest Find the interest rates, or rates of return, on each of the following:
   a. You *borrow* $700 and promise to pay back $749 at the end of 1 year.
   b. You *lend* $700 and receive a promise to be paid $749 at the end of 1 year.
   c. You borrow $85,000 and promise to pay back $201,229 at the end of 10 years.
   d. You borrow $9,000 and promise to make payments of $2,684.80 per year for 5 years.

6-8 Future value for various compounding periods Find the amount to which $500 will grow under each of the following conditions:
   a. 12 percent compounded annually for 5 years.
   b. 12 percent compounded semiannually for 5 years.
   c. 12 percent compounded quarterly for 5 years.
   d. 12 percent compounded monthly for 5 years.

6-9 Present value for various compounding periods Find the present value of $500 due in the future under each of the following conditions:
   a. 12 percent nominal rate, semiannual compounding, discounted back 5 years.
   b. 12 percent nominal rate, quarterly compounding, discounted back 5 years.
   c. 12 percent nominal rate, monthly compounding, discounted back 1 year.

6-10 Future value of an annuity for various compounding periods Find the future values of the following ordinary annuities:
   a. FV of $400 each 6 months for 5 years at a nominal rate of 12 percent, compounded semiannually.
   b. FV of $200 each 3 months for 5 years at a nominal rate of 12 percent, compounded quarterly.
   c. The annuities described in Parts a and b have the same amount of money paid into them during the 5-year period, and both earn interest at the same nominal rate, yet the annuity in Part b earns $101.60 more than the one in Part a over the 5 years. Why does this occur?

6-11 Effective versus nominal interest rates The First City Bank pays 7 percent interest, compounded annually, on time deposits. The Second City Bank pays 6 percent interest, compounded quarterly.
   a. Based on effective, or equivalent, interest rates, in which bank would you prefer to deposit your money?
   b. Could your choice of banks be influenced by the fact that you might want to withdraw your funds during the year as opposed to at the end of the year? In answering this question, assume that funds must be left on deposit during the entire compounding period in order for you to receive any interest.

6-12 Amortization schedule
   a. Set up an amortization schedule for a $25,000 loan to be repaid in equal installments at the end of each of the next 5 years. The interest rate is 10 percent, compounded annually.
   b. How large must each annual payment be if the loan is for $50,000? Assume that the interest rate remains at 10 percent, compounded annually, and that the loan is paid off over 5 years.
   c. How large must each payment be if the loan is for $50,000, the interest rate is 10 percent, compounded annually, and the loan is paid off in equal installments at the end of each of the next 10 years? This loan is for the same amount as the loan in Part b, but the payments are spread out over twice as many periods. Why are these payments not half as large as the payments on the loan in Part b?

6-13 Effective rates of return Assume that AT&T's pension fund managers are considering two alternative securities as investments: (1) Security Z (for zero intermediate year cash flows), which costs $422.41 today, pays nothing during its 10-year life, and then pays $1,000 after 10 years or (2) Security B, which has a cost today of $1,000 and which pays $80 at the end of each of the next 9 years and then $1,080 at the end of Year 10.
   a. What is the rate of return on each security?
   b. Assume that the interest rate AT&T's pension fund managers can earn on the fund's money falls to 6 percent, compounded annually, immediately after the securities are purchased and is expected to remain at that level for the next 10 years. What would the price of each security change to, what would the fund's profit be on each security, and what would be the percentage profit (profit divided by cost) for each security?
   c. Assuming that the cash flows for each security had to be reinvested at the new 6 percent market interest rate, (1) what would be the value attributable to each security at the end of 10 years and (2) what "actual, after-the-fact" rate of return would the fund have earned on each security? (Hint: The "actual" rate of return is found as the interest rate which causes the PV of the compounded Year 10 amount to equal the original cost of the security.)
   d. Now assume all the facts as given in Parts b and c, except assume that the interest rate *rose* to 12 percent rather than fell to 6 percent. What would happen to the profit figures as developed in Part b and to the "actual" rates of return as determined in Part c? Explain your results.

6-14 Required annuity payments A father is planning a savings program to put his daughter through college. His daughter is now 13 years old. She plans to enroll at the university in 5 years, and it should take her 4 years to complete her education. Currently, the cost per year (for everything — food, clothing, tuition, books, transportation, and so forth) is $12,500, but a 5 percent annual inflation rate in these costs is forecasted. The daughter recently received $7,500 from her grandfather's estate; this money, which is invested in a bank account paying 8 percent interest compounded annually, will be used to help meet the costs of the daughter's education. The rest of the costs will be met by money the father will deposit in the savings account. He will make 6 equal deposits to the account, one deposit in each year from now until his daughter starts college. These deposits will begin today and will also earn 8 percent interest, compounded annually.

a. What will be the present value of the cost of 4 years of education at the time the daughter becomes 18? [Hint: Calculate the future value of the cost (at 5%) for each year of her education, then discount 3 of these costs back (at 8%) to the year in which she turns 18, then sum the 4 costs.]

b. What will be the value of the $7,500 which the daughter received from her grandfather's estate when she starts college at age 18? (Hint: Compound for 5 years at an 8 percent annual rate.)

c. If the father is planning to make the first of 6 deposits today, how large must each deposit be for him to be able to put his daughter through college? (Hint: An annuity due assumes interest is earned on all deposits; however, the 6th deposit earns no interest — therefore, the deposits are an ordinary annuity.)

EXAM-TYPE PROBLEMS

The problems included in this section are set up in such a way that they could be used as multiple-choice exam problems.

6-15 Present value comparison Which amount is worth more at 14 percent, compounded annually: $1,000 in hand today or $2,000 due in 6 years?

6-16 Growth rates Shalit Corporation's 1995 sales were $12 million. Sales were $6 million 5 years earlier (in 1990).

a. To the nearest percentage point, at what rate have sales been growing?

b. Suppose someone calculated the sales growth for Shalit Corporation in Part a as follows: "Sales doubled in 5 years. This represents a growth of 100 percent in 5 years, so, dividing 100 percent by 5, we find the growth rate to be 20 percent per year." Explain what is wrong with this calculation.

6-17 Expected rate of return Washington-Atlantic invests $4 million to clear a tract of land and to set out some young pine trees. The trees will mature in 10 years, at which time Washington-Atlantic plans to sell the forest at an expected price of $8 million. What is Washington-Atlantic's expected rate of return?

6-18 Effective rate of interest Your broker offers to sell you a note for $13,250 that will pay $2,345.05 per year for 10 years. If you buy the note, what rate of interest (to the closest percent) will you be earning?

6-19 Effective rate of interest A mortgage company offers to lend you $85,000; the loan calls for payments of $8,273.59 per year for 30 years. What interest rate is the mortgage company charging you?

6-20 Required lump sum payment To complete your last year in business school and then go through law school, you will need $10,000 per year for 4 years, starting next year (that is, you will need to withdraw the first $10,000 one year from today). Your rich uncle offers to put you through school, and he will deposit in a bank paying 7 percent interest, compounded annually, a sum of money that is sufficient to provide the 4 payments of $10,000 each. His deposit will be made today.

a. How large must the deposit be?

b. How much will be in the account immediately after you make the first withdrawal? After the last withdrawal?

6-21 Repaying a loan While you were a student in college, you borrowed $12,000 in student loans at an interest rate of 9 percent, compounded annually. If you repay $1,500 per year, how long, to the nearest year, will it take you to repay the loan?

6-22 Reaching a financial goal You need to accumulate $10,000. To do so, you plan to make deposits of $1,250 per year, with the first payment being made a year from today, in a bank account which pays 12 percent interest, compounded annually. Your last deposit will be less than $1,250 if less is needed to round out to $10,000. How many years will it take you to reach your $10,000 goal, and how large will the last deposit be?

6-23 Present value of a perpetuity What is the present value of a perpetuity of $100 per year if the appropriate discount rate is 7 percent? If interest rates in general were to double and the appropriate discount rate rose to 14 percent, what would happen to the present value of the perpetuity?

6-24 Financial calculator needed; PV and effective annual rate Assume that you inherited some money. A friend of yours is working as an unpaid intern at a local brokerage firm, and her boss is selling some securities which call for 4 payments, $50 at the end of each of the next 3 years, plus a payment of $1,050 at the end of Year 4. Your friend says she can get you some of these securities at a cost of $900 each. Your money is now invested in a bank that pays an 8 percent nominal (quoted) interest rate, but with quarterly compounding. You regard the securities as being just as safe, and as liquid, as your bank deposit, so your required effective annual rate of return on the securities is the same as that on your bank deposit. You must calculate the value of the securities to decide whether they are a good investment. What is their present value to you?

7   Bonds and Their Valuation

Interest rates plunged in 1993, and corporate borrowers were scrambling to lock in low rates by selling long-term bonds. The outer limit for most long-term bonds had been 40 years — investors were unwilling to assume that companies could repay debts due farther in the future, so maturities had to be limited to 40 years to avoid excessive risk premiums.

When interest rates took this nosedive, investors found their old, high-yielding bonds maturing and being called, and they were forced to reinvest their money at new, much lower interest rates. Investors' incomes then plunged — this held true for individual retirees, insurance companies, and pension funds, all of whom invest heavily in the bond market.

How can investors protect themselves against a drop in rates? And how can a corporate borrower lock in a low rate and thus be protected against a later rise in interest rates? The answer, in both cases, is to use longer-term bonds.

Recognizing all this, a large pension fund approached Morgan Stanley & Co., a leading investment banking firm, and asked about the availability of extremely long-term bonds.

This fund wanted to lengthen the average maturity of its portfolio, and 100-year bonds would do the trick. However, almost no 100-year bonds existed; two railroads had sold such bonds in the past, but the dollar amounts of the issues were too small to make much difference to a large fund. Morgan Stanley seized the opportunity and immediately began to call clients who might be interested in selling long-term bonds to lock in the low current rates. Within a week, Disney had agreed to sell $150 million worth of 7.5 percent, 100-year bonds, buyers were clamoring for them, and the offering "flew out the window."

Reaction to the Disney issue has been mixed. The quick sellout is clear evidence that at least some investors liked them, but others have their doubts. According to Glenn Murphy, chief investment officer of Travelers Asset Management, the Disney issue will ultimately be a "historic artifact, a curiosity." And William Gross, head of fixed income investment at Pacific Investment Management, noting the ups and downs of entertainment companies, stated, "It's crazy. Look at the path of Coney Island over the last 50

years and see what happens to amusement parks."

Even if Disney continues to do well and pays interest and principal as they come due, the "100s" could still produce headaches for investors. A relatively small 1 percent increase in interest rates would cause the value of the Disney bonds to fall from the $1,000 offering price to $884, and if long-term interest rates return to the level they were 10 years ago, the bond's value would drop to just $538.

If you had some extra money, would you be willing to invest in Disney's bonds? How might the terms on the Disney bonds affect the company's stock price? If you were running a business and needed debt capital, would Disney's decision to use 100-year debt affect the way you thought about financing your own company? When you finish this chapter, you should at least know how to think about these issues.

Sources: "Disney Amazes Investors with Sale of 100-Year Bonds," The Wall Street Journal, July 21, 1993, C1; and "T-Bill Trauma and the Meaning of Risk," The Wall Street Journal, February 12, 1993, C1.

Bonds are one of the most important types of securities to investors, and a major source of financing for corporations and governments. If you skim through *The Wall Street Journal,* you will see a wide variety of bonds. This variety may seem confusing, but there are actually just a few characteristics which distinguish the various types of bonds. Also, you should note that all bonds can be valued using the principles discussed in Chapter 6.

While bonds are often viewed as relatively safe investments, they can actually be quite risky. Indeed, "riskless" long-term U.S. Treasury bonds declined by more than 20 percent during 1994, and "safe" Mexican government bonds declined by 25 percent in just one day, December 27, 1994. Investors who had regarded bonds as being riskless, or at least fairly safe, learned a sad lesson. In this chapter we will discuss the types of bonds companies and government agencies issue, the kinds of terms that are contained in bond contracts, and the types of risks to which both bond investors and issuers are exposed.

WHO ISSUES BONDS?

Bond
A long-term debt instrument.

A **bond** is a long-term contract under which a borrower agrees to make payments of interest and principal, on specific dates, to the holders of the bond. For example, on January 2, 1996, Allied Food Products borrowed $50 million by selling 50,000 individual bonds for $1,000 each. Allied received the $50 million, and in exchange it promised to make annual interest payments and to repay the $50 million on a specified maturity date.

As noted previously, investors have several choices when investing in bonds, but they are classified into four main types: Treasury, corporate, municipal, and foreign. Each type differs with respect to level of return and degree of risk.

Treasury Bonds
Bonds issued by the federal government, sometimes referred to as government bonds.

Treasury bonds, sometimes referred to as government bonds, are issued by the federal government.[1] It is reasonable to assume that the federal government will make good on its promised payments, so these bonds have no default risk. However, as many investors learned in 1994, Treasury bonds are not free of all risks.

Corporate Bonds
Bonds issued by corporations.

Corporate bonds, as the name implies, are issued by corporations. Unlike Treasury bonds, corporate bonds are exposed to default risk — if the issuing company gets into trouble, it may be unable to make the promised payments on its bonds. Different corporate bonds have different levels of default risk, depending on the issuing company's characteristics and on the terms of the specific bond. Default risk is often referred to as "credit risk," and, as we saw in Chapter 4, the larger the default or credit risk, the higher the interest rate the issuer must pay.

Municipal Bonds
Bonds issued by state and local governments.

Municipal bonds, or "munis," are issued by state and local governments. Like corporate bonds, munis have default risk. However, munis offer one major advantage over all other bonds: As we discussed in Chapter 2, the interest earned on most municipal bonds is exempt from federal taxes, and also from state taxes if the holder is a resident of the issuing state. Consequently, municipal bonds carry interest rates that are considerably lower than those on corporate bonds with the same default risk.

Foreign Bonds
Bonds issued by either foreign governments or foreign corporations.

Foreign bonds are issued by foreign governments or foreign corporations. Foreign corporate bonds are, of course, exposed to default risk, and so are some for-

[1]The U.S. Treasury actually calls its debt issues "bills," "notes," or "bonds." T-bills generally have maturities of 1 year or less at the time of issue, notes generally have original maturities of 2 to 7 years, and bond maturities extend out to 30 years. There are technical differences between bills, notes, and bonds, but they are not important for our purposes, so we generally call all Treasury securities "bonds." Note too that a 30-year T-bond at the time of issue becomes a 1-year bond 29 years later.

set equal to one year's interest if the bonds are called during the first year, and the premium declines at a constant rate of INT/N each year thereafter, where INT = annual interest and N = original maturity in years. For example, the call premium on a $1,000 par value, 10-year, 10 percent bond would generally be $100 if it were called during the first year, $90 during the second year (calculated by reducing the $100, or 10 percent, premium by one-tenth), and so on. However, bonds are often not callable until several years (generally 5 to 10) after they were issued. This is known as a *deferred call,* and the bonds are said to have *call protection.*

Suppose a company sold bonds when interest rates were relatively high. Provided the issue is callable, the company could sell a new issue of low-yielding securities if and when interest rates drop. It could then use the proceeds to retire the high-rate issue and thus reduce its interest expense. This process is called a *refunding operation,* and it is discussed in greater detail in Appendix 11B.

The call privilege is valuable to the firm but potentially detrimental to the investor, especially if the bonds were issued in a period when interest rates were cyclically high. Accordingly, the interest rate on a new issue of callable bonds will exceed that on a new issue of noncallable bonds. For example, on May 2, 1995, Pacific Timber Company sold a bond issue yielding 9.5 percent; these bonds were callable immediately. On the same day, Northwest Milling Company sold an issue of similar risk and maturity which yielded 9.2 percent; its bonds were noncallable for 10 years. Investors were apparently willing to accept a 0.3 percent lower interest rate on Northwest's bonds for the assurance that the 9.2 percent rate of interest would be earned for at least 10 years. Pacific, on the other hand, had to incur a 0.3 percent higher annual interest rate to obtain the option of calling the bonds in the event of a subsequent decline in interest rates.

SINKING FUNDS

Sinking Fund Provision
A provision in a bond contract that requires the issuer to retire a portion of the bond issue each year.

Some corporate bonds also include a **sinking fund provision** that facilitates the orderly retirement of the bond issue. Typically, the sinking fund provision requires the firm to retire a portion of the bond issue each year. On rare occasions the firm may be required to deposit money with a trustee, which invests the funds and then uses the accumulated sum to retire the bonds when they mature. Usually, though, the sinking fund is used to buy back a certain percentage of the issue each year. A failure to meet the sinking fund requirement causes the bond issue to be thrown into default, which may force the company into bankruptcy. Obviously, a sinking fund can constitute a dangerous cash drain on the firm.

In most cases, the firm is given the right to handle the sinking fund in either of two ways:

1. The company can call in for redemption (at par value) a certain percentage of the bonds each year; for example, it might be able to call 2 percent of the total original amount of the issue at a price of $1,000 per bond. The bonds are numbered serially, and those called for redemption are determined by a lottery administered by the trustee.

2. The company may buy the required amount of bonds on the open market.

The firm will choose the least-cost method. If interest rates have risen, causing bond prices to fall, it will buy bonds in the open market at a discount; if interest rates have fallen, it will call the bonds. Note that a call for sinking fund purposes is quite different from a refunding call as discussed above. A sinking fund call typically has a lower call premium,[5] but only a small percentage of the issue is normally callable in any one year.

Although sinking funds are designed to protect bondholders by ensuring that an issue is retired in an orderly fashion, it must be recognized that sinking funds will at times work to the detriment of bondholders. For example, suppose the bond carries a 10 percent interest rate, but yields on similar bonds have fallen to 7.5 percent. A sinking fund call at par would require an investor to give up $100 of interest and then to reinvest in a bond that pays only $75 per year. This obviously disadvantages those bondholders whose bonds are called. On balance, however, bonds that provide for a sinking fund are regarded as being safer than those without such a provision, so at the time they are issued sinking fund bonds have lower coupon rates than otherwise similar bonds without sinking funds.

OTHER FEATURES

Several other types of bonds are used sufficiently often to warrant mention. First, **convertible bonds** are securities that are convertible into shares of common stock, at a fixed price, at the option of the bondholder. Convertibles have a lower coupon rate than nonconvertible debt, but they offer investors a chance for capital gains in exchange for the lower coupon rate. Bonds issued with **warrants** are similar to convertibles. Warrants are options which permit the holder to buy stock for a stated price, thereby providing a capital gain if the price of the stock rises. Bonds that are issued with warrants, like convertibles, carry lower coupon rates than straight bonds. **Income bonds** pay interest only if the interest is earned. Thus, these securities cannot bankrupt a company, but from an investor's standpoint they are riskier than "regular" bonds.

Another type of bond that has been discussed in the United States but is not yet used here to any extent is the **indexed,** or **purchasing power, bond,** which is popular in Brazil, Israel, and a few other countries plagued by high rates of inflation, and also in Great Britain. The interest rate paid on these bonds is based on an inflation index such as the consumer price index, so the interest paid rises automatically when the inflation rate rises, thus protecting the bondholders against inflation. The British bonds' interest rate is set equal to the British inflation rate plus 3 percent. Thus, these bonds provide a "real return" of 3 percent. Also, Mexico used bonds whose interest rate is pegged to the price of oil to finance the development of its huge petroleum reserves; since oil prices and inflation are correlated, these bonds offer some protection to investors against inflation.

Convertible Bond
A bond that is exchangeable, at the option of the holder, for common stock of the issuing firm.

Warrant
A long-term option to buy a stated number of shares of common stock at a specified price.

Income Bond
A bond that pays interest to the holder only if the interest is earned.

Indexed (Purchasing Power) Bond
A bond that has interest payments based on an inflation index so as to protect the holder from inflation.

SELF-TEST QUESTIONS

Define floating rate bonds and zero coupon bonds.

What are the two ways a sinking fund can be handled? Which method will be chosen by the firm if interest rates have risen? If interest rates have fallen?

What is the difference between a call for sinking fund purposes and a refunding call?

Are securities that provide for a sinking fund regarded as being riskier than those without this type of provision? Explain.

Why is a call provision advantageous to a bond issuer? When will the issuer initiate a refunding call? Why?

---

[5]Indeed, most sinking funds do not require the issuer to pay any call premium.

7-5 Financial calculator needed; Interest rate sensitivity A bond trader purchased each of the following bonds at a yield to maturity of 8 percent. Immediately after she purchased the bonds, interest rates fell to 7 percent. What is the percentage change in the price of each bond after the decline in interest rates? Fill in the following table:

	PRICE @ 8%	PRICE @ 7%	PERCENTAGE CHANGE
10-year, 10% annual coupon	_____	_____	_____
10-year zero	_____	_____	_____
5-year zero	_____	_____	_____
30-year zero	_____	_____	_____
$100 perpetuity	_____	_____	_____

7-6 Financial calculator needed; Bond valuation An investor has two bonds in his portfolio. Each bond matures in four years, has a face value of $1,000, and has a yield to maturity equal to 9.6 percent. One bond, Bond C, pays an annual coupon of 10 percent, the other bond, Bond Z, is a zero coupon bond.

a. Assuming that the yield to maturity of each bond remains at 9.6 percent over the next four years, what will be the price of each of the bonds at the following time periods? Fill in the following table:

t	PRICE OF BOND C	PRICE OF BOND Z
0	_____	_____
1	_____	_____
2	_____	_____
3	_____	_____
4	_____	_____

b. Plot the time path of the prices for each of the two bonds.

EXAM-TYPE PROBLEMS

The problems included in this section are set up in such a way that they could be used as multiple-choice exam problems.

7-7 Bond valuation The Garraty Company has two bond issues outstanding. Both bonds pay $100 annual interest plus $1,000 at maturity. Bond L has a maturity of 15 years and Bond S a maturity of 1 year.

a. What will be the value of each of these bonds when the going rate of interest is (1) 5 percent, (2) 8 percent, and (3) 12 percent? Assume that there is only one more interest payment to be made on Bond S.

b. Why does the longer-term (15-year) bond fluctuate more when interest rates change than does the shorter-term bond (1-year)?

7-8 Yield to maturity The Heymann Company's bonds have 4 years remaining to maturity. Interest is paid annually; the bonds have a $1,000 par value; and the coupon interest rate is 9 percent.

a. What is the yield to maturity at a current market price of (1) $829 or (2) $1,104?

b. Would you pay $829 for one of these bonds if you thought that the appropriate rate of interest was 12 percent — that is, if k_d = 12%? Explain your answer.

7-9 Yield to call Six years ago, The Singleton Company sold a 20-year bond issue with a 14 percent annual coupon rate and a 9 percent call premium. Today, Singleton called the bonds. The bonds originally were sold at their face value of $1,000. Compute the realized rate of return for investors who purchased the bonds when they were issued and who surrender them today in exchange for the call price.

7-10 Financial calculator needed; Bond yields A 10-year, 12 percent semiannual coupon bond may be called in four years at a call price of $1,060. The bond sells for $1,100. (Assume that the bond has just been issued.)

a. What is the bond's yield to maturity?

b. What is the bond's current yield?

c. What is the bond's capital gain or loss yield?

d. What is the bond's yield to call?

7-11 Financial calculator needed; Yield to maturity You just purchased a bond which matures in 5 years. The bond has a face value of $1,000, and has an 8 percent annual coupon. The bond has a current yield of 8.21 percent. What is the bond's yield to maturity?

7-12 Financial calculater needed; Current yield A bond which matures in 7 years sells for $1,020. The bond has a face value of $1,000 and a yield to maturity of 10.5883 percent. The bond pays coupons semiannually. What is the bond's current yield?

7-13 Finanical calculator needed; Bond valuation Nungesser Corporation has issued bonds which have a 9 percent coupon rate, payable semiannually. The bonds mature in 8 years, have a face value of $1,000, and a yield to maturity of 8.5 percent. What is the price of the bonds?

7-14 Nominal interest rate Lloyd Corporation's 14 percent coupon rate, semiannual payment, $1,000 par value bonds, which mature in 30 years, are callable 5 years from now at a price of $1,050. The bonds sell at a price of $1,353.54, and the yield curve is flat. Assuming that interest rates in the economy are expected to remain at their current level, what is the best estimate of Lloyd's nominal interest rate on new bonds?

INTEGRATED CASE

WESTERN MONEY MANAGEMENT INC., PART I

7-15 **Bond valuation** Robert Black and Carol Alvarez are vice-presidents of Western Money Management and codirectors of the company's pension fund management division. A major new client, the California League of Cities, has requested that Western present an investment seminar to the mayors of the represented cities, and Black and Alvarez, who will make the actual presentation, have asked you to help them by answering the following questions. Because the Walt Disney Company operates in one of the league's cities, you are to work Disney into the presentation. (See the vignette which opened the chapter for information on Disney.)

a. What are the key features of a bond?

b. What are call provisions and sinking fund provisions? Do these provisions make bonds more or less risky?

c. How is the value of any asset whose value is based on expected future cash flows determined?

d. How is the value of a bond determined? What is the value of a 10-year, $1,000 par value bond with a 10 percent annual coupon if its required rate of return is 10 percent?

e. (1) What would be the value of the bond described in Part d if, just after it had been issued, the expected inflation rate rose by 3 percentage points, causing investors to require a 13 percent return? Would we now have a discount or a premium bond? (If you do not have a financial calculator, $PVIF_{13\%,10} = 0.2946$; $PVIFA_{13\%,10} = 5.4262$.)

(2) What would happen to the bond's value if inflation fell, and k_d declined to 7 percent? Would we now have a premium or a discount bond?

(3) What would happen to the value of the 10-year bond over time if the required rate of return remained at 13 percent, or if it remained at 7 percent? (Hint: With a financial calculator, enter PMT, I, FV, and N, and then change (override) N to see what happens to the PV as the bond approaches maturity.)

f. (1) What is the yield to maturity on a 10-year, 9 percent, annual coupon, $1,000 par value bond that sells for $887.00? That sells for $1,134.20? What does the fact that a bond sells at a discount or at a premium tell you about the relationship between k_d and the bond's coupon rate?

(2) What is the total return, the current yield, and the capital gains yield for the discount bond? (Assume the bond is held to maturity and the company does not default on the bonds.)

g. What is *interest rate (or price) risk?* Which bond has more interest rate risk, an annual payment 1-year bond or a 30-year bond? Why?

h. What is *reinvestment rate risk?* Which has more reinvestment rate risk, a 1-year bond or a 10-year bond?

i. How does the equation for valuing a bond change if semiannual payments are made? Find the value of a 10-year, semiannual payment, 10 percent coupon bond if nominal $k_d = 13\%$. (Hint: $PVIF_{6.5\%,20} = 0.2838$ and $PVIFA_{6.5\%,20} = 11.0185$.)

j. Suppose you could buy, for $1,000, either a 10 percent, 10-year, annual payment bond or a 10 percent, 10-year, semiannual payment bond. They are equally risky. Which would you prefer? If $1,000 is the proper price for the semiannual bond, what is the equilibrium price for the annual payment bond?

k. Suppose a 10-year, 10 percent, semiannual coupon bond with a par value of $1,000 is currently selling for $1,135.90, producing a nominal yield to maturity of 8 percent. However, the bond can be called after 5 years for a price of $1,050.

(1) What is the bond's *nominal yield to call (YTC)?*

(2) If you bought this bond, do you think you would be more likely to earn the YTM or the YTC? Why?

l. Disney's bonds were issued with a yield to maturity of 7.5 percent. Does the yield to maturity represent the promised or expected return on the bond?

m. Disney's bonds were rated AA− by S&P. Would you consider these bonds investment grade or junk bonds?

n. What factors determine a company's bond rating?

o. If Disney were to default on the bonds, would the company be immediately liquidated? Would the bondholders be assured of receiving all of their promised payments?

COMPUTER-RELATED PROBLEM

Work the problem in this section only if you are using the computer problem diskette.

7-16 Yield to call Use the computerized model in the File C7 to solve this problem.

    a. Refer back to Problem 7-4. Suppose that on January 1, 1997, the Racette bond is selling for $1,200. What does this indicate about the level of interest rates in 1997 as compared with interest rates a year earlier? What will be the yield to maturity and the yield to call on the Racette bond on this date? Note that the bond now has 27 years remaining until maturity and 2 years until it can be called. Which rate should an investor expect to receive if he or she buys the bond on this date?

    b. Suppose that instead of increasing the price, the Racette bond falls to $800 on January 1, 1997. What will be the yield to maturity and the yield to call on this date? Which rate should an investor expect to receive?

APPENDIX 7A

ZERO COUPON BONDS

To understand how zeros are used and analyzed, consider the zeros that are going to be issued by Vandenberg Corporation, a shopping center developer. Vandenberg is developing a new shopping center in San Diego, California, and it needs $50 million. The company does not anticipate major cash flows from the project for about 5 years. However, Pieter Vandenberg, the president, plans to sell the center once it is fully developed and rented, which should take about 5 years. Therefore, Vandenberg wants to use a financing vehicle that will not require cash outflows for 5 years, and he has decided on a 5-year zero coupon bond, with a maturity value of $1,000.

Vandenberg Corporation is an A-rated company, and A-rated zeros with 5-year maturities yield 6 percent at this time (5-year coupon bonds also yield 6 percent). The company is in the 40 percent federal-plus-state tax bracket. Pieter Vandenberg wants to know the firm's after-tax cost of debt if it uses 6 percent, 5-year maturity zeros, and he also wants to know what the bond's cash flows will be. Table 7A-1 provides an analysis of the situation, and the following numbered paragraphs explain the table itself.

1. The information in the "Basic Data" section, except the issue price, was given in the preceding paragraph, and the information in the "Analysis" section was calculated using the known data. The maturity value of the bond is always set at $1,000 or some multiple thereof.

2. The issue price is the PV of $1,000, discounted back 5 years at the rate $k_d = 6\%$, annual compounding. Using the tables, we find PV = $1,000(0.7473) = $747.30. Using a financial calculator, we input N = 5, I = 6, PMT = 0, and FV = 1000, then press the PV key to find PV = $747.26. Note that $747.26, compounded annually for 5 years at 6 percent, will grow to $1,000 as shown by the time line on Line 1 in Table 7A-1.

3. The accrued values as shown on Line 1 in the analysis section represent the compounded value of the bond at the end of each year. The accrued value for Year 0 is the issue price; the accrued value for Year 1 is found as $747.26(1.06) = $792.10; the accrued value at the end of Year 2 is $747.26(1.06)^2 = $839.62; and, in general, the value at the end of any Year n is

$$\text{Accrued value at the end of Year n} = \text{Issue price} \times (1 + k_d)^n. \tag{7A-1}$$

4. The interest deduction as shown on Line 2 represents the increase in accrued value during the year. Thus, interest in Year 1 = $792.10 − $747.26 = $44.84. In general,

$$\text{Interest in Year n} = \text{Accrued value}_n - \text{Accrued value}_{n-1}. \tag{7A-2}$$

This method of calculating taxable interest is specified in the Tax Code.

5. The company can deduct interest each year, even though the payment is not made in cash. This deduction lowers the taxes that would otherwise be paid, producing the following savings:

$$\text{Tax savings} = (\text{Interest deduction})(T). \tag{7A-3}$$
$$= \$44.84(0.4)$$
$$= \$17.94 \text{ in Year 1.}$$

6. Line 4 represents cash flows on a time line; it shows the cash flow at the end of Years 0 through 5. At Year 0, the company receives the $747.26 issue price. The company also has positive cash inflows equal to the tax savings during Years 1 through 4. Finally, in Year 5, it must pay the $1,000 maturity value, but it gets one more interest tax savings for the year. Therefore, the net cash flow in Year 5 is −$1,000 + $22.64 = −$977.36.

7. Next, we can determine the after-tax cost (or after-tax yield to maturity) of issuing the bonds. Since the cash flow stream is uneven, the after-tax yield to maturity is found by entering the after-tax cash flows, shown in Line 4 of Table 7A-1, into the

TABLE 7A-1	ANALYSIS OF A ZERO COUPON BOND

Basic Data

Maturity value	$1,000
k_d	6.00%, annual compounding
Maturity	5 years
Corporate tax rate	40.00%
Issue price	$747.26

Analysis

	0 6%	1	2	3	4	5 Years
(1) Year-end accrued value	$747.26	$792.10	$839.62	$890.00	$943.40	$1,000.00
(2) Interest deduction		44.84	47.52	50.38	53.40	56.60
(3) Tax savings (40%)		17.94	19.01	20.15	21.36	22.64
(4) Cash flow to Vandenberg	+747.26	+17.94	+19.01	+20.15	+21.36	−977.36
After-tax cost of debt	3.60%					

Face value of bonds the company must issue to raise $50 million = Amount needed/Issue price as % of par

= $50,000,000/0.74726

≈ $66,911,000.

cash flow register and then pressing the IRR key on the financial calculator. The IRR is the after-tax cost of zero coupon debt to the company. Conceptually, here is the situation:

$$\sum_{t=0}^{n} \frac{CF_n}{(1 + k_{d(AT)})^n} = 0. \tag{7A-4}$$

$$\frac{\$747.26}{(1 + k_{d(AT)})^0} + \frac{\$17.94}{(1 + k_{d(AT)})^1} + \frac{\$19.01}{(1 + k_{d(AT)})^2} + \frac{\$20.15}{(1 + k_{d(AT)})^3} + \frac{\$21.36}{(1 + k_{d(AT)})^4} + \frac{-\$977.36}{(1 + k_{d(AT)})^5} = 0.$$

The value $k_{d(AT)} = 0.036 = 3.6\%$, found with a financial calculator, produces the equality, and it is the cost of this debt. (Input in the cash flow register $CF_0 = 747.26$, $CF_1 = 17.94$, and so forth, out to $CF_5 = -977.36$. Then press the IRR key to find $k_d = 3.6\%$.)

8. Note that $k_d(1 - T) = 6\%(0.6) = 3.6\%$. As we will see in Chapter 9, the cost of capital for regular coupon debt is found using the formula $k_d(1 - T)$. Thus, there is symmetrical treatment for tax purposes for zero coupon and regular coupon debt; that is, both types of debt have the same after-tax cost. This was Congress's intent, and it is why the Tax Code specifies the treatment set forth in Table 7A-1.[1]

---

[1]The purchaser of a zero coupon bond must calculate interest income on the bond in the same manner as the issuer calculates the interest deduction. Thus, in Year 1, a buyer of a bond would report interest income of $44.84 and would pay taxes in the amount of T(Interest income), even though no cash was received. T, of course, would be the bondholder's personal tax rate. Because of the tax situation, most zero coupon bonds are bought by pension funds and other tax-exempt entities. Individuals do, however, buy taxable zeros for their Individual Retirement Accounts (IRAs). Also, state and local governments issue "tax exempt muni zeros," which are purchased by individuals in high tax brackets.

Note too that we have analyzed the bond as if the cash flows accrued annually. Generally, to facilitate comparisons with semiannual payment coupon bonds, the analysis is conducted on a semiannual basis.

Not all original issue discount bonds (OIDs) have zero coupons. For example, Vandenberg might have sold an issue of 5-year bonds with a 5 percent coupon at a time when other bonds with similar ratings and maturities were yielding 6 percent. Such bonds would have had a value of $957.88:

$$\text{Bond value} = \sum_{t=1}^{5} \frac{\$50}{(1.06)^t} + \frac{\$1,000}{(1.06)^5} = \$957.88.$$

If an investor had purchased these bonds at a price of $957.88, the yield to maturity would have been 6 percent. The discount of $1,000 − $957.88 = $42.12 would have been amortized over the bond's 5-year life, and it would have been handled by both Vandenberg and the bondholders exactly as the discount on the zeros was handled.

Thus, zero coupon bonds are just one type of original issue discount bond. Any nonconvertible bond whose coupon rate is set below the going market rate at the time of its issue will sell at a discount, and it will be classified (for tax and other purposes) as an OID bond.

Shortly after corporations began to issue zeros, investment bankers figured out a way to create zeros from U.S. Treasury bonds, which at the time were issued only in coupon form. In 1982, Salomon Brothers bought $1 billion of 12 percent, 30-year Treasuries. Each bond had 60 coupons worth $60 each, which represented the interest payments due every 6 months. Salomon then in effect clipped the coupons and placed them in 60 piles; the last pile also contained the now "stripped" bond itself, which represented a promise of $1,000 in the year 2012. These 60 piles of U.S. Treasury promises were then placed with the trust department of a bank and used as collateral for "zero coupon U.S. Treasury Trust Certificates," which are, in essence, zero coupon Treasury bonds. Treasury zeros are, of course, safer than corporate zeros, so they are very popular with pension fund managers. In response to this demand, the Treasury has also created its own "Strips" program, which allows investors to purchase zeros electronically.

Corporate (and municipal) zeros are generally callable at the option of the issuer, just like coupon bonds, after some stated call protection period. The call price is set at a premium over the accrued value at the time of the call. Stripped U.S. Treasury bonds (Treasury zeros) generally are not callable because the Treasury normally sells noncallable bonds. Thus, Treasury zeros are completely protected against reinvestment risk (the risk of having to invest cash flows from a bond at a lower rate because of a decline in interest rates).

PROBLEMS

7A-1 Zero coupon bonds A company has just issued 4-year zero coupon bonds with a maturity value of $1,000 and a yield to maturity of 9 percent. The company's tax rate is 40 percent. What is the after-tax cost of debt for the company?

7A-2 Zero coupon bonds An investor in the 28 percent bracket purchases the bond discussed in Problem 7A-1. What is the investor's after-tax return?

7A-3 Zero coupon bonds and EAR Assume that the city of Tampa sold tax-exempt (muni), zero coupon bonds 5 years ago. The bonds had a 25-year maturity and a maturity value of $1,000 when they were issued, and the interest rate built into the issue was a nominal 10 percent, but with semiannual compounding. The bonds are now callable at a premium of 10 percent over the accrued value. What effective annual rate of return would an investor who bought the bonds when they were issued and who still owns them earn if they are called today?

APPENDIX 7B

BANKRUPTCY AND REORGANIZATION

In the event of bankruptcy, debtholders have a prior claim to a firm's income and assets over the claims of both common and preferred stockholders. Further, different classes of debtholders are treated differently in the event of bankruptcy. Since bankruptcy is a fairly common occurrence, and since it affects both the bankrupt firm and its customers, suppliers, and creditors, it is important to know who gets what if a firm fails. These topics are discussed in this appendix.[1]

FEDERAL BANKRUPTCY LAWS

Bankruptcy actually begins when a firm is unable to meet scheduled payments on its debt or when the firm's cash flow projections indicate that it will soon be unable to meet payments. As the bankruptcy proceedings go forward, the following central issues arise:

1. Does the firm's inability to meet scheduled payments result from a temporary cash flow problem, or does it represent a permanent problem caused by asset values having fallen below debt obligations?

2. If the problem is a temporary one, then an agreement which stretches out payments may be worked out to give the firm time to recover and to satisfy everyone. However, if basic long-run asset values have truly declined, economic losses will have occurred. In this event, who should bear the losses?

3. Is the company "worth more dead than alive" — that is, would the business be more valuable if it were maintained and continued in operation or if it were liquidated and sold off in pieces?

4. Who should control the firm while it is being liquidated or rehabilitated? Should the existing management be left in control, or should a trustee be placed in charge of operations?

These are the primary issues that are addressed in the federal bankruptcy statutes.

Our bankruptcy laws were first enacted in 1898, modified substantially in 1938, changed again in 1978, and further fine-tuned in 1984. The 1978 Act, which provides the basic laws which govern bankruptcy today, was a major revision designed to streamline and expedite proceedings, and it consists of eight odd-numbered chapters, the even-numbered chapters of the earlier Act having been deleted. Chapters 1, 3, and 5 of the 1978 Act contain general provisions applicable to the other chapters; Chapter 7 details the procedures to be followed when liquidating a firm; Chapter 9 deals with financially distressed municipalities; Chapter 11 is the business reorganization chapter; Chapter 13 covers the adjustment of debts for "individuals with regular income"; and Chapter 15 sets up a system of trustees who help administer proceedings under the Act.

Chapters 11 and 7 are the most important ones for financial management purposes. When you read in the paper that McCrory Corporation or some other company has "filed for Chapter 11," this means that the company is bankrupt and is trying to reorganize under Chapter 11 of the Act. If a reorganization plan cannot be worked out, then the company will be liquidated as prescribed in Chapter 7 of the Act.

The 1978 Act is quite flexible, and it provides a great deal of scope for informal negotiations between a company and its creditors. Under this Act, a case is opened by the filing of a petition with a federal district bankruptcy court. The petition may be either voluntary or involuntary — that is, it may be filed either by the firm's management or by its creditors. A committee of unsecured creditors is then appointed by the court to negotiate with management for a reorganization, which may include the restructuring of debt and other claims against the firm. (A "restructuring" could involve lengthening the maturity of debt, lowering the interest rate on it, reducing the principal amount owed, exchanging common or preferred stock for debt, or some combination of these actions.) A trustee may be appointed by the court if that is deemed to be in the best interests of the creditors and stockholders; otherwise, the existing management will retain control. If no fair and feasible reorganization can be worked out under Chapter 11, the firm will be liquidated under the procedures spelled out in Chapter 7.

This appendix was coauthored by Arthur L. Herrmann of the University of Hartford.

[1]Much of the current work in this area is based on writings by Edward I. Altman. For a summary of his work, and that of others, see Edward I. Altman, "Bankruptcy and Reorganization," in *Handbook of Corporate Finance*, Edward I. Altman, ed. (New York: Wiley, 1986), Chapter 19.

FINANCIAL DECISIONS IN BANKRUPTCY

When a business becomes insolvent, a decision must be made whether to dissolve the firm through *liquidation* or to keep it alive through *reorganization*. To a large extent, this decision depends on a determination of the value of the firm if it is rehabilitated versus the value of its assets if they are sold off individually. The procedure that promises higher returns to the creditors and owners will be adopted. However, the "public interest" will also be considered, and this generally means attempting to salvage the firm, even if the salvaging effort may be costly to bondholders. For example, the bankruptcy court kept Eastern Airlines alive, at the cost of millions of dollars which could have been paid to bondholders, until it was obvious even to the judge that Eastern could not be saved. Note, too, that if the decision is made to reorganize the firm, the courts and possibly the SEC will be called upon to determine the fairness and the feasibility of the proposed reorganization plan.

STANDARD OF FAIRNESS. The basic doctrine of *fairness* states that claims must be recognized in the order of their legal and contractual priority. Carrying out this concept of fairness in a reorganization (as opposed to a liquidation) involves the following steps.

1. Future sales must be estimated.

2. Operating conditions must be analyzed so that the future earnings and cash flows can be predicted.

3. A capitalization (or discount) rate to be applied to these future cash flows must be determined.

4. This capitalization rate must then be applied to the estimated cash flows to obtain a present value figure, which is the indicated value for the reorganized company.

5. Provisions for the distribution of the restructured firm's securities to its claimants must be made.

STANDARD OF FEASIBILITY. The primary test of *feasibility* in a reorganization is whether the fixed charges after reorganization can be covered by cash flows. Adequate coverage generally requires an improvement in operating earnings, a reduction of fixed charges, or both. Among the actions that generally must be taken are the following:

1. Debt maturities are usually lengthened, interest rates may be scaled back, and some debt may be converted into equity.

2. When the quality of management has been substandard, a new team must be given control of the company.

3. If inventories have become obsolete or depleted, they must be replaced.

4. Sometimes the plant and equipment must be modernized before the firm can operate on a competitive basis.

LIQUIDATION PROCEDURES

If a company is too far gone to be reorganized, it must be liquidated. Liquidation should occur if a business is worth more dead than alive, or if the possibility of restoring it to financial health is so remote that the creditors would face a high risk of even greater losses if operations were continued.

Chapter 7 of the Bankruptcy Act is designed to do three things: (1) provide safeguards against the withdrawal of assets by the owners of the bankrupt firm, (2) provide for an equitable distribution of the assets among the creditors, and (3) allow insolvent debtors to discharge all of their obligations and to start over unhampered by a burden of prior debt.

The distribution of assets in a liquidation under Chapter 7 of the Bankruptcy Act is governed by the following priority of claims:

1. **Secured creditors, who are entitled to the proceeds of the sale of specific property pledged for a lien or a mortgage.** If the proceeds do not fully satisfy the secured creditors' claims, the remaining balance is treated as a general creditor claim. (See Item 9.)

2. **Trustee's costs to administer and operate the bankrupt firm.**

3. **Expenses incurred after an involuntary case has begun but before a trustee is appointed.**

4. **Wages due workers if earned within three months prior to the filing of the petition of bankruptcy.** The amount of wages is limited to $2,000 per person.

5. **Claims for unpaid contributions to employee benefit plans that were to have been paid within six months prior to filing.** However, these claims, plus wages in Item 4, are not to exceed the $2,000 per employee limit.

6. **Unsecured claims for customer deposits, not to exceed a maximum of $900 per individual.**

7. **Taxes due to federal, state, county, and any other government agency.**

8 STOCKS AND THEIR VALUATION

SEARCHING FOR THE NEXT DISNEY OR WAL-MART

A $1,000 investment in Disney in 1970 would have grown to $38,653 by 1994. The same $1,000 invested in Wal-Mart would have done even better—by 1994 it would have grown to $577,362! However, as any seasoned investor will tell you, stocks can fall just as fast as they rise. For example, if at the start of 1994 you had put $1,000 in Gitano, a previously high-flying NYSE-listed apparel company, you would have ended the year with just $50.

All boats rise and fall with the tides, but the same does not hold for the stock market — regardless of the trend in the market, some individual stocks always make huge gains, while others experience terrible losses. For example, the Dow Jones Industrial Average was essentially flat in 1994, but IBM gained 40 percent while General Motors suffered a 41 percent decline. These are both large and relatively stable compa-

nies: price swings were even larger for smaller companies. Indeed, literally dozens of publicly traded stocks rose by more than 200 percent or fell by more than 90 percent during 1994.

Some stock price changes are easy to understand, but at first glance other price movements seem irrational. For example, in July 1994, Texas Instruments saw its stock fall by $6.125, or 7 percent, on the day it issued what one analyst called a "superb earnings report." Likewise, most drug stocks fell sharply in 1994, even though the drug companies were generating impressive profits. On the other hand, in December 1994, Intel's stock price rose by more than 5 percent the day it announced an agreement to spend $200 million to replace flawed Pentium chips.

On closer inspection, these price changes were not irrational. In Texas Instru-

ments' case, at the same time it issued its favorable earnings report, the company also noted that the phenomenal growth in chip sales would probably slow in the years ahead. Similarly, the same high earnings that drug companies were reporting in 1994 were leading to fears of profit restrictions under the Clinton administration's proposed health care reforms. Finally, analysts noted that Intel was correcting a major public relations disaster and that the $200 million chip replacement program was much less costly than the damage that would otherwise be inflicted on the chip maker's image.

After studying this chapter, you should have a better understanding of the factors that influence stock prices. With that knowledge — and a little luck — you might be able to use these ideas to find the next Disney or Wal-Mart.

In Chapter 7 we examined bonds. In this chapter, we take up two other important securities, common and preferred stocks. The value of a stock is determined using the time value of money concepts presented in Chapter 6. However, valuing any asset requires a knowledge of the asset's characteristics, so we begin with some background information on common stock.

LEGAL RIGHTS AND PRIVILEGES OF COMMON STOCKHOLDERS

The common stockholders are the *owners* of a corporation, and as such they have certain rights and privileges as described in this section.

CONTROL OF THE FIRM

Its common stockholders have the right to elect a firm's directors, who in turn elect the officers who manage the business. In a small firm, the major stockholder typically assumes the positions of president and chairperson of the board of directors. In a large, publicly owned firm, the managers typically have some stock, but their personal holdings are generally insufficient to give them voting control. Thus, the managements of most publicly owned firms can be removed by the stockholders if they decide the management team is not effective.

Various state and federal laws stipulate how stockholder control is to be exercised. First, corporations must hold an election of directors periodically, usually once a year, with the vote taken at the annual meeting. Frequently, one-third of the directors are elected each year for a three-year term. Each share of stock has one vote; thus, the owner of 1,000 shares has 1,000 votes for each director.[1] Stockholders can appear at the annual meeting and vote in person, but typically they transfer their right to vote to a second party by means of an instrument known as a **proxy.** Management always solicits stockholders' proxies and usually gets them. However, if earnings are poor and stockholders are dissatisfied, an outside group may solicit the proxies in an effort to overthrow management and take control of the business. This is known as a **proxy fight.**

The question of control has become a central issue in finance in recent years. The frequency of proxy fights has increased, as have attempts by one corporation to take over another by purchasing a majority of the outstanding stock. This latter action is called a **takeover.** Some well-known examples of recent takeover battles include KKR's acquisition of RJR Nabisco, Chevron's acquisition of Gulf Oil, and the QVC/Viacom fight to take over Paramount.

Managers who do not have majority control (more than 50 percent of their firms' stock) are very much concerned about proxy fights and takeovers, and many of them are attempting to get stockholder approval for changes in their corporate charters that would make takeovers more difficult. For example, a number of companies have gotten their stockholders to agree (1) to elect only one-third of the directors each year (rather than electing all directors each year), (2) to require 75

Proxy
A document giving one person the authority to act for another, typically the power to vote shares of common stock.

Proxy Fight
An attempt by a person or group to gain control of a firm by getting its stockholders to grant that person or group the authority to vote their shares to place a new management into office.

Takeover
An action whereby a person or group succeeds in ousting a firm's management and taking control of the company.

---

[1]In the situation described, a 1,000-share stockholder could cast 1,000 votes for each of three directors if there were three contested seats on the board. An alternative procedure that may be prescribed in the corporate charter calls for *cumulative voting.* Here the 1,000-share stockholder would get 3,000 votes if there were three vacancies, and he or she could cast all of them for one director. Cumulative voting helps small groups to get representation on the board.

percent of the stockholders (rather than 50 percent) to approve a merger, and (3) to vote in a "poison pill" provision which would allow the stockholders of a firm that is taken over by another firm to buy shares in the second firm at a reduced price. The poison pill makes the acquisition unattractive and, thus, wards off hostile takeover attempts. Managements seeking such changes generally cite a fear that the firm will be picked up at a bargain price, but it often appears that managers' concerns about their own positions might be an even more important consideration.

Management moves to make takeovers more difficult have been countered by stockholders, especially large institutional stockholders, who do not want to see barriers erected to protect incompetent managers. To illustrate, the California Public Employees Retirement System (Calpers), which is one of the largest institutional investors, announced plans in early 1994 to conduct a proxy fight with several corporations whose financial performances were poor in Calpers' judgment. Calpers wants companies to give outside (nonmanagement) directors more clout and to force managers to be more responsive to stockholder complaints.

Prior to 1993, SEC rules prohibited large investors such as Calpers from getting together to force corporate managers to institute policy changes. However, the SEC changed its rules in 1993, and now large investors can work together to force management changes. One can anticipate that this ruling will serve to keep managers focused on stockholder concerns, which means the maximization of stock prices.

THE PREEMPTIVE RIGHT

Preemptive Right
A provision in the corporate charter or bylaws that gives common stockholders the right to purchase on a pro rata basis new issues of common stock (or convertible securities).

Common stockholders often have the right, called the **preemptive right,** to purchase any additional shares sold by the firm. In some states, the preemptive right is automatically included in every corporate charter; in others, it is necessary to insert it specifically into the charter.

The purpose of the preemptive right is twofold. First, it enables current stockholders to maintain control. If it were not for this safeguard, the management of a corporation could issue a large number of additional shares and purchase these shares itself. Management could thereby seize control of the corporation and frustrate the will of the current stockholders.

The second, and by far the most important, reason for the preemptive right is to protect stockholders against a dilution of value. For example, suppose 1,000 shares of common stock, each with a price of $100, were outstanding, making the total market value of the firm $100,000. If an additional 1,000 shares were sold at $50 a share, or for $50,000, this would raise the total market value to $150,000. When total market value is divided by new total shares outstanding, a value of $75 a share is obtained. The old stockholders thus lose $25 per share, and the new stockholders have an instant profit of $25 per share. Thus, selling common stock at a price below the market value would dilute its price and transfer wealth from the present stockholders to those who were allowed to purchase the new shares. The preemptive right prevents such occurrences.

? SELF-TEST QUESTIONS

Identify some actions that companies have taken to make takeovers more difficult.

What are the two primary reasons for the existence of the preemptive right?

TYPES OF COMMON STOCK

Classified Stock
Common stock that is given a special designation, such as Class A, Class B, and so forth, to meet special needs of the company.

Although most firms have only one type of common stock, in some instances **classified stock** is used to meet the special needs of the company. Generally, when special classifications of stock are used, one type is designated *Class A,* another *Class B,* and so on. Small, new companies seeking funds from outside sources frequently use different types of common stock. For example, when Genetic Concepts went public recently, its Class A stock was sold to the public and paid a dividend, but this stock had no voting rights for 5 years. Its Class B stock, which was retained by the organizers of the company, had full voting rights for 5 years, but the legal terms stated that dividends could not be paid on the Class B stock until the company had established its earning power by building up retained earnings to a designated level. The use of classified stock thus enabled the public to take a position in a conservatively financed growth company without sacrificing income, while the founders retained absolute control during the crucial early stages of the firm's development. At the same time, outside investors were protected against excessive withdrawals of funds by the original owners. As is often the case in such situations, the Class B stock was called **founders' shares.**

Founders' Shares
Stock owned by the firm's founders that has sole voting rights but restricted dividends for a specified number of years.

Note that "Class A," "Class B," and so on, have no standard meanings. Most firms have no classified shares, but a firm that does could designate its Class B shares as founders' shares and its Class A shares as those sold to the public, while another could reverse these designations. Still other firms could use stock classifications for entirely different purposes. For example, when General Motors acquired Hughes Aircraft for $5 billion, it paid in part with a new Class H common, GMH, which had limited voting rights and whose dividends are tied to Hughes's performance as a GM subsidiary. The reasons for the new stock were reported to be (1) that GM wanted to limit voting privileges on the new classified stock because of management's concern about a possible takeover and (2) that Hughes employees wanted to be rewarded more directly on Hughes's own performance than would have been possible through regular GM stock.

GM's deal posed a problem for the NYSE, which had a rule against listing any company's common stock if the company had any nonvoting common stock outstanding. GM made it clear that it was willing to delist if the NYSE did not change its rules. The NYSE concluded that such arrangements as GM had made were logical and were likely to be made by other companies in the future, so it changed its rules to accommodate GM. In reality, though, the NYSE had little choice. In recent years, the over-the-counter (OTC) market has proven that it can provide a deep, liquid market for common stocks, and the defection of GM would have hurt the NYSE much more than GM.

 SELF-TEST QUESTION

What are some reasons why a company might use classified stock?

EVALUATION OF COMMON STOCK AS A SOURCE OF FUNDS

Thus far, the chapter has covered the main characteristics of common stock. Now we will appraise stock financing both from the viewpoint of the corporation and from a social perspective.

From the Corporation's Viewpoint

ADVANTAGES.   Common stock offers several advantages to the corporation:

1. Common stock does not obligate the firm to make payments to stockholders: Only if the company generates earnings and has no pressing internal needs for capital will it pay dividends. Had it used debt, it would have incurred a legal obligation to pay interest, regardless of operating conditions and cash flows.

2. Common stock has no fixed maturity date — it never has to be "repaid" as would a debt issue.

3. Since common stock cushions creditors against losses, the sale of common stock increases the creditworthiness of the firm. This, in turn, raises its bond rating, lowers its cost of debt, and increases its future ability to use debt.

4. If a company's prospects look bright, then common stock can often be sold on better terms than debt. Stock appeals to certain groups of investors because (a) it typically carries a higher expected total return (dividends plus expected capital gains) than does preferred stock or debt, and (b) since stock represents the ownership of the firm, it provides the investor with a better hedge against unanticipated inflation, because common dividends tend to rise during inflationary periods.[2]

5. When a company is having operating problems, it often needs new funds to overcome its problems. However, investors are reluctant to supply capital to a troubled company, and, at such times, they generally require some type of security. From a practical standpoint, this often means that a firm which is experiencing problems can only obtain new capital by issuing debt, which is safer from the investor's standpoint. Because corporate treasurers are well aware of this, they often opt to finance with common stock during good times in order to maintain some **reserve borrowing capacity.** Indeed, surveys have indicated that maintenance of an adequate reserve of borrowing capacity is the most important consideration in many financing decisions.

Reserve Borrowing Capacity
Unused debt capacity that permits borrowing if a firm needs capital in troubled times.

DISADVANTAGES.   Disadvantages associated with issuing common stock include the following:

1. The sale of common stock gives some voting rights, and perhaps even control, to new stockholders. For this reason, additional equity financing is often avoided by managers who are concerned about maintaining control. The use of founders' shares, and shares such as those GM issued to acquire Hughes Aircraft, can reduce this problem.

2. Common stock gives new owners the right to share in the income of the firm; if profits soar, then new stockholders will share in this bonanza, whereas if debt had been used, new investors would receive only a fixed return, leaving most of the increased profits for the old stockholders.[3]

3. As we shall see, the costs of underwriting and distributing common stock are usually higher than those for preferred stock or debt. Flotation costs for

---

[2]For an average common stock, the rate of increase in dividends has exceeded the rate of inflation over the last 25 years.

[3]This point has given rise to an important theory: "If a firm sells a large issue of bonds, this is a *signal* that management expects the company to earn high profits on investments financed by the new capital and that it does not wish to share these profits with new stockholders. On the other hand, if the firm issues stock, this is a signal that its prospects are not so bright." This issue will be discussed in Chapters 12 and 13.

common stock are characteristically higher because (a) the costs of investigating an equity security investment are higher than those for a comparable debt security, and (b) stocks are riskier than debt, meaning that investors must diversify their equity holdings, so a given dollar amount of new stock must be sold to a larger number of purchasers than the same amount of debt.

4. As we will see in Chapter 12, if the firm has more equity than is called for in its optimal capital structure, its cost of capital will be higher than necessary. Therefore, a firm would not want to sell stock if the sale would cause its equity ratio to exceed the optimal level.

5. Under current tax laws, dividends on common stock are not deductible for tax purposes, but bond interest is deductible. As we will see in Chapter 9, taxes raise the relative cost of equity as compared with debt.

FROM A SOCIAL VIEWPOINT

From a social viewpoint, common stock is a desirable form of financing because it makes businesses less vulnerable to the consequences of declines in sales and earnings. Common stock financing involves no required payments which might force a faltering firm into bankruptcy. From the standpoint of the economy as a whole, if too many firms used too much debt, business fluctuations would be amplified, and minor recessions could turn into major depressions. Recently, when many leveraged mergers and buyouts were occurring and were raising the aggregate debt ratio (the average debt ratio of all firms), the Federal Reserve and other authorities voiced concern over the situation, and congressional leaders debated the wisdom of social controls over corporations' use of debt. Like most important issues, this one is debatable, and the debate centers around who can better determine "appropriate" capital structures — corporate managers or government officials.[4]

SELF-TEST QUESTIONS

What are the major advantages of common stock financing? The major disadvantages?

From a social viewpoint, why is common stock a desirable form of financing?

Closely Held Corporation
A corporation that is owned by a few individuals who are typically associated with the firm's management.

Publicly Owned Corporation
A corporation that is owned by a relatively large number of individuals who are not actively involved in its management.

THE MARKET FOR COMMON STOCK

Some companies are so small that their common stocks are not actively traded; they are owned by only a few people, usually the companies' managers. Such firms are said to be *privately owned,* or **closely held, corporations,** and their stock is called *closely held stock.* In contrast, the stocks of most larger companies are owned by a large number of investors, most of whom are not active in management. Such companies are called **publicly owned corporations,** and their stock is called *publicly held stock.*

---

[4]When business executives hear someone say, "I'm from Washington and I'm here to help you," they generally cringe, and often with good reason. On the other hand, a stable national economy does require sound businesses, and too much debt can lead to corporate instability.

Over-the-Counter (OTC) Market
The network of dealers that provides for trading in unlisted securities.

Organized Security Exchange
A formal organization, having a tangible physical location, that facilitates trading in designated ("listed") securities. The two major U.S. security exchanges are the New York Stock Exchange (NYSE) and the American Stock Exchange (AMEX).

As we saw in Chapter 4, the stocks of smaller publicly owned firms are not listed on an exchange; they trade in the **over-the-counter (OTC) market,** and the companies and their stocks are said to be *unlisted.* However, larger publicly owned companies generally apply for listing on an **organized security exchange,** and they and their stocks are said to be *listed.* As a general rule, companies are first listed on a regional exchange such as the Pacific Coast or Midwest Exchange. Then, as they grow, they move up to the American Stock Exchange (AMEX). Finally, if they grow large enough, they are listed on the "Big Board," the New York Stock Exchange (NYSE). About 7,000 stocks are traded in the OTC market, but in terms of market value of both outstanding shares and daily transactions, the NYSE is most important, having about 55 percent of the business.

In 1994, institutional investors owned about 46 percent of all publicly held common stocks. Included are pension plans (26 percent), mutual funds (10 percent), foreign investors (6 percent), insurance companies (3 percent), and brokerage firms (1 percent). These institutions buy and sell relatively actively, however, so they account for about 75 percent of all transactions. Thus, institutional investors have a heavy influence on the prices of individual stocks.

Types of Stock Market Transactions

We can classify stock market transactions into three distinct types:

1. **Trading in the outstanding shares of established, publicly owned companies: the secondary market.** Allied Food Products has 50 million shares of stock outstanding. If the owner of 100 shares sells his or her stock, the trade is said to have occurred in the **secondary market.** Thus, the market for outstanding shares, or *used shares,* is the secondary market. The company receives no new money when sales occur in this market.

Secondary Market
The market in which "used" stocks are traded after they have been issued by corporations.

Primary Market
The market in which firms issue new securities to raise corporate capital.

2. **Additional shares sold by established, publicly owned companies: the primary market.** If Allied decides to sell (or issue) an additional 1 million shares to raise new equity capital, this transaction is said to occur in the **primary market.**[5]

3. **Initial public offerings by privately held firms: the IPO market.** Several years ago, the Coors Brewing Company, which was owned by the Coors family at the time, decided to sell some stock to raise capital needed for a major expansion program.[6] This type of transaction is called **going public** — whenever stock in a closely held corporation is offered to the public for the first time, the company is said to be going public. The market for stock that is just being offered to the public is called the **initial public offering (IPO) market.**

Going Public
The act of selling stock to the public at large by a closely held corporation or its principal stockholders.

Initial Public Offering (IPO) Market
The market consisting of stocks of companies that are in the process of going public.

Firms can go public without raising any additional capital. For example, the Ford Motor Company was once owned exclusively by the Ford family. When Henry Ford died, he left a substantial part of his stock to the Ford

---

[5]Recall that Allied has 60 million shares authorized but only 50 million outstanding; thus, it has 10 million authorized but unissued shares. If it had no authorized but unissued shares, management could increase the authorized shares by obtaining stockholders' approval, which would generally be granted without any arguments.

[6]The stock Coors offered to the public was designated Class B, and it was nonvoting. The Coors family retained the founders' shares, called Class A stock, which carried full voting privileges. The company was large enough to obtain an NYSE listing, but at that time the Exchange had a requirement that listed common stocks must have full voting rights, which precluded Coors from obtaining an NYSE listing.

Growth Rate,
The expected
dividends per

Required Rat
The minimun
common stoc
considers acc

Expected Rat
The rate of r
stock that a s
receive.

Actual (Reali
The rate of r
stock actuall
stockholders
less than $\hat{k}_s$

Dividend Yi
The expected
the current $

Capital Gai
The capital g
divided by t

Expected T
The sum of
yield and th
yield.

ARE IPOs FAIRLY PRICED?

Consider the initial public offering (IPO) of Boston Rotisserie Chicken. On November 8, 1993, Merrill Lynch brought out this IPO at $20, but by the end of trading on that same day, the price had risen to $48 1/2. In fact, within the first 2 hours of trading, Boston Chicken's stock had increased 75 percent above the offering price. At the end of the first day, the stock price had risen by 143 percent, and the end-of-day P/E ratio was 263. At the end of its initial trading day, Boston Chicken's market value was $800 million versus sales revenues of only $8.3 million and a net loss of $5 million. Three days later, Boston Chicken filed suit against the underwriter for mispricing (underpricing) its underwriting. Did Merrill Lynch do a bad job of setting the price, or was the market excessively optimistic? We do not know—let a jury decide!

Foundation. When the Foundation later sold some of this stock to the general public, the Ford Motor Company went public, even though the company raised no capital in the transaction.

 SELF-TEST QUESTIONS

Differentiate between a closely held corporation and a publicly owned corporation.

Differentiate between a listed stock and an unlisted stock.

Differentiate between primary and secondary markets.

COMMON STOCK VALUATION

Common stock represents an ownership interest in a corporation, but to the typical investor, a share of common stock is simply a piece of paper characterized by two features:

1. It entitles its owner to dividends, but only if the company has earnings out of which dividends can be paid, and only if management chooses to pay dividends rather than retaining and reinvesting all the earnings. Whereas a bond contains a *promise* to pay interest, common stock provides no such promise to pay dividends—if you own a stock, you may *expect* a dividend, but your expectations may not in fact be met. To illustrate, Long Island Lighting Company (LILCO) had paid dividends on its common stock for more than 50 years, and people expected those dividends to continue. However, when the company encountered severe problems a few years ago, it stopped paying dividends. Note, though, that LILCO continued to pay interest on its bonds; if it had not, then it would have been declared bankrupt, and the bondholders could potentially have taken over the company.

2. Stock can be sold at some future date, hopefully at a price greater than the purchase price. If the stock is actually sold at a price above its purchase price, the investor will receive a *capital gain.* Generally, at the time people buy common stocks, they do expect to receive capital gains; otherwise, they would not buy the stocks. However, after the fact, one can end up with capital losses rather than capital gains. LILCO's stock price dropped from $17.50 to $3.75 in one year, so the *expected* capital gain on that stock turned out to be a huge *actual* capital loss.

If you extended Figure 8-1 on out forever and then added up the present value of each individual dividend, you would end up with the intrinsic value of the stock, $8.58.[9] The actual market price of the stock, P_0, could be greater than, less than, or equal to $8.58, depending on other investors' perceptions of the dividend pattern and riskiness of the stock.

We could transpose the $\hat{P}_0$ and the k_s in Equation 8-2 and solve for k_s to produce Equation 8-3:

$$\hat{k}_s = \frac{D}{P_0}.$$ (8-3)

We could then look up the price of the stock and the latest dividend, P_0 and D, in the newspaper, and D/P_0 would be the rate of return we could expect to earn if we bought the stock. Since we are dealing with an *expected rate of return,* we put a "hat" on the k value. Thus, if we bought the stock at a price of $8.58 and expected to receive a constant dividend of $1.15, our expected rate of return would be

$$\hat{k}_s = \frac{\$1.15}{\$8.58} = 0.134 = 13.4\%.$$

NORMAL, OR CONSTANT, GROWTH

Although the zero growth model is applicable to a few companies, the earnings and dividends of most companies are expected to increase over time. Expected growth rates vary from company to company, but dividend growth on average is expected to continue in the foreseeable future at about the same rate as that of the nominal gross domestic product (real GDP plus inflation). On this basis, one may expect the dividend of an average, or "normal," company to grow at a rate of 6 to 8 percent a year. Thus, if a **normal,** or **constant, growth** company's last dividend, which has already been paid, was D_0, its dividend in any future Year t may be forecasted as $D_t = D_0(1 + g)^t$, where g is the constant expected rate of growth. For example, if Allied Food Products just paid a dividend of $1.15 (that is, $D_0 = \$1.15$), and if investors expect an 8 percent growth rate, then the estimated dividend 1 year hence would be $D_1 = \$1.15(1.08) = \$1.24$; D_2 would be $1.34; and the estimated dividend 5 years hence would be

$$D_t = D_0(1 + g)^t = \$1.15(1.08)^5 = \$1.69.$$

Using this method for estimating future dividends, we can determine the current stock value, $\hat{P}_0$, using Equation 8-1 as set forth previously — in other words, we can find the expected future cash flow stream (the dividends), then calculate the present value of each dividend payment, and finally sum these present values to find the value of the stock. Thus, the intrinsic value of the stock is equal to the present value of its expected future dividends.

Market Price, F
The price at wh the market.

Intrinsic Value
The value of ar mind of a parti justified by the different from market price, it both.

Normal (Constant) Growth
Growth which is expected to continue into the foreseeable future at about the same rate as that of the economy as a whole; g = a constant.

---

[9]If you think that having a stock pay dividends forever is unrealistic, then think of it as lasting only for 50 years. Here you would have an annuity of $1.15 per year for 50 years discounted at 13.4 percent. Enter N = 50, I = 13.4, and PMT = 1.15, and then press PV to find the value of the annuity. It is $8.57, which differs by only a penny from that of the perpetuity. Thus, the dividends from Years 51 to infinity contribute almost nothing to the value of the stock.

If g is constant, Equation 8-1 may be rewritten as follows:[10]

$$\hat{P}_0 = \frac{D_0(1 + g)^1}{(1 + k_s)^1} + \frac{D_0(1 + g)^2}{(1 + k_s)^2} + \cdots + \frac{D_0(1 + g)^\infty}{(1 + k_s)^\infty}$$

$$= \frac{D_0(1 + g)}{k_s - g} = \frac{D_1}{k_s - g}. \tag{8-4}$$

Inserting values into the last version of Equation 8-4, we find the value of our illustrative stock to be $23.00:

$$\hat{P}_0 = \frac{\$1.15(1.08)}{0.134 - 0.08} = \frac{\$1.242}{0.054} = \$23.00.$$

Constant Growth Model
Also called the Gordon Model, it is used to find the value of a constant growth stock.

The **constant growth model** as set forth in the last term of Equation 8-4 is often called the Gordon Model, after Myron J. Gordon, who did much to develop and popularize it.

Note that Equation 8-4 is sufficiently general to encompass the zero growth case described earlier: If growth is zero, this is simply a special case of constant growth, and Equation 8-4 is equal to Equation 8-2. Note also that a necessary condition for the derivation of Equation 8-4 is that k_s be greater than g. If the equation is used in situations where k_s is not greater than g, the results will be both wrong and meaningless.

The concept underlying the valuation process for a constant growth stock is graphed in Figure 8-2. Dividends are growing at the rate g = 8%, but because k_s > g, the present value of each future dividend is declining. For example, the dividend in Year 1 is $D_1 = D_0(1 + g)^1 = \$1.15(1.08) = \$1.242$. However, the present value of this dividend, discounted at 13.4 percent, is $PV(D_1) = \$1.242/(1.134)^1 = \$1.095$. The dividend expected in Year 2 grows to $1.242(1.08) = $1.341, but the present value of this dividend falls to $1.04. Continuing, $D_3 = \$1.449$ and $PV(D_3) = \$0.993$, and so on. Thus, the expected dividends are growing, but the present value of each successive dividend is declining, because the dividend growth rate (8%) is less than the rate used for discounting the dividends to the present (13.4%).

If we summed the present values of each future dividend, this summation would be the value of the stock, $\hat{P}_0$. When g is a constant, this summation is equal to $D_1/(k_s - g)$, as shown in Equation 8-4. Therefore, if we extended the lower step function curve in Figure 8-2 on out to infinity and added up the present values of each future dividend, the summation would be identical to the value given by Equation 8-4, $23.00.

Growth in dividends occurs primarily as a result of growth in *earnings per share (EPS)*. Earnings growth, in turn, results from a number of factors, including (1) inflation, (2) the amount of earnings the company retains and reinvests, and (3) the rate of return the company earns on its equity (ROE). Regarding inflation, if output (in units) is stable, and if both sales prices and input costs rise at the inflation rate, then EPS will also grow at the inflation rate. EPS will also grow as a result of the reinvestment, or plowback, of earnings. If the firm's earnings are not all paid out as dividends (that is, if some fraction of earnings is retained), the dollars of investment behind each share will rise over time, which should lead to growth in earnings and dividends.

---

[10]The last term in Equation 8-4 is derived in Appendix 4A of Eugene F. Brigham and Louis C. Gapenski, *Intermediate Financial Management,* 5th ed. (Fort Worth, Tex.: Dryden Press, 1996). In essence, Equation 8-4 is the sum of a geometric progression, and the final result is the solution value of the progression.

FIGURE 8 - 2

PRESENT VALUES OF DIVIDENDS OF A CONSTANT GROWTH STOCK:
$D_0 = \$1.15$, $g = 8\%$, $k_s = 13.4\%$

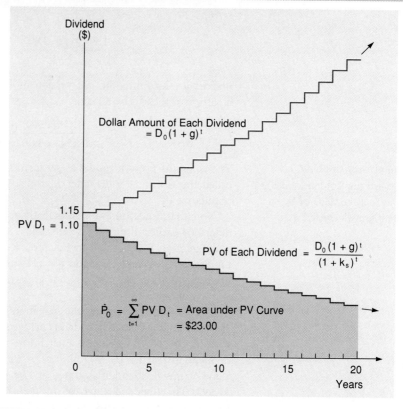

EXPECTED RATE OF RETURN ON A CONSTANT GROWTH STOCK

We can solve Equation 8-4 for k_s, again using the hat to denote that we are dealing with an expected rate of return:[11]

$$
\begin{array}{ccc}
\text{Expected rate} \\
\text{of return}
\end{array}
=
\begin{array}{c}
\text{Expected} \\
\text{dividend} \\
\text{yield}
\end{array}
+
\begin{array}{c}
\text{Expected growth} \\
\text{rate, or capital} \\
\text{gains yield}
\end{array}
$$

$$\hat{k}_s \quad = \quad \frac{D_1}{P_0} \quad + \quad g. \tag{8-5}$$

Thus, if you buy a stock for a price $P_0 = \$23$, and if you expect the stock to pay a dividend $D_1 = \$1.242$ one year from now and to grow at a constant rate $g = 8\%$ in the future, then your expected rate of return will be 13.4 percent:

$$\hat{k}_s = \frac{\$1.242}{\$23} + 8\% = 5.4\% + 8\% = 13.4\%.$$

---

[11]The k_s value in Equation 8-4 is a *required* rate of return, but when we transform to obtain Equation 8-5, we are finding an *expected* rate of return. Obviously, the transformation requires that $k_s = \hat{k}_s$. This equality holds if the stock market is in equilibrium, a condition that will be discussed later in the chapter.

In this form, we see that $\hat{k}_s$ is the *expected total return* and that it consists of an *expected dividend yield*, $D_1/P_0 = 5.4\%$, plus an *expected growth rate or capital gains yield*, $g = 8\%$.

Suppose this analysis had been conducted on January 1, 1996, so $P_0 = \$23$ is the January 1, 1996, stock price and $D_1 = \$1.242$ is the dividend expected at the end of 1996. What is the expected stock price at the end of 1996? We would again apply Equation 8-4, but this time we would use the year-end dividend, $D_2 = D_1$ $(1 + g) = \$1.242(1.08) = \$1.3414$:

$$\hat{P}_{12/31/96} = \frac{D_{1997}}{k_s - g} = \frac{\$1.3414}{0.134 - 0.08} = \$24.84.$$

Now, notice that $\$24.84$ is 8 percent greater than P_0, the $\$23$ price on January 1, 1996:

$$\$23(1.08) = \$24.84.$$

Thus, we would expect to make a capital gain of $\$24.84 - \$23.00 = \$1.84$ during 1996, which would provide a capital gains yield of 8 percent:

$$\text{Capital gains yield}_{1996} = \frac{\text{Capital gain}}{\text{Beginning price}} = \frac{\$1.84}{\$23.00} = 0.08 = 8\%.$$

We could extend the analysis on out, and in each future year the expected capital gains yield would always equal g, the expected dividend growth rate.

Continuing, the dividend yield in 1997 could be estimated as follows:

$$\text{Dividend yield}_{1997} = \frac{D_{1997}}{\hat{P}_{12/31/96}} = \frac{\$1.3414}{\$24.84} = 0.054 = 5.4\%.$$

The dividend yield for 1998 could also be calculated, and again it would be 5.4 percent. Thus, *for a constant growth stock,* the following conditions must hold:

1. The dividend is expected to grow forever at a constant rate, g.
2. The stock price is expected to grow at this same rate.
3. The expected dividend yield is a constant.
4. The expected capital gains yield is also a constant, and it is equal to g.
5. The expected total rate of return, $\hat{k}_s$, is equal to the expected dividend yield plus the expected growth rate: $\hat{k}_s$ = dividend yield + g.

The term *expected* should be clarified — it means expected in a probabilistic sense, as the statistically expected outcome. Thus, if we say the growth rate is expected to remain constant at 8 percent, we mean that the best prediction for the growth rate in any future year is 8 percent, not that we literally expect the growth rate to be exactly 8 percent in each future year. In this sense, the constant growth assumption is a reasonable one for many large, mature companies.

SUPERNORMAL, OR NONCONSTANT, GROWTH

Firms typically go through *life cycles.* During the early part of their lives, their growth is much faster than that of the economy as a whole; then they match the

FIGURE 8-3   ILLUSTRATIVE DIVIDEND GROWTH RATES

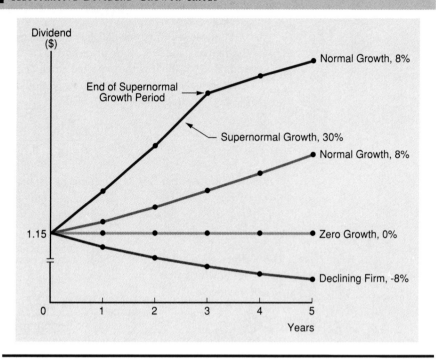

Supernormal (Nonconstant)
Growth
The part of the life cycle of a firm
in which it grows much faster than
the economy as a whole.

economy's growth; and finally their growth is slower than that of the economy.[12]
Automobile manufacturers in the 1920s and computer software firms such as Microsoft in the 1990s are examples of firms in the early part of the cycle; these firms are called **supernormal,** or **nonconstant, growth** firms. Figure 8-3 illustrates nonconstant growth and also compares it with normal growth, zero growth, and negative growth.[13]

In the figure, the dividends of the supernormal growth firm are expected to grow at a 30 percent rate for 3 years, after which the growth rate is expected to fall to 8 percent, the assumed average for the economy. The value of this firm, like any other, is the present value of its expected future dividends as determined by Equation 8-1. In the case in which D_t is growing at a constant rate, we simplified Equation 8-1 to $\hat{P}_0 = D_1/(k_s - g)$. In the supernormal case, however, the expected growth rate is not a constant — it declines at the end of the period of supernormal growth.

To find the value of such a stock, or of any nonconstant growth stock when the growth rate will eventually stabilize, we proceed in three steps:

[12]The concept of life cycles could be broadened to *product cycle,* which would include both small, start-up companies and large companies like Procter & Gamble, which periodically introduce new products that give sales and earnings a boost. We should also mention *business cycles,* which alternately depress and boost sales and profits. The growth rate just after a major new product has been introduced, or just after a firm emerges from the depths of a recession, is likely to be much higher than the "expected long-run average growth rate," which is the proper number for a DCF analysis.

[13]A negative growth rate indicates a declining company. A mining company whose profits are falling because of a declining ore body is an example. Someone buying such a company would expect its earnings, and consequently its dividends and stock price, to decline each year, and this would lead to capital losses rather than capital gains. Obviously, a declining company's stock price will be relatively low, and its dividend yield must be high enough to offset the expected capital loss and still produce a competitive total return. Students sometimes argue that they would not be willing to buy a stock whose price was expected to decline. However, if the annual dividends are large enough to *more than offset* the falling stock price, the stock could still provide a good return.

1. Find the PV of the dividends during the period of nonconstant growth.

2. Find the price of the stock at the end of the nonconstant growth period, at which point it has become a constant growth stock, and discount this price back to the present.

3. Add these two components to find the intrinsic value of the stock, $\hat{P}_0$.

Figure 8-4 can be used to illustrate the process for valuing nonconstant growth stocks, assuming the following five facts exist:

k_s = stockholders' required rate of return = 13.4%. This rate is used to discount the cash flows.

N = years of supernormal growth = 3.

g_s = rate of growth in both earnings and dividends during the supernormal growth period = 30%. (Note: The growth rate during the supernormal growth period could vary from year to year. Also, there could be several different supernormal growth periods, e.g., 30% for 3 years, then 20% for 3 years, and then a constant 8%.) This rate is shown directly on the time line.

g_n = rate of normal, constant growth after the supernormal period = 8%. This rate is also shown on the time line, between periods 3 and 4.

D_0 = last dividend the company paid = $1.15.

The valuation process as diagrammed in Figure 8-4 is explained in the steps set forth below the time line. The value of the supernormal growth stock is calculated to be $39.21.

SELF-TEST QUESTIONS

Explain the following statement: "Whereas a bond contains a promise to pay interest, common stock provides an expectation of but no promise of dividends."

What are the two elements of a stock's expected total return?

Write out and explain the valuation model for a zero growth stock.

Write out and explain the valuation model for a constant growth stock.

How does one calculate the capital gains yield and the dividend yield of a stock?

Explain how one would find the value of a supernormal growth stock.

STOCK MARKET EQUILIBRIUM

Recall from Chapter 5 that the required return on Stock X, k_X, can be found using the Security Market Line (SML) equation as it was developed in our discussion of the Capital Asset Pricing Model (CAPM):

$$k_X = k_{RF} + (k_M - k_{RF}) b_X.$$

If the risk-free rate of return is 8 percent, if the market risk premium is 4 percent, and if Stock X has a beta of 2, then the marginal investor will require a return of 16 percent on Stock X, calculated as follows:

$$k_X = 8\% + (12\% - 8\%) 2.0$$
$$= 16\%.$$

FIGURE 8-4   PROCESS FOR FINDING THE VALUE OF A SUPERNORMAL GROWTH STOCK

Notes to Figure 8-4:

Step 1. Calculate the dividends expected at the end of each year during the super-normal growth period. Calculate the first dividend, $D_1 = D_0(1 + g_s) = \$1.15(1.30) = \$1.4950$. Here g_s is the growth rate during the 3-year super-normal growth period, 30 percent. Show the $1.4950 on the time line as the cash flow at Time 1. Then, calculate $D_2 = D_1(1 + g_s) = \$1.4950(1.30) = \$1.9435$, and then $D_3 = D_2(1 + g_s) = \$1.9435(1.30) = \$2.5266$. Show these values on the time line as the cash flows at Time 2 and Time 3.

Step 2. The price of the stock is the PV of dividends from Time 1 to infinity, so in theory we could project each future dividend, with the normal growth rate, $g_n = 8\%$, used to calculate D_4 and subsequent dividends. However, we know that after D_3 has been paid, which is at Time 3, the stock becomes a constant growth stock. Therefore, we can use the constant growth formula to find $\hat{P}_3$, which is the PV of the dividends from Time 4 to infinity as evaluated at Time 3.

First, we determine $D_4 = \$2.5266(1.08) = \$2.7287$ for use in the formula, and then we calculate $\hat{P}_3$ as follows:

$$\hat{P}_3 = \frac{D_4}{k_s - g_n} = \frac{\$2.7287}{0.134 - 0.08} = \$50.5310.$$

We show this $50.5310 on the time line as a second cash flow at Time 3. The $50.5310 is a Time 3 cash flow in the sense that the owner of the stock could sell it for $50.5310 at Time 3 and also in the sense that $50.5310 is the present value of the dividend cash flows from Time 4 to infinity. Note that the *total cash flow* at Time 3 consists of the sum of $D_3 + \hat{P}_3 = \$2.5266 + \$50.5310 = \$53.0576$.

Step 3. Now that the cash flows have been placed on the time line, we can discount each cash flow at the required rate of return, $k_s = 13.4\%$. We could discount each flow by dividing by $(1.134)^t$, where $t = 1$ for Time 1, $t = 2$ for Time 2, and $t = 3$ for Time 3. This produces the PVs shown to the left below the time line, and the sum of the PVs is the value of the supernormal growth stock, $39.21.

With a financial calculator, you can find the PV of the cash flows as shown on the time line with the cash flow (CFLO) register of your calculator. Enter 0 for CF_0 because you get no cash flow at Time 0, $CF_1 = 1.495$, $CF_2 = 1.9435$, and $CF_3 = 2.5266 + 50.531 = 53.0576$. Then enter $I = 13.4$, and press the NPV key to find the value of the stock, $39.21.

This 16 percent required return is shown as the point on the SML in Figure 8-5 associated with beta = 2.0.

Marginal Investor
A representative investor whose actions reflect the beliefs of those people who are currently trading a stock. It is the marginal investor who determines a stock's price.

The **marginal investor** will want to buy Stock X if its expected rate of return is more than 16 percent, will want to sell it if the expected rate of return is less than 16 percent, and will be indifferent, hence will hold but not buy or sell, if the expected rate of return is exactly 16 percent. Now, suppose the investor's portfolio contains Stock X, and he or she analyzes the stock's prospects and concludes that its earnings, dividends, and price can be expected to grow at a constant rate of 5 percent per year. The last dividend was $D_0 = \$2.8571$, so the next expected dividend is

$$D_1 = \$2.8571(1.05) = \$3.$$

Our marginal investor observes that the present price of the stock, P_0, is $30. Should he or she purchase more of Stock X, sell the stock, or maintain the present position?

The investor can calculate Stock X's *expected rate of return* as follows:

$$\hat{k}_X = \frac{D_1}{P_0} + g = \frac{\$3}{\$30} + 5\% = 15\%.$$

This value is plotted on Figure 8-5 as Point X, which is below the SML. Because the expected rate of return is less than the required return, this marginal investor would want to sell the stock, as would most other holders. However, few people would want to buy at the $30 price, so the present owners would be unable to find buyers unless they cut the price of the stock. Thus, the price would decline, and this decline would continue until the stock's price reached $27.27, at which point the market for this security would be in **equilibrium,** defined as the price at which the expected rate of return, 16 percent, is equal to the required rate of return:

Equilibrium
The condition under which the expected return on a security is just equal to its required return, $\hat{k} = k$. Also, $\hat{P}_0 = P_0$, and the price is stable.

$$\hat{k}_X = \frac{\$3}{\$27.27} + 5\% = 11\% + 5\% = 16\% = k_X.$$

F I G U R E   8 - 5   **EXPECTED AND REQUIRED RETURNS ON STOCK X**

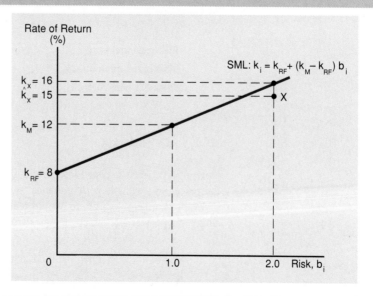

Had the stock initially sold for less than $27.27, say at $25, events would have been reversed. Investors would have wanted to buy the stock because its expected rate of return would have exceeded its required rate of return, and buy orders would have driven the stock's price up to $27.27.

To summarize, in equilibrium two related conditions must hold:

1. A stock's expected rate of return as seen by the marginal investor must equal its required rate of return: $\hat{k}_i = k_i$.

2. The actual market price of the stock must equal its intrinsic value as estimated by the marginal investor: $P_0 = \hat{P}_0$.

Of course, some individual investors may believe that $\hat{k}_i > k$ and $\hat{P}_0 > P_0$, hence they would invest most of their funds in the stock, while other investors may have an opposite view and would sell all of their shares. However, it is the marginal investor who establishes the actual market price, and for this investor, $\hat{k}_i = k_i$ and $P_0 = \hat{P}_0$. If these conditions do not hold, trading will occur until they do hold.

CHANGES IN EQUILIBRIUM STOCK PRICES

Stock market prices are not constant — they undergo violent changes at times. For example, on October 19, 1987, the Dow Jones average dropped 508 points, and the average stock lost about 23 percent of its value on that one day. Some individual stocks lost more than half of their value. To see how such changes can occur, assume that Stock X is in equilibrium, selling at a price of $27.27 per share. If all expectations were exactly met, during the next year the price would gradually rise to $28.63, or by 5 percent. However, many different events could occur to cause a change in the equilibrium price of the stock. To illustrate, consider again the set of inputs used to develop Stock X's price of $27.27, along with a new set of assumed input variables:

	VARIABLE VALUE	
	ORIGINAL	NEW
Risk-free rate, k_{RF}	8%	7%
Market risk premium, $k_M - k_{RF}$	4%	3%
Stock X's beta coefficient, b_X	2.0	1.0
Stock X's expected growth rate, g_X	5%	6%
D_0	$2.8571	$2.8571
Price of Stock X	$27.27	?

Now give yourself a test: How would the change in each variable, by itself, affect the price, and what is your guess as to the new stock price?

Every change, taken alone, would lead to an *increase* in the price. The first three changes all lower k_X, which declines from 16 to 10 percent:

$$\text{Original } k_X = 8\% + 4\%(2.0) = 16\%.$$
$$\text{New } k_X = 7\% + 3\%(1.0) = 10\%.$$

Using these values, together with the new g value, we find that $\hat{P}_0$ rises from \$27.27 to \$75.71.[14]

$$\text{Original } \hat{P}_0 = \frac{\$2.8571(1.05)}{0.16 - 0.05} = \frac{\$3}{0.11} = \$27.27.$$

$$\text{New } \hat{P}_0 = \frac{\$2.8571(1.06)}{0.10 - 0.06} = \frac{\$3.0285}{0.04} = \$75.71.$$

At the new price, the expected and required rates of return will be equal:[15]

$$\hat{k}_X = \frac{\$3.0285}{\$75.71} + 6\% = 10\% = k_X.$$

Evidence suggests that stocks, especially those of large companies, adjust rapidly to disequilibrium situations. Consequently, equilibrium ordinarily exists for any given stock, and required and expected returns are generally equal. Stock prices certainly change, sometimes violently and rapidly, but this simply reflects changing conditions and expectations. There are, of course, times when a stock continues to react for several months to favorable or unfavorable developments, but this does not signify a long adjustment period; rather, it simply illustrates that as more new pieces of information about the situation become available, the market adjusts to them. The ability of the market to adjust to new information is discussed in the next section.

THE EFFICIENT MARKETS HYPOTHESIS

Efficient Markets Hypothesis (EMH)
The hypothesis that securities are typically in equilibrium — that they are fairly priced in the sense that the price reflects all publicly available information on each security.

A body of theory called the **Efficient Markets Hypothesis (EMH)** holds (1) that stocks are always in equilibrium and (2) that it is impossible for an investor to consistently "beat the market." Essentially, those who believe in the EMH note that there are 100,000 or so full-time, highly trained, professional analysts and traders operating in the market, while there are fewer than 3,000 major stocks. Therefore, if each analyst followed 30 stocks (which is about right, as analysts tend to specialize in the stocks in a specific industry), there would on average be 1,000 analysts following each stock. Further, these analysts work for organizations such as Citibank, Merrill Lynch, Prudential Insurance, and the like, which have billions of dollars available with which to take advantage of bargains. In addition, as a result of SEC disclosure requirements and electronic information networks, as new information about a stock becomes available, these 1,000 analysts generally receive and evaluate it at about the same time. Therefore, the price of a stock will adjust almost immediately to any new development.

---

[14]A price change of this magnitude is by no means rare. The prices of *many* stocks double or halve during a year. For example, during 1994, CareNetwork, a health care provider, increased in value by 644 percent; on the other hand, Megafoods Stores, a grocery chain, fell by 97 percent.

[15]It should be obvious by now that *actual realized* rates of return are not necessarily equal to expected and required returns. Thus, an investor might have *expected* to receive a return of 15 percent if he or she had bought CareNetwork or Megafoods stock in 1994, but, after the fact, the realized return on CareNetwork was far above 15 percent, whereas that on Megafoods was far below.

LEVELS OF MARKET EFFICIENCY

If markets are efficient, stock prices will rapidly reflect all available information. This raises an important question: What types of information are available and, therefore, incorporated into stock prices? Financial theorists have discussed three forms, or levels, of market efficiency.

WEAK-FORM EFFICIENCY.   The *weak-form* of the EMH states that all information contained in past price movements is fully reflected in current market prices. If this were true, then information about recent trends in stock prices would be of no use in selecting stocks — the fact that a stock has risen for the past three days, for example, would give us no useful clues as to what it will do today or tomorrow. People who believe that weak-form efficiency exists also believe that "tape watchers" and "chartists" are wasting their time.[16]

For example, after studying the past history of the stock market, a chartist might "discover" the following pattern: If a stock falls three consecutive days, its price typically rises 10 percent the following day. The technician would then conclude that investors could make money by purchasing a stock whose price has fallen three consecutive days.

But if this pattern truly existed, wouldn't other investors also discover it, and if so, why would anyone be willing to sell a stock after it had fallen three consecutive days if they know the stock's price is expected to increase by 10 percent the next day? In other words, if a stock is selling at $40 per share after falling three consecutive days, why would investors sell the stock if they expected it to rise to $44 per share one day later? Those who believe in weak-form efficiency argue that if the stock would really rise to $44 per share tomorrow, its price *today* would actually rise to somewhere near $44 per share immediately, thereby eliminating the trading opportunity. Consequently, weak-form efficiency implies that any information that comes from past stock prices is rapidly incorporated into the current stock price.

SEMISTRONG-FORM EFFICIENCY.   The *semistrong-form* of the EMH states that current market prices reflect all *publicly available* information. Therefore, if semistrong-form efficiency exists, it would do no good to pore over annual reports or other published data because market prices would have adjusted to any good or bad news contained in such reports as soon as the news came out. With semistrong-form efficiency, investors should expect to earn the returns predicted by the SML, but they should not expect to do any better unless they have information that is not publicly available. However, insiders (for example, the presidents of companies) who have information which is not publicly available can earn abnormal returns (returns higher than those predicted by the (SML) even under semistrong-form efficiency.

Another implication of semistrong-form efficiency is that whenever information is released to the public, stock prices will respond only if the information is different from what had been expected. If, for example, a company announces a 30 percent increase in earnings, and if that increase is consistent with what analysts had been expecting, the announcement should have little or no effect on the company's stock price. On the other hand, the stock price would probably fall if ana-

---

[16]Tape watchers are people who watch the NYSE tape, while chartists plot past patterns of stock price movements. Both are called "technicians," and both believe that they can tell if something is happening to the stock that will cause its price to move up or down in the near future.

RUN-UPS BEFORE DEALS: CHICANERY OR COINCIDENCE?

Most studies find that markets are not strong-form efficient — the market can be beaten by those with access to inside information. Inside information is particularly valuable when it comes to corporate takeovers.

A recent article in *Business Week* claims that one out of every three big mergers in 1994 was preceded by suspicious insider trading. For example, the day before American Home Products launched a $95 per share hostile takeover bid for American Cyanamid, there was heavy trading in Cyanamid, and its stock price jumped from $60 5/8 to $63 a share. The article went on to document a number of similar cases, all with sharp run-ups in the target firms' stock prices just before merger announcements.

The Securities and Exchange Commission (SEC), which is responsible for policing insider trading, is currently investigating several of these cases to determine whether there was any illegal insider trading. To be sure, some preannouncement run-ups are undoubtedly legitimate — perhaps a large number of buy orders just randomly came in, or, more likely, perhaps some market professionals guessed correctly that a merger was likely. However, there are cases in which the evidence strongly suggests information was "leaked" prior to the takeover. Harry C. Johnson, chairman and president of Red Eagle Resources Corporation, which was recently acquired by Lomak Petroleum, put it best after he saw the stock price of his company rise 16 percent the day before the deal was announced: "When there are a lot of people involved in a deal, you have to believe in the tooth fairy to think there can't be leakage."

SOURCE: "Insider Trading," *Business Week*, December 12, 1994.

lysts had expected earnings to increase by more than 30 percent, but it probably would rise if they had expected a smaller increase.

STRONG-FORM EFFICIENCY. The *strong-form* of the EMH states that current market prices reflect all pertinent information, whether publicly available or privately held. If this form holds, even insiders would find it impossible to earn abnormal returns in the stock market.[17]

Many empirical studies have been conducted to test for the three forms of market efficiency. Most of these studies suggest that the stock market is indeed highly efficient in the weak form and reasonably efficient in the semistrong form, at least for the larger and more widely followed stocks. However, the strong-form EMH does not hold, so abnormal profits can be made by those who possess inside information. (See box.)

IMPLICATIONS OF MARKET EFFICIENCY

What bearing does the EMH have on financial decisions? Since stock prices do seem to reflect public information, most stocks appear to be fairly valued. This does not mean that new developments could not cause a stock's price to soar or to plummet, but it does mean that stocks in general are neither overvalued nor undervalued — they are fairly priced and in equilibrium. However, there are certainly cases in which corporate insiders have information not known to outsiders.

If the EMH is correct, it is a waste of time for most of us to analyze stocks by looking for those that are undervalued. If stock prices already reflect all publicly

[17]Several cases of illegal insider trading have made the news headlines. These cases involved employees of several major investment banking houses and even an employee of the SEC. In the most famous case, Ivan Boesky admitted to making $50 million by purchasing the stock of firms he knew were about to merge. He went to jail, and he had to pay a large fine, but he helped disprove the strong-form EMH.

available information, and hence are fairly priced, one can "beat the market" only by luck, and it is difficult, if not impossible, for anyone to consistently outperform the market averages. Empirical tests have shown that the EMH is, in its weak and semi-strong forms, valid. However, people such as corporate officers who have inside information can do better than the averages, and individuals and organizations that are especially good at digging out information on small, new companies also seem to do consistently well. Also, some investors may be able to analyze and react more quickly than others to releases of new information, and these investors may have an advantage over others. However, the buy-sell actions of those investors quickly bring market prices into equilibrium. Therefore, it is generally safe to assume that $\hat{k} = k$, that $\hat{P}_0 = P_0$, and that stocks plot on the SML.[18]

Actual Stock Prices and Returns

Our discussion thus far has focused on *expected* stock prices and *expected* rates of return. Anyone who has ever invested in the stock market knows that there can be, and there generally are, large differences between *expected* and *realized* prices and returns.

We can use IBM to illustrate this point. In early 1991, IBM's stock price was about $120 per share. Its 1990 dividend, D_0, had been $4.84, but analysts expected the dividend to grow at a constant rate of about 8 percent in the future. Thus, an average investor who bought IBM at a price of $120 would have expected to earn a return of about 12.4 percent:

$$\hat{k} = \frac{\text{Expected dividend}}{\text{yield}} + \frac{\text{Expected growth rate, which is also}}{\text{the expected capital gains yield}}$$

$$= \frac{D_0(1 + g)}{P_0} + g = \frac{\$5.23}{\$120} + 8\%$$

$$= 4.4\% + 8.0\% = 12.4\%.$$

In fact, things did not work out as expected. IBM's share of the computer market in 1991 was weaker than had been predicted, so IBM's earnings did not grow as fast as expected, and its dividend remained at $4.84. So, rather than growing, IBM's stock price declined, and it closed on December 31, 1991, at $89, down $31

---

[18]Market efficiency also has important implications for managerial decisions, especially those pertaining to common stock issues, stock repurchases, and tender offers. Stocks appear to be fairly valued, so decisions based on the premise that a stock is undervalued or overvalued must be approached with caution. However, managers do have better information about their own companies than outsiders, and this information can legally be used to the companies' (but not the managers') advantage.

We should also note that some Wall Street pros have consistently beaten the market over many years, which is inconsistent with the EMH. An interesting article in the April 3, 1995, issue of *Fortune* (Terence P. Paré, "Yes, You Can Beat the Market") argued strongly against the EMH. Paré suggested that each stock has a fundamental value, but when good or bad news about it is announced, most investors fail to interpret this news correctly. As a result, stocks are generally priced above or below their long-term values.

Think of a graph with stock price on the vertical axis and years on the horizontal axis. A stock's fundamental value might be moving up steadily over time as it retains and reinvests earnings. However, its actual price might fluctuate about the intrinsic value line, overreacting to good or bad news and indicating departures from equilibrium. Successful value investors, according to the article, use fundamental analysis to identify stocks' intrinsic values, and then they buy stocks that are undervalued and sell those that are overvalued.

Paré's argument implies that the market is systematically out of equilibrium and that investors can act on this knowledge to beat the market. That position may turn out to be correct, but it may also be that the superior performance Paré noted simply demonstrates that some people are better at obtaining and interpreting information than others.

| FIGURE 8-6 | S&P 500 Index, 1967–1994 |

Source: Data taken from various issues of *The Wall Street Journal,* "Stock Market Data Bank" section.

for the year. Thus, on a beginning-of-the-year investment of $120, the annual return on IBM for 1991 was −21.8 percent:

$$\bar{k}_s = \text{Actual dividend yield} + \text{Actual capital gains yield}$$

$$= \frac{\$4.84}{\$120} + \frac{-\$31}{\$120} = 4.0\% - 25.8\% = -21.8\%.$$

Many other stocks performed similarly to IBM, or worse, in 1991.

Figure 8-6 shows how the price of a portfolio of stocks has moved in recent years, and Figure 8-7 shows how total realized returns on the portfolio have varied. The market trend has been strongly up, but it has gone up in some years and down in others, and the stocks of individual companies have likewise gone up and down.[19] We know from theory that expected returns, as estimated by a marginal investor, are always positive, but in some years, as Figure 8-7 shows, actual returns are negative. Of course, even in bad years some individual companies do well, so "the name of the game" in security analysis is to pick the winners. Financial managers attempt to take actions which will put their companies into the winners' column, but they don't always succeed. In subsequent chapters, we will examine the actions that managers can take to increase the odds of their firms doing relatively well in the marketplace.

STOCK MARKET REPORTING

Figure 8-8, taken from a daily newspaper, is a section of the stock market page for stocks listed on the NYSE. For each stock, the NYSE report provides specific data on the trading that took place the prior day. Similar information is avail-

---

[19]If we constructed graphs like Figures 8-6 and 8-7 for individual stocks rather than for a large portfolio, far greater variability would be shown. Also, if we constructed a graph like Figure 8-7 for bonds, it would have the same general shape, but the bars would be somewhat smaller, indicating that gains and losses on bonds are generally smaller than those on stocks. Above-average bond returns occur in years when interest rates decline, and losses on bonds occur only when interest rates rise sharply.

FIGURE 8-7	S&P 500 INDEX, TOTAL RETURNS: DIVIDEND YIELD + CAPITAL GAIN OR LOSS, 1967–1994

SOURCE: *Stocks, Bonds, Bills, and Inflation: 1994 Yearbook*, (Chicago: Ibbotson Associates, 1994).

able for stocks listed on the other exchanges as well as for stocks traded over the counter.

Stocks are listed alphabetically, from AAR Industries to Zweig; the data in Figure 8-8 were taken from the top of the listing. We will examine the data for Abbott Laboratories, AbbotLab, shown about halfway down the table. The two columns on the left show the highest and lowest prices at which the stocks have sold during the past year; Abbott Labs has traded in the range from $33 to $25⅜ during the preceding 52 weeks. The figure just to the right of the company's ticker symbol is the dividend; Abbott Labs had a current indicated annual dividend rate of $0.76 per share and a dividend yield (which is the current dividend divided by the closing stock price) of 2.3 percent. Next comes the ratio of the stock's price to its last 12 months' earnings (the P/E ratio), followed by the volume of trading for the day: 643,500 shares of Abbott Labs stock were traded on December 19, 1994. Following the volume come the high and low prices for the day, and then the closing price. On December 19, Abbott Labs traded as high as $32½ and as low as $32, while the last trade was at $32⅜. The last column gives the change from the closing price on the previous day. Abbott Labs' closing price did not change from the previous day's closing price.

SELF-TEST QUESTIONS

When a stock is in equilibrium, what two conditions must hold?

What is the difference between the three forms of the EMH: (1) weak-form, (2) semistrong-form, and (3) strong-form?

If a stock is *not* in equilibrium, explain how financial markets adjust to bring it into equilibrium.

FIGURE 8-8 STOCK MARKET TRANSACTIONS, DECEMBER 19, 1994

Quotations as of 5 p.m. Eastern Time
Monday, December 19, 1994

	52 Weeks Hi	Lo	Stock	Sym	Div	Yld %	PE	Vol 100s	Hi	Lo	Close	Net Chg
					-A-A-A-							
	17⅜	11⅞	AAR	AIR	.48	3.8	23	454	12¾	12½	12⅝	− ⅛
	23⅞	17¼	ABM Indus	ABM	.52	2.2	14	207	23½	23¼	23¼	− ⅛
	12⅝	9	ACM Gvt Fd	ACG	1.10a	11.4	...	1356	9⅝	9½	9⅝	...
	10⅛	6⅞	ACM OppFd	AOF	.80	11.0	...	343	7⅜	7¼	7¼	...
	12¼	7⅝	ACM SecFd	GSF	1.10	12.8	...	1309	8¾	8⅝	8⅝	...
	10⅝	6¼	ACM SpctmFd	SI	.96	12.6	...	1168	7⅝	7½	7⅝	+ ⅛
	15⅛	9¾	ACM Mgmdinc	ADF	1.46	14.2	...	706	10½	10¼	10¼	− ⅛
	11¾	7⅞	ACM MgdincFd	AMF	1.08a	12.7	...	249	8½	8⅜	8½	...
	9⅝	7⅞	ACM MgdMultFd	MMF	.72	8.6	...	191	8½	8⅜	8⅜	...
	14¼	9⅛	ACM MuniSec	AMU	.90a	8.6	...	217	10½	10⅜	10½	+ ⅛
	11⅞	8½	ADT	ADT	...		15	575	10⅜	10⅜	10½	
	36⅛	25¼ ♣	AFLAC	AFL	.46	1.4	12	1544	33⅜	33⅛	33¼	− ¼
s	36¾	18⅝	AGCO Cp	AG	.03	.1	7	1498	29⅝	28½	28⅝	+ ⅛
	72¼	40¾	AGCO pf		1.64	2.8	...	143	57¾	56¼	57¾	− ¼
	18⅛	12⅝	AL Pharma	ALO	.18	1.0	41	446	18⅛	17⅝	18⅛	+ ½
n	23¼	17	AMLI Resdntl	AML	1.68	8.5	...	510	20½	19¾	19¾	− ¼
	79⅝	57⅝ ♣	AMP	AMP	1.68	2.3	22	876	72½	71¾	72½	− ⅝
	72¾	48⅛	AMR	AMR	...		cc	1905	51⅜	50¾	51¼	+ ⅝
	51	43	ARCO Chm	RCM	2.50	5.6	16	248	44⅞	44¾	44¾	
	56½	38⅝	ASA	ASA	2.00	4.5	...	416	44¼	44	44	− ¼
	27⅝	19¾	ATT Cap	TCC	.40f	1.8	10	140	21⅜	21¾	21⅝	− ⅛
	57⅛	47¼	AT&T Cp	T	1.32	2.6	17	15580	51½	51⅛	51⅜	− ¼
	33	25⅜	AbbotLab	ABT	.76	2.3	18	6435	32½	32	32⅜	...
	8¼	2⅞	Abex	ABE	...		10	102	7⅛	7	7⅛	
	15¼	11⅜	Abitibi g	ABY	...	...		94	13⅞	13⅝	13⅝	− ⅛
	18	11⅛ ♣	AcceptIns	AIF	...		10	145	14	13¾	13¾	− ⅛
	31¼	20¾	ACE Ltd	ACL	.44	2.1	dd	674	21¾	20⅞	21⅛	− ½
	15½	8¾	AcmeCleve	AMT	.44	4.1	11	15	10¾	10⅜	10¾	+ ⅛
	14	6½	AcmeElec	ACE	...		dd	41	13⅛	13	13⅛	+ ⅛
	31⅜	23	♣ Acordia	ACO	.60	1.9	16	6	31¼	31⅛	31⅛	+ ⅛
	13¾	5¾	ActavaGp	ACT	.09j	...	dd	117	9⅞	9⅝	9¾	− ⅛
	18⅝	**11¼**	**Acuson**	**ACN**			26	472	16⅝	16	16	− ⅛
	18⅝	15⅜	AdamsExp	ADX	1.60e	10.2	...	429	15⅝	15½	15⅝	...
n	19¾	18⅛	PensnProvdSA ADR	PVD	...	...		347	19½	19⅜	19½	+ ¼
	31¾	16¾	AdvMicro	AMD	...		7	10846	23⅜	22½	22½	− ⅝
	64	46½	AdvMicro pf		3.00	5.9	...	172	51½	50½	50½	− ½
	6⅞	5	Advest	ADV	...		15	64	5⅜	5¼	5¼	− ¼
	20	15	Advo	AD	.10	.6	15	282	16⅜	16	16¼	...
n	11⅝	8¼	Advocat	AVC	...	...		434	11½	11¼	11½	+ ¼
	64	49⅜	AEGON NV	AEG	2.21e	3.5	11	44	63½	63¼	63½	+ ¼
	5	3⅝ ♣	Aeroflex	ARX	...		12	46	3¾	3⅝	3¾	+ ¼
n	26¼	25	AetnaMIPS pfA		.05p	...	...	230	26	25¾	26	...
	65¾	42¼	AetnaLife	AET	2.76	6.0	dd	1783	46	45½	45¾	+ ⅛
	14¾	8¼ ♣	AgnicoEgl	AEM	.10	1.0	...	646	9¾	9½	9⅝	...
n▼	19⅝	15½	AgreeRlty	ADC	1.80	11.4	...	47	15⅜	15⅝	15¾	+ ⅛
	22¾	15¼	Ahmanson	AHM	.88	5.3	10	2746	16⅝	16¼	16⅜	+ ¼
	27¼	22⅛	Ahmanson pfC		2.10	9.0	...	18	23¾	23¼	23⅝	− ⅜
	52	39¾	Ahmanson pfD		3.00	7.3	...	216	41	40½	41	+ ¼
	28¼	24½			2.40	9.5	...	50	25⅜	25⅛	25¼	

Notes: The "pf" following the stock name of the second AGCO listing tells us that this one is a preferred stock rather than a common stock. A "▲" preceding the columns containing a stock's 52-week high and low prices indicates that the price hit a new 52-week high, whereas a "▼" indicates a new 52-week low. AgreeRlty hit a new low on December 19, 1994. An "x" preceding the columns containing the 52-week high and low prices indicates that the stock went ex-dividend that day; this means that someone who buys the stock will not receive the next dividend. An "s" preceding the 52-week high and low prices indicates that the stock was split within the past 52 weeks. (See Chapter 13 for a discussion of stock splits.) AGCO Corp. had a stock split during the past 52-week period. An "n" preceding the 52-week high and low prices indicates that the stock is newly issued within the past 52 weeks. There were five stocks in Figure 8-8 that were newly issued within the past 52 weeks; AgreeRlty was one of them. Those companies whose listings are underlined have had large changes in volume compared with average trading volume; Advocat is an example. An "a" following the dividend column indicates an extra dividend in addition to the regular dividend, while an "f" following the dividend column indicates that the annual dividend was increased on the last declaration date. An "e" following the dividend column indicates that a dividend was declared or paid in the preceding 12 months, but there is no regular dividend rate; AEGON NV is an example. A "j" following the dividend column indicates the dividend paid this year; however, at the last dividend meeting a dividend was omitted or deferred. Finally, a "club" appearing before the company name indicates that *Journal* readers can obtain a copy of the company's annual report.
SOURCE: *The Wall Street Journal,* December 20, 1994, C3.

EVALUATING STOCKS THAT DON'T PAY DIVIDENDS

In this chapter, we presented several equations for valuing a firm's common stock. These equations had one common element: they all assumed that the firm is currently paying a dividend. However, many firms, even highly profitable ones, have never paid a dividend. If a firm is expected to begin paying dividends in the future, we can modify the equations presented in the chapter and use them to determine the value of the stock.

A new business often expects to have low sales during its first few years of operation as it develops its product. Then, if the product catches on, sales will grow rapidly for several years. For example, Compaq Computer Company had only three employees when it was incorporated in 1982. Its first year was devoted to product development, and 1982 sales were zero. In 1983, however, Compaq began marketing its personal computer, and its sales hit $111 million, a record first-year volume for any new firm. By 1986 Compaq was included in Fortune's 500 largest U.S. industrial firms. Obviously, Compaq has been more successful than most new businesses, but it is common for small firms to have growth rates of 100 percent, 500 percent, or even 1,000 percent during their first few years of operation.

Sales growth brings with it the need for additional assets — Compaq could not have increased sales as it did without also increasing its assets, and asset growth requires an increase in liability and/or equity accounts. Small firms can generally obtain some bank credit, but they must maintain a reasonable balance between debt and equity. Thus, additional bank borrowings require increases in equity, and getting the equity capital needed to support growth can be difficult for small firms. They have limited access to the capital markets, and, even when they can sell common stock, the owners of small firms are reluctant to do so for fear of losing voting control. Therefore, the best source of equity for most small businesses is retained earnings, and for this reason most small firms pay no dividends during their rapid growth years. Eventually, though, successful small firms do pay dividends, and those dividends generally grow rapidly at first but slow down to a sustainable constant rate once the firm reaches maturity.

If a firm currently pays no dividend but is expected to pay dividends in the future, the value of its stock can be found as follows:

1. Estimate when dividends will be paid, the amount of the first dividend, the growth rate during the supernormal growth period, the length of the supernormal period, the long-run (constant) growth rate, and the rate of return required by investors.
2. Use the constant growth model to determine the price of the stock after the firm reaches a stable growth situation.
3. Set out on a time line the cash flows (dividends during the supernormal growth period and the stock price once the constant growth state is reached), and then find the present value of these cash flows. That present value represents the value of the stock today.

To illustrate this process, consider the situation for MarvelLure Inc., a company that was set up in 1994 to produce and market a new high-tech fishing lure. MarvelLure's sales are currently growing at a rate of 200 percent per year. The company expects to experience a high but declining rate of growth in sales and earnings during the next 10 years, after which analysts estimate that it will grow at a steady 10 percent per year. The firm's management has announced that it will pay no dividends for 5 years, but if earnings materialize as forecasted, it will pay a dividend of $0.20 per share at the end of Year 6, $0.30 in Year 7, $0.40 in Year 8, $0.45 in Year 9, and $0.50 in Year 10. After Year 10, current plans are to increase the dividend by 10 percent per year.

MarvelLure's investment bankers estimate that investors require a 15 percent return on similar stocks. Therefore, we find the value of a share of MarvelLure's stock as follows:

$$
\begin{aligned}
P_0 = {} & \frac{\$0}{(1.15)^1} + \cdots + \frac{\$0}{(1.15)^5} \\
& + \frac{\$0.20}{(1.15)^6} + \frac{\$0.30}{(1.15)^7} \\
& + \frac{\$0.40}{(1.15)^8} + \frac{\$0.45}{(1.15)^9} + \frac{\$0.50}{(1.15)^{10}} \\
& + \left(\frac{\$0.50(1.10)}{0.15 - 0.10}\right)\left(\frac{1}{(1.15)^{10}}\right) \\
= {} & \$3.30.
\end{aligned}
$$

The last term finds the expected price of the stock in Year 10 and then finds the present value of that price. Thus, we see that the valuation concepts discussed in the chapter can be applied to firms which currently pay no dividends, provided an estimate of future dividends can be made. Clearly, though, these estimates are uncertain, hence stocks such as MarvelLure are very risky.

PREFERRED STOCK[20]

Preferred stock is a *hybrid* — it is similar to bonds in some respects and to common stock in others. The hybrid nature of preferred stock becomes apparent when we try to classify it in relation to bonds and common stock. Like bonds, preferred stock has a par value and a fixed amount of dividends which must be paid before dividends can be paid on the common stock. However, if the preferred dividend is not earned, the directors can omit (or "pass") it without throwing the company into bankruptcy. So, although preferred stock has a fixed payment like bonds, a failure to make this payment will not lead to bankruptcy.

Accountants define preferred stock to be equity and report it in the equity portion of the balance sheet under "preferred stock" or "preferred equity." However, financial analysts sometimes treat preferred stock as debt and at other times treat it as equity, depending on the type of analysis being conducted. If the analysis is being made from the viewpoint of a common stockholder, the key consideration is the fact that the preferred dividend is a fixed charge which reduces earnings on the common. Therefore, from the common stockholder's point of view, preferred stock is similar to debt. Suppose, however, that the analysis is being made by a bondholder studying the firm's vulnerability to failure in the event of a decline in sales and income. If the firm's income declines, the bondholders have a prior claim to the available income ahead of preferred stockholders, and if the firm fails, bondholders have a prior claim to assets when the firm is liquidated. Thus, to a bondholder, preferred stock is similar to common equity.

From management's perspective, preferred stock lies between debt and common equity. Since failure to pay dividends on preferred stock will not force the firm into bankruptcy, preferred stock is safer to use than debt. At the same time, if the firm is highly successful, the common stockholders will not have to share that success with the preferred stockholders, because preferred dividends are fixed. Remember, however, that the preferred stockholders do have a higher priority claim than the common stockholders. We see, then, that preferred stock has some of the characteristics of debt and some of the characteristics of common stock, and it is used in situations in which neither debt nor common stock is entirely appropriate.

MAJOR PROVISIONS OF PREFERRED STOCK ISSUES

Preferred stock has a number of features, the most important of which are discussed in the following sections.

PRIORITY CLAIM ON ASSETS AND EARNINGS. Preferred stockholders have priority over common stockholders with regard to earnings and assets. Thus, dividends must be paid on preferred stock before they can be paid on the common stock, and, in the event of bankruptcy, the claims of the preferred shareholders must be satisfied before the common stockholders receive anything. To reinforce these features, most preferred stocks have coverage requirements similar to those on bonds. These restrictions limit the amount of preferred stock a company can use, and they also require a minimum level of retained earnings before common dividends can be paid.

---

[20]The material on preferred stock is not difficult, but if time pressures are great, instructors may elect to omit it without loss of continuity.

PAR VALUE.   Unlike common stock, preferred stock always has a par value (or its equivalent under some other name), and this value is important. First, the par value establishes the amount due the preferred stockholders in the event a firm is liquidated. Second, the preferred dividend is frequently stated as a percentage of the par value. For example, an issue of Duke Power's preferred stock has a par value of $100 and a stated dividend of 7.8 percent of par. The same results would, of course, be produced if this issue of Duke's preferred stock simply called for an annual dividend of $7.80.

Cumulative Dividends

A protective feature on preferred stock that requires preferred dividends previously not paid to be paid before any common dividends can be paid.

CUMULATIVE DIVIDENDS.   Most preferred stock provides for **cumulative dividends;** that is, any preferred dividends not paid in previous periods (that is, "in arrears") must be paid before common dividends can be paid. The cumulative feature is a protective device, for if the preferred stock dividends were not cumulative, a firm could avoid paying preferred and common stock dividends for, say, 10 years, plowing back all of its earnings, and then pay a huge common stock dividend but pay only the stipulated annual dividend to the preferred stockholders. Obviously, such an action would effectively void the preferred position which preferred stockholders are supposed to enjoy. The cumulative feature helps prevent such abuses.[21]

CONVERTIBILITY.   About half of all preferred stock issued in recent years is convertible into common stock. For example, each share of Enron's $10.50 Class J preferred stock can be converted into 3.413 shares of its common stock at the option of the preferred shareholders.

OTHER PROVISIONS.   Some other provisions occasionally encountered in preferred stocks include the following:

1. **Voting rights.** Preferred stockholders are generally given the right to vote for directors if the company has not paid the preferred dividend for a specified period, such as ten quarters. This feature motivates management to make every effort to pay preferred dividends.

2. **Participating.** A rare type of preferred stock is one that participates with the common stock in sharing the firm's earnings. Participating preferred stocks generally work as follows: (a) the stated preferred dividend is paid — for example, $5 a share; (b) the common stock is then entitled to a dividend in an amount up to the preferred dividend; (c) if the common dividend is raised, say, to $5.50, the preferred dividend must likewise be raised to $5.50.

3. **Sinking fund.** In the past (before the mid-1970s), few preferred issues had sinking funds. Today, however, most newly issued preferred stocks have sinking funds which call for the purchase and retirement of a given percentage of the issue each year. If the amount is 2 percent, which is used frequently, the preferred issue will have an average life of 25 years and a maximum life of 50 years.

4. **Call provision.** A call provision gives the issuing corporation the right to call in the preferred stock for redemption. As in the case of bonds, call provisions generally state that the company must pay an amount greater than the par value of the preferred stock, the additional sum being termed a

---

[21]Note, however, that compounding is absent in most cumulative plans — in other words, the unpaid preferred dividends themselves earn no return. Also, many preferred issues have a limited cumulative feature; for example, unpaid preferred dividends might accumulate for only three years.

Call Premium
The amount in excess of par value that a company must pay when it calls a security.

call premium. For example, Trivoli Corporation's 12 percent, $100 par value preferred stock, issued in 1990, is noncallable for 10 years, but it may be called at a price of $112 after 2000.

5. **Maturity.** Before the mid-1970s, most preferred stock was *perpetual* — it had no maturity and never needed to be paid off. However, today most new preferred stock has a sinking fund and thus an effective maturity date.

PROS AND CONS OF PREFERRED STOCK

As noted below, there are both advantages and disadvantages to financing with preferred stock.

ISSUER'S VIEWPOINT. By using preferred stock, a firm can fix its financial costs and thus keep more of the potential future profits for its existing common stockholders, yet still avoid the danger of bankruptcy if earnings are too low to meet these fixed charges. Also, by selling preferred rather than common stock, the firm avoids sharing control with new investors.

However, preferred stock does have a major disadvantage from the issuer's standpoint: It has a higher after-tax cost of capital than debt. The major reason for this higher cost is taxes: Preferred dividends are not deductible as a tax expense, whereas interest expense is deductible.

One would think that a given firm's preferred stock would carry a higher coupon rate than its bonds because of the preferred's greater risk from the holder's viewpoint. However, 70 percent of preferred dividends received by corporate owners are exempt from income taxes, and this has made preferred stock very attractive to corporate investors. Therefore, most preferred stock is owned by corporations, and, in recent years, high-grade preferreds, on average, have sold on a lower-yield basis than high-grade bonds. As an example, Alabama Power several years ago sold a preferred issue yielding 11 percent to investors. On the day the preferred was issued, Alabama Power's bonds yielded 13 percent, or 2 percentage points more than the preferred. The tax treatment accounted for this differential. For a corporate investor in the 40 percent tax bracket,

$$\text{After-tax yield on bonds} = \text{Yield} - \text{Yield}(T)$$
$$= \text{Yield}(1 - T) = 13\%(0.6) = 7.8\%.$$
$$\text{After-tax yield on preferred} = \text{Yield} - \text{Yield}(1 - \text{Exclusion})(T)$$
$$= 11\% - 11\%(0.3)(0.4)$$
$$= 11\%(1 - 0.12) = 11\%(0.88) = 9.68\%.$$

Thus, the *after-tax* yield to a corporate investor was greater on the preferred stock than on the bonds.

As we shall see in Chapter 9, the corporate tax situation makes the component cost of preferred stock much greater than that of bonds — the after-tax cost of debt is approximately two-thirds of the stated coupon rate for profitable firms, whereas the cost of preferred stock is the full percentage amount of the preferred dividend. Of course, the deductibility differential is most important for issuers that are in relatively high tax brackets. If a company pays little or no taxes because it is unprofitable or because it has a great deal of accelerated depreciation, the deductibility of interest does not make much difference. Thus, the lower a company's tax bracket, the more likely it is to issue preferred stock.

INVESTOR'S VIEWPOINT.   In designing securities, the financial manager must consider the investor's point of view. It is sometimes asserted that preferred stock has so many disadvantages to both the issuer and the investor that it should never be issued. Nevertheless, preferred stock is being issued in substantial amounts. It provides investors with steadier and more assured income than common stock, and it has a preference over common in the event a firm is liquidated. In addition, 70 percent of the preferred dividends received by corporations are not taxable. For this reason, most preferred stock is owned by corporations.

The principal disadvantage of preferred stock from an investor's standpoint is that although preferred stockholders bear some of the ownership risks, their returns are limited. Other disadvantages are that (1) preferred stockholders have no legally enforceable right to dividends, even if a company earns a profit, and (2) for individual as opposed to corporate investors, after-tax bond yields are generally higher than those on preferred stock, even though the preferred is riskier. Because of this last point, it is generally unwise for individuals to own preferred stocks, except possibly convertible preferreds.

RECENT TRENDS

Because preferred dividends are not deductible expenses for the issuing corporation, many companies have retired their preferred stocks and replaced them with debentures or subordinated debentures. However, as the following examples illustrate, preferred is still being used to raise long-term capital under a number of different conditions, including situations where neither common stock nor long-term debt can be issued on reasonable terms.

1. Chrysler's issue of preferred stock with warrants several years ago proved a successful means of raising capital in the face of adverse circumstances. Because of its losses, Chrysler's common stock was depressed and very much out of favor. Investors were so worried about the company's ability to survive that they were unwilling to make additional commitments without receiving some sort of senior position. Therefore, common stock was ruled out. Chrysler had already borrowed to the hilt, and it could not obtain any more debt without first building its equity base (and preferred is equity from the bondholders' viewpoint). Various incentives were offered to the brokers who handled the preferred issue, and a relatively high yield was set. As a result, the issue was so successful that its size was raised from $150 to $200 million while the underwriting was under way. Chrysler got the money it needed, and that money helped the company survive.

2. Utility companies often use preferred stock to bolster the equity component of their capital structures. These companies are capital intensive, and they make heavy use of debt financing. However, lenders and rating agencies require minimum equity ratios as a condition for maintaining bond ratings. Also, the utilities have made very heavy investments in fixed assets and thus have high depreciation charges, which has held down their effective tax rates. These low tax rates have lowered the tax disadvantage of preferred stock in relation to debt.

3. In recent years there has been much use of convertible preferred in connection with mergers. For example, when Belco Petroleum was negotiating its acquisition by Enron, it was pointed out that if the buyout were for cash, Belco's stockholders (one of whom owned 40 percent of the stock and thus

could block the merger) would be required to immediately pay huge capital gains taxes. However, under U.S. tax laws, if preferred stock is exchanged for the acquired company's common, this constitutes a tax-free exchange of securities. Thus, Belco's stockholders could obtain a fixed-income security yet postpone the payment of taxes on their capital gains.

Enron actually offered a choice of straight or convertible preferred to Belco's stockholders. Those stockholders who were interested primarily in income could take the straight preferred, whereas those interested in capital gains could take the convertible preferred.

Floating Rate Preferred Stock
Preferred stock whose dividend rate fluctuates with changes in the general level of interest rates.

4. In 1984, Alabama Power introduced a new type of security, **floating rate preferred stock.** Since this stock had a floating rate, its price would stay relatively constant, making it suitable for liquid asset portfolios (marketable securities held by corporations to provide funds either for planned expenditures or to meet emergencies). The combination of a floating rate, hence a stable price, plus the 70 percent dividend exclusion for corporations, made this preferred quite attractive, and it enabled Alabama Power to obtain capital at a low cost. Many other companies have since used various types of floating rate preferred stocks.

 SELF-TEST QUESTIONS

Explain the following statement: "Preferred stock is a hybrid security."

Identify and briefly explain some of the key features of preferred stock.

What are the advantages and disadvantages of preferred stock from an issuer's viewpoint?

What are the advantages and disadvantages of preferred stock from an investor's viewpoint?

PREFERRED STOCK VALUATION

Most preferred stocks entitle their owners to regular, fixed dividend payments. If the payments last forever, the issue is a perpetuity whose value, V_{ps}, is found as follows:

$$V_{ps} = \frac{D_{ps}}{k_{ps}}. \tag{8-6}$$

V_{ps} is the value of the preferred stock, D_{ps} is the preferred dividend, and k_{ps} is the required rate of return. Allied Food Products has preferred stock outstanding which pays a dividend of \$10 per year. If the required rate of return on this preferred stock is 10 percent, its value is \$100, found by solving Equation 8-6 as follows:

$$V_{ps} = \frac{\$10.00}{0.10} = \$100.00.$$

If we know the current price of a preferred stock and its dividend, we can solve for the current rate being earned, as follows:

$$k_{ps} = \frac{D_{ps}}{V_{ps}}. \tag{8-6a}$$

Most preferred stock pays dividends quarterly. This is true for Allied Food, so we could find the effective rate of return on its preferred stock as follows:

$$\text{EFF\%} = \text{EAR}_{ps} = \left(1 + \frac{k_{Nom}}{m}\right)^m - 1 = \left(1 + \frac{0.10}{4}\right)^4 - 1 = 10.38\%.$$

If an investor wanted to compare the returns on Allied's bonds and its preferred stock, it would be best to convert the nominal rates on each security to effective rates and then compare these "equivalent annual rates."

SUMMARY

Corporate decisions should be analyzed in terms of how alternative courses of action are likely to affect the value of a firm. However, it is necessary to know how preferred and common stock prices are established before attempting to measure how a given decision will affect a specific firm's value. This chapter showed how preferred and common stock values are determined, and also how investors go about estimating the rates of return they expect to earn. The key concepts covered are summarized below.

- A **proxy** is a document which gives one person the power to act for another person, typically the power to vote shares of common stock. A proxy fight occurs when an outside group solicits stockholders' proxies in an effort to vote a new management team into office.

- A **takeover** occurs when a person or group succeeds in ousting a firm's management and taking control of the company.

- Stockholders often have the right to purchase any additional shares sold by the firm. This right, called the **preemptive right,** protects the control of the present stockholders and prevents dilution of their stock's value.

- Although most firms have only one type of common stock, in some instances **classified stock** is used to meet the special needs of the company. One type of classified stock is **founders' shares.** This is stock owned by the firm's founders that carries sole voting rights but restricted dividends for a specified number of years.

- The major **advantages of common stock financings** are as follows: (1) there is no obligation to make fixed payments, (2) common stock never matures, (3) the use of common stock increases the creditworthiness of the firm, (4) stock can often be sold on better terms than debt, and (5) using stock helps the firm maintain a reserve borrowing capacity.

- The major **disadvantages of common stock financings** are (1) they extend voting privileges to new stockholders, (2) new stockholders share in the firm's profits, (3) the flotation costs of stock financings are high, (4) using stock can raise the firm's cost of capital, and (5) dividends paid on common stock are not tax deductible.

- A **closely held corporation** is one that is owned by a few individuals who are typically associated with the firm's management.

- A **publicly owned corporation** is one that is owned by a relatively large number of individuals who are not actively involved in its management.

- Whenever stock in a closely held corporation is offered to the public for the first time, the company is said to be **going public.** The market for stock that is just being offered to the public is called the **initial public offering (IPO) market.**

■ The **value of a share of stock** is calculated as the **present value of the stream of dividends** the stock is expected to provide in the future.

■ The equation used to find the **value of a constant growth stock** is:

$$\hat{P}_0 = \frac{D_1}{k_s - g}.$$

■ The **expected total rate of return** from a stock consists of an **expected dividend yield** plus an **expected capital gains yield.** For a constant growth firm, both the expected dividend yield and the expected capital gains yield are constant.

■ The equation for $\hat{k}_s$, **the expected rate of return on a constant growth stock,** can be expressed as follows:

$$\hat{k}_s = \frac{D_1}{P_0} + g.$$

■ A **zero growth stock** is one whose future dividends are not expected to grow at all, while a **supernormal growth stock** is one whose earnings and dividends are expected to grow much faster than the economy as a whole over some specified time period and then to grow at the "normal" rate.

■ To find the **present value of a supernormal growth stock,** (1) find the dividends expected during the supernormal growth period, (2) find the price of the stock at the end of the supernormal growth period, (3) discount the dividends and the projected price back to the present, and (4) sum these PVs to find the current value of the stock, $\hat{P}_0$.

■ The **Efficient Markets Hypothesis (EMH)** holds (1) that stocks are always in equilibrium and (2) that it is impossible for an investor who does not have inside information to consistently "beat the market." Therefore, according to the EMH, stocks are always fairly valued ($\hat{P}_0 = P_0$), the required return on a stock is equal to its expected return ($k = \hat{k}$), and all stocks' expected returns plot on the SML.

■ We saw that differences can and do exist between expected and realized returns in the stock and bond markets — only for short-term, risk-free assets are expected and actual (or realized) returns equal.

■ **Preferred stock** is a hybrid security having some characteristics of debt and some of equity.

■ Most preferred stocks are **perpetuities,** and the value of a share of perpetual preferred stock is found as the dividend divided by the required rate of return:

$$V_{ps} = \frac{D_{ps}}{k_{ps}}.$$

QUESTIONS

8-1 Two investors are evaluating AT&T's stock for possible purchase. They agree on the expected value of D_1 and also on the expected future dividend growth rate. Further, they agree on the riskiness of the stock. However, one investor normally holds stocks for 2 years, while the other normally holds stocks for 10 years. On the basis of the type of analysis done in this chapter, they should both be willing to pay the same price for AT&T's stock. True or false? Explain.

we adjust the interest rate downward to take account of the preferential tax treatment of debt.[4]

Note that the cost of debt is the interest rate on *new* debt, not that on already outstanding debt; in other words, we are interested in the *marginal* cost of debt. Our primary concern with the cost of capital is to use it for capital budgeting decisions — for example, would a new machine earn a return greater than the cost of the capital needed to acquire the machine? The rate at which the firm has borrowed in the past is irrelevant for cost of capital purposes.

❓ SELF-TEST QUESTIONS

Why is the after-tax cost of debt rather than the before-tax cost used to calculate the weighted average cost of capital?

Is the relevant cost of debt the interest rate on already *outstanding* debt or that on *new* debt? Why?

COST OF PREFERRED STOCK, k_{ps}

Cost of Preferred Stock, k_{ps}
The rate of return investors require on the firm's preferred stock. k_{ps} is calculated as the preferred dividend, D_{ps}, divided by the net issuing price, P_n.

The component **cost of preferred stock, k_{ps}**, used to calculate the weighted average cost of capital is the preferred dividend, D_{ps}, divided by the net issuing price, P_n, or the price the firm receives after deducting flotation costs:

$$\text{Component cost of preferred stock} = k_{ps} = \frac{D_{ps}}{P_n}. \qquad (9\text{-}2)$$

For example, Allied has preferred stock that pays a $10 dividend per share and sells for $100 per share in the market. If Allied issues new shares of preferred, it will

---

[4]The tax rate is *zero* for a firm with losses. Therefore, for a company that does not pay taxes, the cost of debt is not reduced; that is, in Equation 9-1, the tax rate equals zero, so the after-tax cost of debt is equal to the interest rate.

It should also be noted that we have ignored flotation costs (the costs incurred for new issuances) on debt. The reason is that the vast majority of debt (over 99 percent) is privately placed, hence has no flotation cost. However, if bonds are publicly placed and do involve flotation costs, the solution value of k_d in this formula is used as the after-tax cost of debt:

$$M(1 - F) = \sum_{t=1}^{N} \frac{INT(1 - T)}{(1 + k_d)^t} + \frac{M}{(1 + k_d)^N}.$$

Here F is the percentage amount of the bond flotation cost, N is the number of periods to maturity, INT is the dollars of interest per period, T is the corporate tax rate, M is the maturity value of the bond, and k_d is the after-tax cost of debt adjusted to reflect flotation costs. If we assume that the bond in the example calls for annual payments, that it has a 20-year maturity, and that F = 2%, then the flotation-adjusted, after-tax cost of debt is 6.18 percent versus 6 percent before the flotation adjustment.

Strictly speaking, the after-tax cost of debt should relect the *expected* cost of debt. While Allied's bonds have a promised return of 10 percent, there is some chance of default, so its bondholders' expected return (and consequently Allied's cost) is a bit less than 10 percent. For a relatively strong company such as Allied, this difference is quite small. Note too that Allied must incur flotation costs when it issues debt, but like the difference between the promised and the expected rate of return, flotation costs are generally small. Finally, note that these two factors tend to offset one another — not including the possibility of default leads to an overstatement of the cost of debt, but not including flotation costs leads to an understatement. For all these reasons, k_d is generally a good approximation of the before-tax cost of debt capital.

incur an underwriting (or flotation) cost of 2.5 percent, or $2.50 per share, so it will net $97.50 per share. Therefore, Allied's cost of preferred stock is 10.3 percent:

$$k_{ps} = \$10/\$97.50 = 10.3\%.$$

No tax adjustments are made when calculating k_{ps} because preferred dividends, unlike interest expense on debt, are *not* deductible, hence there are no tax savings associated with the use of preferred stock.

SELF-TEST QUESTIONS

Does the component cost of preferred stock include or exclude flotation costs? Explain.

Is a tax adjustment made to the cost of preferred stock? Why or why not?

COST OF RETAINED EARNINGS, k_s

Cost of Retained Earnings, k_s
The rate of return required by stockholders on a firm's common stock.

The costs of debt and preferred stock are based on the returns investors require on these securities. Similarly, the **cost of retained earnings, k_s,** is the rate of return stockholders require on equity capital the firm obtains by retaining earnings.[5]

The reason we must assign a cost of capital to retained earnings involves the *opportunity cost principle.* The firm's after-tax earnings literally belong to its stockholders. Bondholders are compensated by interest payments, and preferred stockholders by preferred dividends. All earnings remaining after interest and preferred dividends belong to the common stockholders, and these earnings serve to compensate stockholders for the use of their capital. Management may either pay out earnings in the form of dividends or else retain earnings and reinvest them in the business. If management decides to retain earnings, there is an *opportunity cost* involved — stockholders could have received the earnings as dividends and invested this money in other stocks, in bonds, in real estate, or in anything else. Thus, the firm should earn on its retained earnings at least as much as the stockholders themselves could earn on alternative investments of comparable risk.

What rate of return can stockholders expect to earn on equivalent-risk investments? First, recall from Chapter 8 that stocks are normally in equilibrium, with the expected and required rates of return being equal: $\hat{k}_s = k_s$. Thus, we can assume that Allied's stockholders expect to earn a return of k_s on their money. *Therefore, if the firm cannot invest retained earnings and earn at least k_s, it should pay these funds to its stockholders and let them invest directly in other assets that do provide this return.*[6]

Whereas debt and preferred stocks are contractual obligations that have easily determined costs, it is difficult to measure k_s. However, we can employ the principles developed in Chapters 5 and 8 to produce reasonably good cost of equity

---

[5]The term *retained earnings* can be interpreted to mean either the balance sheet item "retained earnings," consisting of all the earnings retained in the business throughout its history, or the income statement item "additions to retained earnings." The income statement item is used in this chapter; for our purpose, *retained earnings* refers to that part of the current year's earnings not paid out in dividends, hence available for reinvestment in the business this year.

[6]Dividends and capital gains are taxed differently, with long-term capital gains being taxed at a lower rate than dividends for many stockholders. That makes it beneficial for companies to retain earnings rather than to pay them out as dividends, and that, in turn, results in a relatively low cost of capital for retained earnings. This point is discussed in detail in Chapter 13.

estimates. Recall that if a stock is in equilibrium, then its required rate of return, k_s, must be equal to its expected rate of return, $\hat{k}_s$. Further, its *required* return is equal to a risk-free rate, k_{RF}, plus a risk premium, RP, whereas the *expected* return on a constant growth stock is equal to the stock's dividend yield, D_1/P_0, plus its expected growth rate, g:

$$\text{Required rate of return} = \text{Expected rate of return}$$
$$k_s = k_{RF} + RP \quad = \quad D_1/P_0 + g = \hat{k}_s. \tag{9-3}$$

Therefore, we can estimate k_s either as $k_s = k_{RF} + RP$ or as $k_s = D_1/P_0 + g$.

THE CAPM APPROACH

One approach to estimating the cost of retained earnings is to use the Capital Asset Pricing Model (CAPM) as developed in Chapter 5, proceeding as follows:

Step 1. Estimate the risk-free rate, k_{RF}, generally taken to be either the U.S. Treasury bond rate or the short-term (30-day) Treasury bill rate.

Step 2. Estimate the stock's beta coefficient, b_i, and use this as an index of the stock's risk. The i signifies the *i*th company's beta.

Step 3. Estimate the expected rate of return on the market, or on an "average" stock, k_M.

Step 4. Substitute the preceding values into the CAPM equation to estimate the required rate of return on the stock in question:

$$k_s = k_{RF} + (k_M - k_{RF})b_i. \tag{9-4}$$

Equation 9-4 shows that the CAPM estimate of k_s begins with the risk-free rate, k_{RF}, to which is added a risk premium set equal to the risk premium on an average stock, $k_M - k_{RF}$, scaled up or down to reflect the particular stock's risk as measured by its beta coefficient.

To illustrate the CAPM approach, assume that $k_{RF} = 8\%$, $k_M = 13\%$, and $b_i = 0.7$ for a given stock. This stock's k_s is calculated as follows:

$$k_s = 8\% + (13\% - 8\%)(0.7)$$
$$= 8\% + (5\%)(0.7)$$
$$= 8\% + 3.5\%$$
$$= 11.5\%.$$

Had b_i been 1.8, indicating that the stock was riskier than average, its k_s would have been

$$k_s = 8\% + (5\%)(1.8)$$
$$= 8\% + 9\%$$
$$= 17\%.$$

For an average stock when k_{RF} is 8 percent and the market risk premium is 5 percent,

$$k_s = k_M = 8\% + (5\%)(1.0) = 13\%.$$

It should be noted that although the CAPM approach appears to yield accurate, precise estimates of k_s, there are actually several problems with it. First, as we saw in Chapter 5, if a firm's stockholders are not well diversified, they may be concerned with *stand-alone risk* rather than with market risk only. In that case, the firm's true investment risk will not be measured by its beta, and the CAPM procedure will understate the correct value of k_s. Further, even if the CAPM method is valid, it is hard to obtain correct estimates of the inputs required to make it operational: (1) there is controversy about whether to use long-term or short-term Treasury yields for k_{RF}; (2) it is hard to estimate the beta that investors expect the company to have in the future; and (3) it is difficult to estimate the market risk premium.

BOND-YIELD-PLUS-RISK-PREMIUM APPROACH

Analysts who do not have confidence in the CAPM often use a subjective, ad hoc procedure to estimate a firm's cost of common equity: they simply add a judgmental risk premium of three to five percentage points to the interest rate on the firm's own long-term debt. It is logical to think that firms with risky, low-rated, and consequently high-interest-rate debt will also have risky, high-cost equity, and the procedure of basing the cost of equity on a readily observable debt cost utilizes this precept. For example, if an extremely strong firm such as Southern Bell had bonds which yielded 8 percent, its cost of equity might be estimated as follows:

$$k_s = \text{Bond yield} + \text{Risk premium} = 8\% + 4\% = 12\%.$$

The debt of a riskier company such as Continental Airlines might carry a yield of 12 percent, making its estimated cost of equity 16 percent:

$$k_s = 12\% + 4\% = 16\%.$$

Because the 4 percent risk premium is a judgmental estimate, the estimated value of k_s is also judgmental. Empirical work in recent years suggests that the risk premium over a firm's own bond yield has generally ranged from 3 to 5 percentage points, so this method is not likely to produce a precise cost of equity — about all it can do is get us "into the right ballpark."

DIVIDEND-YIELD-PLUS-GROWTH-RATE, OR DISCOUNTED CASH FLOW (DCF), APPROACH

In Chapter 8, we learned that both the price and the expected rate of return on a share of common stock depend, ultimately, on the dividends expected on the stock:

$$P_0 = \frac{D_1}{(1 + k_s)^1} + \frac{D_2}{(1 + k_s)^2} + \cdots$$

$$= \sum_{t=1}^{\infty} \frac{D_t}{(1 + k_s)^t}. \tag{9-5}$$

Here P_0 is the current price of the stock; D_t is the dividend expected to be paid at the end of Year t; and k_s is the required rate of return. If dividends are expected to grow at a constant rate, then, as we saw in Chapter 8, Equation 9-5 reduces to this important formula:

$$P_0 = \frac{D_1}{k_s - g}. \tag{9-6}$$

We can solve for k_s to obtain the required rate of return on common equity, which, for the marginal investor, is also equal to the expected rate of return:

$$k_s = \hat{k}_s = \frac{D_1}{P_0} + \text{Expected g.} \tag{9-7}$$

Thus, investors expect to receive a dividend yield, D_1/P_0, plus a capital gain, g, for a total expected return of $\hat{k}_s$, and in equilibrium this expected return is also equal to the required return, k_s. This method of estimating the cost of equity is called the *discounted cash flow, or DCF, method.* Henceforth, we will assume that equilibrium exists, and we will use the terms k_s and $\hat{k}_s$ interchangeably.

It is relatively easy to determine the dividend yield, but it is difficult to establish the proper growth rate. If past growth rates in earnings and dividends have been relatively stable, and if investors appear to be projecting a continuation of past trends, then g may be based on the firm's historic growth rate. *However, if the company's past growth has been abnormally high or low, either because of its own unique situation or because of general economic fluctuations, then investors will not project the past growth rate into the future.* In this case, g must be estimated in some other manner.

Security analysts regularly make earnings and dividend growth forecasts, looking at such factors as projected sales, profit margins, and competitive factors. For example, *Value Line,* which is available in most libraries, provides growth rate forecasts for 1,700 companies, and Merrill Lynch, Salomon Brothers, and other organizations make similar forecasts. Therefore, someone making a cost of capital estimate can obtain several analysts' forecasts, average them, use the average as a proxy for the growth expectations of investors in general, and then combine this g with the current dividend yield to estimate $\hat{k}_s$ as follows:

$$\hat{k}_s = \frac{D_1}{P_0} + \text{Growth rate as projected by security analysts.}$$

Again, note that this estimate of $\hat{k}_s$ is based on the assumption that g is expected to remain constant in the future.[7]

Another method for estimating g involves first forecasting the firm's average future dividend payout ratio and its complement, the *retention rate,* and then multiplying the retention rate by the company's expected future rate of return on equity (ROE):

$$g = (\text{Retention rate})(\text{ROE}) = (1.0 - \text{Payout rate})(\text{ROE}). \tag{9-8}$$

---

[7]Analysts' growth rate forecasts are usually for five years into the future, and the rates provided represent the average growth rate over that five-year horizon. Studies have shown that analysts' forecasts represent the best source of growth rate data for DCF cost of capital estimates. See Robert Harris, "Using Analysts' Growth Rate Forecasts to Estimate Shareholder Required Rates of Return," *Financial Management,* Spring 1986.

Note also that two organizations—IBES and Zacks—collect the forecasts of leading analysts for most larger companies, average these forecasts, and then publish the averages. The IBES and Zacks data are available through on-line computer data services.

Security analysts often use this procedure when they estimate growth rates. For example, suppose a company is expected to have a constant ROE of 13.4 percent, and it is expected to pay out 40 percent of its earnings and to retain 60 percent. In this case, its forecasted growth rate would be g = (0.60)(13.4%) = 8.0%.

To illustrate the DCF approach, suppose Allied's stock sells for $23; its next expected dividend is $1.24; and its expected growth rate is 8 percent. Allied's expected and required rate of return, hence its cost of retained earnings, would then be 13.4 percent:

$$\hat{k}_s = k_s = \frac{\$1.24}{\$23} + 8.0\%$$

$$= 5.4\% + 8.0\%$$

$$= 13.4\%.$$

This 13.4 percent is the minimum rate of return that management must expect to earn to justify retaining earnings and plowing them back into the business rather than paying them out to stockholders as dividends. Put another way, investors have an *opportunity* to earn 13.4 percent if earnings are paid to them as dividends, so the company's *opportunity cost* of equity from retained earnings is 13.4 percent.

People experienced in estimating equity capital costs recognize that both careful analysis and sound judgment are required. It would be nice to pretend that judgment is unnecessary and to specify an easy, precise way of determining the exact cost of equity capital. Unfortunately, this is not possible — finance is in large part a matter of judgment, and we simply must face that fact.

SELF-TEST QUESTIONS

Why must a cost be assigned to retained earnings?

What are the three approaches for estimating the cost of retained earnings?

Identify some problems with the CAPM approach.

What is the reasoning behind the bond-yield-plus-risk-premium approach?

Which of the components of the constant growth DCF formula, the dividend yield or the growth rate, is more difficult to estimate? Why?

COST OF NEWLY ISSUED COMMON STOCK, OR EXTERNAL EQUITY, k_e

Cost of New Common Equity, k_e
The cost of external equity; based on the cost of retained earnings, but increased for flotation costs.

The **cost of new common equity, k_e,** or external equity, is higher than the cost of retained earnings, k_s, because of flotation costs involved in issuing new common stock. What rate of return must be earned on funds raised by selling stock to make issuing new stock worthwhile? To put it another way, what is the cost of new common stock?

Target (Optimal) Capital Structure
The percentages of debt, preferred stock, and common equity that will maximize the price of the firm's stock.

Weighted Average Cost of Capital, WACC
A weighted average of the component costs of debt, preferred stock, and common equity.

maximized. Therefore, a value-maximizing firm will establish a **target (optimal) capital structure** and then raise new capital in a manner that will keep the actual capital structure on target over time. In this chapter, we assume that the firm has identified its optimal capital structure, that it uses this optimum as the target, and that it finances so as to remain constantly on target. How the target is established will be examined in Chapter 12.

The target proportions of debt, preferred stock, and common equity, along with the component costs of capital, are used to calculate the firm's **weighted average cost of capital, WACC.** To illustrate, suppose Allied Food has a target capital structure calling for 45 percent debt, 2 percent preferred stock, and 53 percent common equity (retained earnings plus common stock). Its before-tax cost of debt, k_d, is 10 percent; its after-tax cost of debt $= k_d(1 - T) = 10\%(0.6) = 6.0\%$; its cost of preferred stock, k_{ps}, is 10.3 percent; its cost of common equity from retained earnings, k_s, is 13.4 percent; its marginal tax rate is 40 percent, and all of its new equity will come from retained earnings. Now we can calculate Allied's weighted average cost of capital, WACC, as follows:

$$\text{WACC} = w_d k_d(1 - T) + w_{ps} k_{ps} + w_{ce} k_s \tag{9-11}$$
$$= 0.45(10\%)(0.6) + 0.02(10.3\%) + 0.53(13.4\%)$$
$$= 10.0\%.$$

Here w_d, w_{ps}, and w_{ce} are the weights used for debt, preferred, and common equity, respectively.

Every dollar of new capital that Allied obtains consists of 45 cents of debt with an after-tax cost of 6 percent, 2 cents of preferred stock with a cost of 10.3 percent, and 53 cents of common equity (all from additions to retained earnings) with a cost of 13.4 percent. The average cost of each whole dollar, WACC, is 10 percent.

The weights could be based either on the accounting values shown on the firm's balance sheet (book values) or on the market values of the different securities. Theoretically, the weights should be based on market values, but if a firm's book value weights are reasonably close to its market value weights, book value weights can be used as a proxy for market value weights. This point is discussed further in Chapter 12, but in the remainder of this chapter, we shall assume that the firm's market values are reasonably close to its book values, and we will use book value capital structure weights.

SELF-TEST QUESTION

How does one calculate the weighted average cost of capital? Write out the equation.

MARGINAL COST OF CAPITAL, MCC

Marginal Cost of Capital (MCC)
The cost of obtaining another dollar of new capital; the weighted average cost of the last dollar of new capital raised.

The *marginal cost* of any item is the cost of another unit of that item; for example, the marginal cost of labor is the cost of adding one additional worker. The marginal cost of labor may be $25 per person if 10 workers are added but $35 per person if the firm tries to hire 100 new workers, because it will be harder to find 100 people willing and able to do the work. The same concept applies to capital. As the firm tries to attract more new dollars, the cost of each dollar will at some point rise. *Thus, the* **marginal cost of capital (MCC)** *is defined as the cost of the*

Flotati
The pe
new cc

last dollar of new capital the firm raises, and the marginal cost rises as more and more capital is raised during a given period.

We can use Allied Food Products to illustrate the marginal cost of capital concept. The company's target capital structure and other data follow:

Long-term debt	$ 754,000,000	45%
Preferred stock	40,000,000	2
Common equity	896,000,000	53
Total capital	$1,690,000,000	100%

k_d = 10%.

k_{ps} = 10.3%.

T = 40%.

P_0 = $23.

g = 8%, and it is expected to remain constant.

D_0 = $1.15 = dividends per share in the *last* period. D_0 has already been paid, so someone who purchased this stock today would *not* receive D_0 — rather, he or she would receive D_1, the *next* dividend.

D_1 = $D_0(1 + g)$ = $1.15(1.08) = $1.24.

k_s = $D_1/P_0 + g$ = ($1.24/$23) + 0.08 = 0.054 + 0.08 = 0.134 = 13.4%.

On the basis of these data, the weighted average cost of capital, WACC, is 10 percent:

$$WACC = \left(\begin{array}{c}\text{Fraction}\\\text{of}\\\text{debt}\end{array}\right)\left(\begin{array}{c}\text{Interest}\\\text{rate}\end{array}\right)(1 - T) + \left(\begin{array}{c}\text{Fraction}\\\text{of}\\\text{preferred}\\\text{stock}\end{array}\right)\left(\begin{array}{c}\text{Cost}\\\text{of}\\\text{preferred}\\\text{stock}\end{array}\right) + \left(\begin{array}{c}\text{Fraction of}\\\text{common}\\\text{equity}\end{array}\right)\left(\begin{array}{c}\text{Cost}\\\text{of}\\\text{equity}\end{array}\right)$$

= (0.45)(10%)(0.6) + (0.02)(10.3%) + (0.53)(13.4%)

= 2.7% + 0.2% + 7.1%

= 10.0%.

Note that short-term debt is not included in the capital structure. Allied uses its cost of capital in the capital budgeting process, which involves long-term assets, and it finances those assets with long-term capital. Thus, current liabilities do not enter the calculation. We will discuss this point in more detail in Chapter 12.[10]

As long as Allied keeps its capital structure on target, and as long as its debt has an after-tax cost of 6 percent, preferred stock a cost of 10.3 percent, and common equity a cost of 13.4 percent, then its weighted average cost of capital will be WACC = 10%. Each dollar the firm raises will consist of some long-term debt, some preferred stock, and some common equity, and the cost of the whole dollar will be 10 percent.

A graph which shows how the WACC changes as more and more new capital is raised during a given year is called the **marginal cost of capital schedule.** The graph shown in Figure 9-1 is Allied's MCC schedule. Here the dots represent dollars raised, and because each dollar of new capital has a cost of 10 percent, the marginal cost

Marginal Cost of Capital (MCC) Schedule

A graph that relates the firm's weighted average cost of each dollar of capital to the total amount of new capital raised.

[10]Also see Eugene F. Brigham and Louis C. Gapenski, *Intermediate Financial Management,* 5th ed., Chapter 6.

FIGURE 9-1

MARGINAL COST OF CAPITAL (MCC) SCHEDULE
FOR ALLIED FOOD PRODUCTS

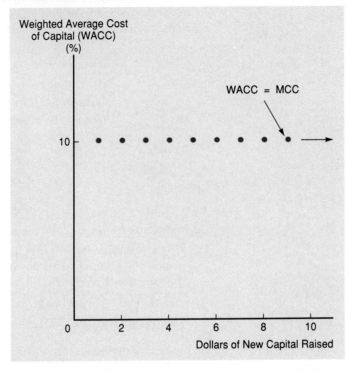

of capital (MCC) for Allied is constant at 10 percent under the assumptions we
have used thus far.[11]

THE RETAINED EARNINGS BREAK POINT

Could Allied raise an unlimited amount of new capital at the 10 percent cost? The
answer is no. As a practical matter, as a company raises larger and larger sums
during a given time period, the costs of debt, preferred stock, and common equity
begin to rise, and as this occurs, the weighted average cost of each new dollar also
rises. Thus, just as corporations cannot hire unlimited numbers of workers at a
constant wage, they cannot raise unlimited amounts of capital at a constant cost.
At some point, the cost of each new dollar will increase.

Where will this point occur for Allied? As a first step to determining the point
at which the MCC begins to rise, recognize that although the company's balance
sheet shows total long-term capital of $1,690,000,000, all of this capital was raised
in the past, and it has been invested in assets which are being used in operations.
New (or marginal) capital presumably will be raised so as to maintain the 45/2/53
debt/preferred/common relationship. Therefore, if Allied wants to raise $1,000,000
in new capital, it should obtain $450,000 of debt, $20,000 of preferred stock, and

---

[11]Allied's MCC schedule in Figure 9-1 would be different (higher) if the company used any capital
structure other than 45 percent debt, 2 percent preferred, and 53 percent common equity. This point
will be developed in Chapter 12. However, as a general rule, a different MCC schedule exists for every
possible capital structure, and the optimal structure is the one that produces the lowest MCC schedule.

TABLE 9-1	ALLIED'S WACC USING NEW RETAINED EARNINGS AND NEW COMMON STOCK

I. WACC when Equity Is from New Retained Earnings

	WEIGHT ×	COMPONENT COST =	PRODUCT
Debt	0.45	6.0%	2.7%
Preferred stock	0.02	10.3	0.2
Common equity (Re-tained earnings)	0.53	13.4	7.1
	1.00	WACC₁ =	10.0%

II. WACC when Equity Is from Sale of New Common Stock

	WEIGHT ×	COMPONENT COST =	PRODUCT
Debt	0.45	6.0%	2.7%
Preferred stock	0.02	10.3	0.2
Common equity (New common stock)	0.53	14.0	7.4
	1.00	WACC₂ =	10.3%

$530,000 of common equity. The new common equity could come from two sources: (1) retained earnings, defined as that part of this year's profits which management decides to retain in the business rather than use for dividends (but not earnings retained in the past, for these have already been invested in plant, equipment, inventories, and so on); or (2) proceeds from the sale of new common stock.

The debt will have an interest rate of 10 percent, or an after-tax cost of 6 percent, and the preferred stock will have a cost of 10.3 percent. *The cost of common equity will be $k_s = 13.4\%$ as long as the equity is obtained as retained earnings, but it will jump to $k_e = 14\%$ once the company uses up all of its retained earnings and is thus forced to sell new common stock.*

Allied's weighted average cost of capital, when it uses new retained earnings (earnings retained this year, not in the past) and also when it uses new common stock, is shown in Table 9-1. We see that the weighted average cost of each dollar is 10 percent as long as retained earnings are used, but the WACC jumps to 10.3 percent as soon as the firm exhausts its retained earnings and is forced to sell new common stock.

How much new capital can Allied raise before it exhausts its retained earnings and is forced to sell new common stock; that is, where will an increase in the MCC schedule occur? We find this point as follows:[12]

1. Assume that the company expects to have total earnings of $137.8 million in 1996. Further, it has a target payout ratio of 45 percent, so it plans to pay out 45 percent of its earnings as dividends. Thus, the retained earnings for the year are projected to be $137.8(1.0 − 0.45) = $75.8 million.

2. We know that Allied expects to have $75.8 million of retained earnings for the year. We also know that if the company is to remain at its optimal capital

---

[12]The numbers in this set of calculations are rounded. Since the inputs are estimates, it makes little sense to carry estimates out to very many decimal places — this is "spurious accuracy."

structure, it must raise each dollar as 45 cents of debt, 2 cents of preferred, and 53 cents of common equity. Therefore, each 53 cents of retained earnings will support $1 of capital, and the $75.8 million of retained earnings will not be exhausted, hence the WACC will not rise, until $75.8 million of retained earnings, plus some additional amount of debt and preferred stock, have been used up.

Break Point (BP)
The dollar value of new capital that can be raised before an increase in the firm's weighted average cost of capital occurs.

3. We now want to know how much *total new capital* — debt, preferred stock, and retained earnings — can be raised before the $75.8 million of retained earnings is exhausted and Allied is forced to sell new common stock. In effect, we are seeking some amount of capital, X, which is called a **break point (BP)** and which represents the total financing that can be done before Allied is forced to sell new common stock.

4. We know that 53 percent, or 0.53, of X, the total capital raised, will be retained earnings, whereas 47 percent will be debt plus preferred. We also know that retained earnings will amount to $75.8 million. Therefore,

$$\text{Retained earnings} = 0.53X = \$75,800,000.$$

5. Solving for X, which is the *retained earnings break point*, we obtain $BP_{RE} = \$143$ million:

$$X = BP_{RE} = \frac{\text{Retained earnings}}{\text{Equity fraction}} = \frac{\$75,800,000}{0.53} = \$143,018,868 \approx 143 \text{ million.}$$

6. Thus, given $75.8 million of retained earnings, Allied can raise a total of $143 million, consisting of 0.53($143 million) = $75.8 million of retained earnings plus 0.02($143 million) = $2.9 million of preferred stock plus 0.45($143 million) = $64.3 million of new debt supported by these new retained earnings, without altering its capital structure (dollars in millions):

New debt supported by retained earnings	$64.3	45%
Preferred stock supported by retained earnings	2.9	2
Retained earnings	75.8	53
Total capital supported by retained earnings, or break point for retained earnings	$143.0	100%

7. The value of X, or $BP_{RE} = \$143$ million, is defined as the *retained earnings break point*, and it is the amount of total capital at which a break, or jump, occurs in the MCC schedule.

Figure 9-2 graphs Allied's marginal cost of capital schedule with the retained earnings break point. Each dollar has a weighted average cost of 10 percent until the company has raised a total of $143 million. This $143 million will consist of $64.3 million of new debt with an after-tax cost of 6 percent, $2.9 million of preferred stock with a cost of 10.3 percent, and $75.8 million of retained earnings with a cost of 13.4 percent. However, if Allied raises one dollar over $143 million, each new dollar will contain 53 cents of equity *obtained by selling new common equity at a cost of 14 percent;* therefore, WACC jumps from 10 percent to 10.3 percent, as calculated in Table 9-1.

Note that we don't really think the MCC jumps by precisely 0.3 percent when we raise $1 over $143 million. Thus, Figure 9-2 should be regarded as an approxi-

FIGURE 9-2	MARGINAL COST OF CAPITAL SCHEDULE BEYOND THE RETAINED EARNINGS BREAK POINT FOR ALLIED FOOD PRODUCTS

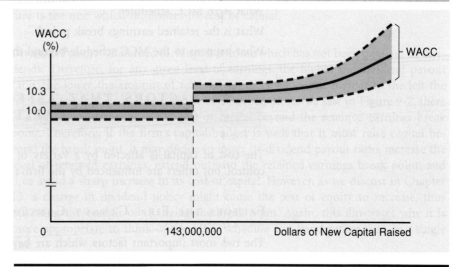

mation rather than as a precise representation of reality. We will return to this point later in the chapter.

THE MCC SCHEDULE BEYOND THE RETAINED EARNINGS BREAK POINT

There is a jump, or break, in Allied's MCC schedule at $143 million of new capital. Could there be other breaks in the schedule? Yes, there could. The cost of capital could also rise due to increases in the cost of debt or the cost of preferred stock, or as a result of further increases in flotation costs as the firm issues more and more common stock. Some people have asserted that the costs of capital components other than common stock should not rise. Their argument is that as long as the capital structure does not change, and presuming that the firm uses new capital to invest in profitable projects with the same degree of risk as its existing projects, investors should be willing to invest unlimited amounts of additional capital at the same rate. However, this argument assumes an infinitely elastic demand for a firm's securities. In practice, the demand curve for securities is downward sloping, so the more securities issued during a given period, the lower the price received for the securities, and the higher the required rate of return. Therefore, the more new financing required, the higher the firm's WACC.

As a result of all this, firms face increasing MCC schedules, such as the one shown in Figure 9-2. Here we have identified a specific retained earnings break point, but because of estimation difficulties, we have not attempted to identify precisely any additional break points. However, we have (1) shown the MCC schedule to be upward sloping, reflecting a positive relationship between capital raised and capital costs and (2) indicated our inability to measure these costs precisely by using a band of costs rather than a single line. Note that this band exists even over the whole range of capital raised — our component costs are only estimates, these estimates become more uncertain as the firm requires more and more capital, and thus the band widens as the amount of new capital raised increases.

yet its payback and discounted payback make it look worse than Project X. Consequently, both payback methods have serious deficiencies. Therefore, we will not dwell on the finer points of payback analysis.[2]

Although the payback method has some serious faults as a ranking criterion, it does provide information on how long funds will be tied up in a project. Thus, the shorter the payback period, other things held constant, the greater the project's *liquidity*. Also, since cash flows expected in the distant future are generally riskier than near-term cash flows, the payback is often used as one indicator of a project's *riskiness*.

NET PRESENT VALUE (NPV)

Net Present Value (NPV) Method
A method of ranking investment proposals using the NPV, which is equal to the present value of future net cash flows, discounted at the marginal cost of capital.

Discounted Cash Flow (DCF) Techniques
Methods of ranking investment proposals that employ time value of money concepts.

As the flaws in the payback and other early methods were recognized, people began to search for ways to improve the effectiveness of project evaluations. One such method is the **net present value (NPV) method,** which relies on **discounted cash flow (DCF) techniques.** To implement this approach, we proceed as follows:

1. Find the present value of each cash flow, including both inflows and outflows, discounted at the project's cost of capital.

2. Sum these discounted cash flows; this sum is defined as the project's NPV.

3. If the NPV is positive, the project should be accepted, while if the NPV is negative, it should be rejected. If two projects are mutually exclusive, the one with the higher NPV should be chosen, provided its NPV is positive.

The NPV can be expressed as follows:

$$NPV = CF_0 + \frac{CF_1}{(1 + k)^1} + \frac{CF_2}{(1 + k)^2} + \cdots + \frac{CF_n}{(1 + k)^n}$$

$$= \sum_{t = 0}^{n} \frac{CF_t}{(1 + k)^t}. \tag{10-1}$$

Here CF_t is the expected net cash flow at Period t, and k is the project's cost of capital. Cash outflows (expenditures such as the cost of buying equipment or building factories) are treated as *negative* cash flows. In evaluating Projects S and L, only CF_0 is negative, but for many large projects such as the Alaska Pipeline, an electric generating plant, or IBM's laptop computer project, outflows occur for several years before operations begin and cash flows turn positive.

At a 10 percent cost of capital, Project S's NPV is $78.82:

---

[2]Another capital budgeting technique that was once used widely is the *accounting rate of return (ARR)*, which examines a project's contribution to the firm's net income. Although some companies still calculate an ARR, it really has no redeeming features, so we will not discuss it in this text. See Eugene F. Brigham and Louis C. Gapenski, *Intermediate Financial Management*, 5th ed., Chapter 7. Yet another technique which we omit here is the *profitability index*, or *benefit/cost ratio*. Brigham and Gapenski also discuss this criterion.

By a similar process, we find $NPV_L = \$49.18$. On this basis, both projects should be accepted if they are independent, but S should be chosen if they are mutually exclusive.

It is not hard to calculate the NPV as was done in the time line by using Equation 10-1 and a regular calculator, along with the interest rate tables. However, it is more efficient to use a financial calculator. Different calculators are set up somewhat differently, but they all have a section of memory called the "cash flow register" which is used for uneven cash flows such as those in Projects S and L (as opposed to equal annuity cash flows). A solution process for Equation 10-1 is literally programmed into financial calculators, and all you have to do is enter the cash flows (being sure to observe the signs), along with the value of $k = I$. At that point, you have (in your calculator) this equation:

$$NPV_S = -1,000 + \frac{500}{(1.10)^1} + \frac{400}{(1.10)^2} + \frac{300}{(1.10)^3} + \frac{100}{(1.10)^4}.$$

Notice that the equation has one unknown, NPV. Now, all you need to do is to ask the calculator to solve the equation for you, which you do by pressing the NPV button (and, on some calculators, the "compute" button). The answer, 78.82, will appear on the screen.[3]

RATIONALE FOR THE NPV METHOD

The rationale for the NPV method is straightforward. An NPV of zero signifies that the project's cash flows are just sufficient to repay the invested capital and to

---

[3]The *Technology Supplement* provided to instructors and available for copying by users explains this and other commonly used calculator applications. For those who do not have the *Supplement*, the steps for two popular calculators, the HP-10B and the HP-17B, are shown below. If you have another type of financial calculator, see its manual or the *Supplement*.

HP-10B:

1. Clear the memory.
2. Enter CF_0 as follows: 1000 `+/−` `CF_j`.
3. Enter CF_1 as follows: 500 `CF_j`.
4. Repeat the process to enter the other cash flows. Note that CF 0, CF 1, and so forth flash on the screen as you press the `CF_j` button. If you hold the button down, CF 0 and so forth will remain on the screen until you release it.
5. Once the CFs have been entered, enter $k = I = 10\%$: 10 `I/YR`.
6. Now that all of the inputs have been entered, you can press ▌ `NPV` to get the answer, NPV = $78.82.
7. If a cash flow is repeated for several years, you can avoid having to enter the CFs for each year. For example, if the $500 cash flow for Year 1 had also been the CF for Years 2 through 10, making 10 of these $500 cash flows, then after entering 500 `CF_j` the first time, you could enter 10 ▌ `N_j`. This would automatically enter 10 CFs of 500.

HP-17B:

1. Go to the cash flow (CFLO) menu, clear if FLOW(0) = ? does not appear on the screen.
2. Enter CF_0 as follows: 1000 `+/−` `INPUT`.
3. Enter CF_1 as follows: 500 `INPUT`.
4. Now, the calculator will ask you if the 500 is for Period 1 only or if it is also used for several following periods. Since it is only used for Period 1, press `INPUT` to answer "1." Alternatively, you could press `EXIT` and then `#T?` to turn off the prompt for the remainder of the problem. For some problems, you will want to use the repeat feature.
5. Enter the remaining CFs, being sure to turn off the prompt or else to specify "1" for each entry.
6. Once the CFs have all been entered, press `EXIT` and then `CALC`.
7. Now enter $k = I = 10\%$ as follows: 10 `I%`.
8. Now press `NPV` to get the answer, NPV = $78.82.

Multiple IRRs

Multiple IRRs
The situation where a project has two or more IRRs.

There is one other situation in which the IRR approach may not be usable — this is when projects with nonnormal cash flows are involved. A project has *normal* cash flows if one or more cash outflows (costs) are followed by a series of cash inflows. If, however, a project calls for a large cash outflow either sometime during or at the end of its life, then the project has *nonnormal* cash flows. Projects with nonnormal cash flows can present unique difficulties when they are evaluated by the IRR method, with the most common problem being the existence of **multiple IRRs.**

When one solves Equation 10-2 to find the IRR for a project with nonnormal cash flows,

$$\sum_{t=0}^{n} \frac{CF_t}{(1 + IRR)^t} = 0, \tag{10-2}$$

it is possible to obtain more than one value of IRR, which means that multiple IRRs occur. Notice that Equation 10-2 is a polynomial of degree n, so it has n different roots, or solutions. All except one of the roots are imaginary numbers when investments have normal cash flows (one or more cash outflows followed by cash inflows), so in the normal case, only one value of IRR appears. However, the possibility of multiple real roots, hence multiple IRRs, arises when the project has nonnormal cash flows (negative net cash flows occur during some year after the project has been placed in operation).

To illustrate this problem, suppose a firm is considering the expenditure of $1.6 million to develop a strip mine (Project M). The mine will produce a cash flow of $10 million at the end of Year 1. Then, at the end of Year 2, $10 million must be expended to restore the land to its original condition. Therefore, the project's expected net cash flows are as follows (in millions of dollars):

EXPECTED NET CASH FLOWS

YEAR 0	END OF YEAR 1	END OF YEAR 2
−$1.6	+$10	−$10

These values can be substituted into Equation 10-2 to derive the IRR for the investment:

$$NPV = \frac{-\$1.6 \text{ million}}{(1 + IRR)^0} + \frac{\$10 \text{ million}}{(1 + IRR)^1} + \frac{-\$10 \text{ million}}{(1 + IRR)^2} = 0.$$

When solved, we find that NPV = 0 when IRR = 25% and also when IRR = 400%.[12] Therefore, the IRR of the investment is both 25 and 400 percent. This

---

[12]If you attempted to find the IRR of Project M with many financial calculators, you would get an error message. This same message would be given for all projects with multiple IRRs. However, you can still find Project M's IRRs by first calculating NPVs using several different values for k and then plotting the NPV profile. The intersections with the X-axis give a rough idea of the IRR values. Finally, you can use trial-and-error to find the exact values of k which force NPV = 0.

Note, too, that some calculators, including the HP-10B and 17B, can find the IRR. At the error message, key in a guess, store it, and repress the IRR key. With the HP-10B, type 10 ■ STO ■ IRR, and the answer, 25.00, appears. If you enter as your guess a cost of capital less than the one at which NPV in Figure 10-5 is maximized (about 100%), the lower IRR, 25%, is displayed. If you guess a high rate, say 150, the higher IRR is shown.

| FIGURE 10-5 | NPV PROFILE FOR PROJECT M |

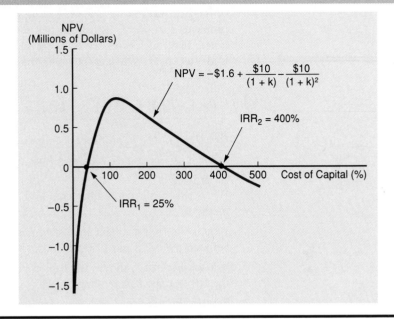

relationship is depicted graphically in Figure 10-5.[13] Note that no dilemma would arise if the NPV method were used; we would simply use Equation 10-1, find the NPV, and use this to evaluate the project. If Project M's cost of capital were 10 percent, then its NPV would be −$0.77 million, and the project should be rejected. If k were between 25 and 400 percent, the NPV would be positive.

One of the authors encountered another example of multiple internal rates of return when a major California bank *borrowed* funds from an insurance company and then used these funds (plus an initial investment of its own) to buy a number of jet engines, which it then leased to a major airline. The bank expected to receive positive net cash flows (lease payments plus tax savings minus interest on the insurance company loan) for a number of years, then several large negative cash flows as it repaid the insurance company loan, and, finally, a large inflow from the sale of the engines when the lease expired.

The bank discovered two IRRs and wondered which was correct. It could not ignore the IRR and use the NPV method since the lease was already on the books, and the bank's senior loan committee, as well as Federal Reserve bank examiners, wanted to know the return on the lease. The bank's solution called for calculating and then using the "modified internal rate of return" as discussed in the next section.

---

[13]Does Figure 10-5 suggest that the firm should try to *raise* its cost of capital to about 100 percent in order to maximize the NPV of the project? Certainly not. The firm should seek to *minimize* its cost of capital; this will cause the price of its stock to be maximized. Actions taken to raise the cost of capital might make this particular project look good, but those actions would be terribly harmful to the firm's more numerous projects with normal cash flows. Only if the firm's cost of capital is high in spite of efforts to keep it down will the illustrative project have a positive NPV.

The examples just presented illustrate one problem, multiple IRRs, that can arise when the IRR criterion is used with a project that has nonnormal cash flows. Use of the IRR method on projects having nonnormal cash flows could produce other problems such as no IRR or an IRR which leads to an incorrect accept/reject decision. In all such cases, the NPV criterion could be easily applied, and this method leads to conceptually correct capital budgeting decisions.

 ## SELF-TEST QUESTIONS

Describe how NPV profiles are constructed.

What is the crossover rate, and how does it affect the choice between mutually exclusive projects?

What two basic conditions can lead to conflicts between the NPV and IRR methods?

Why is the "reinvestment rate" considered to be the underlying cause of conflicts between the NPV and IRR methods?

If a conflict exists, should the capital budgeting decision be made on the basis of the NPV or the IRR ranking? Why?

Explain the difference between normal and nonnormal cash flows.

What is the "multiple IRR problem," and what condition is necessary for its occurrence?

MODIFIED INTERNAL RATE OF RETURN (MIRR)

In spite of a strong academic preference for NPV, surveys indicate that executives prefer IRR over NPV. Apparently, managers find it intuitively more appealing to evaluate investments in terms of percentage rates of return than dollars of NPV. Given this fact, can we devise a percentage evaluator that is better than the regular IRR? The answer is yes — we can modify the IRR and make it a better indicator of relative profitability, hence better for use in capital budgeting. The new measure is called the **modified IRR,** or **MIRR,** and it is defined as follows:

Modified IRR (MIRR)
The discount rate at which the present value of a project's cost is equal to the present value of its terminal value, where the terminal value is found as the sum of the future values of the cash inflows, compounded at the firm's cost of capital.

$$PV \text{ costs} = PV \text{ terminal value}$$

$$\sum_{t=0}^{n} \frac{COF_t}{(1 + k)^t} = \frac{\sum_{t=0}^{n} CIF_t(1 + k)^{n-t}}{(1 + MIRR)^n}$$

$$PV \text{ costs} = \frac{TV}{(1 + MIRR)^n}. \tag{10-2a}$$

Here COF refers to cash outflows (negative numbers), or the cost of the project, and CIF refers to cash inflows (positive numbers). The left term is simply the PV of the investment outlays when discounted at the cost of capital, and the numerator of the right term is the future value of the inflows, assuming that the cash inflows are reinvested at the cost of capital. The future value of the cash inflows is also called the *terminal value,* or *TV.* The discount rate that forces the PV of the TV to equal the PV of the costs is defined as the MIRR.[14]

If the investment costs are all incurred at t = 0, and if the first operating inflow occurs at t = 1, as is true for our illustrative Projects S and L which we first presented in Figure 10-1, then this equation may be used:

$$\text{Cost} = \frac{TV}{(1 + MIRR)^n} = \frac{\displaystyle\sum_{t=1}^{n} CIF_t(1 + k)^{n-t}}{(1 + MIRR)^n}. \qquad \textbf{(10-2b)}$$

We can illustrate the calculation with Project S:

Using the cash flows as set out on the time line, first find the terminal value by compounding each cash inflow at the 10 percent cost of capital. Then enter N = 4, PV = −1000, PMT = 0, FV = 1579.5, and then press the I button to find MIRR$_S$ = 12.1%. Similarly, we find MIRR$_L$ = 11.3%.[15]

The modified IRR has a significant advantage over the regular IRR. MIRR assumes that cash flows from all projects are reinvested at the cost of capital, while the regular IRR assumes that the cash flows from each project are reinvested at the project's own IRR. Since reinvestment at the cost of capital is generally more correct, the modified IRR is a better indicator of a project's true profitability. MIRR also solves the multiple IRR problem. To illustrate, with k = 10%, Project M (the strip mine project) has MIRR = 5.6% versus its 10 percent cost of capital, so it should be rejected. This is consistent with the decision based on the NPV method, because at k = 10%, NPV = −$0.77 million.

Is MIRR as good as NPV for choosing between mutually exclusive projects? If two projects are of equal size and have the same life, then NPV and MIRR will always lead to the same decision. Thus, for any set of projects like our Projects S and L, if NPV$_S$ > NPV$_L$, then MIRR$_S$ > MIRR$_L$, and the kinds of conflicts we encountered between NPV and the regular IRR will not occur. Also, if the projects

---

[14]There are several alternative definitions for the MIRR. The differences primarily relate to whether negative cash flows which occur after positive cash flows begin should be compounded and treated as part of the TV or discounted and treated as a cost. A related issue is whether negative and positive flows in a given year should be netted or treated separately. For a complete discussion, see William R. McDaniel, Daniel E. McCarty, and Kenneth A. Jessell, "Discounted Cash Flow with Explicit Reinvestment Rates: Tutorial and Extension," *The Financial Review,* August 1988, 369–385, and David M. Shull, "Interpreting Rates of Return: A Modified Rate of Return Approach," *Financial Practice and Education,* Fall 1993, 67–71.

[15]With some calculators, including the HP-17B, you could enter the cash inflows in the cash flow register (being sure to enter CF$_0$ = 0), enter I = 10, and then press the NFV key to find TV = 1,579.50. The HP-10B does not have an NFV key, but you can still use the cash flow register to find TV. Enter the cash flows in the cash flow register (with CF$_0$ = 0), then enter I = 10, then press ■ NPV to find the PV of the inflows, which is 1,078.82. Now, with the regular time value keys, enter N = 4, I = 10, PV = −1078.82, PMT = 0, and press FV to find TV = 1,579.50. Similar procedures can be used with other financial calculators.

ments to reflect divisional risk. We will cover risk analysis in capital budgeting in Chapter 11.

5. An examination of surveys done by other authors led Bierman to conclude that there has been a strong trend toward the acceptance of academic recommendations, at least by large companies.

A second 1993 study, conducted by Joe Walker, Richard Burns, and Chad Denson (WBD), focused on small companies.[17] WBD began by noting the same trend toward the use of DCF that Bierman cited, but they reported that only 21 percent of their companies used DCF versus 100 percent for Bierman's large companies. WBD also noted that within their sample, the smaller the firm, the smaller the likelihood that DCF would be used. The focal point of the WBD study was *why* small companies use DCF so much less frequently than large firms. WBD actually based their questionnaire on our box entitled "Capital Budgeting in the Small Firm" on pages 370 and 371, and they concluded that the reasons given in that section do indeed explain why DCF is used infrequently by small firms. The three most frequently cited reasons, according to their survey, were (1) small firms' preoccupation with liquidity, which is best indicated by payback, (2) a lack of familiarity with DCF methods, and (3) a belief that small project sizes make DCF not worth the effort.

The general conclusion one can reach from these studies is that large firms should and do use the procedures we recommend, and that managers of small firms, especially managers with aspirations for future growth, should at least understand DCF procedures well enough to make rational decisions about using or not using them. Moreover, as computer technology makes it easier and less expensive for small firms to use DCF methods, and as more and more of their competitors begin using these methods, survival will necessitate increased DCF usage.

SELF-TEST QUESTIONS

What were Bierman's findings from his survey of capital budgeting methods used by the Fortune 500 industrial companies?

How did the WBD study's findings differ from Bierman's findings?

What general considerations can be reached from these studies?

THE POST-AUDIT

Post-audit
A comparison of the actual versus the expected results for a given capital project.

An important aspect of the capital budgeting process is the **post-audit,** which involves (1) comparing actual results with those predicted by the project's sponsors and (2) explaining why any differences occurred. For example, many firms require that the operating divisions send a monthly report for the first six months after a project goes into operation, and a quarterly report thereafter, until the project's results are up to expectations. From then on, reports on the project are handled like those of other operations.

The post-audit has two main purposes:

1. **Improve forecasts.** When decision makers are forced to compare their projections to actual outcomes, there is a tendency for estimates to improve. Con-

---

[17]Joe Walker, Richard Burns, and Chad Denson, "Why Small Manufacturing Firms Shun DCF," *Journal of Small Business,* 1993, 233–249.

scious or unconscious biases are observed and eliminated; new forecasting methods are sought as the need for them becomes apparent; and people simply tend to do everything better, including forecasting, if they know that their actions are being monitored.

2. **Improve operations.** Businesses are run by people, and people can perform at higher or lower levels of efficiency. When a divisional team has made a forecast about an investment, its members are, in a sense, putting their reputations on the line. If costs are above predicted levels, sales below expectations, and so on, executives in production, sales, and other areas will strive to improve operations and to bring results into line with forecasts. In a discussion related to this point, one executive made this statement: "You academicians worry only about making good decisions. In business, we also worry about making decisions good."

The post-audit is not a simple process — a number of factors can cause complications. First, we must recognize that each element of the cash flow forecast is subject to uncertainty, so a percentage of all projects undertaken by any reasonably aggressive firm will necessarily go awry. This fact must be considered when appraising the performances of the operating executives who submit capital expenditure requests. Second, projects sometimes fail to meet expectations for reasons beyond the control of the operating executives and for reasons that no one could realistically be expected to anticipate. For example, the 1990–1991 recession adversely affected many projects. Third, it is often difficult to separate the operating results of one investment from those of a larger system. Although some projects stand alone and permit ready identification of costs and revenues, the actual cost savings that result from a new computer system, for example, may be very hard to measure. Fourth, it is often hard to hand out blame or praise because the executives who were responsible for launching a given long-term investment may have moved on by the time the results are known.

Because of these difficulties, some firms tend to play down the importance of the post-audit. However, observations of both businesses and governmental units suggest that the best-run and most successful organizations are the ones that put the greatest emphasis on post-audits. Accordingly, we regard the post-audit as being one of the most important elements in a good capital budgeting system.

SELF-TEST QUESTIONS

What is done in the post-audit?

Identify several purposes of the post-audit.

What are some factors which can cause complications in the post-audit?

SUMMARY

This chapter discussed the capital budgeting process, and the key concepts covered are listed below.

- **Capital budgeting** is the process of analyzing potential fixed asset investments. Capital budgeting decisions are probably the most important ones financial managers must make.

CAPITAL BUDGETING IN THE SMALL FIRM

The allocation of capital in small firms is as important as it is in large ones. In fact, given their lack of access to the capital markets, it is often more important in the small firm, because the funds necessary to correct a mistake may not be available. Also, large firms allocate capital to numerous projects, so a mistake on one can be offset by successes with others.

In spite of the importance of capital expenditures to small business, studies of the way capital budgeting decisions are made generally suggest that many small firms use "back-of-the-envelope" analysis, or perhaps even no analysis at all. For example, when L. R. Runyon studied 214 firms with net worths of from $500,000 to $1,000,000, he found that almost 70 percent relied upon either payback or some other questionable criteria; only 14 percent used a discounted cash flow analysis; and about 9 percent indicated that they used no formal analysis at all.[18] Studies of larger firms, on the other hand, generally find that most analyze capital budgeting decisions using discounted cash flow techniques.

We are left with a puzzle. Capital budgeting is clearly important to small firms, yet these firms neglect to use the tools that have been developed to improve these decisions. Why does this situation exist? One argument is that

managers of small firms are simply not well trained; they are unsophisticated. This argument suggests that the managers would use the more sophisticated techniques if they understood them better.

Another argument relates to the fact that management talent is a scarce resource in small firms. That is, even if the managers were exceptionally sophisticated, perhaps the demands on their time are such that they simply cannot take the time to use elaborate techniques to analyze proposed projects. In other words, small-business managers may be capable of doing careful discounted cash flow analysis, but it would be irrational for them to allocate the time required for such an analysis.

A third argument relates to the cost of analyzing capital projects. To some extent, these costs are fixed; the costs of analysis may be larger for bigger projects, but not by much. To the extent that these costs are indeed fixed, it may not be economical to incur them if the project itself is relatively small. This argument suggests that small firms with small projects may in some cases be making the sensible decision when they rely on management's "gut feeling."

Note also that a major part of the capital budgeting process in large firms

involves lower-level analysts' marshalling facts needed by higher-level decision makers. This step is less necessary in the small firm. Thus, a cursory examination of a small firm's decision process might suggest that capital budgeting decisions are based on snap judgment, but if that judgment is exercised by someone with a total knowledge of the firm and its markets, it could represent a better decision than one based on an elaborate analysis by a lower-level employee in a large firm.

Also, as Runyon reported in his study of manufacturing firms, small firms tend to be cash oriented. They are concerned with basic survival, so they tend to look at expenditures from the standpoint of their near-term effects on cash. This cash and survival orientation leads firms to focus on a relatively short time horizon, and this, in turn, may lead to an emphasis on the payback method. The limitations of payback are well known, but in spite of those limitations, the technique is popular in small business, as it gives the firm a feel for when the cash committed to an investment will be recovered and thus available to repay loans or for new opportunities. Therefore, small firms that are cash oriented and have limited managerial resources may find the payback method an appealing compromise

- The **payback period** is defined as the expected number of years required to recover a project's cost. The payback method ignores cash flows beyond the payback period, and it does not consider the time value of money. The payback does, however, provide an indication of a project's risk and liquidity, because it shows how long the invested capital will be "at risk."

- The **discounted payback method** is similar to the regular payback method except that it discounts cash flows at the project's cost of capital. Like the regular payback method, it ignores cash flows beyond the discounted payback period.

- The **net present value (NPV) method** discounts all cash flows at the project's cost of capital and then sums those cash flows. The project is accepted if this sum, called the NPV, is positive.

between the need for extensive analysis on the one hand and the high costs of analysis on the other.

Small firms also face greater uncertainty in the cash flows they might generate beyond the immediate future. Large firms such as AT&T and General Motors have "staying power" — they can make an investment and then ride out business downturns or situations of excess capacity in an industry. Such periods are called "shakeouts," and it is the smaller firms that are generally shaken out. Therefore, most small-business managers are uncomfortable making forecasts beyond a few years. Since discounted cash flow techniques require explicit estimates of cash flows through the life of the project, small-business managers may not take seriously an analysis that hinges on "guesstimate" numbers which, if wrong, could lead to bankruptcy.

THE VALUE OF THE FIRM AND CAPITAL BUDGETING

The single most appealing argument for the use of net present value in capital expenditure decisions is that NPV gives an explicit measure of the effect the investment will have on the value of the firm: if NPV is positive, the investment will increase the value of the firm and make its owners wealthier. In small firms, however, the stock is often not traded in public markets, so its value cannot be observed. Also, for reasons of control, many small-business owners and managers may not want to broaden ownership by going public.

It is difficult to argue for value-based techniques when the value of the firm itself is unobservable. Furthermore, in a closely held firm, the objectives of the individual owner-manager may extend beyond the firm's monetary value. For example, the owner-manager may value the firm's reputation for quality and service and therefore may make an investment that would be rejected on purely economic grounds. In addition, the owner-manager may not hold a well-diversified investment portfolio but may instead have all of his or her eggs in this one basket. In that case, the manager would logically be sensitive to the stand-alone risk of the firm, not just to its undiversifiable component. Thus, one project might be viewed as desirable because of its contribution to risk reduction in the firm as a whole, whereas another project with a low beta but high diversifiable risk might be unacceptable, even though in a CAPM framework it would be judged superior.

Another problem faced by a firm that is not publicly traded is that its cost of equity capital is not easily determined — the P_0 term in the cost of equity equation $k = D_1/P_0 + g$ is not observable, nor is its beta. Since a cost of capital estimate is required to use either the NPV or the IRR method, a small firm in an industry of small firms may simply have no basis for estimating its cost of capital.

CONCLUSIONS

Small firms make less extensive use of DCF techniques than larger firms. This may be a rational decision resulting from a conscious or subconscious conclusion that the costs of sophisticated analyses outweigh their benefits; it may reflect nonmonetary goals of small businesses' owner-managers; or it may reflect difficulties in estimating the cost of capital, which is required for DCF analyses but not for payback. However, nonuse of DCF methods may also reflect a weakness in many small-business organizations. We simply do not know. We do know that small businesses must do all they can to compete effectively with big business, and to the extent that a small business fails to use DCF methods because its manager is unsophisticated or uninformed, it may be putting itself at a serious competitive disadvantage.

[18]L. R. Runyon, "Capital Expenditure Decision Making in Small Firms," *Journal of Business Research,* September 1983, 389–397.

- The **internal rate of return (IRR)** is defined as the discount rate which forces a project's NPV to equal zero. The project is accepted if its IRR is greater than its cost of capital.

- The NPV and IRR methods make the same accept/reject decisions for **independent projects,** but if projects are **mutually exclusive,** then ranking conflicts can arise. If conflicts arise, the NPV method should be used. The NPV and IRR methods are both superior to the payback, but NPV is the single best measure of a project's profitability.

- The NPV method assumes that cash flows will be reinvested at the firm's cost of capital, while the IRR method assumes reinvestment at the project's IRR. Because **reinvestment at the cost of capital is generally a better (closer to reality) assumption,** the NPV is superior to the IRR.

- The **modified IRR (MIRR) method** corrects some of the problems with the regular IRR. MIRR involves finding the terminal value (TV) of the cash inflows, compounded at the firm's cost of capital, and then determining the discount rate which forces the present value of the TV to equal the present value of the outflows.

- Sophisticated managers consider all of the project evaluation measures because the different measures provide different types of information.

- The **post-audit** is a key element of capital budgeting. By comparing actual results with predicted results, and then determining why differences occurred, decision makers can improve both their operations and their forecasts of projects' outcomes.

- Small firms tend to use the payback method rather than a discounted cash flow method. This may be a rational decision, because (1) the **cost** of the DCF analysis **may outweigh the benefits** for the project being considered, (2) **the firm's cost of capital cannot be estimated accurately,** or (3) the small-business owner may be considering **nonmonetary goals.**

Although this chapter has presented the basic elements of the capital budgeting process, there are many other aspects of this crucial topic. Some of the more important ones are discussed in the following chapter.

QUESTIONS

10-1 How is a project classification scheme (for example, replacement, expansion into new markets, and so forth) used in the capital budgeting process?

10-2 Explain why the NPV of a relatively long-term project, defined as one for which a high percentage of its cash flows are expected in the distant future, is more sensitive to changes in the cost of capital than is the NPV of a short-term project.

10-3 Explain why, if two mutually exclusive projects are being compared, the short-term project might have the higher ranking under the NPV criterion if the cost of capital is high, but the long-term project might be deemed better if the cost of capital is low. Would changes in the cost of capital ever cause a change in the IRR ranking of two such projects?

10-4 In what sense is a reinvestment rate assumption embodied in the NPV, IRR, and MIRR methods? What is the assumed reinvestment rate of each method?

10-5 "If a firm has no mutually exclusive projects, only independent ones, and it also has both a constant cost of capital and projects with normal cash flows in the sense that each project has one or more outflows followed by a stream of inflows, then the NPV and IRR methods will always lead to identical capital budgeting decisions." Discuss this statement. What does it imply about using the IRR method in lieu of the NPV method? If each of the assumptions made in the question were changed (one by one), how would these changes affect your answer?

10-6 Are there conditions under which a firm might be better off if it were to choose a machine with a rapid payback rather than one with a larger NPV?

10-7 A firm has $100 million available for capital expenditures. It is considering investing in one of two projects; each has a cost of $100 million. Project A has an IRR of 20 percent and an NPV of $9 million. It will be terminated at the end of 1 year at a profit of $20 million, resulting in an immediate increase in earnings per share (EPS). Project B, which cannot be postponed, has an IRR of 30 percent and an NPV of $50 million. However, the firm's short-run EPS will be reduced if it accepts Project B, because no revenues will be generated for several years.
   a. Should the short-run effects on EPS influence the choice between the two projects?
   b. How might situations like the one described here influence a firm's decision to use payback as a part of the capital budgeting process?

SELF-TEST PROBLEMS *(Solutions Appear in Appendix B)*

ST-1 Key terms Define each of the following terms:
  a. The capital budget; capital budgeting; strategic business plan
  b. Regular payback period; discounted payback period
  c. Independent projects; mutually exclusive projects
  d. DCF techniques; net present value (NPV) method
  e. Internal rate of return (IRR) method
  f. Modified internal rate of return (MIRR) method
  g. NPV profile; crossover rate
  h. Nonnormal cash flow projects; normal cash flow projects; multiple IRRs
  i. Project cost of capital, or discount rate
  j. Reinvestment rate assumption
  k. Post-audit

ST-2 Project analysis You are a financial analyst for Damon Electronics Company. The director of capital budgeting has asked you to analyze two proposed capital investments, Projects X and Y. Each project has a cost of $10,000, and the cost of capital for each project is 12 percent. The projects' expected net cash flows are as follows:

	EXPECTED NET CASH FLOWS	
YEAR	PROJECT X	PROJECT Y
0	($10,000)	($10,000)
1	6,500	3,500
2	3,000	3,500
3	3,000	3,500
4	1,000	3,500

  a. Calculate each project's payback period, net present value (NPV), internal rate of return (IRR), and modified internal rate of return (MIRR).
  b. Which project or projects should be accepted if they are independent?
  c. Which project should be accepted if they are mutually exclusive?
  d. How might a change in the cost of capital produce a conflict between the NPV and IRR rankings of these two projects? Would this conflict exist if k were 5%? (Hint: Plot the NPV profiles.)
  e. Why does the conflict exist?

PROBLEMS

10-1 Payback, NPV, IRR, and MIRR calculations Project K has a cost of $52,125, and its expected net cash inflows are $12,000 per year for 8 years.
  a. What is the project's payback period (to the closest year)?
  b. The cost of capital is 12 percent. What is the project's NPV?
  c. What is the project's IRR? (Hint: Recognize that the project is an annuity.)
  d. What is the project's discounted payback period, assuming a 12 percent cost of capital?
  e. Calculate the project's MIRR assuming a 12 percent cost of capital.

10-2 NPV and IRR analysis Cummings Products Company is considering two mutually exclusive investments. The projects' expected net cash flows are as follows:

CHANGES IN NET WORKING CAPITAL

Change in Net Working Capital
The increased current assets resulting from a new project, minus the spontaneous increase in accounts payable and accruals.

Normally, additional inventories are required to support a new operation, and expanded sales also lead to additional accounts receivable. Both of these asset increases must be financed. However, payables and accruals will increase spontaneously as a result of the expansion, and this will reduce the net cash needed to finance inventories and receivables. The difference between the required increase in current assets and the spontaneous increase in current liabilities is the **change in net working capital.** If this change is positive, as it generally is for expansion projects, this indicates that additional financing, over and above the cost of the fixed assets, will be needed to fund the increase in current assets.

As the project approaches termination, inventories will be sold off and not replaced, and receivables will be collected. As these changes occur, the firm will receive an end-of-project cash inflow that is equal to the net working capital requirement that occurred when the project was begun. Thus, the working capital investment will be returned at the end of the project's life.

 SELF-TEST QUESTIONS

How is an increase in net working capital dealt with in capital budgeting?

Does the company get back the dollars it invests in working capital? How?

EVALUATING CAPITAL BUDGETING PROJECTS

Up to this point, we have discussed several important aspects of cash flow analysis, but we have not seen how they affect capital budgeting decisions. In this section, we illustrate these effects by examining two types of capital budgeting decisions — expansion projects and replacement projects.

EXPANSION PROJECTS

Expansion Project
A project that is intended to increase sales.

An **expansion project** is defined as one where the firm invests in new assets to increase sales. We will illustrate the expansion project analysis by examining a project being considered by Brandt-Quigley Corporation (BQC), an Atlanta-based technology company. BQC's research and development department has been applying its expertise in microprocessor technology to develop a small computer designed to control home appliances. Once programmed, the computer will automatically control the heating and air-conditioning systems, security system, hot water heater, and even small appliances such as a coffee maker. By increasing a home's energy efficiency, the computer can save enough on costs to pay for itself within a few years. Developments have now reached the stage where a decision must be made about whether or not to go forward with full-scale production.

BQC's marketing department plans to target sales of the appliance computer toward the owners of larger homes; the computer is cost effective only in homes with 2,000 or more square feet of heated/air-conditioned space. The marketing vice-president believes that annual sales would be 20,000 units if the units were priced at $2,000 each, so annual sales are estimated at $40 million. The engineering department has reported that the firm would need additional manufacturing capability, and BQC currently has an option to purchase an existing building, at a cost of $12 million, which would meet this need. The building would be bought and paid for in 1 year, on December 31, 1996, and for depreciation purposes it would fall into the MACRS 39-year class.

The necessary equipment would be purchased and installed late in 1996, and it would also be paid for on December 31, 1996. The equipment would fall into the MACRS 5-year class, and it would cost $8 million, including transportation and installation.

The project would also require an initial investment of $6 million in net working capital. The initial working capital investment would also be made on December 31, 1996. The project's estimated economic life is 4 years. At the end of that time, the building is expected to have a market value of $7.5 million and a book value of $10.908 million, whereas the equipment would have a market value of $2 million and a book value of $1.36 million. The production department has estimated that variable manufacturing costs would total 60 percent of sales, and that fixed overhead costs, excluding depreciation, would be $5 million a year. Depreciation expenses would vary from year to year in accordance with the MACRS rates (which are discussed in Appendix 11A).

BQC's marginal federal-plus-state tax rate is 40 percent; its cost of capital is 12 percent; and, for capital budgeting purposes, the company's policy is to assume that operating cash flows occur at the end of each year. Because the plant would begin operations on January 1, 1997, the first operating cash flows would occur on December 31, 1997.

Assume that you are one of the company's financial analysts, and you have been assigned the task of supervising the capital budgeting analysis. For now, you may assume that the project has the same risk as an average project, and you may use the corporate weighted average cost of capital, 12 percent, for this project.

ANALYSIS OF THE CASH FLOWS.   The first step in the analysis is to summarize the investment outlays required for the project; this is done in the 1996 column of Table 11-2. For BQC's computer project, the cash outlays consist of the purchase price of the building, the price of the needed equipment, and the required investment in net working capital (NWC).

Having estimated the capital requirements, we must now estimate the cash flows that will occur once production begins; these are set forth in the remaining columns of Table 11-2. The operating cash flow estimates are based on information provided by BQC's various departments. The depreciation amounts were obtained by multiplying the depreciable basis by the MACRS recovery allowance rates as set forth in Note b to Table 11-2.

The investment in net working capital will be recovered in 2000. Also, estimates of the cash flows from the salvage values are required, and Table 11-3 summarizes this analysis. The building has an estimated salvage value which is less than its book value — it will be sold at a loss for tax purposes. This loss will reduce taxable income and thus will generate a tax savings. In effect, the company will have been depreciating the building too slowly, and it will write off the loss against its ordinary income, saving taxes that it would otherwise have to pay. The equipment, on the other hand, will be sold for more than its book value, and the company will have to pay taxes on the $640,000 profit. In both cases, the book value is calculated as the initial cost minus the accumulated depreciation. The total cash flow from

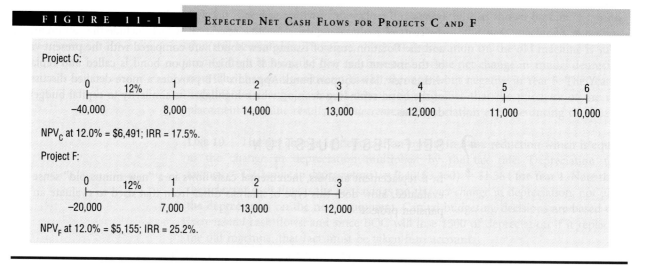

FIGURE 11-1	EXPECTED NET CASH FLOWS FOR PROJECTS C AND F

the overall life of the combined projects to 6 years. Here we assume (1) that Project F's cost and annual cash inflows will not change if the project is repeated in 3 years and (2) that BQC's cost of capital will remain at 12 percent:

NPV at 12% = $8,824; IRR = 25.2%.

The NPV of this extended Project F is $8,824, and its IRR is 25.2 percent. (The IRR of two Project Fs is the same as the IRR for one Project F.) Since the $8,824 extended NPV of Project F over the common life of 6 years is greater than the $6,491 NPV of Project C, Project F should be selected.[7]

Equivalent Annual Annuity (EAA) Method

A method which calculates the annual payments a project would provide if it were an annuity. When comparing projects of unequal lives, the one with the higher equivalent annual annuity should be chosen.

EQUIVALENT ANNUAL ANNUITY (EAA) APPROACH

Although the preceding example illustrates why an extended analysis is necessary if we are comparing mutually exclusive projects with different lives, the arithmetic is generally more complex in practice. For example, one project might have a 6-year life versus a 10-year life for the other. This would require a replacement chain analysis over 30 years, the lowest common denominator of the two lives. In such a situation, it is often simpler to use a second procedure, the **equivalent annual annuity (EAA) method,** which involves three steps:

---

[7]Alternatively, we could recognize that the value of the cash flow stream of two consecutive Project Fs can be summarized by two NPVs: one at Year 0 representing the value of the initial project, and one at Year 3 representing the value of the replication project:

5,155   5,155

NPV ≈ $8,824.

Ignoring rounding differences, the present value of these two cash flows, when discounted at 12 percent, is $8,824, so we again come to the conclusion that Project F should be selected.

1. Find each project's NPV over its initial life. In Figure 11-1, we found NPV_C = \$6,491 and NPV_F = \$5,155.

2. There is some constant annuity cash flow (the equivalent annual annuity [EAA]) that has the same present value as a project's NPV. For Project F, here is the time line:

To find the value of EAA_F with a financial calculator, enter N = 3, k = I = 12, PV = -5155, and FV = 0, and solve for PMT. The answer is \$2,146. This cash flow stream, when discounted back 3 years at 12 percent, has a present value equal to Project F's original NPV, \$5,155. The \$2,146 is called the project's "equivalent annual annuity (EAA)." The EAA for Project C can be found similarly, and it is \$1,579. Thus, Project C has an NPV which is equivalent to an annuity of \$1,579 per year, while Project F's NPV is equivalent to an annuity of \$2,146.[8]

3. The project with the higher EAA will always have the higher NPV when extended out to any common life. Therefore, since F's EAA is larger than C's, we would choose Project F.

The EAA method is often easier to apply than the replacement chain method, but the replacement chain method is easier to explain to decision makers. Still, the two methods always lead to the same decision if consistent assumptions are used.

When should we worry about unequal life analysis? As a general rule, the unequal life issue (1) does not arise for independent projects, but (2) it can arise if mutually exclusive projects with significantly different lives are being compared. However, even for mutually exclusive projects, it is not always appropriate to extend the analysis to a common life. This should only be done if there is a high probability that the projects will actually be repeated at the end of their initial lives.

We should note several potentially serious weaknesses inherent in this type of analysis: (1) If inflation is expected, then replacement equipment will have a higher price, and both sales prices and operating costs will probably change. Thus, the static conditions built into the analysis would be invalid. (2) Replacements that occur down the road would probably employ new technology, which in turn might change the cash flows. This factor is not built into either replacement chain analysis or the EAA approach. (3) It is difficult enough to estimate the lives of most projects, so estimating the lives of a series of projects is often just a speculation.

In view of these problems, no experienced financial analyst would be too concerned about comparing mutually exclusive projects with lives of, say, 8 years and 10 years. Given all the uncertainties in the estimation process, such projects would, for all practical purposes, be assumed to have the same life. Still, it is important to recognize that a problem does exist if mutually exclusive projects have substantially different lives. When we encounter such problems in practice, we use a computer spreadsheet and build expected inflation and/or possible efficiency gains

---

[8]Some financial calculators have the EAA feature programmed in. For example, the HP-17B has the function in its cash flow register. One simply keys in the cash flows, enters the interest rate, and then presses the "NUS" key to get the EAA. Hewlett-Packard uses the term NUS (for "net uniform series") in lieu of the term EAA.

directly into the cash flow estimates, and then use the replacement chain approach (but not the equivalent annual annuity method). The cash flow estimation is more complicated, but the concepts involved are exactly the same as in our example.

 SELF-TEST QUESTIONS

Why is it not always necessary to adjust project cash flow analyses for unequal lives?

Briefly describe the replacement chain (common life) approach.

Briefly describe the equivalent annual annuity (EAA) approach.

DEALING WITH INFLATION

Inflation is a fact of life, and it should be recognized in capital budgeting decisions. Some important points follow:

1. Recall from Chapter 4 that inflationary expectations are built into interest rates and money costs: $k_i = k^* + IP + LP + MRP + DRP$, with IP being the inflation factor. This factor is reflected in the WACC used to find the NPV and as the hurdle rate if the IRR or MIRR method is used. Therefore, inflation is reflected in the cost of capital used in a capital budgeting analysis.

2. The NPV method involves finding the PV of each future CF, discounted at the cost of capital, as follows:

$$NPV = \sum_{t=0}^{n} \frac{CF_t}{(1 + k)^t}.$$

Note that k, which is the WACC, includes a premium for expected inflation, so the higher the expected inflation rate, the larger the value of k, and, other things held constant, the smaller the NPV.

3. If inflation is expected, but this expectation is not built into the forecasted cash flows as shown in Table 11-2, then the calculated NPV will be incorrect — it will be downward biased. To see this, recognize that sales prices over the life of the project are built into the sales revenues shown in Table 11-2, hence into the cash flow projections for BQC's expansion project. If projected sales prices do not reflect expected inflation, this bias will be present — the denominator of the NPV equation will be increased because expected inflation is automatically built into the cost of capital by participants in the capital market, but the cash flows in the numerator will not be increased. Therefore, the NPV will be biased downward.

It is easy to avoid the inflation bias — simply build inflationary expectations into the cash flows used in the analysis. In other words, when making a table such as Table 11-2, simply reflect expected inflation in the revenue and cost figures, hence in the annual net cash flow forecasts. Then the NPV will be unbiased.

 SELF-TEST QUESTIONS

How can inflation cause a downward bias in a project's estimated NPV?

What is the best way of handling inflation in a capital budgeting analysis, and how does this procedure eliminate the potential bias?

INCORPORATING PROJECT RISK AND CAPITAL STRUCTURE INTO CAPITAL BUDGETING

Capital budgeting can affect a firm's market risk, its corporate risk, or both, but it is extremely difficult to quantify either type of risk. Although it may be possible to reach the general conclusion that one project is riskier than another, it is difficult to develop a really good *quantitative measure* of project risk. This makes it difficult to incorporate differential risk into capital budgeting decisions.

Two methods are used to incorporate project risk into capital budgeting. One is the *certainty equivalent* approach, where all cash flows that are not known with certainty are scaled down, and the riskier the flows, the lower their certainty equivalent values. The other method, and the one we focus on, is the **risk-adjusted discount rate** approach, under which differential project risk is dealt with by changing the discount rate. Average-risk projects are discounted at the firm's average cost of capital, higher-risk projects are discounted at a higher cost of capital, and lower-risk projects are discounted at a rate below the firm's average cost of capital.

One way to estimate the cost of capital for projects whose risk differs from that of an average asset is to estimate the beta of each project and then use the CAPM to estimate each project's cost of capital. For example, suppose the risk-free rate is 7 percent, the market risk premium is 5 percent, and a project is estimated to have a beta of 1.0. In this case, the CAPM estimate of the project's cost of capital would be 7% + (5%)(1.0) = 12%. However, if a riskier project with a beta of 1.2 were being considered, it would be evaluated with a 13 percent cost of capital: 7% + (5%)(1.2) = 13.0%.

Unfortunately, project betas are difficult to estimate, and the use of the CAPM for an individual project is questionable. Given the state of the art, risk adjustments are necessarily judgmental and somewhat arbitrary, and the details of the risk adjustment process are best left to advanced finance courses.

Capital structure must also be taken into account if a firm finances different assets in different ways. For example, one division might have a lot of real estate which is well suited as collateral for loans, whereas some other division might have most of its capital tied up in research and development (R&D), which is not good collateral. As a result, the division with the real estate might have a higher *debt capacity* than the division with the R&D, hence an optimal capital structure which contains a higher percentage of debt. In this case, the financial staff might calculate the cost of capital differently for the two divisions.[9]

Although the process is not exact, many companies use a two-step procedure to develop risk-adjusted discount rates for use in capital budgeting. First, *divisional costs of capital* are established for each of the major operating divisions on the basis of each division's estimated average riskiness and its capital structure. Second, within each division all projects are classified into three categories — high risk, average risk, and low risk. Then, each division uses its basic divisional cost of capital for average risk projects, reduces the divisional cost of capital by one or two percentage points when evaluating low-risk projects, and raises the cost of capital by several percentage points for high-risk projects. For example, if a division's basic cost of capital is estimated to be 10 percent, a 12 percent discount rate might be

Risk-Adjusted Discount Rate
The discount rate that applies to a particular risky stream of income; the riskier the project's income stream, the higher the discount rate.

---

[9]We will say more about optimal capital structure and debt capacity in Chapter 12.

able costs (for gas) would be high. Thus, by its capital budgeting decisions, the utility (or any other company) can influence its operating leverage and hence its basic business risk.

The concept of operating leverage was in fact originally developed for use in capital budgeting. Alternative methods for making a given product often have different degrees of operating leverage and hence different breakeven points and different degrees of risk. Bigbee Electronics and other companies regularly undertake a breakeven analysis as part of their capital budgeting process. Still, once a corporation's operating leverage has been established, this factor influences its capital structure decisions.

FINANCIAL RISK

Financial Leverage
The extent to which fixed-income securities (debt and preferred stock) are used in a firm's capital structure.

Financial Risk
An increase in stockholders' risk, over and above the firm's basic business risk, resulting from the use of financial leverage.

Financial leverage refers to the use of fixed-income securities — debt and preferred stock — and **financial risk** is the additional risk placed on the common stockholders as a result of financial leverage. Conceptually, the firm has a certain amount of risk inherent in its operations; this is its business risk, which is defined as the uncertainty inherent in projections of future ROA. If it uses debt and preferred stock (financial leverage), the firm concentrates its business risk on the common stockholders. To illustrate, suppose 10 people decide to form a corporation to manufacture running shoes. There is a certain amount of business risk in the operation. If the firm is capitalized only with common equity, and if each person buys 10 percent of the stock, then each investor will bear an equal share of the business risk. However, suppose the firm is capitalized with 50 percent debt and 50 percent equity, with 5 of the investors putting up their capital as debt and the other 5 putting up their money as equity. In this case, the investors who put up the equity will have to bear essentially all of the business risk, so their common stock will be twice as risky as it would have been had the firm been financed only with equity. *Thus, the use of debt concentrates the firm's business risk on its stockholders.*

In the next section, we will explain how financial leverage affects a firm's expected earnings per share, the riskiness of those earnings, and, consequently, the price of its stock. As you will see, the value of a firm that has no debt first rises as it substitutes debt for equity, then hits a peak, and finally declines as the use of debt becomes excessive. The objective is to determine the capital structure at which value is maximized; this point is then used as the *target capital structure.*[5]

SELF-TEST QUESTIONS

Explain the difference between business risk and financial risk.

Identify some of the more important factors which affect business risk.

Why does business risk vary from industry to industry?

What is financial risk, and how does it arise?

---

[5]In this chapter, we examine capital structures on a *book value* (or *balance sheet*) *basis*. An alternative approach is to calculate the market values of debt, preferred stock, and common equity and then to reconstruct the balance sheet on a *market value basis*. Although the market value approach is more consistent with financial theory, bond rating agencies and most financial executives focus on book values. Moreover, the conversion from book to market values is a complicated process, and since market value capital structures change with stock market fluctuations, they are thought by many to be too unstable to serve as operationally useful targets. Finally, exactly the same insights are gained from the book and market value analyses. For all these reasons, a market value analysis of capital structure is best left for advanced finance courses.

DETERMINING THE OPTIMAL CAPITAL STRUCTURE

We can illustrate the effects of financial leverage using the data shown in Table 12-1 for Firm B. As shown in the top section of the table, the company has no debt. Should it continue the policy of using no debt, or should it start using financial leverage? If it does substitute debt for equity, how far should it go? *It should choose the capital structure that maximizes the price of its stock.*

EBIT/EPS ANALYSIS

Changes in the use of debt will cause changes in earnings per share (EPS) and, consequently, in the stock price. To understand the relationship between financial leverage and EPS, first consider Table 12-2, which shows how Firm B's cost of debt would vary if it used different percentages of debt. The higher the percentage of debt, the riskier the debt, hence the higher the interest rate lenders will charge.

Now consider Table 12-3, which shows how expected EPS varies with changes in financial leverage. Section I of the table begins with a probability distribution of sales; we assume for simplicity that sales can take on only three values, $100,000, $200,000, or $300,000. In the remainder of Section I, we calculate EBIT at each sales level. We assume that both sales and operating costs are independent of fi-

---

TABLE 12-1   DATA ON FIRM B

I. Balance Sheet on 12/31/95

Current assets	$100,000	Debt	$ 0
Net fixed assets	100,000	Common equity (10,000 shares)	200,000
Total assets	$200,000	Total liabilities and equity	$200,000

II. Income Statement for 1995

Sales		$200,000
Fixed operating costs	$ 40,000	
Variable operating costs	120,000	160,000
Earnings before interest and taxes (EBIT)		$ 40,000
Interest		0
Earnings before taxes		$ 40,000
Taxes (40%)		16,000
Net income		$ 24,000

III. Other Data

1. Earnings per share = EPS = $24,000/10,000 shares = $2.40.
2. Dividends per share = DPS = $24,000/10,000 shares = $2.40. (Thus, Firm B pays out all of its earnings as dividends.)
3. Book value per share = $200,000/10,000 shares = $20.
4. Market price per share = P_0 = $20. (Thus, the stock sells at its book value, so M/B = 1.0.)
5. Price/earnings ratio = P/E = $20/$2.40 = 8.33 times.

TABLE 12-2	INTEREST RATES FOR FIRM B WITH DIFFERENT DEBT/ASSETS RATIOS

AMOUNT BORROWED[a]	DEBT/ASSETS RATIO	INTEREST RATE, k_d, ON ALL DEBT
$ 20,000	10%	8.0%
40,000	20	8.3
60,000	30	9.0
80,000	40	10.0
100,000	50	12.0
120,000	60	15.0

[a]We assume that the firm must borrow in increments of $20,000. We also assume that Firm B is unable to borrow more than $120,000, which is 60 percent of assets, because of restrictions in its corporate charter.

nancial leverage, so the three EBIT figures ($0, $40,000, and $80,000) will always remain the same, no matter how much debt Firm B uses.[6]

Section II of Table 12-3, the zero debt case, calculates Firm B's earnings per share at each sales level under the assumption that the company continues to use no debt. Net income is divided by the 10,000 shares outstanding to obtain EPS. If sales are as low as $100,000, EPS will be zero, but EPS will rise to $4.80 at a sales level of $300,000. The EPS at each sales level is then multiplied by the probability of that sales level to calculate the expected EPS, which is $2.40 if Firm B uses no debt. We also calculate the standard deviation of EPS and the coefficient of variation as indicators of the firm's risk at a zero debt ratio: $\sigma_{EPS} = \$1.52$, and $CV_{EPS} = 0.63$.[7]

Section III shows the results if Firm B financed with a debt/assets ratio of 50 percent. In this situation, $100,000 of the $200,000 total capital would be debt. The interest rate on the debt, 12 percent, is taken from Table 12-2. With $100,000 of 12 percent debt outstanding, the company's interest expense in Table 12-3 would be $12,000 per year. This is a fixed cost — it is the same regardless of the level of sales — and it is deducted from the EBIT values as calculated in the top section. Next, taxes are taken out to calculate net income. EPS is then calculated as net income divided by shares outstanding. With debt = 0, there would be 10,000 shares outstanding. However, if half of the equity were replaced by debt (debt = $100,000), there would be only 5,000 shares outstanding, and we must use this fact to deter-

---

[6]In the real world, capital structure *does* at times affect EBIT. First, if debt levels are excessive, the firm will probably find it difficult to obtain financing if its earnings are low at a time when interest rates are high. This could lead to stop-start construction and R&D programs, as well as to having to pass up good investment opportunities. Second, a weak financial condition (i.e., too much debt) could cause a firm to lose sales. For example, prior to the time that its huge debt forced Eastern Airlines into bankruptcy, many people refused to buy Eastern tickets because they were afraid the company would go bankrupt and leave them holding unusable tickets. Third, financially strong companies are able to bargain hard with their unions and suppliers, whereas weaker ones may have to give in simply because they do not have the financial resources to carry on the fight. Finally, a company with so much debt that bankruptcy is a serious threat will have difficulty attracting and retaining managers and employees, or it will have to pay premium salaries. People value job security, and financially weak companies simply cannot provide such protection. For all these reasons, it is not totally correct to say that a firm's financial policy has no effect on its operating income.

[7]See Chapter 5 for a review of procedures for calculating the standard deviation and coefficient of variation. Recall that the advantage of the coefficient of variation is that it permits better comparisons when the expected values of EPS vary, as they do here for the two capital structures.

TABLE 12-3	FIRM B: EPS WITH DIFFERENT AMOUNTS OF FINANCIAL LEVERAGE (THOUSANDS OF DOLLARS, EXCEPT PER-SHARE FIGURES)

I. Calculation of EBIT

Probability of indicated sales	0.2	0.6	0.2
Sales	$100.0	$200.0	$300.0
Fixed costs	40.0	40.0	40.0
Variable costs (60% of sales)	60.0	120.0	180.0
Total costs (except interest)	$100.0	$160.0	$220.0
Earnings before interest and taxes (EBIT)	$ 0.0	$ 40.0	$ 80.0

II. Situation if Debt/Assets (D/A) = 0%

EBIT (from Section I)	$ 0.0	$ 40.0	$ 80.0
Less interest	0.0	0.0	0.0
Earnings before taxes (EBT)	$ 0.0	$ 40.0	$ 80.0
Taxes (40%)	0.0	(16.0)	(32.0)
Net income	$ 0.0	$ 24.0	$ 48.0
Earnings per share (EPS) on 10,000 shares[a]	$ 0.0	$ 2.40	$ 4.80
Expected EPS		$ 2.40	
Standard deviation of EPS		$ 1.52	
Coefficient of variation		0.63	

III. Situation if Debt/Assets (D/A) = 50%

EBIT (from Section I)	$ 0.0	$ 40.0	$ 80.0
Less interest (0.12 × $100,000)	12.0	12.0	12.0
Earnings before taxes (EBT)	($ 12.0)	$ 28.0	$ 68.0
Taxes (40%; tax credit on losses)	4.8	(11.2)	(27.2)
Net income	($ 7.2)	$ 16.8	$ 40.8
Earnings per share (EPS) on 5,000 shares[a]	($ 1.44)	$ 3.36	$ 8.16
Expected EPS		$ 3.36	
Standard deviation of EPS		$ 3.04	
Coefficient of variation		0.90	

[a]The EPS figures can also be obtained using the following formula, in which the numerator amounts to an income statement at a given sales level laid out horizontally:

$$\text{EPS} = \frac{(\text{Sales} - \text{Fixed costs} - \text{Variable costs} - \text{Interest})(1 - \text{Tax rate})}{\text{Shares outstanding}} = \frac{(\text{EBIT} - \text{I})(1 - \text{T})}{\text{Shares outstanding}}.$$

For example, with zero debt and Sales = $200,000, EPS is $2.40:

$$\text{EPS}_{D/A=0} = \frac{(\$200,000 - \$40,000 - \$120,000 - 0)(0.6)}{10,000} = \$2.40.$$

With 50 percent debt and Sales = $200,000, EPS is $3.36:

$$\text{EPS}_{D/A=0.5} = \frac{(\$200,000 - \$40,000 - \$120,000 - \$12,000)(0.6)}{5,000} = \$3.36.$$

The sales level at which EPS will be equal under the two financing policies, or the indifference level of sales, S_I, can be found by setting $\text{EPS}_{D/A=0}$ equal to $\text{EPS}_{D/A=0.5}$ and solving for S_I:

$$\text{EPS}_{D/A=0} = \frac{(S_I - \$40,000 - 0.6S_I - 0)(0.6)}{10,000} = \frac{(S_I - \$40,000 - 0.6S_I - \$12,000)(0.6)}{5,000} = \text{EPS}_{D/A=0.5}.$$

$$S_I = \$160,000.$$

By substituting this value of sales into either equation, we can find EPS_I, the earnings per share at this indifference point. In our example, $\text{EPS}_I = \$1.44$.

CORPORATE GET-RICH-SLOWLY PLANS

For investors who do not need immediate cash income, more than 900 public companies offer a plan that is an almost guaranteed money-maker. It is a dividend reinvestment plan (DRP), which allows stockholders to use their dividends to buy more stock. Instead of receiving checks, they automatically get additional shares of firm's stock.

Participants in DRPs benefit whether the market moves up or down because a DRP is a form of dollar-cost averaging—a proven way to lower the cost of investments. If dividends are reinvested regularly (and the payment period for most companies is every quarter), the same dividend buys more shares when the price is low and fewer when it is high. Over time, the result for a reasonably stable company is an average cost per share that is lower than the stock's average market price.

The shareholder gets another important advantage—some 600 DRPs involve no brokerage fees, so the entire dividend check goes toward more shares of stock. Although investors must own at least one share in a company to be eligible for its reinvestment plan, they pay a stockbroker only for that first purchase, and they do not need to work with the broker again. Regular purchases through a broker can cost a minimum of $35 to $55 per transaction, so the savings in a reinvestment plan can be substantial.

However, if you agree to have dividends reinvested, a handful of companies, such as Bank of New York, Minnesota Power & Light, Texaco, Citibank, and W. R. Grace, will sell you your first shares directly, up to a set dollar amount. "From the corporate point of view, it's a goodwill gesture," says the editor of a reinvestment-plan directory. "Most of those are consumer-oriented companies trying to attract long-term shareholders."

The advantages of keeping shares for a long time are demonstrated by the profits enjoyed by a retired Texas engineer. In 25 years, his 700 shares of a utility stock, purchased for just under $10,000, grew to 5,000 shares, worth about $102,500, through dividend reinvestment alone—a 925 percent gain with no work involved. Still more can be amassed if a stockholder adds cash to the dividend reinvestments. Many companies allow this practice, with $3,000 being the typical maximum per quarter, but in some cases, the maximum can be in the hundreds of thousands.

Corporations also benefit from DRPs because the plans strengthen shareholders' commitment to the company. Most firms prefer to have small investors as shareholders because they are loyal, and they make good customers. Also, the plans can be used to raise capital when firms keep the cash and issue new shares.

As an additional lure to stockholders, about 100 companies offer stock through DRPs at a discount of from 3 to 5 percent below market price. However, Chemical Bank and Chase Manhattan Bank both had to change their discount policies when traders figured out that they could sell shares short and then cover their positions by buying the stock at a 5 percent discount. This short selling caused the banks' stock prices to fluctuate. As a result, Chemical lowered its discount for cash purchases from 5 percent to 2.5 percent, and then eliminated it altogether. Similarly, Chase Manhattan amended its cash option plan to 3 percent from 5 percent, and it reduced the maximum amount of stock a shareholder could buy from $250,000 a quarter to $40,000 a month. Traders had not only been selling Chase shares short and covering this action with discount purchases, but they also avoided the $250,000 limit by buying the discounted shares under multiple names. Even so, neither Chase nor Chemical Bank is thinking of eliminating their DRPs.

Although investors continue to respond well to DRPs, these plans do have some drawbacks. For example, all reinvested dividends are taxable in the year they were paid, even though no cash goes directly to the shareholder. Obviously, the plans are inappropriate for people who need cash income for living expenses or for tax payments. Second, these direct investment plans are not aimed at the active trader who wants to buy and sell quickly. Rather, they are aimed at the small investor who has only a limited amount to invest.

The latest trend appears to be the revamping of companies' plans from "limited" DRPs to plans that offer shareholders services that are similar to those provided by mutual funds. Exxon offers these expanded investment services, permitting people to buy the stock directly, to open individual retirement accounts, and even to set up automatic transfers from their bank accounts to buy Exxon stock. The response to its new services has been tremendous.

SOURCES: "Chase Drops Parts of Dividend Plan Due to Stock Fall," *The Wall Street Journal*, February 16, 1990; "Chemical Banking Cuts Reinvestment Plan Following Stock Drop," *The Wall Street Journal*, February 23, 1990; "Chemical Banking Ends Discount on Stock Buys," *The Wall Street Journal*, March 29, 1990; "DRIPs Can Help Your Dividends Multiply," *Money*, May 1990; "Smart Money—Replanting Dividends: It's Easy and Cheap," *Business Week*, February 24, 1992; "Bookshelf: Investing Wisely," *The Wall Street Journal*, January 15, 1993; "Dividend Reinvestment Plans Take on New Look," *The Wall Street Journal*, March 3, 1993; "How You Can Make Money in the Stock Market—DRIP by DRIP," *Money*, Forecast 1994.

DIVIDEND REINVESTMENT PLANS

Dividend Reinvestment Plan (DRP)

A plan that enables a stockholder to automatically reinvest dividends received back into the stock of the paying firm.

In recent years most larger companies have instituted **dividend reinvestment plans (DRPs),** whereby stockholders can automatically reinvest dividends received in the stock of the paying corporation.[7] There are two types of DRPs: (1) plans which involve only "old" stock that is already outstanding and (2) plans which involve newly issued stock. In either case, the stockholder must pay income taxes on the amount of the dividends even though stock, rather than cash, is received.

Under the "old-stock" type of plan, the stockholder chooses between receiving dividend checks or having the company use the dividends to buy more stock in the corporation. If the stockholder elects reinvestment, a bank, acting as trustee, takes the total funds available for reinvestment, purchases the corporation's stock on the open market, and allocates the shares purchased to the participating stockholders' accounts on a pro rata basis. The transactions costs of buying shares (brokerage costs) are low because of volume purchases, so these plans benefit small stockholders who do not need cash dividends for current consumption.

The "new-stock" type of DRP provides for dividends to be invested in newly issued stock; hence, these plans raise new capital for the firm. AT&T, Florida Power & Light, Union Carbide, and many other companies have had such plans in effect in recent years, using them to raise substantial amounts of new equity capital. No fees are charged to stockholders, and many companies offer stock at a discount of 5 percent below the actual market price. The companies absorb these costs as a trade-off against the flotation costs that would have been incurred had they sold stock through investment bankers rather than through the dividend reinvestment plans.[8] See the accompanying box for more information on DRPs.

SELF-TEST QUESTIONS

Explain the logic of the residual dividend policy, the steps a firm would take to implement it, and why it is more likely to be used to establish a long-run payout target than to set the actual year-by-year payout ratio.

Describe the constant, or steadily increasing, dividend policy, and give two reasons why a firm might follow such a policy.

Explain what a low-regular-dividend-plus-extras policy is and why a firm might follow such a policy.

Describe the constant payout ratio dividend policy. Why is this policy not as popular as a constant, or steadily increasing, dividend policy?

Why is the ex-dividend date important to investors?

Describe the two types of dividend reinvestment plans.

---

[7]See Richard H. Pettway and R. Phil Malone, "Automatic Dividend Reinvestment Plans," *Financial Management*, Winter 1973, 11–18, for an excellent discussion of this topic.

[8]One interesting aspect of DRPs is that they are forcing corporations to reexamine their basic dividend policies. A high participation rate in a DRP suggests that stockholders might be better off if the firm simply reduced cash dividends, as this would save stockholders some personal income taxes. Quite a few firms are surveying their stockholders to learn more about their preferences and to find out how they would react to a change in dividend policy. A more rational approach to basic dividend policy decisions may emerge from this research.

    Also, it should be noted that companies either start or stop using new-stock DRPs depending on their need for equity capital. Florida Power & Light recently stopped offering a new-stock DRP with a 5 percent discount because its need for equity capital declined once it had completed a nuclear power plant. FP&L simply switched to an old-stock plan.

SUMMARY OF FACTORS INFLUENCING DIVIDEND POLICY

Thus far in the chapter, we have described the major theories that deal with the effects of dividend policy on the value of a firm, and we have discussed alternative payment policies. Firms choose a particular policy based on managements' beliefs concerning which dividend theory is most correct, but they also consider a host of other factors as described below. All of the factors firms take into account may be grouped into four broad categories: (1) constraints on dividend payments, (2) investment opportunities, (3) availability and cost of alternative sources of capital, and (4) effects of dividend policy on k_s. Each of these categories has several subparts, which we discuss in the following paragraphs.

CONSTRAINTS

1. **Bond indentures.** Debt contracts often limit dividend payments to earnings generated after the loan was granted. Also, contracts often stipulate that no dividends can be paid unless the current ratio, times-interest-earned ratio, and other safety ratios exceed stated minimums.

2. **Impairment of capital rule.** Dividend payments cannot exceed the balance sheet item "retained earnings." This legal restriction, known as the *impairment of capital rule,* is designed to protect creditors. Without the rule, a company that was in trouble might distribute most of its assets to stockholders and leave its debtholders out in the cold. (*Liquidating dividends* can be paid out of capital, but they must be indicated as such, and they must not reduce capital below the limits stated in debt contracts.)

3. **Availability of cash.** Cash dividends can be paid only with cash. Thus, a shortage of cash in the bank can restrict dividend payments. However, the ability to borrow can offset this factor.

4. **Penalty tax on improperly accumulated earnings.** To prevent wealthy individuals from using corporations to avoid personal taxes, the Tax Code provides for a special surtax on improperly accumulated income. Thus, if the IRS can demonstrate that a firm's dividend payout ratio is being deliberately held down to help its stockholders avoid personal taxes, the firm is subject to heavy penalties. This factor is generally relevant only to privately owned firms.

INVESTMENT OPPORTUNITIES

1. **Location of the IOS schedule.** If a firm's "typical" IOS schedule as shown earlier in Figure 13-4 is far to the right, this will tend to produce a low target payout ratio, and vice versa if the IOS is far to the left.

2. **Possibility of accelerating or delaying projects.** The ability to accelerate or to postpone projects will permit a firm to adhere more closely to a stable dividend policy.

ALTERNATIVE SOURCES OF CAPITAL

1. **Cost of selling new stock.** If a firm needs to finance a given level of investment, it can obtain equity by retaining earnings or by issuing new common stock. If flotation costs (including any negative signaling effects of a stock offering) are high, k_e will be well above k_s, making it better to set a low payout ratio and to finance through retention rather than through sale of new common stock. On the other hand, a high dividend payout ratio is more feasible for a firm whose flotation costs are low. Flotation costs differ among firms—for example, the flotation percentage is generally higher for small firms, so they tend to set low payout ratios.

2. **Ability to substitute debt for equity.** A firm can finance a given level of investment with either debt or equity. As noted above, low stock flotation costs permit a more flexible dividend policy because equity can be raised either by retaining earnings or by selling new stock. A similar situation holds for debt policy: if the firm can adjust its debt ratio without raising costs sharply, it can pay the expected dividend, even if earnings fluctuate, by using a variable debt ratio. The shape of the average cost of capital curve (in the left-hand panel of Figure 13-2) determines the practical extent to which the debt ratio can be varied. If the average cost of capital curve is relatively flat over a wide range, then a higher payout ratio is more feasible than it would be if the curve had a sharp V shape.

3. **Control.** If management is concerned about maintaining control, it may be reluctant to sell new stock, hence the company may retain more earnings than it otherwise would. However, if stockholders want higher dividends and a proxy fight looms, then the dividend will be increased.

EFFECTS OF DIVIDEND POLICY ON k_s

The effects of dividend policy on k_s may be considered in terms of four factors: (1) stockholders' desire for current versus future income, (2) perceived riskiness of dividends versus capital gains, (3) the tax advantage of capital gains over dividends, and (4) the information content of dividends (signaling). Since we discussed each of these factors in detail earlier, we need only note here that the importance of each factor in terms of its effect on k_s varies from firm to firm depending on the makeup of its current and possible future stockholders.

It should be apparent from our discussion thus far that dividend policy decisions are truly exercises in informed judgment, not decisions that can be quantified precisely. Even so, to make rational dividend decisions, financial managers must take account of all the points discussed in the preceding sections.

⁇ SELF-TEST QUESTIONS

Identify the four broad sets of factors which affect dividend policy.

What constraints affect dividend policy?

How do investment opportunities affect dividend policy?

How does the availability and cost of outside capital affect dividend policy?

STOCK DIVIDENDS AND STOCK SPLITS

Stock dividends and stock splits are related to the firm's cash dividend policy. The rationale for stock dividends and splits can best be explained through an example. We will use Porter Electronic Controls Inc., a $700 million electronic components manufacturer, for this purpose. Since its inception, Porter's markets have been expanding, and the company has enjoyed growth in sales and earnings. Some of its earnings have been paid out in dividends, but some are also retained each year, causing its earnings per share and stock price to grow. The company began its life with only a few thousand shares outstanding, and, after some years of growth, each of Porter's shares had a very high EPS and DPS. When a "normal" P/E ratio was applied, the derived market price was so high that few people could afford to buy a "round lot" of 100 shares. This limited the demand for the stock and thus kept the total market value of the firm below what it would have been if more shares, at a lower price, had been outstanding. To correct this situation, Porter "split its stock," as described in the next section.

STOCK SPLITS

Although there is little empirical evidence to support the contention, there is nevertheless a widespread belief in financial circles that an *optimal price range* exists for stocks. "Optimal" means that if the price is within this range, the price/earnings ratio, hence the value of the firm, will be maximized. Many observers, including Porter's management, believe that the best range for most stocks is from $20 to $80 per share. Accordingly, if the price of Porter's stock rose to $80, management would probably declare a two-for-one **stock split,** thus doubling the number of shares outstanding, halving the earnings and dividends per share, and thereby lowering the price of the stock. Each stockholder would have more shares, but each share would be worth less. If the post-split price were $40, Porter's stockholders would be exactly as well off as they were before the split. However, if the price of the stock were to stabilize above $40, stockholders would be better off. Stock splits can be of any size — for example, the stock could be split two-for-one, three-for-one, one-and-a-half-for-one, or in any other way.[9]

Stock Split
An action taken by a firm to increase the number of shares outstanding, such as doubling the number of shares outstanding by giving each stockholder two new shares for each one formerly held.

STOCK DIVIDENDS

Stock dividends are similar to stock splits in that they "divide the pie into smaller slices" without affecting the fundamental position of the current stockholders. On a 5 percent stock dividend, the holder of 100 shares would receive an additional 5 shares (without cost); on a 20 percent stock dividend, the same holder would receive 20 new shares; and so on. Again, the total number of shares is increased, so earnings, dividends, and price per share all decline. If a firm wants to reduce the price of its stock, should it use a stock split or a stock dividend? Stock splits are generally used after a sharp price run-up to produce a large price reduction. Stock

Stock Dividend
A dividend paid in the form of additional shares of stock rather than in cash.

---

[9]*Reverse splits,* which reduce the shares outstanding, can even be used. For example, a company whose stock sells for $5 might employ a one-for-five reverse split, exchanging 1 new share for 5 old ones and raising the value of the shares to about $25, which is within the optimal price range. LTV Corporation did this after several years of losses had driven its stock price down below the optimal range.

dividends used on a regular annual basis will keep the stock price more or less constrained. For example, if a firm's earnings and dividends were growing at about 10 percent per year, its stock price would tend to go up at about that same rate, and it would soon be outside the desired trading range. A 10 percent annual stock dividend would maintain the stock price within the optimal trading range. Note, though, that small stock dividends create bookkeeping problems, so firms today use stock splits far more often than stock dividends.[10]

PRICE EFFECTS

Several empirical studies have examined the effects of stock splits and stock dividends on stock prices.[11] These studies suggest that investors see stock splits and stock dividends for what they are — simply additional pieces of paper. If stock dividends and splits are accompanied by higher earnings and cash dividends, then investors will bid up the price of the stock. However, if stock dividends are not accompanied by increases in earnings and cash dividends, the dilution of earnings and dividends per share causes the price of the stock to drop by the same percentage as the stock dividend. Thus, the fundamental determinants of price are the underlying earnings and cash dividends per share, and stock splits and stock dividends merely cut the pie into thinner slices.

 ## SELF-TEST QUESTIONS

What is the rationale for a stock split?

What is the effect of stock splits and stock dividends on stock prices?

STOCK REPURCHASES

Several years ago, a *Fortune* article entitled "Beating the Market by Buying Back Stock" discussed the fact that during a one-year period, more than 600 major corporations repurchased significant amounts of their own stock. It also gave illustrations of some specific companies' repurchase programs and their effects on stock prices. The article's conclusion was that "buybacks have made a mint for shareholders who stay with the companies carrying them out." This section explains what a **stock repurchase** is, how a repurchase is carried out, and how the financial manager should analyze a possible repurchase program.

Stock Repurchase
A transaction in which a firm buys back shares of its own stock, thereby decreasing shares outstanding, increasing EPS, and, often, increasing the price of the stock.

---

[10]Accountants treat stock splits and stock dividends somewhat differently. For example, in a 2-for-1 stock split, the number of shares outstanding is doubled and the par value is halved, and that is about all there is to it. With a stock dividend, a bookkeeping entry is made transferring "retained earnings" to "common stock." For example, if a firm had 1,000,000 shares outstanding, if the stock price was $10, and if it wanted to pay a 10 percent stock dividend, then (1) each stockholder would be given 1 new share of stock for each 10 shares held, and (2) the accounting entries would involve showing 100,000 more shares outstanding and transferring 100,000($10) = $1,000,000 from "retained earnings" to "common stock." The retained earnings transfer limits the size of stock dividends, but that is not important because companies can always split their stock in any way they choose.

[11]See C. A. Barker, "Evaluation of Stock Dividends," *Harvard Business Review,* July–August 1958, 99–114. Barker's study has been replicated several times in recent years, and his results are still valid — they have withstood the test of time. Another excellent study, using an entirely different methodology, reached similar conclusions; see Eugene F. Fama, Lawrence Fisher, Michael C. Jensen, and Richard Roll, "The Adjustment of Stock Prices to New Information," *International Economic Review,* February 1969, 1–21.

There are two principal types of repurchases: (1) situations in which the firm has cash available for distribution to its stockholders, and it distributes this cash by repurchasing shares rather than by paying cash dividends; and (2) situations in which the firm concludes that its capital structure is too heavily weighted with equity, and then it sells debt and uses the proceeds to buy back its stock.

Stock that has been repurchased by a firm is called *treasury stock.* If some of the outstanding stock is repurchased, fewer shares will remain outstanding. Assuming that the repurchase does not adversely affect the firm's future earnings, the earnings per share on the remaining shares will increase, resulting in a higher market price per share. As a result, capital gains will have been substituted for dividends.

THE EFFECTS OF STOCK REPURCHASES

Many companies have been repurchasing their stock in recent years. Until the 1980s, most repurchases amounted to a few million dollars, but in 1985, Phillips Petroleum announced plans for the largest repurchase on record — 81 million of its shares with a market value of $4.1 billion. Other large repurchases have been made by Texaco, IBM, CBS, Coca-Cola, Teledyne, Atlantic Richfield, Goodyear, and Xerox. Indeed, since 1985, more shares have been repurchased than issued.

The effects of a repurchase can be illustrated with data on American Development Corporation (ADC). The company expects to earn $4.4 million in 1996, and 50 percent of this amount, or $2.2 million, has been allocated for distribution to common shareholders. There are 1.1 million shares outstanding, and the market price is $20 a share. ADC believes that it can either use the $2.2 million to repurchase 100,000 of its shares through a tender offer at $22 a share or else pay a cash dividend of $2 a share.[12]

The effect of the repurchase on the EPS and market price per share of the remaining stock can be analyzed in the following way:

1. Current EPS $= \dfrac{\text{Total earnings}}{\text{Number of shares}} = \dfrac{\$4.4\text{ million}}{1.1\text{ million}} = \$4$ per share.

2. P/E ratio $= \dfrac{\$20}{\$4} = 5\times$.

3. EPS after repurchase of 100,000 shares $= \dfrac{\$4.4\text{ million}}{1\text{ million}}$
$= \$4.40$ per share.

4. Expected market price after repurchase $= (\text{P/E})(\text{EPS}) = (5)(\$4.40)$
$= \$22$ per share.

---

[12]Stock repurchases are generally made in one of three ways: (1) A publicly owned firm can simply buy its own stock through a broker on the open market. (2) It can make a *tender offer,* under which it permits stockholders to send in (that is, "tender") their shares to the firm in exchange for a specified price per share. In this case, it generally indicates that it will buy up to a specified number of shares within a particular time period (usually about two weeks); if more shares are tendered than the company wishes to purchase, purchases are made on a pro rata basis. (3) The firm can purchase a block of shares from one large holder on a negotiated basis. If a negotiated purchase is employed, care must be taken to ensure that this one stockholder does not receive preferential treatment over other stockholders or that any preference given can be justified by "sound business reasons." Texaco's management was sued by stockholders who were unhappy over the company's repurchase of about $600 million of stock from the Bass Brothers' interests at a substantial premium over the market price. The suit charged that Texaco's management, afraid the Bass Brothers would attempt a takeover, used the buyback to get them off its back. Such payments have been dubbed "greenmail."

It should be noted from this example that investors would receive before-tax benefits of $2 per share in any case, either in the form of a $2 cash dividend or a $2 increase in the stock price. This result would occur because we assumed, first, that shares could be repurchased at exactly $22 a share and, second, that the P/E ratio would remain constant. If shares could be bought for less than $22, the operation would be even better for *remaining* stockholders, but the reverse would hold if ADC had to pay more than $22 a share. Furthermore, the P/E ratio might change as a result of the repurchase operation, rising if investors viewed it favorably and falling if they viewed it unfavorably. Some factors that might affect P/E ratios are considered next.

ADVANTAGES OF REPURCHASES

The advantages of repurchases are as follows:

1. Repurchase announcements are viewed as positive signals by investors because the repurchase is often motivated by management's belief that the firm's shares are undervalued.

2. The stockholders have a choice when the firm distributes cash by repurchasing stock — they can sell or not sell. With a cash dividend, on the other hand, stockholders must accept a dividend payment and pay the tax. Thus, those stockholders who need cash can sell back some of their shares, while those who do not want additional cash can simply retain their stock. From a tax standpoint, a repurchase permits both types of stockholders to get what they want.

3. A third advantage is that a repurchase can remove a large block of stock that is "overhanging" the market and keeping the price per share down.

4. Dividends are "sticky" in the short run because managements are reluctant to raise the dividend if the increase cannot be maintained in the future — managements dislike cutting cash dividends because of the negative signal a cut gives. Hence, if the excess cash flow is thought to be only temporary, management may prefer to make the distribution in the form of a share repurchase rather than to declare an increased cash dividend that cannot be maintained.

5. Repurchases can be used to produce large-scale changes in capital structures. For example, several years ago, Consolidated Edison decided to repurchase $400 million of its common stock in order to increase its debt ratio. The repurchase was necessary because even if the company financed its capital budget only with debt, it would still have taken years to get the debt ratio up to the target level. Con Ed used the repurchase to produce an instantaneous change in its capital structure.

DISADVANTAGES OF REPURCHASES

Disadvantages of repurchases include the following:

1. Stockholders may not be indifferent between dividends and capital gains, and the price of the stock might benefit more from cash dividends than from repurchases. Cash dividends are generally dependable, but repurchases are not. Further, if a firm announced a regular, dependable repurchase program, the improper accumulation tax might become a threat.

fixed assets in 1995 were being utilized to only 96 percent of capacity. If fixed assets had been used to full capacity, 1995 sales could have been as high as $3,125 million, versus the $3,000 million in actual sales:

$$\begin{matrix} \text{Full} \\ \text{capacity} \\ \text{sales} \end{matrix} = \frac{\text{Actual sales}}{\begin{matrix}\text{Percentage of capacity}\\\text{at which fixed assets}\\\text{were operated}\end{matrix}} = \frac{\$3,000 \text{ million}}{0.96} = \$3,125 \text{ million.} \quad \textbf{(14-2)}$$

This suggests that Allied's Fixed assets/Sales ratio should be 32 percent:

$$\text{Target fixed assets/Sales ratio} = \frac{\text{Actual fixed assets}}{\text{Full capacity sales}} \quad \textbf{(14-3)}$$

$$= \frac{\$1,000}{\$3,125} = 0.32 = 32\%.$$

Therefore, if sales are to increase to $3,300 million, then fixed assets would have to increase to $1,056 million:

$$\begin{matrix}\text{Required level}\\\text{of fixed assets}\end{matrix} = (\text{Target fixed assets/Sales ratio})(\text{Projected sales}) \quad \textbf{(14-4)}$$

$$= 0.32(\$3,300) = \$1,056 \text{ million.}$$

We had previously forecasted that Allied would need to increase fixed assets at the same rate as sales, or by 10 percent, which meant an increase from $1,000 million to $1,100 million, or by $100 million. Now we see that the actual required increase is only from $1,000 million to $1,056 million, or by $56 million. Thus, the capacity-adjusted forecast is $100 million − $56 million = $44 million less than the earlier forecast. Therefore, the projected AFN would decline from an estimated $112 million (before financing feedback effects) to $112 million − $44 million = $68 million.

Note also that when excess capacity exists, sales can grow to the capacity sales as determined above with no increase whatever in fixed assets, but sales beyond that level will require fixed asset additions as calculated in our example. The same situation could occur with respect to inventories, and the required additions would be determined in exactly the same manner as for fixed assets. Theoretically, the same situation could occur with other types of assets, but as a practical matter, excess capacity normally exists primarily with respect to fixed assets and inventories.

❓ SELF-TEST QUESTIONS

Would it be more important to use the regression method of forecasting asset requirements if the true situation were like that in Panel a or b in Figure 14-3?

If excess capacity exists, how will that affect the target asset/sales ratio?

COMPUTERIZED FINANCIAL PLANNING MODELS

Although financial forecasting as described in this chapter can be done with a calculator, virtually all corporate forecasts are made using computerized forecasting models. Many computerized financial forecasting models are based on a spreadsheet program such as *Lotus 1-2-3* or *Microsoft Excel*. Spreadsheet models have two major advantages over pencil-and-paper calculations. First, it is much faster to construct a spreadsheet model than to make a "by hand" forecast if the forecast period extends beyond two or three years. Second, and more important, a spreadsheet model can recompute the projected financial statements and ratios almost instantaneously when one of the input variables is changed, thus making it easy for managers to determine the effects of changes in variables such as sales.

We developed the forecasts for Allied using a 5-year financial planning model based on a spreadsheet model which uses 5 years of historical data. We used the spreadsheet's linear regression capability to develop Allied's historical sales growth rate and the historical relationships between accounts receivable, inventories, and sales. Other input data include forecasted sales growth rates, the financing mix to apply to any additional funds needed, the cost rates on incremental debt financing, and the tax rate. The model calculates projected financial statements for 5 years, including financing feedback effects, along with some key financial ratios. Thus, it was quite easy to examine the effects of alternative assumptions on Allied's forecasts.[6]

? SELF-TEST QUESTION

Why are computerized planning models playing an increasingly important role in corporate management?

SUMMARY

This chapter described in broad outline how firms project their financial statements and determine their capital requirements. The key concepts covered are listed below.

- Management establishes a **target balance sheet** on the basis of ratio analysis.

- **Financial forecasting** generally begins with a forecast of the firm's sales, in terms of both units and dollars, for some future period.

- **The projected,** or **pro forma, financial statement method** and the **formula method** are used to forecast financial requirements.

- A firm can determine its **additional funds needed (AFN)** by estimating the amount of new assets necessary to support the forecasted level of sales and then subtracting from that amount the spontaneous funds that will be gen-

---

[6]It is becoming increasingly easy for companies to develop planning models as a result of the dramatic recent improvements in computer hardware and software. *Lotus 1-2-3* and *Excel* are the most widely used systems, although many companies also employ more complex and elaborate modeling systems. Increasingly, a knowledge of *Lotus 1-2-3, Excel,* or some similar spreadsheet program is becoming a requirement for getting even an entry-level job in many corporations. Indeed, surveys indicate that the probability of a business student getting an attractive job offer increases dramatically if he or she has a working knowledge of spreadsheets. In addition, starting salaries are materially higher for those students who have such a knowledge.

Note also that we have concentrated on long-run, or strategic, financial planning. Within the framework of the long-run strategic plan, firms also develop short-run financial plans. For example, in Table 14-2, we saw that Allied Food Products expects to need $119 million by the end of 1996, and that it plans to raise this capital by using short-term debt, long-term debt, and common stock. However, we do not know when during the year the funds will be needed, or when Allied will obtain each of its different types of capital. To address these issues, the firm must develop a short-run financial plan, the centerpiece of which is the *cash budget*, which is a projection of cash inflows and outflows on a daily, weekly, or monthly basis during the coming year (or other budget period). We will discuss cash budgeting in Chapter 15, where we consider cash and marketable securities.

c. Now calculate the following ratios, based on your projected December 31, 1996, balance sheet. Tozer's 1995 ratios and industry average ratios are shown here for comparison:

	TOZER COMPUTERS		INDUSTRY AVERAGE
	12/31/96	12/31/95	12/31/95
Current ratio	_____	2.5×	3×
Debt/total assets	_____	33.9%	30%
Rate of return on equity	_____	13.0%	12%

d. Now assume that Tozer grows by the same $70 million but that the growth is spread over 5 years — that is, that sales grow by $14 million each year. Do not consider any financing feedback effects.
   (1) Calculate total additional financial requirements over the 5-year period. (Hint: Use 1995 ratios, ΔS = $70, but *total* sales for the 5-year period.)
   (2) Construct a pro forma balance sheet as of December 31, 2000, using notes payable as the balancing item.
   (3) Calculate the current ratio, total debt/total assets ratio, and rate of return on equity as of December 31, 2000. [Hint: Be sure to use *total sales*, which amount to $1,960 million, to calculate retained earnings, but 2000 profits to calculate the rate of return on equity — that is, return on equity = (2000 profits)/(12/31/00 equity).]

e. Do the plans outlined in Parts b and/or d seem feasible to you? That is, do you think Tozer could borrow the required capital, and would the company be raising the odds on its bankruptcy to an excessive level in the event of some temporary misfortune?

14-2 Additional funds needed Cooley Textile's 1995 financial statements are shown below.

QUE

14-1

14-2

14-3

14-4

14-5

COOLEY TEXTILE:
BALANCE SHEET AS OF DECEMBER 31, 1995
(THOUSANDS OF DOLLARS)

Cash	$ 1,080	Accounts payable	$ 4,320
Receivables	6,480	Accruals	2,880
Inventory	9,000	Notes payable	2,100
Total current assets	$16,560	Total current liabilities	$ 9,300
Net fixed assets	12,600	Mortgage bonds	3,500
		Common stock	3,500
		Retained earnings	12,860
Total assets	$29,160	Total liabilities and equity	$29,160

COOLEY TEXTILE:
INCOME STATEMENT FOR DECEMBER 31, 1995
(THOUSANDS OF DOLLARS)

Sales	$36,000
Operating costs	32,440
Earnings before interest and taxes	$ 3,560
Interest	560
Earnings before taxes	$ 3,000
Taxes (40%)	1,200
Net income	$ 1,800
Dividends (45%)	$810
Addition to retained earnings	$990

a. Suppose 1996 sales are projected to increase by 15 percent over 1995 sales. Determine the additional funds needed. Assume that the company was operating at full capacity in 1995, that it cannot sell off any of its fixed assets, and that any required financing will be borrowed as notes payable. Also, assume that assets, spontaneous liabilities, and operating costs are expected to increase by the same percentage as sales. Use the projected financial statement method to develop a pro forma balance sheet and income statement for December 31, 1996. (Do not incorporate any financing feedback effects. Use the pro forma income statement to determine the addition to retained earnings.)

b. Use the financial statements developed in Part a to incorporate the financing feedback as a result of the addition to notes payable. (That is, do the next financial statement iteration.) For the purpose of this part, assume that the notes payable interest rate is 10 percent. What is the AFN for this iteration?

14-3 Excess capacity Krogh Lumber's 1995 financial statements are shown below.

KROGH LUMBER:
BALANCE SHEET AS OF DECEMBER 31, 1995
(THOUSANDS OF DOLLARS)

Cash	$ 1,800	Accounts payable	$ 7,200
Receivables	10,800	Notes payable	3,472
Inventory	12,600	Accruals	2,520
Total current assets	$25,200	Total current liabilities	$13,192
		Mortgage bonds	5,000
		Common stock	2,000
Net fixed assets	21,600	Retained earnings	26,608
Total assets	$46,800	Total liabilities and equity	$46,800

KROGH LUMBER:
INCOME STATEMENT FOR DECEMBER 31, 1995
(THOUSANDS OF DOLLARS)

Sales	$36,000
Operating costs	30,783
Earnings before interest and taxes	$ 5,217
Interest	1,017
Earnings before taxes	$ 4,200
Taxes (40%)	1,680
Net income	$ 2,520
Dividends (60%)	$1,512
Addition to retained earnings	1,008

a. Assume that the company was operating at full capacity in 1995 with regard to all items *except* fixed assets; fixed assets in 1995 were being utilized to only 75 percent of capacity. By what percentage could 1996 sales increase over 1995 sales without the need for an increase in fixed assets?

b. Now suppose 1996 sales increase by 25 percent over 1995 sales. How much additional external capital will be required? Assume that Krogh cannot sell any fixed assets. (Hint: Use the projected financial statement method to develop a pro forma balance sheet and income statement as in Tables 14-1 and 14-2.) Assume that any required financing is borrowed as notes payable. Do not include any financing feedbacks, and use a pro forma income statement to determine the addition to retained earnings. (Another hint: Notes payable = $6,021.)

c. Use the financial statements developed in Part b to incorporate the financing feedback which results from the addition to notes payable. (That is, do the next financial statement iteration.) For purposes of this part, assume that the notes payable interest rate is 12 percent. What is the AFN for this iteration?

d. Suppose the industry average DSO and inventory turnover ratio are 90 days and 3.33, respectively, and that Krogh Lumber matches these figures in 1996 and then uses the funds released to reduce equity. (It pays a special dividend out of retained earnings.) What would this do to the rate of return on year-end 1996 equity? Use the second-pass balance sheet and income statement as developed in Part c, and assume that the additional AFN amount calculated in that iteration is added to notes payable. (Hint: Notes payable is now $6,094.)

14-4 Additional funds needed Morrissey Technologies Inc.'s 1995 financial statements are shown below.

MORRISSEY TECHNOLOGIES INC.:
BALANCE SHEET AS OF DECEMBER 31, 1995

Cash	$ 180,000	Accounts payable	$ 360,000
Receivables	360,000	Notes payable	156,000
Inventory	720,000	Accruals	180,000
Total current assets	$1,260,000	Total current liabilities	$ 696,000
Fixed assets	1,440,000	Common stock	1,800,000
		Retained earnings	204,000
Total assets	$2,700,000	Total liabilities and equity	$2,700,000

MORRISSEY TECHNOLOGIES INC.:
INCOME STATEMENT FOR DECEMBER 31, 1995

Sales	$3,600,000
Operating costs	3,279,720
EBIT	$ 320,280
Interest	20,280
EBT	$ 300,000
Taxes (40%)	120,000
Net income	$ 180,000

Per share data:

Common stock price	$24.00
Earnings per share (EPS)	$ 1.80
Dividends per share (DPS)	$ 1.08

a. Suppose that in 1996 sales increase by 10 percent over 1995 sales and that 1996 DPS will increase to $1.12. Construct the pro forma financial statements using the projected financial statement method. How much additional capital will be required? Assume the firm operated at full capacity in 1995. Do not include any financing feedbacks.
b. Now assume that 50 percent of the additional capital required will be financed by selling common stock and the remainder by borrowing as notes payable. Assume that the interest rate on notes payable is 13 percent. Do the next iteration of financial statements incorporating financing feedbacks. What is the AFN for this iteration?
c. If the profit margin were to remain at 5 percent and the dividend payout rate were to remain at 60 percent, at what growth rate in sales would the additional financing requirements be exactly zero? (Hint: Set AFN equal to zero and solve for g.)

14-5 External financing requirements The 1995 balance sheet and income statement for the Lewis Company are shown below.

LEWIS COMPANY:
BALANCE SHEET AS OF DECEMBER 31, 1995
(THOUSANDS OF DOLLARS)

Cash	$ 80	Accounts payable	$ 160
Accounts receivable	240	Accruals	40
Inventory	720	Notes payable	252
Total current assets	$1,040	Total current liabilities	$ 452
Fixed assets	3,200	Long-term debt	1,244
		Total debt	$1,696
		Common stock	1,605
		Retained earnings	939
Total assets	$4,240	Total liabilities and equity	$4,240

LEWIS COMPANY:
INCOME STATEMENT FOR DECEMBER 31, 1995
(THOUSANDS OF DOLLARS)

Sales	$8,000
Operating costs	7,450
EBIT	$ 550
Interest	150
EBT	$ 400
Taxes (40%)	160
Net income	$ 240

Per share data:

Common stock price	$16.96
Earnings per share (EPS)	$ 1.60
Dividends per share (DPS)	$ 1.04

a. The firm operated at full capacity in 1995. It expects sales to increase by 20 percent during 1996 and expects 1996 dividends per share to increase to $1.10. Use the projected financial statement method to determine how much outside financing is required, developing the firm's pro forma balance sheet and income statement, and use AFN as the balancing item.

b. If the firm must maintain a current ratio of 2.3 and a debt ratio of 40 percent, how much financing, after the first pass, will be obtained using notes payable, long-term debt, and common stock?

c. Make the second-pass financial statements incorporating financing feedbacks, using the ratios in Part b. Assume that the interest rate on debt averages 10 percent.

EXAM-TYPE PROBLEMS

The problems included in this section are set up in such a way that they could be used as multiple-choice exam problems.

14-6 Long-term financing needed At year-end 1995, total assets for Ambrose Inc. were $1.2 million and accounts payable were $375,000. Sales, which in 1995 were $2.5 million, are expected to increase by 25 percent in 1996. Total assets and accounts payable are proportional to sales and that relationship will be maintained. Ambrose typically uses no current liabilities other than accounts payable. Common stock amounted to $425,000 in 1995, and retained earnings were $295,000. Ambrose plans to sell new common stock in the amount of $75,000. The firm's profit margin on sales is 6 percent; 40 percent of earnings will be paid out as dividends.

a. What was Ambrose's total debt in 1995?

b. How much new, long-term debt financing will be needed in 1996? (Hint: AFN − New stock = New long-term debt.) Do not consider any financing feedback effects.

14-7 Additional funds needed The Flint Company's sales are forecasted to increase from $1,000 in 1995 to $2,000 in 1996. Here is the December 31, 1995, balance sheet:

Cash	$ 100	Accounts payable	$ 50
Accounts receivable	200	Notes payable	150
Inventory	200	Accruals	50
Total current assets	$ 500	Total current liabilities	$ 250
Net fixed assets	500	Long-term debt	400
		Common stock	100
		Retained earnings	250
Total assets	$1,000	Total liabilities and equity	$1,000

Flint's fixed assets were used to only 50 percent of capacity during 1995, but its current assets were at their proper levels. All assets except fixed assets increase at the same rate as sales, and fixed assets would also increase at the same rate if the current excess capacity did not exist. Flint's after-tax profit margin is forecasted to be 5 percent, and its payout ratio will be 60 percent. What is Flint's additional funds needed (AFN) for the coming year? Ignore financing feedback effects.

INTEGRATED CASE

NEW WORLD CHEMICALS INC.

14-8 Financial forecasting Sue Wilson, the new financial manager of New World Chemicals (NWC), a California producer of specialized chemicals for use in fruit orchards, must prepare a financial forecast for 1996. NWC's 1995 sales were $2 billion, and the marketing department is forecasting a 25 percent increase for 1996. Wilson thinks the company was operating at full capacity in 1995, but she is not sure about this. The 1995 financial statements, plus some other data, are given in Table IC14-1.

Assume that you were recently hired as Wilson's assistant, and your first major task is to help her develop the forecast. She asked you to begin by answering the following set of questions.

a. Assume (1) that NWC was operating at full capacity in 1995 with respect to all assets, (2) that all assets must grow proportionally with sales, (3) that accounts payable and accruals will also grow in proportion to sales, and (4) that the 1995 profit margin and dividend payout will be maintained. Under these conditions, what will the company's financial requirements be for the coming year? Use the AFN equation to answer this question.

b. Now estimate the 1996 financial requirements using the projected financial statement approach, making an initial ("first-pass") forecast plus one additional "pass" to determine the effects of financing feedbacks. Assume (1) that each type of asset, as well as payables, accruals, and fixed and variable costs, grow at the same rate as sales; (2) that the payout ratio is held constant at 30 percent; (3) that external funds needed are financed 50 percent by notes payable and 50 percent by long-term debt (no new common stock will be issued); and (4) that all debt carries an interest rate of 8 percent.

c. Why do the two methods produce somewhat different AFN forecasts? Which method provides the more accurate forecast?

d. Calculate NWC's forecasted ratios, and compare them with the company's 1995 ratios and with the industry averages. How does NWC compare with the average firm in its industry, and is the company expected to improve during the coming year?

e. Suppose you now learn that NWC's 1995 receivables and inventory were in line with required levels, given the firm's credit and inventory policies, but that excess capacity existed with regard to fixed assets. Specifically, fixed assets were operated at only 75 percent of capacity.

(1) What level of sales could have existed in 1995 with the available fixed assets? What would the fixed assets/sales ratio have been if NWC had been operating at full capacity?

(2) How would the existence of excess capacity in fixed assets affect the additional funds needed during 1996?

f. Without actually working out the numbers, how would you expect the ratios to change in the situation where excess capacity in fixed assets exists? Explain your reasoning.

g. Based on comparisons between NWC's days sales outstanding (DSO) and inventory turnover ratios with the industry average figures, does it appear that NWC is operating efficiently with respect to its inventory and accounts receivable? If the company were able to bring these ratios into line with the industry averages, what effect would this have on its AFN and its financial ratios? (Note: Inventory and receivables will be discussed in detail in Chapter 15.)

h. The relationship between sales and the various types of assets is important in financial forecasting. The financial statement method, under the assumption that each asset item grows at the same rate as sales, leads to an AFN forecast that is reasonably close to the forecast using the AFN equation. Explain how each of the following factors would affect the accuracy of financial forecasts based on the AFN equation: (1) excess capacity; (2) base stocks of assets, such as shoes in a shoe store; (3) economies of scale in the use of assets; and (4) lumpy assets.

i. (1) How could regression analysis be used to detect the presence of the situations described above and then to improve the financial forecasts? Plot a graph of the following data, which is for a typical well-managed company in NWC's industry, to illustrate your answer.

Year	Sales	Inventories
1993	$1,280	$118
1994	1,600	138
1995	2,000	162
1996E	2,500	192

(2) On the same graph that plots the above data, draw a line which shows how the regression line would have to appear to justify the use of the AFN formula and the projected financial statement forecasting method. As a part of your answer, show the growth rate in inventory that results from a 10 percent increase in sales from a sales level of (a) $200 and (b) $2,000 based on both the actual regression line and a *hypothetical* regression line which is linear and which goes through the origin.

j. How would changes in these items affect the AFN? (1) The dividend payout ratio, (2) the profit margin, (3) the capital intensity ratio, and (4) if NWC begins buying from its suppliers on terms which permit it to pay after 60 days rather than after 30 days. (Consider each item separately and hold all other things constant.)

TABLE IC14-1	FINANCIAL STATEMENTS AND OTHER DATA ON NWC (MILLIONS OF DOLLARS)

A. 1995 Balance Sheet

Cash and securities	$ 20	Accounts payable and accruals	$ 100
Accounts receivable	240	Notes payable	100
Inventory	240	Total current liabilities	$ 200
Total current assets	$ 500	Long-term debt	100
Net fixed assets	500	Common stock	500
		Retained earnings	200
Total assets	$ 1,000	Total liabilities and equity	$1,000

B. 1995 Income Statement

Sales	$2,000.00
Less: Variable costs	1,200.00
Fixed costs	700.00
Earnings before interest and taxes	$ 100.00
Interest	16.00
Earnings before taxes	$ 84.00
Taxes (40%)	33.60
Net income	$ 50.40
Dividends (30%)	15.12
Addition to retained earnings	$ 35.28

C. Key Ratios

	NWC	INDUSTRY	COMMENT
Basic earnings power	10.00%	20.00%	
Profit margin	2.52	4.00	
Return on equity	7.20	15.60	
Days sales outstanding (360 days)	43.20 days	32.00 days	
Inventory turnover	8.33×	11.00×	
Fixed assets turnover	4.00	5.00	
Total assets turnover	2.00	2.50	
Debt/assets	30.00%	36.00%	
Times interest earned	6.25×	9.40×	
Current ratio	2.50	3.00	
Payout ratio	30.00%	30.00%	

COMPUTER-RELATED PROBLEM

Work the problem in this section only if you are using the computer problem diskette.

14-9 Forecasting Use the model in File C14 to solve this problem. Pettijohn Industries' 1995 financial statements are shown below.

PETTIJOHN INDUSTRIES:
BALANCE SHEET AS OF DECEMBER 31, 1995
(MILLIONS OF DOLLARS)

Cash	$ 4.0	Accounts payable	$ 8.0
Receivables	12.0	Notes payable	5.0
Inventory	16.0	Total current liabilities	$13.0
Total current assets	$32.0	Long-term debt	12.0
Net fixed assets	40.0	Common stock	20.0
		Retained earnings	27.0
Total assets	$72.0	Total liabilities and equity	$72.0

PETTIJOHN INDUSTRIES:
INCOME STATEMENT FOR DECEMBER 31, 1995
(MILLIONS OF DOLLARS)

Sales	$80.0
Operating costs	71.3
EBIT	$ 8.7
Interest	2.0
EBT	$ 6.7
Taxes (40%)	2.7
Net income	$ 4.0
Dividends (40%)	$1.60
Addition to retained earnings	$2.40

Assume that the firm has no excess capacity in fixed assets, that the average interest rate for debt is 12 percent, and that the projected annual sales growth rate for the next 5 years is 15 percent.

a. Pettijohn plans to finance its additional funds needed with 50 percent short-term debt and 50 percent long-term debt. Using the projected financial statement method, prepare the pro forma financial statements for 1996 through 2000, and then determine (1) additional funds needed, (2) the current ratio, (3) the debt ratio, and (4) the return on equity.

b. Sales growth could be 5 percentage points above or below the projected 15 percent. Determine the effect of such variances on AFN and the key ratios.

c. Perform an analysis to determine the sensitivity of AFN and the key ratios for the year 2000 to changes in the dividend payout ratio as specified in the following, assuming sales grow at a constant 15 percent. What happens to AFN if the dividend payout ratio (1) is raised from 40 to 70 percent or (2) is lowered from 40 to 20 percent?

MANAGING CURRENT ASSETS 15

WORKING CAPITAL IMPROVEMENTS LIFT STOCK PRICE

Core Industries Inc. is a $200 million electrical equipment manufacturer whose stock is listed on the NYSE. The stock traded in the range of $12 to $17 per share during most of the 1980s, but during the recession of 1990, earnings plunged and the stock dropped to $4. Then Core's directors made several key managerial changes, including the chief financial officer (CFO), and things improved dramatically.

At Core's 1994 annual meeting of stockholders, the new CFO, Ray Steben, kicked off the presentations, informing stockholders that 1993 sales had increased by 12 percent, while profits rose 29 percent and the stock price 79 percent.

What caused this dramatic improvement? According to Steben, the improvement resulted primarily from the company's renewed focus on stockholder value:

> These strong sales and earnings figures are further evidence that shareholder value will continue to be focused upon, and your management will be stewards of the capital entrusted to it. Return on beginning equity jumped from 7.2 percent to 13.3 percent, a level not exceeded since 1981. As you know, our stated objective is to better 15 percent. Return on average capital employed improved almost 50 percent, from 4.5 percent to 6.8

percent. And the company was considerably more efficient in its use of working capital. As a direct result of a companywide program, operating working capital was reduced from $0.50 to $0.40 per dollar of sales. Operating working capital is basically receivables and inventory less payables and accruals. The cash freed up by this program was used to reduce debt and to invest in operations and acquisitions that will return better than our cost of capital.

Following Steben's address, Core's president, Dave Zimmer, elaborated on Core's 1993 improvement and the ways that management planned to keep the momentum going in the coming years. Like Steben, Zimmer stressed the improvement in working capital management, and the fact that capital previously locked up in excessive inventories and receivables had been freed up and was now earning returns for stockholders. Zimmer also informed the stockholders that "your top management has placed a significant portion of its compensation at risk both through the annual bonus plan and the new, long-term incentive plan." He then explained that management's future compensation will be tied directly to stock price performance, so managers will do well only if stockholders do well.

A year later, at the 1995 annual meeting, Zimmer had good news and bad news to report. The good news was that sales and earnings had continued to increase, and working capital had been lowered even further. The bad news was that "in spite of all that we accomplished in 1994, the stock market treated the company poorly — an obvious disappointment to investors in Core Industries." Actually, the decline in Core's stock price was similar to that of other small capitalization firms during 1994, and despite the decline, the stock still traded at a level substantially higher than the level that existed before the company's turnaround.

Zimmer was not discouraged, and he was resolute in his desire to improve operations. The company plans to continue shrinking working capital. In addition, Zimmer announced that Core has adopted the Economic Value Added (EVA) concept, discussed in Chapter 3, under which employees throughout the corporation will see their overall compensation tied to the EVA level in their division.

Clearly, Core Industries has taken some important steps to improve its operations. However, it remains to be seen how things will turn out. If the steps taken are successful, they should propel the stock price upward.

About 60 percent of a typical financial manager's time is devoted to working capital management, and many students' first jobs will involve working capital. This is particularly true in smaller businesses, where the most new jobs are being created.

Working capital policy involves two basic questions: (1) What is the appropriate amount of current assets for the firm to carry, both in total and for each specific account, and (2) how should current assets be financed? This chapter addresses the first question, and Chapter 16 addresses the second.

WORKING CAPITAL TERMINOLOGY

We begin our discussion of working capital policy by reviewing some basic definitions and concepts:

Working Capital
A firm's investment in short-term assets — cash, marketable securities, inventory, and accounts receivable.

Net Working Capital
Current assets minus current liabilities.

1. **Working capital,** sometimes called *gross working capital,* simply refers to current assets.

2. **Net working capital** is defined as current assets minus current liabilities.

3. The *current ratio,* which was discussed in Chapter 3, is calculated by dividing current assets by current liabilities, and it is intended to measure a firm's liquidity. However, a high current ratio does not ensure that a firm will have the cash required to meet its needs. If inventories cannot be sold, or if receivables cannot be collected in a timely manner, then the apparent safety reflected in a high current ratio could be illusory.

4. The *quick ratio,* or *acid test,* also attempts to measure liquidity, and it is found by subtracting inventories from current assets and then dividing by current liabilities. The quick ratio removes inventories from current assets because they are the least liquid of current assets; therefore, it is an "acid test" of a company's ability to meet its current obligations.

5. The best and most comprehensive picture of a firm's liquidity position is shown by its *cash budget.* This statement, which forecasts cash inflows and outflows, focuses on what really counts, the firm's ability to generate sufficient cash inflows to meet its required cash outflows. We will discuss cash budgeting in detail later in the chapter.

Working Capital Policy
Basic policy decisions regarding (1) target levels for each category of current assets and (2) how current assets will be financed.

6. **Working capital policy** refers to the firm's policies regarding (1) target levels for each category of current assets and (2) how current assets will be financed.

7. *Working capital management* involves the administration, within policy guidelines, of current assets and current liabilities.

The term *working capital* originated with the old Yankee peddler, who would load up his wagon with goods and then go off on his route to peddle his wares. The merchandise was called working capital because it was what he actually sold, or "turned over," to produce his profits. The wagon and horse were his fixed assets. He generally owned the horse and wagon, so they were financed with "equity" capital, but he borrowed the funds to buy the merchandise. These borrowings were called *working capital loans,* and they had to be repaid after each trip to demonstrate to the bank that the credit was sound. If the peddler was able to repay the loan, then the bank would make another loan, and banks that followed this procedure were said to be employing "sound banking practices."

SELF-TEST QUESTIONS

Why is the quick ratio also called an acid test?

Where did the term "working capital" originate?

ALTERNATIVE CURRENT ASSET INVESTMENT POLICIES

Relaxed Current Asset Investment Policy
A policy under which relatively large amounts of cash, marketable securities, and inventories are carried and under which sales are stimulated by a liberal credit policy, resulting in a high level of receivables.

Figure 15-1 shows three alternative policies regarding the total amount of current assets carried. Essentially, these policies differ in that different amounts of current assets are carried to support any given level of sales, and they differ in the turnover of those assets. The line with the steepest slope represents a **relaxed current asset investment** (or "fat cat") **policy,** where relatively large amounts of cash, marketable securities, and inventories are carried, and where sales are stimulated by the use of a credit policy that provides liberal financing to customers and a correspond-

FIGURE 15-1	ALTERNATIVE CURRENT ASSET INVESTMENT POLICIES (MILLIONS OF DOLLARS)

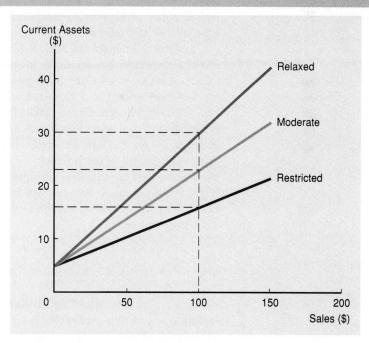

POLICY	CURRENT ASSETS TO SUPPORT SALES OF $100	TURNOVER OF CURRENT ASSETS
Relaxed	$30	3.3×
Moderate	23	4.3×
Restricted	16	6.3×

Note: The sales/current assets relationship is shown here as being linear, but the relationship is often curvilinear.

Restricted Current Asset Investment Policy
A policy under which holdings of cash, securities, inventories, and receivables are minimized.

Moderate Current Asset Investment Policy
A policy that is between the relaxed and restricted policies.

ing high level of receivables. Conversely, with the **restricted current asset investment** (or "lean-and-mean") **policy,** the holdings of cash, securities, inventories, and receivables are minimized. Under the restricted policy, current assets are turned over more frequently, so each dollar of current assets is forced to "work harder." The **moderate current asset investment policy** is between the two extremes.

Under conditions of certainty — when sales, costs, lead times, payment periods, and so on, are known for sure — all firms would hold only minimal levels of current assets. Any larger amounts would increase the need for external funding without a corresponding increase in profits, while any smaller holdings would involve late payments to labor and suppliers, and lost sales due to inventory shortages and an overly restrictive credit policy.

However, the picture changes when uncertainty is introduced. Here the firm requires some minimum amount of cash and inventories based on expected payments, expected sales, expected order lead times, and so on, plus additional holdings, or *safety stocks,* which enable it to deal with departures from the expected values. Similarly, accounts receivable levels are determined by credit terms, and the tougher the credit terms, the lower the receivables for any given level of sales. With a restricted current asset investment policy, the firm would hold minimal levels of safety stocks for cash and inventories, and it would have a tight credit policy even though this would mean running the risk of losing sales. A restricted, lean-and-mean current asset investment policy generally provides the highest expected return on investment, but it entails the greatest risk, while the reverse is true under a relaxed policy. The moderate policy falls in between the two extremes in terms of expected risk and return.

Changing technology can lead to dramatic changes in the optimal current asset investment policy. For example, if new technology makes it possible for a manufacturer such as Core Industries to speed up the production of a given product from 10 days to 5 days, then its work-in-progress inventory can be cut in half. Similarly, retailers such as Wal-Mart or Home Depot have installed systems under which bar codes on all merchandise are read at the cash register. The information on the sale is electronically transmitted to a computer which maintains a record of the inventory of each item, and the computer automatically transmits orders to suppliers' computers when stocks fall to prescribed levels. With such a system, inventories will be held at optimal levels; orders will reflect exactly what styles, colors, and sizes consumers are buying; and the firm's profits will be maximized.

MANAGING THE COMPONENTS OF WORKING CAPITAL

Working capital consists of four main components: cash, marketable securities, inventory, and accounts receivable. The remainder of this chapter will focus on the issues involved with managing each of these components. As you will see, a common thread underlies all current asset management. For each type of asset, firms face a fundamental trade-off: current assets (that is, working capital) are necessary to conduct business, and the greater the holdings of current assets, the smaller the danger of running out, hence the lower the firm's operating risk. However, holding working capital is costly — for example, if inventories are too large, then the firm will have assets which earn a zero or even negative return if storage and spoilage costs are high. And, of course, firms must acquire capital to buy assets such as inventory, and this capital has a cost, which increases the downward drag from excessive inventories (or receivables or even cash). So, there is pressure to hold the amount of working capital carried to the minimum consistent with running the business without interruption.

Firms typically follow a cycle in which they purchase inventory, sell goods on credit, and then collect accounts receivable. This cycle is referred to as the cash conversion cycle and is discussed in detail in Appendix 15A. Sound working policy is designed to minimize the time between cash expenditures on materials and the collection of cash on sales.

 ## SELF-TEST QUESTIONS

Identify and explain three alternative current asset investment policies.

What are the principal components of working capital?

What are the reasons for not wanting to hold too little working capital? For not wanting to hold too much?

What is the fundamental trade-off that managers face when managing working capital?

CASH MANAGEMENT

Approximately 1.5 percent of the average industrial firm's assets are held in the form of cash, which is defined as demand deposits plus currency. Cash is often called a "nonearning asset." It is needed to pay for labor and raw materials, to buy fixed assets, to pay taxes, to service debt, to pay dividends, and so on. However, cash itself (and also commercial checking accounts) earns no interest. Thus, the goal of the cash manager is to minimize the amount of cash the firm must hold for use in conducting its normal business activities, yet, at the same time, to have sufficient cash (1) to take trade discounts, (2) to maintain its credit rating, and (3) to meet unexpected cash needs. We begin our analysis with a discussion of the reasons for holding cash.

RATIONALE FOR HOLDING CASH

Firms hold cash for two primary reasons:

Transactions Balance
A cash balance associated with payments and collections; the balance necessary for day-to-day operations.

Compensating Balance
A bank balance that a firm must maintain to compensate the bank for services rendered or for granting a loan.

1. **Transactions.** Cash balances are necessary in business operations. Payments must be made in cash, and receipts are deposited in the cash account. Cash balances associated with routine payments and collections are known as **transactions balances.**

2. **Compensation to banks for providing loans and services.** A bank makes money by lending out funds that have been deposited with it, so the larger its deposits, the better the bank's profit position. In addition, if a bank is providing services to a customer, it may require the customer to leave a minimum balance on deposit to help offset the costs of providing the services. This type of balance, defined as a **compensating balance,** is discussed in detail later in this chapter.

Two other reasons for holding cash have been noted in the finance and economics literature: for *precaution* and for *speculation.* Cash inflows and outflows are somewhat unpredictable, with the degree of predictability varying among firms and

Precautionary Balance
A cash balance held in reserve for random, unforeseen fluctuations in cash inflows and outflows.

industries. Therefore, firms need to hold some cash in reserve for random, unforeseen fluctuations in inflows and outflows. These "safety stocks" are called **precautionary balances,** and the less predictable the firm's cash flows, the larger such balances should be. However, if the firm has easy access to borrowed funds — that is, if it can borrow on short notice — its need for precautionary balances is reduced. Also, as we note later in this chapter, firms that would otherwise need large precautionary balances tend to hold highly liquid marketable securities rather than cash per se; marketable securities serve many of the purposes of cash, but they provide greater interest income than bank deposits.

Some cash balances may be held to enable the firm to take advantage of bargain purchases that might arise; these funds are called **speculative balances.** However, firms today are more likely to rely on reserve borrowing capacity and/or marketable securities portfolios than on cash per se for speculative purposes.

Speculative Balance
A cash balance that is held to enable the firm to take advantage of any bargain purchases that might arise.

Although the cash accounts of most firms can be thought of as consisting of transactions, compensating, precautionary, and speculative balances, we cannot calculate the amount needed for each purpose, sum them, and produce a total desired cash balance because the same money often serves more than one purpose. For instance, precautionary and speculative balances can also be used to satisfy compensating balance requirements. Firms do, however, consider all four factors when establishing their target cash positions.

ADVANTAGES OF HOLDING ADEQUATE CASH AND NEAR-CASH ASSETS

In addition to the four motives just discussed, sound working capital management requires that an ample supply of cash be maintained for several specific reasons:

Trade Discount
A price reduction that suppliers offer customers for early payment of bills.

1. It is essential that the firm have sufficient cash and near-cash assets to take **trade discounts.** Suppliers frequently offer customers discounts for early payment of bills. As we will see in the next chapter, the cost of not taking discounts is very high, so firms should have enough cash and near-cash assets to permit payment of bills in time to take discounts.

2. Adequate holdings of cash and near-cash assets can help the firm maintain its credit rating by keeping its current and acid test ratios in line with those of other firms in its industry. A strong credit rating enables the firm both to purchase goods from suppliers on favorable terms and to maintain an ample line of credit with its bank.

3. Cash and near-cash assets are useful for taking advantage of favorable business opportunities, such as special offers from suppliers or the chance to acquire another firm.

4. The firm should have sufficient cash and near-cash assets to meet such emergencies as strikes, fires, or competitors' marketing campaigns, and to weather seasonal and cyclical downturns.

? SELF-TEST QUESTIONS

Why is cash management important?

What are the two primary motives for holding cash?

What are the two secondary motives for holding cash as noted in the finance and economics literature?

THE CASH BUDGET

The firm estimates its needs for cash as a part of its general budgeting, or forecasting, process. First, it forecasts both fixed asset and inventory requirements, along with the times when payments must be made. This information is combined with projections about the delay in collecting accounts receivable, tax payment dates, dividend and interest payment dates, and so on. All of this information is summarized in the **cash budget,** which shows the firm's projected cash inflows and outflows over some specified period. Generally, firms use a monthly cash budget forecasted over the next year, plus a more detailed daily or weekly cash budget for the coming month. The monthly cash budgets are used for planning purposes, and the daily or weekly budgets for actual cash control.

Cash Budget
A table showing cash flows (receipts, disbursements, and cash balances) for a firm over a specified period.

The cash budget provides much more detailed information concerning a firm's future cash flows than do the forecasted financial statements. In the previous chapter, we developed Allied Food Products' 1996 forecasted financial statements. Allied's projected 1996 sales were $3,300 million, resulting in a net cash flow from operations of $162 million. When all expenditures and financing flows are considered, Allied's cash account is projected to increase by $1 million in 1996. Does this mean that Allied will not have to worry about cash shortages during 1996? To answer this question, we must construct Allied's cash budget for 1996.

To simplify the example, we will only consider Allied's cash budget for the last half of 1996. Further, we will not list every cash flow but rather focus on the operating cash flows. Allied's sales peak is in September, shortly after the majority of its raw food inputs have been harvested. All sales are made on terms of 2/10, net 40, meaning that a 2 percent discount is allowed if payment is made within 10 days, and, if the discount is not taken, the full amount is due in 40 days. However, like most companies, Allied finds that some of its customers delay payment up to 90 days. Experience has shown that payment on 20 percent of Allied's dollar sales is made during the month in which the sale is made — these are the discount sales. On 70 percent of sales, payment is made during the month immediately following the month of sale, and on 10 percent of sales payment is made in the second month following the month of sale.

The costs to Allied of foodstuffs, spices, preservatives, and packaging materials average 70 percent of the sales prices of the finished products. These purchases are generally made 1 month before the firm expects to sell the finished products, but Allied's purchase terms with its suppliers allow it to delay payments for 30 days. Accordingly, if July sales are forecasted at $300 million, then purchases during June will amount to $210 million, and this amount will actually be paid in July.

Target Cash Balance
The desired cash balance that a firm plans to maintain in order to conduct business.

Such other cash expenditures as wages and rent are also built into the cash budget, and Allied must make estimated tax payments of $30 million on September 15 and $20 million on December 15, while a $100 million payment for a new plant must be made in October. Assuming that Allied's **target cash balance** is $10 million, and that it projects $15 million to be on hand on July 1, 1996, what will the firm's monthly cash surpluses or shortfalls be for the period from July to December?

The monthly cash flows are shown in Table 15-1. Section I of the table provides a worksheet for calculating both collections on sales and payments on purchases. Line 1 gives the sales forecast for the period from May through December. (May and June sales are necessary to determine collections for July and August.) Next, Lines 2 through 5 show cash collections. Line 2 shows that 20 percent of the sales during any given month are collected during that month. Customers who pay in

TABLE 15-1	ALLIED FOOD PRODUCTS: CASH BUDGET (MILLIONS OF DOLLARS)							

	MAY	JUN	JUL	AUG	SEP	OCT	NOV	DEC
I. COLLECTIONS AND PURCHASES WORKSHEET								
(1) Sales (gross)[a]	$200	$250	$300	$400	$500	$350	$250	$200
Collections								
(2) During month of sale: (0.2)(0.98)(month's sales)			59	78	98	69	49	39
(3) During first month after sale: 0.7 (previous month's sales)			175	210	280	350	245	175
(4) During second month after sale: 0.1 (sales 2 months ago)			20	25	30	40	50	35
(5) Total collections (2 + 3 + 4)			$254	$313	$408	$459	$344	$249
Purchases								
(6) 0.7(next month's sales)		$210	$280	$350	$245	$175	$140	
(7) Payments (1-month lag)			$210	$280	$350	$245	$175	$140
II. CASH GAIN OR LOSS FOR MONTH								
(8) Collections (from Section I)			$254	$313	$408	$459	$344	$249
(9) Payments for purchases (from Section I)			$210	$280	$350	$245	$175	$140
(10) Wages and salaries			30	40	50	40	30	30
(11) Rent			15	15	15	15	15	15
(12) Other expenses			10	15	20	15	10	10
(13) Taxes					30			20
(14) Payment for plant construction						100		
(15) Total payments			$265	$350	$465	$415	$230	$215
(16) Net cash gain (loss) during month (Line 8 − Line 15)			($ 11)	($ 37)	($ 57)	$ 44	$114	$ 34
III. CASH SURPLUS OR LOAN REQUIREMENT								
(17) Cash at start of month if no borrowing is done[b]			$ 15	$ 4	($ 33)	($ 90)	($ 46)	$ 68
(18) Cumulative cash (cash at start, +gain or −loss = Line 16 + Line 17)			$ 4	($ 33)	($ 90)	($ 46)	$ 68	$102
(19) Target cash balance			10	10	10	10	10	10
(20) Cumulative surplus cash (or loans outstanding) to maintain $10 target cash balance: (Line 18 − Line 19)[c]			($ 6)	($ 43)	($100)	($ 56)	$ 58	$ 92

[a]Although the budget period is July through December, sales and purchases data for May and June are needed to determine collections and payments during July and August.

[b]The amount shown on Line 17 for July, the $15 balance (in millions), is assumed to be on hand initially. The values shown for each of the following months on Line 17 are equal to the cumulative cash as shown on Line 18 for the preceding month; for example, the $4 shown on Line 17 for August is taken from Line 18 in the July column.

[c]When the target cash balance of $10 (Line 19) is deducted from the cumulative cash balance (Line 18), a resulting negative figure on Line 20 represents a required loan, whereas a positive figure represents surplus cash. Loans are required from July through October, and surpluses are expected during November and December. Note also that firms can borrow or pay off loans on a daily basis, so the $6 borrowed during July would be done on a daily basis, as needed, and during October the $100 loan that existed at the beginning of the month would be reduced daily to the $56 ending balance, which in turn would be completely paid off during November.

the first month, however, typically take the discount, so the cash collected in the month of sale is reduced by 2 percent; for example, collections during July for the $300 million of sales in that month will be 20 percent times sales times 1.0 minus the 2 percent discount = (0.20)($300)(0.98) ≈ $59 million. Line 3 shows the collections on the previous month's sales, or 70 percent of sales in the preceding month; for example, in July, 70 percent of the $250 million June sales, or $175 million, will be collected. Line 4 gives collections from sales 2 months earlier, or 10 percent of sales in that month; for example, the July collections for May sales are (0.10)($200) = $20 million. The collections during each month are summed and shown on Line 5; thus, the July collections represent 20 percent of July sales (minus the discount) plus 70 percent of June sales plus 10 percent of May sales, or $254 million in total.

Next, payments for purchases of raw materials are shown. July sales are forecasted at $300 million, so Allied will purchase $210 million of materials in June (Line 6) and pay for these purchases in July (Line 7). Similarly, Allied will purchase $280 million of materials in July to meet August's forecasted sales of $400 million.

With Section I completed, Section II can be constructed. Cash from collections is shown on Line 8. Lines 9 through 14 list payments made during each month, and these payments are summed on Line 15. The difference between cash receipts and cash payments (Line 8 minus Line 15) is the net cash gain or loss during the month; for July there is a net cash loss of $11 million, as shown on Line 16.

In Section III, we first determine Allied's cash balance at the start of each month, assuming no borrowing is done; this is shown on Line 17. We assume that Allied will have $15 million on hand on July 1. The beginning cash balance (Line 17) is then added to the net cash gain or loss during the month (Line 16) to obtain the cumulative cash that would be on hand if no financing were done (Line 18); at the end of July, Allied forecasts a cumulative cash balance of $4 million in the absence of borrowing.

The target cash balance, $10 million, is then subtracted from the cumulative cash balance to determine the firm's borrowing requirements, shown in parentheses, or its surplus cash. Because Allied expects to have cumulative cash, as shown on Line 18, of only $4 million in July, it will have to borrow $6 million to bring the cash account up to the target balance of $10 million. Assuming that this amount is indeed borrowed, loans outstanding will total $6 million at the end of July. (Allied did not have any loans outstanding on July 1.) The cash surplus or required loan balance is given on Line 20; a positive value indicates a cash surplus, whereas a negative value indicates a loan requirement. Note that the surplus cash or loan requirement shown on Line 20 is a *cumulative amount*. Thus, Allied must borrow $6 million in July; it has an additional cash shortfall during August of $37 million as reported on Line 16, so its total loan requirement at the end of August is $6 + $37 = $43 million, as reported on Line 20. Allied's arrangement with the bank permits it to increase its outstanding loans on a daily basis, up to a prearranged maximum, just as you could increase the amount you owe on a credit card. Allied will use any surplus funds it generates to pay off its loans, and because the loan can be paid down at any time, on a daily basis, the firm will never have both a cash surplus and an outstanding loan balance.

This same procedure is used in the following months. Sales will peak in September, accompanied by increased payments for purchases, wages, and other items. Receipts from sales will also go up, but the firm will still be left with a $57 million net cash outflow during the month. The total loan requirement at the end of September will hit a peak of $100 million, the cumulative cash plus the target cash balance. This amount is also equal to the $43 million needed at the end of August plus the $57 million cash deficit for September.

Sales, purchases, and payments for past purchases will fall sharply in October, but collections will be the highest of any month because they will reflect the high September sales. As a result, Allied will enjoy a healthy $44 million net cash gain during October. This net gain can be used to pay off borrowings, so loans outstanding will decline by $44 million, to $56 million.

Allied will have an even larger cash surplus in November, which will permit it to pay off all of its loans. In fact, the company is expected to have $58 million in surplus cash by the month's end, and another cash surplus in December will swell the excess cash to $92 million. With such a large amount of unneeded funds, Allied's treasurer will certainly want to invest in interest-bearing securities or to put the funds to use in some other way.

Before concluding our discussion of the cash budget, we should make some additional points:

1. For simplicity, our illustrative budget for Allied omitted many important cash flows that are anticipated for 1996, such as dividends, proceeds from stock and bond sales, and fixed asset additions. Some of these are projected to occur in the first half of the year, but those that are projected for the July–December period could easily be added to the example. The final cash budget should contain all projected cash inflows and outflows.

2. Our cash budget example does not reflect interest on loans or income from investing surplus cash. This refinement could easily be added.

3. If cash inflows and outflows are not uniform during the month, we could seriously understate the firm's peak financing requirements. The data in Table 15-1 show the situation expected on the last day of each month, but on any given day during the month, it could be quite different. For example, if all payments had to be made on the fifth of each month, but collections came in uniformly throughout the month, the firm would need to borrow much larger amounts than those shown in Table 15-1. In this case, we would have to prepare a cash budget which determined requirements on a daily basis.

4. Since depreciation is a noncash charge, it does not appear on the cash budget other than through its effect on taxable income, hence on taxes paid.

5. Since the cash budget represents a forecast, all the values in the table are *expected* values. If actual sales, purchases, and so on are different from the forecasted levels, then the projected cash deficits and surpluses will also be incorrect. Thus, Allied might end up needing to borrow larger amounts than are indicated on Line 20, so it should arrange a line of credit in excess of that amount. For example, if Allied's monthly sales turn out to be only 80 percent of their forecasted levels, the firm's maximum cumulative borrowing requirement will turn out to be $126 million rather than $100 million, a 26 percent increase from the expected cash budget.

6. Computerized spreadsheet programs are particularly well suited for constructing and analyzing cash budgets, especially with respect to the sensitivity of cash flows to changes in sales levels, collection periods, and the like. We could change any assumption, say, the projected monthly sales or the lag before customers pay, and the cash budget would automatically and instantly be recalculated. This would show us exactly how the firm's borrowing requirements would change if different things changed. Also, with a computer model, it is easy to add features like interest paid on loans, interest earned

on marketable securities, and so on. We have written such a model for the computer-related problem at the end of the chapter.

7. Finally, we should note that the target cash balance probably will be adjusted over time, rising and falling with seasonal patterns and with long-term changes in the scale of the firm's operations. Thus, Allied will probably plan to maintain larger cash balances during August and September than at other times, and as the company grows, so will its required cash balance. Also, the firm might even set the target cash balance at zero — this could be done if it carried a portfolio of marketable securities which could be sold to replenish the cash account, or if it had an arrangement with its bank that permitted it to borrow any funds needed on a daily basis. In that event, the cash budget would simply stop with Line 18, and the amounts on that line would represent projected loans outstanding or surplus cash. Note, though, that most firms would find it difficult to operate with a zero-balance bank account, just as you would, and the costs of such an operation would in most instances offset the costs associated with maintaining a positive cash balance. Therefore, most firms do set a positive target cash balance.

Statistics are not available on whether transactions balances or compensating balances actually control most firms' target cash balances, but compensating balance requirements do often dominate, especially during periods of high interest rates and tight money.[1]

SELF-TEST QUESTIONS

What is the purpose of a cash budget?

What are the three major sections of a cash budget?

Suppose a firm's cash flows do not occur uniformly throughout the month. What impact would this have on the accuracy of the forecasted borrowing requirements?

How could uncertainty be handled in a cash budget?

Does depreciation appear in a cash budget? Explain.

CASH MANAGEMENT TECHNIQUES

Cash management has changed significantly over the last 20 years as a result of two factors. First, from the early 1970s to the mid-1980s, there was an upward trend in interest rates which increased the opportunity cost of holding cash and, therefore, encouraged financial managers to search for more efficient ways of managing the firm's cash. Second, technological developments, particularly computerized electronic funds transfer mechanisms, have improved cash management.

---

[1]This point was underscored by an incident that occurred at a professional finance meeting. A professor presented a scholarly paper that used operations research techniques to determine "optimal cash balances" for a sample of firms. He then reported that the firms' actual cash balances greatly exceeded their optimal balances, suggesting inefficiency and the need for more refined techniques. The discussant of the paper made her comments short and sweet. She reported that she had written each of the sample firms and asked them why they had so much cash; they had uniformly replied that their cash holdings were set by compensating balance requirements. Thus, the model might have been useful to determine the optimal cash balance in the absence of compensating balance requirements, but it was precisely those requirements that determined actual balances.

Most cash management activities are performed jointly by the firm and its primary bank. Effective cash management encompasses proper management of both the cash inflows and the cash outflows, which entails (1) synchronizing cash flows, (2) using float, (3) accelerating collections, (4) getting available funds to where they are needed, and (5) controlling disbursements. Most business is conducted by large firms, many of which operate regionally, nationally, or even globally. They collect cash from many sources and make payments from a number of different cities. For example, companies like IBM, General Motors, and Hewlett-Packard have manufacturing plants all around the world, even more sales offices, and bank accounts in virtually every city where they do business. Their collection points are located to follow sales patterns. Some disbursements are made from local offices, but most disbursements are made in the areas where manufacturing occurs, or else from the home office (dividend and interest payments, taxes, debt repayments, and the like). Thus, a major corporation might have hundreds or even thousands of bank accounts, and since there is no reason to think that inflows and outflows will balance in each account, a system must be in place to transfer funds from where they currently are to where they are needed, to arrange loans to cover net corporate shortfalls, and to invest net corporate surpluses without delay. We discuss the most commonly used techniques for accomplishing these tasks in the following sections.

CASH FLOW SYNCHRONIZATION

If you as an individual were to receive income once a year, you would probably put it in the bank, draw down your account periodically, and have an average balance during the year equal to about half your annual income. If you received income monthly instead of once a year, you would operate similarly, but now your average balance would be much smaller. If you could arrange to receive income daily and to pay rent, tuition, and other charges on a daily basis, and if you were quite confident of your forecasted inflows and outflows, then you could hold a very small average cash balance.

Exactly the same situation holds for business firms — by improving their forecasts and by arranging things so that cash receipts coincide with cash requirements, firms can reduce their transactions balances to a minimum. Recognizing all this, utility companies, oil companies, credit card companies, and so on arrange to bill customers, and to pay their own bills, on regular "billing cycles" throughout the month. This improves the **synchronization of cash flows,** which in turn enables firms to reduce their cash balances, decrease their bank loans, lower interest expenses, and boost profits.

Synchronized Cash Flows
A situation in which inflows coincide with outflows, thereby permitting a firm to hold low transactions balances.

CHECK-CLEARING PROCESS

When a customer writes and mails a check, this *does not* mean that the funds are immediately available to the receiving firm. Most of us have been told by someone that "the check is in the mail," and we have also deposited a check in our account and then been told that we cannot write our own checks against this deposit until the **check-clearing** process has been completed. Our bank must first make sure that the check we deposited is good and then receive funds itself from the customer's bank before it will give us cash.

In practice, it may take a long time for a firm to process incoming checks and obtain the use of the money. A check must first be delivered through the mail and then be cleared through the banking system before the money can be put to use.

Check Clearing
The process of converting a check that has been written and mailed into cash in the payee's account.

Checks received from customers in distant cities are especially subject to delays because of mail time and also because more parties are involved. For example, assume that we receive a check and deposit it in our bank. Our bank must send the check to the bank on which it was drawn. Only when this latter bank transfers funds to our bank are the funds available for us to use. Checks are generally cleared through the Federal Reserve System or through a clearinghouse set up by the banks in a particular city. Of course, if the check is deposited in the same bank on which it was drawn, that bank merely transfers funds by bookkeeping entries from one of its depositors to another. The length of time required for checks to clear is thus a function of the distance between the payer's and the payee's banks. In the case of private clearinghouses, it can range from one to three days. The maximum time required for checks to clear through the Federal Reserve System is two days, but mail delays can slow down things on each end of the Fed's involvement in the process.

USING FLOAT

Float is defined as the difference between the balance shown in a firm's (or individual's) checkbook and the balance on the bank's records. Suppose a firm writes, on average, checks in the amount of $5,000 each day, and it takes six days for these checks to clear and to be deducted from the firm's bank account. This will cause the firm's own checkbook to show a balance $30,000 smaller than the balance on the bank's records; this difference is called **disbursement float.** Now suppose the firm also receives checks in the amount of $5,000 daily, but it loses four days while they are being deposited and cleared. This will result in $20,000 of **collections float.** In total, the firm's **net float** — the difference between $30,000 positive disbursement float and the $20,000 negative collections float — will be $10,000.

If the firm's own collection and clearing process is more efficient than that of the recipients of its checks — which is generally true of larger, more efficient firms — then the firm could actually show a *negative* balance on its own books but have a *positive* balance on the records of its bank. Some firms indicate that they *never* have positive book cash balances. One large manufacturer of construction equipment stated that while its account, according to its bank's records, shows an average cash balance of about $20 million, its *book* cash balance is *minus* $20 million — it has $40 million of net float. Obviously, the firm must be able to forecast its disbursements and collections accurately in order to make such heavy use of float.

E. F. Hutton provides an example of pushing cash management too far. Hutton, a leading brokerage firm at the time, did business with banks across the country, and it had to keep compensating balances in these banks. The sizes of the required compensating balances were known, and any excess funds in these banks were sent electronically, on a daily basis, to New York and San Francisco banks, where they were immediately invested in interest-bearing securities. However, rather than waiting to see what the end-of-day balances actually were, Hutton began estimating inflows and outflows, and it transferred out for investment the *estimated* end-of-day excess. But then Hutton got greedy and began *kiting* checks. Hutton deliberately overestimated its deposits and underestimated clearings of its own checks, thereby deliberately overstating its estimated end-of-day balances. As a result, Hutton was chronically overdrawn at its local banks, and it was in effect earning interest on funds which really belonged to those local banks. It is entirely proper to forecast what your bank will have recorded as your balance and then to make de-

Disbursement Float
The value of the checks which we have written but which are still being processed and thus have not been deducted from our account balance by the bank.

Collections Float
The amount of checks that we have received but which have not yet been credited to our account.

Net Float
The difference between our checkbook balance and the balance shown on the bank's books.

cisions based on the estimate, even if that balance is different from the balance your own books show. However, it is illegal to forecast an overdrawn situation but then to tell the bank that you expect to have a positive balance.[2]

Delays that cause float arise because it takes time for checks (1) to travel through the mail (mail float), (2) to be processed by the receiving firm (processing float), and (3) to clear through the banking system (clearing, or availability, float). Basically, the size of a firm's net float is a function of its ability to speed up collections on checks received and to slow down collections on checks written. Efficient firms go to great lengths to speed up the processing of incoming checks, thus putting the funds to work faster, and they try to stretch their own payments out as long as possible.

ACCELERATION OF RECEIPTS

Financial managers have searched for ways to collect receivables faster since credit transactions began. Although cash collection is the financial manager's responsibility, the speed with which checks are cleared is dependent on the banking system. Several techniques are now used both to speed collections and to get funds where they are needed. Included are (1) lockbox plans established close to customers and (2) requiring large customers to pay by wire.

Lockbox Plan

A procedure used to speed up collections and reduce float through the use of post office boxes in payers' local areas.

LOCKBOXES.   A **lockbox plan** is one of the oldest cash management tools. In a lockbox system, incoming checks are sent to post office boxes rather than to corporate headquarters. For example, a firm headquartered in New York City might have its West Coast customers send their payments to a box in San Francisco, its customers in the Southwest send their checks to Dallas, and so on, rather than having all checks sent to New York City. Several times a day a local bank will collect the contents of the lockbox and deposit the checks into the company's local account. The bank would then provide the firm with a daily record of the receipts collected, usually via an electronic data transmission system in a format that permits on-line updating of the firm's receivables accounts.

A lockbox system reduces the time required for a firm to receive incoming checks, to deposit them, and to get them cleared through the banking system so that the funds are available for use. Lockbox services can often increase the availability of funds by two to five days over the "regular" system.

PAYMENT BY WIRE.   Firms are increasingly demanding payments of larger bills by wire, or even by automatic electronic debits. This is, of course, the ultimate in a speeded-up collection process, and computer technology is making such a process increasingly feasible and efficient.

---

[2]A question raised during the Hutton investigation was this: "Why didn't the banks recognize that Hutton was systematically overdrawing its account and call the company to task?" The answer is that some banks, with tight controls, did exactly that — they refused to let Hutton get away with the practice. Other banks were lax. Still other banks apparently let Hutton get away with being chronically overdrawn out of fear of losing its business: Hutton used its economic muscle to force the banks to let it get away with an illegal act. In many people's opinion, the banks were as much at fault as Hutton. Still, in business dealings, honesty is presumed, and Hutton was dishonest in its dealings with the banks. This dishonesty severely damaged Hutton's reputation, cost the company profits totaling hundreds of millions of dollars, cost its top managers their jobs, and contributed to the ultimate demise of the company.

SELF-TEST QUESTIONS

What is float? How do firms use float to increase cash management efficiency? What are some methods firms can use to accelerate receipts?

MARKETABLE SECURITIES

Marketable Securities
Securities that can be sold on short notice.

Realistically, the management of cash and marketable securities cannot be separated — management of one implies management of the other. In the first part of the chapter, we focused on cash management. Now, we turn to **marketable securities.**

Marketable securities typically provide much lower yields than operating assets. For example, recently Chrysler held a $7.3 billion portfolio of short-term marketable securities that yielded about 6 percent, but its operating assets provided a return of about 14 percent. Why would a company such as Chrysler have such large holdings of low-yielding assets?

In many cases, companies hold marketable securities for the same reasons that they hold cash. Although these securities are not as liquid as cash, in most cases they can be converted to cash in a very short period of time (often just a few minutes) with a single telephone call. Moreover, while cash yields nothing, marketable securities provide at least a modest return. For this reason, many firms hold at least some marketable securities in lieu of larger cash balances, liquidating part of the portfolio to increase the cash account when cash outflows exceed inflows. In such situations, the marketable securities could be used as a substitute for transactions balances, for precautionary balances, for speculative balances, or for all three. In most cases, the securities are held primarily for precautionary purposes — most firms prefer to rely on bank credit to make temporary transactions or to meet speculative needs, but they may still hold some liquid assets to guard against a possible shortage of bank credit.

A few years ago, Chrysler had essentially no cash — it was incurring huge losses, and those losses had drained its cash account. Then a new management team took over, improved operations, and began generating positive cash flows. By April 1995, Chrysler's cash (and marketable securities) was up to $7.3 billion, and analysts were forecasting a further buildup over the next 2 years to more than $10 billion. Management indicated, in various statements, that the cash hoard was necessary to enable the company to weather the next downturn in auto sales.

But some stockholders, notably Kirk Kerkorian (its largest stockholder) and Lee Iacocca (its former chairman), felt that management was too conservative, and they offered to buy the company for about $22 billion. They also stated that they would reduce Chrysler's cash account to about $2 billion, in effect using the company's own cash to help pay for it. Chrysler's management immediately countered that the Kerkorian/Iacocca plan would weaken the company to a dangerous degree. Who is right, and what will happen? We do not know. However, the example does show that the right amount of cash to hold is a judgmental issue, and one on which successful, intelligent people can disagree.

Although setting the target cash balance is, to a large extent, judgmental, analytical rules can be applied to help formulate better judgments. For example, years ago William Baumol recognized that the trade-off between cash and marketable securities is similar to the one firms face when setting the optimal level of inventory.[3] Baumol then applied the EOQ inventory model to determine the optimal level of cash balances.[4] His model suggests that cash holdings should be higher if costs are high and the time to liquidate marketable securities is long, but that those holdings should be lower if interest rates are low. His logic was that if it is expensive and time consuming to convert securities to cash, and if securities do not earn much because interest rates are low, then it does not pay to hold securities as opposed to cash. It does pay to hold securities if interest rates are high and the securities can be converted to cash quickly and cheaply.

SELF-TEST QUESTIONS

Why might a company hold low-yielding marketable securities when it could earn a much higher return on operating assets?

Why might a low interest rate environment lead to larger cash balances?

How might improvements in telecommunications technology affect the level of corporations' holding of cash?

INVENTORY

Inventories, which may be classified as (1) *raw materials,* (2) *work-in-process,* and (3) *finished goods,* are an essential part of virtually all business operations. As is the case with accounts receivable, inventory levels depend heavily upon sales. However, whereas receivables build up *after* sales have been made, inventory must be acquired *ahead* of sales. This is a critical difference, and the necessity of forecasting sales before establishing target inventory levels makes inventory management a difficult task. Also, since errors in the establishment of inventory levels quickly lead either to lost sales or to excessive carrying costs, inventory management is as important as it is difficult.

Inventory management techniques are covered in depth in production management courses. Still, since financial managers have a responsibility both for raising the capital needed to carry inventory and for the overall profitability of the firm, we need to cover the financial aspects of inventory management here. Two examples will make clear the types of issues involved in inventory management, and the financial problems poor inventory control can cause.

RETAIL CLOTHING STORE

Chicago Discount Clothing Company (CDCC) must order swimsuits for summer sales in January, and it must take delivery by April to be sure of having enough suits to meet the heavy May–June demand. Bathing suits come in many styles, colors, and sizes, and if CDCC stocks incorrectly, either in total or in terms of the style-color-size distribution, then the store will have trouble. It will lose potential sales if it stocks too few suits, and it will be forced to lower prices and take losses if it stocks too many or the wrong types.

---

[3]William J. Baumol, "The Transactions Demand for Cash: An Inventory Theoretic Approach," *Quarterly Journal of Economics,* November 1952, 545–556.

[4]A more complete description of the Economic Ordering Quantity (EOQ) model can be found in Eugene F. Brigham and Louis C. Gapenski, *Intermediate Financial Management,* 5th ed., 1996, Chapter 22.

The effects of inventory changes on the balance sheet are important. For simplicity, assume that CDCC has a $10,000 base stock of inventory which is financed by common stock. Its balance sheet is as follows:

Inventory (base stock)	$10,000	Common stock	$10,000
Total assets	$10,000	Total claims	$10,000

Now it anticipates that it will sell $5,000 worth of swimsuit inventory this summer. Dollar sales will actually be greater than $5,000, since CDCC makes about $200 in profits for every $1,000 of inventory sold. CDCC finances its seasonal inventory with bank loans, so its pre-summer balance sheet would look like this:

Inventory (seasonal)	$ 5,000	Notes payable to bank	$ 5,000
Inventory (base stock)	10,000	Common stock	10,000
Total assets	$15,000	Total claims	$15,000

If everything works out as planned, sales will be made, inventory will be converted to cash, the bank loan will be retired, and the company will earn a profit. The balance sheet, after a successful season, might look like this:

Cash	$ 1,000	Notes payable to bank	$ 0
Inventory (seasonal)	0	Common stock	10,000
Inventory (base stock)	10,000	Retained earnings	1,000
Total assets	$11,000	Total claims	$11,000

The company is now in a highly liquid position and is ready to begin a new season.

But suppose the season had not gone well, and CDCC had only sold $1,000 of its inventory. As fall approached, the balance sheet would look like this:

Cash	$ 200	Notes payable to bank	$ 4,000
Inventory (seasonal)	4,000	Common stock	10,000
Inventory (base stock)	10,000	Retained earnings	200
Total assets	$14,200	Total claims	$14,200

Now suppose the bank insists on repayment of the $4,000 outstanding on the loan, and it wants cash, not swimsuits. But if the swimsuits did not sell well in the summer, how will out-of-style suits sell in the fall? Assume that CDCC is forced to mark the suits down to half their cost (not half the selling price) in order to sell them to raise cash to repay the bank loan. The result will be as follows:

Cash	$ 2,200	Notes payable to bank	$ 4,000
Inventory (base stock)	10,000	Common stock	10,000
		Retained earnings	(1,800)
Total assets	$12,200	Total claims	$12,200

At this point, CDCC is in serious trouble. It does not have the cash to pay off the loan, and the firm's shareholders have lost $1,800 of their equity. If the bank will not extend the loan, and if other sources of cash are not available, CDCC will have to mark down its base stock prices in an effort to stimulate sales, and if this does not work, CDCC could be forced into bankruptcy. Clearly, poor inventory decisions can spell trouble.

APPLIANCE MANUFACTURER

Now consider a different type of situation, that of Housepro Corporation, a well-established appliance manufacturer whose inventory position, in millions of dollars, follows:

Raw materials	$ 200
Work-in-process	200
Finished goods	600
Total inventory	$1,000

Suppose Housepro anticipates that the economy is about to get much stronger and that the demand for appliances will rise sharply. If it is to share in the expected boom, Housepro will have to increase production. This means it will have to increase inventory, and, since the inventory buildup must precede sales, additional financing will be required — some liability account, perhaps notes payable, will have to be increased in order to support the additional inventory.

Proper inventory management requires close coordination among the sales, purchasing, production, and finance departments. The sales/marketing department is generally the first to spot changes in demand. These changes must be worked into the company's purchasing and manufacturing schedules, and the financial manager must arrange any financing that will be needed to support the inventory buildup. Lack of coordination among departments, poor sales forecasts, or both, can lead to disaster.

INVENTORY COSTS

The goal of inventory management is to ensure that the inventories needed to sustain operations are available while at the same time holding the costs of ordering and carrying inventories to the lowest possible level. Table 15-2 gives a listing of the typical costs associated with inventory. These costs are divided into three categories: carrying costs, ordering and receiving costs, and the costs that are incurred if the firm runs short of inventory.

Inventory is costly to store; therefore, there is always pressure to reduce inventory as part of firms' overall cost-containment strategies. A recent article in *Fortune* highlights the fact that an increasing number of corporations are taking drastic steps to control inventory costs.[5] For example, Trane Corporation, which makes air conditioners, recently adopted many of the just-in-time inventory principles which are described in more detail in the next section.

In the past, Trane produced parts on a steady basis, stored them as inventory, and had them ready whenever the company received an order for a batch of air conditioners or a large commercial air-conditioning system. However, the company reached the point where its inventory covered an area equal to three football fields, and it sometimes took as long as 15 days to find the necessary parts and to complete an order. To make matters worse, occasionally some of the necessary components simply could not be located, while in other instances the components were located but found to have been damaged from long storage.

Then Trane adopted a new inventory policy — it began producing components only after an order is received, and then sending the parts directly from the ma-

---

[5]Shawn Tully, "Raiding a Company's Hidden Cash," *Fortune*, August 22, 1994, 82–87.

TABLE 15-2	COSTS ASSOCIATED WITH INVENTORY	APPROXIMATE ANNUAL COST AS A PERCENTAGE OF INVENTORY VALUE
I. Carrying Costs		
	Cost of capital tied up	12.0%
	Storage and handling costs	0.5
	Insurance	0.5
	Property taxes	1.0
	Depreciation and obsolescence	12.0
	Total	26.0%
II. Ordering, Shipping, and Receiving Costs		
	Cost of placing orders, including production and set-up costs	Varies
	Shipping and handling costs	2.5%
III. Costs of Running Short		
	Loss of sales	Varies
	Loss of customer goodwill	Varies
	Disruption of production schedules	Varies

Note: These costs vary from firm to firm, from item to item, and also over time. The figures shown are U.S. Department of Commerce estimates for an average manufacturing firm. Where costs vary so widely that no meaningful numbers can be assigned, the term "Varies" is reported.

chines which make them to the final assembly line. The net effect: Inventories fell nearly 40 percent even as sales increased by 30 percent.

However, as Table 15-2 indicates, there are costs associated with holding too little inventory, and these costs can be severe. Generally, if a business carries small inventories, it must reorder frequently. This increases ordering costs. Even more important, firms can face large costs (for example, an immediate loss of sales and a loss of goodwill which can lead to lower sales in the future) if they do not have the inventory on hand to meet customer demands.

Consider a company which has developed a new line of notebook computers. How much inventory should it produce and have on hand when the marketing campaign is launched? If the company has too much inventory, it will incur unnecessarily high carrying costs. In addition, other problems may arise, particularly if the product has mediocre sales. For example, in 1995 some companies had too many 486 computers in stock and were forced to discount them to make room for new Pentium-based computers. These discounts not only reduced profit margins on the older models but also depressed prices on the newer models.

 ## SELF-TEST QUESTIONS

What are the three categories of inventory costs?

What are some components of inventory carrying costs?

What are some components of inventory ordering costs?

INVENTORY CONTROL SYSTEMS

Inventory management also involves the establishment of an *inventory control system.* Inventory control systems run the gamut from very simple to extremely complex, depending on the size of the firm and the nature of its inventory. For example, one simple control procedure is the **red-line method** — inventory items are stocked in a bin, a red line is drawn around the inside of the bin at the level of the reorder point, and the inventory clerk places an order when the red line shows. The **two-bin method** has inventory items stocked in two bins. When the working bin is empty, an order is placed and inventory is drawn from the second bin. These procedures work well for parts such as bolts in a manufacturing process, or for many items in retail businesses.

Red-Line Method
An inventory control procedure in which a red line is drawn around the inside of an inventory-stocked bin to indicate the reorder point level.

Two-Bin Method
An inventory control procedure in which an order is placed when one of two inventory-stocked bins is empty.

Computerized Inventory Control System
A system of inventory control in which a computer is used to determine reorder points and to adjust inventory balances.

COMPUTERIZED SYSTEMS

Larger companies employ **computerized inventory control systems.** The computer starts with an inventory count in memory. As withdrawals are made, they are recorded by the computer, and the inventory balance is revised. When the reorder point is reached, the computer automatically places an order, and when the order is received, the recorded balance is increased. As we noted earlier, retailers such as Wal-Mart have carried this system quite far — each item has a bar code, and, as an item is checked out, the code is read, a signal is sent to the computer, and the inventory balance is adjusted at the same time the price is fed into the cash register tape. When the balance drops to the reorder point, an order is placed. In Wal-Mart's case, the order goes directly from its computers to those of its suppliers.

A good inventory control system is dynamic, not static. A company such as Wal-Mart or General Motors stocks hundreds of thousands of different items. The sales (or use) of these various items can rise or fall quite separately from rising or falling overall corporate sales. As the usage rate for an individual item begins to rise or fall, the inventory manager must adjust its balance to avoid running short or ending up with obsolete items. If the change in the usage rate appears to be permanent, the safety stock level should be reconsidered, and the computer model used in the control process should be reprogrammed.

JUST-IN-TIME SYSTEMS

Just-in-Time (JIT) System
A system of inventory control in which a manufacturer coordinates production with suppliers so that raw materials or components arrive just as they are needed in the production process.

A relatively new approach to inventory control called the **just-in-time (JIT) system** has been developed by Japanese firms and is gaining popularity throughout the world. Toyota provides a good example of the just-in-time system. Eight of Toyota's ten factories, along with most of Toyota's suppliers, dot the countryside around Toyota City. Delivery of components is tied to the speed of the assembly line, and parts are generally delivered no more than a few hours before they are used. The just-in-time system reduces the need for Toyota and other manufacturers to carry large inventories, but it requires a great deal of coordination between the manufacturer and its suppliers, both in the timing of deliveries and the quality of the parts. It also requires that component parts be perfect; otherwise, some bad parts could stop the entire production line. Therefore, JIT inventory management has been developed in conjunction with total quality management (TQM).

Not surprisingly, U.S. automobile manufacturers were among the first domestic firms to move toward just-in-time systems. Ford has been restructuring its production system with a goal of increasing its inventory turnover from 20 times a year to 30 or 40 times. Of course, just-in-time systems place considerable pressure on suppliers. GM formerly kept a 10-day supply of seats and other parts made by Lear Siegler; now GM sends in orders at four- to eight-hour intervals and expects immediate shipment. A Lear Siegler spokesman stated, "We can't afford to keep things sitting around either," so Lear Siegler has had to be tougher on its own suppliers.

Just-in-time systems are also being adopted by smaller firms. In fact, some production experts say that small companies are better positioned than large ones to use just-in-time methods, because it is easier to redefine job functions and to educate people in small firms. One small-firm example is Fireplace Manufacturers Inc., a manufacturer of prefabricated fireplaces. The company was recently having cash flow problems, and it was carrying $1.1 million in inventory to support annual sales of about $8 million. The company went to a just-in-time system to trim its raw material and work-in-process inventory to $750,000, freeing up $350,000 of cash, even as sales doubled.

It has been argued that just-in-time inventory controls do not really increase overall economic efficiency because they merely shift costs of purchases to other firms further up the supply chain. However, this view is probably incorrect — the close coordination required between the parties has led to an overall reduction of inventory throughout the production-distribution system, and hence to a general improvement in economic efficiency. This point is made by companies such as Wal-Mart and Toyota, and it is borne out by economic statistics, which indicate that inventory as a percentage of sales has been declining since the use of just-in-time procedures began.

Out-Sourcing

Out-Sourcing
The practice of purchasing components rather than making them in-house.

Another important development related to inventory is **out-sourcing**, which is the practice of purchasing components rather than making them in-house. Thus, if GM arranged to buy radiators, axles, and other parts from suppliers rather than making them itself, it would be increasing its use of out-sourcing. Out-sourcing is often combined with just-in-time systems to reduce inventory levels. However, perhaps the major reason for out-sourcing has nothing to do with inventory policy — a bureaucratic, unionized company like GM can often buy parts from a smaller, non-unionized supplier at a lower cost than if it made them itself.

The Relationship between Production Scheduling and Inventory Levels

A final point relating to inventory levels is *the relationship between production scheduling and inventory levels.* A firm like a greeting card manufacturer has highly seasonal sales. Such a firm could produce on a steady, year-round basis, or it could let production rise and fall with sales. If it established a level production schedule, its inventory would rise sharply during periods when sales were low and then would decline during peak sales periods, but the average inventory held would be substantially higher than if production rose and fell with sales.

Our discussions of just-in-time systems, out-sourcing, and production scheduling all point out the necessity of coordinating inventory policy with manufacturing/procurement policies. Companies try to minimize *total production and*

KEEPING INVENTORY LEAN

What do just-in-time (JIT) inventory methods and supercomputers have in common? The answer is that both are being used, in a coordinated manner, to keep U.S. business inventories remarkably lean. Recent statistics show that retail, wholesale, and factory inventories — taken together and adjusted for inflation — amount to just 1.4 times monthly sales, the lowest reading in the 40 years that records have been kept. And leaner inventories mean lower inventory carrying costs for businesses, hence greater profits.

JIT became the watchword for many U.S. manufacturers in the mid-1980s, as they began to adopt this Japanese method of inventory delivery. JIT involves redesigning production so that parts and raw materials flow into the factory just as they are needed, thus allowing manufacturers to save the cost of carrying inventories. Large firms, including General Motors, Campbell Soup, Motorola, Hewlett-Packard, and Intel, as well as dozens of small firms such as Omark Industries, an Oregon manufacturer of power saw chains, have converted to JIT. A recent survey of 385 manufacturing plants in the United States, conducted for the National Association of Manufacturers, found that more than 16 percent were "extremely skilled" in JIT procedures, and another 44 percent had plans under way to "ex-

cel" in JIT operations. Importantly, the inventory turnover ratios of plants using JIT procedures were twice as high as those for the survey groups as a whole.

Large corporations started the just-in-time trend in the United States, but Robert W. Hall of Indiana University, who has written several books on the subject, says smaller companies are actually better positioned to adopt the method. Hall points out that small firms usually have only one plant to convert, and they usually have simpler accounting and planning systems. Also, their management groups are smaller and can make faster decisions than can larger firms. Another advantage for many small firms is that smaller, nonunionized labor forces make it easier to redesign job functions.

Worker attitudes toward these changes have generally been the greatest stumbling block for companies — large or small — that convert to JIT methods. One company president says employee acceptance depends on management. "It's just a matter of managers getting their mind-sets correct." This can be difficult, though, since managers must give up the security of large inventories and trust their suppliers more than they ever have before. It is essential for managers to work closely with suppliers to ensure that parts or materials get to the

plant at the right time and in the right sequence for the assembly line.

Cadbury Schweppes PLC, the London food and beverage producer, has inventory levels that are a fraction of what they were in the mid-1980s as a result of "closer cooperation with a smaller but better informed set of suppliers." The Schweppes unit gets 80 percent of its glass containers from a single supplier, as compared with 30 percent seven years ago. The firm's director of purchasing commented, "We used to play one off against the other and keep them guessing, but now we work very closely together, providing sales forecasts and other data we once kept to ourselves." By working in this way, the Schweppes unit has been able to reduce its inventory carrying costs, including financing and warehousing costs, dramatically.

When a company adopts the JIT method, it is essential that managers be concerned not only with their own problems but also with those faced by their suppliers. Xerox, for instance, went into the new system with the idea that "this was an inventory reduction program for our benefit," according to the materials manager for the copier division, "and we treated it that way, asking suppliers to hold inventories without compensation." Suppliers protested, and good relationships built over many

---

distribution costs, and inventory costs are just one part of total costs. Still, they are an important cost, and financial managers should be aware of the determinants of inventory costs and how they can be minimized.

 SELF-TEST QUESTIONS

Describe some inventory control systems used in practice.

What are just-in-time systems? What are their advantages? Why is quality especially important if a JIT system is used?

What is out-sourcing?

Describe the relationship between production scheduling and inventory levels.

years began to deteriorate. To improve the situation, Xerox reorganized its production and ordering schedules so suppliers could plan better. It also formed classes about JIT for the suppliers. One supplier, Rockford Dynatorq, reduced the time needed to make one brake part from three and a half weeks to just one day with the help of Xerox. Rockford's inventory dropped by 10 percent in just six months.

Improvement in quality control is a common by-product of JIT. First, with smaller inventories it is more critical than ever that there be few unusable units. In addition, many wasteful procedures are also uncovered when manufacturers reevaluate their production processes for JIT conversion. Costs that add nothing to a product's value are incurred every time an item is moved, inspected, or stored in inventory, and JIT helps trim these costs.

Retailers such as Kmart, Wal-Mart, and Dayton Hudson are using a sophisticated approach to maintaining lean inventories and reducing carrying costs. These firms are using supercomputers, extraordinarily powerful parallel computers, to help managers decide what to buy, where to stock it, and when to cut prices. Wayne Hood, a retail analyst with Prudential Securities, states that "Technology like this is absolutely critical . . . It's going to separate the win-

ners from the losers in retailing in the 1990s. Companies that don't invest in technology — even in the hard times — won't make it."

The parallel design of these supercomputers, where thousands of small processors work as one, instead of having two to four large processors as in mainframe computers, permits the retailing managers to quickly access data. For example, managers can obtain data through on-line searches instantly from every register, in every store, during the last year: What was sold, when, and what were the colors, styles, sizes, and prices? These managers can then act on this information. Mainframe computers would choke on this terabyte (a trillion characters of information) of data. In addition to having the capability of accessing such information, the supercomputers are less costly than the mainframes.

Supercomputers have been especially effective in managing seasonal inventory items. Seasonal merchandise, such as Christmas and Valentine's Day items, have high profit margins, so it is bad to have them go out of stock, but they also have a "death date" — a time at which they need to be completely sold out. Therefore, such items need to be tightly managed. By using the supercomputers, Kmart was able to determine that it sold 50 percent of its Valen-

tine inventory in a particular store in the last two days, hence that there was no need to panic and mark down prices to move the stock. Thus, the store managers were able to avoid unnecessary price cuts, and this increased the stores' profits.

It is apparent from firms' statements and from reported statistics that the trend to lower inventory levels represents a long-term, serious commitment. According to Geoffrey Moore, a Columbia University economist, the trend toward leaner inventories will reduce the volatility of U.S. business cycles because with smaller stockpiles of inventories, inventory draw-downs during recessions cannot last as long; hence, production must pick up sooner than would be the case if initial inventories were larger. Thus, it appears that JIT procedures, combined with supercomputers, will lower companies' costs and help stabilize the economy. But they will also make life increasingly difficult for smaller, less efficient firms.

SOURCES: "Small Manufacturers Shifting to 'Just-in-Time' Techniques," *The Wall Street Journal*, December 21, 1987; "Having a Hard Time," *Fortune*, June 9, 1986; "General Motors' Little Engine That Could," *Business Week*, August 3, 1987; "Firms' Inventories Are Remarkably Lean," *The Wall Street Journal*, November 3, 1992; "Supercomputers Manage Holiday Stock," *The Wall Street Journal*, December 23, 1992.

RECEIVABLES MANAGEMENT

Account Receivable
A balance due from a customer.

Firms would, in general, rather sell for cash than on credit, but competitive pressures force most firms to offer credit. Thus, goods are shipped, inventories are reduced, and an **account receivable** is created.[6] Eventually, the customer will pay the

[6]Whenever goods are sold on credit, two accounts are created — an asset item entitled *accounts receivable* appears on the books of the selling firm, and a liability item called *accounts payable* appears on the books of the purchaser. At this point, we are analyzing the transaction from the viewpoint of the seller, so we are concentrating on the variables under its control, in this case, the receivables. We will examine the transaction from the viewpoint of the purchaser in Chapter 16, where we discuss accounts payable as a source of funds and consider their cost relative to the cost of funds obtained from other sources.

account, at which time (1) the firm will receive cash and (2) its receivables will decline. Carrying receivables has both direct and indirect costs, but it also has an important benefit — granting credit will increase sales.

Receivables management begins with the decision of whether or not to grant credit. In this section, we discuss the manner in which a firm's receivables build up, and we also discuss several alternative ways to monitor receivables. A monitoring system is important, because without it receivables will build up to excessive levels, cash flows will decline, and bad debts will offset the profits on sales. Corrective action is often needed, and the only way to know whether the situation is getting out of hand is to set up and then follow a good receivables control system.

THE ACCUMULATION OF RECEIVABLES

The total amount of accounts receivable outstanding at any given time is determined by two factors: (1) the volume of credit sales and (2) the average length of time between sales and collections. For example, suppose the Boston Lumber Company (BLC), a wholesale distributor of lumber products, opens a warehouse on January 1 and, starting the first day, makes sales of $1,000 each day. For simplicity, we assume that all sales are on credit, and customers are given 10 days in which to pay. At the end of the first day, accounts receivable will be $1,000; they will rise to $2,000 by the end of the second day; and by January 10, they will have risen to 10($1,000) = $10,000. On January 11, another $1,000 will be added to receivables, but payments for sales made on January 1 will reduce receivables by $1,000, so total accounts receivable will remain constant at $10,000. In general, once the firm's operations have stabilized, this situation will exist:

$$\frac{\text{Accounts}}{\text{receivable}} = \frac{\text{Credit sales}}{\text{per day}} \times \frac{\text{Length of}}{\text{collection period}} \qquad (15\text{-}1)$$

$$= \quad \$1,000 \quad \times \quad 10 \text{ days} \quad = \$10,000.$$

If either credit sales or the collection period changes, such changes will be reflected in accounts receivable.

Notice that the $10,000 investment in receivables must be financed. To illustrate, suppose that when the warehouse opened on January 1, BLC's shareholders had put up $800 as common stock and used this money to buy the goods sold the first day. The $800 worth of inventory will be sold for $1,000; thus, BLC's gross profit on the $800 investment is $200, or 25 percent. In this situation, the initial balance sheet would be as follows:[7]

Inventories	$800	Common equity	$800
Total assets	$800	Total liabilities and equity	$800

At the end of the day, the balance sheet would look like this:

Accounts receivable	$1,000	Common equity	$ 800
Inventories	0	Retained earnings	200
Total assets	$1,000	Total liabilities and equity	$1,000

---

[7]Note that the firm would need other assets such as cash, fixed assets, and a permanent stock of inventory. Also, overhead costs and taxes would have to be deducted, so retained earnings would be less than the figures shown here. We abstract from these details here so that we may focus on receivables.

In order to remain in business, BLC must replenish inventories. To do so requires that $800 of goods be purchased, and this requires $800 in cash. Assuming that BLC borrows the $800 from the bank, the balance sheet at the start of the second day will be as follows:

Accounts receivable	$1,000	Notes payable to bank	$ 800
Inventories	800	Common equity	800
		Retained earnings	200
Total assets	$1,800	Total liabilities and equity	$1,800

At the end of the second day, the inventories will have been converted to receivables, and the firm will have to borrow another $800 to restock for the third day.

This process will continue, provided the bank is willing to lend the necessary funds, until the beginning of the 11th day, when the balance sheet reads as follows:

Accounts receivable	$10,000	Notes payable to bank	$ 8,000
Inventories	800	Common equity	800
		Retained earnings	2,000
Total assets	$10,800	Total liabilities and equity	$10,800

From this point on, $1,000 of receivables will be collected every day, and $800 of these funds can be used to purchase new inventories.

This example should make it clear (1) that accounts receivable depend jointly on the level of credit sales and the collection period, (2) that any increase in receivables must be financed in some manner, but (3) that the entire amount of receivables does not have to be financed because the profit portion ($200 of each $1,000 of sales) does not represent a cash outflow. In our example, we assumed bank financing, but, as we demonstrate in Chapter 16, there are many alternative ways to finance current assets.

MONITORING THE RECEIVABLES POSITION

Investors — both stockholders and bank loan officers — should pay close attention to accounts receivable management, for, as we shall see, one can be misled by reported financial statements and later suffer serious losses on an investment.

When a credit sale is made, the following events occur: (1) Inventories are reduced by the cost of goods sold, (2) accounts receivable are increased by the sales price, and (3) the difference is profit, which is added to retained earnings. If the sale is for cash, then the cash from the sale has actually been received by the firm, but if the sale is on credit, the firm will not receive the cash from the sale unless and until the account is collected. Firms have been known to encourage "sales" to very weak customers in order to report high profits. This could boost the firm's stock price, at least until credit losses begin to lower earnings, at which time the stock price will fall. Analyses along the lines suggested in the following sections will detect any such questionable practice, as well as any unconscious deterioration in the quality of accounts receivable. Such early detection could help both investors and bankers avoid losses.[8]

---

[8]Accountants are increasingly interested in these matters. Investors have sued several of the major accounting firms for substantial damages when (1) profits were overstated and (2) it could be shown that the auditors should have conducted an analysis along the lines described here and then should have reported the results to stockholders in their audit opinion.

Days Sales Outstanding (DSO)
The average length of time required to collect credit sales.

DAYS SALES OUTSTANDING (DSO). Suppose Super Sets Inc., a television manufacturer, sells 200,000 television sets a year at a price of $198 each. Further, assume that all sales are on credit, with terms of 2/10, net 30. Finally, assume that 70 percent of the customers take discounts and pay on Day 10, while the other 30 percent pay on Day 30.

Super Sets's **days sales outstanding (DSO),** sometimes called the *average collection period (ACP),* is 16 days:

$$DSO = ACP = 0.7(10 \text{ days}) + 0.3(30 \text{ days}) = 16 \text{ days.}$$

Super Sets's *average daily sales (ADS),* assuming a 360-day year, is $110,000:

$$ADS = \frac{\text{Annual sales}}{360} = \frac{(\text{Units sold})(\text{Sales price})}{360} \tag{15-2}$$

$$= \frac{200,000(\$198)}{360} = \frac{\$39,600,000}{360} = \$110,000.$$

Super Sets's accounts receivable, assuming a constant, uniform rate of sales throughout the year, will at any point in time be $1,760,000:

$$\text{Receivables} = (ADS)(DSO) \tag{15-3}$$

$$= (\$110,000)(16) = \$1,760,000.$$

Note also that its DSO, or average collection period, is a measure of the average length of time it takes Super Sets's customers to pay off their credit purchases, and the DSO is often compared with an industry average DSO. For example, if all television manufacturers sell on the same credit terms, and if the industry average DSO is 25 days versus Super Sets's 16 days, then Super Sets either has a higher percentage of discount customers or else its credit department is exceptionally good at ensuring prompt payment.

Finally, note that if you know both the annual sales and the receivables balance, you can calculate DSO as follows:

$$DSO = \frac{\text{Receivables}}{\text{Sales per day}} = \frac{\$1,760,000}{\$110,000} = 16 \text{ days.}$$

The DSO can also be compared with the firm's own credit terms. For example, suppose Super Sets's DSO had been running at a level of 35 days versus its 2/10, net 30 credit terms. With a 35-day DSO, some customers would obviously be taking more than 30 days to pay their bills. In fact, if many customers were paying within 10 days to take advantage of the discount, the others would, on average, be taking much longer than 35 days. One way to check this possibility is to use an aging schedule as described in the next section.

Aging Schedule
A report showing how long accounts receivable have been outstanding.

AGING SCHEDULES. An **aging schedule** breaks down a firm's receivables by age of account. Table 15-3 contains the December 31, 1995, aging schedules of two television manufacturers, Super Sets and Wonder Vision. Both firms offer the same credit terms, 2/10, net 30, and both show the same total receivables. However, Super Sets's aging schedule indicates that all of its customers pay on time — 70 percent pay on Day 10 while 30 percent pay on Day 30. Wonder Vision's schedule, which is more typical, shows that many of its customers are not abiding by its credit terms — some 27 percent of its receivables are more than 30 days past due, even though Wonder Vision's credit terms call for full payment by Day 30.

| TABLE 15-3 | AGING SCHEDULES |

	SUPER SETS		WONDER VISION	
AGE OF ACCOUNT (DAYS)	VALUE OF ACCOUNT	PERCENTAGE OF TOTAL VALUE	VALUE OF ACCOUNT	PERCENTAGE OF TOTAL VALUE
0–10	$1,232,000	70%	$ 825,000	47%
11–30	528,000	30	460,000	26
31–45	0	0	265,000	15
46–60	0	0	179,000	10
Over 60	0	0	31,000	2
Total receivables	$1,760,000	100%	$1,760,000	100%

Aging schedules cannot be constructed from the type of summary data that are reported in financial statements; they must be developed from the firm's accounts receivable ledger. However, well-run firms have computerized their accounts receivable records, so it is easy to determine the age of each invoice, to sort electronically by age categories, and thus to generate an aging schedule.

Management should constantly monitor both the DSO and the aging schedule to detect trends, to see how the firm's collection experience compares with its credit terms, and to see how effectively the credit department is operating in comparison with other firms in the industry. If the DSO starts to lengthen, or if the aging schedule begins to show an increasing percentage of past-due accounts, then the firm's credit policy may need to be tightened.

Although a change in the DSO or the aging schedule should be a signal to the firm to investigate its credit policy, a deterioration in either of these measures does not necessarily indicate that the firm's credit policy has weakened. In fact, if a firm experiences sharp seasonal variations, or if it is growing rapidly, then both the aging schedule and the DSO may be distorted. The DSO is calculated as follows:

$$\text{DSO} = \frac{\text{Accounts receivable}}{\text{Sales}/360}$$

Since receivables at a given point in time reflect sales in the last month or so, but sales as shown in the denominator of the equation are for the last 12 months, a seasonal increase in sales will increase the numerator more than the denominator, hence will raise the DSO. This will occur even if customers are still paying exactly as before. Similar problems arise with the aging schedule if sales fluctuate widely. Therefore, a change in either the DSO or the aging schedule should be taken as a signal to investigate further, but not necessarily as a sign that the firm's credit policy has weakened. Still, days sales outstanding and the aging schedule are useful tools for reviewing the credit department's performance.[9]

---

[9]See Eugene F. Brigham and Louis C Gapenski, *Intermediate Financial Management,* 5th ed., Chapter 23, for a more complete discussion of the problems with the DSO and aging schedule and ways to correct for them.

SELF-TEST QUESTIONS

Explain how a new firm's receivables balance is built up over time.

Define days sales outstanding (DSO). What can be learned from it? How is it affected by sales fluctuations?

What is an aging schedule? What can be learned from it? How is it affected by sales fluctuations?

CREDIT POLICY

The success or failure of a business depends primarily on the demand for its products — as a rule, the higher its sales, the larger its profits and the higher the value of its stock. Sales, in turn, depend on a number of factors, some exogenous but others under the control of the firm. The major controllable determinants of demand are sales prices, product quality, advertising, and the firm's **credit policy.** Credit policy, in turn, consists of these four variables:

Credit Policy
A set of decisions that include a firm's credit period, credit standards, collection procedures, and discounts offered.

1. *Credit period,* which is the length of time buyers are given to pay for their purchases.
2. *Credit standards,* which refer to the minimum financial strength of acceptable credit customers and the amount of credit available to different customers.
3. *Collection policy,* which is measured by its toughness or laxity in following up on slow-paying accounts.
4. *Discounts* given for early payment, including the discount amount and period.

The credit manager has the responsibility for administering the firm's credit policy. However, because of the pervasive importance of credit, the credit policy itself is normally established by the executive committee, which usually consists of the president plus the vice-presidents in charge of finance, marketing, and production.

SELF-TEST QUESTION

What are the four credit policy variables?

SETTING THE CREDIT PERIOD AND STANDARDS

Credit Terms
A statement of the credit period and any discounts offered — for example, 2/10, net 30.

Credit Period
The length of time for which credit is granted.

A firm's regular **credit terms,** which include the **credit period** and *discount,* might call for sales on a 2/10, net 30 basis to all "acceptable" customers. Here customers who paid within 10 days would be given a 2 percent discount, and others would be required to pay within 30 days. Its *credit standards* would be applied to determine which customers are qualified for the regular credit terms, and the amount of credit available to each customer.

CREDIT STANDARDS

Credit Standards

Standards that stipulate the minimum financial strength that an applicant must demonstrate in order to be granted credit.

Credit standards refer to the strength and creditworthiness a customer must exhibit in order to qualify for credit. If a customer does not qualify for the regular credit terms, it can still purchase from the firm, but under more restrictive terms. For example, a firm's "regular" credit terms might call for payment after 30 days, and these terms might be extended to all qualified customers. The firm's credit standards would be applied to determine which customers qualified for the regular credit terms and how much credit each customer should receive. The major factors considered when setting credit standards relate to the likelihood that a given customer will pay slowly or perhaps even end up as a bad debt loss.

Setting credit standards implicitly requires a measurement of *credit quality,* which is defined in terms of the probability of a customer's default. The probability estimate for a given customer is, for the most part, a subjective judgment. Nevertheless, credit evaluation is a well-established practice, and a good credit manager can make reasonably accurate judgments of the probability of default by different classes of customers.

Managing a credit department requires fast, accurate, up-to-date information, and to help get such information, the National Association of Credit Management (a group with 43,000 member firms) persuaded TRW, a large credit-reporting agency, to develop a computer-based telecommunications network for the collection, storage, retrieval, and distribution of credit information. A typical business credit report would include the following pieces of information:

1. A summary balance sheet and income statement.
2. A number of key ratios, with trend information.
3. Information obtained from the firm's suppliers telling whether it has been paying promptly or slowly, and whether it has recently failed to make any payments.
4. A verbal description of the physical condition of the firm's operations.
5. A verbal description of the backgrounds of the firm's owners, including any previous bankruptcies, lawsuits, divorce settlement problems, and the like.
6. A summary rating, ranging from A for the best credit risks down to F for those that are deemed likely to default.

Although a great deal of credit information is available, it must still be processed in a judgmental manner. Computerized information systems can assist in making better credit decisions, but, in the final analysis, most credit decisions are really exercises in informed judgment.[10]

---

[10]Credit analysts use procedures ranging from highly sophisticated, computerized "credit-scoring" systems, which actually calculate the statistical probability that a given customer will default, to informal procedures, which involve going through a checklist of factors that should be considered when processing a credit application. The credit-scoring systems use various financial ratios such as the current ratio and the debt ratio (for businesses) and income, years with the same employer, and the like (for individuals) to determine the statistical probability of default. Credit is then granted to those with low default probabilities. The informal procedures often involve examining the "5 C's of Credit": character, capacity, capital, collateral, and conditions. Character is obvious; capacity is a subjective estimate of ability to repay; capital means how much net worth the borrower has; collateral means assets pledged to secure the loan; and conditions refers to business conditions, which affects ability to repay.

SETTING THE COLLECTION POLICY

Collection Policy
The procedures that a firm follows to collect accounts receivable.

Collection policy refers to the procedures the firm follows to collect past-due accounts. For example, a letter might be sent to customers when a bill is 10 days past due; a more severe letter, followed by a telephone call, would be sent if payment is not received within 30 days; and the account would be turned over to a collection agency after 90 days.

The collection process can be expensive in terms of both out-of-pocket expenditures and lost goodwill — customers dislike being turned over to a collection agency. However, at least some firmness is needed to prevent an undue lengthening of the collection period and to minimize outright losses. A balance must be struck between the costs and benefits of different collection policies.

Changes in collection policy influence sales, the collection period, and the bad debt loss percentage. The effects of a change in collection policy, along with changes in the other credit policy variables, will be analyzed later in the chapter.

CASH DISCOUNTS

Cash Discount
A reduction in the price of goods given to encourage early payment.

The last element in the credit policy decision, the use of **cash discounts** for early payment, is analyzed by balancing the costs and benefits of different cash discounts. For example, a firm might decide to change its credit terms from "net 30," which means that customers must pay within 30 days, to "2/10, net 30." This change should produce two benefits: (1) It should attract new customers who consider the discount to be a price reduction, and (2) the discount should cause a reduction in the days sales outstanding, because some existing customers will pay more promptly in order to take advantage of the discount. Offsetting these benefits is the dollar cost of the discounts. The optimal discount percentage is established at the point where the marginal costs and benefits are exactly offsetting.

Seasonal Dating
Terms to induce customers to buy early by not requiring payment until the purchaser's selling season, regardless of when the goods are shipped.

If sales are seasonal, a firm may use **seasonal dating** on discounts. For example, Slimware Inc., a swimsuit manufacturer, sells on terms of 2/10, net 30, May 1 dating. This means that the effective invoice date is May 1, even if the sale was made back in January. The discount may be taken up to May 10; otherwise, the full amount must be paid on May 30. Slimware produces throughout the year, but retail sales of bathing suits are concentrated in the spring and early summer, and by offering seasonal dating, the company induces some of its customers to stock up early, saving Slimware storage costs and also "nailing down sales."

SELF-TEST QUESTIONS

How can cash discounts be used to influence sales volume and the DSO?

What is seasonal dating?

OTHER FACTORS INFLUENCING CREDIT POLICY

In addition to the factors discussed in the previous sections, several other points should be made regarding credit policy.

PROFIT POTENTIAL

We have emphasized the costs of granting credit. *However, if it is possible to sell on credit and also to impose a carrying charge on the receivables that are outstanding, then credit sales can actually be more profitable than cash sales.* This is especially true for consumer durables (autos, appliances, and so on), but it is also true for certain types of industrial equipment. Thus, GM's General Motors Acceptance Corporation (GMAC) unit, which finances automobiles, is highly profitable, as is Sears's credit subsidiary.[11] Some encyclopedia companies are even reported to lose money on cash sales but to more than make up these losses from the carrying charges on their credit sales. Obviously, such companies would rather sell on credit than for cash!

The carrying charges on outstanding credit are generally about 18 percent on a nominal basis: 1.5 percent per month, so $1.5\% \times 12 = 18\%$. This is equivalent to an effective annual rate of $(1.015)^{12} - 1.0 = 19.6\%$. Having receivables outstanding that earn more than 18 percent is highly profitable.

LEGAL CONSIDERATIONS

It is illegal, under the Robinson-Patman Act, for a firm to charge prices that discriminate between customers unless these differential prices are cost-justified. The same holds true for credit — it is illegal to offer more favorable credit terms to one customer or class of customers than to another, unless the differences are cost-justified.

SELF-TEST QUESTION

How do profit potential and legal considerations affect a firm's credit policy?

SUMMARY

This chapter discussed the management of current assets, particularly cash, marketable securities, inventory, and receivables. The key concepts are listed below.

- **Working capital** refers to current assets, and **net working capital** is defined as current assets minus current liabilities. **Working capital policy** refers to decisions relating to the level of and the financing of current assets.

- Under a **relaxed current asset investment policy,** a firm would hold relatively large amounts of each type of current asset. Under a **restricted current asset investment policy,** the firm would hold minimal amounts of these items.

- The **primary goal of cash management** is to reduce the amount of cash held to the minimum necessary to conduct business.

- The **transactions balance** is the cash necessary to conduct day-to-day business, whereas the **precautionary balance** is a cash reserve held to meet ran-

---

[11]Companies that do a large volume of sales financing typically set up subsidiary companies called *captive finance companies* to do the actual financing. Thus, General Motors, Chrysler, and Ford all have captive finance companies, as do Sears, Montgomery Ward, and General Electric.

dom, unforeseen needs. A **compensating balance** is a minimum checking account balance that a bank requires as compensation either for services provided or as part of a loan agreement. Firms also hold **speculative balances,** which allow them to take advantage of bargain purchases. Note, though, that borrowing capacity and marketable security holdings reduce the need for both precautionary and speculative balances.

■ A **cash budget** is a schedule showing projected cash inflows and outflows over some period. The cash budget is used to predict cash surpluses and shortages, and thus it is the primary cash management planning tool.

■ **Cash management techniques** generally fall into five categories: (1) synchronizing cash flows, (2) using float, (3) accelerating collections, (4) determining where and when funds will be needed, and (5) controlling disbursements.

■ **Disbursement float** is the amount of funds associated with checks written by a firm that are still in process and hence have not yet been deducted from the firm's bank account.

■ **Collections float** is the amount of funds associated with checks written to a firm that have not been cleared, hence are not yet available for the firm's use.

■ **Net float** is the difference between disbursement float and collections float, and it also is equal to the difference between the balance in the firm's own checkbook and the balance on the bank's records. The larger the net float, the smaller the cash balance the firm must maintain, so net float is good.

■ Two techniques that can be used to speed up collections are (1) **lockboxes** and (2) **wire transfers.**

■ Firms can reduce their cash balances by holding **marketable securities,** which can be sold on short notice at close to their quoted prices. Marketable securities serve both as a substitute for cash and as a temporary investment for funds that will be needed in the near future. Safety is the primary consideration when selecting marketable securities.

■ **Inventory management** involves determining how much inventory to hold, when to place orders, and how many units to order.

■ **Inventory** can be grouped into three categories: (1) raw materials, (2) work-in-process, and (3) finished goods.

■ **Inventory costs** can be divided into three types: carrying costs, ordering costs, and stock-out costs. In general, carrying costs increase as the level of inventory rises, but ordering costs and stock-out costs decline with larger inventory holdings.

■ Firms use inventory control systems such as the **red-line method** and the **two-bin method,** as well as **computerized inventory control systems,** to help them keep track of actual inventory levels and to ensure that inventory levels are adjusted as sales change. **Just-in-time (JIT) systems** are also used to hold down inventory costs and, simultaneously, to improve the production process.

■ When a firm sells goods to a customer on credit, an **account receivable** is created.

■ Firms can use an **aging schedule** and the **days sales outstanding (DSO)** to help keep track of their receivables position and to help avoid an increase in bad debts.

- A firm's **credit policy** consists of four elements: (1) credit period, (2) discounts given for early payment, (3) credit standards, and (4) collection policy. The first two, when combined, are called the **credit terms.**

- Two major sources of external credit information are **credit associations,** which are local groups that meet frequently and correspond with one another to exchange information on credit customers, and **credit-reporting agencies,** which collect credit information and sell it for a fee.

- Additional factors that influence a firm's overall credit policy are (1) **profit potential** and (2) **legal considerations.**

- The basic objective of the credit manager is to increase profitable sales by extending credit to worthy customers and therefore adding value to the firm.

As we demonstrated in this chapter, working capital policy involves two basic issues. The first, determining the appropriate level for each current asset, was addressed in this chapter. The second, how current assets should be financed, will be addressed in Chapter 16.

QUESTIONS

15-1 Assuming the firm's sales volume remained constant, would you expect it to have a higher cash balance during a tight-money period or during an easy-money period? Why?

15-2 What are the two principal reasons for holding cash? Can a firm estimate its target cash balance by summing the cash held to satisfy each of the two?

15-3 Explain how each of the following factors would probably affect a firm's target cash balance if all other factors were held constant.
a. The firm institutes a new billing procedure which better synchronizes its cash inflows and outflows.
b. The firm develops a new sales forecasting technique which improves its forecasts.
c. The firm reduces its portfolio of U.S. Treasury bills.
d. The firm arranges to use an overdraft system for its checking account.
e. The firm borrows a large amount of money from its bank and also begins to write far more checks than it did in the past.
f. Interest rates on Treasury bills rise from 5 percent to 10 percent.

15-4 Why would a lockbox plan make more sense for a firm that makes sales all over the United States than for a firm with the same volume of business but concentrated in its home city?

15-5 Is it true that when one firm sells to another on credit, the seller records the transaction as an account receivable while the buyer records it as an account payable and that, disregarding discounts, the receivable typically exceeds the payable by the amount of profit on the sale?

15-6 What are the four elements of a firm's credit policy? To what extent can firms set their own credit policies as opposed to having to accept policies that are dictated by "the competition"?

15-7 Suppose that a firm makes a purchase and receives the shipment on February 1. The terms of trade as stated on the invoice read "2/10, net 40, May 1 dating." What is the latest date on which payment can be made and the discount still be taken? What is the date on which payment must be made if the discount is not taken?

15-8 a. What is the days sales outstanding (DSO) for a firm whose sales are $2,880,000 per year and whose accounts receivable are $312,000? (Use 360 days per year.)
b. Is it true that if this firm sells on terms of 3/10, net 40, its customers probably all pay on time?

15-9 Is it true that if a firm calculates its days sales outstanding, it has no need for an aging schedule?

15-10 Firm A had no credit losses last year, but 1 percent of Firm B's accounts receivable proved to be uncollectible and resulted in losses. Should Firm B fire its credit manager and hire A's?

15-11 Indicate by a (+), (−), or (0) whether each of the following events would probably cause accounts receivable (A/R), sales, and profits to increase, decrease, or be affected in an indeterminant manner:

	A/R	SALES	PROFITS
The firm tightens its credit standards.	_____	_____	_____
The terms of trade are changed from 2/10, net 30, to 3/10, net 30.	_____	_____	_____
The terms are changed from 2/10, net 30, to 3/10, net 40.	_____	_____	_____
The credit manager gets tough with past-due accounts.	_____	_____	_____

15-12 A firm can reduce its investment in inventory by having its suppliers hold raw materials inventory and its customers hold finished goods inventory. Explain actions a firm can take which would result in larger inventory for its suppliers and customers and smaller inventory for itself. What are the limitations of such actions?

SELF-TEST PROBLEMS *(Solutions Appear in Appendix B)*

ST-1 Key terms Define each of the following terms:
  a. Working capital; net working capital; working capital policy
  b. Relaxed current asset investment policy; restricted current asset investment policy; moderate current asset investment policy
  c. Transactions balance; compensating balance; precautionary balance; speculative balance
  d. Cash budget; target cash balance
  e. Trade discounts
  f. Synchronized cash flows
  g. Check clearing; net float; disbursement float; collections float
  h. Lockbox plan
  i. Marketable securities
  j. Red-line method; two-bin method; computerized inventory control system
  k. Just-in-time system; out-sourcing
  l. Account receivable; days sales outstanding
  m. Aging schedule
  n. Credit policy; credit period; credit standards; collection policy; credit terms
  o. Cash discounts
  p. Seasonal dating

ST-2 Working capital policy The Calgary Company is attempting to establish a current assets policy. Fixed assets are $600,000, and the firm plans to maintain a 50 percent debt-to-assets ratio. The interest rate is 10 percent on all debt. Three alternative current asset policies are under consideration: 40, 50, and 60 percent of projected sales. The company expects to earn 15 percent before interest and taxes on sales of $3 million. Calgary's effective federal-plus-state tax rate is 40 percent. What is the expected return on equity under each alternative?

ST-3 Float The Upton Company is setting up a new checking account with Howe National Bank. Upton plans to issue checks in the amount of $1 million each day and to deduct them from its own records at the close of business on the day they are written. On average, the bank will receive and clear the checks at 5 P.M. the third day after they are written; for example, a check written on Monday will be cleared on Thursday afternoon. The firm's agreement with the bank requires it to maintain a $500,000 average compensating balance; this is $250,000 greater than the cash balance the firm would otherwise have on deposit. It makes a $500,000 deposit at the time it opens the account.
  a. Assuming that the firm makes deposits at 4 P.M. each day (and the bank includes them in that day's transactions), how much must it deposit daily in order to maintain a sufficient balance once it reaches a steady state? Indicate the required deposit on Day 1, Day 2, Day 3, if any, and each day thereafter, assuming that the company will write checks for $1 million on Day 1 and each day thereafter.
  b. How many days of float does Upton have?
  c. What ending daily balance should the firm try to maintain (1) on the bank's records and (2) on its own records?

PROBLEMS

15-1 Working capital policy The Rentz Corporation is attempting to determine the optimal level of current assets for the coming year. Management expects sales to increase to approximately $2 million as a result of an asset expansion presently being undertaken. Fixed assets total $1 million, and the firm wishes to maintain a 60 percent debt ratio. Rentz's interest cost is currently 8 percent on both short-term and longer-term debt (which the firm uses in its permanent structure). Three alternatives regarding the projected current asset level are available to the firm: (1) a tight policy requiring current assets of only 45 percent of projected sales, (2) a moderate policy of 50 percent of sales in current assets, and (3) a relaxed policy requiring current assets of 60 percent of sales. The firm expects to generate earnings before interest and taxes at a rate of 12 percent on total sales.

    a. What is the expected return on equity under each current asset level? (Assume a 40 percent effective federal-plus-state tax rate.)

    b. In this problem, we have assumed that the level of expected sales is independent of current asset policy. Is this a valid assumption?

    c. How would the overall riskiness of the firm vary under each policy?

15-2 Net float The Stendardi-Stephens Company (SSC) is setting up a new checking account with National Bank. SSC plans to issue checks in the amount of $1.6 million each day and to deduct them from its own records at the close of business on the day they are written. On average, the bank will receive and clear (that is, deduct from the firm's bank balance) the checks at 5 P.M. the fourth day after they are written; for example, a check written on Monday will be cleared on Friday afternoon. The firm's agreement with the bank requires it to maintain a $1.2 million average compensating balance; this is $400,000 greater than the cash balance the firm would otherwise have on deposit. It makes a $1.2 million deposit at the time it opens the account.

    a. Assuming that the firm makes deposits at 4 P.M. each day (and the bank includes them in that day's transactions), how much must it deposit daily in order to maintain a sufficient balance once it reaches a steady state? Indicate the required deposit on Day 1, Day 2, Day 3, Day 4, if any, and each day thereafter, assuming that the company will write checks for $1.6 million on Day 1 and each day thereafter.

    b. How many days of float does SSC carry?

    c. What ending daily balance should the firm try to maintain (1) on the bank's records and (2) on its own records?

    d. Explain how net float can help increase the value of the firm's common stock.

15-3 Lockbox system The Hardin-Gehr Corporation (HGC) began operations 5 years ago as a small firm serving customers in the Detroit area. However, its reputation and market area grew quickly, so that today HGC has customers throughout the entire United States. Despite its broad customer base, HGC has maintained its headquarters in Detroit and keeps its central billing system there. HGC's management is considering an alternative collection procedure to reduce its mail time and processing float. On average, it takes 5 days from the time customers mail payments until HGC is able to receive, process, and deposit them. HGC would like to set up a lockbox collection system, which it estimates would reduce the time lag from customer mailing to deposit by 3 days — bringing it down to 2 days. HGC receives an average of $1,400,000 in payments per day.

    a. How many days of collection float now exist (HGC's customers' disbursement float) and what would it be under the lockbox system? What reduction in cash balances could HGC achieve by initiating the lockbox system?

    b. If HGC has an opportunity cost of 10 percent, how much is the lockbox system worth on an annual basis?

    c. What is the maximum monthly charge HGC should pay for the lockbox system?

15-4 Cash budgeting Dorothy Koehl recently leased space in the Southside Mall and opened a new business, Koehl's Doll Shop. Business has been good, but Koehl has frequently run out of cash. This has necessitated late payment on certain orders, which in turn is beginning to cause a problem with suppliers. Koehl plans to borrow from the bank to have cash ready as needed, but first she needs a forecast of just how much she must borrow. Accordingly, she has asked you to prepare a cash budget for the critical period around Christmas, when needs will be especially high.

    Sales are made on a cash basis only. Koehl's purchases must be paid for during the following month. Koehl pays herself a salary of $4,800 per month, and the rent is $2,000 per month. In addition, she must make a tax payment of $12,000 in December. The current cash on hand (on December 1) is $400, but Koehl has agreed to maintain an average bank balance of $6,000 — this is her target cash balance. (Disregard till cash, which is insignificant because Koehl keeps only a small amount on hand in order to lessen the chances of robbery.)

    The estimated sales and purchases for December, January, and February are shown below. Purchases during November amounted to $140,000.

	SALES	PURCHASES
December	$160,000	$40,000
January	40,000	40,000
February	60,000	40,000

a. Prepare a cash budget for December, January, and February.

b. Now, suppose Koehl were to start selling on a credit basis on December 1, giving customers 30 days to pay. All customers accept these terms, and all other facts in the problem are unchanged. What would the company's loan requirements be at the end of December in this case? (Hint: The calculations required to answer this question are minimal.)

15-5 Cash budgeting Helen Bowers, owner of Helen's Fashion Designs, is planning to request a line of credit from her bank. She has estimated the following sales forecasts for the firm for parts of 1996 and 1997:

May 1996	$180,000
June	180,000
July	360,000
August	540,000
September	720,000
October	360,000
November	360,000
December	90,000
January 1997	180,000

Collection estimates obtained from the credit and collection department are as follows: collections within the month of sale, 10 percent; collections the month following the sale, 75 percent; collections the second month following the sale, 15 percent. Payments for labor and raw materials are typically made during the month following the one in which these costs have been incurred. Total labor and raw materials costs are estimated for each month as follows:

May 1996	$ 90,000
June	90,000
July	126,000
August	882,000
September	306,000
October	234,000
November	162,000
December	90,000

General and administrative salaries will amount to approximately $27,000 a month; lease payments under long-term lease contracts will be $9,000 a month; depreciation charges will be $36,000 a month; miscellaneous expenses will be $2,700 a month; income tax payments of $63,000 will be due in both September and December; and a progress payment of $180,000 on a new design studio must be paid in October. Cash on hand on July 1 will amount to $132,000, and a minimum cash balance of $90,000 will be maintained throughout the cash budget period.

a. Prepare a monthly cash budget for the last 6 months of 1996.

b. Prepare an estimate of the required financing (or excess funds) — that is, the amount of money Bowers will need to borrow (or will have available to invest) — for each month during that period.

c. Assume that receipts from sales come in uniformly during the month (that is, cash receipts come in at the rate of $\frac{1}{30}$ each day), but all outflows are paid on the fifth of the month. Will this have an effect on the cash budget — in other words, would the cash budget you have prepared be valid under these assumptions? If not, what can be done to make a valid estimate of peak financing requirements? No calculations are required, although calculations can be used to illustrate the effects.

d. Bowers produces on a seasonal basis, just ahead of sales. Without making any calculations, discuss how the company's current ratio and debt ratio would vary during the year assuming all financial requirements were met by short-term bank loans. Could changes in these ratios affect the firm's ability to obtain bank credit?

EXAM-TYPE PROBLEMS

The problems included in this section are set up in such a way that they could be used as multiple-choice exam problems.

15-6 Lockbox system I. Malitz and Associates Inc. operates a mail-order firm doing business on the West Coast. Malitz receives an average of $325,000 in payments per day. On average, it takes 4 days from the time customers mail checks until Malitz receives and processes them. Malitz is considering the use of a lockbox system to reduce collection and processing float. The system will cost $6,500 per month and will consist of 10 local depository banks and a concentration bank located in San Francisco. Under this system, customers' checks should be received at the lockbox locations 1 day after they are mailed, and daily totals will be transferred to San Francisco using wire transfers costing $9.75 each. Assume that Malitz has an opportunity cost of 10 percent and that there are 52 × 5 = 260 working days, hence 260 transfers from each lockbox location, in a year.

    a. What is the total annual cost of operating the lockbox system?

    b. What is the benefit of the lockbox system to Malitz?

    c. Should Malitz initiate the system?

15-7 Receivables investment   McDowell Industries sells on terms of 3/10, net 30. Total sales for the year are $900,000. Forty percent of the customers pay on the 10th day and take discounts; the other 60 percent pay, on average, 40 days after their purchases.

    a. What is the days sales outstanding?

    b. What is the average amount of receivables?

    c. What would happen to average receivables if McDowell toughened up on its collection policy with the result that all nondiscount customers paid on the 30th day?

INTEGRATED CASE

SKI EQUIPMENT INC.

15-8 Managing current assets   Dan Barnes, financial manager of Ski Equipment Inc. (SKI), is excited, but apprehensive. The company's founder recently sold his 51 percent controlling block of stock to Kent Koren, who is a big fan of EVA (Economic Value Added). EVA is found by taking the after-tax operating profit and then subtracting the dollar cost of all the capital the firm uses:

$$\text{EVA} = \text{Sales revenues} - \text{Operating costs} - \text{Taxes}$$
$$- \text{Capital costs}$$

$$= \text{Sales} - \text{Operating costs} - \text{Taxes}$$
$$- \text{WACC (Capital employed)}.$$

If EVA is positive, then the firm is creating value. On the other hand, if EVA is negative, the firm is not covering its cost of capital, and stockholders' value is being eroded. Koren rewards managers handsomely if they create value, but those whose operations produce negative EVAs are soon looking for work. Koren frequently points out that if a company can generate its current level of sales with less assets, it would need less capital. That would, other things held constant, lower capital costs and increase its EVA.

Shortly after he took control of SKI, Kent Koren met with SKI's senior executives to tell them of his plans for the company. First, he presented some EVA data which convinced everyone that SKI had not been creating value in recent years. He then stated, in no uncertain terms, that this situation must change. He noted that SKI's designs of skis, boots, and clothing are acclaimed throughout the industry, but something is seriously amiss elsewhere in the company. Costs are too high, prices are too low, or the company employs too much capital, and he wants SKI's managers to correct the problem or else.

Barnes has long felt that SKI's working capital situation should be studied—the company may have the optimal amounts of cash, securities, receivables, and inventories, but it may also have too much or too little of these items. In the past, the production manager resisted Dan's efforts to question his holdings of raw materials inventories, the marketing manager resisted questions about finished goods, the sales staff resisted questions about credit policy (which affects accounts receivable), and the treasurer did not want to talk about her cash and securities balances. Koren's speech made it clear that such resistance would no longer be tolerated.

Dan also knows that decisions about working capital cannot be made in a vacuum. For example, if inventories could be lowered without adversely affecting operations, then less capital would be required, the dollar cost of capital would decline, and EVA would increase. However, lower raw materials inventories might lead to production slowdowns and higher costs, while lower finished goods inventories might lead to the loss of profitable sales. So, before inventories are changed, it will be necessary to study operating as well as financial effects. The situation is the same with regard to cash and receivables.

    a. Dan plans to use the ratios in Table IC15-1 as the starting point for discussions with SKI's operating executives. He wants everyone to think about the pros and cons of changing each type of current asset and how changes would interact to affect profits and EVA. Based on the Table IC15-1 data, does SKI seem to be following a conservative, moderate, or aggressive working capital policy?

    b. How can one distinguish between a conservative but rational working capital policy and a situation where a firm simply has a lot of current assets because it is inefficient? Does SKI's working capital policy seem appropriate?

    c. What might SKI do to reduce its cash and securities without harming operations?

    d. What is "float," and how is it affected by the firm's cash manager (treasurer)?

In an attempt to better understand SKI's cash position, Dan developed a cash budget. Data for the first two months of the year are shown in Table IC15-2. (Note that Dan's preliminary

TABLE IC15-1   SELECTED RATIOS: SKI AND INDUSTRY AVERAGE

	SKI	INDUSTRY
Current	1.75	2.25
Quick	0.83	1.20
Debt/assets	58.76%	50.00%
Turnover of cash and securities	16.67	22.22
Days sales outstanding	45.00	32.00
Inventory turnover	4.82	7.00
Fixed assets turnover	11.35	12.00
Total assets turnover	2.08	3.00
Profit margin on sales	2.07%	3.50%
Return on equity (ROE)	10.45%	21.00%

TABLE IC15-2   SKI'S CASH BUDGET FOR JANUARY AND FEBRUARY

	NOV	DEC	JAN	FEB	MAR	APR
I. COLLECTIONS AND PURCHASES WORKSHEET						
(1) Sales (gross)	$71,218	$68,212	$65,213	$52,475	$42,909	$30,524
Collections						
(2) During month of sale (0.2)(0.98)(month's sales)			12,781.75	10,285.10		
(3) During first month after sale (0.7)(previous month's sales)			47,748.40	45,649.10		
(4) During second month after sale (0.1)(sales 2 months ago)			7,121.80	6,821.20		
(5) Total collections (Lines 2 + 3 + 4)			$67,651.95	$62,755.40		
Purchases						
(6) (0.85)(forecasted sales 2 months from now)		$44,603.75	$36,472.65	$25,945.40		
(7) Payments (1-month lag)			44,603.75	36,472.65		
II. CASH GAIN OR LOSS FOR MONTH						
(8) Collections (from Section I)			$67,651.95	$62,755.40		
(9) Payments for purchases (from Section I)			44,603.75	36,472.65		
(10) Wages and salaries			6,690.56	5,470.90		
(11) Rent			2,500.00	2,500.00		
(12) Taxes						
(13) Total payments			$53,794.31	$44,443.55		
(14) Net cash gain (loss) during month (Line 8 − Line 13)			$13,857.64	$18,311.85		
III. CASH SURPLUS OR LOAN REQUIREMENT						
(15) Cash at beginning of month if no borrowing is done			$3,000.00	$16,857.64		
(16) Cumulative cash (cash at start, + gain or − loss = Line 14 + Line 15)			16,857.64	35,169.49		
(17) Target cash balance			1,500.00	1,500.00		
(18) Cumulative surplus cash or loans outstanding to maintain $1,500 target cash balance (Line 16 − Line 17)			$15,357.64	$33,669.49		

cash budget does not account for interest income or interest expense.) He has the figures for the other months, but they are not shown in Table IC15-2.

e. Should depreciation expense be explicitly included in the cash budget? Why or why not?

f. In his preliminary cash budget, Dan has assumed that all sales are collected and, thus, that SKI has no bad debts. Is this realistic? If not, how would bad debts be dealt with in a cash budgeting sense? (Hint: Bad debts will affect collections but not purchases.)

g. Dan's cash budget for the entire year, although not given here, is based heavily on his forecast for monthly sales. Sales are expected to be extremely low between May and September but then increase dramatically in the fall and winter. November is typically the firm's best month, when SKI ships equipment to retailers for the holiday season. Interestingly, Dan's forecasted cash budget indicates that the company's cash holdings will exceed the targeted cash balance every month except for October and November, when shipments will be high but collections will not be coming in until later. Based on the ratios in Table IC15-1, does it appear that SKI's target cash balance is appropriate? In addition to possibly lowering the target cash balance, what actions might SKI take to better improve its cash management policies, and how might that affect its EVA?

h. What reasons might SKI have for maintaining a relatively high amount of cash?

i. What are the three categories of inventory costs? If the company takes steps to reduce its inventory, what effect would this have on the various costs of holding inventory?

j. Is there any reason to think that SKI may be holding too much inventory? If so, how would that affect EVA and ROE?

k. If the company reduces its inventory without adversely affecting sales, what effect should this have on the company's cash position (1) in the short run and (2) in the long run? Explain in terms of the cash budget and the balance sheet.

l. Dan knows that SKI sells on the same credit terms as other firms in its industry. Use the ratios presented in Table IC15-1 to explain whether SKI's customers pay more or less promptly than those of its competitors. If there are differences, does that suggest that SKI should tighten or loosen its credit policy? What four variables make up a firm's credit policy, and in what direction should each be changed by SKI?

m. Does SKI face any risks if it tightens its credit policy?

n. If the company reduces its DSO without seriously affecting sales, what effect would this have on its cash position (1) in the short run and (2) in the long run? Answer in terms of the cash budget and the balance sheet. What effect should this have on EVA in the long run?

COMPUTER-RELATED PROBLEM

Work the problem in this section only if you are using the computer problem diskette.

15-9 Cash budgeting Use the model in the File C15 to solve this problem.

a. Refer back to Problem 15-5. Suppose that by offering a 2 percent cash discount for paying within the month of sale, the credit manager of Helen's Fashion Designs has revised the collection percentages to 50 percent, 35 percent, and 15 percent, respectively. How will this affect the loan requirements?

b. Return the payment percentages to their base-case values: 10 percent, 75 percent, and 15 percent, respectively, and the discount to zero percent. Now suppose sales fall to only 70 percent of the forecasted level. Production is maintained, so cash outflows are unchanged. How does this affect Bowers's financial requirements?

c. Return sales to the forecasted level (100%), and suppose collections slow down to 3 percent, 10 percent, and 87 percent for the 3 months, respectively. How does this affect financial requirements? If Bowers went to a cash-only sales policy, how would that affect requirements, other things held constant?

APPENDIX 15A

THE CASH CONVERSION CYCLE

As we noted earlier in the chapter, the concept of working capital management originated with the old Yankee peddler, who would borrow to buy inventory, sell the inventory to pay off the bank loan, and then repeat the cycle. That concept has been applied to more complex businesses, where it is used to analyze the effectiveness of a firm's working capital management.

We can illustrate the process with data from Real Time Computer Corporation (RTC), which in early 1995 introduced a new super-minicomputer that can perform 500 million instructions per second and that will sell for $250,000. The effects of this new product on RTC's working capital position were analyzed in terms of the following five steps:

1. RTC will order and then receive the materials it needs to produce the 100 computers it expects to sell. Because RTC and most other firms purchase materials on credit, this transaction will create an account payable. However, the purchase will have no immediate cash flow effect.

2. Labor will be used to convert the materials into finished computers. However, wages will not be fully paid at the time the work is done, so, like accounts payable, accrued wages will also build up.

3. The finished computers will be sold, but on credit. Therefore, sales will create receivables, not immediate cash inflows.

4. At some point before cash comes in, RTC must pay off its accounts payable and accrued wages. This outflow must be financed.

5. The cycle will be completed when RTC's receivables have been collected. At that time, the company can pay off the credit that was used to finance production, and it can then repeat the cycle.

The *cash conversion cycle* model, which focuses on the length of time between when the company makes payments and when it receives cash inflows, formalizes the steps outlined above.[1] The following terms are used in the model:

1. *Inventory conversion period,* which is the average time required to convert materials into finished goods and then to sell those goods. Note that the inventory conversion period is calculated by dividing inventory by sales per day. For example, if average inventories are $2 million and sales are $10 million, then the inventory conversion period is 72 days:

$$\text{Inventory conversion period} = \frac{\text{Inventory}}{\text{Sales per day}} \qquad (15A\text{-}1)$$

$$= \frac{\$2,000,000}{\$10,000,000/360}$$

$$= 72 \text{ days.}$$

Thus, it takes an average of 72 days to convert materials into finished goods and then to sell those goods.

2. *Receivables collection period,* which is the average length of time required to convert the firm's receivables into cash, that is, to collect cash following a sale. The receivables collection period is also called the *days sales outstanding (DSO),* and it is calculated by dividing accounts receivable by the average credit sales per day. If receivables are $666,667 and sales are $10 million, the receivables collection period is

$$\frac{\text{Receivables}}{\text{collection period}} = \text{DSO} = \frac{\text{Receivables}}{\text{Sales}/360} \qquad (15A\text{-}2)$$

$$= \frac{\$666,667}{\$10 \text{ million}/360} = 24 \text{ days.}$$

Thus, it takes 24 days after a sale to convert the receivables into cash.

[1] See Verlyn D. Richards and Eugene J. Laughlin, "A Cash Conversion Cycle Approach to Liquidity Analysis," *Financial Management,* Spring 1980, 32–38.

3. *Payables deferral period,* which is the average length of time between the purchase of materials and labor and the payment of cash for them. For example, if the firm on average has 30 days to pay for labor and materials, if its cost of goods sold are $8 million per year, and if its accounts payable average $666,667, then its payables deferral period can be calculated as follows:

$$\begin{aligned}
\text{Payables deferral period} &= \frac{\text{Payables}}{\text{Purchases per day}} \\[6pt]
&= \frac{\text{Payables}}{\text{Cost of goods sold}/360} \\[6pt]
&= \frac{\$666,667}{\$8,000,000/360} \\[6pt]
&= 30 \text{ days.}
\end{aligned} \tag{15A-3}$$

The calculated figure is consistent with the stated 30-day payment period.

4. *Cash conversion cycle,* which nets out the three periods just defined and which therefore equals the length of time between the firm's actual cash expenditures to pay for productive resources (materials and labor) and its own cash receipts from the sale of products (that is, the length of time between paying for labor and materials and collecting on receivables). The cash conversion cycle thus equals the average length of time a dollar is tied up in current assets.

We can now use these definitions to analyze the cash conversion cycle. First, the concept is diagrammed in Figure 15A-1. Each component is given a number, and the cash conversion cycle can be expressed by this equation:

$$\underset{\substack{\text{Inventory} \\ \text{conversion} \\ \text{period}}}{(1)} + \underset{\substack{\text{Receivables} \\ \text{collection} \\ \text{period}}}{(2)} - \underset{\substack{\text{Payables} \\ \text{deferral} \\ \text{period}}}{(3)} = \underset{\substack{\text{Cash} \\ \text{conversion.} \\ \text{cycle}}}{(4)} \tag{15A-4}$$

To illustrate, suppose it takes Real Time an average of 72 days to convert raw materials to computers and then to sell them, and another 24 days to collect on receivables. However, 30 days normally elapse between receipt of raw materials and payment for them. In this case, the cash conversion cycle would be 66 days:

$$72 \text{ days} + 24 \text{ days} - 30 \text{ days} = 66 \text{ days.}$$

To look at it another way,

$$\text{Cash inflow delay} - \text{Payment delay} = \text{Net delay}$$

$$(72 \text{ days} + 24 \text{ days}) - 30 \text{ days} = 66 \text{ days.}$$

Given these data, RTC knows when it starts producing a computer that it will have to finance the manufacturing costs for a 66-day period. The firm's goal should be to shorten its cash conversion cycle as much as possible without hurting operations. This

FIGURE 15A-1   THE CASH CONVERSION CYCLE MODEL

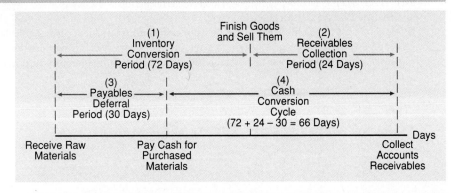

would improve profits, because the longer the cash conversion cycle, the greater the need for external financing, and that financing has a cost.

The cash conversion cycle can be shortened (1) by reducing the inventory conversion period by processing and selling goods more quickly; (2) by reducing the receivables collection period by speeding up collections; or (3) by lengthening the payables deferral period by slowing down the firm's own payments. To the extent that these actions can be taken *without increasing costs or depressing sales,* they should be carried out.

We can illustrate the benefits of shortening the cash conversion cycle by looking again at Real Time Computer Corporation. Suppose RTC must spend $200,000 on materials and labor to produce 1 computer, and it takes 3 days to produce a computer. Thus, it must invest $200,000/3 = $66,667 for each day's production. This investment must be financed for 66 days — the length of the cash conversion cycle — so the company's working capital financing needs will be 66 × $66,667 = $4.4 million. If RTC could reduce the cash conversion cycle to 56 days, say, by deferring payment of its accounts payable an additional 10 days, or by speeding up either the production process or the collection of its receivables, it could reduce its working capital financing requirements by $666,667. We see, then, that actions which affect the inventory conversion period, the receivables collection period, and the payables deferral period all affect the cash conversion cycle, hence they influence the firm's need for current assets and current asset financing. You should keep the cash conversion cycle concept in mind as you go through the other chapters on working capital management.

PROBLEMS

15A-1 Working capital investment The Prestopino Corporation is a leading U.S. producer of automobile batteries. Prestopino turns out 1,500 batteries a day at a cost of $6 per battery for materials and labor. It takes the firm 22 days to convert raw materials into a battery. Prestopino allows its customers 40 days in which to pay for the batteries, and the firm generally pays its suppliers in 30 days.
   a. What is the length of Prestopino's cash conversion cycle?
   b. At a steady state in which Prestopino produces 1,500 batteries a day, what amount of working capital must it finance?
   c. By what amount could Prestopino reduce its working capital financing needs if it was able to stretch its payables deferral period to 35 days?
   d. Prestopino's management is trying to analyze the effect of a proposed new production process on the working capital investment. The new production process would allow Prestopino to decrease its inventory conversion period to 20 days and to increase its daily production to 1,800 batteries. However, the new process would cause the cost of materials and labor to increase to $7. Assuming the change does not affect the receivables collection period (40 days) or the payables deferral period (30 days), what will be the length of the cash conversion cycle and the working capital financing requirement if the new production process is implemented?

15A-2 Cash conversion cycle The Zocco Corporation has an inventory conversion period of 75 days, a receivables collection period of 38 days, and a payables deferral period of 30 days.
   a. What is the length of the firm's cash conversion cycle?
   b. If Zocco's annual sales are $3,375,000 and all sales are on credit, what is the firm's investment in accounts receivable?
   c. How many times per year does Zocco turn over its inventory?

15A-3 Working capital cash flow cycle The Christie Corporation is trying to determine the effect of its inventory turnover ratio and days sales outstanding (DSO) on its cash flow cycle. Christie's 1995 sales (all on credit) were $150,000, and it earned a net profit of 6 percent, or $9,000. It turned over its inventory 6 times during the year, and its DSO was 36 days. The firm had fixed assets totaling $40,000. Christie's payables deferral period is 40 days.
   a. Calculate Christie's cash conversion cycle.
   b. Assuming Christie holds negligible amounts of cash and marketable securities, calculate its total assets turnover and ROA.
   c. Suppose Christie's managers believe that the inventory turnover can be raised to 8 times. What would Christie's cash conversion cycle, total assets turnover, and ROA have been if the inventory turnover had been 8 for 1995?

FINANCING CURRENT ASSETS 16

SOUND WORKING CAPITAL POLICY
REQUIRES APPROPRIATE FINANCING

In the last chapter we discussed steps Core Industries has taken to improve its working capital management. Core reduced its cash, receivables, and inventories, and, as a result, lowered its operating costs and raised its profits. Even so, Core still has substantial holdings of current assets, and the funds invested in these assets must be obtained from some source. This involves "working capital financing policy," the focus of the current chapter.

Most firms use several types of short-term funds to finance their working capital requirements. Included are bank loans, trade credit, commercial paper, and accruals. Well-run companies structure their current liabilities in a manner that depends on the nature of their business. For example, the sales of Toys R Us are very seasonal—

nearly half of all sales occur in the final three months of the year. To meet holiday demands, Toys R Us must dramatically increase its inventories during the summer and early fall. This inventory buildup must be financed until after Christmas, when collections bring cash into the till and debts can be reduced. The company relies on trade credit, loans from U.S. and foreign banks, and commercial paper, and it sells off marketable securities built up during the prior year.

Short-term credit is generally cheaper than long-term capital, but it is a riskier, less dependable source of financing. Interest rates can increase dramatically, and changes in a company's financial position can affect both the cost and availability of short-term credit.

In recent years, Core Industries financed its working capital very conservatively. It uses trade credit and accruals because such credit is essentially free, but it paid off its short-term bank debt. The company was able to reduce its debt as a result of its reduction of receivables and inventories, which freed up cash that was then used to pay off bank loans. Currently, Core is highly liquid, and it is in a good position to finance internal growth, to acquire other companies, or both.

After you have completed this chapter, you will have a better understanding of the various ways corporations can finance their current assets, and of the costs associated with each type of financing.

In the previous chapter, we discussed the first step in working capital management — determining the optimal level for each type of current asset. Now we turn to the second step — financing current assets. We begin with a discussion of some alternative financing policies.

ALTERNATIVE CURRENT ASSET FINANCING POLICIES

Most businesses experience seasonal and/or cyclical fluctuations. For example, construction firms have peaks in the spring and summer, retailers peak around Christmas, and the manufacturers who supply both construction companies and retailers follow similar patterns. Similarly, virtually all businesses must build up current assets when the economy is strong, but they then sell off inventories and reduce receivables when the economy slacks off. Still, current assets rarely drop to zero, and this fact has led to the development of the idea of **permanent current assets,** which are the current assets on hand at the low point of the cycle. Then, as sales increase during the upswing, current assets must likewise increase, and these additional current assets are defined as **temporary current assets.** The manner in which the permanent and temporary current assets are financed is called the firm's *current asset financing policy.*

MATURITY MATCHING, OR "SELF-LIQUIDATING," APPROACH

The **maturity matching, or "self-liquidating," approach** calls for matching asset and liability maturities as shown in Panel a of Figure 16-1. This strategy minimizes the risk that the firm will be unable to pay off its maturing obligations. To illustrate, suppose a company borrows on a 1-year basis and uses the funds obtained to build and equip a plant. Cash flows from the plant (profits plus depreciation) would not be sufficient to pay off the loan at the end of only 1 year, so the loan would have to be renewed. If for some reason the lender refused to renew the loan, then the company would have problems. Had the plant been financed with long-term debt, however, the required loan payments would have been better matched with cash flows from profits and depreciation, and the problem of renewal would not have arisen.

At the limit, a firm could attempt to match exactly the maturity structure of its assets and liabilities. Inventory expected to be sold in 30 days could be financed with a 30-day bank loan; a machine expected to last for 5 years could be financed by a 5-year loan; a 20-year building could be financed by a 20-year mortgage bond; and so forth. Actually, of course, two factors prevent this exact maturity matching: (1) there is uncertainty about the lives of assets, and (2) some common equity must be used, and common equity has no maturity. To illustrate the uncertainty factor, a firm might finance inventories with a 30-day loan, expecting to sell the inventories and to use the cash generated to retire the loan. But if sales were slow, the cash would not be forthcoming, and the use of short-term credit could end up causing a problem. Still, if a firm makes an attempt to match asset and liability maturities, we would define this as a moderate current asset financing policy.

Permanent Current Assets
Current assets that are still on hand at the trough of a firm's cycles.

Temporary Current Assets
Current assets that fluctuate with seasonal or cyclical variations in a firm's business.

Maturity Matching, or "Self-Liquidating," Approach
A financing policy that matches asset and liability maturities. This is a moderate policy.

FIGURE 16-1   ALTERNATIVE CURRENT ASSET FINANCING POLICIES

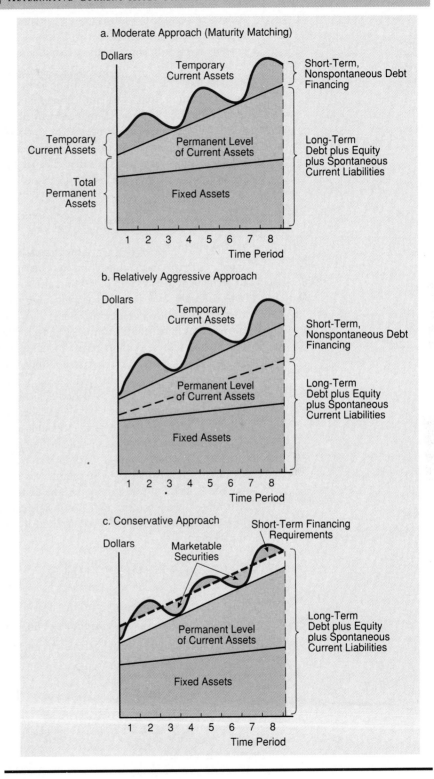

AGGRESSIVE APPROACH

Panel b of Figure 16-1 illustrates the situation for a relatively aggressive firm which finances all of its fixed assets with long-term capital and part of its permanent current assets with short-term, nonspontaneous credit. Note that we used the term "relatively" in the title for Panel b because there can be different *degrees* of aggressiveness. For example, the dashed line in Panel b could have been drawn *below* the line designating fixed assets, indicating that all of the permanent current assets and part of the fixed assets were financed with short-term credit; this would be a highly aggressive, extremely nonconservative position, and the firm would be very much subject to dangers from rising interest rates as well as to loan renewal problems. However, short-term debt is often cheaper than long-term debt, and some firms are willing to sacrifice safety for the chance of higher profits.

CONSERVATIVE APPROACH

In Panel c of Figure 16-1, we show the dashed line *above* the line designating permanent current assets, indicating that permanent capital is being used to finance all permanent asset requirements and also to meet some or all of the seasonal needs. In this situation, the firm uses a small amount of short-term, nonspontaneous credit to meet its peak requirements, but it also meets a part of its seasonal needs by "storing liquidity" in the form of marketable securities. The humps above the dashed line represent short-term financing, while the troughs below the dashed line represent short-term security holdings. Panel c represents a very safe, conservative current asset financing policy.

Chrysler, which in May 1995 had $7.3 billion of cash and marketable securities, fits the Panel c pattern. Its chairman, Robert Eaton, stated that these liquid assets will be needed during the next recession, and he cited as evidence the fact that Chrysler had an operating cash deficit of more than $4 billion during the 1991–1992 recession. However, some of Chrysler's stockholders, notably Lee Iacocca and Kirk Kerkorian, argued that only $2 billion was necessary — since Chrysler could borrow funds in the future if need be, the extra $5.3 billion should be redeployed to earn more than 3 percent after taxes. This example illustrates the fact that there is no clear, precise answer to the question of how much cash and securities a firm should hold.

SELF-TEST QUESTIONS

What is meant by the term "current asset financing policy"?

What are three alternative current asset financing policies? Is one best?

What is meant by the term "permanent current assets"?

What is meant by the term "temporary current assets"?

ADVANTAGES AND DISADVANTAGES OF SHORT-TERM FINANCING

The three possible financing policies described above were distinguished by the relative amounts of short-term debt used under each policy. The aggressive policy called for the greatest use of short-term debt, while the conservative policy called for the least. Maturity matching fell in between. Although using short-term credit is generally riskier than using long-term credit, short-term credit does have some significant advantages. The pros and cons of short-term financing are considered in this section.

SPEED

A short-term loan can be obtained much faster than long-term credit. Lenders will insist on a more thorough financial examination before extending long-term credit, and the loan agreement will have to be spelled out in considerable detail because a lot can happen during the life of a 10- to 20-year loan. Therefore, if funds are needed in a hurry, the firm should look to the short-term markets.

FLEXIBILITY

If its needs for funds are seasonal or cyclical, a firm may not want to commit itself to long-term debt for three reasons: (1) Flotation costs are generally high when raising long-term debt but trivial for short-term credit. (2) Although long-term debt can be repaid early, provided the loan agreement includes a prepayment provision, prepayment penalties can be expensive. Accordingly, if a firm thinks its need for funds will diminish in the near future, it should choose short-term debt for the flexibility it provides. (3) Long-term loan agreements always contain provisions, or covenants, which constrain the firm's future actions. Short-term credit agreements are generally much less onerous in this regard.

COST OF LONG-TERM VERSUS SHORT-TERM DEBT

The yield curve is normally upward sloping, indicating that interest rates are generally lower on short-term than on long-term debt. Thus, under normal conditions, interest costs at the time the funds are obtained will be lower if the firm borrows on a short-term rather than a long-term basis.

RISK OF LONG-TERM VERSUS SHORT-TERM DEBT

Even though short-term debt is often less expensive than long-term debt, short-term credit is riskier to the firm for two reasons: (1) If a firm borrows on a long-term basis, its interest costs will be relatively stable over time, but if it uses short-term credit, its interest expense will fluctuate widely, at times going quite high. For example, the rate banks charge large corporations for short-term debt more than tripled over a two-year period in the 1980s, rising from 6.25 to 21 percent. Many firms that had borrowed heavily on a short-term basis simply could not meet their rising interest costs, and, as a result, bankruptcies hit record levels during that period. (2) If a firm borrows heavily on a short-term basis, it may find itself unable to repay this debt, and it may be in such a weak financial position that the lender will not extend the loan; this too could force the firm into bankruptcy. Braniff Airlines, which failed during a credit crunch in the 1980s, is an example.

   Another good example of the riskiness of short-term debt is provided by Transamerica Corporation, a major financial services company. Transamerica's chairman, Mr. Beckett, described how his company was moving to reduce its dependency on short-term loans whose costs vary with short-term interest rates. According to Beckett, Transamerica had reduced its variable-rate (short-term) loans by about $450 million over a two-year period. "We aren't going to go through the enormous increase in debt expense again that had such a serious impact on earnings," he said. The company's earnings fell sharply because money rates rose to record highs. "We were almost entirely in variable-rate debt," he said, but currently "about 65 percent is fixed rate and 35 percent variable. We've come a long way, and we'll keep plugging away at it." Transamerica's earnings were badly depressed by the increase in short-term rates, but other companies were even less fortunate — they simply could not pay the rising interest charges, and this forced them into bankruptcy.

 ## SELF-TEST QUESTION

What are some advantages and disadvantages of short-term debt over long-term debt?

SOURCES OF SHORT-TERM FINANCING

Statements about the flexibility, cost, and riskiness of short-term versus long-term debt depend, to a large extent, on the type of short-term credit that is actually used. There are numerous sources of short-term funds, and in the following sections, we describe four major types: (1) accruals, (2) accounts payable (trade credit), (3) bank loans, and (4) commercial paper. In addition, we discuss the cost of bank loans and the factors that influence a firm's choice of a bank.

ACCRUALS

Firms generally pay employees on a weekly, biweekly, or monthly basis, so the balance sheet will typically show some accrued wages. Similarly, the firm's own estimated income taxes, the social security and income taxes withheld from employee payrolls, and the sales taxes collected are generally paid on a weekly, monthly, or quarterly basis, hence the balance sheet will typically show some accrued taxes along with accrued wages.

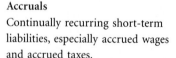
Accruals
Continually recurring short-term liabilities, especially accrued wages and accrued taxes.

    Accruals increase automatically, or spontaneously, as a firm's operations expand. Further, this type of debt is "free" in the sense that no explicit interest is paid on funds raised through accruals. However, a firm cannot ordinarily control its accruals: The timing of wage payments is set by economic forces and industry custom, while tax payment dates are established by law. Thus, firms use all the accruals they can, but they have little control over the levels of these accounts.

 ## SELF-TEST QUESTIONS

What types of short-term credit are classified as accruals?

What is the cost of accruals?

How much control do financial managers have over the dollar amount of accruals?

ACCOUNTS PAYABLE
(TRADE CREDIT)

Trade Credit
Debt arising from credit sales and recorded as an account receivable by the seller and as an account payable by the buyer.

Firms generally make purchases from other firms on credit, recording the debt as an *account payable*. Accounts payable, or **trade credit,** is the largest single category of short-term debt, representing about 40 percent of the current liabilities of the average nonfinancial corporation. The percentage is somewhat larger for smaller firms: Because small companies often do not qualify for financing from other sources, they rely especially heavily on trade credit.[1]

Trade credit is a spontaneous source of financing in the sense that it arises from ordinary business transactions. For example, suppose a firm makes average purchases of $2,000 a day on terms of net 30, meaning that it must pay for goods 30 days after the invoice date. On average, it will owe 30 times $2,000, or $60,000, to its suppliers. If its sales, and consequently its purchases, were to double, then its accounts payable would also double, to $120,000. So, simply by growing, the firm would have spontaneously generated an additional $60,000 of financing. Similarly, if the terms under which it bought were extended from 30 to 40 days, its accounts payable would expand from $60,000 to $80,000. Thus, lengthening the credit period, as well as expanding sales and purchases, generates additional financing.

THE COST OF TRADE CREDIT

Firms that sell on credit have a *credit policy* that includes certain *terms of credit*. For example, Microchip Electronics sells on terms of 2/10, net 30, meaning that a 2 percent discount is given if payment is made within 10 days of the invoice date, with the full invoice amount being due and payable within 30 days if the discount is not taken.

Note that the true price of Microchip's products is the net price, or 0.98 times the list price, because any customer can purchase an item at a 2 percent "discount" as long as the customer pays within 10 days. Now consider Personal Computer Company (PCC), which buys its memory chips from Microchip. One commonly used memory chip is listed at $100, so the "true" price to PCC is $98. Now, if PCC wants an additional 20 days of credit beyond the 10-day discount period, it must incur a finance charge of $2 per chip for that credit. Thus, the $100 list price can be thought of as follows:

List price = $98 true price + $2 finance charge.

The question that PCC must ask before it turns down the discount to obtain the additional 20 days of credit from Microchip is whether the firm could obtain similar credit under better terms from some other lender, say, a bank. In other words, could 20 days of credit be obtained for less than $2 per chip?

PCC buys an average of $11,760,000 of memory chips from Microchip each year at the net, or true, cost of $11,760,000/360 = $32,666.67 per day. For simplicity, assume that Microchip is PCC's only supplier. If PCC decides not to take the

---

[1]In a credit sale, the seller records the transaction as a receivable, the buyer as a payable. We examined accounts receivable as an asset investment in Chapter 15. Our focus in this chapter is on accounts payable, a liability item. We might also note that if a firm's accounts payable exceed its receivables, it is said to be *receiving net trade credit*, whereas if its receivables exceed its payables, it is *extending net trade credit*. Smaller firms frequently receive net credit; larger firms generally extend it.

additional trade credit — that is, if it pays on the 10th day and takes the discount — its payables will average 10($32,666.67) = $326,667. Thus, PCC will be receiving $326,667 of credit from its only supplier, Microchip.

Now suppose PCC decides to take the additional 20 days credit and thus must pay the finance charge. Since PCC will now pay on the 30th day, its accounts payable will increase to 30($32,666.67) = $980,000.[2] Microchip will now be supplying PCC with an additional $653,333 of credit, which it could use to build up its cash account, to pay off debt, to expand inventories, or even to extend more credit to its own customers, hence increasing its own accounts receivable.

The additional credit offered by Microchip has a cost — PCC must pay the finance charge by forgoing the 2 percent discount on its purchases from Microchip. Since PCC buys $11,760,000 of chips at the true price of 0.98(list price), the added finance charge increases the total cost to PCC to $11,760,000/0.98 = $12 million, so the annual financing cost is $12,000,000 − $11,760,000 = $240,000. Dividing the $240,000 financing cost by the $653,333 of additional credit, we find the nominal annual cost rate of the additional trade credit to be 36.7 percent:

$$\text{Nominal annual cost} = \frac{\$240,000}{\$653,333} = 36.7\%.$$

Assuming that PCC can borrow from its bank (or from other sources) at an interest rate less than 36.7 percent, it should take discounts and forgo the additional trade credit.

The following equation can be used to calculate the nominal cost, on an annual basis, of not taking discounts, illustrated with terms of 2/10, net 30:

$$\begin{matrix} \text{Nominal} \\ \text{annual} \\ \text{cost} \end{matrix} = \frac{\text{Discount percent}}{100 - \begin{matrix}\text{Discount} \\ \text{percent}\end{matrix}} \times \frac{360}{\begin{matrix}\text{Days credit is} \\ \text{outstanding}\end{matrix} - \begin{matrix}\text{Discount} \\ \text{period}\end{matrix}}. \qquad \textbf{(16-1)}$$

$$= \frac{2}{98} \times \frac{360}{20} = 2.04\% \times 18 = 36.7\%.$$

The numerator of the first term, Discount percent, is the cost per dollar of credit, while the denominator in this term, 100 − Discount percent, represents the funds made available by not taking the discount. Thus, the first term, 2.04%, is the periodic cost of the trade credit. The denominator of the second term is the number of days of extra credit obtained by not taking the discount, so the entire second term shows how many times each year the cost is incurred, 18 times in this example.

The nominal annual cost formula does not take account of compounding, and in effective annual interest terms, the cost of trade credit is much higher. The discount amounts to interest, and with terms of 2/10, net 30, the firm gains use of the funds for 30 − 10 = 20 days, so there are 360/20 = 18 "interest periods" per year. Remember that the first term in Equation 16-1, (Discount percent)/ (100 − Discount percent) = 0.02/0.98 = 0.0204, is the periodic interest rate. This rate is paid 18 times each year, so the effective annual cost rate of trade credit is

---

[2]A question arises here: Should accounts payable reflect gross purchases or purchases net of discounts? Generally accepted accounting principles permit either treatment if the difference is not material, but if the discount is material, then the transaction must be recorded net of discounts, or at "true" prices. Then, the higher payments that result from not taking discounts is reported as an additional expense called "discounts lost." Thus, we show accounts payable net of discounts even if the company does not expect to take the discount.

$$\text{Effective annual rate} = (1.0204)^{18} - 1.0 = 1.439 - 1.0 = 43.9\%.$$

Thus, the 36.7 percent nominal cost calculated with Equation 16-1 understates the true cost of trade credit.

Notice, however, that the cost of trade credit can be reduced by paying late. Thus, if PCC could get away with paying in 60 days rather than in the specified 30, then the effective credit period would become $60 - 10 = 50$ days, the number of times the discount would be lost would fall to $360/50 = 7.2$, and the nominal cost would drop from 36.7 percent to $2.04\% \times 7.2 = 14.7\%$. The effective annual rate would drop from 43.9 to 15.7 percent:

$$\text{Effective annual rate} = (1.0204)^{7.2} - 1.0 = 1.157 - 1.0 = 15.7\%.$$

Stretching Accounts Payable
The practice of deliberately paying accounts payable late.

In periods of excess capacity, firms may be able to get away with late payments, but they will also suffer a variety of problems associated with **stretching accounts payable** and being branded a "slow payer." These problems are discussed later in the chapter.

The cost of the additional trade credit from forgoing discounts under some other purchase terms are shown below:

	COST OF ADDITIONAL CREDIT IF THE CASH DISCOUNT IS NOT TAKEN	
CREDIT TERMS	NOMINAL COST	EFFECTIVE COST
1/10, net 20	36.4%	43.6%
1/10, net 30	18.2	19.8
2/10, net 20	73.5	106.9
3/15, net 45	37.1	44.1

As these figures show, the cost of not taking discounts can be substantial. Incidentally, throughout the chapter, we assume that payments are made either on the *last day* for taking discounts or on the *last day* of the credit period, unless otherwise noted. It would be foolish to pay, say, on the fifth day or on the twentieth day if the credit terms were 2/10, net 30.

EFFECTS OF TRADE CREDIT ON THE FINANCIAL STATEMENTS

A firm's policy with regard to taking or not taking discounts can have a significant effect on its financial statements. To illustrate, let us assume that PCC is just beginning its operations. On the first day, it makes net purchases of $32,666.67. This amount is recorded on its balance sheet under accounts payable.[3] The second day it buys another $32,666.67. The first day's purchases are not yet paid for, so at the end of the second day, accounts payable total $65,333.34. Accounts payable increase by another $32,666.67 on the third day, for a total of $98,000, and after 10 days, accounts payable are up to $326,667.

If PCC takes discounts, then on the 11th day it will have to pay for the $32,666.67 of purchases made on the first day, which will reduce accounts payable. However, it will buy another $32,666.67, which will increase payables. Thus, after the 10th day of operations, PCC's balance sheet will level off, showing a balance of $326,667

---

[3]Inventories also increase by $32,666.67, but we are not now concerned with inventories. Again note that both inventories and receivables are recorded net of discounts regardless of whether discounts are taken.

THE COST OF BANK LOANS

Prime Rate
A published interest rate charged by commercial banks to large, strong borrowers.

The cost of bank loans varies for different types of borrowers at any given point in time and for all borrowers over time. Interest rates are higher for riskier borrowers, and rates are also higher on smaller loans because of the fixed costs involved in making and servicing loans. If a firm can qualify as a "prime credit" because of its size and financial strength, it can borrow at the **prime rate,** which has traditionally been the lowest rate banks charge. Rates on other loans are generally scaled up from the prime rate, but loans to very large, strong customers are made at rates below prime.

Bank rates vary widely over time depending on economic conditions and Federal Reserve policy. When the economy is weak, then (1) loan demand is usually slack, (2) inflation is low, and (3) the Fed also makes plenty of money available to the system. As a result, rates on all types of loans are relatively low. Conversely, when the economy is booming, loan demand is typically strong, the Fed restricts the money supply, and the result is high interest rates. As an indication of the kinds of fluctuations that can occur, the prime rate during 1980 rose from 11 percent to 21 percent in just four months, and it rose from 6 to 9 percent during 1994. Interest rates on other bank loans also vary, generally moving with the prime rate.

Interest rates on bank loans are calculated in three ways: (1) *simple interest,* (2) *discount interest,* and (3) *add-on interest.* These three methods are explained in the following sections.

REGULAR, OR SIMPLE, INTEREST

Simple Interest
The situation when interest is not compounded, that is, interest is not earned on interest.

In a **simple interest** loan, the borrower receives the face value of the loan and repays the principal and interest at maturity. For example, in a simple interest loan of $10,000 at 12 percent for 1 year, the borrower receives the $10,000 upon approval of the loan and pays back the $10,000 principal plus $10,000(0.12) = $1,200 in interest at maturity (1 year later). The 12 percent is the quoted, or nominal, rate. On this 1-year loan, the effective annual rate is also 12 percent:

$$\text{Effective annual rate}_{\text{Simple}} = \frac{\text{Interest paid}}{\text{Amount received}} \qquad (16\text{-}2)$$

$$= \frac{\$1,200}{\$10,000} = 12\%.$$

Here is the time line setup:

```
     0        i = ?    1 Year
     ├─────────────────┤
  10,000           −10,000
                    −1,200
                   ─────────
                   −11,200
```

Although it is not necessary, you could solve this with a financial calculator. Enter N = 1, PV = 10000, PMT = 0, and FV = −11200, and then press I to obtain 12%.

THE TRAVAILS OF JAMESWAY

The recent travails of Jamesway Corporation, a retailer which operates primarily in the northeastern United States, provides a vivid illustration of the difficulty of maintaining an inexpensive source of funds. After 28 profitable years, Jamesway's financial position deteriorated as a result of unforeseen problems when it implemented a new automated merchandise ordering system. Order errors led to excessive inventory buildup, which in turn required the firm to mark down its goods and to book large losses.

Jamesway's lead lender, who had been providing the company with short-term credit to finance its inventories, cut its line of credit in half. The problems were exacerbated because a considerable amount of long-term debt was coming due in the near future. This situation caused suppliers to restrict credit to Jamesway, squeezing it still further. In the end, the company was unable to finance the purchase of inventory needed for the "Back-to-School" and Christmas holiday seasons, and it was forced to declare bankruptcy.

After working out a plan of reorganization, the company emerged from bankruptcy in early 1995. Needless to say, a key element of the reorganization plan was to obtain a secure line of credit.

On a simple interest loan of 1 year, the nominal rate equals the effective rate. However, if the loan had a term of less than 1 year, say, 90 days, then the effective annual rate would be calculated as follows:

$$\text{Effective annual rate}_{\text{Simple}} = \left(1 + \frac{k_{\text{Nom}}}{m}\right)^m - 1.0 \qquad (16\text{-}3)$$

$$= (1 + 0.12/4)^4 - 1.0 = 12.55\%.$$

Here k_{Nom} is the nominal, or quoted, rate and m is the number of loan periods per year, or 360/90 = 4. The bank gets the interest sooner than under a 1-year loan, hence the effective rate is higher.

Note that the interest payment on a $10,000 90-day loan is $10,000(0.12) (90/360) = $300, so the time line looks like this:

```
       0   i = ?   1        2        3      4 Quarters
       +---------+--------+--------+--------+
    10,000  -10,000
             -300
            -10,300
```

To solve with a financial calculator, enter N = 1, PV = 10000, PMT = 0, and FV = −10300, and then press I to obtain 3%. But this is a quarterly rate, so the effective annual rate = $(1.03)^4 - 1.0 = 12.55\%$.

DISCOUNT INTEREST

Discount Interest
Interest that is calculated on the face amount of a loan but is paid in advance.

In a **discount interest** loan, the bank deducts the interest in advance (*discounts* the loan). Thus, the borrower receives less than the face value of the loan. On a 1-year, $10,000 loan with a 12 percent (nominal) rate, discount basis, the interest is $10,000(0.12) = $1,200, so the borrower obtains the use of only $10,000 −

Prior to the passage of the truth in lending laws in the 1970s, most banks would have called this a 12 percent loan, period. The truth in lending laws apply primarily to consumer as opposed to business loans.

SIMPLE INTEREST WITH COMPENSATING BALANCES

Compensating balances tend to raise the effective rate on a loan. To illustrate, suppose a firm needs $10,000 to pay for some equipment that it recently purchased. A bank offers to lend the company money for 1 year at a 12 percent simple rate, but the company must maintain a *compensating balance (CB)* equal to 20 percent of the loan amount. If the firm did not take the loan, it would keep no deposits with the bank. What is the effective annual rate on the loan?

First, note that if the firm requires $10,000, it must, assuming it does not currently have cash balances that can be used as all or part of the compensating balance, borrow $12,500:

$$\text{Face value} = \frac{\text{Funds required}}{1.0 - \text{CB (decimal)}} \qquad (16\text{-}6)$$

$$= \frac{\$10,000}{1.0 - 0.20} = \$12,500.$$

The interest paid at the end of the year will be $12,500(0.12) = $1,500, but the firm will only get the use of $10,000. Therefore, the effective annual rate is 15 percent:

$$\text{Effective annual rate}_{\text{Simple/CB}} = \frac{\text{Interest paid}}{\text{Amount received}} \qquad (16\text{-}7)$$

$$= \frac{\$1,500}{\$10,000} = 15\%.$$

An alternative formula is

$$\text{Effective annual rate}_{\text{Simple/CB}} = \frac{\text{Nominal rate (decimal)}}{1.0 - \text{CB (decimal)}} \qquad (16\text{-}7a)$$

$$= \frac{0.12}{1.0 - 0.2} = 0.15 = 15\%.$$

Here's the time line solution:

	0	i = ?	1 Year	
Face Value	12,500		−12,500	Principal repayment
Less CB	−2,500		2,500	CB returned
Amount received	10,000		−1,500	Interest payment
			−11,500	Amount repaid

With a financial calculator, enter N = 1, PV = 10000, PMT = 0, and FV = −11500, and then press I to obtain 15%.

Note that if a firm normally carries cash balances with the bank, then those balances can be used to meet all or part of the compensating balance requirement, and this will reduce the effective cost of the loan. In this case, the calculations required to determine the effective annual rate are a bit more complicated, and we must go through the following three-step process:

1. $$\begin{array}{l}\text{Additional funds}\\\text{needed to meet}\\\text{compensating balance}\\\text{requirement}\end{array} = \left(\begin{array}{c}\text{Compensating}\\\text{balance}\\\text{percentage}\end{array} \times \text{Loan}\right) - \left(\begin{array}{c}\text{Cash available}\\\text{for compensating}\\\text{balance}\end{array}\right).$$

2. $$\text{Loan} = \left(\begin{array}{c}\text{Funds}\\\text{needed}\end{array}\right) + \left(\begin{array}{c}\text{Required additional funds}\\\text{for compensating balance}\end{array}\right)$$

    $$= \left(\begin{array}{c}\text{Funds}\\\text{needed}\end{array}\right) + \left(\begin{array}{c}\text{Compensating}\\\text{balance percentage}\end{array} \times \text{Loan}\right) - \left(\begin{array}{c}\text{Available}\\\text{cash}\end{array}\right).$$

3. $$\text{Effective annual rate} = \frac{\text{Nominal rate(Loan)}}{\text{Funds needed}}.$$

To illustrate, if our firm normally carried a working balance of $1,000, then the effective annual cost of a $10,000 loan requiring a 20 percent compensating balance would be found as follows:

Step 1. $$\begin{array}{l}\text{Additional funds to meet}\\\text{compensating balance}\end{array} = 0.2(\text{Loan}) - \$1,000.$$

Step 2. $$\text{Loan} = \$10,000 + 0.2(\text{Loan}) - \$1,000$$

$$0.8(\text{Loan}) = \$9,000$$

$$\text{Loan} = \$11,250.$$

Step 3. $$\text{Effective annual rate} = \frac{\text{Nominal rate(Loan)}}{\text{Funds needed}}$$

$$= \frac{0.12(\$11,250)}{\$10,000} = 13.5\%.$$

Thus, the firm will borrow $11,250, use $10,000 of this amount to meet its obligations, leave $1,250 on deposit as part of the compensating balance requirement, meet the remainder of the compensating balance requirement with the currently available $1,000, and pay an effective interest rate of 13.5 percent for the $10,000 net usable funds it received.

We can confirm the interest cost with a financial calculator. Note that when the loan matures at year-end, the firm must pay the $11,250 loan amount plus interest of 0.12($11,250) = $1,350, or $12,600 in total, but it can use for the payment the $11,250 − $10,000 = $1,250 borrowed compensating balance, so its net repayment will be $12,600 − $1,250 = $11,350. Therefore, we can enter N = 1, PV = 10000, PMT = 0, FV = −11350, and then press I to find the effective rate, 13.5%.

In our experience, most firms that require significant bank loans do not have much in the way of cash balances available for compensating balances. Therefore, in most situations, Equation 16-7a can be used to find the cost of a bank loan with compensating balance requirements. However, if cash balances are available, it is easy enough to go through the three-step process described above.

DISCOUNT INTEREST WITH COMPENSATING BALANCES

The analysis can be extended to the case where compensating balances are required and the loan is on a discount basis. Assume that a firm needs $10,000 for 1 year, and a 20 percent compensating balance (CB) is required on a 12 percent discount loan. The firm must borrow $14,705.88:

$$\text{Face value} = \frac{\text{Funds required}}{1.0 - \text{Nominal rate (decimal)} - \text{CB (decimal)}} \quad (16\text{-}8)$$

$$= \frac{\$10,000}{1.0 - 0.12 - 0.2} = \$10,000/0.68 = \$14,705.88.$$

The firm would record this $14,705.88 as a note payable, and it would be offset by these asset accounts (note that a small rounding difference occurs):

To working cash account	$10,000.00
Prepaid interest (12% of $14,705.88)	1,764.71
Compensating balance (20% of $14,705.88)	2,941.18
	$14,705.89

Now the effective annual rate is 17.65 percent:

$$\text{Effective annual rate}_{\text{Discount/CB}} = \frac{\text{Nominal rate (decimal)}}{1.0 - \text{Nominal rate (decimal)} - \text{CB (decimal)}} \quad (16\text{-}9)$$

$$= \frac{0.12}{1.0 - 0.12 - 0.2} = 0.12/0.68 = 0.1765 = 17.65\%.$$

On a time line, the situation looks like this:

```
                    0        i = ?      1 Year
                    |-------------------|
Face value          14,705.89   -14,705.89   Principal repayment
Less interest       -1,764.71     2,941.18   CB returned
Less CB             -2,941.18   -11,764.71   Amount repaid
Amount received     10,000.00
```

With a financial calculator, enter N = 1, PV = 10000, PMT = 0, and FV = −11764.71, and then press I to obtain 17.65%.

In our example, compensating balances and discount interest combined to push the effective interest rate up from 12 to 17.65 percent. Note, however, that in this analysis we assumed that the compensating balance requirement forced the firm to increase its bank deposits. If the company normally carried cash balances which could be used to supply all or part of the compensating balances, we would adjust the calculations along the lines discussed in the preceding section, and the effective annual rate would be less than 17.65 percent. Also, if the firm earns interest on its bank deposits, including the compensating balance, then the effective annual rate would be further decreased.

SELF-TEST QUESTIONS

What are some different ways that banks can calculate interest on loans?

What is a compensating balance? What effect does a compensating balance requirement have on the effective interest rate on a loan?

CHOOSING A BANK

Individuals whose only contact with their bank is through the use of its checking services generally choose a bank for the convenience of its location and the competitive cost of its services. However, a business that borrows from banks must look at other criteria, and a potential borrower seeking banking relations should recognize that important differences exist among banks. Some of these differences are considered next.

WILLINGNESS TO ASSUME RISKS

Banks have different basic policies toward risk. Some are inclined to follow relatively conservative lending practices, while others engage in what are properly termed "creative banking practices." These policies reflect partly the personalities of bank officers and partly the characteristics of the bank's deposit liabilities. Thus, a bank with fluctuating deposit liabilities in a static community will tend to be a conservative lender, while a bank whose deposits are growing with little interruption may follow more liberal credit policies. Similarly, a large bank with broad diversification over geographic regions and across industries can obtain the benefit of combining and averaging risks. Thus, marginal credit risks that might be unacceptable to a small or specialized bank can be pooled by a branch banking system to reduce the overall risk of a group of marginal accounts.[10]

ADVICE AND COUNSEL

Some bank loan officers are active in providing counsel and in stimulating development loans to firms in their early and formative years. Certain banks have specialized departments which make loans to firms expected to grow and thus to become more important customers. The personnel of these departments can provide valuable counseling to customers: The bankers' experience with other firms in growth situations may enable them to spot, and then to warn their customers about, developing problems.

LOYALTY TO CUSTOMERS

Banks differ in the extent to which they will support the activities of borrowers in bad times. This characteristic is referred to as the degree of *loyalty* of the bank. Some banks may put great pressure on a business to liquidate its loans when the firm's outlook becomes clouded, whereas others will stand by the firm and work diligently to help it get back on its feet. An especially dramatic illustration of this

---

[10]Bank deposits are insured by a federal agency, and banks are required to pay premiums to cover the cost of this insurance. Logically, riskier banks should pay higher premiums, but to date political forces have limited the use of risk-based insurance premiums. As an alternative, banks with riskier loan portfolios are required to have more equity capital per dollar of deposits than less risky banks. The savings and loan industry, until the 1980s, had federal insurance, no differential capital requirements, and lax regulations. As a result, some S&L operators wrote very high interest rate, but very risky, loans using low-cost, insured deposits. If the loans paid off, the S&L owners would get rich. If they went into default, the taxpayers would have to pay off the deposits. Those government policies ended up costing taxpayers many billions of dollars, and the bill will continue to come due for many more years.

point was Bank of America's bailout of Memorex Corporation. The bank could have forced Memorex into bankruptcy, but instead it loaned the company additional capital and helped it survive a bad period. Memorex's stock price subsequently rose on the New York Stock Exchange from $1.50 to $68, so Bank of America's help was indeed beneficial.

SPECIALIZATION

Banks differ greatly in their degrees of loan specialization. Larger banks have separate departments that specialize in different kinds of loans — for example, real estate loans, farm loans, and commercial loans. Within these broad categories, there may be a specialization by line of business, such as steel, machinery, cattle, or textiles. The strengths of banks are also likely to reflect the nature of the business and the economic environment in which they operate. For example, some California banks have become specialists in lending to electronics companies, while many Midwestern banks are agricultural specialists. A sound firm can obtain more creative cooperation and more active support by going to a bank that has experience and familiarity with its particular type of business. Therefore, a bank that is excellent for one firm may be unsatisfactory for another.

MAXIMUM LOAN SIZE

The size of a bank can be an important factor. Since the maximum loan a bank can make to any one customer is limited to 15 percent of the bank's capital accounts (capital stock plus retained earnings), it is generally not appropriate for large firms to develop borrowing relationships with small banks.

MERCHANT BANKING

The term "merchant bank" was originally applied to banks which not only loaned depositors' money but also provided customers with equity capital and financial advice. Prior to 1933, U.S. commercial banks performed all types of merchant banking functions. However, about one-third of the U.S. banks failed during the Great Depression, in part because of these activities, so in 1933 the Glass-Steagall Act was passed in an effort to reduce banks' exposure to risk. In recent years, commercial banks have been attempting to get back into merchant banking, in part because their foreign competitors offer such services, and U.S. banks need to be able to compete with their foreign counterparts for multinational corporations' business. Currently, the larger banks, often through holding companies, are being permitted to get back into merchant banking, at least to a limited extent. This trend will probably continue, and, if it does, corporations will need to consider a bank's ability to provide a full range of commercial and merchant banking services when choosing a bank.

OTHER SERVICES

Banks can also provide cash management services, assist with electronic funds transfers, help firms obtain foreign exchange, and the like, and the availability of such services should be taken into account when selecting a bank. Also, if the firm is a small business whose manager owns most of its stock, the bank's willingness and ability to provide trust and estate services should also be considered.

SELF-TEST QUESTION

What are some of the factors that should be considered when choosing a bank?

COMMERCIAL PAPER

Commercial Paper
Unsecured, short-term promissory notes of large firms, usually issued in denominations of $100,000 or more and having an interest rate somewhat below the prime rate.

Commercial paper is a type of unsecured promissory note issued by large, strong firms and sold primarily to other business firms, to insurance companies, to pension funds, to money market mutual funds, and to banks. Although the amount of commercial paper outstanding is smaller than bank loans outstanding, this form of financing has grown rapidly in recent years. In fall 1994, there was approximately $575 billion of commercial paper outstanding, versus about $635 billion of regular business loans.

MATURITY AND COST

Maturities of commercial paper generally vary from one to nine months, with an average of about five months.[11] The interest rate on commercial paper fluctuates with supply and demand conditions — it is determined in the marketplace, varying daily as conditions change. Recently, commercial paper rates have ranged from 1½ to 3 percentage points below the stated prime rate, and about ⅛ to ½ of a percentage point above the T-bill rate. For example, on February 3, 1995, the average rate on 3-month commercial paper was 6.2 percent, the stated prime rate was 9 percent, and the 3-month T-bill rate was about 5.8 percent.

USE OF COMMERCIAL PAPER

The use of commercial paper is restricted to a comparatively small number of very large concerns that are exceptionally good credit risks. Dealers prefer to handle the paper of firms whose net worth is $100 million or more and whose annual borrowing exceeds $10 million. One potential problem with commercial paper is that a debtor who is in temporary financial difficulty may receive little help because commercial paper dealings are generally less personal than are bank relationships. Thus, banks are generally more able and willing to help a good customer weather a temporary storm than is a commercial paper dealer. On the other hand, using commercial paper permits a corporation to tap a wide range of credit sources, including financial institutions outside its own area and industrial corporations across the country, and this can reduce interest costs.

SELF-TEST QUESTIONS

What is commercial paper?

What types of companies can use commercial paper to meet their short-term financing needs?

---

[11]The maximum maturity without SEC registration is 270 days. Also, commercial paper can only be sold to "sophisticated" investors; otherwise, SEC registration would be required even for maturities of 270 days or less.

How does the cost of commercial paper compare to the cost of short-term bank loans? To the cost of Treasury bills?

USE OF SECURITY IN SHORT-TERM FINANCING

Thus far, we have not addressed the question of whether or not loans should be secured. Commercial paper is never secured, but all other types of loans can be secured if this is deemed necessary or desirable. Given a choice, it is ordinarily better to borrow on an unsecured basis, since the bookkeeping costs of **secured loans** are often high. However, weak firms may find that they can borrow only if they put up some type of collateral to protect the lender, or that by using security they can borrow at a much lower rate.

Secured Loan
A loan backed by collateral, often inventories or receivables.

Several different kinds of collateral can be employed, including marketable stocks or bonds, land or buildings, equipment, inventory, and accounts receivable. Marketable securities make excellent collateral, but few firms that need loans also hold portfolios of stocks and bonds. Similarly, real property (land and buildings) and equipment are good forms of collateral, but they are generally used as security for long-term loans rather than for working capital loans. Therefore, most secured short-term business borrowing involves the use of accounts receivable and inventories as collateral.

To understand the use of security, consider the case of a Chicago hardware dealer who wanted to modernize and expand his store. He requested a $200,000 bank loan. After examining his business's financial statements, the bank indicated that it would lend him a maximum of $100,000 and that the interest rate would be 12 percent, discount interest, for an effective rate of 13.6 percent. The owner had a substantial personal portfolio of stocks, and he offered to put up $300,000 of high-quality stocks to support the $200,000 loan. The bank then granted the full $200,000 loan, and at a rate of only 10 percent, simple interest. The store owner might also have used his inventories or receivables as security for the loan, but processing costs would have been high. Procedures for using accounts receivable and inventories as security for short-term credit are described in Appendix 16A.[12]

 SELF-TEST QUESTIONS

What is a secured loan?

What are some types of current assets that are pledged as security for short-term loans?

SUMMARY

This chapter examined the financing of current assets. The key concepts covered are listed below.

---

[12]The term "asset-based financing" is often used as a synonym for "secured financing." In recent years, accounts receivable have been used as security for long-term bonds, and this permits corporations to borrow from lenders such as pension funds rather than being restricted to banks and other traditional short-term lenders.

■ **Permanent current assets** are those current assets that the firm holds even during slack times, whereas **temporary current assets** are the additional current assets that are needed during seasonal or cyclical peaks. The methods used to finance permanent and temporary current assets define the firm's **current asset financing policy.**

■ A **moderate** approach to current asset financing involves matching, to the extent possible, the maturities of assets and liabilities, so that temporary current assets are financed with short-term nonspontaneous debt, and permanent current assets and fixed assets are financed with long-term debt or equity, plus spontaneous debt. Under an **aggressive** approach, some permanent current assets, and perhaps even some fixed assets, are financed with short-term debt. A **conservative** approach would be to use long-term capital to finance all permanent assets and some of the temporary current assets.

■ The advantages of short-term credit are (1) the **speed** with which short-term loans can be arranged, (2) increased **flexibility,** and (3) the fact that short-term **interest rates** are generally **lower** than long-term rates. The principal disadvantage of short-term credit is the **extra risk** that the borrower must bear because (1) the lender can demand payment on short notice and (2) the cost of the loan will increase if interest rates rise.

■ **Short-term credit** is defined as any liability originally scheduled for payment within one year. The four major sources of short-term credit are (1) accruals, (2) accounts payable, (3) loans from commercial banks and finance companies, and (4) commercial paper.

■ **Accruals,** which are continually recurring short-term liabilities, represent free, spontaneous credit.

■ **Accounts payable,** or **trade credit,** is the largest category of short-term debt. Trade credit arises spontaneously as a result of credit purchases. Firms should use all the **free trade credit** they can obtain, but they should use **costly trade credit** only if it is less expensive than other forms of short-term debt. Suppliers often offer discounts to customers who pay within a stated discount period. The following equation may be used to calculate the nominal cost, on an annual basis, of not taking discounts:

$$\frac{\text{Nominal}}{\text{cost}} = \frac{\text{Discount percent}}{100 - \frac{\text{Discount}}{\text{percent}}} \times \frac{360}{\frac{\text{Days credit}}{\text{is outstanding}} - \frac{\text{Discount}}{\text{period}}}.$$

■ **Bank loans** are an important source of short-term credit. Interest on bank loans may be quoted as **simple interest, discount interest,** or **add-on interest.** The effective rate on a discount or add-on loan always exceeds the quoted nominal rate.

■ When a bank loan is approved, a **promissory note** is signed. It specifies: (1) the amount borrowed, (2) the percentage interest rate, (3) the repayment schedule, (4) the collateral, and (5) any other conditions to which the parties have agreed.

■ Banks sometimes require borrowers to maintain **compensating balances,** which are deposit requirements set at between 10 and 20 percent of the loan amount. Compensating balances raise the effective interest rate on bank loans.

■ **A line of credit** is an understanding between the bank and the borrower indicating the maximum amount of credit the bank will extend to the borrower.

- A **revolving credit agreement** is a formal line of credit often used by large firms; it involves a **commitment fee.**
- **Commercial paper** is unsecured short-term debt issued by large, financially strong corporations. Although the cost of commercial paper is lower than the cost of bank loans, commercial paper's maturity is limited to 270 days, and it can be used only by large firms with exceptionally strong credit ratings.
- Sometimes a borrower will find that it is necessary to borrow on a **secured basis,** in which case the borrower pledges assets such as real estate, securities, equipment, inventories, or accounts receivable as collateral for the loan.

QUESTIONS

16-1 How does the seasonal nature of a firm's sales influence its decision regarding the amount of short-term credit to use in its financial structure?

16-2 What are the advantages of matching the maturities of assets and liabilities? What are the disadvantages?

16-3 From the standpoint of the borrower, is long-term or short-term credit riskier? Explain. Would it ever make sense to borrow on a short-term basis if short-term rates were above long-term rates?

16-4 If long-term credit exposes a borrower to less risk, why would people or firms ever borrow on a short-term basis?

16-5 "Firms can control their accruals within fairly wide limits; depending on the cost of accruals, financing from this source will be increased or decreased." Discuss.

16-6 Is it true that both trade credit and accruals represent a spontaneous source of capital for financing growth? Explain.

16-7 Is it true that most firms are able to obtain some free trade credit and that additional trade credit is often available, but at a cost? Explain.

16-8 The availability of bank credit is often more important to a small firm than to a large one. Why?

16-9 What kinds of firms use commercial paper? Could Mama and Papa Gus's Corner Grocery borrow using this form of credit?

16-10 Given that commercial paper interest rates are generally lower than bank loan rates to a given borrower, why might firms which are capable of selling commercial paper also use bank credit?

16-11 Suppose a firm can obtain funds by borrowing at the prime rate or by selling commercial paper.
a. If the prime rate is 9 percent, what is a reasonable estimate for the cost of commercial paper?
b. If a substantial cost differential exists, why might a firm like this one actually borrow some of its funds in each market?

SELF-TEST PROBLEMS *(Solutions Appear in Appendix B)*

ST-1 Key terms Define each of the following terms:
a. Permanent current assets; temporary current assets
b. Moderate current asset financing policy; aggressive current asset financing policy; conservative current asset financing policy
c. Maturity matching, or "self-liquidating," approach
d. Accruals
e. Trade credit; stretching accounts payable; free trade credit; costly trade credit
f. Promissory note; line of credit; revolving credit agreement
g. Prime rate
h. Simple interest; discount interest; add-on interest
i. Compensating balance (CB)
j. Commercial paper
k. Secured loan

ST-2 Current asset financing Vanderheiden Press Inc. and the Herrenhouse Publishing Company had the following balance sheets as of December 31, 1995 (thousands of dollars):

	VANDERHEIDEN PRESS	HERRENHOUSE PUBLISHING
Current assets	$100,000	$ 80,000
Fixed assets (net)	100,000	120,000
Total assets	$200,000	$200,000
Current liabilities	$ 20,000	$ 80,000
Long-term debt	80,000	20,000
Common stock	50,000	50,000
Retained earnings	50,000	50,000
Total liabilities and equity	$200,000	$200,000

Earnings before interest and taxes for both firms are $30 million, and the effective federal-plus-state tax rate is 40 percent.

a. What is the return on equity for each firm if the interest rate on current liabilities is 10 percent and the rate on long-term debt is 13 percent?

b. Assume that the short-term rate rises to 20 percent. While the rate on new long-term debt rises to 16 percent, the rate on existing long-term debt remains unchanged. What would be the return on equity for Vanderheiden Press and Herrenhouse Publishing under these conditions?

c. Which company is in a riskier position? Why?

PROBLEMS

16-1 Cash discounts Suppose a firm makes purchases of $3.6 million per year under terms of 2/10, net 30, and takes discounts.

a. What is the average amount of accounts payable net of discounts? (Assume that the $3.6 million of purchases is net of discounts — that is, gross purchases are $3,673,469, discounts are $73,469, and net purchases are $3.6 million. Also, use 360 days in a year.)

b. Is there a cost of the trade credit the firm uses?

c. If the firm did not take discounts but it did pay on the due date, what would be its average payables and the cost of this nonfree trade credit?

d. What would its cost of not taking discounts be if it could stretch its payments to 40 days?

16-2 Trade credit versus bank credit The Thompson Corporation projects an increase in sales from $1.5 million to $2 million, but it needs an additional $300,000 of current assets to support this expansion. The money can be obtained from the bank at an interest rate of 13 percent, discount interest; no compensating balance is required. Alternatively, Thompson can finance the expansion by no longer taking discounts, thus increasing accounts payable. Thompson purchases under terms of 2/10, net 30, but it can delay payment for an additional 35 days — paying in 65 days and thus becoming 35 days past due — without a penalty because of its suppliers' current excess capacity problems.

a. Based strictly on effective, or equivalent, annual interest rate comparisons, how should Thompson finance its expansion?

b. What additional qualitative factors should Thompson consider before reaching a decision?

16-3 Bank financing The Raattama Corporation had sales of $3.5 million last year, and it earned a 5 percent return, after taxes, on sales. Recently, the company has fallen behind in its accounts payable. Although its terms of purchase are net 30 days, its accounts payable represent 60 days' purchases. The company's treasurer is seeking to increase bank borrowings in order to become current in meeting its trade obligations (that is, to have 30 days' payables outstanding). The company's balance sheet is as follows (thousands of dollars):

Cash	$ 100	Accounts payable	$ 600
Accounts receivable	300	Bank loans	700
Inventory	1,400	Accruals	200
Current assets	$1,800	Current liabilities	$1,500
Land and buildings	600	Mortgage on real estate	700
Equipment	600	Common stock, $0.10 par	300
		Retained earnings	500
Total assets	$3,000	Total liabilities and equity	$3,000

a. How much bank financing is needed to eliminate the past-due accounts payable?

b. Would you as a bank loan officer make the loan? Why?

16-4 Cost of bank loans Gifts Galore Inc. borrowed $1.5 million from National City Bank. The loan was made at a simple annual interest rate of 9 percent a year for 3 months. A 20 percent compensating balance requirement raised the effective interest rate.

a. The nominal interest rate on the loan was 11.25 percent. What is the true effective rate?

b. What would be the effective cost of the loan if the note required discount interest?

c. What would be the nominal annual interest rate on the loan if National City Bank required Gifts Galore to repay the loan and interest in 3 equal monthly installments?

16-5 Short-term financing analysis Malone Feed and Supply Company buys on terms of 1/10, net 30, but it has not been taking discounts and has actually been paying in 60 rather than 30 days. Malone's balance sheet follows (thousands of dollars):

Cash	$ 50	Accounts payable[a]	$ 500
Accounts receivable	450	Notes payable	50
Inventory	750	Accruals	50
Current assets	$1,250	Current liabilities	$ 600
		Long-term debt	150
Fixed assets	750	Common equity	1,250
Total assets	$2,000	Total liabilities and equity	$2,000

[a]Stated net of discounts.

Now, Malone's suppliers are threatening to stop shipments unless the company begins making prompt payments (that is, paying in 30 days or less). The firm can borrow on a 1-year note (call this a current liability) from its bank at a rate of 15 percent, discount interest, with a 20 percent compensating balance required. (Malone's $50,000 of cash is needed for transactions; it cannot be used as part of the compensating balance.)

a. Determine what action Malone should take by calculating (1) the cost of nonfree trade credit and (2) the cost of the bank loan.

b. Assume that Malone forgoes discounts and then borrows the amount needed to become current on its payables from the bank. How large will the bank loan be?

c. Based on your conclusion in Part b, construct a pro forma balance sheet. (Hint: You will need to include an account entitled "prepaid interest" under current assets.)

16-6 Alternative financing arrangements Suncoast Boats Inc. estimates that because of the seasonal nature of its business, it will require an additional $2 million of cash for the month of July. Suncoast Boats has the following 4 options available for raising the needed funds:

(1) Establish a 1-year line of credit for $2 million with a commercial bank. The commitment fee will be 0.5 percent per year on the unused portion, and the interest charge on the used funds will be 11 percent per annum. Assume that the funds are needed only in July, and that there are 30 days in July and 360 days in the year.

(2) Forgo the trade discount of 2/10, net 40, on $2 million of purchases during July.

(3) Issue $2 million of 30-day commercial paper at a 9.5 percent per annum interest rate. The total transactions fee, including the cost of a backup credit line, on using commercial paper is 0.5 percent of the amount of the issue.

(4) Issue $2 million of 60-day commercial paper at a 9 percent per annum interest rate, plus a transactions fee of 0.5 percent. Since the funds are required for only 30 days, the excess funds ($2 million) can be invested in 9.4 percent per annum marketable securities for the month of August. The total transactions cost of purchasing and selling the marketable securities is 0.4 percent of the amount of the issue.

a. What is the dollar cost of each financing arrangement?

b. Is the source with the lowest expected cost necessarily the one to select? Why or why not?

EXAM-TYPE PROBLEMS

The problems included in this section are set up in such a way that they could be used as multiple-choice exam problems.

16-7 Cost of trade credit Calculate the nominal annual cost of nonfree trade credit under each of the following terms. Assume payment is made either on the due date or on the discount date.

a. 1/15, net 20.

b. 2/10, net 60.

    c. 3/10, net 45.

    d. 2/10, net 45.

    e. 2/15, net 40.

16-8 Cost of trade credit

    a. If a firm buys under terms of 3/15, net 45, but actually pays on the 20th day and *still takes the discount*, what is the nominal cost of its nonfree trade credit?

    b. Does it receive more or less credit than it would if it paid within 15 days?

16-9 Cost of bank loans Del Hawley, owner of Hawley's Hardware, is negotiating with First City Bank for a $50,000, 1-year loan. First City has offered Hawley the following alternatives. Calculate the effective annual interest rate for each alternative. Which alternative has the lowest effective annual interest rate?

    a. A 12 percent annual rate on a simple interest loan, with no compensating balance required and interest due at the end of the year.

    b. A 9 percent annual rate on a simple interest loan, with a 20 percent compensating balance required and interest again due at the end of the year.

    c. An 8.75 percent annual rate on a discounted loan, with a 15 percent compensating balance.

    d. Interest is figured as 8 percent of the $50,000 amount, *payable at the end of the year,* but the $50,000 is repayable in monthly installments during the year.

16-10 Cost of trade credit Grunewald Industries sells on terms of 2/10, net 40. Gross sales last year were $4.5 million, and accounts receivable averaged $437,500. Half of Grunewald's customers paid on the 10th day and took discounts. What are the nominal and effective costs of trade credit to Grunewald's nondiscount customers? (Hint: Calculate sales/day based on a 360-day year; then get average receivables of discount customers; then find the DSO for the non-discount customers.)

16-11 Effective cost of short-term credit The D. J. Masson Corporation needs to raise $500,000 for 1 year to supply working capital to a new store. Masson buys from its suppliers on terms of 3/10, net 90, and it currently pays on the 10th day and takes discounts, but it could forego discounts, pay on the 90th day, and get the needed $500,000 in the form of costly trade credit. Alternatively, Masson could borrow from its bank on a 12 percent discount interest rate basis. What is the effective annual interest rate of the lower-cost source?

16-12 Effective cost of short-term credit Yonge Corporation must arrange financing for its working capital requirements for the coming year. Yonge can (a) borrow from its bank on a simple interest basis (interest payable at the end of the loan) for 1 year at a 12 percent nominal rate; (b) borrow on a 3-month, but renewable, loan at an 11.5 percent nominal rate; (c) borrow on an installment loan basis at a 6 percent add-on rate with 12 end-of-month payments; or (d) obtain the needed funds by no longer taking discounts and thus increasing its accounts payable. Yonge buys on terms of 1/15, net 60. What is the effective annual cost (*not* the nominal cost) of the *least expensive* type of credit, assuming 360 days per year?

INTEGRATED CASE

BATS AND BALLS INC.

16-13 Working capital financing policy Bats and Balls (B&B) Inc., a baseball equipment manufacturer, is a small company with seasonal sales. Each year before the baseball season, B&B purchases inventory which is financed through a combination of trade credit and short-term bank loans. At the end of the season, B&B uses sales revenues to repay its short-term obligations. The company is always looking for ways to become more profitable, and senior management has asked one of its employees, Ann Taylor, to review the company's current asset financing policies. Putting together her report, Ann is trying to answer each of the following questions:

a. B&B tries to match the maturity of its assets and liabilities. Describe how B&B could adopt either a more aggressive or more conservative financing policy.

b. What are the advantages and disadvantages of using short-term credit as a source of financing?

c. Is it likely that B&B could make significantly greater use of accruals?

d. Assume that B&B buys on terms of 1/10, net 30, but that it can get away with paying on the 40th day if it chooses not to take discounts. Also, assume that it purchases $3 million of components per year, net of discounts. How much free trade credit can the company get, how much costly trade credit can it get, and what is the percentage cost of the costly credit? Should B&B take discounts?

e. Would it be feasible for B&B to finance with commercial paper?

f. Suppose B&B decided to raise an additional $100,000 as a one-year loan from its bank, for which it was quoted a rate of 8 percent. What is the effective annual cost rate assuming (1) simple interest, (2) discount interest, (3) discount interest with a 10 percent compensating balance, and (4) add-on interest on a 12-month installment loan? For the first three of these assumptions, would it matter if the loan were for 90 days, but renewable, rather than for a year?

g. How large would the loan actually be in each of the cases in Part f?

h. What are the pros and cons of borrowing on a secured versus an unsecured basis? If inventories or receivables are to be used as collateral, how would the loan be handled?

COMPUTER-RELATED PROBLEM

Work the problem in this section only if you are using the computer problem diskette.

16-14 Working capital financing Three companies — Aggressive, Moderate, and Conservative — have different working capital management policies as implied by their names. For example, Aggressive employs only minimal current assets, and it finances almost entirely with current liabilities plus equity. This restricted approach has a dual effect. It keeps total assets low, which tends to increase return on assets; but because of stock-outs and credit rejections, total sales are reduced, and because inventory is ordered more frequently and in smaller quantities, variable costs are increased. Condensed balance sheets for the three companies follow:

	AGGRESSIVE	MODERATE	CONSERVATIVE
Current assets	$225,000	$300,000	$450,000
Fixed assets	300,000	300,000	300,000
Total assets	$525,000	$600,000	$750,000
Current liabilities (12%)	$300,000	$150,000	$ 75,000
Long-term debt (10%)	0	150,000	300,000
Total debt	$300,000	$300,000	$375,000
Equity	225,000	300,000	375,000
Total liabilities and equity	$525,000	$600,000	$750,000
Current ratio	0.75:1	2:1	6:1

The cost of goods sold functions for the three firms are as follows:

$$\text{Cost of goods sold} = \text{Fixed costs} + \text{Variable costs.}$$

Aggressive: Cost of goods sold = $300,000 + 0.70(Sales).

Moderate: Cost of goods sold = $405,000 + 0.65(Sales).

Conservative: Cost of goods sold = $577,500 + 0.60(Sales).

Because of the working capital differences, sales for the three firms under different economic conditions are expected to vary as follows:

	AGGRESSIVE	MODERATE	CONSERVATIVE
Strong economy	$1,800,000	$1,875,000	$1,950,000
Average economy	1,350,000	1,500,000	1,725,000
Weak economy	1,050,000	1,200,000	1,575,000

a. Construct income statements for each company for strong, average, and weak economies using the following format:

> Sales
> Less cost of goods sold
> Earnings before interest and taxes (EBIT)
> Less interest expense
> Earnings before taxes (EBT)
> Less taxes (40%)
> Net income

b. Compare the basic earning power (EBIT/assets) and return on equity for the companies. Which company is best in a strong economy? In an average economy? In a weak economy?

c. Suppose that, with sales at the average-economy level, short-term interest rates rose to 20 percent. How would this affect the three firms?

d. Suppose that because of production slowdowns caused by inventory shortages, the aggressive company's variable cost ratio rose to 80 percent. What would happen to its ROE? Assume a short-term interest rate of 12 percent.

e. What considerations for management of working capital are indicated by this problem?

APPENDIX 16A

SECURED SHORT-TERM FINANCING

This appendix discusses procedures for using accounts receivable and inventories as security for short-term loans. As noted earlier in the chapter, secured loans involve quite a bit of paperwork and other administrative costs, which make them relatively expensive. However, this is often the only type of financing available to weaker firms.

ACCOUNTS RECEIVABLE FINANCING

Accounts receivable financing involves either the pledging of receivables or the selling of receivables (called factoring). The *pledging of accounts receivable,* or putting accounts receivable up as security for a loan, is characterized by the fact that the lender not only has a claim against the receivables but also has *recourse* to the borrower: If the person or firm that bought the goods does not pay, the selling firm must take the loss. Therefore, the risk of default on the pledged accounts receivable remains with the borrower. The buyer of the goods is not ordinarily notified about the pledging of the receivables, and the financial institution that lends on the security of accounts receivable is generally either a commercial bank or one of the large industrial finance companies.

Factoring, or selling accounts receivable, involves the purchase of accounts receivable by the lender, generally without recourse to the borrower, which means that if the purchaser of the goods does not pay for them, the lender rather than the seller of the goods takes the loss. Under factoring, the buyer of the goods is typically notified of the transfer and is asked to make payment directly to the financial institution. Since the factoring firm assumes the risk of default on bad accounts, it must make the credit check. Accordingly, factors provide not only money, but also a credit department for the borrower. Incidentally, the same financial institutions that make loans against pledged receivables also serve as factors. Thus, depending on the circumstances and the wishes of the borrower, a financial institution will provide either form of receivables financing.

PROCEDURE FOR PLEDGING ACCOUNTS RECEIVABLE. The financing of accounts receivable is initiated by a legally binding agreement between the seller of the goods and the financing institution. The agreement sets forth in detail the procedures to be followed and the legal obligations of both parties. Once the working relationship has been established, the seller periodically takes a batch of invoices to the financing institution. The lender reviews the invoices and makes credit appraisals of the buyers. Invoices of companies that do not meet the lender's credit standards are not accepted for pledging.

The financial institution seeks to protect itself at every phase of the operation. First, selection of sound invoices is one way the lender safeguards itself. Second, if the buyer of the goods does not pay the invoice, the lender still has recourse against the seller. Third, additional protection is afforded the lender because the loan will generally be less than 100 percent of the pledged receivables; for example, the lender may advance the selling firm only 75 percent of the amount of the pledged invoices.

PROCEDURE FOR FACTORING ACCOUNTS RECEIVABLE. The procedures used in factoring are somewhat different from those for pledging. Again, an agreement between the seller and the factor specifies legal obligations and procedural arrangements. When the seller receives an order from a buyer, a credit approval slip is written and immediately sent to the factoring company for a credit check. If the factor approves the credit, shipment is made and the invoice is stamped to notify the buyer to make payment directly to the factoring company. If the factor does not approve the sale, the seller generally refuses to fill the order; if the sale is made anyway, the factor will not buy the account.

The factor normally performs three functions: (1) credit checking, (2) lending, and (3) risk bearing. However, the seller can select various combinations of these functions by changing provisions in the factoring agreement. For example, a small- or medium-sized firm may have the factor perform the risk-bearing function and thus avoid having to establish a credit department. The factor's service is often less costly than a credit department that would have excess capacity for the firm's credit volume. At the same time, if the selling firm uses someone who is not really qualified for the job to perform credit checking, then that person's lack of education, training, and experience could result in excessive losses.

The seller may have the factor perform the credit-checking and risk-taking functions without performing the lending function. The following procedure illustrates the handling of a $10,000 order under this arrangement. The factor checks and approves the invoices. The goods are shipped on terms of net 30. Payment is made to the factor, who remits to the seller. If the buyer defaults, however, the $10,000 must still be remitted to the seller, and if the $10,000 is never paid, the factor sustains a $10,000 loss. Note that in this situation, the factor does not remit funds to the seller until either they are received from the buyer of the goods or the credit period has expired. Thus, the factor does not supply any credit.

Now consider the more typical situation in which the factor performs the lending, risk-bearing, and credit-checking functions. The goods are shipped, and even though payment is not due for 30 days, the factor immediately makes funds available to the seller. Suppose $10,000 worth of goods are shipped. Further, assume that the factoring commission for credit checking and risk bearing is 2.5 percent of the invoice price, or $250, and that the interest expense is computed at a 9 percent annual rate on the invoice balance, or $75.[1] The selling firm's accounting entry is as follows:

Cash	$9,175	
Interest expense	75	
Factoring commission	250	
Reserve due from factor on collection of account	500	
Accounts receivable		$10,000

The $500 due from the factor upon collection of the account is a reserve established by the factor to cover disputes between the seller and buyers over damaged goods, goods returned by the buyers to the seller, and the failure to make an outright sale of goods. The reserve is paid to the selling firm when the factor collects on the account.

Factoring is normally a continuous process instead of the single cycle just described. The firm that sells the goods receives an order; it transmits this order to the factor for approval; upon approval, the firm ships the goods; the factor advances the invoice amount minus withholdings to the seller; the buyer pays the factor when payment is due; and the factor periodically remits any excess in the reserve to the seller of the goods. Once a routine has been established, a continuous circular flow of goods and funds takes place between the seller, the buyers of the goods, and the factor. Thus, once the factoring agreement is in force, funds from this source are *spontaneous* in the sense that an increase in sales will automatically generate additional credit.

COST OF RECEIVABLES FINANCING.   Both accounts receivable pledging and factoring are convenient and advantageous, but they can be costly. The credit-checking and risk-bearing fee is 1 to 3 percent of the amount of invoices accepted by the factor, and it may be even more if the buyers are poor credit risks. The cost of money is reflected in the interest rate (usually 2 to 3 percentage points over the prime rate) charged on the unpaid balance of the funds advanced by the factor.

EVALUATION OF RECEIVABLES FINANCING.   It cannot be said categorically that accounts receivable financing is always either a good or a poor way to raise funds. Among the advantages is, first, the flexibility of this source of financing: As the firm's sales expand, more financing is needed, but a larger volume of invoices, and hence a larger amount of receivables financing, is generated automatically. Second, receivables can be used as security for loans that would not otherwise be granted. Third, factoring can provide the services of a credit department that might otherwise be available only at a higher cost.

Accounts receivable financing also has disadvantages. First, when invoices are numerous and relatively small in dollar amount, the administrative costs involved may be excessive. Second, since receivables represent the firm's most liquid noncash assets, some trade creditors may refuse to sell on credit to a firm that factors or pledges its receivables on the grounds that this practice weakens the position of other creditors.

FUTURE USE OF RECEIVABLES FINANCING.   We may make a prediction at this point: In the future, accounts receivable financing will increase in relative importance. Computer technology is rapidly advancing toward the point where credit records of individuals and firms can be kept on disks and magnetic tapes. For example, one device used by retailers consists of a box which, when an individual's magnetic credit card is inserted, gives a signal that the credit is "good" and that a bank is willing to "buy" the receivable created as soon as the store completes the sale. The cost of handling invoices will be greatly reduced over present-day costs because the new systems will be so highly automated. This will make it possible to use accounts receivable financing for very small sales, and it will reduce the cost of all receivables financing. The net result will be a marked expansion of accounts receivable financing. In fact, when consumers use credit cards such as MasterCard or Visa, the seller is in effect factoring receivables. The seller receives the amount of the purchase, minus a percentage fee, the next working day. The buyer receives 30 days' (or so) credit, at which time he or she remits payment directly to the credit card company or sponsoring bank.

---

[1]Since the interest is only for 1 month, we multiply 1/12 of the quoted rate (9 percent) by the $10,000 invoice price:

$$(1/12)(0.09)(\$10,000) = \$75.$$

The effective annual interest rate is above 9 percent because (1) the term is for less than 1 year and (2) a discounting procedure is used and the borrower does not get the full $10,000. In many instances, however, the factoring contract calls for interest to be calculated on the invoice price minus the factoring commission and the reserve account.

INVENTORY FINANCING

A substantial amount of credit is secured by business inventories. If a firm is a relatively good credit risk, the mere existence of the inventory may be a sufficient basis for receiving an unsecured loan. However, if the firm is a relatively poor risk, the lending institution may insist upon security in the form of a *lien* against the inventory. Methods for using inventories as security are discussed in this section.

BLANKET LIENS.   The *inventory blanket lien* gives the lending institution a lien against all of the borrower's inventories. However, the borrower is free to sell inventories, and thus the value of the collateral can be reduced below the level that existed when the loan was granted.

TRUST RECEIPTS.   Because of the inherent weakness of the blanket lien, another procedure for inventory financing has been developed — the *trust receipt,* which is an instrument acknowledging that the goods are held in trust for the lender. Under this method, the borrowing firm, as a condition for receiving funds from the lender, signs and delivers a trust receipt for the goods. The goods can be stored in a public warehouse or held on the premises of the borrower. The trust receipt states that the goods are held in trust for the lender or are segregated on the borrower's premises on the lender's behalf, and that any proceeds from the sale of the goods must be transmitted to the lender at the end of each day. Automobile dealer financing is one of the best examples of trust receipt financing.

One defect of trust receipt financing is the requirement that a trust receipt be issued for specific goods. For example, if the security is autos in a dealer's inventory, the trust receipts must indicate the cars by registration number. In order to validate its trust receipts, the lending institution must send someone to the borrower's premises periodically to see that the auto numbers are correctly listed because auto dealers who are in financial difficulty have been known to sell cars backing trust receipts and then use the funds obtained for other operations rather than to repay the bank. Problems are compounded if the borrower has a number of different locations, especially if they are separated geographically from the lender. To offset these inconveniences, *warehousing* has come into wide use as a method of securing loans with inventory.

WAREHOUSE RECEIPTS.   *Warehouse receipt financing* is another way to use inventory as security. It is a method of financing which uses inventory as a security and which requires public notification, physical control of the inventory, and supervision by a custodian of the field warehousing concern. A *public warehouse* is an independent third-party operation engaged in the business of storing goods. Items which must age, such as tobacco and liquor, are often financed and stored in public warehouses. Sometimes a public warehouse is not practical because of the bulkiness of goods and the expense of transporting them to and from the borrower's premises. In such cases, a *field warehouse* may be established on the borrower's grounds. To provide inventory supervision, the lending institution employs a third party in the arrangement, the field warehousing company, which acts as its agent.

Field warehousing can be illustrated by a simple example. Suppose a firm which has iron stacked in an open yard on its premises needs a loan. A field warehousing concern can place a temporary fence around the iron, erect a sign stating "This is a field warehouse supervised by the Smith Field Warehousing Corporation," and then assign an employee to supervise and control the fenced-in inventory.

This example illustrates the three essential elements for the establishment of a field warehouse: (1) public notification, (2) physical control of the inventory, and (3) supervision by a custodian of the field warehousing concern. When the field warehousing operation is relatively small, the third condition is sometimes violated by hiring an employee of the borrower to supervise the inventory. This practice is viewed as undesirable by most lenders because there is no control over the collateral by a person independent of the borrowing firm.[2]

The field warehouse financing operation is best described by an actual case. A California tomato cannery was interested in financing its operations by bank borrowing. It had sufficient funds to finance 15 to 20 percent of its operations during the canning season. These funds were adequate to purchase and process an initial batch of tomatoes. As the cans were put into boxes and rolled into the storerooms, the cannery needed additional funds for both raw materials and labor. Because of the cannery's poor credit rating, the bank decided that a field warehousing operation was necessary to secure its loans.

The field warehouse was established, and the custodian notified the bank of the description, by number, of the boxes of canned tomatoes in storage and under warehouse control. With this inventory as collateral, the lending institution established for the cannery a deposit on which it could draw. From this point on, the bank financed the operations. The cannery needed only enough

---

[2]This absence of independent control was the main cause of the breakdown that resulted in more than $200 million of losses on loans to the Allied Crude Vegetable Oil Company by Bank of America and other banks. American Express Field Warehousing Company was handling the operation, but it hired men from Allied's own staff as custodians. Their dishonesty was not discovered because of another breakdown — the fact that the American Express touring inspector did not actually take a physical inventory of the warehouses. As a consequence, the swindle was not discovered until losses running into the hundreds of millions of dollars had been suffered.

cash to initiate the cycle. The farmers brought in more tomatoes; the cannery processed them; the cans were boxed; the boxes were put into the field warehouse; field warehouse receipts were drawn up and sent to the bank; the bank established further deposits for the cannery on the basis of the additional collateral, and the cannery could draw on the deposits to continue the cycle.

Of course, the cannery's ultimate objective was to sell the canned tomatoes. As it received purchase orders, it transmitted them to the bank, and the bank directed the custodian to release the inventories. It was agreed that as remittances were received by the cannery, they would be turned over to the bank. These remittances thus paid off the loans.

Note that a seasonal pattern existed. At the beginning of the tomato harvesting and canning season, the cannery's cash needs and loan requirements began to rise, and they reached a peak just as the season ended. It was expected that well before the new canning season began, the cannery would have sold a sufficient volume to pay off the loan. If the cannery had experienced a bad year, the bank might have carried the loan over for another year to enable the company to work off its inventory.

ACCEPTABLE PRODUCTS.   In addition to canned foods, which account for about 17 percent of all field warehouse loans, many other types of products provide a basis for field warehouse financing. Some of these are miscellaneous groceries, which represent about 13 percent; lumber products, about 10 percent; and coal and coke, about 6 percent. These products are relatively nonperishable and are sold in well-developed, organized markets. Nonperishability protects the lender if it should have to take over the security. For this reason, a bank would not make a field warehousing loan on perishables such as fresh fish, but frozen fish, which can be stored for a long time, can be field warehoused.

COST OF FINANCING.   The fixed costs of a field warehousing arrangement are relatively high; such financing is therefore not suitable for a very small firm. If a field warehousing company sets up a field warehouse, it will typically set a minimum charge of about $5,000 per year, plus about 1 to 2 percent of the amount of credit extended to the borrower. Furthermore, the financing institution will charge an interest rate of two to three percentage points over the prime rate. An efficient field warehousing operation requires a minimum inventory of at least $1 million.

EVALUATION OF INVENTORY FINANCING.   The use of inventory financing, especially field warehouse financing, as a source of funds has many advantages. First, the amount of funds available is flexible because the financing is tied to inventory growth, which in turn is related directly to financing needs. Second, the field warehousing arrangement increases the acceptability of inventories as loan collateral; some inventories simply would not be accepted by a bank as security without such an arrangement. Third, the necessity for inventory control and safekeeping, as well as the use of specialists in warehousing, often results in improved warehouse practices, which in turn save handling costs, insurance charges, theft losses, and so on. Thus, field warehousing companies often save money for firms in spite of the costs of financing that we have discussed. The major disadvantages of field warehousing include the paperwork, physical separation requirements, and, for small firms, the fixed-cost element.

PROBLEMS

16A-1 Receivables financing Finnerty's Funtime Company manufactures plastic toys. It buys raw materials, manufactures the toys in the spring and summer, and ships them to department stores and toy stores by late summer or early fall. Funtime factors its receivables; if it did not, its October 1995 balance sheet would appear as follows (thousands of dollars):

Cash	$ 40	Accounts payable	$1,200
Receivables	1,200	Notes payable	800
Inventory	800	Accruals	80
Current assets	$2,040	Current liabilities	$2,080
		Mortgages	200
		Common stock	400
Fixed assets	800	Retained earnings	160
Total assets	$2,840	Total liabilities and equity	$2,840

Funtime provides extended credit to its customers, so its receivables are not due for payment until January 31, 1996. Also, Funtime would have been overdue on some $800,000 of its accounts payable if the preceding situation had actually existed.

Funtime has an agreement with a finance company to factor the receivables for the period October 31 through January 31 of each selling season. The factoring company charges a flat commission of 2 percent of the invoice price, plus 6 percent per year interest on the outstanding balance; it deducts a reserve of 8 percent for returned and damaged materials. Interest and commissions are paid in advance. No interest is charged on the reserved funds or on the commission.

a. Show Funtime's balance sheet on October 31, 1995, including the purchase of all the receivables by the factoring company and the use of the funds to pay accounts payable.

b. If the $1.2 million is the average level of outstanding receivables, and if they turn over 4 times a year (hence the commission is paid 4 times a year), what are the total dollar costs of receivables financing (factoring) and the effective annual interest rate?

16A-2 Factoring arrangement Merville Industries needs an additional $500,000, which it plans to obtain through a factoring arrangement. The factor would purchase Merville's accounts receivable and advance the invoice amount, minus a 2 percent commission, on the invoices purchased each month. Merville sells on terms of net 30 days. In addition, the factor charges a 12 percent annual interest rate on the total invoice amount, to be deducted in advance.

a. What amount of accounts receivable must be factored to net $500,000?

b. If Merville can reduce credit expenses by $3,500 per month and avoid bad debt losses of 2.5 percent on the factored amount, what is the total dollar cost of the factoring arrangement?

c. What would be the total cost of the factoring arrangement if Merville's funds needed rose to $750,000? Would the factoring arrangement be profitable under these circumstances?

16A-3 Field warehousing arrangement Because of crop failures last year, the San Joaquin Packing Company has no funds available to finance its canning operations during the next 6 months. It estimates that it will require $1,200,000 from inventory financing during the period. One alternative is to establish a 6-month, $1,500,000 line of credit with terms of 9 percent annual interest on the used portion, a 1 percent commitment fee on the unused portion, and a $300,000 compensating balance at all times. The other alternative is to use field warehouse financing. The costs of the field warehouse arrangement in this case would be a flat fee of $2,000, plus 8 percent annual interest on all outstanding credit, plus 1 percent of the maximum amount of credit extended.

Expected inventory levels to be financed are as follows:

MONTH	AMOUNT
July 1996	$ 250,000
August	1,000,000
September	1,200,000
October	950,000
November	600,000
December	0

a. Calculate the cost of funds from using the line of credit. Be sure to include interest charges and commitment fees. Note that each month's borrowings will be $300,000 greater than the inventory level to be financed because of the compensating balance requirement.

b. Calculate the total cost of the field warehousing operation.

c. Compare the cost of the field warehousing arrangement to the cost of the line of credit. Which alternative should San Joaquin choose?

APPENDIX A

MATHEMATICAL TABLES

| TABLE A-1 | | PRESENT VALUE OF $1 DUE AT THE END OF n PERIODS | | | | | | | | |

Equation:

Financial Calculator Keys:

$$PVIF_{i,n} = \frac{1}{(1 + i)^n}$$

| n | i | | 0 | 1.0 |
| N | I | PV | PMT | FV |

TABLE
VALUE

PERIOD	1%	2%	3%	4%	5%	6%	7%	8%	9%	10%
1	.9901	.9804	.9709	.9615	.9524	.9434	.9346	.9259	.9174	.9091
2	.9803	.9612	.9426	.9246	.9070	.8900	.8734	.8573	.8417	.8264
3	.9706	.9423	.9151	.8890	.8638	.8396	.8163	.7938	.7722	.7513
4	.9610	.9238	.8885	.8548	.8227	.7921	.7629	.7350	.7084	.6830
5	.9515	.9057	.8626	.8219	.7835	.7473	.7130	.6806	.6499	.6209
6	.9420	.8880	.8375	.7903	.7462	.7050	.6663	.6302	.5963	.5645
7	.9327	.8706	.8131	.7599	.7107	.6651	.6227	.5835	.5470	.5132
8	.9235	.8535	.7894	.7307	.6768	.6274	.5820	.5403	.5019	.4665
9	.9143	.8368	.7664	.7026	.6446	.5919	.5439	.5002	.4604	.4241
10	.9053	.8203	.7441	.6756	.6139	.5584	.5083	.4632	.4224	.3855
11	.8963	.8043	.7224	.6496	.5847	.5268	.4751	.4289	.3875	.3505
12	.8874	.7885	.7014	.6246	.5568	.4970	.4440	.3971	.3555	.3186
13	.8787	.7730	.6810	.6006	.5303	.4688	.4150	.3677	.3262	.2897
14	.8700	.7579	.6611	.5775	.5051	.4423	.3878	.3405	.2992	.2633
15	.8613	.7430	.6419	.5553	.4810	.4173	.3624	.3152	.2745	.2394
16	.8528	.7284	.6232	.5339	.4581	.3936	.3387	.2919	.2519	.2176
17	.8444	.7142	.6050	.5134	.4363	.3714	.3166	.2703	.2311	.1978
18	.8360	.7002	.5874	.4936	.4155	.3503	.2959	.2502	.2120	.1799
19	.8277	.6864	.5703	.4746	.3957	.3305	.2765	.2317	.1945	.1635
20	.8195	.6730	.5537	.4564	.3769	.3118	.2584	.2145	.1784	.1486
21	.8114	.6598	.5375	.4388	.3589	.2942	.2415	.1987	.1637	.1351
22	.8034	.6468	.5219	.4220	.3418	.2775	.2257	.1839	.1502	.1228
23	.7954	.6342	.5067	.4057	.3256	.2618	.2109	.1703	.1378	.1117
24	.7876	.6217	.4919	.3901	.3101	.2470	.1971	.1577	.1264	.1015
25	.7798	.6095	.4776	.3751	.2953	.2330	.1842	.1460	.1160	.0923
26	.7720	.5976	.4637	.3607	.2812	.2198	.1722	.1352	.1064	.0839
27	.7644	.5859	.4502	.3468	.2678	.2074	.1609	.1252	.0976	.0763
28	.7568	.5744	.4371	.3335	.2551	.1956	.1504	.1159	.0895	.0693
29	.7493	.5631	.4243	.3207	.2429	.1846	.1406	.1073	.0822	.0630
30	.7419	.5521	.4120	.3083	.2314	.1741	.1314	.0994	.0754	.0573
35	.7059	.5000	.3554	.2534	.1813	.1301	.0937	.0676	.0490	.0356
40	.6717	.4529	.3066	.2083	.1420	.0972	.0668	.0460	.0318	.0221
45	.6391	.4102	.2644	.1712	.1113	.0727	.0476	.0313	.0207	.0137
50	.6080	.3715	.2281	.1407	.0872	.0543	.0339	.0213	.0134	.0085
55	.5785	.3365	.1968	.1157	.0683	.0406	.0242	.0145	.0087	.0053

TABLE A-1 CONTINUED

PERIOD	12%	14%	15%	16%	18%	20%	24%	28%	32%	36%
1	.8929	.8772	.8696	.8621	.8475	.8333	.8065	.7813	.7576	.7353
2	.7972	.7695	.7561	.7432	.7182	.6944	.6504	.6104	.5739	.5407
3	.7118	.6750	.6575	.6407	.6086	.5787	.5245	.4768	.4348	.3975
4	.6355	.5921	.5718	.5523	.5158	.4823	.4230	.3725	.3294	.2923
5	.5674	.5194	.4972	.4761	.4371	.4019	.3411	.2910	.2495	.2149
6	.5066	.4556	.4323	.4104	.3704	.3349	.2751	.2274	.1890	.1580
7	.4523	.3996	.3759	.3538	.3139	.2791	.2218	.1776	.1432	.1162
8	.4039	.3506	.3269	.3050	.2660	.2326	.1789	.1388	.1085	.0854
9	.3606	.3075	.2843	.2630	.2255	.1938	.1443	.1084	.0822	.0628
10	.3220	.2697	.2472	.2267	.1911	.1615	.1164	.0847	.0623	.0462
11	.2875	.2366	.2149	.1954	.1619	.1346	.0938	.0662	.0472	.0340
12	.2567	.2076	.1869	.1685	.1372	.1122	.0757	.0517	.0357	.0250
13	.2292	.1821	.1625	.1452	.1163	.0935	.0610	.0404	.0271	.0184
14	.2046	.1597	.1413	.1252	.0985	.0779	.0492	.0316	.0205	.0135
15	.1827	.1401	.1229	.1079	.0835	.0649	.0397	.0247	.0155	.0099
16	.1631	.1229	.1069	.0930	.0708	.0541	.0320	.0193	.0118	.0073
17	.1456	.1078	.0929	.0802	.0600	.0451	.0258	.0150	.0089	.0054
18	.1300	.0946	.0808	.0691	.0508	.0376	.0208	.0118	.0068	.0039
19	.1161	.0829	.0703	.0596	.0431	.0313	.0168	.0092	.0051	.0029
20	.1037	.0728	.0611	.0514	.0365	.0261	.0135	.0072	.0039	.0021
21	.0926	.0638	.0531	.0443	.0309	.0217	.0109	.0056	.0029	.0016
22	.0826	.0560	.0462	.0382	.0262	.0181	.0088	.0044	.0022	.0012
23	.0738	.0491	.0402	.0329	.0222	.0151	.0071	.0034	.0017	.0008
24	.0659	.0431	.0349	.0284	.0188	.0126	.0057	.0027	.0013	.0006
25	.0588	.0378	.0304	.0245	.0160	.0105	.0046	.0021	.0010	.0005
26	.0525	.0331	.0264	.0211	.0135	.0087	.0037	.0016	.0007	.0003
27	.0469	.0291	.0230	.0182	.0115	.0073	.0030	.0013	.0006	.0002
28	.0419	.0255	.0200	.0157	.0097	.0061	.0024	.0010	.0004	.0002
29	.0374	.0224	.0174	.0135	.0082	.0051	.0020	.0008	.0003	.0001
30	.0334	.0196	.0151	.0116	.0070	.0042	.0016	.0006	.0002	.0001
35	.0189	.0102	.0075	.0055	.0030	.0017	.0005	.0002	.0001	*
40	.0107	.0053	.0037	.0026	.0013	.0007	.0002	.0001	*	*
45	.0061	.0027	.0019	.0013	.0006	.0003	.0001	*	*	*
50	.0035	.0014	.0009	.0006	.0003	.0001	*	*	*	*
55	.0020	.0007	.0005	.0003	.0001	*	*	*	*	*

*The factor is zero to four decimal places.

TABLE A-2	**PRESENT VALUE OF AN ANNUITY OF $1 PER PERIOD FOR n PERIODS**

Equation:

Financial Calculator Keys:

$$PVIFA_{i,n} = \sum_{t=1}^{n} \frac{1}{(1+i)^t} = \frac{1 - \dfrac{1}{(1+i)^n}}{i} = \frac{1}{i} - \frac{1}{i(1+i)^n}$$

n   i   1.0   0

N   **I**   **PV**   **PMT**   **FV**

TABLE VALUE

NUMBER OF PERIODS	1%	2%	3%	4%	5%	6%	7%	8%	9%
1	0.9901	0.9804	0.9709	0.9615	0.9524	0.9434	0.9346	0.9259	0.9174
2	1.9704	1.9416	1.9135	1.8861	1.8594	1.8334	1.8080	1.7833	1.7591
3	2.9410	2.8839	2.8286	2.7751	2.7232	2.6730	2.6243	2.5771	2.5313
4	3.9020	3.8077	3.7171	3.6299	3.5460	3.4651	3.3872	3.3121	3.2397
5	4.8534	4.7135	4.5797	4.4518	4.3295	4.2124	4.1002	3.9927	3.8897
6	5.7955	5.6014	5.4172	5.2421	5.0757	4.9173	4.7665	4.6229	4.4859
7	6.7282	6.4720	6.2303	6.0021	5.7864	5.5824	5.3893	5.2064	5.0330
8	7.6517	7.3255	7.0197	6.7327	6.4632	6.2098	5.9713	5.7466	5.5348
9	8.5660	8.1622	7.7861	7.4353	7.1078	6.8017	6.5152	6.2469	5.9952
10	9.4713	8.9826	8.5302	8.1109	7.7217	7.3601	7.0236	6.7101	6.4177
11	10.3676	9.7868	9.2526	8.7605	8.3064	7.8869	7.4987	7.1390	6.8052
12	11.2551	10.5753	9.9540	9.3851	8.8633	8.3838	7.9427	7.5361	7.1607
13	12.1337	11.3484	10.6350	9.9856	9.3936	8.8527	8.3577	7.9038	7.4869
14	13.0037	12.1062	11.2961	10.5631	9.8986	9.2950	8.7455	8.2442	7.7862
15	13.8651	12.8493	11.9379	11.1184	10.3797	9.7122	9.1079	8.5595	8.0607
16	14.7179	13.5777	12.5611	11.6523	10.8378	10.1059	9.4466	8.8514	8.3126
17	15.5623	14.2919	13.1661	12.1657	11.2741	10.4773	9.7632	9.1216	8.5436
18	16.3983	14.9920	13.7535	12.6593	11.6896	10.8276	10.0591	9.3719	8.7556
19	17.2260	15.6785	14.3238	13.1339	12.0853	11.1581	10.3356	9.6036	8.9501
20	18.0456	16.3514	14.8775	13.5903	12.4622	11.4699	10.5940	9.8181	9.1285
21	18.8570	17.0112	15.4150	14.0292	12.8212	11.7641	10.8355	10.0168	9.2922
22	19.6604	17.6580	15.9369	14.4511	13.1630	12.0416	11.0612	10.2007	9.4424
23	20.4558	18.2922	16.4436	14.8568	13.4886	12.3034	11.2722	10.3711	9.5802
24	21.2434	18.9139	16.9355	15.2470	13.7986	12.5504	11.4693	10.5288	9.7066
25	22.0232	19.5235	17.4131	15.6221	14.0939	12.7834	11.6536	10.6748	9.8226
26	22.7952	20.1210	17.8768	15.9828	14.3752	13.0032	11.8258	10.8100	9.9290
27	23.5596	20.7069	18.3270	16.3296	14.6430	13.2105	11.9867	10.9352	10.0266
28	24.3164	21.2813	18.7641	16.6631	14.8981	13.4062	12.1371	11.0511	10.1161
29	25.0658	21.8444	19.1885	16.9837	15.1411	13.5907	12.2777	11.1584	10.1983
30	25.8077	22.3965	19.6004	17.2920	15.3725	13.7648	12.4090	11.2578	10.2737
35	29.4086	24.9986	21.4872	18.6646	16.3742	14.4982	12.9477	11.6546	10.5668
40	32.8347	27.3555	23.1148	19.7928	17.1591	15.0463	13.3317	11.9246	10.7574
45	36.0945	29.4902	24.5187	20.7200	17.7741	15.4558	13.6055	12.1084	10.8812
50	39.1961	31.4236	25.7298	21.4822	18.2559	15.7619	13.8007	12.2335	10.9617
55	42.1472	33.1748	26.7744	22.1086	18.6335	15.9905	13.9399	12.3186	11.0140

TABLE A - 2   CONTINUED

Number of Periods	10%	12%	14%	15%	16%	18%	20%	24%	28%	32%
1	0.9091	0.8929	0.8772	0.8696	0.8621	0.8475	0.8333	0.8065	0.7813	0.7576
2	1.7355	1.6901	1.6467	1.6257	1.6052	1.5656	1.5278	1.4568	1.3916	1.3315
3	2.4869	2.4018	2.3216	2.2832	2.2459	2.1743	2.1065	1.9813	1.8684	1.7663
4	3.1699	3.0373	2.9137	2.8550	2.7982	2.6901	2.5887	2.4043	2.2410	2.0957
5	3.7908	3.6048	3.4331	3.3522	3.2743	3.1272	2.9906	2.7454	2.5320	2.3452
6	4.3553	4.1114	3.8887	3.7845	3.6847	3.4976	3.3255	3.0205	2.7594	2.5342
7	4.8684	4.5638	4.2883	4.1604	4.0386	3.8115	3.6046	3.2423	2.9370	2.6775
8	5.3349	4.9676	4.6389	4.4873	4.3436	4.0776	3.8372	3.4212	3.0758	2.7860
9	5.7590	5.3282	4.9464	4.7716	4.6065	4.3030	4.0310	3.5655	3.1842	2.8681
10	6.1446	5.6502	5.2161	5.0188	4.8332	4.4941	4.1925	3.6819	3.2689	2.9304
11	6.4951	5.9377	5.4527	5.2337	5.0286	4.6560	4.3271	3.7757	3.3351	2.9776
12	6.8137	6.1944	5.6603	5.4206	5.1971	4.7932	4.4392	3.8514	3.3868	3.0133
13	7.1034	6.4235	5.8424	5.5831	5.3423	4.9095	4.5327	3.9124	3.4272	3.0404
14	7.3667	6.6282	6.0021	5.7245	5.4675	5.0081	4.6106	3.9616	3.4587	3.0609
15	7.6061	6.8109	6.1422	5.8474	5.5755	5.0916	4.6755	4.0013	3.4834	3.0764
16	7.8237	6.9740	6.2651	5.9542	5.6685	5.1624	4.7296	4.0333	3.5026	3.0882
17	8.0216	7.1196	6.3729	6.0472	5.7487	5.2223	4.7746	4.0591	3.5177	3.0971
18	8.2014	7.2497	6.4674	6.1280	5.8178	5.2732	4.8122	4.0799	3.5294	3.1039
19	8.3649	7.3658	6.5504	6.1982	5.8775	5.3162	4.8435	4.0967	3.5386	3.1090
20	8.5136	7.4694	6.6231	6.2593	5.9288	5.3527	4.8696	4.1103	3.5458	3.1129
21	8.6487	7.5620	6.6870	6.3125	5.9731	5.3837	4.8913	4.1212	3.5514	3.1158
22	8.7715	7.6446	6.7429	6.3587	6.0113	5.4099	4.9094	4.1300	3.5558	3.1180
23	8.8832	7.7184	6.7921	6.3988	6.0442	5.4321	4.9245	4.1371	3.5592	3.1197
24	8.9847	7.7843	6.8351	6.4338	6.0726	5.4509	4.9371	4.1428	3.5619	3.1210
25	9.0770	7.8431	6.8729	6.4641	6.0971	5.4669	4.9476	4.1474	3.5640	3.1220
26	9.1609	7.8957	6.9061	6.4906	6.1182	5.4804	4.9563	4.1511	3.5656	3.1227
27	9.2372	7.9426	6.9352	6.5135	6.1364	5.4919	4.9636	4.1542	3.5669	3.1233
28	9.3066	7.9844	6.9607	6.5335	6.1520	5.5016	4.9697	4.1566	3.5679	3.1237
29	9.3696	8.0218	6.9830	6.5509	6.1656	5.5098	4.9747	4.1585	3.5687	3.1240
30	9.4269	8.0552	7.0027	6.5660	6.1772	5.5168	4.9789	4.1601	3.5693	3.1242
35	9.6442	8.1755	7.0700	6.6166	6.2153	5.5386	4.9915	4.1644	3.5708	3.1248
40	9.7791	8.2438	7.1050	6.6418	6.2335	5.5482	4.9966	4.1659	3.5712	3.1250
45	9.8628	8.2825	7.1232	6.6543	6.2421	5.5523	4.9986	4.1664	3.5714	3.1250
50	9.9148	8.3045	7.1327	6.6605	6.2463	5.5541	4.9995	4.1666	3.5714	3.1250
55	9.9471	8.3170	7.1376	6.6636	6.2482	5.5549	4.9998	4.1666	3.5714	3.1250

TABLE A - 3   FUTURE VALUE OF $1 AT THE END OF n PERIODS

Equation: Financial Calculator Keys:

$$FVIF_{i,n} = (1 + i)^n$$

	n	i	1.0	0	
	N	**I**	**PV**	**PMT**	**FV**

TABLE
VALUE

Period	1%	2%	3%	4%	5%	6%	7%	8%	9%	10%
1	1.0100	1.0200	1.0300	1.0400	1.0500	1.0600	1.0700	1.0800	1.0900	1.1000
2	1.0201	1.0404	1.0609	1.0816	1.1025	1.1236	1.1449	1.1664	1.1881	1.2100
3	1.0303	1.0612	1.0927	1.1249	1.1576	1.1910	1.2250	1.2597	1.2950	1.3310
4	1.0406	1.0824	1.1255	1.1699	1.2155	1.2625	1.3108	1.3605	1.4116	1.4641
5	1.0510	1.1041	1.1593	1.2167	1.2763	1.3382	1.4026	1.4693	1.5386	1.6105
6	1.0615	1.1262	1.1941	1.2653	1.3401	1.4185	1.5007	1.5869	1.6771	1.7716
7	1.0721	1.1487	1.2299	1.3159	1.4071	1.5036	1.6058	1.7138	1.8280	1.9487
8	1.0829	1.1717	1.2668	1.3686	1.4775	1.5938	1.7182	1.8509	1.9926	2.1436
9	1.0937	1.1951	1.3048	1.4233	1.5513	1.6895	1.8385	1.9990	2.1719	2.3579
10	1.1046	1.2190	1.3439	1.4802	1.6289	1.7908	1.9672	2.1589	2.3674	2.5937
11	1.1157	1.2434	1.3842	1.5395	1.7103	1.8983	2.1049	2.3316	2.5804	2.8531
12	1.1268	1.2682	1.4258	1.6010	1.7959	2.0122	2.2522	2.5182	2.8127	3.1384
13	1.1381	1.2936	1.4685	1.6651	1.8856	2.1329	2.4098	2.7196	3.0658	3.4523
14	1.1495	1.3195	1.5126	1.7317	1.9799	2.2609	2.5785	2.9372	3.3417	3.7975
15	1.1610	1.3459	1.5580	1.8009	2.0789	2.3966	2.7590	3.1722	3.6425	4.1772
16	1.1726	1.3728	1.6047	1.8730	2.1829	2.5404	2.9522	3.4259	3.9703	4.5950
17	1.1843	1.4002	1.6528	1.9479	2.2920	2.6928	3.1588	3.7000	4.3276	5.0545
18	1.1961	1.4282	1.7024	2.0258	2.4066	2.8543	3.3799	3.9960	4.7171	5.5599
19	1.2081	1.4568	1.7535	2.1068	2.5270	3.0256	3.6165	4.3157	5.1417	6.1159
20	1.2202	1.4859	1.8061	2.1911	2.6533	3.2071	3.8697	4.6610	5.6044	6.7275
21	1.2324	1.5157	1.8603	2.2788	2.7860	3.3996	4.1406	5.0338	6.1088	7.4002
22	1.2447	1.5460	1.9161	2.3699	2.9253	3.6035	4.4304	5.4365	6.6586	8.1403
23	1.2572	1.5769	1.9736	2.4647	3.0715	3.8197	4.7405	5.8715	7.2579	8.9543
24	1.2697	1.6084	2.0328	2.5633	3.2251	4.0489	5.0724	6.3412	7.9111	9.8497
25	1.2824	1.6406	2.0938	2.6658	3.3864	4.2919	5.4274	6.8485	8.6231	10.835
26	1.2953	1.6734	2.1566	2.7725	3.5557	4.5494	5.8074	7.3964	9.3992	11.918
27	1.3082	1.7069	2.2213	2.8834	3.7335	4.8223	6.2139	7.9881	10.245	13.110
28	1.3213	1.7410	2.2879	2.9987	3.9201	5.1117	6.6488	8.6271	11.167	14.421
29	1.3345	1.7758	2.3566	3.1187	4.1161	5.4184	7.1143	9.3173	12.172	15.863
30	1.3478	1.8114	2.4273	3.2434	4.3219	5.7435	7.6123	10.063	13.268	17.449
40	1.4889	2.2080	3.2620	4.8010	7.0400	10.286	14.974	21.725	31.409	45.259
50	1.6446	2.6916	4.3839	7.1067	11.467	18.420	29.457	46.902	74.358	117.39
60	1.8167	3.2810	5.8916	10.520	18.679	32.988	57.946	101.26	176.03	304.48

TABLE A-3   CONTINUED

PERIOD	12%	14%	15%	16%	18%	20%	24%	28%	32%	36%
1	1.1200	1.1400	1.1500	1.1600	1.1800	1.2000	1.2400	1.2800	1.3200	1.3600
2	1.2544	1.2996	1.3225	1.3456	1.3924	1.4400	1.5376	1.6384	1.7424	1.8496
3	1.4049	1.4815	1.5209	1.5609	1.6430	1.7280	1.9066	2.0972	2.3000	2.5155
4	1.5735	1.6890	1.7490	1.8106	1.9388	2.0736	2.3642	2.6844	3.0360	3.4210
5	1.7623	1.9254	2.0114	2.1003	2.2878	2.4883	2.9316	3.4360	4.0075	4.6526
6	1.9738	2.1950	2.3131	2.4364	2.6996	2.9860	3.6352	4.3980	5.2899	6.3275
7	2.2107	2.5023	2.6600	2.8262	3.1855	3.5832	4.5077	5.6295	6.9826	8.6054
8	2.4760	2.8526	3.0590	3.2784	3.7589	4.2998	5.5895	7.2058	9.2170	11.703
9	2.7731	3.2519	3.5179	3.8030	4.4355	5.1598	6.9310	9.2234	12.166	15.917
10	3.1058	3.7072	4.0456	4.4114	5.2338	6.1917	8.5944	11.806	16.060	21.647
11	3.4785	4.2262	4.6524	5.1173	6.1759	7.4301	10.657	15.112	21.199	29.439
12	3.8960	4.8179	5.3503	5.9360	7.2876	8.9161	13.215	19.343	27.983	40.037
13	4.3635	5.4924	6.1528	6.8858	8.5994	10.699	16.386	24.759	36.937	54.451
14	4.8871	6.2613	7.0757	7.9875	10.147	12.839	20.319	31.691	48.757	74.053
15	5.4736	7.1379	8.1371	9.2655	11.974	15.407	25.196	40.565	64.359	100.71
16	6.1304	8.1372	9.3576	10.748	14.129	18.488	31.243	51.923	84.954	136.97
17	6.8660	9.2765	10.761	12.468	16.672	22.186	38.741	66.461	112.14	186.28
18	7.6900	10.575	12.375	14.463	19.673	26.623	48.039	85.071	148.02	253.34
19	8.6128	12.056	14.232	16.777	23.214	31.948	59.568	108.89	195.39	344.54
20	9.6463	13.743	16.367	19.461	27.393	38.338	73.864	139.38	257.92	468.57
21	10.804	15.668	18.822	22.574	32.324	46.005	91.592	178.41	340.45	637.26
22	12.100	17.861	21.645	26.186	38.142	55.206	113.57	228.36	449.39	866.67
23	13.552	20.362	24.891	30.376	45.008	66.247	140.83	292.30	593.20	1178.7
24	15.179	23.212	28.625	35.236	53.109	79.497	174.63	374.14	783.02	1603.0
25	17.000	26.462	32.919	40.874	62.669	95.396	216.54	478.90	1033.6	2180.1
26	19.040	30.167	37.857	47.414	73.949	114.48	268.51	613.00	1364.3	2964.9
27	21.325	34.390	43.535	55.000	87.260	137.37	332.95	784.64	1800.9	4032.3
28	23.884	39.204	50.066	63.800	102.97	164.84	412.86	1004.3	2377.2	5483.9
29	26.750	44.693	57.575	74.009	121.50	197.81	511.95	1285.6	3137.9	7458.1
30	29.960	50.950	66.212	85.850	143.37	237.38	634.82	1645.5	4142.1	10143.
40	93.051	188.88	267.86	378.72	750.38	1469.8	5455.9	19427.	66521.	*
50	289.00	700.23	1083.7	1670.7	3927.4	9100.4	46890.	*	*	*
60	897.60	2595.9	4384.0	7370.2	20555.	56348.	*	*	*	*

*FVIF > 99,999.

TABLE A-4	FUTURE VALUE OF AN ANNUITY OF $1 PER PERIOD FOR n PERIODS

Equation:

$$FVIFA_{i,n} = \sum_{t=1}^{n} (1 + i)^{n-t} = \frac{(1 + i)^n - 1}{i}$$

Financial Calculator Keys:

n   i   0   1.0

[N]   [I]   [PV]   [PMT]   [FV]

TABLE
VALUE

NUMBER OF PERIODS	1%	2%	3%	4%	5%	6%	7%	8%	9%	10%
1	1.0000	1.0000	1.0000	1.0000	1.0000	1.0000	1.0000	1.0000	1.0000	1.0000
2	2.0100	2.0200	2.0300	2.0400	2.0500	2.0600	2.0700	2.0800	2.0900	2.1000
3	3.0301	3.0604	3.0909	3.1216	3.1525	3.1836	3.2149	3.2464	3.2781	3.3100
4	4.0604	4.1216	4.1836	4.2465	4.3101	4.3746	4.4399	4.5061	4.5731	4.6410
5	5.1010	5.2040	5.3091	5.4163	5.5256	5.6371	5.7507	5.8666	5.9847	6.1051
6	6.1520	6.3081	6.4684	6.6330	6.8019	6.9753	7.1533	7.3359	7.5233	7.7156
7	7.2135	7.4343	7.6625	7.8983	8.1420	8.3938	8.6540	8.9228	9.2004	9.4872
8	8.2857	8.5830	8.8923	9.2142	9.5491	9.8975	10.260	10.637	11.028	11.436
9	9.3685	9.7546	10.159	10.583	11.027	11.491	11.978	12.488	13.021	13.579
10	10.462	10.950	11.464	12.006	12.578	13.181	13.816	14.487	15.193	15.937
11	11.567	12.169	12.808	13.486	14.207	14.972	15.784	16.645	17.560	18.531
12	12.683	13.412	14.192	15.026	15.917	16.870	17.888	18.977	20.141	21.384
13	13.809	14.680	15.618	16.627	17.713	18.882	20.141	21.495	22.953	24.523
14	14.947	15.974	17.086	18.292	19.599	21.015	22.550	24.215	26.019	27.975
15	16.097	17.293	18.599	20.024	21.579	23.276	25.129	27.152	29.361	31.772
16	17.258	18.639	20.157	21.825	23.657	25.673	27.888	30.324	33.003	35.950
17	18.430	20.012	21.762	23.698	25.840	28.213	30.840	33.750	36.974	40.545
18	19.615	21.412	23.414	25.645	28.132	30.906	33.999	37.450	41.301	45.599
19	20.811	22.841	25.117	27.671	30.539	33.760	37.379	41.446	46.018	51.159
20	22.019	24.297	26.870	29.778	33.066	36.786	40.995	45.762	51.160	57.275
21	23.239	25.783	28.676	31.969	35.719	39.993	44.865	50.423	56.765	64.002
22	24.472	27.299	30.537	34.248	38.505	43.392	49.006	55.457	62.873	71.403
23	25.716	28.845	32.453	36.618	41.430	46.996	53.436	60.893	69.532	79.543
24	26.973	30.422	34.426	39.083	44.502	50.816	58.177	66.765	76.790	88.497
25	28.243	32.030	36.459	41.646	47.727	54.865	63.249	73.106	84.701	98.347
26	29.526	33.671	38.553	44.312	51.113	59.156	68.676	79.954	93.324	109.18
27	30.821	35.344	40.710	47.084	54.669	63.706	74.484	87.351	102.72	121.10
28	32.129	37.051	42.931	49.968	58.403	68.528	80.698	95.339	112.97	134.21
29	33.450	38.792	45.219	52.966	62.323	73.640	87.347	103.97	124.14	148.63
30	34.785	40.568	47.575	56.085	66.439	79.058	94.461	113.28	136.31	164.49
40	48.886	60.402	75.401	95.026	120.80	154.76	199.64	259.06	337.88	442.59
50	64.463	84.579	112.80	152.67	209.35	290.34	406.53	573.77	815.08	1163.9
60	81.670	114.05	163.05	237.99	353.58	533.13	813.52	1253.2	1944.8	3034.8

TABLE   A-4   CONTINUED

NUMBER OF PERIODS	12%	14%	15%	16%	18%	20%	24%	28%	32%	36%
1	1.0000	1.0000	1.0000	1.0000	1.0000	1.0000	1.0000	1.0000	1.0000	1.0000
2	2.1200	2.1400	2.1500	2.1600	2.1800	2.2000	2.2400	2.2800	2.3200	2.3600
3	3.3744	3.4396	3.4725	3.5056	3.5724	3.6400	3.7776	3.9184	4.0624	4.2096
4	4.7793	4.9211	4.9934	5.0665	5.2154	5.3680	5.6842	6.0156	6.3624	6.7251
5	6.3528	6.6101	6.7424	6.8771	7.1542	7.4416	8.0484	8.6999	9.3983	10.146
6	8.1152	8.5355	8.7537	8.9775	9.4420	9.9299	10.980	12.136	13.406	14.799
7	10.089	10.730	11.067	11.414	12.142	12.916	14.615	16.534	18.696	21.126
8	12.300	13.233	13.727	14.240	15.327	16.499	19.123	22.163	25.678	29.732
9	14.776	16.085	16.786	17.519	19.086	20.799	24.712	29.369	34.895	41.435
10	17.549	19.337	20.304	21.321	23.521	25.959	31.643	38.593	47.062	57.352
11	20.655	23.045	24.349	25.733	28.755	32.150	40.238	50.398	63.122	78.998
12	24.133	27.271	29.002	30.850	34.931	39.581	50.895	65.510	84.320	108.44
13	28.029	32.089	34.352	36.786	42.219	48.497	64.110	84.853	112.30	148.47
14	32.393	37.581	40.505	43.672	50.818	59.196	80.496	109.61	149.24	202.93
15	37.280	43.842	47.580	51.660	60.965	72.035	100.82	141.30	198.00	276.98
16	42.753	50.980	55.717	60.925	72.939	87.442	126.01	181.87	262.36	377.69
17	48.884	59.118	65.075	71.673	87.068	105.93	157.25	233.79	347.31	514.66
18	55.750	68.394	75.836	84.141	103.74	128.12	195.99	300.25	459.45	700.94
19	63.440	78.969	88.212	98.603	123.41	154.74	244.03	385.32	607.47	954.28
20	72.052	91.025	102.44	115.38	146.63	186.69	303.60	494.21	802.86	1298.8
21	81.699	104.77	118.81	134.84	174.02	225.03	377.46	633.59	1060.8	1767.4
22	92.503	120.44	137.63	157.41	206.34	271.03	469.06	812.00	1401.2	2404.7
23	104.60	138.30	159.28	183.60	244.49	326.24	582.63	1040.4	1850.6	3271.3
24	118.16	158.66	184.17	213.98	289.49	392.48	723.46	1332.7	2443.8	4450.0
25	133.33	181.87	212.79	249.21	342.60	471.98	898.09	1706.8	3226.8	6053.0
26	150.33	208.33	245.71	290.09	405.27	567.38	1114.6	2185.7	4260.4	8233.1
27	169.37	238.50	283.57	337.50	479.22	681.85	1383.1	2798.7	5624.8	11198.0
28	190.70	272.89	327.10	392.50	566.48	819.22	1716.1	3583.3	7425.7	15230.3
29	214.58	312.09	377.17	456.30	669.45	984.07	2129.0	4587.7	9802.9	20714.2
30	241.33	356.79	434.75	530.31	790.95	1181.9	2640.9	5873.2	12941.	28172.3
40	767.09	1342.0	1779.1	2360.8	4163.2	7343.9	22729.	69377.	*	*
50	2400.0	4994.5	7217.7	10436.	21813.	45497.	*	*	*	*
60	7471.6	18535.	29220.	46058.	*	*	*	*	*	*

*FVIFA > 99,999.

APPENDIX B

SOLUTIONS TO SELF-TEST PROBLEMS

Note: Except for Chapter 1, we do not show an answer for ST-1 problems because they are verbal rather than quantitative in nature.

CHAPTER 1

ST-1 Refer to the marginal glossary definitions or relevant chapter sections to check your responses.

CHAPTER 2

ST-2	Henderson's Taxes as a Corporation	1996	1997	1998
	Income before salary and taxes	$52,700	$90,000	$150,000
	Less: salary	(40,000)	(40,000)	(40,000)
	Taxable income, corporate	$12,700	$50,000	$110,000
	Total corporate tax	1,905[a]	7,500	26,150
	Salary	$40,000	$40,000	$ 40,000
	Less exemptions and deductions	(17,050)	(17,050)	(17,050)
	Taxable personal income	$22,950	$22,950	$ 22,950
	Total personal tax	3,443[b]	3,443	3,443
	Combined corporate and personal tax:	$ 5,348	$10,943	$ 29,593
	Henderson's Taxes as a Proprietorship			
	Total income	$52,700	$90,000	$150,000
	Less: exemptions and deductions	(17,050)	(17,050)	(17,050)
	Taxable personal income	$35,650	$72,950	$132,950
	Tax liability of proprietorship	$ 5,348[c]	$15,486	$ 33,519
	Advantage to being a corporation:	$ 0	$ 4,543	$ 3,926

[a]Corporate tax in 1996 = (0.15)($12,700) = $1,905.
[b]Personal tax (if Henderson incorporates) in 1996 = (0.15)($22,950) = $3,443.
[c]Proprietorship tax in 1996 = (0.15)($35,650) = $5,348.

Notice that in 1996, both the corporate form of organization and the proprietorship form have the same tax liability; however, in 1997 and 1998, the corporate form has the lower tax liability. Thus, the corporate form of organization allows Henderson to pay the lowest taxes in each year. Therefore, on the basis of taxes over the 3-year period, Henderson should incorporate her business. However, note that to get additional money out of the corporation so she can spend it, Henderson will have to have the corporation pay dividends, which will be taxed to Henderson, and thus she will, sometime in the future, have to pay additional taxes.

CHAPTER 3

ST-2 Billingsworth paid $2 in dividends and retained $2 per share. Since total retained earnings rose by $12 million, there must be 6 million shares outstanding. With a book value of $40 per share, total common equity must be $40(6 million) = $240 million. Since Billingsworth has $120 million of debt, its debt ratio must be 33.3 percent:

$$\frac{Debt}{Assets} = \frac{Debt}{Debt + Equity} = \frac{\$120 \text{ million}}{\$120 \text{ million} + \$240 \text{ million}}$$

$$= 0.333 = 33.3\%.$$

ST-3 a. In answering questions such as this, always begin by writing down the relevant definitional equations, then start filling in numbers. Note that the extra zeros indicating millions have been deleted in the calculations below.

(1)
$$DSO = \frac{Accounts\ receivable}{Sales/360}$$

$$40 = \frac{A/R}{\$1,000/360}$$

$$A/R = 40(\$2.778) = \$111.1 \text{ million.}$$

(2)
$$Quick\ ratio = \frac{Current\ assets - Inventories}{Current\ liabilities} = 2.0$$

$$= \frac{Cash\ and\ marketable\ securities + A/R}{Current\ liabilities} = 2.0$$

$$2.0 = \frac{\$100 + \$111.1}{Current\ liabilities}$$

$$Current\ liabilities = (\$100 + \$111.1)/2 = \$105.5 \text{ million.}$$

(3)
$$Current\ ratio = \frac{Current\ assets}{Current\ liabilities} = 3.0$$

$$= \frac{Current\ assets}{\$105.5} = 3.0$$

$$Current\ assets = 3.0(\$105.5) = \$316.50 \text{ million.}$$

(4)
$$Total\ assets = Current\ assets + Fixed\ assets$$

$$= \$316.5 + \$283.5 = \$600 \text{ million.}$$

(5)
$$ROA = Profit\ margin \times Total\ assets\ turnover$$

$$= \frac{Net\ income}{Sales} \times \frac{Sales}{Total\ assets}$$

$$= \frac{\$50}{\$1,000} \times \frac{\$1,000}{\$600}$$

$$= 0.05 \times 1.667 = 0.0833 = 8.33\%.$$

(6)
$$ROE = ROA \times \frac{Assets}{Equity}$$

$$12.0\% = 8.33\% \times \frac{\$600}{Equity}$$

$$Equity = \frac{(8.33\%)(\$600)}{12.0\%}$$

$$= \$416.50 \text{ million.}$$

(7)   Total assets = Total claims = $600 million

Current liabilities + Long-term debt + Equity = $600 million

$105.5 + Long-term debt + $416.5 = $600 million

Long-term debt = $600 − $105.5 − $416.5 = $78 million.

Note: We could have found equity as follows:

$$ROE = \frac{Net\ income}{Equity}$$

$$12.0\% = \frac{\$50}{Equity}$$

$$Equity = \$50/0.12$$

$$= \$416.67\ million\ (rounding\ difference).$$

Then we could have gone on to find current liabilities and long-term debt.

b. Kaiser's average sales per day were $1,000/360 = $2.8 million. Its DSO was 40, so A/R = 40($2.8) = $111.1 million. Its new DSO of 30 would cause A/R = 30($2.8) = $83.3 million. The reduction in receivables would be $111.1 − $83.3 = $27.8 million, which would equal the amount of cash generated.

(1)   New equity = Old equity − Stock bought back

$$= \$416.5 − \$27.8$$

$$= \$388.7\ million.$$

Thus,

$$New\ ROE = \frac{Net\ income}{New\ equity}$$

$$= \frac{\$50}{\$388.7}$$

$$= 12.86\%\ (versus\ old\ ROE\ of\ 12.0\%).$$

(2) $$New\ ROA = \frac{Net\ income}{Total\ assets − Reduction\ in\ A/R}$$

$$= \frac{\$50}{\$600 − \$27.8}$$

$$= 8.74\%\ (versus\ old\ ROA\ of\ 8.33\%).$$

(3) The old debt is the same as the new debt:

$$Debt = Total\ claims − Equity$$

$$= \$600 − \$416.5 = \$183.5\ million.$$

$$Old\ total\ assets = \$600\ million.$$

New total assets = Old total assets − Reduction in A/R

$$= \$600 − \$27.8$$

$$= \$572.2\ million.$$

Therefore,

$$\frac{Debt}{Old\ total\ assets} = \frac{\$183.5}{\$600} = 30.6\%,$$

while

$$\frac{New\ debt}{New\ total\ assets} = \frac{\$183.5}{\$572.2} = 32.1\%.$$

CHAPTER 4

ST-2 a. Average = (4% + 5% + 6% + 7%)/4 = 22%/4 = 5.5%.

b. $k_{T\text{-bond}}$ = k* + IP = 2% + 5.5% = 7.5%.

c. If the 5-year T-bond rate is 8 percent, the inflation rate is expected to average approximately 8% − 2% = 6% during the next 5 years. Thus, the implied Year 5 inflation rate is 8 percent:

$$6\% = (4\% + 5\% + 6\% + 7\% + I_5)/5$$
$$30\% = 22\% + I_5$$
$$I_5 = 8\%.$$

CHAPTER 5

ST-2 a. The average rate of return for each stock is calculated simply by averaging the returns over the 5-year period. The average return for each stock is 18.90 percent, calculated for Stock A as follows:

$$k_{Avg} = (-10.00\% + 18.50\% + 38.67\% + 14.33\% + 33.00\%)/5$$
$$= 18.90\%.$$

The realized rate of return on a portfolio made up of Stock A and Stock B would be calculated by finding the average return in each year as k_A(% of Stock A) + k_B(% of Stock B) and then averaging these yearly returns:

YEAR	PORTFOLIO AB's RETURN, k_{AB}
1991	(6.50%)
1992	19.90
1993	41.46
1994	9.00
1995	30.65
	k_{Avg} = 18.90%

b. The standard deviation of returns is estimated, using Equation 5-3a, as follows (see Footnote 5):

$$\text{Estimated } \sigma = S = \sqrt{\frac{\sum_{t=1}^{n} (\overline{k}_t - \overline{k}_{Avg})^2}{n-1}}. \tag{5-3a}$$

For Stock A, the estimated σ is 19.0 percent:

$$\sigma_A = \sqrt{\frac{(-10.00 - 18.9)^2 + (18.50 - 18.9)^2 + \cdots + (33.00 - 18.9)^2}{5-1}}$$
$$= \sqrt{\frac{1,445.92}{4}} = 19.0\%.$$

The standard deviation of returns for Stock B and for the portfolio are similarly determined, and they are as follows:

	STOCK A	STOCK B	PORTFOLIO AB
Standard deviation	19.0	19.0	18.6

c. Since the risk reduction from diversification is small (σ_{AB} falls only from 19.0 to 18.6 percent), the most likely value of the correlation coefficient is 0.9. If the correlation coefficient were −0.9, the risk reduction would be much larger. In fact, the correlation coefficient between Stocks A and B is 0.92.

d. If more randomly selected stocks were added to the portfolio, σ_p would decline to somewhere in the vicinity of 21 percent; see Figure 5-8. σ_p would remain constant only if the correlation coefficient were +1.0, which is most unlikely. σ_p would decline to zero only if the correlation coefficient, r, were equal to zero and a large number of stocks were added to the portfolio, or if the proper proportions were held in a two-stock portfolio with r = −1.0.

Chapter 6

ST-2 a.

```
1/1/96   8%   1/1/97      1/1/98       1/1/99       1/1/00
  ├──────────────┼────────────┼────────────┼────────────┤
     -1,000                                          FV = ?
```

$1,000 is being compounded for 3 years, so your balance on January 1, 2000, is $1,259.71:

$$FV_n = PV(1 + i)^n = \$1,000(1 + 0.08)^3 = \$1,259.71.$$

Alternatively, using a financial calculator, input N = 3, I = 8, PV = -1000, PMT = 0, and FV = ? FV = $1,259.71.

b.

```
1/1/96              1/1/97           1/1/98            1/1/99           1/1/00
  2%
  ├──┼──┼──┼──┼──┼──┼──┼──┼──┼──┼──┼──┤
     -1,000                                                          FV = ?
```

Use FVIF for 2%, 3 × 4 = 12 periods:

$$FV_{12} = \$1,000(FVIF_{2\%,12}) = \$1,000(1.2682) = \$1,268.20.$$

Alternatively, using a financial calculator, input N = 12, I = 2, PV = -1000, PMT = 0, and FV = ? FV = $1,268.24. (Note that since the interest factor is carried to only 4 decimal places, a rounding difference occurs.)

c.

```
1/1/96   8%   1/1/97      1/1/98       1/1/99       1/1/00
  ├──────────────┼────────────┼────────────┼────────────┤
                  250          250          250          250
                                                        FV = ?
```

As you work this problem, keep in mind that the tables assume that payments are made at the end of each period. Therefore, you may solve this problem by finding the future value of an annuity of $250 for 4 years at 8 percent:

$$FVA_4 = PMT(FVIFA_{i,n}) = \$250(4.5061) = \$1,126.53.$$

Alternatively, using a financial calculator, input N = 4, I = 8, PV = 0, PMT = -250, and FV = ? FV = $1,126.53.

d.

```
1/1/96   8%   1/1/97      1/1/98       1/1/99       1/1/00
  ├──────────────┼────────────┼────────────┼────────────┤
                   ?            ?            ?            ?
                                                    FV = 1,259.71
```

N = 4; I = 8; PV = 0; FV = 1259.71; PMT = ?; PMT = $279.56.

$$PMT(FVIFA_{8\%,4}) = FVA_4$$
$$PMT(4.5061) = \$1,259.71$$
$$PMT = \$1,259.71/4.5061 = \$279.56.$$

Therefore, you would have to make 4 payments of $279.56 each to have a balance of $1,259.71 on January 1, 2000.

ST-3 a. Set up a time line like the one in the preceding problem:

```
1/1/96   8%   1/1/97      1/1/98       1/1/99       1/1/00
  ├──────────────┼────────────┼────────────┼────────────┤
     PV = ?                                          1,000
```

Note that your deposit will grow for 3 years at 8 percent. The fact that it is now January 1, 1996, is irrelevant. The deposit on January 1, 1997, is the PV, and the FV is $1,000. Here is the solution:

$$N = 3; I = 8; PMT = 0; FV = 1000; PV = ?; PV = \$793.83.$$
$$FV_3(PVIF_{8\%,3}) = PV$$
$$PV = \$1,000(0.7938) = \$793.80 = \text{Initial deposit to accumulate } \$1,000.$$

(Difference due to rounding.)

b.

```
1/1/96   8%   1/1/97      1/1/98       1/1/99       1/1/00
  ├──────────────┼────────────┼────────────┼────────────┤
                   ?            ?            ?            ?
                                                    FV = 1,000
```

Here we are dealing with a 4-year annuity whose first payment occurs 1 year from today, on 1/1/97, and whose future value must equal $1,000. You should modify the time line to help visualize the situation. Here is the solution:

$$N = 4; I = 8; PV = 0; FV = 1000; PMT = ?; PMT = \$221.92.$$

$$PMT(FVIFA_{8\%,4}) = FVA_4$$

$$PMT = \frac{FVA_4}{(FVIFA_{8\%,4})}$$

$$= \frac{\$1,000}{4.5061} = \$221.92 = \text{Payment necessary to accumulate \$1,000.}$$

c. This problem can be approached in several ways. Perhaps the simplest is to ask this question: "If I received $750 on 1/1/97 and deposited it to earn 8 percent, would I have the required $1,000 on 1/1/00?" The answer is no:

1/1/96	8%	1/1/97	1/1/98	1/1/99	1/1/00
		−750			FV = ?

$$FV_3 = \$750(1.08)(1.08)(1.08) = \$944.78.$$

This indicates that you should let your father make the payments rather than accept the lump sum of $750.

You could also compare the $750 with the PV of the payments:

1/1/96	8%	1/1/97	1/1/98	1/1/99	1/1/00
		221.92	221.92	221.92	221.92
		PV = ?			

$$N = 4; I = 8; PMT = -221.92; FV = 0; PV = ?; PV = \$735.03.$$

$$PMT(PVIFA_{8\%,4}) = PVA_4$$

$$\$221.92(3.3121) = \$735.02 = \text{Present value of the required payments.}$$

(Difference due to rounding.)

This is less than the $750 lump sum offer, so your initial reaction might be to accept the lump sum of $750. However, this would be a mistake. The problem is that when you found the $735.02 PV of the annuity, you were finding the value of the annuity *today*, on January 1, 1996. You were comparing $735.02 today with the lump sum of $750 1 year from now. This is, of course, invalid. What you should have done was take the $735.02, recognize that this is the PV of an annuity as of January 1, 1996, multiply $735.02 by 1.08 to get $793.82, and compare $793.82 with the lump sum of $750. You would then take your father's offer to make the payments rather than take the lump sum on January 1, 1997.

d.

1/1/96	i = ?	1/1/97	1/1/98	1/1/99	1/1/00
		−750			1,000

$$N = 3; PV = -750; PMT = 0; FV = 1000; I = ?; I = 10.0642\%.$$

$$PV(FVIF_{i,3}) = FV$$

$$FVIF_{i,3} = \frac{FV}{PV}$$

$$= \frac{\$1,000}{\$750} = 1.3333.$$

Use the Future Value of $1 table (Table A-3 in Appendix A) for 3 periods to find the interest rate corresponding to an FVIF of 1.3333. Look across the Period 3 row of the table until you come to 1.3333. The closest value is 1.3310, in the 10 percent column. Therefore, you would require an interest rate of approximately 10 percent to achieve your $1,000 goal. The exact rate required, found with a financial calculator, is 10.0642 percent.

e.

1/1/96	i = ?	1/1/97	1/1/98	1/1/99	1/1/00
		186.29	186.29	186.29	186.29
					FV = 1,000

$N = 4$; $PV = 0$; $PMT = -186.29$; $FV = 1000$; $I = ?$; $I = 19.9997\%$.

$$PMT(FVIFA_{i,4}) = FVA_4$$

$$\$186.29(FVIFA_{i,4}) = \$1,000$$

$$FVIFA_{i,4} = \frac{\$1,000}{\$186.29} = 5.3680.$$

Using Table A-4 in Appendix A, we find that 5.3680 corresponds to a 20 percent interest rate. You might be able to find a borrower willing to offer you a 20 percent interest rate, but there would be some risk involved — he or she might not actually pay you your $1,000!

f.

Find the future value of the original $400 deposit:

$$FV_6 = PV(FVIF_{4\%,6}) = \$400(1.2653) = \$506.12.$$

This means that on January 1, 2000, you need an additional sum of $493.88:

$$\$1,000.00 - \$506.12 = \$493.88.$$

This will be accumulated by making 6 equal payments which earn 8 percent compounded semiannually, or 4 percent each 6 months:

$$N = 6; I = 4; PV = 0; FV = 493.88; PMT = ?; PMT = \$74.46.$$

$$PMT(FVIFA_{4\%,6}) = FVA_6$$

$$PMT = \frac{FVA_6}{(FVIFA_{4\%,6})}$$

$$= \frac{\$493.88}{6.6330} = \$74.46.$$

Alternatively, using a financial calculator, input $N = 6$, $I = 4$, $PV = -400$, $FV = 1000$, and $PMT = ?$ $PMT = \$74.46$.

g.

$$\text{Effective annual rate} = \left(1 + \frac{i_{Nom}}{m}\right)^m - 1.0$$

$$= \left(1 + \frac{0.08}{2}\right)^2 - 1 = (1.04)^2 - 1$$

$$= 1.0816 - 1 = 0.0816 = 8.16\%.$$

h. There is a reinvestment rate risk here because we assumed that funds will earn an 8 percent return in the bank. In fact, if interest rates in the economy fall, the bank will lower its deposit rate because it will be earning less when it lends out the funds you deposited with it. If you buy certificates of deposit (CDs) that mature on the date you need the money (1/1/00), you will avoid the reinvestment risk, but that would work only if you were making the deposit today. Other ways of reducing reinvestment rate risk will be discussed later in the text.

ST-4 Bank A's effective annual rate is 8.24 percent:

$$\text{Effective annual rate} = \left(1 + \frac{0.08}{4}\right)^4 - 1.0$$

$$= (1.02)^4 - 1 = 1.0824 - 1$$

$$= 0.0824 = 8.24\%.$$

Now Bank B must have the same effective annual rate:

$$\left(1 + \frac{i}{12}\right)^{12} - 1.0 = 0.0824$$

$$\left(1 + \frac{i}{12}\right)^{12} = 1.0824$$

$$1 + \frac{i}{12} = (1.0824)^{1/12}$$

$$1 + \frac{i}{12} = 1.00662$$

$$\frac{i}{12} = 0.00662$$

$$i = 0.07944 = 7.94\%.$$

Thus, the two banks have different quoted rates — Bank A's quoted rate is 8 percent, while Bank B's quoted rate is 7.94 percent; however, both banks have the same effective annual rate of 8.24 percent. The difference in their quoted rates is due to the difference in compounding frequency.

CHAPTER 7

ST-2   a. Pennington's bonds were sold at par; therefore, the original YTM equaled the coupon rate of 12%.

b.
$$V_B = \sum_{t=1}^{50} \frac{\$120/2}{\left(1 + \frac{0.10}{2}\right)^t} + \frac{\$1,000}{\left(1 + \frac{0.10}{2}\right)^{50}}$$

$$= \$60(\text{PVIFA}_{5\%,50}) + \$1,000(\text{PVIF}_{5\%,50})$$

$$= \$60(18.2559) + \$1,000(0.0872)$$

$$= \$1,095.35 + \$87.20 = \$1,182.55.$$

Alternatively, with a financial calculator, input the following: N = 50, I = 5, PMT = 60, FV = 1000, and PV = ? PV = $1,182.56.

c.
$$\text{Current yield} = \text{Annual coupon payment/Price}$$

$$= \$120/\$1,182.55$$

$$= 0.1015 = 10.15\%.$$

$$\text{Capital gains yield} = \text{Total yield} - \text{Current yield}$$

$$= 10\% - 10.15\% = -0.15\%.$$

d.
$$\$916.42 = \sum_{t=1}^{13} \frac{\$60}{(1 + k_d/2)^t} + \frac{\$1,000}{(1 + k_d/2)^{13}}.$$

Try $k_d = 14\%$:

$$V_B = \text{INT}(\text{PVIFA}_{7\%,13}) + M(\text{PVIF}_{7\%,13})$$

$$\$916.42 = \$60(8.3577) + \$1,000(0.4150)$$

$$= \$501.46 + \$415.00 = \$916.46.$$

Therefore, the YTM on July 1, 1995, was 14 percent. Alternatively, with a financial calculator, input the following: N = 13, PV = −916.42, PMT = 60, FV = 1000, and $k_{d/2}$ = I = ? Calculator solution = $k_{d/2}$ = 7.00%; therefore, k_d = 14.00%.

e.
$$\text{Current yield} = \$120/\$916.42 = 13.09\%.$$

$$\text{Capital gains yield} = 14\% - 13.09\% = 0.91\%.$$

f. The following time line illustrates the years to maturity of the bond:

Thus, on March 1, 1995, there were $13\frac{2}{3}$ periods left before the bond matured. Bond traders actually use the following procedure to determine the price of the bond:

(1) Find the price of the bond on the next coupon date, July 1, 1995.

$$V_{B\ 7/1/95} = \$60(PVIFA_{7.75\%,13}) + \$1,000(PVIF_{7.75\%,13})$$
$$= \$60(8.0136) + \$1,000(0.3789)$$
$$= \$859.72.$$

Note that we could use a calculator to solve for $V_{B\ 7/1/95}$ or we could substitute $i = 7.75\%$ and $n = 13$ periods into the equations for PVIFA and PVIF:

$$PVIFA = \frac{1 - \dfrac{1}{(1+i)^n}}{i} = \frac{1 - \dfrac{1}{(1+0.0775)^{13}}}{0.0775} = 8.0136.$$

$$PVIF = \frac{1}{(1+k)^n} = \frac{1}{(1+0.0775)^{13}} = 0.3789.$$

(2) Add the coupon, $60, to the bond price to get the total value, TV, of the bond on the next interest payment date: TV = $859.72 + $60.00 = $919.72.

(3) Discount this total value back to the purchase date:

$$\text{Value at purchase date (March 1, 1995)} = \$919.72(PVIF_{7.75\%,4/6})$$
$$= \$919.72(0.9515)$$
$$= \$875.11.$$

Here

$$PVIF_{7.75\%,2/3} = \frac{1}{(1+0.0775)^{2/3}} = \frac{1}{1.0510} = 0.9515.$$

(4) Therefore, you would have written a check for $875.11 to complete the transaction. Of this amount, $20 = ($\frac{1}{3}$)($60) would represent accrued interest and $855.11 would represent the bond's basic value. This breakdown would affect both your taxes and those of the seller.

(5) This problem could be solved *very* easily using a financial calculator with a bond valuation function, such as the HP-12C or the HP-17B. This is explained in the calculator manual under the heading, "Bond Calculations."

ST-3 a. $100,000,000/10 = $10,000,000 per year, or $5 million each 6 months. Since the $5 million will be used to retire bonds immediately, no interest will be earned on it.

b. The debt service requirements will decline. As the amount of bonds outstanding declines, so will the interest requirements (amounts given in millions of dollars):

SEMIANNUAL PAYMENT PERIOD (1)	SINKING FUND PAYMENT (2)	OUTSTANDING BONDS ON WHICH INTEREST IS PAID (3)	INTEREST PAYMENT[a] (4)	TOTAL BOND SERVICE (2) + (4) = (5)
1	$5	$100	$6.0	$11.0
2	5	95	5.7	10.7
3	5	90	5.4	10.4

SEMIANNUAL PAYMENT PERIOD (1)	SINKING FUND PAYMENT (2)	OUTSTANDING BONDS ON WHICH INTEREST IS PAID (3)	INTEREST PAYMENT[a] (4)	TOTAL BOND SERVICE (2) + (4) = (5)
.	.	.	.	.
.	.	.	.	.
.	.	.	.	.
20	5	5	0.3	5.3

[a]Interest is calculated as $(0.5)(0.12)$(Column 3); for example: interest in Period 2 $= (0.5)(0.12)(\$95) = \$5.7$.

The company's total cash bond service requirement will be $21.7 million per year for the first year. The requirement will decline by $0.12(\$10,000,000) = \$1,200,000$ per year for the remaining years.

c. Here we have a 10-year, 9 percent annuity whose compound value is $100 million, and we are seeking the annual payment, PMT. The solution can be obtained with a financial calculator. Input $N = 10$, $I = 9$, $PV = 0$, and $FV = 100000000$, and press the PMT key to obtain $6,582,009.

We could also find the solution using this equation:

$$\$100,000,000 = \sum_{t=1}^{10} PMT(1 + k)^t$$

$$= PMT(FVIFA_{9\%,10})$$

$$= PMT(15.193)$$

$$PMT = \$6,581,979 = \text{sinking fund payment.}$$

The difference is due to rounding the FVIFA to 3 decimal places.

d. Annual debt service costs will be $\$100,000,000(0.12) + \$6,582,009 = \$18,582,009$.

e. If interest rates rose, causing the bond's price to fall, the company would use open market purchases. This would reduce its debt service requirements.

CHAPTER 8

ST-2 a. This is not necessarily true. Because G plows back two-thirds of its earnings, its growth rate should exceed that of D, but D pays higher dividends ($6 versus $2). We cannot say which stock should have the higher price.

b. Again, we just do not know which price would be higher.

c. This is false. The changes in k_d and k_s would have a greater effect on G; its price would decline more.

d. The total expected return for D is $\hat{k}_D = D_1/P_0 + g = 15\% + 0\% = 15\%$. The total expected return for G will have D_1/P_0 less than 15 percent and g greater than 0 percent, but $\hat{k}_G$ should be neither greater nor smaller than D's total expected return, 15 percent, because the two stocks are stated to be equally risky.

e. We have eliminated a, b, c, and d, so e should be correct. On the basis of the available information, D and G should sell at about the same price, $40; thus, $\hat{k}_s = 15\%$ for both D and G. G's current dividend yield is $2/$40 = 5%. Therefore, g = 15% − 5% = 10%.

ST-3 The first step is to solve for g, the unknown variable, in the constant growth equation. Since D_1 is unknown but D_0 is known, substitute $D_0(1 + g)$ as follows:

$$\hat{P}_0 = P_0 = \frac{D_1}{k_s - g} = \frac{D_0(1 + g)}{k_s - g}$$

$$\$36 = \frac{\$2.40(1 + g)}{0.12 - g}.$$

Solving for g, we find the growth rate to be 5 percent:

$$\$4.32 - \$36g = \$2.40 + \$2.40g$$

$$\$38.4g = \$1.92$$

$$g = 0.05 = 5\%.$$

The next step is to use the growth rate to project the stock price 5 years hence:

$$\hat{P}_5 = \frac{D_0(1 + g)^6}{k_s - g}$$

$$= \frac{\$2.40(1.05)^6}{0.12 - 0.05}$$

$$= \$45.95.$$

[Alternatively, $\hat{P}_5 = \$36(1.05)^5 = \$45.95$.]

Therefore, Ewald Company's expected stock price 5 years from now, $\hat{P}_5$, is $45.95.

ST-4 a. (1) Calculate the PV of the dividends paid during the supernormal growth period:

$$D_1 = \$1.1500(1.15) = \$1.3225.$$

$$D_2 = \$1.3225(1.15) = \$1.5209.$$

$$D_3 = \$1.5209(1.13) = \$1.7186.$$

$$PV\ D = \$1.3225(0.8929) + \$1.5209(0.7972) + \$1.7186(0.7118)$$

$$= \$1.1809 + \$1.2125 + \$1.2233$$

$$= \$3.6167 \approx \$3.62.$$

(2) Find the PV of Snyder's stock price at the end of Year 3:

$$\hat{P}_3 = \frac{D_4}{k_s - g} = \frac{D_3(1 + g)}{k_s - g}$$

$$= \frac{\$1.7186(1.06)}{0.12 - 0.06}$$

$$= \$30.36.$$

$$PV\ \hat{P}_3 = \$30.36(0.7118) = \$21.61.$$

(3) Sum the two components to find the value of the stock today:

$$\hat{P}_0 = \$3.62 + \$21.61 = \$25.23.$$

Alternatively, the cash flows can be placed on a time line as follows:

Enter the cash flows into the cash flow register, I = 12, and press the NPV key to obtain $P_0 = \$25.23$.

b.

$$\hat{P}_1 = \$1.5209(0.8929) + \$1.7186(0.7972) + \$30.36(0.7972)$$

$$= \$1.3580 + \$1.3701 + \$24.2030$$

$$= \$26.9311 \approx \$26.93.$$

(Calculator solution: $26.93.)

$$\hat{P}_2 = \$1.7186(0.8929) + \$30.36(0.8929)$$

$$= \$1.5345 + \$27.1084$$

$$= \$28.6429 \approx \$28.64.$$

(Calculator solution: $28.64.)

ST-4 a. *Cost using retained earnings:*

$$k_s = \hat{k}_s = \frac{D_1}{P_0} + g = \frac{(\$1.85)(1.08)}{\$50} + 0.08 = 12.0\%.$$

$$WACC_1 = 0.3(8\%)(0.6) + 0.7(12.0\%) = 9.84\%.$$

Cost using new common stock:

$$k_e = \hat{k}_e = \frac{D_1}{P_0(1 - F)} + g = \frac{(\$1.85)(1.08)}{(\$50)(0.85)} + 0.08 = 12.7\%.$$

$$WACC_2 = 0.3(8\%)(0.6) + 0.7(12.7\%) = 10.33\%.$$

Break point:

$$\text{Break point} = \frac{\$105,000(0.5)}{0.7} = \$75,000.$$

b. The MCC and IOS schedules are shown next:

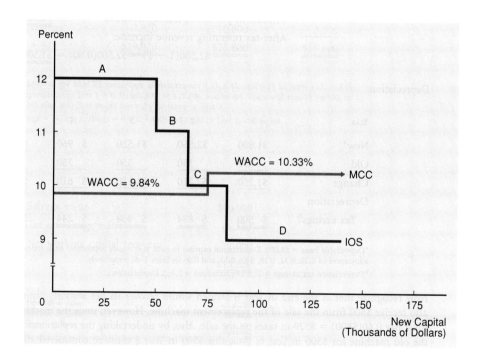

c. From this graph, we conclude that the firm should definitely undertake Projects A and B, assuming that these projects have about "average risk" in relation to the rest of the firm. Now, to evaluate Project C, recognize that one half of its capital would cost 9.84 percent, while the other half would cost 10.33 percent. Thus, the cost of the capital required for Project C is 10.09 percent:

$$0.5(9.84\%) + 0.5(10.33\%) = 10.09\%.$$

Since the cost is greater than Project C's return of 10 percent, the firm should not accept Project C.

d. The solution implicitly assumes (1) that all of the projects are equally risky and (2) that these projects are as risky as the firm's existing assets. If the accepted projects (A and B) were of above-average risk, this could raise the company's overall risk, and hence its cost of capital. Taking on these projects could result in a decline in the company's value.

e. If the payout ratio were lowered to zero, this would shift the break point to the right, from $75,000 to $150,000:

$$\text{Break point} = \frac{\$105,000(1.0)}{0.7} = \$150,000.$$

As the problem is set up, this would make Project C acceptable. If the payout were changed to 100 percent, the break point would shift to the left, from $75,000 to $0:

$$\text{Break point} = \frac{\$105,000(0.0)}{0.7} = \$0.$$

The optimal capital budget would still consist of Projects A and B. This assumes that the change in payout would not affect k_s or k_d; as we shall see in Chapter 13, this assumption may not be correct.

CHAPTER 12

ST-2 a.

EBIT	$4,000,000
Interest ($2,000,000 × 0.10)	200,000
Earnings before taxes (EBT)	$3,800,000
Taxes (35%)	1,330,000
Net income	$2,470,000

$$\text{EPS} = \$2,470,000/600,000 = \$4.12.$$
$$P_0 = \$4.12/0.15 = \$27.47.$$

b.

$$\text{Equity} = 600,000 \times (\$10) = \$6,000,000.$$
$$\text{Debt} = \$2,000,000.$$
$$\text{Total capital} = \$8,000,000.$$
$$\text{WACC} = w_d k_d (1 - T) + w_{ce} k_s$$
$$= (2/8)(10\%)(1 - 0.35) + (6/8)(15\%)$$
$$= 1.63\% + 11.25\%$$
$$= 12.88\%.$$

c.

EBIT	$4,000,000
Interest ($10,000,000 × 0.12)	1,200,000
Earnings before taxes (EBT)	$2,800,000
Taxes (35%)	980,000
Net income	$1,820,000

Shares bought and retired:

$$\Delta N = \Delta \text{Debt}/P_0 = \$8,000,000/\$27.47 = 291,227.$$

New outstanding shares:

$$N_1 = N_0 - \Delta N = 600,000 - 291,227 = 308,773.$$

New EPS:

$$\text{EPS} = \$1,820,000/308,773 = \$5.89.$$

New price per share:

$$P_0 = \$5.89/0.17 = \$34.65 \text{ versus } \$27.47.$$

Therefore, Gentry should change its capital structure.

d. In this case, the company's net income would be higher by $(0.12 - 0.10)(\$2,000,000)(1 - 0.35) = \$26,000$ because its interest charges would be lower. The new price would be

$$P_0 = \frac{(\$1,820,000 + \$26,000)/308,773}{0.17} = \$35.18.$$

In the first case, in which debt had to be refunded, the bondholders were compensated for the increased risk of the higher debt position. In the second case, the old bondholders were not compensated; their 10 percent coupon perpetual bonds would now be worth

$$\$100/0.12 = \$833.33,$$

or $1,666,667 in total, down from the old $2 million, or a loss of $333,333. The stockholders would have a gain of

$$(\$35.18 - \$34.65)(308,773) = \$163,650.$$

This gain would, of course, be at the expense of the old bondholders. (There is no reason to think that bondholders' losses would exactly offset stockholders' gains.)

e.
$$\text{TIE} = \frac{\text{EBIT}}{\text{I}}.$$

$$\text{Original TIE} = \frac{\$4,000,000}{\$200,000} = 20 \text{ times.}$$

$$\text{New TIE} = \frac{\$4,000,000}{\$1,200,000} = 3.33 \text{ times.}$$

ST-3 a. (1) Determine the variable cost per unit at present, using the following definitions and equations:

$$Q = \text{units of output (sales)} = 5,000.$$
$$P = \text{average sales price per unit of output} = \$100.$$
$$F = \text{fixed operating costs} = \$200,000.$$
$$V = \text{variable costs per unit.}$$
$$\text{EBIT} = P(Q) - F - V(Q)$$
$$\$50,000 = \$100(5,000) - \$200,000 - V(5,000)$$
$$5,000V = \$250,000$$
$$V = \$50.$$

(2) Determine the new EBIT level if the change is made:

$$\text{New EBIT} = P_2(Q_2) - F_2 - V_2(Q_2)$$
$$= \$95(7,000) - \$250,000 - \$40(7,000)$$
$$= \$135,000.$$

(3) Determine the incremental EBIT:

$$\Delta\text{EBIT} = \$135,000 - \$50,000 = \$85,000.$$

(4) Estimate the approximate rate of return on the new investment:

$$\Delta\text{ROA} = \frac{\Delta\text{EBIT}}{\text{Investment}} = \frac{\$85,000}{\$400,000} = 21.25\%.$$

Since the ROA exceeds Olinde's average cost of capital, this analysis suggests that Olinde should go ahead and make the investment.

b.
$$\text{DOL} = \frac{Q(P - V)}{Q(P - V) - F}$$

$$\text{DOL}_{\text{Old}} = \frac{5,000(\$100 - \$50)}{5,000(\$100 - \$50) - \$200,000} = 5.00.$$

$$\text{DOL}_{\text{New}} = \frac{7,000(\$95 - \$40)}{7,000(\$95 - \$40) - \$250,000} = 2.85.$$

This indicates that operating income will be less sensitive to changes in sales if the production process is changed; thus, the change would reduce risks. However, the change would increase the breakeven point. Still, with a lower sales price, it might be easier to achieve the higher new breakeven volume.

$$\text{Old: } Q_{BE} = \frac{F}{P - V} = \frac{\$200,000}{\$100 - \$50} = 4,000 \text{ units.}$$

$$\text{New: } Q_{BE} = \frac{F}{P_2 - V_2} = \frac{\$250,000}{\$95 - \$40} = 4,545 \text{ units.}$$

c. The incremental ROA is:

$$\text{ROA} = \frac{\Delta\text{Profit}}{\Delta\text{Sales}} \times \frac{\Delta\text{Sales}}{\Delta\text{Assets}}.$$

Using debt financing, the incremental profit associated with the investment is equal to the incremental profit found in Part a minus the interest expense incurred as a result of the investment:

$$\Delta\text{Profit} = \text{New profit} - \text{Old profit} - \text{Interest}$$

$$= \$135,000 - \$50,000 - 0.10(\$400,000)$$

$$= \$45,000.$$

The incremental sales is calculated as:

$$\Delta\text{Sales} = P_2Q_2 - P_1Q_1$$

$$= \$95(7,000) - \$100(5,000)$$

$$= \$665,000 - \$500,000$$

$$= \$165,000.$$

$$\text{ROA} = \frac{\$45,000}{\$165,000} \times \frac{\$165,000}{\$400,000} = 11.25\%.$$

The return on the new equity investment still exceeds the average cost of capital, so Olinde should make the investment.

CHAPTER 13

ST-2 a.

Projected net income	$2,000,000
Less projected capital investments	800,000
Available residual	$1,200,000
Shares outstanding	200,000

DPS = $1,200,000/200,000 shares = $6 = D_1.

b.   EPS = $2,000,000/200,000 shares = $10.

Payout ratio = DPS/EPS = $6/$10 = 60%, or

Total dividends/NI = $1,200,000/$2,000,000 = 60%.

c. $$\text{Currently, } P_0 = \frac{D_1}{k_s - g} = \frac{\$6}{0.14 - 0.05} = \frac{\$6}{0.09} = \$66.67.$$

Under the former circumstances, D_1 would be based on a 20 percent payout on $10 EPS, or $2. With $k_s = 14\%$ and $g = 12\%$, we solve for P_0:

$$P_0 = \frac{D_1}{k_s - g} = \frac{\$2}{0.14 - 0.12} = \frac{\$2}{0.02} = \$100.$$

Although CMC has suffered a severe setback, its existing assets will continue to provide a good income stream. More of these earnings should now be passed on to the shareholders, as the slowed internal growth has reduced the need for funds. However, the net result is a 33 percent decrease in the value of the shares.

d. If the payout ratio were continued at 20 percent, even after internal investment opportunities had declined, the price of the stock would drop to $2/(0.14 − 0.06) = $25 rather than to $66.67. Thus, an increase in the dividend payout is consistent with maximizing shareholder wealth.

Because of the downward-sloping IOS curve (see Figure 13-4), the greater the firm's level of investment, the lower the average ROE. Thus, the more money CMC retains and invests, the lower its average ROE will be. We can determine the average ROE under different conditions as follows:

Old situation (with founder active and a 20 percent payout):

$$g = (1.0 - \text{Payout ratio})(\text{Average ROE})$$

$$12\% = (1.0 - 0.2)(\text{Average ROE})$$

$$\text{Average ROE} = 12\%/0.8 = 15\% > k_s = 14\%.$$

Note that the *average* ROE is 15 percent, whereas the *marginal* ROE is presumably equal to 14 percent. In terms of a graph like Figure 13-4, the intersection of the MCC and IOS curves would be 14 percent, and the average of the IOS curve above the intersection would be 15 percent.

New situation (with founder retired and a 60 percent payout):

$$g = 6\% = (1.0 - 0.6)(\text{ROE})$$

$$\text{ROE} = 6\%/0.4 = 15\% > k_s = 14\%.$$

This suggests that the new payout is appropriate and that the firm is taking on investments down to the point at which marginal returns are equal to the cost of capital. In terms of a graph like Figure 13-4, the IOS curve shifted to the left after the founder retired. Note that if the 20 percent payout was maintained, the *average* ROE would be only 7.5 percent, which would imply a marginal ROE far below the 14 percent cost of capital.

Chapter 14

ST-2 To solve this problem, we will define ΔS as the change in sales and g as the growth rate in sales, and then we use the three following equations:

$$\Delta S = S_0 g.$$

$$S_1 = S_0(1 + g).$$

$$\text{AFN} = (A^*/S)(\Delta S) - (L^*/S)(\Delta S) - MS_1(1 - d).$$

Set AFN = 0, substitute in known values for A^*/S, L^*/S, M, d, and S, and then solve for g:

$$0 = 1.6(\$100g) - 0.4(\$100g) - 0.10[\$100(1 + g)](0.55)$$

$$= \$160g - \$40g - 0.055(\$100 + \$100g)$$

$$= \$160g - \$40g - \$5.5 - \$5.5g$$

$$\$114.5g = \$5.5$$

$$g = \$5.5/\$114.5 = 0.048 = 4.8\%$$

$$= \text{Maximum growth rate without external financing.}$$

ST-3 Assets consist of cash, marketable securities, receivables, inventories, and fixed assets. Therefore, we can break the A^*/S ratio into its components — cash/sales, inventories/sales, and so forth. Then,

$$\frac{A^*}{S} = \frac{A^* - \text{Inventories}}{S} + \frac{\text{Inventories}}{S} = 1.6.$$

We know that the inventory turnover ratio is sales/inventories = 3 times, so inventories/sales = 1/3 = 0.3333. Further, if the inventory turnover ratio can be increased to 4 times, then the inventory/sales ratio will fall to 1/4 = 0.25, a difference of 0.3333 − 0.2500 = 0.0833. This, in turn, causes the A^*/S ratio to fall from $A^*/S = 1.6$ to $A^*/S = 1.6 - 0.0833 = 1.5167$.

This change has two effects: First, it changes the AFN equation, and second, it means that Weatherford currently has excessive inventories. Because it is costly to hold excess inventories, Weatherford will want to reduce its inventory holdings by not replacing inventories until the excess amounts have been used. We can account for this by setting up the revised AFN equation (using the new A*/S ratio), estimating the funds that will be needed next year if no excess inventories are currently on hand, and then subtracting out the excess inventories which are currently on hand:

Present conditions:

$$\frac{Sales}{Inventories} = \frac{\$100}{Inventories} = 3,$$

so

$$Inventories = \$100/3 = \$33.3 \text{ million at present.}$$

New conditions:

$$\frac{Sales}{Inventories} = \frac{\$100}{Inventories} = 4,$$

so

$$\text{New level of inventories} = \$100/4 = \$25 \text{ million.}$$

Therefore,

$$\text{Excess inventories} = \$33.3 - \$25 = \$8.3 \text{ million.}$$

Forecast of funds needed, first year:

$$\Delta S \text{ in first year} = 0.2(\$100 \text{ million}) = \$20 \text{ million.}$$
$$AFN = 1.5167(\$20) - 0.4(\$20) - 0.1(0.55)(\$120) - \$8.3$$
$$= \$30.3 - \$8 - \$6.6 - \$8.3$$
$$= \$7.4 \text{ million.}$$

Forecast of funds needed, second year:

$$\Delta S \text{ in second year} = gS_1 = 0.2(\$120 \text{ million}) = \$24 \text{ million.}$$
$$AFN = 1.5167(\$24) - 0.4(\$24) - 0.1(0.55)(\$144)$$
$$= \$36.4 - \$9.6 - \$7.9$$
$$= \$18.9 \text{ million.}$$

ST-4

ALLIED FOOD PRODUCTS:
PRO FORMA INCOME STATEMENT
(MILLIONS OF DOLLARS)

	SECOND PASS	FEEDBACK EFFECTS	THIRD PASS
EBIT	$312		$312
Interest	93		93
EBT	$219		$219
Taxes (40%)	88		88
Net income before preferred dividends	$131		$131
Dividends to preferred	4		4
Net income available to common	$127		$127
Common dividends	$66		$66
Addition to retained earnings	$61		$61

$$\text{Change in interest expense} = (\$2 \times 0.08) + (\$2 \times 0.10)$$
$$= 0.36 \approx \$0.$$

13-4 Payout = 20%.

13-5 Payout = 52%.

13-6 D_0 = $3.44.

13-7 Payout = 31.39%.

14-1 a. $13.44 million.
  b. Notes payable = $31.44 million.
  c. Current ratio = 2.00×; ROE = 14.2%.
  d(1). −$14.28 million (surplus).
   (2). Total assets = $147 million; Notes payable = $3.72 million.
   (3). Current ratio = 4.25×; ROE = 10.84%.

14-2 a. Total assets = $33,534; AFN = $2,128.
  b. Notes payable = $4,228; AFN = $70; ΔInterest = $213.

14-3 a. 33%.
  b. AFN = $2,549.
  c. ΔInterest = $306; AFN = $73.
  d. ROE = 12.3%.

14-4 a. AFN = $128,783.
  b. Notes payable = $220,392; ΔInterest = $8,371; AFN = $8,028.
  c. 3.45%.

14-5 a. AFN = $667.
  b. Increase in notes payable = $51; Increase in C/S = $368.

14-6 a. $480,000.
  b. $18,750.

14-7 AFN = $360.

15-1 a. ROE_T = 11.75%; ROE_M = 10.80%; ROE_R = 9.16%.

15-2 a. $1,600,000.
  c. Bank = $1,200,000; Books = −$5,200,000.

15-3 b. $420,000.
  c. $35,000.

15-4 a. Feb. surplus = $2,000.

15-5 a. Oct. loan = $22,800.

15-6 a. $103,350.
  b. $97,500.

15-7 a. DSO = 28 days.
  b. $70,000.

15A-1 a. 32.
  b. $288,000.
  c. $45,000.
  d(1). 30.
   (2). $378,000.

15A-2 a. 83.
  b. $356,250.
  c. 4.8×.

15A-3 a. 56.
  b(1). 1.875×.
   (2). 11.25%.
  c(1). 41.

    (2). $2.03\times$.
    (3). 12.2%.

16-1 a. $100,000.
   c(1). $300,000.
    (2). Nominal cost = 36.73%; Effective cost = 43.86%.

16-3 a. $300,000.

16-4 a. 11.73%.
   b. 12.09%.
   c. 18%.

16-5 b. $384,615.
   c. Cash = $126.90; NP = $434.60.

16-6 a(1). $27,500.
    (3). $25,833.

16-7 b. 14.69%.
   d. 20.99%.

16-8 a. 44.54%.

16-9 a. k_d = 12%.
   b. k_d = 11.25%.
   c. k_d = 11.48%.
   d. k_d = 16%. Alternative b has lowest interest rate.

16-10 Nominal cost = 14.69%; Effective cost = 15.66%.

16-11 Bank loan = 13.64%.

16-12 d. 8.3723%.

16A-1 b. Total dollar cost = $160,800; 15.12%.

16A-2 a. $515,464.

16A-3 a. $46,167.
    b. $40,667.

CHAPTER 3

$$\text{Current ratio} = \frac{\text{Current assets}}{\text{Current liabilities}}.$$

$$\text{Quick, or acid test, ratio} = \frac{\text{Current assets} - \text{Inventories}}{\text{Current liabilities}}.$$

$$\text{Inventory turnover ratio} = \frac{\text{Sales}}{\text{Inventories}}.$$

$$\text{DSO} = \begin{matrix}\text{Days}\\\text{sales}\\\text{outstanding}\end{matrix} = \frac{\text{Receivables}}{\text{Average sales per day}} = \frac{\text{Receivables}}{\text{Annual sales}/360}.$$

$$\text{Fixed assets turnover ratio} = \frac{\text{Sales}}{\text{Net fixed assets}}.$$

$$\text{Total assets turnover ratio} = \frac{\text{Sales}}{\text{Total assets}}.$$

$$\text{Debt ratio} = \frac{\text{Total debt}}{\text{Total assets}}.$$

$$\text{D/E} = \frac{\text{D/A}}{1 - \text{D/A}}, \text{ and D/A} = \frac{\text{D/E}}{1 + \text{D/E}}.$$

$$\text{Times-interest-earned (TIE) ratio} = \frac{\text{EBIT}}{\text{Interest charges}}.$$

$$\begin{matrix}\text{Fixed charge}\\\text{coverage ratio}\end{matrix} = \frac{\text{EBIT} + \text{Lease payments}}{\text{Interest charges} + \text{Lease payments} + \dfrac{\text{Sinking fund payments}}{(1 - \text{Tax rate})}}.$$

$$\text{Profit margin on sales} = \frac{\text{Net income available to common stockholders}}{\text{Sales}}.$$

$$\text{Basic earning power ratio} = \frac{\text{EBIT}}{\text{Total assets}}.$$

$$\text{Return on total assets (ROA)} = \frac{\text{Net income available to common stockholders}}{\text{Total assets}}.$$

$$\text{ROA} = \left(\begin{matrix}\text{Profit}\\\text{margin}\end{matrix}\right)(\text{Total assets turnover}).$$

$$\text{Return on common equity (ROE)} = \frac{\text{Net income available to common stockholders}}{\text{Common equity}}.$$

$$\text{Price/earnings (P/E) ratio} = \frac{\text{Price per share}}{\text{Earnings per share}}.$$

$$\text{Book value per share} = \frac{\text{Common equity}}{\text{Shares outstanding}}.$$

$$\text{Market/book (M/B) ratio} = \frac{\text{Market price per share}}{\text{Book value per share}}.$$

$$\text{ROE} = \text{ROA} \times \text{Equity multiplier}$$

$$= \left(\frac{\text{Profit}}{\text{margin}}\right)\left(\frac{\text{Total assets}}{\text{turnover}}\right)\left(\frac{\text{Equity}}{\text{multiplier}}\right)$$

$$= \left(\frac{\text{Net income}}{\text{Sales}}\right)\left(\frac{\text{Sales}}{\text{Total assets}}\right)\left(\frac{\text{Total assets}}{\text{Common equity}}\right)$$

$$= \frac{\text{Net income}}{\text{Common equity}}.$$

CHAPTER 4

$$k = k^* + IP + DRP + LP + MRP.$$

$$k_{RF} = k^* + IP.$$

$$IP_n = \frac{I_1 + I_2 + \cdots + I_n}{n}.$$

CHAPTER 5

$$\text{Expected rate of return} = \hat{k} = \sum_{i=1}^{n} P_i k_i.$$

$$\text{Variance} = \sigma^2 = \sum_{i=1}^{n} (k_i - \hat{k})^2 P_i.$$

$$\text{Standard deviation} = \sigma = \sqrt{\sum_{i=1}^{n} (k_i - \hat{k})^2 P_i}.$$

$$CV = \frac{\sigma}{\hat{k}}.$$

$$\hat{k}_p = \sum_{i=1}^{n} w_i \hat{k}_i.$$

$$\sigma_p = \sqrt{\sum_{i=j}^{n} (k_{pj} - \hat{k}_p)^2 P_j}.$$

$$b_p = \sum_{i=1}^{n} w_i b_i.$$

$$SML = k_i = k_{RF} + (k_M - k_{RF}) b_i.$$

$$RP_i = (RP_M) b_i.$$

$$b = \frac{Y_2 - Y_1}{X_2 - X_1} = \text{slope coefficient in } \bar{k}_{it} = a + b\,\bar{k}_{Mt} + e_t.$$

CHAPTER 6

$$FV_n = PV(1 + i)^n = PV(FVIF_{i,n}).$$

$$PV = FV_n\left(\frac{1}{1+i}\right)^n = FV_n(1 + i)^{-n} = FV_n(PVIF_{i,n}).$$

$$PVIF_{i,n} = \frac{1}{FVIF_{i,n}}.$$

$$FVIFA_{i,n} = [(1 + i)^n - 1]/i.$$

$$PVIFA_{i,n} = [1 - (1/(1 + i)^n)]/i.$$

$$FVA_n = PMT(FVIFA_{i,n}).$$

$$FVA_n \text{ (Annuity due)} = PMT(FVIFA_{i,n})(1 + i).$$

$$PVA_n = PMT(PVIFA_{i,n}).$$

$$PVA_n \text{ (Annuity due)} = PMT(PVIFA_{i,n})(1 + i).$$

$$PV \text{ (Perpetuity)} = \frac{Payment}{Interest\ rate} = \frac{PMT}{i}.$$

$$PV_{Uneven\ stream} = \sum_{t=1}^{n} CF_t\left(\frac{1}{1+i}\right)^t = \sum_{t=1}^{n} CF_t(PVIF_{i,t}).$$

$$FV_{Uneven\ stream} = \sum_{t=1}^{n} CF_t (1 + i)^{n-t} = \sum_{t=1}^{n} CF_t(FVIF_{i,n-t}).$$

$$FV_n = PV\left(1 + \frac{i_{Nom}}{m}\right)^{mn}.$$

$$Effective\ annual\ rate = \left(1 + \frac{i_{Nom}}{m}\right)^m - 1.0.$$

$$Periodic\ rate = i_{Nom}/m.$$

$$i_{Nom} = APR = (Periodic\ rate)(m).$$

$$FV_n = PVe^{in}.$$

$$PV = FV_n e^{-in}.$$

CHAPTER 7

$$V_B = \sum_{t=1}^{N} \frac{INT}{(1 + k_d)^t} + \frac{M}{(1 + k_d)^N}$$

$$= INT(PVIFA_{k_d,N}) + M(PVIF_{k_d,N}).$$

$$V_B = \sum_{t=1}^{2N} \frac{INT/2}{(1 + k_{d/2})^t} + \frac{M}{(1 + k_{d/2})^{2N}} = \frac{INT}{2}(PVIFA_{k_{d/2},2N}) + M(PVIF_{k_{d/2},2N}).$$

$$Price\ of\ callable\ bond = \sum_{t=1}^{N} \frac{INT}{(1 + k_d)^t} + \frac{Call\ price}{(1 + k_d)^N}.$$

$$\text{Discount or premium} = \sum_{t=1}^{n} \frac{\text{Interest on old bond} - \text{Interest on new bond}}{(1 + k_d)^t}.$$

Accrued value at end of Year n = Issue price $\times (1 + k_d)^n$.

Interest in Year n = Accrued value$_n$ − Accrued value$_{n-1}$.

Tax savings = (Interest deduction)(T).

CHAPTER 8

$$\hat{P}_0 = \text{PV of expected future dividends} = \sum_{t=1}^{\infty} \frac{D_t}{(1 + k_s)^t}.$$

$$\hat{P}_0 = \frac{D_0(1 + g)}{k_s - g} = \frac{D_1}{k_s - g}.$$

$$\hat{k}_s = \frac{D_1}{P_0} + g.$$

$$V_{ps} = \frac{D_{ps}}{k_{ps}}.$$

$$k_{ps} = \frac{D_{ps}}{V_{ps}}.$$

CHAPTER 9

After-tax component cost of debt = $k_d(1 - T)$.

$$\text{Component cost of preferred stock} = k_{ps} = \frac{D_{ps}}{P_n}.$$

$$k_s = \hat{k}_s = k_{RF} + RP = D_1/P_0 + g.$$

$$k_s = k_{RF} + (k_M - k_{RF})b_i.$$

$$k_s = \text{Bond yield} + \text{Risk premium}.$$

$$k_e = \frac{D_1}{P_0(1 - F)} + g.$$

$$g = (\text{Retention rate})(\text{ROE}) = (1.0 - \text{Payout rate})(\text{ROE}).$$

$$\text{WACC} = w_d k_d(1 - T) + w_{ps}k_{ps} + w_{ce}(k_s \text{ or } k_e).$$

$$BP_{RE} = \frac{\text{Retained earnings}}{\text{Equity fraction}}.$$

CHAPTER 10

$$\text{NPV} = CF_0 + \frac{CF_1}{(1 + k)^1} + \frac{CF_2}{(1 + k)^2} + \cdots + \frac{CF_n}{(1 + k)^n}$$

$$= \sum_{t=0}^{n} \frac{CF_t}{(1 + k)^t}.$$

$$\text{IRR: } CF_0 + \frac{CF_1}{(1 + IRR)^1} + \frac{CF_2}{(1 + IRR)^2} + \cdots + \frac{CF_n}{(1 + IRR)^n} = 0$$

$$\sum_{t=0}^{n} \frac{CF_t}{(1 + IRR)^t} = 0.$$

$$\text{MIRR: PV costs} = \sum_{t=0}^{n} \frac{COF_t}{(1 + k)^t} = \frac{\sum_{t=0}^{n} CIF_t(1 + k)^{n-t}}{(1 + MIRR)^n} = \frac{TV}{(1 + MIRR)^n}.$$

CHAPTER 11

Net cash flow = Net income + Depreciation.

RECOVERY ALLOWANCE PERCENTAGE FOR PERSONAL PROPERTY

OWNERSHIP YEAR	CLASS OF INVESTMENT			
	3-YEAR	5-YEAR	7-YEAR	10-YEAR
1	33%	20%	14%	10%
2	45	32	25	18
3	15	19	17	14
4	7	12	13	12
5		11	9	9
6		6	9	7
7			9	7
8			4	7
9				7
10				6
11				3
	100%	100%	100%	100%

CHAPTER 12

$$Q_{BE} = \frac{F}{P - V}.$$

$$EBIT = PQ - VQ - F.$$

$$EPS = \frac{(S - FC - VC - I)(1 - T)}{\text{Shares outstanding}} = \frac{(EBIT - I)(1 - T)}{\text{Shares outstanding}}.$$

$$DOL_Q = \frac{\dfrac{\Delta EBIT}{EBIT}}{\dfrac{\Delta Q}{Q}} = \frac{Q(P - V)}{Q(P - V) - F}.$$

$$DOL_S = \frac{S - VC}{S - VC - F}.$$

$$DFL = \frac{EBIT}{EBIT - I}.$$

$$DTL = \frac{Q(P - V)}{Q(P - V) - F - I} = \frac{S - VC}{S - VC - F - I} = (DOL)(DFL).$$

$$EPS_1 = EPS_0[1 + (DTL)(\%\Delta Sales)].$$

Chapter 14

$$AFN = (A^*/S)\Delta S - (L^*/S)\Delta S - MS_1(1 - d).$$

$$\text{Full capacity sales} = \frac{\text{Actual sales}}{\begin{array}{c}\text{Percentage of capacity at}\\\text{which fixed assets were operated}\end{array}}.$$

$$\text{Target FA/Sales ratio} = \frac{\text{Actual fixed assets}}{\text{Full capacity sales}}.$$

Required level of FA = (Target FA/Sales ratio) (Projected sales).

Chapter 15

$$A/R = \begin{array}{c}\text{Credit sales}\\\text{per day}\end{array} \times \begin{array}{c}\text{Length of}\\\text{collection period}\end{array}.$$

$$ADS = \text{Annual sales}/360 = \frac{(\text{Units sold})(\text{Sales price})}{360}.$$

Receivables = (ADS)(DSO).

$$\begin{array}{c}\text{Inventory conversion}\\\text{period}\end{array} = \frac{\text{Inventory}}{\text{Sales}/360}.$$

$$\begin{array}{c}\text{Receivables collection}\\\text{period}\end{array} = DSO = \frac{\text{Receivables}}{\text{Sales}/360}.$$

$$\text{Payables deferral period} = \frac{\text{Payables}}{\text{Cost of goods sold}/360}.$$

$$\begin{array}{c}\text{Inventory}\\\text{conversion}\\\text{period}\end{array} + \begin{array}{c}\text{Receivables}\\\text{collection}\\\text{period}\end{array} - \begin{array}{c}\text{Payables}\\\text{deferral}\\\text{period}\end{array} = \begin{array}{c}\text{Cash}\\\text{conversion}.\\\text{cycle}\end{array}$$

Chapter 16

$$\text{Nominal cost of payables} = \frac{\text{Discount percent}}{100 - \begin{array}{c}\text{Discount}\\\text{percent}\end{array}} \times \frac{360}{\begin{array}{c}\text{Days credit is}\\\text{outstanding}\end{array} - \begin{array}{c}\text{Discount}\\\text{period}\end{array}}.$$

$$EAR_{Simple} = \frac{\text{Interest paid}}{\text{Amount received}} = \left(1 + \frac{k_{Nom}}{m}\right)^m - 1.0.$$

$$EAR_{Discount} = \frac{\text{Interest paid}}{\text{Amount received}} = \frac{\text{Interest paid}}{\text{Face value} - \text{Interest paid}}$$

$$= \frac{\text{Nominal rate (decimal)}}{1.0 - \text{Nominal rate (decimal)}}.$$

$$\text{Face value}_{\text{Discount}} = \frac{\text{Funds received}}{1.0 - \text{Nominal rate (decimal)}}.$$

$$\text{EAR}_{\text{Simple/CB}} = \frac{\text{Interest paid}}{\text{Amount received}} = \frac{\text{Nominal rate (decimal)}}{1.0 - \text{CB (decimal)}}.$$

$$\text{Face value}_{\text{Simple/CB}} = \frac{\text{Funds required}}{1.0 - \text{CB (decimal)}}.$$

$$\text{EAR}_{\text{Discount/CB}} = \frac{\text{Nominal rate (decimal)}}{1 - \text{Nominal rate (decimal)} - \text{CB (decimal)}}.$$

$$\text{Face value}_{\text{Discount/CB}} = \frac{\text{Funds required}}{1.0 - \text{Nominal rate (decimal)} - \text{CB (decimal)}}.$$

$$\text{Approximate annual rate}_{\text{Add-on}} = \frac{\text{Interest paid}}{(\text{Amount received})/2}.$$

$$\begin{array}{l}\text{Additional funds needed}\\ \text{to meet CB requirement}\end{array} = \left(\text{CB\%} \times \text{Loan} \right) - \begin{array}{l}\text{Cash available}\\ \text{for CB}\end{array}.$$

$$\text{Loan} = \text{Funds needed} + (\text{CB\%} \times \text{Loan}) - \text{Available cash}.$$

$$\text{EAR}_{\text{With cash balances}} = \frac{\text{Nominal rate (decimal)} \times \text{Loan}}{\text{Funds needed}}.$$

INDEX